GW00715445

Australian Film 1900–1977

Australian Film 1900-1977

A Guide to Feature Film Production

by
Andrew Pike and Ross Cooper

Melbourne
OXFORD UNIVERSITY PRESS
in association with
The Australian Film Institute
1980

Oxford University Press
OXFORD LONDON GLASGOW
NEW YORK TORONTO MELBOURNE WELLINGTON
KUALA LUMPUR SINGAPORE HONG KONG TOKYO
DELHI BOMBAY CALCUTTA MADRAS KARACHI
NAIROBI DAR ES SALAAM CAPE TOWN

First published 1980

Pike, Andrew Franklin, 1946-
Australian film 1900–1977.

Index
Bibliography
ISBN 0 19 554213 4

1. Moving-pictures – Australia – History. I. Cooper, Ross Francis, 1944-, joint author. II. Australian Film Institute. III. Title.

791.43'0994

NATIONAL LIBRARY OF AUSTRALIA CATALOGUING IN PUBLICATION DATA
Published with the assistance of the Literature Board of the Australia Council

Designed by Vicki Hamilton and Lauren Statham
Edited by John Bangsund
Produced by Hyland House Publishing Pty Ltd, Melbourne
Typeset by Computer Graphics Corporation Pty Ltd, Adelaide
Printed and bound by Griffin Press Limited, Adelaide
Published by Oxford University Press, 7 Bowen Crescent, Melbourne

Contents

Preface

This book began in 1970 when four people conducting research into early Australian film history decided to pool their findings. It is our regret that our original collaborators, Mervyn Wasson and Lyndsay Wasson, had to withdraw from the project because of other professional commitments. For their major contribution to the research, and to their early drafting of entries, their stimulating friendship and their encouragement, we are deeply indebted.

The intended scope of the book gradually shrank as the volume of production grew during the 1970s, and it became impossible to cover many areas of cinema that were of interest to us, especially documentary and experimental films. In the introductions to each of the seven periods in this book we have made some brief comments about these other areas of film. The main body of the book covers feature film production in Australia from its beginnings in 1900 to the end of 1977. Definitions of 'feature' film inevitably vary and our approach has been flexible, bending the definition from period to period to allow us to include films of interest, but we hope that we have provided a survey of one aspect of Australian film, the one best known to the public and of greatest importance to the film industry—the narrative film intended for theatrical screening. We have included many 16mm features from the 1970s that were shown in co-operative cinemas rather than conventional commercial theatres. Our intention is to give an idea of the depth and range of fiction film in Australia and to suggest something of the spirit of the film community in this country, rather than restrict ourselves to a history of the industry as such.

In preparing the book over so many years we have been helped and supported by many people. We thank especially the Film, Radio and Television Board of the Australia Council, and the Australian Film Institute, for financial aid, which at certain points enabled us to work full-time on the book, to employ research assistants and to recover typing costs. We also wish to thank Merrilyn Fitzpatrick for her major research and editorial assistance over the full span of the book's preparation. Ken G. Hall has given us constant encouragement and been a valuable and tolerant friend, making frank criticisms of several drafts. Karla Sigel gave long and dedicated service as a research assistant in Canberra. We are also grateful to Tim Blakely, Maureen Kupinsky, Rick Williams and Christine Johnson for their research assistance in Melbourne, and to the many friends who contributed hours along the way.

Scores of film-makers and their relatives have corresponded with us, given us interviews, and helped us with information in other ways, and in this regard we thank especially Joan Long, Elsa Chauvel, Tim Burstall, John B. Murray, Reg Perry, Gwen Oatley, A. R. Harwood, R. Maslyn Williams, Cecil Holmes and Nigel Buesst.

Chris Collier has supported us throughout with information, and his fund of knowledge about Australian film has been invaluable. The time he devoted to a thorough reading of the final draft prevented many embarrassing errors from appearing. Joan Long, Graham Shirley, Ray Edmondson and Elvey Drummond also devoted many days to reading drafts and gave valuable and frank comments, for which we are grateful.

Rosamunde Walsh carried the burden of the typing. Keith Pardy prepared most of the stills, and we warmly appreciate his patience and professional skill. Nigel Buesst, Sandy Edwards, and the staff of the photographics unit at the National Library of Australia, also provided important assistance with stills.

The staff of the National Film Archive, especially Ray Edmondson, Karen Foley, Kate McLoughlin, Glenda Marsh Wright, May Meyer and Pam Hill, provided service, advice and friendship far beyond the call of duty; the book would have been impossible without their help. We would also like to thank the staff of the Mitchell Library, Sydney, the La Trobe Library, Melbourne, the Australian Archives and the Archives Authority of New South Wales, for their assistance over the years.

Suzanne Ridley did most of the work on the index, and her professional skill was invaluable. Richard and Margaret Ruhfus and Sally de Tores also spent many weeks on the index.

Finally, the manuscript was edited by John Bangsund, and the book designed by Vicki Hamilton and Lauren Statham, in association with Anne Godden and Al Knight. Their enthusiasm for the book was most heartening.

We need hardly say that the book's errors and omissions are our own responsibility. We are painfully aware of many areas inadequately covered here, and of more checking that could have been done. However, our intention has been to open up the field of Australian film history by establishing a factual framework on which others may build. We hope that readers who find errors will get in touch with us or the National Film Archive, or will write articles or books themselves, to fill in the gaps and to develop the themes that we have only tentatively proposed.

Andrew Pike
Ross Cooper

How to use this book

Sequence of entries. Films have been arranged chronologically according to the date of their release. A release date has generally been taken to be the date of the first public screening. Where a film experienced a substantial delay between production and release, it has been dated by its first recorded preview for the film trade or press, or by its known completion date. Where release dates are unknown, films have been placed at the end of the month or year of their known completion.

Range of films. The definition of 'feature' film varies from period to period. Up to 1913, any narrative film, of any length, has been included, since short films were often 'featured' on a programme at this time. From 1914 to 1930, only films of 4000 feet or more have been included. From 1931 to 1977, only films that run for 50 minutes or more have been included, whether on 16mm or 35mm, provided that they have a significant fictional or acted component, and received public or commercial screenings. Films made on 8mm, telemovies (i.e., feature-length films made exclusively for television), television plays, feature-length documentaries and experimental films have been excluded.

Credits. Wherever possible, credits have been based directly on the text of the films themselves. Obvious misspellings have been corrected, but variant names of people (and fictional characters) from film to film have generally been maintained. Where a noteworthy contribution has been uncredited on the film itself, we have added the name to the credits (where we are aware of the person's work). The following abbreviations have been used.

ART D	art director
ASSOC P	associate producer
ASST D	assistant director
CAM OP	camera operator
CHOREOG	choreography
ED	editor
LOC M	location manager
M	music
MD	musical director
P	producer
P ASST	production assistant
PC	production company
P DES	production design
PM	production manager
PRE-P	pre-production
SC	scenario, screenplay, script
SD	sound
SD R	sound recording
SD RE-R	sound re-recording

The director of each film is named immediately beneath the film title. The word 'Scope' used in the credits refers to any form of process requiring an anamorphic lens for projection — for example, CinemaScope, Panavision, Tohoscope. Unless otherwise indicated, all films were made in 35mm and black-and-white, although they may have been released in other forms. Films made before 1930 were silent, and their length is indicated by feet (approximately 11 minutes to 1000 feet) or by reels (exact length unknown).

The other main abbreviations used in the book are:

NFA	National Film Archive (see Appendix A)
RCE	Minutes of Evidence of the Royal Commission on the Moving Picture Industry in Australia (published 1927)

The Index. The titles of the 488 films covered in the book, and their numbers, are set in bold type. All other films mentioned in the book are set in italics. The figures given, in all cases, refer to film numbers, not page numbers—except the roman numerals I to VII, which refer to the seven period introductions in the book.

Availability of Films. Readers who wish to view films listed in this book will find the most recent of them available from commercial distribution companies or from non-commercial libraries such as the Australian Film Institute or the Sydney Filmmakers' Co-operative. Hiring charges and conditions of access vary from place to place and depend upon the nature of the proposed screening.

For most films, however, the best starting point is the National Film Archive, attached to the National Library of Australia, Canberra. The Archive is Australia's major centre for film preservation and research. It has a long history of involvement in these activities (see Appendix A), and has a large collection of stills, posters and other publicity materials, memorabilia, production papers, scripts and tape-recorded interviews to supplement its holdings of films. Subject to the requirements of preservation technology, and to the wishes of copyright owners, films may be viewed at the Archive.

The survival of films until the late 1960s was usually a matter of chance. Once a film's commercial life was over, producers often lost interest in it: prints were junked by distributors, and negatives were destroyed, lost or simply thrown away. Films before 1950 were made on an unstable nitrate stock and often films from earlier decades suffered chemical deterioration, which impaired the image or sound quality, or which, in the most severe cases, made restoration impossible. The physical quality of films in the Archive is therefore variable, depending on the condition of the original material located by the Archive staff.

The following key is used in this book to indicate holdings of the Archive. Only the existence of a film, and its relative completeness, is indicated, not the quality of its sound or image. The symbols, appearing against the film title, are:

*	Substantially complete.
**	Incomplete: has major gaps, several reels missing, or exists only in fragments.

This key is employed only until 1945 in the text. For films made after that date the Archive's holdings are changing too rapidly to make the key meaningful. If the Archive does not hold any particular film from this later period it can generally direct inquirers to the appropriate source. Films not held by the Archive, whether before or after 1945, may still be represented in the Archive by posters, scripts or other materials, and it is recommended that readers not hesitate in beginning any research project by contacting the Archive.

In addition to the Film Archive, but quite separate from it, the National Library of Australia operates a Film Study Collection from which 16mm prints of numerous Australian films may be borrowed, free of charge, for non-commercial screenings. Details of the Collection's conditions of loan and its holdings may be obtained from the Film Study Officer, National Library of Australia, Parkes Place, Canberra, A.C.T. 2600.

Acknowledgements

The authors wish to thank the following people and organisations for permission to reproduce photographs in this book. Photographs are identified by the numbers of film entries. Most photographs were copied from the collection of the National Film Archive, in the National Library of Australia, Canberra.

1 Reg Perry
2, 11, 18, 19, 24, 27, 39, 49 National Film Archive
71 The Collection of the Western Australian Art Gallery
88 National Film Archive
98, 99, 101, 103 Australian Archives
104 Australian Archives (for stills); National Gallery of Victoria (for the painting)
110, 118 Australian Archives
120 National Film Archive
122, 124, 125 Australian Archives
133, 134 National Film Archive
135 Ric Throssell
141 National Film Archive
142 Australian Archives
148, 149 National Film Archive
165 Agnes Dobson
166 Jack Tauchert
168 Agnes Dobson
174, 176 National Film Archive
177 Elsa Chauvel
180, 182, 183, 187, 189 National Film Archive
199 Jack Tauchert
206 Gordon Collingridge
209 Jack Tauchert
212 National Film Archive
217 Paulette McDonagh
218 National Film Archive
222 Gordon Collingridge
223 Elsa Chauvel
228, 231 National Film Archive
234 Elsa Chauvel
235 Paulette McDonagh
236 Gordon Collingridge
238 Dorothy Tayler
239 National Film Archive
242 A. R. Harwood
244 National Film Archive
249 Jack Tauchert
251 Paulette McDonagh
253 Young and District Historical Society
256 National Film Archive
260 Paulette McDonagh
261 Jack Tauchert
264 Ian Hanna
265 Jack Tauchert
266 National Film Archive
267 Cinesound Productions
268 National Film Archive
269 Ian Hanna
271 Elsa Chauvel
272 Cinesound Productions
273 Paulette McDonagh
274 Ian Hanna
275 J. C. Williamson Theatres
277 A. R. Harwood
278 Cinesound Productions
281 National Film Archive
282 Cinesound Productions
283 J. C. Williamson Theatres
285 Cinesound Productions
286 Elsa Chauvel
288 Cinesound Productions
289 Denison Estates
290 Elsa Chauvel
291 Zane Grey Inc.
292, 294, 297, 299, 300, 301 Cinesound Productions
303 Joy Jobbins
304, 306, 307, 308, 310 Cinesound Productions
312 Elsa Chauvel
314 Denison Estates
316 Hartney Arthur
317 Elsa Chauvel
318 National Film Archive
319 Supreme Films
320 Columbia Pictures
321 Eric Porter Productions
322 EMI Film Distributors
323 Children's Film Foundation
324 National Film Archive
325 EMI Film Distributors
328 Elsa Chauvel
329 EMI Film Distributors
330 Joan Sheil
331 EMI Film Distributors
333 Film Australia
336 Cecil Holmes
337, 338 Lee Robinson
339 John Heyer
343 Lee Robinson
344 Cecil Holmes, Edmund Allison
345 Cinema International Corporation
346 The Rank Organisation
347 Lee Robinson
351 United Artists
353 EMI Film Distributors
354 World Wide Pictures
355 Warner Bros
356 Children's Film Foundation
358 Giorgio Mangiamele
360 Lee Robinson
361 Brian Davies
362 Australian-American Pictures
363 Ludwik Dutkiewicz
366 Amalgamated Television Services
367 Columbia Pictures
368 Tim Burstall
370 Lee Robinson
373 Phillip Adams
375 Peter Carmody
376 Warner Bros
379 United Artists
382 John B. Murray
385 Film Australia
387 Act One Productions, Freeman-Fishburn International
388 Peter Weir (photo by Jennifer Steele)
390 Twentieth Century-Fox
392 Dusan Marek
393 Nigel Buesst
394 Hans Pomeranz
395 Tim Burstall
398 Jim Sharman
400 Phillip Adams
401 Tom Cowan
402 Jack Neary
403 Eric Porter Productions
404, 405 Film Australia
407 John B. Murray
412 Nigel Buesst
415 Tim Burstall
418 Cash Harmon Television
419 Smart Street Films
420 McElroy and McElroy
421 Sandy Harbutt
423 Tim Burstall
424 Michael Thornhill
425 Tim Burstall
426 Reg Grundy Productions
429 Tom Cowan
430 Richard Franklin
432 South Australian Film Corporation
433 The Movie Company, Golden Harvest
434 David Baker
435 Crawford Productions
436 McElroy and McElroy, Patricia Lovell
441 Terry Bourke
443 Margaret Fink
445 Carolyn Strachan
448 United Telecasters
449 Walt Disney Productions
450 Tim Burstall
451 Anthony Buckley
452 Paul Cox
455 South Australian Film Corporation (photo by David Kynoch)
456 Antony I. Ginnane
457 John Ruanne
458 Count Features
459 The Film House
462 Phillip Adams
463 South Australian Film Corporation (photo by David Kynoch)
466 Tim Burstall
468 Michael Thornhill
469 Patricia Lovell
470 Homestead Films
471 Gillian Armstrong
472 Michael Thornhill
473 Joan Long
474 Phil Noyce (photo of Noyce by Leon Saunders)
475 Ken Cameron
476 Stephen Wallace
477 Tim Burstall
478 Phillip Adams
479 Tom Cowan
480 Robert Hill
481 Patricia Lovell
484 Michael Pate
486 McElroy and McElroy
488 Antony I. Ginnane

For colour reproductions:
The Adventures of Barry McKenzie Phillip Adams
Barry McKenzie Holds his Own Reg Grundy Productions
Between Wars Michael Thornhill
Caddie Anthony Buckley
The Cars that Ate Paris McElroy and McElroy
Dad Rudd, M.P. Cinesound Productions
The Dinkum Bloke National Film Archive, Jack Tauchert
Dot and the Kangaroo Yoram Gross
Eliza Fraser Tim Burstall
Jedda Elsa Chauvel
The Last Wave McElroy and McElroy
Mad Dog Morgan Peter Beilby
Marco Polo Jnr Eric Porter Productions
Ned Kelly United Artists
On Our Selection Cinesound Productions
Petersen Tim Burstall
Picnic at Hanging Rock McElroy and McElroy, Patricia Lovell
Soldiers of the Cross Reg Perry
Stone Sandy Harbutt
Walkabout Twentieth Century-Fox

Part 1:

1900–1913

Actuality films recording daily life in Australian cities were made as early as 1896, and they provided a staple income for early Australian film-makers. By 1899, films were also being made that added new dimensions to the presentation of evangelical religion (such as *Soldiers of the Cross,* 1900), and others that served as moving backgrounds to stage plays (such as *Besieged at Port Arthur,* 1906—a 'magnificent Russo-Japanese war spectacle').

In 1906 the first continuous narrative film of any substantial length, *The Story of the Kelly Gang,* was made in Melbourne. Debate about whether it was the first feature film in Australia, or even in the world, has tended to obscure the important fact that in Australia there was an early flowering of feature film production from 1906 to 1912, pre-dating the regular appearance of narrative films of similar length (4000 feet or more) in other countries, especially Britain and the U.S.A. In Britain, for example, the longest film made in 1911 was 2500 feet; in Australia in the same year at least twenty films were over 3000 feet, and of those nearly half were over 4000 feet. In these early years it was essentially an indigenous cinema, reflecting the producers' direct responses to the Australian audience, without reliance on established models from overseas. It was perhaps the most acutely 'national' period in Australian cinema, and many of the recurring themes and motifs of the local cinema were first explored and defined at this time.

Many of the films in the pre-war years were produced by theatrical companies based in Sydney, using film as a means of penetrating their market more thoroughly than had been possible before. E. J. Cole's Bohemian Dramatic Company and George Marlow's company were two such groups. By recording its repertoire on film, a theatrical troupe could send its work to remote country towns and could saturate the city suburbs by using several prints. There soon emerged other troupes that specialized in film, that had no theatrical basis, but employed a regular staff of players and technicians (for example, the Australian Photo-Play Company and the Australian Life Biograph Company).

Whether made by theatre or film specialists, the early films tended to be closely allied to theatrical experiences: while the film 'unwound', performers on stage or behind the screen would provide music, sound effects and dialogue, or descriptions of the action. The moving image provided a simple means not only of illustrating the plays but also of opening them up, and it allowed action scenes to be performed outdoors in surroundings that looked more authentic. Accordingly, producers tended to favour subjects with open-air Australian settings—stories of the convict days or of the gold rushes, sporting dramas, tales of station life in the outback, and above all, bushranging adventures. Other popular subjects in local theatre were sometimes filmed, as diverse as Deep South racial melodramas (*The Octoroon,* 1912), American Westerns (*The Luck of Roaring Camp,* 1911), Irish romances (*Colleen Bawn,* 1911) and British dramas of class, religion and sex (*The Christian,* 1911), but none of these triggered off the same degree of public enthusiasm as the Australian outdoor subjects.

The urban dramas were often centred upon new technological phenomena—for example, telegrams and telephones (*A Silent Witness,* 1912), police detection methods such as finger-printing (*Whose Was the Hand?,* 1912), and fast cars and trains (*All for Gold,* 1911)—but were nevertheless rooted in the recognizable contemporary life of the city. Films of the bush, however, tended to be romantic fantasies, made by city-dwellers about a vanishing or extinct life-style. Chief among them were the bushranging films, which established themselves as a distinctive genre before the Hollywood Western swept the world. These films had stock characters and actions that appeared repeatedly, regardless of historical accuracy or physical possibility. Raymond Longford wrote: 'All they needed was horses hired from stables in Redfern, some uniforms, guns, a stagecoach, and enough men to play troopers and rangers. They would take their gear down to the bush at Brookvale, outside Manly, camp out for a week, and—without any script—make a film. Their action was usually a stagecoach hold-up, a lot of galloping, and a shooting-match.' (*Daily Telegraph,* 9 November 1946) Bushrangers usually included at least one daring leap in their adventures, whether alone or on horseback, from a cliff into the ocean or from a bridge into a flooded river, and they often had a quick-witted 'black boy' as faithful ally.

Women also followed a romantic pattern in outback films. Bush heroines were always accomplished horsewomen, knowledgeable about bush lore and cattle mustering, but they were not tomboys. While they could ride the range with the best of the men, they maintained a dainty and demure appearance and flirted happily with the men of their choice. They were simultaneously loyal mates and good wives. Such a woman was often the protagonist of the film. Unlike some Hollywood Westerns in later decades, there was in these films no question of women being 'tamed' by marriage: they were presented as emotionally balanced characters, their ability to play both 'male' and 'female' roles in the bush creating no signs of psychological stress. The tradition established in these early years of 'the squatter's daughter' or 'the girl of the bush' continued through to the 1950s in the local cinema.

Outback films rivalled each other in the authenticity of their action scenes. Spectacular feats of horsemanship by rodeo roughriders would sometimes be interpolated into a bush yarn to give it distinction, and the promise of 'real rides' was often highlighted in film advertising to lure audiences away from the theatre into the cinema (for example, *The Squatter's Daughter,* 1910). Injuries often occurred in the staging of fight scenes, especially in the bravura stunt-work of John Gavin's films (such as *The Assigned Servant,* 1911). The urge to find 'real' scenery led film-makers into distant or almost inaccessible parts of the continent, not only for outback films but also for a melodrama like *The Bells*

(1911), for which the film unit ventured under difficult conditions into the Snowy Mountains to secure background scenery to represent the countryside of Alsace in the mid-nineteenth century.

Sustained portraits of little-seen corners of Australia also attracted an enormous public following, far beyond the numerous short 'actualities' of city and country life. In 1911 Francis Birtles made *Across Australia*, the first of several long records of journeys around the continent and into 'unknown' Australia. Travelling first by bicycle, and later by car and aeroplane, Birtles's adventures in central Australia and in the tropical north established armchair travelling as a popular form of commercial cinema, and his example was followed by other film-makers, from Frank Hurley and J. E. Ward later in the decade to the wave of 'safari' documentaries in the late 1960s.

The years before the First World War were the most productive for Australian cinema, with a quantitative peak in 1911 that has not been equalled since. But by 1913 production had declined, and it did not recover until the heavy input of government finance in the 1970s. The cultural imperialism of the U.S.A. and Britain has often been blamed for causing the failure of the feature film industry by acquiring a stranglehold over Australian theatres and denying local film-makers access to the screen. While such arguments may help to explain the problems of the industry in later decades, they do not explain the sudden and sharp fall in production in 1912, several years before Hollywood gained primacy in world production.

The collapse in production had nothing to do with audience response; it was a myth spread by the enemies of local production that Australian films were 'below standard' and that Australian audiences did not want to see them. On the contrary, the feature film industry was the victim of a struggle for power within the distribution and exhibition trades. Early in 1912 several film exchanges and theatre-owning companies began to merge their interests in a combine made up of Australasian Films for distribution, equipment and production, and Union Theatres for exhibition. Under the direction of businessmen such as Henry Gee, Australasian and Union Theatres systematically set about consolidating their hold over the Australian trade. By mid-1912 independent production units, including larger operations such as the Australian Photo-Play Company and the Australian Life Biograph Company, were beginning to go out of business because the theatres they normally supplied had signed to screen nothing but films from Australasian. For sheer lack of theatre outlets, production fell into decay. *Theatre*, 2 November 1914, estimated that eight out of ten exhibitors in New South Wales were dependent on Australasian for film supplies and were tied to contracts that gave them no freedom in programming. On 1 January 1915 an editorial in the same magazine asserted that 'Whether deliberate or accidental, [Australasian's] contract with exhibitors has done more to kill local picture production than anything else.' Thus the first major blow against production came from Australian businessmen in a situation of unfettered free enterprise. The monopoly of Australasian Films and Union Theatres was dominant in the industry for the next decade, and the companies remained powerful forces in the industry into the 1970s.

The production industry was also hampered by the banning of the bushranging genre by the New South Wales Police Department in 1912. Bushranging had been the most popular subject for films in 1911, and New South Wales was the largest market for them, so the ban was a body-blow to the industry. The police claimed that the bushranging films made a mockery of the law and glorified outlawry to audiences that were largely composed of young adults and children. Bushranging stories remained in a less spectacular form on the stage, but the police did not consider the predominantly adult audience for live theatre to be endangered by exposure to them. The ban remained in force until the 1940s and had a powerful influence on Australian popular culture: the entire folklore relating to bushrangers was effectively removed from the most popular form of cultural expression, and for more than thirty years Australians were left ignorant of the exploits of bushrangers. A ready substitute was found in the American Western, and Australians became more familiar with Tom Mix and Bill Hart than with Frank Morgan or the Captains Midnight, Moonlite and Starlight.

During these early years of Australian cinema, many people drifted in and out of production, moving back into live theatre or departing overseas when conditions toughened in 1912. But the period also constituted the formative years for a handful of film-makers who persevered with production during the war and after: Raymond Longford and Lottie Lyell displayed an acute sense of the medium's power to express emotion, but like John Gavin and Franklyn Barrett, their best work was yet to come. The most important figures in the early production industry, the men with vision, were the entrepreneurs—Cozens Spencer, J. D. Williams, T. J. West, Stanley Crick, the Frasers and others. Their rivalry in exploring the possibilities of film 'showmanship' stimulated a healthy climate of ingenuity and enthusiasm in production as well as exhibition, and the rapid development of the commercial uses of film in Australia owed much to them.

1 Soldiers of the Cross

1900 JOSEPH PERRY, HERBERT BOOTH

P: The Salvation Army.

Many claims have been made about *Soldiers of the Cross*—that it was the first feature film in the world, the first full-length film, the first religious film, the first propaganda film, and even the first 'spectacle'—all of which depend entirely on definition. Discussion of it as a 'feature film', however, obscures the fact that it was *not* a continuous film, but rather a complex display of inter-related films, slides, music and the spoken word. Also, discussion of it as the 'first' of anything obscures the fact that it was by no means an isolated experiment. It was rather the culmination of a series of illustrated lectures prepared and presented by the Salvation Army in the late 1890s.

The Salvation Army had long been harnessing the new technology of mass entertainment for their own purpose of saving souls. Magic lanterns, recorded music devices (the phonograph, the graphophone and others) and the cinematograph were all part of the Army's weaponry. As Herbert Booth wrote in 1901: 'These means are employed by the worldling; they form a source of attraction in the theatres and music halls. Why should they be usurped by the enemy of souls? The magic power of light . . . is the creation of God, and it can only honour Him, and glorify His own handiwork, to utilize this invention for the salvation and blessing of mankind.' (*Victory*, September 1901) The Army established a Limelight Department in Melbourne in 1892 to produce lantern slides on biblical and social subjects, and to develop equipment and effects that could wring the maximum emotional value from the slides. The key figure in the Department was Joseph Perry, showman, scientist and Salvationist. He was born in England in 1862 and went to New Zealand as a boy; he joined the Salvation Army in 1883 and two years later was sent by the Army to Australia. He worked for the Army in various mining districts, and in Ballarat began to develop the use of lantern slides and photographs for propaganda effect. His slide shows became popular, and in 1892 he was brought to Melbourne to help establish the Limelight Department and to extend his special talents for nation-wide use.

1 Joseph Perry and his sons: (*from left*) Orrie, Stan, Joseph, Reg

In September 1896 Commandant Herbert Booth, a son of the Salvation Army's founder, General William Booth, arrived in Australia and immediately recognized the value of Perry's work. Under his impetus, the Limelight Department was expanded even further, and early in 1897 the Department bought its first film projector. The purchase was made less than a year after the first films had been shown in Australia. Booth was a forceful orator and an able administrator, but he came to rely heavily on Perry for the bravura pyrotechnics that he used extensively in his campaigns. At first the films shown by the Army were Lumière productions—views of people and places from around the world—but by August 1897 Perry had started to shoot his own 75-foot films. These short films subsequently became the basis of the *Social Lecture*, which Booth and others gave around Australia and New Zealand in 1898 to raise funds for the social welfare work of the Army. This cluster of films mainly consisted of unadorned actuality footage, such as a Salvation Army procession and women cadets selling the Army magazine, the *War Cry*, but it also included a brief enacted drama of a man convicted for stealing bread and being helped by the Army's 'prison-gate brigade' on his release from jail. This drama, running for barely three minutes and having no specific title, was probably the first fiction film ever made in Australia.

Late in 1899 Booth and Perry developed their film and lecture programme by making a series of biblical stories. Thirteen short films (each probably less than three minutes) were made about the birth of Christ, the flight into Egypt, the Last Supper, the trial before Herod and other episodes from the Bible. Known collectively as the *Passion Films*, they were taken on tour by the Army in January 1900, and their popularity inspired the Army's most ambitious project, *Soldiers of the Cross*.

Credit for the creation of *Soldiers of the Cross* cannot be apportioned with certainty, but it is likely that Booth and Perry wrote the scenario together and that, because of Booth's ill-health and heavy administrative work-load, Perry had effective control over the making of the films. Thirteen short films (possibly including some items from the *Passion Films*) were prepared. Shooting took place in June, July and August 1900, mainly in the grounds of a Salvation Army girls' home at Murrumbeena, on the outskirts of Melbourne. Canvas backdrops were hung from the fence around the tennis court, and girls from the home made the costumes and acted in the films, along with volunteers from the Army's male cadets. No-one in the cast was a professional actor. Other scenes were shot at the Richmond baths (for the drowning of a Christian martyr in the River Tiber) and in the bush at Murrumbeena.

On 13 September 1900 the lecture (as the Army always referred to it) was first performed at the Melbourne Town Hall, with the thirteen films, some 200 slides and an elaborate music score using themes from hymns and the popular classics. Booth's intention was to convey the suffering and the sorrow, the gladness and the triumph of the early Christian martyrs, and through his emotional presentation not only to win souls but to raise funds and attract new recruits for the Army. A packed audience responded with emotion as Booth used his most powerful rhetoric to tell them about the life and death of Jesus and the martyrdom of his early followers in Rome. As he spoke, images flowed smoothly from slide to film and from film to slide. Scenes depicted the stoning of Stephen, the massacre in the Catacombs, the burning of Polycarp at the stake, and as a climax, the events in the Colosseum, where the Christians were devoured by lions and tigers. Nothing like this panoramic view of early Christian history, lasting two and a quarter hours, had been seen before, and in the days that followed the press applauded the event. The *Age* said on 14 September: 'To have some of the most tragic episodes of Christian history carried out in all savage but soul-stirring realism is an accomplishment essentially of today. . . . As the audience witnessed martyrdom enacted as though grimly real before their eyes, fervent questions as to the enduring quality of their own faith were put by the commandant, and, at intervals rousing hymns were sung by the whole gathering.'

After the enormous success of the première, attended by 4000 people, the lecture toured widely in Australia and New Zealand, frequently being altered or expanded as new material was made. In 1902 Booth resigned from the Army and went to the U.S.A., taking the films and slides with him, to become a private evangelist. After his departure, the use of film for propagating the Army's message began to decline, and Perry became increasingly involved in the photographing of secular activities, hiring his services out to government bodies and private companies. Among the many actuality films that he made were several especially popular items—a naval contingent leaving Melbourne in 1900 to help put down the Boxer Rebellion, the visit of the Duke and Duchess of York to Australia in 1901, the inauguration of the Commonwealth in 1901, and above all, the visit to Australia and New Zealand of the 'Great White Fleet' from the U.S.A. in 1908.

In 1908 it was decided to erect a new studio and laboratory for the Limelight Department in Melbourne, and in 1909 the production of religious films resumed with two major projects, *Heroes of the Cross* (which owed much of its content to *Soldiers of the Cross*) and *The Scottish Covenanters* (a drama set in England at the time of Oliver Cromwell), both personally supervised by Perry. But the work of the Department soon ceased. In 1910 it was disbanded, partly because of the abundant availability of films from other sources, partly because of the increasing belief of the Army leadership that the medium of film was no longer appropriate to the Army's work, film being now too firmly associated with entertainments of an undesirable type. Finding his principal work curtailed, Perry resigned from the Army and joined the commercial film trade, working with Co-operative Films and later as a distribution representative in the Dutch East Indies from 1918 to 1930. He died in Sydney in April 1943.

Perry's sons also joined the film trade and had long and successful careers: Orizaba (usually known as Orrie), born in 1887, and Reginald, born in 1890, had helped their father in the making of *Soldiers of the Cross* (among other roles they had played the fore and aft legs of a lion in the Colosseum scenes). Orrie became a photographer for Johnson and Gibson, and in 1913 turned to cinema management, eventually managing Union Theatres' most prestigious houses, in turn the Capitol Theatre and the State Theatre in Sydney. Reg became the South Australian manager for Universal Pictures and worked in that position from 1920 to 1962. Another brother, Stan, worked primarily in exhibition, and was manager for Hoyts Theatres in Western Australia for many years.

2 The Story of the Kelly Gang**

1906 CHARLES TAIT

P: J. and N. Tait/Johnson and Gibson. SC: Charles Tait. PH: Millard Johnson, Orrie Perry, Reg Perry. ASST D: Sam Crewes. Approx. 4000 ft.
CAST: Elizabeth Tait (Kate Kelly), John Tait (schoolmaster), E.J. and Frank Tait (extras).

The longest narrative film then seen in Australia, and quite possibly in the world, opened on 26 December 1906 at the Athenaeum Hall, Melbourne. In 1904, two young entrepreneurs, John and Nevin Tait, from a family of five brothers in show business, had begun to include film programmes among their concert bookings at the Athenaeum Hall. Their screenings of imported 'scenics' had been profitable, and they became eager to expand their film activities. In making their first film, *The Story of the Kelly Gang*, they were joined by Millard Johnson and William Gibson, two chemists who had become interested in film when they acquired a second-hand projector from a vaudeville show. Johnson and Gibson soon began showing films to large crowds around Melbourne, in the open air on the beach at St Kilda, and at the Melbourne Cricket Ground, and through their knowledge of chemistry they became proficient in handling technical aspects of photography and processing.

The film was financed jointly by the two partnerships, and after thorough planning, was directed by the Taits' older brother, Charles, who had had wider experience in theatrical presentations. The direct inspiration probably lay in the popularity of the Kelly exploits on the stage. A series of plays on the Kellys had been appearing for a decade or more, and some reports attributed the original initiative for the film to an actor-manager, Sam Crewes. Costumes and some of the cast for the film were secured from one of the existing stage productions (possibly from E. J. Cole's Bohemian Dramatic Company).

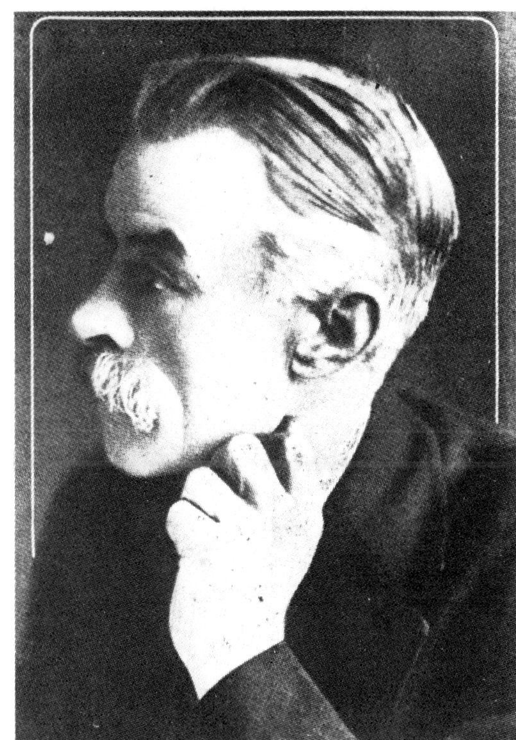
2 W. A. Gibson

The chief location was the family estate of Charles Tait's wife, Elizabeth, at Heidelberg on the outskirts of Melbourne. The Tait family provided enthusiastic support, both in the cast and behind the camera. Elizabeth appeared as Kate Kelly, and all of the Tait brothers and Charles Tait's children took part in crowd scenes. A local circus provided some fifty horses and a team of roughriders. An actor hired to play Ned Kelly deserted the production after a few scenes had been shot, and to avoid reshooting, various understudies appeared in his place, on horseback or wearing armour, so that his face was never seen. Millard Johnson operated the camera with technical supervision and laboratory work provided by Gibson. One of the dramatic highlights—the bushrangers' attempt to derail a train-load of police—was staged with the help of the Victorian Railways Commissioners, who provided a train as well as a team of gangers to tear up the track. This gesture of support from the government tells much about the Taits' infectious enthusiasm and powers of persuasion, for government authorities were later notorious for their obstruction to any film-making proposal that involved public utilities. Interiors, including the Glenrowan hotel, were staged in the back yard of Charles Tait's home in Melbourne, using sunlight as the sole light source. Tinting was applied for dramatic effect throughout the film, for example with a red glow for the scene in which Ned's armour was made by a blacksmith.

At the time the Taits were unaware of the historical importance of the film, and only much later, when film production was more established, did their work appear in perspective as a significant pioneering feat. The Tait brothers, Gibson and others poured forth their memories of the event but the passage of time and the desire to make a good story of it created a maze of contradictory information. It is possible, for example, that Elizabeth Tait did not play Kate Kelly throughout the film but merely doubled for another actress in the horse-riding scenes, since Elizabeth was an expert horsewoman. Estimates of the production cost also varied widely: John Tait claimed that the total cost rose to just over £1000; Gibson spoke of £400, but it is possible that he was referring only to his share of the total. The confusion was not helped by the Taits' decision to improve and extend the film, so that its length and its content continually varied. It was advertised as 4000 feet in length at the original Melbourne season, but in February 1907, when it opened in Sydney at the Palace Theatre, it already boasted at least one new scene, exclusive to New South Wales, depicting the Kellys' raid on a bank at Jerilderie. When re-released in 1910, it again

2 *The Story of the Kelly Gang* Frame enlargements

carried new scenes shot by Orrie and Reg Perry.

In the hour or more that it lasted on the screen, *The Story of the Kelly Gang* presented the highlights from the bushranging career of the Kelly brothers. Using no intertitles, it was entirely dependent on an on-stage lecturer, or often a group of actors, to provide continuity and to identify the characters. Later films on the Kellys took a defensive stand against the threat of censorship by adopting a stridently moralistic tone, offering the story as a tribute to the police and as an example of the dangers of anti-social behaviour, but the 1906 film openly presented the Kellys as gallant heroes, with the police as the enemy, and no attempt was made to apologize for the cheerful celebration of outlawry. The synopsis offered a clear contrast between the Kellys and the police: Ned and his men were proud of their boast, 'We Do Not Rob Ladies or Children,' while the police thought nothing of treating Ned's old mother roughly or of exploiting their position of power, as one proposed, 'Just One Kiss, Katie, Dear, and I'll Let Dan Go'. In the spirit of myth-making, the film refrained from humiliating Ned by showing his execution (an obligatory display of a just reward in later films) and the film closed on a note of sadness with his capture by police, as though the moment symbolized the passing of a romantic era: 'Thus Fell the Last of the Kelly Gang, and With the Fall of Ned Kelly, the Last of the Bushrangers.' A contributor to the *Bulletin*, 24 January 1907, described the film's romantic image of the Kellys: 'These splendid bushrangers never come within a hundred yards of a woman without taking off their hats, and on occasions they remove their hats as often as nine times to one woman. This is held to be a glorious characteristic, and justifies all Ned Kelly's viciousness and villainies.'

The film's capacity to stir its audience was reflected in its extraordinary attendance records. For five weeks it ran to full houses at the Athenaeum Hall (transferring occasionally to the larger Town Hall near by when it was available) and then moved to other Melbourne theatres. At the same time it was screened in Sydney and Adelaide, and reports of its success soon drew a young Queensland entrepreneur, E. J. Carroll, to Melbourne to purchase the Queensland rights; Carroll proceeded to make his fortune by touring with the film around the state, and he remained involved in film exhibition and occasionally production from that time on. Gibson later claimed that the film had returned no less than £25 000 to the producers, which he regarded as a record percentage profit for any Australian production.

The Taits approached the marketing of the film with the same efficiency that marked the production. Before its Athenaeum release it was tried out in several country towns and was probably re-edited according to audience reaction. A biograph company was employed by the Taits to tour with the film around Australia, controlling publicity, accounts and the elaborate stage presentation that accompanied each screening. As the film unwound, an orchestra provided music, an actor (sometimes two) provided voices and a description of the actions, and young boys were employed to provide sound effects behind the screen. Sometimes effects were delivered with more vigour than taste and the *Bulletin* reviewer, quoted earlier, complained that 'there is a deal too much racket in connection with the show—sometimes you can't see the pictures for the noise of horses, trains, gunshots, and wild cries'. By September 1907 it was screening in New Zealand, and had reached England, where it toured as 'the longest film ever made'. In all of its screenings the film was presented with a programme of curtain-raisers—scenics, comedy items and news topics—while intervals during the screening of the feature, as reels were being changed, were filled with songs by one of the actors on stage.

The bushranging genre on the screen habitually attracted the attention of the censors, and the Taits' experience in 1907 did not augur well for the future: in April the Victorian Chief Secretary banned screenings of the film in Kelly's own territory, around Benalla and Wangaratta in the central north of the state, partly for fear of public disorder and rioting, and partly because of representations to the police from relatives and friends of the Kelly family, who feared that their names would be hurt by a renewal of the family scandal. In April 1912 the Victorian government went further, and prevented the screening of a revised version of the film throughout the state.

Buoyed by the continuing profitability of the film, J. and N. Tait and Johnson and Gibson eventually merged their interests in March 1911 in a company, Amalgamated Pictures, and continued to produce films on a modest scale until they joined the combine of Australasian Films in 1912. Their main interest, however, was exhibition, and neither party had a deep commitment to production. In the light of Australasian's later impact on the production industry, it is ironic that Gibson continued to refer back to his work on *The Story of the Kelly Gang* and to himself as the 'father' of the Australian film industry. Like the Taits, he was a shrewd and adventurous businessman, and the achievement of Amalgamated Pictures under his guidance included the construction of the Majestic Theatre in Flinders Street, Melbourne, in 1912, the first luxury theatre built specifically for films in Australia. He was born in England in 1870 and came to Australia as a young man. After 1906 he devoted much energy to the promotion of the novelty, Kinemacolor, which greatly consolidated his financial strength. With the formation of the combine, he became general manager of Australasian and a managing director of Union Theatres, and remained there until his death in October 1929. He was awarded an O.B.E. in 1919 for his services to the industry and to Australian society. His partner, Millard Johnson, spent many years in America as Australasian's film buyer, from 1913 until his retirement in the late 1920s.

The Taits did not maintain their interest in film and eventually severed their connection with Amalgamated to focus on theatrical activity. All five brothers (Charles, John, Nevin, E. J. and Frank) became powerful entrepreneurial figures in Australian theatre, with a dominant position in the J. C. Williamson empire after 1920.

1900/13 **3** **Eureka Stockade**

1907 GEORGE CORNWELL, ARTHUR CORNWELL

PC: Australasian Cinematograph Company.

The Australasian Cinematograph Company was formed in 1907 by George Cornwell, a motor mechanic, and his brother Arthur, with a group of Melbourne businessmen and capital of £1500. Their only film was this story of rebellion on the Ballarat goldfields. A writer in the *Bulletin*, 31 October 1907, was greatly taken by it: 'However short of the possible the Eureka scenes might be, they stirred me to the core . . . What tremendous possibilities there are in the biograph!'

The first screening was at the Athenaeum Hall, Melbourne, on 19 October 1907, and it ran there for two weeks. Public reaction does not seem to have been enough to interest the Cornwells in further production, and the company was wound up in March 1908.

EUREKA STOCKADE

Reproduced with Faithful Fidelity to Detail, and Throbbing with the Pulse and Memories of the "ROARING FIFTIES."

The soldiers of Britain pressed forward, whilst high on the rude barricade
Brave Lalor stood calmly directing the diggers within the stockade:
'Twas a sight for the Gods; such a picture an artist would die to have drawn,
A fragile stockade, rebel leader, the red coats, and glimmering dawn.

"Gold Seekers Leaving London"

Shipping Office in London. On the Road.
Wheelbarrows and Handcarts.
New Churns arriivng at Poverty Flat footsore and weary, A Lonely Bush Road.
Poverty Flat. A Butcher's Shop,
Diggers' Washing Day.

ISSUING LICENSES

The Road-Side Shanty. How they get the Gold. The Windlass.
The Whim. Cradling (Zealous Diggers). Panning Off. Puddling.
The Rush at Canadian Gully.
Arrival of First Woman on Goldfields. . Gold Stealing.
The Petticoat on the Line.
Road to Sulky Gully. The Departure for a New Rush. New Chum's Dance.
License Hunting.
Diggers Chained to Logs and Rescued by Mates.
Letters from Home. Lost in the Bush. How the Lucky Diggers Spent their Money. Bentley's Hotel. Scobie and Martin.
Murder of Scobie. Discovey of Scobie's Body.
Indignation Meeting outside Eureka Hotel. Arrival of Troopers.
Diggers Burning Bentley's Hotel.
Ruins of Bently's Hotel. Flight of Bentley and his Wife.

THE GREAT EUREKA REBELLION

Lalor Addressing the Diggers. A Stormy Meeting on a Stormy Night.
Burning the Licenses. **Building the Stockade.**
Goodenough the Spy at the Stockade. Inside the Guard Room.
Captain Wise and the Spy. Diggers Taking the Oath. The Diggers' Flag.
Flight and Death of Goodenongh the Spy. Soldiers Advancing on the Stockade. Alarm and First shot.
Troops Storming the Stockade.
Hidiug Lalor at Dusk. Returning to Camp with Captured Diggers.
Stockade in Ruins.

FIFTY-FIVE YEARS AFTER.

A Trip Trough the City of Ballarat. Bridge Street. Sturt Street.
Unveiling the Lalor Statue. Up-to-Date Hydraulic Sluicing.
A Glimpse of the Eureka Monument.
A Grand Military March Past of the 7th Infantry Regiment.

4 Robbery Under Arms

1907 CHARLES MACMAHON

PC: MacMahon's Exquisite Pictures. SC: Charles MacMahon. From the novel by Rolf Boldrewood. PH: Byers Coates, William Duff. 5000 ft.

CAST: Jim Gerald (Warrigal), George Merriman (warder), Lance Vane (Inspector of Police), William Duff (trooper), Arthur Guest (curate), Rhoda Dendron.

The story of the young Marston brothers, who are led into a bushranging life by the notorious Captain Starlight, had been popular as a novel and a stage play for many years, and it became a favourite of Australian film producers. It inspired Spencer's *Captain Starlight, or Gentleman of the Road* (1911), and was refilmed in 1920 by Kenneth Brampton and in 1957 by the Rank Organisation. It was also frequently proposed as a feature by Raymond Longford and Ken G. Hall, but they were hampered by the New South Wales ban on bushranging films after 1912.

A relatively lavish production, *Robbery Under Arms* ran for over an hour and cost £1000. The action was staged by Charles MacMahon in bush locations near Sydney and further afield. The *Bulletin*, 14 November 1907, said: 'Charles MacMahon roamed the Western Plains, accompanied by a band of appropriately dressed mummers; and so soon as a spot was reached whereon Starlight had stuck-up someone, the apparatus was fixed, and wild, bloodsome proceedings began.' Other papers commented less flippantly that the film 'had evidently been prepared with the minutest care as to detail, particularly with respect to the scenery' (*Advertiser*, 11 May 1908), and that 'the scenes are laid in a rugged Australian background and pains have been taken to impart local colour, together with the atmosphere of the bushranging days' (*Register*, 11 May 1908). The cast included the juvenile actor Jim Gerald (later a vaudeville star) in blackface as Warrigal, the black tracker, and another young actor, William Duff, who began as a camera technician with the firm of Osborne and Jerdan in Melbourne and grew up to prominence in film distribution in Australia and New Zealand. The actors who played Starlight and the Marston brothers are not known.

The initial presentations of the film were elaborate: on 9 May 1908, at the Adelaide Town Hall, Alfred Boothman, a 'well-known actor', stood beside the screen and narrated the story, accompanied by 'realistic sound effects' by George Rocks, and an orchestra of piano and strings. The film was premièred by the Taits at the Athenaeum Hall, Melbourne, on 2 November 1907, and it followed a week later at the Oxford Theatre, Sydney. Audience response was enthusiastic. The *Sydney Morning Herald*, 11 November 1907, wrote that at the Oxford the film 'drew so large a crowd that the box-office was literally stormed, and the sale of tickets had to be stopped'. The film ran for a month in both Sydney and Melbourne and was frequently revived in the following years.

Charles MacMahon was a theatrical entrepreneur born in Bendigo, Victoria, in 1853. In partnership with his brother James he produced numerous plays and stage shows in Melbourne, including the comic opera *Paul Jones* with Nellie Stewart in 1890. Among many overseas celebrities whom they brought to Australia for theatrical tours was the American boxer, John L. Sullivan. As early as 1896, the MacMahons extended their theatrical repertoire to include film exhibition. After the production experiments of *Robbery Under Arms* and *For the Term of his Natural Life* (1908), Charles concentrated on film exhibition in Australia and New Zealand until he returned briefly to production in 1916 with a feature-length travelogue, *London by Day and Night*. He died in Melbourne on 27 June 1917.

5 For the Term of his Natural Life

1908 CHARLES MACMAHON

P: Charles MacMahon, E. J. Carroll, Messrs Gunn, Osborne and Jerdan. From the novel by Marcus Clarke. PH: Byers Coates. 2000 ft.

CAST: Martyn Keith (Rufus Dawes), Rosie Knight Phillips (Sylvia Vickers), Mrs Barry Lane (Mrs Vickers), Frank Kenny (Lord Bellasis), Augustus Neville (Gabbett), Roland Conway (Reverend North), Mr Jerdan (Reverend Meekin), Fred Francis (Lieutenant Frere), Charles Morse (Jemmy Vetch).

This collection of highlights from Marcus Clarke's complex novel of the convict days was the first of several adaptations for the screen. It was based on a popular stage version, and according to the *Bulletin*, 13 August 1908, the story had been 'severely edited, but the boiling-down was evidently done by a man who knew his business, for the continuity of the yarn is quite unbroken'. The film begins in England with a murder on Hampstead Heath for which Rufus Dawes is wrongly arrested and sentenced to transportation as a convict to Van Diemen's Land. The bitter life of the convicts is depicted, culminating in Dawes's escape. In disguise, he joins a boat to sail to freedom, and on board meets his long-lost love, Sylvia. In a raging storm, the boat founders, and as it sinks, Dawes and Sylvia are united in an eternal embrace.

For all its brevity, no expense was spared in the production, and the cost rose to the enormous sum of £7000. Cameramen and cast travelled to Port Arthur in Tasmania to shoot scenes in the ruins of the convict settlement. A much-publicized sequence showing the burning of a sailing ship was staged with a model ship in a tank; overhead views of the scene made the *Bulletin*, 31 December 1908, wonder whether they had been 'flicker-graphed from a captive balloon'.

The returns more than justified the expense, for when it was released in Sydney at the Queen's Hall on 8 August 1908 it became an immediate hit, and ran for an extraordinary eight weeks. The *Bulletin*, 31 December 1908, found the film 'marred by some unconsciously funny effects . . . the melancholy perish of Rufus Dawes and Sylvia on the sinking ship—the same carried out with agonising gyrations by earnest impersonators—was almost laughable, though it would have been impious to laugh'. In its first release in Victoria through the Tait brothers, the screening was accompanied by Alfred Boothman, who provided a resonant descriptive commentary, which the *Bulletin* found far in excess of the action on the screen: Boothman would 'split the dark with a remark, such as "A terrific struggle takes place"—whereupon a number of persons on the sheeting entered into a life-and-death grapple with the fury of listless undertakers'. For all its faults, the film was an enduring success, and was frequently revived.

6 The Life and Adventures of John Vane, the Notorious Australian Bushranger

1910 S. A. FITZGERALD

PC: Spencer's Pictures. PH: Ernest Higgins. CAST: Jim Gerald, Lance Vane, Max Clifton.

John Vane is a member of Ben Hall's gang of bushrangers; after a succession of criminal activities he decides to reform; he surrenders to a priest and expiates his sins in prison; fifteen years later he emerges from jail at peace with the world, a living example of the moral lesson, 'Often from evil cometh good'.

The film, made by an experienced theatre showman, S. A. (Stephen Australia) Fitzgerald, screened to large audiences at Spencer's Olympia Theatre, Melbourne, from 12 March 1910. The *Bulletin*, 17 March 1910, reviewed it with customary brevity and wit: 'The picture is an admirable work of local production, and, as Vane becomes an admirable person after his career of crime, the whole film is a rare hash of saintliness and sensation.'

6 Cozens Spencer

Although a routine story, *The Life and Adventures of John Vane* figures as a landmark in Australian cinema, as the first recorded involvement in narrative film production by Charles Cozens Spencer, one of the boldest and most visionary showmen in the early years of the industry. Born in London as Spencer Cozens, he began exhibiting films in Canada, and there married Eleanor Huntley, who played an active part in his business affairs under the romantic name of Senora Spencer. They took their limelight equipment and films to New Zealand and then to Australia in June 1905. Spencer travelled around Australia as an exhibitor, and after a film-buying trip to Europe, returned early in 1908 to lease the Lyceum Hall in Sydney, which he remodelled as a permanent venue for film presentations. Promoting his Lyceum shows with a wide range of ingenious gimmicks (including Senora Spencer as Australia's only woman projectionist), he quickly established primacy in the trade. From this profitable base he soon ventured into other areas of the film business, and in June 1908 established a production unit, headed by the photographer Ernest Higgins (later joined by his brothers Arthur and Tasman), making topical newsreels and 'scenics' for inclusion in his programmes. The production unit also ventured into occasional narrative films in 1910 and 1911, most of them under the direction of Raymond Longford. Spencer's operations, both as exhibitor and film producer, gradually spread around Australia, and he trained an efficient and respected staff who later became prominent in the film trade, including Herc

McIntyre, Stanley N. Wright, and Alan J. Williamson.

In 1912 Spencer planned a major extension of his film production activity and constructed an £8000 studio at Rushcutters Bay, Sydney. Employing Raymond Longford as his production supervisor, Spencer opened the studio on 16 August 1912 with a grand public ceremony and the production of a costume romance, *The Midnight Wedding*. To safeguard his new empire, Spencer formed a public company to manage his affairs. The decision was a fundamental error: Spencer was an aggressive individualist and found it difficult to work with a board of directors. While he was absent on a trip abroad his directors elected to merge the company with the combine of Australasian Films. With this action, the most lavishly equipped of all Australian film studios became the property of the organization least interested in local production. Longford was dismissed and production scaled down. Only at Spencer's insistence did Australasian agree to the production of *The Shepherd of the Southern Cross* (1914), but when it failed, the board voted against any continuation of feature production. Emotionally defeated by the decision, Spencer resigned from the board and withdrew from any further direct involvement in the film trade. His wife, however, ventured into business deals of her own, as an exhibitor in Newcastle and Brisbane, and bitter litigation followed in which Australasian sued Spencer for alleged breach of contract. The case was finally settled out of court when Senora Spencer's exhibition interests were sold to Australasian. Following the court case, the Spencers left Australia and settled in Canada. Nothing more was heard from them until September 1930 when Spencer's nerves collapsed; he ran amok, shooting others and then himself.

6 Senora Spencer

7 The Squatter's Daughter, or The Land of the Wattle

1910 BERT BAILEY

P: William Anderson. From the play by Bert Bailey and Edmund Duggan. PH: Orrie Perry. 6000(?) ft.

CAST: Olive Wilton (Violet Enderby), Bert Bailey (Archie McPherson), Edmund Duggan (Ben Hall), J. H. Nunn (James Harrington), Rutland Beckett (Dudley Harrington), George Cross (Tom Bathurst), George Mackenzie (Nick Harvey), Temple Harrison (Nulla Nulla), Edwin Campbell (Billy), Fred Kehoe, C. Rossmore, W. Chainey and C. Moore (Ben Hall's gang), Max Clifton (Jim S. Kenit), Kathleen Lorimer (Biddy), Fanny Erris (Jenny Thornton), Lily Bryer (Virginia Spraggins), Florence Ritcher (Sarah Lynch).

Edmund Duggan and Bert Bailey (sometimes using the joint pseudonym of Albert Edmunds) were actors who teamed together in 1905 to write a stage melodrama, *The Squatter's Daughter*, which became an immediate commercial success. Productions were staged by the William Anderson company, usually with Duggan as Ben Hall, his sister Eugenie as the heroine, and Bailey as the hero, Archie, a 'new chum' from England. Years later, in 1933, the play was still well enough known to lend its title and basic situation to a film by Ken G. Hall.

The story depicted the rivalry between two neighbouring sheep stations, Enderby (managed by a woman, Violet) and Waratah (managed by a weak-willed rich boy who is manipulated by a villainous overseer). The plot introduced several exploits of the bushranger Ben Hall, and showed the moment of his death. Other scenes included a dramatic shearing competition and 'an Aboriginal wedding'.

The film cost an estimated £1000 to produce. The star was Olive Wilton, an English actress whom William Anderson had brought to Australia in 1910. She remained in Australia as a star for J. C. Williamson, and later was a leading figure in Tasmanian theatre. Shooting began in June or July 1910 on locations near Melbourne, with Anderson's troupe under the personal supervision of Bert

7 Bert Bailey

Bailey. A *Bulletin* correspondent, on 14 July 1910, noted the delight of the local residents in receiving 'Bilanderson shows for nothing'. In the cause of realism, an expert horsewoman, Mrs Hassett, stood in for Olive Wilton in the riding scenes, and the *Bulletin's* observer wrote with enthusiasm that 'one thing the picture-audience will have that the theatre is done out of—*real rides*'. The greater advantage of film for staging action scenes was also evident in the escape of the Aboriginal boy, Nulla Nulla, from Ben Hall's camp; the boy is seen running through the bush with Hall's men on horseback in close pursuit, with far more excitement generated than had been possible on the stage.

Anderson first 'unwound' the film on 4 August 1910 at the Victorian country town of Colac, and after a short tour through other rural centres, it opened on 29 October at the Athenaeum Hall, Melbourne, for a remarkably successful season. Billed as 'The Longest Picture Ever Filmed', it appeared in Sydney at an open-air theatre, the Olympia, on 5 November. The *Bulletin*, 17 November 1910, found 'enough horse and girl in it to appeal to crowded houses six nights a week', and recorded much cheering and laughter from the audience.

Bailey and Duggan collaborated on several more plays, all reliant on melodrama, slapstick and Australian sentiment. By far the most successful commercially was *On Our Selection*, which they adapted from Steele Rudd's stories in 1912. Bailey was born in New Zealand on 11 June 1868 and was raised in Sydney. He first entered vaudeville as a tambourine player and singer, and in 1889 joined a touring theatrical company led by Duggan. In 1900 he became a comedian with William Anderson's company in Sydney, but retained a close working relationship with Duggan. His most famous role by far was the part of Dad Rudd in *On Our Selection*, which he played repeatedly from 1912 until 1940, initially on stage and later on screen. He died in Sydney on 30 March 1953.

8 Thunderbolt

1910 JOHN GAVIN

PC: Southern Cross Motion Pictures. P: H. A. Forsyth. From the novel *Three Years with Thunderbolt* by Ambrose Pratt. PH: A. J. Moulton. Over 3000 ft.

CAST: John Gavin (Thunderbolt), Ruby Butler, H. A. Forsyth.

Frederick Ward is a young citizen of Windsor, N.S.W., who goes droving to earn money for his wedding. He is suspected of cattle duffing, is arrested and sentenced to seven years' imprisonment. He escapes from prison on Cockatoo Island in a daring and historic swim across the waters to freedom. He soon learns that grief has caused the death of his fiancée and he vows to wreak vengeance on the law, which has caused so much suffering. The film continues with the story of his life as the notorious bushranger, Captain Thunderbolt; he is rescued from a police trap by a half-caste girl, raids a country hotel, and dies after a gallant struggle with the police.

The story was filmed in Lithgow and Hartley Vale in the Blue Mountains, with historic buildings in the area as backgrounds. Extras were recruited from among local miners, who were then on strike; they received the generous fee of £1 per day and free meals for riding their own horses as bushrangers and troopers. The producer, H. A. (Bert) Forsyth, was himself an expert horseman and took part in the riding scenes. The film opened in Sydney at the Queen's Theatre on 12 November 1910 for a long season of one month, and it was frequently revived.

John Francis Henry Gavin was born in 1875 in Sydney, and entered production after a long career on the stage as an actor, including ten years with the Bland Holt company and much experience in vaudeville. After making three bushranging films for Forsyth, he was engaged to direct a series of films in the early months of 1911 for the new production partnership of Crick and Finlay. In mid-1911 Gavin branched out on his own and

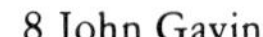

8 John Gavin

8 *Thunderbolt*

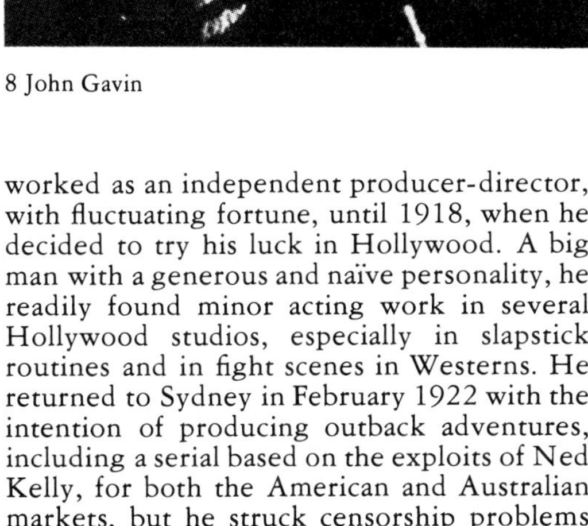

worked as an independent producer-director, with fluctuating fortune, until 1918, when he decided to try his luck in Hollywood. A big man with a generous and naïve personality, he readily found minor acting work in several Hollywood studios, especially in slapstick routines and in fight scenes in Westerns. He returned to Sydney in February 1922 with the intention of producing outback adventures, including a serial based on the exploits of Ned Kelly, for both the American and Australian markets, but he struck censorship problems and failed to raise the necessary capital, and in May 1923 he went back to work in Hollywood. Late in 1925 he returned again to Sydney and directed his last film, *Trooper O'Brien* (1928). He died in Sydney on 6 January 1938. In all of his work he was supported by his wife Agnes, who occasionally acted in his films but more often wrote them. Making a team with more enthusiasm and stubborn persistence than talent, the Gavins occasionally hit upon the right formula for commercial success, most notably with *The Martyrdom of Nurse Cavell* (1916), but most of their productions were 'quickies', and Gavin emerges clearly as a colourful lone wolf, lured onwards by the romance of production but lacking any marked ability to fulfil his ambition.

9 Moonlite [Captain Moonlite]

1910 JOHN GAVIN

PC: Southern Cross Motion Pictures. P, SC: H. A. Forsyth. PH: A. J. Moulton. 3750 ft.
CAST: John Gavin (Captain Moonlite), H. A. Forsyth, Ruby Butler, Agnes Gavin (Bunda).

The film depicts the career of Captain Moonlite, the 'gentleman bushranger . . . who robbed the rich for the poor, and never wronged a woman'. Highlights include Moonlite's arrest by the Victorian police, his escape from jail, and the robbery of gold escorts and banks.

Location scenes were shot at Victoria Barracks, Sydney, and in the bush around Lithgow. Gavin's wife, Agnes, played a supporting role in blackface as an Aboriginal 'gin', Bunda. Gavin described the film as 'a bushranging saga in the grand manner, with enough dead troopers to warrant a later severe censorship'. In addition to violence done to the police, the film was far from condemnatory of Moonlite's life of crime, as the Brisbane *Daily Mail*, 13 March 1911, commented: 'notwithstanding the lawlessness of Moonlite's career, there is so much genuine kindness to his nature and so much true manliness that he gained the appreciation and won the hearts of all those present'.

The film was premièred by Forsyth at an open-air theatre in the centre of Sydney on 31 December 1910. Audiences were warmly responsive and Gavin later recalled (in *Everyones*, 9 May 1923) that the film 'earned a fortune' for its backers. The production cost was advertised as over £1000.

9 Shooting *Moonlite* in the streets of Lithgow

10 It is Never Too Late to Mend

1911 W. J. LINCOLN

PC: J. and N. Tait. From the novel by Charles Reade. SC: W. J. Lincoln. PH: Orrie Perry. 4000ft.
CAST: Stanley Walpole.

Charles Reade's novel (published in 1856) had long been a popular exposé of the misery of the prison system in England and in Australian convict settlements. It had been dramatized by Reade himself and for several decades was widely performed on the stage in Britain and Australia. This film adaptation of the play was made in Melbourne and portrayed 'with the greatest realism' the trial of the hero and his experiences in British prisons and as a convict transported to Australia. It opened at the Olympia Theatre, Sydney, on 7 January 1911, and attracted record crowds.

W. J. Lincoln began as a playwright and stage actor in Melbourne and developed into one of Australia's earliest specialists in screen-writing. He became involved in film first as an exhibitor, managing tours of J. C. Williamson's Bio-Tableau (a presentation of various imported film items) in New Zealand and Australia with substantial success in 1904 and 1905. He later managed an outdoor cinema in Melbourne, the St Kilda Paradise Gardens. After his first feature for J. and N. Tait, he became the main director for their new company, Amalgamated Pictures, and later in 1911 made at least six films for them in their Melbourne studio. Amalgamated withdrew from feature production early in 1912, and in July 1913 Lincoln formed his own company with the actor Godfrey Cass and produced a series of short features, also in Melbourne. This enterprise failed and Lincoln's career began to falter, partly because of his problems with alcohol. When J. C. Williamson bought the Lincoln-Cass studio, Lincoln was hired by them to write (but not direct) scenarios for several films in 1915. Lincoln's last films as director in 1916 were his own productions, but none succeeded commercially. He died in August 1917 while working on a scenario called *The Worst Woman in Sydney.*

11 Stanley Crick at Pathé Frères

11 Ben Hall and his Gang

1911 JOHN GAVIN

PC: Crick and Finlay. SC: Agnes Gavin. PH: Herbert Finlay. 3000 ft.
CAST: John Gavin (Ben Hall).

This tale about the bushranger Ben Hall was screened first at the Colonial Theatre, Sydney, for a three-day season, commencing on 30 January 1911.

Gavin announced early in January that he had severed his connection with H. A. Forsyth and intended to produce his own bushranging films. He quickly found new backers in Stanley Crick and Herbert Finlay, both of whom were on the staff of Pathé Frères in Sydney, Crick as manager and Finlay as chief cameraman, working mainly on newsreel assignments. Crick and Finlay formed a partnership and commissioned Gavin to produce for them, giving him considerable freedom to select his own casts and to find his own scripts (most of which were written by his wife, Agnes). *Ben Hall and his Gang* was the first of four films that Gavin made for Crick and Finlay in quick succession in the first half of the year. Despite distribution problems, Crick and Finlay decided to expand their operation and establish production on a far more intensive basis in the Australian Photo-Play Company, formed in June 1911. Gavin, however, did not stay long with the new company; he later claimed (in *Everyones*, 9 May 1923) that he regarded the expansion as excessive given the limitations of the local market, and he continued production on his own on a more modest and erratic level.

Stanley Sadler Crick was born in Tasmania on 9 October 1888. He joined the Melbourne office of Pathé Frères and became manager of the Sydney branch in 1909. After his production venture failed in mid-1912 with the closing of the Australian Photo-Play Company, Crick turned to distribution as managing director of the Express Film Service, and in 1914 became the partner of John C. Jones in another distribution service. In 1919 he was appointed Victorian manager of the Fox Film Corporation, soon became managing director of Fox's Australian operation and held that post until his retirement in 1938. Through his position in Fox he also served for many years as the chairman of directors of Hoyts Theatres. In addition to his work in the film trade, Crick was active in local government; he was elected an alderman on the Sydney City Council in 1935 and was Lord Mayor of Sydney from 1940 to 1942.

His original partner, Herbert Finlay, began in films as a photographer and exhibitor of topical news items in Melbourne in the late 1890s. He was a member of the biograph company employed by Johnson and Gibson to tour with *The Story of the Kelly Gang* around Australia in 1907, and in 1910 he joined Pathé to produce the Sydney edition of their weekly newsreel. After his involvement in the Australian Photo-Play Company, he photographed the 1912 production of *The Life Story of John Lee.* He was seriously injured in a film fire and spent several years on the fringe of the industry as a travelling exhibitor. He eventually renewed his association with John Gavin in the production of *Trooper O'Brien* (1928).

12 Captain Midnight, the Bush King

1911 ALFRED ROLFE

PC: Spencer's Pictures. PH: Ernest Higgins. CAST: Alfred Rolfe (Edgar Dalmore/Captain Midnight), Lily Dampier (Elsa), Raymond Longford.

This bushranging drama was the first of three films made for Spencer by Alfred Rolfe (real name Alfred Roker) and his wife Lily Dampier. Both had acted on the stage in *The Bush King* as members of the famous theatrical troupe managed by her father, Alfred Dampier. The three films appeared in close succession during the first half of 1911, at a time when the Dampier company was disintegrating, and the cast of each film employed 'all that is left of the Dampier combination'.

The setting is colonial Australia: Edgar Dalmore, the son of a wealthy station-owner, is wrongfully accused of murdering his father, and is sentenced to jail for life. Later he escapes and becomes the leader of a bushranging gang, using the name of Captain Midnight. In a raid on a gold escort, Midnight is recognized by the police and is forced to hide in the cottage of a girl, Elsa, who has long nurtured love for him. Edgar, however, loves another, Thelma Warren, and after several further adventures he renounces his life of crime and marries her. At the church he is unexpectedly denounced as an escaped criminal, but 'his good angel', Elsa, appears with evidence to prove that he is innocent of the murder of his father. At last free to build a new life with Thelma, Edgar departs with his bride, leaving the pathetic figure of Elsa alone and forsaken, 'finding consolation in the sympathy of her faithful horse'. A few lines of soulful verse by Joseph L. Goodman appeared on the screen as a final touch of sentiment, which drew a 'hearty outburst of applause' from the audience (*Sydney Morning Herald*, 8 February 1911).

Shooting took place in and around Sydney, with scenes at Manly and in the Blue Mountains. The dramatic highlights included Midnight's daring leap from a cliff into a river, a scene that soon became obligatory for bushrangers in Australian cinema folklore. His escape by swimming away amid a hail of bullets from the police was warmly applauded by audiences.

12 Alfred Rolfe

The film open at the Lyceum Theatre, Sydney, on 9 February 1911. The *Sydney Morning Herald* regretted that Australian melodramas were so 'frequently identified with the murderous doings of ruffians carefully whitewashed, and presented as heroes', but admitted that *Captain Midnight* represented 'a cleverly contrived example of its class'.

Release in England was also promptly arranged by Spencer, and a print was previewed there in August. The London trade paper, *Bioscope*, 31 August 1911, commended it with enthusiasm: 'This is an excellent film, with a beautiful ending, and we think it will have a very considerable vogue amongst all who love wonderful scenery and the freedom of true life.' The paper even predicted that if the film attracted the success it deserved, England might witness 'a sudden exodus of photographers and stock companies to the Land of the Rabbits'.

After his initial trio of filmed plays for Spencer, Rolfe turned from his career as an actor to specialize in film direction, and quickly became one of Australia's most prolific craftsmen. In mid-1911 he joined the Australian Photo-Play Company as their principal director, and in quick succession over the next year made a total of twenty-five features (not all of which have been identified). His next major engagement as director was with Australasian Films in 1915 and 1916, where he directed 'industrials', short programme fillers (including a series of 'picture songs', which offered visual settings of popular melodies) and narrative films, including *The Hero of the Dardanelles* and *The Loyal Rebel* (both 1915). He eventually abandoned show business and became associated with amateur athletic organizations in Sydney. He died on 9 September 1943 aged 81.

13 Frank Gardiner, the King of the Road

1911 JOHN GAVIN

PC: Crick and Finlay. SC: Agnes Gavin. PH: Herbert Finlay. 3500 (4000?) ft.
CAST: John Gavin (Frank Gardiner).

This adventure was the second that Gavin made quickly and cheaply (probably for less than £300) for the Crick and Finlay partnership. The film surveyed the main events in the bushranging career of Gardiner, including his daring leap from a cliff to escape pursuers. The tale ended with a view of a ship in full sail outside Sydney Heads to represent Gardiner's final exile to America. A review in the Hobart *Daily Post*, 21 August 1911, commented: 'The scene in which Gardiner and the gang bail up the police is about the best piece of acting in the picture, the audience being shown in a marvellously realistic manner how that notorious action was performed. The picture is typically Australian, and the bush scenes which are brought into being are very fine indeed.' The film was released in Sydney by Victoria Pictures on 27 February 1911.

14 The Mystery of a Hansom Cab

1911 W. J. LINCOLN

PC: Amalgamated Pictures. From the novel by Fergus Hume. PH: Orrie Perry. 4000(?) ft.

The Mystery of a Hansom Cab was the first film released under the banner of Amalgamated Pictures, a new company formed in March 1911 by the producer-exhibitor combination of Johnson and Gibson, and J. and N. Tait. The company produced numerous newsreels and features during 1911 and early 1912, before withdrawing from feature production and merging with its main competitors in the combine of Australasian Films in November 1912.

The story had long been popular as a novel (published in 1886) and as a play. It begins with the murder of a playboy, Oliver White, as he is driven home late at night in a hansom cab. The steps leading to the solution of the crime are then staged in front of well-known Melbourne landmarks, including the Orient Hotel, the Melbourne Club, the Esplanade at St Kilda, the Melbourne Gaol and several prominent St Kilda homes. The *Bulletin*, 9 March 1911, had some reservations about the adaptation: the murder, which was supposed to occur at one o'clock in the morning, had been staged in the afternoon for the sake of better photography, and the secret of the murderer's identity was revealed too soon before the end; nevertheless 'the acting in the picture is generally good, and makes dumb show look more like an art than an aberration'.

The film, which ran for more than an hour, was screened at West's Glaciarium, Melbourne, on 4 March 1911 and proved a major success, even attracting unexpected patronage from the Governor of Victoria. In 1925 the story was refilmed by Arthur Shirley.

15 Captain Starlight, or Gentleman of the Road

1911 ALFRED ROLFE

PC: Spencer's Pictures. From the play by Alfred Dampier, based on the novel *Robbery Under Arms* by Rolf Boldrewood. PH: Ernest Higgins. Over 3000 ft.
CAST: Alfred Rolfe, Lily Dampier, Raymond Longford, Stanley Walpole, Augustus Neville.

The second of the Alfred Dampier stage productions recorded on film by Alfred Rolfe was loosely based on the novel *Robbery Under Arms* and told the story of the young Marston boys, who are led into a life of bushranging by the gallant outlaw, Captain Starlight. The *Sydney Morning Herald*, 18 March 1911, described it as an 'elaborate series of clearly-screened pictures . . . [which] open at the home of the Marstons, passes on to an exciting race for the Gold Cup, won by Rainbow, shows how the bushrangers stick up the mail coach at the Rocky Rises, and exhibits Sir Ferdinand Morringer threatened with death in Terrible Hollow at the hands of the brutal Dan Moran, and his rescue by Starlight. One of the most applauded of the scenes . . . was the burning of the stables and the rescue of the horses, and Starlight's Last Stand also excited enthusiasm.'

In advertising the film, Spencer took a defensive stand against a current wave of criticism of the supposedly immoral bushranging genre: 'The work from which the main incidents . . . are taken may be given a place amongst the CLASSICS OF AUSTRALIAN FICTION, and in using the story for motion picture illustration Mr Spencer is persuaded that, whilst it naturally contains elements that perhaps conflict with strict LEGAL AND MORAL RECTITUDE, yet this adaptation, though it preserves the healthy, vigorous and breezy atmosphere of the Australian bush, and reveals courageous traits and heroic impulses in desperate men, throws no HALO OF ROMANCE OVER CRIME, but, on the contrary, brings home the oft-told truths that the WAY OF THE TRANSGRESSOR IS HARD; and that still, for the evil doer—though his sins were as scarlet—there is yet open the path of redemption, leading to REPENTANCE! PARDON! PEACE!' (*Age*, 5 April 1911).

The film opened at Spencer's Lyceum Theatre, Sydney, on 16 March 1911 and ran for a profitable extended season.

16 A Tale of the Australian Bush
[Ben Hall, the Notorious Bushranger]

1911 GASTON MERVALE

PC: Australian Life Biograph Company. SC: P. W. Marony. 2500 ft.
CAST: A. J. Patrick (Ben Hall), Godfrey Cass (Melville), Harry Beaumont (Gilbert), James Martin (Keightley), Gilbert Emery (Chief of Police), Harrie Ireland (Mrs Keightley), Isma Owen (Robbie Hall), Louise Carbasse (Mrs Hall).

This bushranging adventure promised 'a sensational, clean tale . . . that will please the masses and not offend anybody'. The highlights were advertised as: 'Ben Hall and his Wife and Child at Home—the Duel between Ben Hall and Melville—Ben Hall accused of Stealing a Horse—Ben Hall's Last Stand—The Death of Ben Hall' (*Brisbane Courier*, 3 October 1911).

It was privately previewed at the Glaciarium, Sydney, in mid-March 1911, under the title, *Ben Hall, the Notorious Bushranger*, but the first recorded public screening was not until 3 October at the Earl's Court, Brisbane, as *A Tale of the Australian Bush*. It made a quiet début for the Australian Life Biograph Company, a new enterprise based at a 'studio and factory' at Manly in Sydney, and using a regular troupe of players under the direction of a well-known actor, Gaston Mervale. Like other producers, the company foundered in May 1912 because of difficulties in placing its work on the market. One of the company's financial backers, Rhodes Speight, later commented (in *Theatre*, 1 January 1915): 'At one time the company was turning over £300 a week, and employing six lecturers. This shows that Australian productions were a success, and would have continued so, had it not been for—among other things—the methods adopted by [the] Australian combine.'

16 Gaston Mervale

16 Louise Lovely (Louise Carbasse)

Mervale's career as a film director was brief. After Australian Life Biograph closed down in 1912 he went to New York and worked in the U.S.A. for five years as an actor with various stage companies. He returned to Australia in 1917 under engagement to J. and N. Tait to produce new American plays for them in Australia and New Zealand. He continued to make minor film appearances until the late 1920s.

Mervale's stock acting company at Australian Life Biograph included Louise Carbasse, a teenage actress already playing adult roles, who later became one of the most successful of all Australians in establishing a Hollywood career. She had been working with George Marlow's theatrical company in Western Australia when Mervale sent her a telegram asking her to act in his films. In February 1912 she married Wilton Welch, a comedian and writer of melodramas and vaudeville sketches, and acted with him in local vaudeville after the film company failed. Late in 1914 she and Welch went to the U.S.A., and after further vaudeville performances she won a contract with Universal Pictures and her Hollywood career began. Carl Laemmle gave her the name Louise Lovely, and with Welch as her manager, she starred in numerous features for Universal, Fox and other companies. During the height of her fame, her success helped to lure many other young Australians to Hollywood in search of film careers. By 1923 her career had begun to wane, and she and Welch returned to vaudeville and eventually to Sydney, where they formed their own company and produced *Jewelled Nights* (1925).

Mervale's company also included a colourful Australian character actor, Gilbert Emery (sometimes billed as Gilbert Warren Emery). Of the many roles he played on stage and screen, his most popular by far was Ginger Mick in Raymond Longford's films of *The Sentimental Bloke* (1919) and *Ginger Mick* (1920). He later went to the U.S.A, and taught in an acting school until his death in Los Angeles on 24 December 1934, aged 52. He bore no relation to the British actor of the same name who made many films in Hollywood from the late 1920s.

17 The Luck of Roaring Camp

1911 W. J. LINCOLN

PC: Amalgamated Pictures. SC: W. J. Lincoln. From the story by Francis Bret Harte. PH: Orrie Perry. 4000 ft.
CAST: The George Marlow Dramatic Company, including Ethel Buckley, Robert Inman, John Cosgrove.

Only the title of this tale of the American West was related to the story by Bret Harte: the film was based more directly on a stage adaptation that had been performed for some time in Australia by George Marlow's Dramatic Company. Marlow's company provided the leading players for the film, with Marlow's wife, Ethel Buckley, as the heroine. The story, as the *Sydney Morning Herald*, 10 April 1911, noted, was well suited to screen adaptation; not only was the action 'complete in itself without the words', but also it teemed with 'thrilling incidents in the life of the hard-living westerners'. Set on the Californian goldfields, the story rose to a dramatic highlight with the seizure of the hero by an angry mob that wrongly believes him guilty of murder. He is on the point of being lynched when his sweetheart rides to the rescue, and he lives to round up the villains who tried to destroy him. Sequences included 'a splendid exhibition of horsemanship' by a group of roughriders especially recruited to the film for their skill. The film opened at the Glaciarium, Melbourne, on 25 March 1911, and in Sydney at the Palace Theatre on 8 April. Bret Harte's story inspired several other films with the same title by American producers, in 1910 and 1917 by Edison, and in 1937 by Monogram.

18 The Golden West

1911 GEORGE YOUNG

PC: Australian Film Syndicate. PH: Lacey Percival. 2500 ft.

'A romance of the west Australian goldfields', featuring 'magnificent scenery' and 'sensational rides', *The Golden West* was privately screened at the King's Theatre, Sydney, on 27 March 1911.

The Australian Film Syndicate was formed early in 1911 with the financial backing of a draper, a doctor and a squatter from Goulburn, N.S.W. The producer of the company's films was George Young, a retired stage manager from J. C. Williamson's, and brother of the comic opera star Florence Young. The technical department was run by Jack Wainwright and a young cinematographer, Lacey Percival. A camera and processing plant were bought and a small studio and laboratory set up in North Sydney. The enterprise was not, however, commercially viable; Alec Hellmrich, a distributor who tried to sell some of the syndicate's films, later recalled (in *Everyones*, 4 March 1925) that 'these pictures were very crude . . . and although I was successful in placing them, they had no drawing power, and were turned down by a number of exhibitors on account of their crudeness and unsuitability'.

Lacey Percival had worked in a photographic studio in West Wyalong before coming to Sydney in 1908 to find work as a projectionist. After gaining experience in cinematography with the Australian Film Sydicate, he was offered a contract with the Australian Photo-Play Company and worked there until the company closed down production. He then joined West's Pictures as a newsreel photographer, and when that company joined Australasian Films he remained in charge of its weekly newsreel, *Australasian Gazette*, as well as photographing numerous scenic novelties, sponsored documentaries and feature films. In 1925 he left Australasian to work as a freelance photographer and in 1927 took a position with Automatic Film Laboratories in Sydney. In 1935 he established his own laboratory, Percival Film Laboratories, which he operated until his retirement in 1948.

18 Lacey Percival

19 E. J. Cole

19 A Bushranger's Ransom, or A Ride for a Life

1911 E. J. COLE (?)

PC: Pathé Frères.
CAST: E. J. Cole's Bohemian Dramatic Company.

This bushranging drama was one of a series of 'purely Australian' films made by Pathé Frères early in 1911. It told the story of an incident that occurred near Bathurst, N.S.W., in 1863—the raid by Ben Hall upon the Keightley homestead. The Keightley family barricade themselves in the house and resist the attack of Hall's gang for six hours. In the fight one member of the gang, Mick Bourke, is accidentally shot by one of his comrades, and in severe pain begs to be put out of his misery, which Hall himself reluctantly does. Later when the Keightleys run out of ammunition they surrender, and Hall and his gang spend a night of feasting and drinking in the house. Hall offers to spare Keightley's life if his wife can bring a ransom payment of £500; he gives her eight hours to ride the thirty miles to Bathurst to collect the money from her father at the bank. Just as the time limit expires Mrs Keightley returns triumphantly with the money. Hall honours his word and departs, leaving the Keightleys in peace.

E. J. Cole and his Bohemian Company had long included the story of Ben Hall in their stage repertoire. Advertising boasted that the film had been shot where the events had actually taken place, and great emphasis was placed on the thrilling spectacle of Mrs Keightley's extraordinary ride at breakneck speed across the rough bush terrain. The film screened in Sydney at the Coliseum Theatre on 28 March 1911.

20 The Assigned Servant

1911 JOHN GAVIN

PC: Crick and Finlay. SC: Agnes Gavin. PH: Herbert Finlay. 4000 ft.
CAST: John Gavin, Alf Scarlett, Charles Woods, Dore Kurtz, Sid Harrison, Agnes Gavin.

This 'life story of a deported convict' was filmed during a month on location in the National Park near Sydney. The staging of the action there involved some authentic injuries, all of them captured by Gavin's camera: a fight on the brink of a 25-foot cliff resulted in one actor falling into the water below and being stunned; another actor fell badly from a horse and suffered severe cuts; and a 'bushranger' knocked out several teeth of a 'policeman' during a fist fight.

The story begins in England with the arrest of Ralph Frawley for rabbit poaching, and his transportation to Van Diemen's Land as a convict. There he is assigned as a servant to a settler and falls in love with the daughter of the house. He marries her in secret but when this forbidden act is discovered he is sent back to prison for the rest of his term. One day he manages to escape in a spectacular leap for his life and a swim to liberty. Taking to the bush, he robs the Royal Mail and embarks on a life of crime. Later, in a fight with police, he is saved by an Aboriginal friend, and learning that his wife has died, he makes his way back to England.

The film was offered to exhibitors in March 1911, but the first recorded screening was not until 26 August at the Academy of Music, Launceston. A season at the Star Theatre, Melbourne, followed on 16 October.

21 Three Strings to her Bow

1911 GEORGE YOUNG

PC: Australian Film Syndicate.

'A fine farcical comedy', released at the King's Theatre, Sydney, on 10 April 1911.

22 Called Back

1911 W. J. LINCOLN

PC: Amalgamated Pictures. SC: W. J. Lincoln. From the novel by Hugh Conway. PH: Orrie Perry. 4000 ft.
CAST: Arthur Styan.

This melodrama about international intrigue and murder was based on a play derived from a novel published in England in 1883. The story is set in Italy in the days of Garibaldi. Dr Ceneri gives money to support the Italian cause, including funds entrusted to him for the future welfare of his orphaned niece and nephew, Pauline and Anthony. When the children come of age they learn of his mishandling of the money, and a series of tragic events ensue, culminating in the murder of Anthony by the villain, Macari. The murder is witnessed by Pauline, who loses her reason. Gilbert Vaughan, a blind man who is lost, is also present when the crime is committed. He later regains his sight and finds evidence to prove that Macari is guilty. Pauline recovers her reason and she and Gilbert are married.

The film was staged in the Melbourne studio of Amalgamated Pictures, and it opened at the Glaciarium, Melbourne, on 15 April 1911. It was accompanied there by J. Ennis, 'a baritone lecturer [who] described the stirring incidents in organ tones', and Daisy Young, a vocalist (for scenes set in an Italian opera house). The *Bulletin*, 27 April 1911, commented that the film was 'very creditable' and that 'the cast is not pretentious, but does fairly'.

23 The Squatter's Son

1911 E. J. COLE (?)

PC: Pathé Frères.
CAST: E. J. Cole's Bohemian Dramatic Company.

The film tells a melodramatic tale in twenty-five scenes of the pioneering days in the outback. The main characters are two cousins representing 'the True and the False'. Their conflict involves a forged will, murder and a bushranging gang. In a climactic horseback escape, the hero is helped by an obedient 'Black Boy' who destroys a bridge to delay the pursuers. The Bijou Theatre, Melbourne, screened the film on 22 April 1911.

24 The Fatal Wedding

1911 RAYMOND LONGFORD

PC: Spencer's Pictures. SC: Raymond Longford.
PH: Arthur Higgins. 3500 ft.
CAST: Raymond Longford (Howard Wilson), Lottie Lyell (Mabel Wilson), Walter Vincent (Robert Curtis), Tom Cosgrove (Toto), Harry Saville (Peter Schwartz), George Ellis (Constable O'Reilly), Mr Henderson (Reverend Dr Lanceford), Miss Clare (Cora Williams), Helen Fergus (Bridget), Elsie Rennie (Jessie), Master Anson (Frankie), Jack Goodall.

An adventuress, Cora Williams, tries to destroy the happy marriage of Howard and Mabel Wilson so that she can have Howard for herself. She sows 'the seeds of suspicion' and succeeds in driving Howard and Mabel to divorce. Howard has custody of the children, Jessie and Frankie, but desperate to see them, Mabel enlists the aid of friends and abducts them. Five years later, Mabel and her children are living in poverty when she is discovered by Cora, who attempts to complete Mabel's destruction by poisoning her. Cora's plan fails and she next tries to frame little Jessie on a charge of theft, but that too fails. Eventually Cora is vanquished; the children make a tearful farewell to their slum friends (who form a 'tin can band' to play a song of farewell) and join their reconciled parents on a wealthier level of society.

One of the major films of 1911, *The Fatal Wedding* had been a stage favourite for many years, and Raymond Longford and Lottie Lyell had toured in New Zealand in the starring roles with the Clarke and Meynell company. The film production was staged largely indoors, in an artists' studio in Bondi; the roof was removed and six-foot reflectors (made with silver paper stretched over wooden frames) were used to improve the lighting. It opened at Spencer's Lyceum on 24 April 1911 and ran for an unprecedented five weeks. Similar commercial results occurred around Australia, and Longford later estimated (in *RCE* p.145) that for an outlay of £600 the film had netted some £16 000 in Australasia and England. The highlight of the screening in most major centres was the performance on stage of a children's chorus and a 'tin can band' to synchronize with the sentimental farewell scene on the screen.

Quite apart from the significance of the film in boosting Spencer's confidence in narrative production (leading to increasingly lavish productions as the year progressed), the film brought together three central figures in Australian film history—Raymond Longford, Lottie Lyell and Arthur Higgins—and it is a reflection of Spencer's business acumen that he recognized their talents and gathered such a gifted team in his service.

Longford's career as director began strongly with a series of commercially successful productions for Spencer, including *The Romantic Story of Margaret Catchpole* and *Sweet Nell of Old Drury* (both 1911). Born John Walter Longford on 23 September 1878 in Hawthorn, Victoria, the son of a prison warder, he later dropped his father's names of John Walter and adopted the names Raymond Hollis (after his mother's maiden name of Hollis). He had an active early life at sea and in the Boer War before becoming an actor with various touring stage companies in Australia and New Zealand. He acted in three films produced by Spencer early in 1911, and under Spencer's sponsorship he quickly became the most adventurous and capable of

24 Raymond Longford

24 Lottie Lyell

24 Arthur Higgins

Australian film directors. When Spencer's operations were absorbed into Australasian Films, Longford joined the Fraser film company as supervisor of its productions, and in 1914 directed *The Silence of Dean Maitland*, which became one of his biggest commercial successes. When the Frasers cancelled most of their production programme, allegedly because of pressure from Australasian, Longford spent the rest of his film career buffeted from company to company, growing progressively paranoid about the influence of the combine. His abilities continued at peak level into the 1920s: *The Sentimental Bloke* (1919) and *On Our Selection* (1920) became enduring works of art as well as impressive commercial successes, but nowhere did he find continuity of work. By the early 1930s he was employed only on minor productions, usually as associate director or as a character actor, and he soon turned his back on the film world to spend his last years working as a nightwatchman on the Sydney waterfront. He died on 2 April 1959 in Sydney, still calling himself 'the sentimental bloke'.

Through his most creative years Longford was closely associated with Lottie Lyell, until her death from tuberculosis on 21 December 1925. Born in Sydney on 23 February 1890 as Lottie Edith Cox, she acted with touring stage companies before joining Spencer in 1911 to play leading roles in Longford's film productions. She was an accomplished horsewoman and opportunities were often contrived in her films to display her riding skills. Her exact contribution to Longford's work can never be properly assessed; certainly she worked with him variously as actress, writer, associate director, art director and co-producer when his most important films were made, and the loss of her support was possibly a key factor in his creative decline after her death.

Arthur Embrey Higgins was another close associate of Longford's for many years. He was born in Tasmania on 25 October 1891, the brother of two other cinematographers, Ernest and Tasman. He followed Ernest to Sydney and was barely twenty when *The Fatal*

24 Raymond Longford in the 1950s

Wedding was shot. His career as a newsreel and documentary photographer flourished and he also worked on several features. He joined Longford again on the South Australian production, *The Woman Suffers* (1918), and remained with him to photograph *The Sentimental Bloke*, *On Our Selection* and others. In the late 1920s he turned briefly to feature film direction and production, but without marked success. After a long and active career as one of Australia's best known and most poetic cameramen, he died in Sydney on 22 September 1963.

25 Keane of Kalgoorlie

1911 JOHN GAVIN

PC: Crick and Finlay. SC: Agnes Gavin. From the play by E. W. O'Sullivan, based on the novel by Arthur Wright. PH: Herbert Finlay. 2500 ft.
CAST: John Gavin (Frank Keane), Agnes Gavin, Alf Scarlett.

Arthur Wright's novel first appeared as a serial in the Sydney sporting weekly, the *Referee*, and was dramatized for the stage by E. W. O'Sullivan, a Tasmanian author and parliamentarian. Set in the racing and gambling circles of Sydney, the story involves a mysterious murder in the Sydney Domain for which the hero is wrongly arrested. Highlights include the running of the Sydney Cup race and a scene in a 'two-up' gambling school. The film was offered to exhibitors in April 1911 but the first recorded screening was not until early October at the Town Hall, Hobart.

In 1927 Arthur Wright recalled the production of the film: 'The producer had to overcome many difficulties. There were no studios then, no Klieg lights to take the place of the sun. Interiors were taken in the open mostly, with the walls of rooms—canvas, etc.—at the mercy of the weather, and likely to collapse if the wind blew strongly. But he got through with it. Mob scenes did not cost a great deal . . . [For the two-up scene] the by-ways were scoured and a crowd secured willing to act for the fun of the thing. The Sydney Cup had to be included. The authorities would not allow Randwick course to be used for picture purposes, so a "scenic" picture of the running of a race in W.A. (the Perth Cup, I think) was joined up in the film . . . One scene had to show the hero . . . being released from Darlinghurst Gaol. Producer Gavin wished to show Keane actually emerging from the prison through the great gates. He discovered that at a certain hour the baker's cart was admitted into the gaol daily, so one morning he had his camera man ready with himself in character adjacent to the gates. The cart came along. The gates swung inward and as it passed within, Gavin, crouching close behind out of the sight of the warder, followed. The gates were closed and Gavin straightened up to confront a surprised and enraged attendant, who promptly conferred upon the picture hero the order of the boot. Again the gate swung open and Frank Keane emerged into focus and the cranking camera did the rest.' (*Everyones*, 5 January 1927)

26 One Hundred Years Ago

1911 GASTON MERVALE

PC: Australian Life Biograph Company. STORY: P. W. Marony. 2000 ft.
CAST: Louise Carbasse (Judith), Harrie Ireland, A. J. Patrick, Godfrey Cass, Alf Scarlett, James Martin, Harry Beaumont.

In this romantic melodrama, a convict on Norfolk Island is saved by the undying love of a woman in far-off England. She secures a free pardon for him and they are reunited happily back in the 'Old Country'.

One Hundred Years Ago was filmed at the Australian Life Biograph studio at Manly and screened at West's Princess and Palace Theatres, Sydney, for a week, commencing 8 May 1911.

27 The Five of Hearts, or Buffalo Bill's Love Story** [A Maiden's Distress]

1911 E. J. COLE (?)

PC: Pathé Frères.
CAST: E. J. Cole's Bohemian Dramatic Company.

This Western was presented by Empire Pictures at the Town Hall, Perth, on 10 May 1911, offering the following highlights: 'On the trail . . . In the Indian Camp; Rose Tortured; Surrounded by Daggers; Rescued; Buffalo Bill at the Stake; The Indian Chief's Fight with Knives; Black Bill's Lair . . . ' A report of the screening in the *West Australian* on 11 May described it as 'A dramatic picture, in which all the actors are Australians, [depicting] an exciting episode on the outskirts of the Indian reservation, made famous by the exploits of Buffalo Bill and his cowboys.'

E. J. Cole and his Bohemian Dramatic Company were renowned for their noisy and action-packed stage productions of tales from the American West, and Buffalo Bill was a Cole speciality. It is likely that footage from an E. J. Cole production held in the National Film Archive under the title of *A Maiden's Distress* is actually from this 1911 film.

28 The Lost Chord

1911 W. J. LINCOLN

PC: Amalgamated Pictures. PH: Orrie Perry.

Inspiration for the film lay in the sentimental song of the same name, which had long been a standard favourite in England and Australia. The music had been written by Sir Arthur Sullivan as a tribute to his dying brother, and the words ('Seated one day at the organ . . . ') were written by Adelaide Procter. The film was screened at Tait's Glaciarium, Melbourne, on 13 May 1911, with 'descriptive singing' on stage by Isabella Bull, accompanied by the 'Grand Organ'. Sullivan's ballad also provided the basis for a British film released in 1917.

27 *The Five of Hearts* Frame enlargement

29 Dan Morgan

1911

PC: Spencer's Pictures.

This bushranging drama opened at Spencer's Lyceum Theatre, Sydney, on 22 May 1911. A day later, a review in the *Daily Telegraph* praised both its moral and technical qualities: 'there isn't in the picture a single feature to attract sympathy for the ruthless robber and murderer . . . [Spencer] has apparently taken the raw official records of the heartless Dan Morgan and constructed the picture story in all its natural horrors. One is shown a series of sensational encounters, in which Morgan murders his colleagues in cold blood, shoots wholesale his pursuers from behind safe shelter, and robs, burns, and outrages indiscriminately throughout his brief career . . . His ignominious end, when he is shot by a dozen bullets and sinks convulsively imprecating in a mean pool, closes the story. The pictures have been finely prepared, and are amongst the most successful samples of moving photography that Mr. Spencer has so far exhibited in Sydney.'

30 Sentenced for Life

1911 E. J. COLE (?)

PC: Pathé Frères (?).
CAST: E. J. Cole's Bohemian Dramatic Company (?).

This 'Australian drama of the convict days' was possibly an earlier production under a new title. It screened in Perth at the Shaftesbury Picture Gardens on 10 June 1911.

31 The Life of Rufus Dawes

1911 ALFRED ROLFE

PC: Spencer's Pictures. SC: Alfred Rolfe. From the novel, *For the Term of his Natural Life*, by Marcus Clarke. PH: Ernest Higgins. 4000 ft.
CAST: Alfred Rolfe, Lily Dampier, Raymond Longford (Gabbett).

These highlights from Marcus Clarke's novel of the convict days in Van Diemen's Land were shot in and around Sydney, with Raymond Longford in the role of the convict cannibal, Gabbett. The film opened at the Broadway Theatre, Sydney, on 19 June 1911.

32 A Ticket in Tatts

1911 GASTON MERVALE

PC: Australian Life Biograph Company. STORY: P. W. Marony. 2000 ft.
CAST: A. J. Patrick (John Hare), Alf Scarlett (Dick Fallon), Godfrey Cass (Fred Wynne), James Martin (clergyman), Louise Carbasse (Mrs Fallon), Harrie Ireland (Mrs Hare), Harry Beaumont.

A Ticket in Tatts was made by the Australian Life Biograph Company in its Manly studio in Sydney, and aimed 'to show how racing, if carried to excess, can run away with a man's balance, and make him unfit for the stern side of life' (*Daily Telegraph*, 17 June 1911). A penniless and unemployed wastrel, John Hare, wins a lottery and spends his fortune on alcohol and race-track gambling. Mixing in unsavoury society, he is framed for a murder and suffers much mental agony before the real culprit is exposed. Now a repentant man, John returns to a sober life and is reunited with his family.

The film was shown at the Lyric Theatre, Sydney, from 19 June 1911.

33 Attack on the Gold Escort

1911

A drama of the Australian goldfields, screened at the Alhambra Theatre, Sydney, on 26 June 1911.

34 The Miner's Daughter

1911

A drama of the gold diggings, screened in Adelaide by the People's Picture Company on 28 June 1911.

35 In the Days of 49

1911

Set in the days of 'gold fever' on the early Australian goldfields, the film told the story of a 'fickle woman' and how she was saved from herself. It was presented by Empire Pictures at the Town Hall, Perth, on 26 July 1911, and it screened in Hobart on 12 August.

36 Moora Neya, or The Message of the Spear

1911 ALFRED ROLFE

PC: Australian Photo-Play Company. 1500 ft.
CAST: Ethel Phillips, Stanley Walpole, Charles Villiers.

The Australian Photo-Play Company was established in June 1911 under the management of Stanley Crick. The company had arisen out of the Crick and Finlay partnership, which had produced four films by John Gavin earlier in the year. Crick's new company was an ambitious undertaking, with capital of £20 000, offices in Sydney and Melbourne, and two studios planned for construction in Sydney. By November 1911 Crick claimed to be employing about forty staff, with a camera department in the charge of Herbert Finlay, a laboratory managed by A. O. Segerberg, and an acting troupe under the direction of Alfred Rolfe. The staff was young (only one of the principal members was over 30) and their work often displayed an ingenuity that set them far ahead of their local contemporaries, many of whom still regarded film as an adjunct to stage productions.

The company did not survive long, but it was prolific, making a score of films in less than a year. Crick had hoped for government support in the form of a protective tariff to limit the number of imported films, but as many later film-makers found, governments were reluctant to act. Because of the inadequacy of theatre outlets, especially after the merging of the main competition forces in the combine of Australasian Films and Union Theatres, the company never became financially stable. In March 1912 the marketing of the films was assigned to Gaumont, but with no evident improvement, and production ground to a halt in mid-1912.

Their first melodrama offered forty-one scenes of bush and station life, 'with a reality so intense that the audience wants to get up and boil a billy' (*Bulletin*, 17 August 1911). On a station west of the Darling, an evil overseer makes advances to the station-owner's daughter, but Harry Earl, the girl's lover, gives him a thrashing. In revenge, the overseer urges some local Aborigines to kill Harry in his remote hut. After 'a weird and fantastic' corroboree, the tribe departs to capture Harry, but one responsible tribesman, Budgerie, manages to alert the station men by writing a message on a spear: 'Blacks kill Harry tonight 30 Miles Hut, HELP!' The stockmen ride to the rescue and save Harry just as the Aborigines perform a 'Death Dance' around him. The overseer is killed and the lovers reunited.

Advertisements claimed that this was 'the first film introducing the Aboriginals in their native haunts and war dances'. Alfred Rolfe and his crew travelled to Brewarrina on the Darling River, in the central north of New South Wales, to film scenes with 'one of the wildest tribes of the Never Never Land'. One advertisement described some of the 'dangers' braved in making the film: 'after much trouble, the blacks were induced to face the camera. During the corroboree the natives became excited, and threw spears and boomerangs, one hitting the machine. Then, again, where the natives attack the hut, they hit the man who was acting the part of the Old Shepherd on the head with a nulla nulla, stunning him, and severely handled Mr Rolfe' (unidentified cutting, Crick scrapbook, NFA).

The film opened at the Broadway Theatre, Sydney, on 31 July 1911, and in August at the Lyric Theatre, Prahran, in Melbourne.

37 The Mark of the Lash

1911 JOHN GAVIN

PC: Australian Photo-Play Company. SC: Agnes Gavin. PH: A. J. Moulton. 3000 ft.
CAST: John Gavin.

This convict drama was the only film that Gavin made for the new Australian Photo-Play Company before he broke off his connection with them and established his own company. The film was announced as completed and available to exhibitors in July 1911, but no public screening has been traced.

38 The Drover's Sweetheart

1911 JOHN GAVIN

PC: John F. Gavin Productions. SC: Agnes Gavin. PH: A. J. Moulton. Over 3000 ft.
CAST: John Gavin.

This film was the first that John and Agnes Gavin made for their own company after announcing their severance from the Australian Photo-Play Company on 19 July 1911. An advertisement in the *Referee* on this date promised the film for early release, and Gavin later claimed (in *Everyones*, 9 May 1923) that the film had been completed, but no public screening has been traced.

39 The Romantic Story of Margaret Catchpole**

1911 RAYMOND LONGFORD

PC: Spencer's Pictures. PH: Ernest Higgins. 3000 (?) ft.
CAST: Lottie Lyell (Margaret Catchpole), Raymond Longford (Will Laud), Augustus Neville (Lieutenant Barry), Sybil Wilde (little Kitty), William Coulter (Lord Chief Justice), E. Melville (Justice Heath), Fred Hardy (Chaloner Archdeckne), Walter Vincent (Captain Luff, a smuggler), Fred Twitcham (Mr Cobbold), Jack Goodall (Edward Catchpole), J. Howard (Reverend O'Gharty), H. Parker (Lieutenant Bourne), J. Eldridge (landlord of the Bull Inn), C. Swain (landlord of the Chester Inn), and Arno, Mr Spencer's dapple grey horse.

The story is founded on fact. In a village on the south coast of England, young Margaret Catchpole is being courted by two rivals, Will Laud, a smuggler, and Lieutenant Barry of the coast guards. She favours Laud, and when he escapes from custody after a government raid on the smugglers, Margaret steals a horse and tries to join him. In a fight with the coast guards, Laud is killed and Margaret is arrested for horse-stealing and transported to Botany Bay. During her seven years as a convict she begins working in a children's hospital. Meanwhile, Barry resigns from the guards and comes to settle in Sydney. Eventually he finds Margaret, woos and weds her, and they live happily at Windsor, where Margaret is well-loved and respected for her hospital work.

About half of the film survives today, and from it one can see Longford's astute use of a wide range of picturesque backgrounds, carefully chosen in and around Sydney to represent the 'Old Country', with an imposing rocky coastline and crashing waves effectively supporting the mood of the romance. Elsewhere a grim corner of a slum street is used as a suitably sordid setting for a meeting between informers. In addition, the leading performances show some sign that Longford

39 *The Romantic Story of Margaret Catchpole* Lottie Lyell on Mr Spencer's famous dapple grey horse, Arno. Frame enlargement

1900/13

39 *The Romantic Story of Margaret Catchpole* Raymond Longford (*l*), Lottie Lyell, Augustus Neville. Frame enlargement

was attempting to reduce stage mannerisms in favour of a more naturalistic acting style. Although some of the supporting players are theatrical grotesques, Lottie Lyell's performance in particular is a convincing portrayal of an energetic, forthright and wilful young woman. Her skill at horse-riding is very much in evidence, and the early part of the film contains several shots accentuating her horsemanship. Longford's own performance makes the 'unworthy' character of Will Laud thoroughly sympathetic compared with the insipid Barry.

A première was held at Spencer's Lyceum Theatre, Sydney, on 7 August 1911, and the film earned a healthy commercial return.

40 Only a Factory Girl

1911

The son of a millionaire industrialist is in love with a girl who works in his father's factory. Her devotion to the son during a period of strife changes the millionaire's attitude to the girl from contempt to admiration, and he consents to their marriage. Billed as 'an Australian drama', it screened as the main feature at the Victoria Theatre, Sydney, in the week commencing 14 August 1911.

41 The Squatter and the Clown

1911

This Australian drama was shown by the People's Picture Company, Adelaide, on 16 August 1911.

42 The Sundowner

1911 E. J. COLE (?)

PC: Pathé Frères.
CAST: Vera Remée, Frank Mills and members of E. J. Cole's Bohemian Dramatic Company.

The Launceston *Weekly Courier*, 14 September 1911, described the film as follows: 'The story revealed how a happy-go-lucky tramp or "sundowner" frustrated the evil designs of a scoundrel, who, to avenge himself on the heroine and her husband, stole their infant daughter. The little drama was capably presented, the work of the actor who portrayed the jovial sundowner being particularly noteworthy.' The story ended with 'an exciting chase', with the villain pursued by mounted police and stockmen. It opened at the Victoria Theatre, Sydney, on 21 August 1911.

43 The Lady Outlaw

1911 ALFRED ROLFE

PC: Australian Photo-Play Company.
CAST: Charles Villiers.

Although shot in and around Sydney, the film was set in Van Diemen's Land in the convict days. When her lover is transported to Hobart for a trivial offence, Dorothy follows him to the colony, only to learn that he has been assigned as a servant to a malicious land-owner and has fled into the hills, where the police believed he has died. Determined to seek revenge, Dorothy joins a group of escaped convicts and leads a raid on the land-owner's house. To her dismay she finds her lover still alive and married to another woman. Embittered and disillusioned, she decides to remain with the outlaws and become a bushranger. In one encounter with the army, she and her gang are trapped by the sea, and after a duel on the beach between a lieutenant and Dorothy's sole surviving follower, 'the lady bushranger' is captured and taken to stand trial.

The film screened quietly at the Star Theatre, Melbourne, from 28 August 1911, but won a far more positive response in Hobart in September.

44 In the Nick of Time

1911 ALFRED ROLFE

PC: Australian Photo-Play Company. 1200 ft.

This 'sensational railway drama' screened in Sydney at the Victoria Theatre on 4 September 1911, and later in the same month at the Star Theatre, Melbourne. A notice in the *Age*, 25 September 1911, promised 'an exciting race, horse against motor car, and a fight on the footboard of a moving train'. A film with the same title was shown in Sydney in December, but it seems likely that this later film was American.

45 Mates of the Murrumbidgee

1911 ALFRED ROLFE

PC: Australian Photo-Play Company. 2500 ft.

The story ranges from a homestead on the banks of the Murrumbidgee to South Africa during the Boer War, where thirty stirring scenes of mateship and war are depicted, including a spirited charge by a hundred New South Wales Lancers at Majuba Hill. The film ends with the triumphant return of the Australian contingent to Sydney.

The film was selected as the main feature to open the Lyric Theatre in the Melbourne suburb of Brunswick on 4 September 1911. Like its companion theatre, the Lyric at Prahran, it became a major outlet for Australian films in Melbourne. The film screened in Tasmania in October, and the press recorded much cheering from audiences and commended the film as 'a healthy departure from the beaten track, which Australian audiences should welcome' (*Weekly Courier*, Launceston, 26 October 1911); this 'realistic' drama should help 'to keep fresh the memory of those brave Australian boys who fought their way to victory' (*Mercury*, Hobart, 28 October 1911).

46 The Colleen Bawn

1911 GASTON MERVALE

PC: Australian Life Biograph Company. From the play by Dion Boucicault. 3500 ft.
CAST: Louise Carbasse (the colleen), James Martin (Danny Mann).

This sentimental Irish melodrama was based on one of Dion Boucicault's most popular plays, about an aristocrat who marries a peasant girl and cannot bring himself to tell his mother. His mother had wanted him to marry an heiress in order to prevent the ancestral home from being sold. The family tries to murder the girl but she is rescued by a villager and hidden away. Her husband is persuaded that she is dead, and he is reluctantly leading the heiress to the altar when the colleen suddenly reappears; the villains are disgraced and the lovers happily reunited.

Despite the competition of a British film based on the same play and released in Australia in the same year, the Australian Life Biograph Company proceeded with their own version, shot in their Manly studio in Sydney and on locations near by. A cliff and cave on the foreshores of Sydney Harbour were used for the scene of the attempted murder and subsequent rescue of the colleen. The film was screened in Melbourne at the Exhibition Building on 25 September 1911.

47 Way Outback

1911 ALFRED ROLFE

PC: Australian Photo-Play Company. 1000 ft.
CAST: Charles Villiers.

A bush romance, screened at the Victoria Theatre, Sydney, on 25 September 1911.

48 What Women Suffer

1911 ALFRED ROLFE

PC: Australian Photo-Play Company. 2500 ft.
CAST: Alfred Rolfe (Lieutenant Coventry), Ethel Phillips (the heroine), Stanley Walpole (Standish), Charles Villiers.

A beautiful young girl is betrothed to a dashing naval officer, Lieutenant Coventry. A ruthless scoundrel, Standish, who has designs upon her, commits a murder and frames Coventry for the crime. The hapless Lieutenant is thrown into prison. Standish then forges a letter to lure the girl and her little brother to a lonely sawmill. There he ties her to a post, then stuns the boy and places him on a moving sawbench, threatening to cut him in pieces if she does not consent to marry him. Luckily, Coventry escapes from jail and arrives at the mill in time to fell the villain and rescue the boy and his beloved.

This unabashed Victorian melodrama was screened to large audiences in Melbourne at the two Lyric Theatres, at Brunswick and Prahran, for a season that commenced on 2 October 1911. The *Bulletin*, 12 October 1911, found it a 'long and rather disjointed story [containing] some delightful violence and hugger-mugger'.

49 The Bells

1911 W. J. LINCOLN

PC: Amalgamated Pictures. SC: W. J. Lincoln. From the adaptation by Leopold Lewis of the play *Le Juif Polonais* by Erckmann-Chatrian. PH: Orrie Perry. ART D: Sam Crewes. STAGE MANAGER: J. Ennis. 4000 ft.
CAST: Arthur Styan (Mathias), Nellie Bramley (Annette), Miss Grist (Catherine), J. Ennis (Walter), Ward Lyons (Hans), Charles Lawrence (Christian), Mr Johns (mesmerist), Mr Ebbsmith (Dr Zimmer), George Kensington (notary), Mr Devon (Tony), Mr Devine (Fritz), Mr Cullenane (the Polish Jew), Mr Coleridge (judge), Mr Sinclair (clerk), Marion Willis (Sozel).

Mathias is a poor innkeeper in a village in Alsace. His happy life with Catherine and their little daughter, Annette, is in jeopardy, for he is seriously in debt to the landlord and faces eviction. On Christmas Day 1833 Mathias murders a wealthy Polish Jew who visits the inn, and with his gold pays off his debts and rapidly rises in society, eventually becoming Burgomeister of the town. Fifteen years later on Christmas Eve in the same tavern, the villagers remember the old mystery surrounding the disappearance of the Polish Jew. Mathias, who has been tormented for years by guilt and has become subject to strange visions, becomes delirious and hears again the sound of the Jew's sleighbells. He dreams he is being tried in a court for the murder and violently denies the accusations. The judge calls for a mesmerist and under his hypnosis Mathias is made to re-enact the whole dreadful crime. The verdict of the court is death, whereupon Mathias awakes, raving helplessly, and soon dies in the presence of his family, leaving the mystery of the Polish Jew unsolved forever.

The Bells was based on a well established stage melodrama written by Erckmann-Chatrian and first performed in London in 1871. The film offered sixty 'Grand Tableaux' in telling the tale, but it was no mere representation of a stage production, for considerable pains were taken to use outdoor locations. The snow scenes were shot on the slopes of Mount Donna Buang in the Victorian ranges, which the film company ascended on horseback under difficult winter conditions. The film offered the first and only screen appearance of Nellie Bramley, a stage actress then in her late teens and already renowned for the sentimental sweetness of her theatrical *persona*. *The Bells* opened at Tait's Glaciarium, Melbourne, on 7 October 1911, with a 'descriptive lecture' by J. Ennis, who appeared in the drama as Walter, a villager who frequents the inn.

Other film versions of the play abounded: in the U.S.A. in 1918, in England in 1923 and 1931, in Belgium in 1925, and again in Australia in 1935, the last under the title of *The Burgomeister*.

49 *The Bells*

50 All for Gold, or Jumping the Claim

1911 FRANKLYN BARRETT (?)

PC: West's Pictures. SC: W. S. Percy. PH: Franklyn Barrett. 3000 ft.

CAST: Herbert J. Bentley (Jack Cardigan), Hilliard Vox (Ralph Blackstone), Lilian Teece (Nora Fraser), Ronald McLeod (Bert Fraser), E. Melville (warden), Walter Bastin (Jim Carey).

In mid-1911 West's Pictures offered a prize of £25 for the best story suitable for screen adaptation. Two hundred entries were received, and the prize went to a well-known stage comedian, W. S. Percy, for a story that brought the romance of the gold diggings into a modern setting. A young Englishman, Jack Cardigan, strikes gold on his claim, and writes at once to share the news with his sweetheart, Nora. He entrusts the letter to a friend, Ralph Blackstone, who concocts a plan to murder Cardigan and take possession of the claim. He poisons Cardigan's drink and hurls his body into a river. On his return to Sydney he unwittingly allows Jack's letter to fall into Nora's hands and she decides to investigate. While the villainous Blackstone travels by train back to the mine with a business promoter, she tries to get there ahead of him; in a tense and exciting race with the train, she takes a speedboat across Sydney Harbour and then daringly drives a fast car by herself into the country. She manages to arrive in time to expose Blackstone's treachery, and to find Jack Cardigan alive and recovering from the effects of the poison. All ends happily with Cardigan reassured in his claim over both the gold and Nora.

In a remarkable instance of early split-screen technology, Barrett made three separate exposures to cover the action of the heroine making a telephone call to order the speedboat to take her across Sydney Harbour: on the left side of the screen, Nora was shown making the call, with the boatman receiving the call on the right, the two separated by a wide view of the boat harbour. The *Bulletin*,

50 T. J. West

12 October 1911, found the chase scene 'a triumph of photo art' and one of the most exciting moments in a 'wild and whirling tale'. The film was screened at West's Glaciarium, Sydney, on 9 October 1911, and seems to have been a modest success.

West's Pictures did not have a pronounced interest in production, although the company did employ a newsreel team and financed several narrative films, which Franklyn Barrett photographed and possibly directed. The main focus of the company's activity was film marketing and between 1908 and 1913 it was Spencer's biggest rival in exhibition. Thomas James West was born in England in 1855. As a theatrical entrepreneur he worked extensively in England and took stage companies on tour in the U.S.A., New Zealand and Australia. With substantial capital behind him, he established himself in film exhibition in Australia, and by early 1908 was operating regular screenings at the huge circus auditorium, the Olympic, Melbourne, and in a converted skating rink, the Glaciarium, Sydney. A less flamboyant showman than Spencer, West nevertheless bought his films carefully to provide variety and sensation for his audiences. He had an ability to think big and his theatres tended to be the largest and his prices the highest; by 1911 he had theatres operating successfully throughout Australia as well as in New Zealand. London served as his headquarters and he never stayed in Australia for long; from London he purchased his films and they were sold in Australia by his agents. He had nothing to lose and a lot to gain by merging his interests with Australasian Films, and he did so in 1912, thereby giving himself access to a much wider range of outlets and reducing his overhead expenses. He did not enjoy the profits for long, however, for he died in England in November 1916.

Franklyn Barrett (real name Walter Franklyn Brown) was one of Australia's finest cinematographers and a prolific director of feature films. Born in 1873 in England, he went to New Zealand about 1895 and worked as a press photographer and as a violinist in touring theatre orchestras. He also gained experience in film as a newsreel photographer and shot his own 'scenics' of New Zealand. In an early use of film for dramatic purposes, he shot an 800-foot narrative film, *A Message from Mars*, in Wellington in 1903. Over the next decade he travelled widely in New Zealand, Australia and England, shooting newsreels and travelogues for various sponsors, including Pathé Frères, whom he joined in Sydney in 1908. He was with Pathé when West's Pictures took over the company and he remained to photograph productions for them, including *All for Gold*. In 1913, after West's had merged with Australasian Films, he joined the Fraser company as a film-maker and film-buyer and his career flourished thereafter as his reputation as a director grew.

50 Franklyn Barrett

His features, whether made for himself or for other companies, revealed a flair for realism in the setting of conventional plots, and *The Breaking of the Drought* (1920) and *A Girl of the Bush* (1921) survive today as evidence of his sensitive eye as a photographer of Australian landscapes. His efforts to remain active as a film-maker in the face of Australasian's monopoly over theatres eventually defeated him, and in 1922 he made a clean break from production and settled into life as an exhibitor in Sydney and Canberra. He died in Sydney on 16 July 1964 at the age of 91.

51 Assigned to his Wife

1911 JOHN GAVIN

PC: John F. Gavin Productions. SC: Agnes Gavin. PH: A. J. Moulton. 4000 (?) ft.
CAST: John Gavin (Jack Throsby), Agnes Gavin (Bess Wilmot), Carr Austin (Colonel McGregor), J. Harris (Sandy McDougal), F. Henderson (Trooper McGuire), Miss Daphne (Bertha McGregor), H. Harding (Captain Danvers), Wilton Power (Harry Wilmot), H. Benson (The Governor), A. Delaware (Yacka).

England in the 1840s: a British army officer, Captain Danvers, discovers that his lover, Bess Wilmot, is already married to the hapless Jack Throsby. In revenge, Danvers frames Throsby on a charge of treason, and Throsby is transported as a convict to Van Diemen's Land. Filled with remorse, Bess follows Jack to Australia. Danvers is transferred to the colonies, and appeases Bess by arranging for Jack to be assigned to her as a servant. Later, however, when Jack prevents Danvers from molesting Bess, Danvers has Jack thrown into prison again. In the dramatic highlight of the film, Jack's faithful Aboriginal friend, Yacka, contrives to rescue him with a 'Dive for Life' in which the Aboriginal boy dives 250 feet over a precipice into a river. Evidence is eventually found that exonerates Jack and condemns Danvers, and at last Jack is free to return to England with Bess and Yacka.

The film was made cheaply, for less than £500, and shot in the bush near Sydney and in Gavin's own improvised studio in Waverley. Distribution was undertaken by Gavin himself, and the film opened in Sydney at the Lyric and Colonial Theatres on 9 October 1911.

52 The Double Event

1911 W. J. LINCOLN

PC: Amalgamated Pictures. SC: W. J. Lincoln. From the novel by Nat Gould. PH: Orrie Perry.
CAST: The Bland Holt Company, including Martyn Hagen.

The story was based on the first novel by the prolific English writer of racing stories, Nat Gould, who had spent twelve years in Australia from 1884 to 1896. *The Double Event* was first published in 1891 and was dramatized soon after, appearing on the stage in Melbourne in 1893. The story follows a familiar pattern in which the Australian bush provides a refuge and a new start for an Englishman who has left home after an affair of honour.

To save the name of his wealthy family, Jack Drayton refrains from denouncing his wastrel brother for various misdeeds (including attempted murder) and leaves England in secrecy, bound for Australia. There he assumes the name of Jack Marston and becomes involved in the world of the turf. He falls in love with Edith, the daughter of a Sydney bookmaker, John Kingdon, and makes a bid 'for Love and Fortune' by entering his horse, Caloola, in the Melbourne Cup. Despite attempted interference by Fletcher, a

crooked trainer, Caloola wins the race. A celebratory ball is disturbed by Fletcher who is seeking to blackmail a high-society lady who formerly moved in gambling circles. Rebuffed by the lady, Fletcher shoots her. A chase ensues and the villain is tracked down to a Chinese den in the city where he falls from a rooftop and dies. Jack marries Edith and returns to England to be welcomed back by his family.

The drama was performed by members of the recently disbanded Bland Holt theatrical company (Holt had retired from the theatre in 1909) and several racing scenes were shot at the Flemington racecourse in Melbourne. It was released in Melbourne on Caulfield Cup day, 21 October 1911, at Tait's Glaciarium.

53 The Girl from Outback

1911

PC: Australian Life Biograph Company. 3000 ft.

'A thrilling story of real Australian life', first offered to exhibitors in October 1911.

54 The Cup Winner

1911 ALFRED ROLFE

PC: Australian Photo-Play Company. From the play by Phillip Lytton and William J. Lee. 3000 ft.
CAST: Charles Villiers.

When Richard Avenal mistakenly believes his wife to be unfaithful, he orders her out of the house, divorces her, and gives away their young son to an Italian organ-grinder. The Italian in turn places the baby in a stable where he is found by the stable's owner and adopted into his family. In time the boy grows up to become a jockey and is set to ride the favourite in the Melbourne Cup. The favourite happens to be owned by Richard Avenal, the jockey's real father. The villain who years earlier had caused the misunderstanding that disrupted the family, and his comic Jewish bookmaker, try to force the jockey to dope the horse, but they are outwitted by the boy, who rides the horse to victory in the Cup. The story ends with the family reunited and posing together within a giant horseshoe, a symbol of future peace and good fortune.

The main distinction of the film was the inclusion of actual footage of the Melbourne Cup race for 1911. Newsreel companies had traditionally competed with each other to bring the race to the screen at the earliest possible time, but this year, Stanley Crick, the managing director of Australian Photo-Play, tried a new gimmick, presenting the newsreel footage in a dramatic context. The narrative scenes were shot in Sydney well before the race, and six cameramen were hired to shoot scenes of the Cup Day crowds and the main racing events. The film was immediately processed and printed, and the completed drama was shown that night, 7 November 1911, at five Melbourne theatres. Copies were rushed to Sydney by express train to screen there the next day, and to Adelaide a day later. The gimmick was effective, for hundreds were reportedly turned away from the crowded theatres on the opening night, and even months later, in February 1912, when the film ran in Hobart, it could still attract 'immense audiences'.

55 Caloola, or The Adventures of a Jackeroo

1911 ALFRED ROLFE

PC: Australian Photo-Play Company. From the novel by Clement Pratt. 2700 ft.
CAST: Charles Villiers.

'The story concerned a tribe of aborigines who capture the daughter of a struggling settler. Her parents become worried and a search party sets out to teach Jacky and his brethren a lesson. They take no risks and shoot the blacks on sight. Enter the hero jackeroo, who spots the chief of the tribe ready to fling the girl over the cliff. Dashing to the rescue he saves the girl's life and puts finis to the body-snatching habits of the black chief.' (*Everyones*, 12 May 1937) The Aborigines were played by members of several Sydney boat crews with blackened faces. Despite this conventional artifice, the film was promoted as 'a Real Thriller . . . which positively breathes with panting realism'. It screened in Melbourne at the Lyric Theatre, Brunswick, for a season commencing on 20 November 1911.

56 Driving a Girl to Destruction

1911 GEORGE MARLOW (?)

PC: Australian Picturised Drama Company. P: George Marlow. From the play by Mrs Morton Powell. PH: Bert Ive. 3000 ft.
CAST: Louise Hampton (Ruby), Nellie Ferguson (Ruth), Ethel Buckley, Beth Murdoch, Robert Inman, Herbert Linden, Frank Reis, John Cosgrove.

The production company was based at the Adelphi Theatre, Sydney, and was controlled by George Marlow, whose acting troupe (including his wife, Ethel Buckley) appeared in the film. The play had been popular in England, and Marlow imported the British star of the play, Louise Hampton, to appear in both the play and the film in Australia. It rapidly became one of the most successful plays in Marlow's repertoire, after a première in June 1911 at the Adelphi, but as a film it was a failure; it was offered to exhibitors in November 1911 but no screenings are known to have taken place.

The story, about alcoholism, prostitution, rape and murder, begins when the wealthy hero, Robert Ray, wakens from a drinking bout to find himself married to Ruth, a 'brandy nymph', who announces later that she is pregnant. In the course of the play Robert's

56 George Marlow

former fiancée, an upright schoolteacher named Ruby, drifts through the seamy side of London in search of her beloved. She unwittingly takes lodgings in a brothel and escapes 'without her hat or blouse, but with her purity unsullied'. She is found alone and starving in a garret by a dishonourable villain from whom she escapes only when he is murdered by the drunken Ruth. Later Ruth too is killed by a prostitute, and Robert and Ruby are reunited.

Marlow was renowned for his sensationalistic melodramas, and the *Sun*, 19 June 1911, attacked the play for being 'every bit as lurid as it sounds . . . What the heroine did to deserve this treatment is not made at all clear.' Despite such criticism, productions of the play continued to be highly profitable for Marlow, even after the film was completed.

Marlow clearly lacked expertise in both film production and marketing, and his second film, *Angel of his Dreams* (1912), fared no better commercially. One film businessman wrote sternly to Marlow on 13 March 1912: 'Re the two films of yours . . . The great trouble in booking these pictures has been this, the photography is good, very good in fact . . . but the acting, "ugh" it is awful. With regard to pictures, these dramatic stars and "would be's" are no earthly use for picture work at all . . . Another thing it is no earthly use me trying to book "The Angel of His Dreams" when there is no paper for it . . . If these pictures are to be hired out you must have paper for your clients to advertise them.' (Bert Ive scrapbook, NFA)

57 The Christian

1911 FRANKLYN BARRETT (?)

PC: West's Pictures. From the play by Hall Caine.
PH: Franklyn Barrett. 2500 ft.

CAST: Roy Redgrave (John Storm), Eugenie Duggan (Glory Quayle), Rutland Beckett (Lord Robert Ure), Olive Wilton (Polly Love), Marie D'Alton (Lady Robert Ure), Lily Bryer (Mrs James Callender), Alfred Harford (Lord Storm), Edmund Duggan (Father Enderby), Fred Kehoe (Parson Quayle), Bert Bailey (Archdeacon Wealthy), George Kensington (Brother Paul), Max Clifton (Horatio Drake), Gus Franks (Mr Jupe), Mabs Howth (Liza).

A conflict between holy and human passions, the story follows the love of a zealous clergyman, John Storm, for the actress Glory Quayle. Storm is devoted to mission work in the slums of London, where he meets Glory, a naïve country girl who has been persuaded by an aristocrat, Lord Robert Ure, to seek a career on the stage. Storm tries to dissuade her, but she rejects his advice. Storm clashes angrily with Lord Robert, and consumed with hatred, Lord Robert hires a scoundrel to set fire to the mission hall while Storm lies unconscious inside. Storm is rescued at the last moment and goes to Glory's flat determined to save her soul, by killing her if necessary. Her passionate pleading awakens the love that he has always had for her, and the film closes with them both kneeling before a shrine, promising their lives to each other.

Hall Caine's play had been a major success in many countries, and the film arose directly from a production of the play by the William Anderson Dramatic Company at the Palace Theatre, Sydney, in September 1911. Indoor scenes were shot on the stage of the theatre with the full cast of the play, and other scenes on outdoor locations in and around Sydney.

The *Daily Telegraph*, 4 December 1911, commended the production warmly: Eugenie Duggan 'succeeded beyond expectation in her work for the camera, giving one of those life-like pictures that are the exception rather than the rule . . . The work of the cinematographer, Mr W. Franklyn Barrett, was up to the best traditions of the West, Ltd. management, the fire scene being a strikingly well-arranged piece of stagecraft.' It opened at West's Glaciarium, Sydney, on 2 December 1911. An English film based on the same play and starring the author's son, Derwent Hall Caine, was released in 1915, and an American version, directed by Maurice Tourneur, appeared in 1923.

The star of the Australian version was G. E. (stage name Roy) Redgrave, father of the English actor, Sir Michael Redgrave. He came to Australia at the turn of the century under engagement to J. C. Williamson, and remained to appear with other companies including William Anderson's. He died in Australia in May 1922 at the age of 50.

1900/13

57 Roy Redgrave as John Storm in a stage production of *The Christian*

58 Sweet Nell of Old Drury

1911 RAYMOND LONGFORD

PC: Spencer's Pictures. P: George Musgrove.
SC: Raymond Longford. From the play by Paul Kester.
PH: Ernest Higgins. 4800 ft.
CAST: Nellie Stewart (Nell Gwynne), Augustus Neville (King Charles), Charles Lawrence (Lord Jeffries), Stewart Clyde (Lord Rochester), W. Ladd (Lord Lovelace), Leslie Woods (Sir Robert Fairfax), W. Edgeworth (Lacey, Lord Jeffries' servant), Walter Bastin and Fred Pettit (Percival and Rollins, strolling players), Henry Westall (Lord Winchester), A. Kendall (Mercer), Walter Vincent (William), Master Eric Montaigne (Nebuchadnezzar), P. Francis (Captain Clavering), W. Flindt (Captain of the Guard), Miss Neville Vane (Tiffin), Elsie Rennie (page), Miss P. Laing (Lady Clivebrook), Dorothy Clarke (Duchess of Portsmouth), Agnes Keogh (Lady Castlemaine), Roslyn Vane (Lady Olivia Vernon).

Nellie Stewart's only screen appearance, made at the age of 53, was in a role that she had made her own for many years on the stage, that of Nell Gwynne. Born in 1858 to an acting family, Nellie Stewart began on the stage as a child and rose to fame in both Australia and London for her performances in Gilbert and Sullivan, musical comedy, and as principal boy in pantomime. She first played Nell Gwynne in Melbourne in 1902, in the play by an American writer, Paul Kester, and the role quickly became indelibly associated with her until her death in 1931. Her business partner and close friend through most of her long acting career was the entrepreneur George Musgrove (1854-1916), who managed her appearances and produced many of her plays as well as supervising her sole film performance.

The setting of the story is the Restoration court of Charles II: Judge Jeffries tries to persuade his ward, Lady Olivia Vernon, to marry Lord Rochester, but she refuses and flees. The actress Nell Gwynne takes Lady Olivia under her wing and shelters her at the Drury Lane theatre until she can arrange to join her true love, Sir Robert Fairfax. Meanwhile, Nell's lampoons of the nobility attract the attention of King Charles, who visits her theatre and proceeds to woo her. Her popularity with the king incurs the jealousy of the court, and Jeffries determines to destroy her. He forges a letter to try to compromise Nell and Fairfax, and the king is momentarily duped and spurns Nell, while Fairfax is arrested for treason. Nell retaliates by impersonating Jeffries and releasing Fairfax so that he is reunited with Olivia. She also finds enough evidence to secure the dismissal of Jeffries. The young lovers receive the king's blessing and Nell is welcomed back into the king's favour.

Shooting began in September 1911 at Spencer's 'Wonderland City' studio, Bondi, with exteriors in the grounds of Sydney's mansions. The work was initially under the direction of George Musgrove himself, whom Longford later described (in *Everyones*, 1 July 1931) as a 'martinet . . . inexorable and egotistic to a degree'. According to Longford's account of the production, Musgrove shot some 15 000 feet of film on Act One alone, guided only by a rigorous but inappropriate concept of filmed theatre. 'Then came the big day when we all saw that first act screened, and that put the lid on properly. Even the great G. M. himself laughed and finally capitulated. The whole contract was revised, as were his ideas of picture-making; Spencer developed a back-bone; even the star herself accepted direction; and the writer [Longford] took sole control and started all over again.'

Nellie Stewart received a reported £1000 (half of the total budget) for appearing in the film, a sum that no other screen star in Australia could match for several decades. She did, however, work hard to promote the film, making numerous personal appearances, and it was a major success when it opened at Spencer's Lyceum Theatre, Sydney, on 2 December 1911. Twelve thousand people reportedly saw the film during the first seven sessions. The star's coquetry was fully exploited by Longford's camera; a writer in the *Daily Telegraph*, 4 December 1911, reported that 'when the figure of Miss Nellie Stewart, as the bare-footed orange girl, was descried in the distant perspective of a narrow rural track, there was great applause; and as she advanced into the foreground and coyly held out an orange, as if offering it to the audience, she had a fine reception'.

58 Nellie Stewart

Given the dominance of her presence, it was inevitable that faults would be more easily found in her co-stars: the *Daily Telegraph* found Augustus Neville miscast as Charles II, because his face possessed 'too much strength of character for the easy-going, dissolute monarch'. Furthermore, some of the cast 'had not quite mastered the art of making-up for the camera', and there were defects in the presentation of off-screen sound effects to accompany the film on the opening night:

58 A *Bulletin* cartoon of the main characters in the film of *Sweet Nell of Old Drury*

'People walking on a garden path, for example, were accompanied by noise such as might have been caused by tramping on a wooden floor; and even Nell Gwynne, mincing in her bare feet on the cobble stones outside Drury-lane in mimicry of Mrs Barry, was represented as producing aggressively loud footsteps.'

59 Gambler's Gold

1911 GEORGE YOUNG

PC: Australian Film Syndicate. From the novel by Arthur Wright. PH: George Wilkins. 4500 ft.
CAST: Roland Conway, Evelyn St Jermyn, E. B. Russell, Casper Middleton.

This racing melodrama, depicting the Sydney Cup race meeting and 'a sensational motor boat chase' on Sydney Harbour, was screened on 7 December 1911 at the Broadway Theatre, Sydney. George Wilkins became cinematographer for the Australian Film Syndicate after Lacey Percival's departure for the Australian Photo-Play Company. Formerly a projectionist and exhibitor in North Sydney, Wilkins later achieved distinction in the war and in polar exploration, and became better known as Sir Hubert Wilkins.

60 The Miner's Curse

1911 ALFRED ROLFE

PC: Australian Photo-Play Company. 1200 ft.

A drama of the gold diggings, shown in Melbourne at the Lyric Theatre, Prahran, from 7 December 1911.

61 King of the Coiners

1912 ALFRED ROLFE

PC: Australian Photo-Play Company. 3000 ft.
CAST: Charles Villiers.

Filmed in two acts and sixty-one scenes, this melodrama about a double life was distinguished by 'a sensational and realistic motor accident' at its climax. The story follows the career of Luke Holt, a police sergeant who doubles as the head of a gang of counterfeiters. One day he tries to recruit a young engraver, Ned Truman, to the gang but Ned is too honest to give in to temptation. Counterfeit coins are planted in Ned's room, and he is arrested by Holt in his guise as a policeman and is sent to jail. Ned's wife, Nellie, is turned into the streets without money or friends, but a detective comes to her aid and manages to uncover the truth. Holt escapes from the police in a fast car, but it crashes over a cliff and he is killed.

The film screened at the Lyric Theatre, Prahran, for a season commencing on 8 January 1912.

62 Do Men Love Women?

1912 ALFRED ROLFE

PC: Australian Photo-Play Company. 3000 ft.
CAST: Charles Villiers.

The highlight of this melodrama was a 'realistic railway collision', forming the climax of a story about a drunkard's reformation through the love of a good woman. It screened at the Star Theatre, Melbourne, on 25 January 1912.

63 The Sin of a Woman

1912 ALFRED ROLFE

PC: Australian Photo-Play Company.
CAST: Charles Villiers.

This 'purely Australian story, enacted by Australian artists amid typical Australian scenery' was released in several suburban cinemas in Sydney on 29 January 1912.

64 Angel of his Dreams

1912 GEORGE MARLOW (?)

PC: Australian Picturised Drama Company. P: George Marlow. PH: Bert Ive.

Murder, adultery, surprise confessions, theft and alcoholism were all integral to this melodrama of a bad woman and her seduction of an innocent young clergyman. With its overtones of *The Silence of Dean Maitland*, the film was a close adaptation of a play that George Marlow had first produced in Australia early in 1911 and it was clearly part of his notorious repertoire of sex and scandal. The film version was screened at Thiele's Star Pictures in the Sydney suburb of Rozelle on 5 February 1912.

65 The Strangler's Grip

1912

PC: West's Pictures. PH: Franklyn Barrett.
CAST: Sydney Stirling (John Dalton, squatter), Cyril Mackay (Frank Wood, his friend), Leonard Willey (Mike Logan, tramp), Charles Lawrence (Old Simon, John's butler), Master Willey (Billy Dalton, John's son), Irby Marshall (Mrs Dalton, John's wife).

In 1912 four films were made by the actors Cyril Mackay, Leonard Willey and Sydney Stirling for West's Pictures. All of the films were photographed by Franklyn Barrett, but only on the last, *A Silent Witness*, did he claim (in *Theatre*, 1 January 1917) to have had 'a free hand' in the production. The other films were probably directed jointly by the principals in the cast. The first, *The Strangler's Grip*, featured 'a furious motor drive', and its story was written especially for the screen. It opened at the Victoria Theatre, Sydney, on 5 February 1912.

Cyril Mackay was a stage actor born in London and brought to Australia around 1906 by J. C. Williamson. He died in Brisbane in July 1923 at the age of 43. His colleagues in the 1912 venture, Leonard Willey and his wife, Irby Marshall, went to the U.S.A. in 1914 to further their careers and both found extensive work on the stage there.

66 Hands across the Sea

1912 GASTON MERVALE

PC: Australian Life Biograph Company. 2000 ft.
CAST: Louise Carbasse.

Like other productions of this company, the film was made at its Manly studio in Sydney and was based on a popular stage play. The climax of the film came with the hero's escape in an open boat from the French penal settlement of New Caledonia and his rescue in mid-ocean by a British naval vessel. Billed as 'A beautiful nautical drama, showing the love of a good woman and the hate of a bad man', it screened for a short season at the Lyric Theatre, Adelaide, commencing on 8 February 1912.

67 A Daughter of Australia

1912 GASTON MERVALE (?)

PC: Australian Life Biograph Company. SC: Harry Beaumont (?). 3000 ft.
CAST: Harry Beaumont (?), Louise Carbasse.

This romance of the Australian gold diggings screened in Sydney at the Alhambra Theatre from 12 February 1912, accompanied by a lecture read by Harry Beaumont, who was described as the 'producer' of the film. Gaston Mervale, however, was usually responsible for the productions of the Australian Life Biograph Company, and it seems more likely that Beaumont was the author or leading actor.

68 The Crime and the Criminal

1912 ALFRED ROLFE

PC: Australian Photo-Play Company. 3000 ft.
CAST: Charles Villiers.

This story of crime and romance in Sydney was told in '2 acts and 37 scenes' and climaxed with 'an awful and realistic railway wreck'. The film was released at the Alhambra Theatre, Sydney, on 19 February 1912, a few weeks after another Australian Photo-Play production featuring a railway collision as its climax, *Do Men Love Women?* The plots of the two films seem to have been quite different, and presumably the company was using the same train footage to maximize the dramatic potential of what was possibly originally a newsreel segment.

69 The Octoroon

1912 GEORGE YOUNG

PC: Australian Film Syndicate. From the play by Dion Boucicault.

Boucicault's stage melodrama, set in the Deep South of the U.S.A. in the 1850s, told the story of Zoe, a beautiful octoroon (of one-eighth Negro blood) who is given her freedom by her white father but is later bought as a slave by the evil Jacob McCloskey. This local version was made near Sydney, with an old paddle steamer, *Narrabeen*, serving as a Mississippi river boat. It opened for a three-day season at Waddington's Grand Theatre, Sydney, on 19 February 1912.

70 A. O. Segerberg, with his camera mounted on his Harley-Davidson motorcycle

70 Cooee and the Echo

1912 ALFRED ROLFE

PC: Australian Photo-Play Company. From the play by E. W. O'Sullivan. PH: A. O. Segerberg. 3000 ft.
CAST: Ethel Phillips, Stanley Walpole, Charles Villiers, Charles Woods.

A *Bulletin* correspondent wrote of the film as 'a rather misguided story of Binghis and bushrangers, jerky in its action and tiresome in its length' (11 April 1912). The story followed the efforts of a young miner to avenge the murder of his brother. The lad falls in love with the daughter of the mine manager, but finds that he has a rival for her hand, none other than the man who had killed his brother. A climax is reached on the diggings deep in the bush, with a knife fight and a spectacular leap by a man on horseback from a bridge into a river hundreds of feet below. A happy ending is only reached when a 'faithful' Aboriginal boy (played by Charles Woods in blackface) arrives in time to rescue the hero.

Although set in northern Queensland, the film was shot near Sydney, with bush scenes in the near-by National Park. The film opened at Waddington's Grand Theatre, Sydney, on 11 March 1912 for a routine three-day season.

It was the first feature film definitely known to be photographed by A. O. (Albert Oscar) Segerberg, one of the staff technicians with the Australian Photo-Play Company. He had begun shooting 'actuality' footage in Australia as early as 1896, and later joined Pathé Frères to work on their weekly news gazette. After the demise of the Australian Photo-Play Company he made newsreels for the Fraser brothers in Sydney and later numerous industrial and educational documentaries, including a series that he produced himself, *Australia at Work*.

71 Breaking the News

1912 W. J. LINCOLN

PC: Amalgamated Pictures. SC: W. J. Lincoln. PH: Orrie Perry (?). 3500 ft.
CAST: Harrie Ireland, Arthur Styan.

The story was inspired by a famous painting by Sir John Longstaff, and the moment of 'breaking the news' came as the climax to a melodrama about frontier life in 'the never-never land'. After fighting for water in the outback, a prospector stakes a claim on a lead mine and attempts to win a new bride for his desert home. Scenes in the Melbourne stock exchange are followed by the miner's marriage to his loved one, but back at the mine a crisis arises with a murder and a flood; miners are trapped, and the scene is set for a heroic ride to alert rescuers. The mining scenes were shot at Diamond Creek, near Melbourne, and the *Age*, 18 March 1912, recorded audience enthusiasm for the 'realistic' scenes of the tapping of an underground stream and the flooding of the mine. The film was released at Tait's Glaciarium, Melbourne, on 16 March 1912.

72 The Mystery of the Black Pearl
[The Black Pearl Mystery]

1912

PC: West's Pictures. PH: Franklyn Barrett.
CAST: Cyril Mackay (Dick Weston), Sydney Stirling (Dudley Segrave), Leonard Willey (Sam Grimm), Charles Lawrence, Joseph Brennan, Irby Marshall.

A detective drama, screened as a supporting film at Spencer's Lyceum Theatre, Sydney, on 25 March 1912.

73 Conn, the Shaughraun

1912 GASTON MERVALE

PC: Australian Life Biograph Company. From the play *The Shaughraun* by Dion Boucicault. 3000 ft.
CAST: Louise Carbasse.

More Irish sentiment from another popular play by Dion Boucicault: a villainous magistrate in an Irish village wrongfully sentences a young man to penal servitude in Australia. The young man is rescued from the prison ship by Conn, a puckish prankster (or shaughraun), and they return to the village. There, after several dramatic confrontations, the magistrate is killed, and the young man is reunited with his loved one. The film screened in Sydney at Waddington's Grand Theatre on 28 March 1912. The same play inspired at least two other films, both American, one in 1907, and another, *My Wild Irish Rose*, in 1922.

74 Strike

1912 GEORGE YOUNG

PC: Australian Film Syndicate. From a story by Casper Middleton. 3000 ft.
CAST: Casper Middleton, Roland Conway.

The villain is a foreigner, Von Haeke, who charms the daughter of a mine-owner in order to gain access to her house and steal money from her father. Von Haeke is about to marry the deluded girl when his deserted wife arrives and exposes him as a fraud. In revenge, he induces the miners to go on strike, forcibly abducts the girl and imprisons her in an old mineshaft. An explosion follows and the mine is flooded. The hero, Jack, arrives in time to save the girl and tackles Von Haeke in a cliff-top struggle. The villain falls to his death, and Jack and the girl are happily united.

Scenes were shot at a coal mine on the New South Wales south coast in January 1912, and the film opened at the Lyric Theatre, Sydney, on 1 April 1912.

71 'Breaking the News', the painting by John Longstaff that inspired the film by W. J. Lincoln

75 The Love Tyrant [Love, the Tyrant]

1912 ALFRED ROLFE

PC: Australian Photo-Play Company. 1800 ft.
CAST: Charles Villiers.

This 'thrilling and exciting Australian drama' was selected as the main feature to open the new Glenferrie Theatre in Melbourne, on 6 April 1912, where it was advertised as *The Love Tyrant*. The Victoria Theatre, Sydney, presented it as *Love, the Tyrant* for a week commencing on 8 April 1912, and it seems safe to assume that it was the same film.

76 Rip Van Winkle

1912 W. J. LINCOLN

PC: Amalgamated Pictures. Based on the story by Washington Irving. PH: Orrie Perry.
CAST: Arthur Styan (Rip Van Winkle).

The tale of Rip Van Winkle and his twenty years' slumber had been adapted into a play by Joseph Jefferson and Dion Boucicault in the 1890s. This local film version was made in the wake of the play's success in Australia and screened at the Glaciarium, Melbourne, on 6 April 1912.

The universal popularity of *Rip Van Winkle* as a play and story prompted many other film versions, in England in 1903 and 1914, in France in 1912, and in America in 1914 and 1921.

77 The Eleventh Hour

1912

PC: West's Pictures. From the play by Leonard Willey. PH: Franklyn Barrett.
CAST: Cyril Mackay, Sydney Stirling, Leonard Willey, Charles Lawrence, Loris Brown, Irby Marshall.

This four-act melodrama, by the actor-playwright Leonard Willey, narrated 'the adventures and vicissitudes in the life of a Girl Telegraphist'. Advertisements named the title of each act thus: 'Pangs of Jealousy', 'Bad Blood', 'The Distress Call' and 'The Eleventh Hour' (*Sydney Morning Herald*, 13 April 1912). The film was shot in Sydney and presented as the main feature at two of West's theatres in Sydney, the New Olympia and the Glaciarium, on 13 April 1912. It was released in London in September 1913 under a new title, *Saved by Telegram.*

78 The Tide of Death

1912 RAYMOND LONGFORD

PC: Spencer's Pictures. SC: Raymond Longford. PH: Tasman Higgins, Arthur Higgins. 3000 ft.
CAST: Augustus Neville (Philip Maxwell), Lottie Lyell (Sylvia Grey), Frank Harcourt (Black Dan), Bert Harvey, D. L. Dalziel and D. Sweeney (Dan's gang), G. Flinn, Fred Twitcham and Arthur Steel (bushmen), Joe Hamilton (Mat Davis, Maxwell's groom), Lois Cumming (Jenny, housemaid), Little Annie Gentile (Little Edna), Jack Goodall and F. Laurence (burglars), Robert Henry (Sub-Inspector Milverton), Olive Cottey (Nurse Briar), Ada Clyde and E. Olliffe (Sisters of Mercy), E. Melville (Dr Hollis), Alice Holroyd (Miss Barry), Reggie Rennie (schoolboy), and Arno, Mr Spencer's dapple grey horse.

The Tide of Death and 'how it was stemmed by a devoted woman' was an original story by Longford, a grand conception tracing the fortunes of two ill-fated lovers over a period of many years and sweeping through settings in the bush and the high and low strata of city life. A young mining contractor, Philip Maxwell, is attacked by a gang of ruffians led by Black Dan, but he manages to hide the money they are looking for. To force him to reveal where the money is, Dan ties Philip to a stake in the middle of a tidal creek, but Philip is rescued just in time by his mining crew after they have been alerted by Dan's own stepdaughter, Sylvia. Years pass, and Sylvia and Philip marry and settle in the city with their baby daughter, Edna. One day, Dan reappears, still bent on revenge. He kidnaps Sylvia, and Philip assumes that she has deserted him. Heartbroken, he sells their house and goes abroad with Edna. When Sylvia escapes from Dan she finds herself alone and lost and seeks refuge in a convent where she becomes a teacher. More years pass; Philip returns to Australia with Edna, and the chance discovery by Sylvia of a lost bangle belonging to Edna serves to bring about the tearful reunion of the little family.

The *Bulletin*, 18 April 1912, found much to enjoy in the film: 'The acting and mountings show an improvement on the previous pictures; plainly the Spencer co. means to hold its own with Yankee and European cos. The riding scenes in the bush are certainly improvements on most imported films, where the actors seem to be totally unaccustomed to horses. Miss Lyell in particular is a gladsome centaur.' The film opened at Spencer's Lyceum Theatre, Sydney, on 13 April 1912.

79 The Cheat

1912 ALFRED ROLFE

PC: Australian Photo-Play Company.
CAST: Ethel Phillips, Stanley Walpole, Charles Villiers.

A young Englishman is wrongly accused of a crime and leaves his home for Australia. On the boat he befriends the daughter of a wealthy Australian squatter, and saves her in a daring rescue when she accidentally falls overboard from the speeding liner. In gratitude, the girl's father gives the Englishman a position on his station, and later the young couple are engaged. The station manager, however, dislikes the young man and many adventures follow before the villainous manager receives his just deserts and the lovers are united.

The formula plot, relieved only by the incident at sea, was produced in and around Sydney and the film was screened at the Victoria Theatre, Sydney, on 29 April 1912.

80 Percy Gets a Job

1912

CAST: W. S. Percy.

This comedy screened as a supporting short at the Victoria Theatre, Sydney, on 29 April 1912. Authorship of the film is unknown, but the star, W. S. (William Stratford) Percy, was well-known on the Australian stage in comic opera, pantomime and farce. In 1914 he travelled to the U.S.A. and there made another comedy short, *Percy's First Holiday*, released in Sydney on 30 March 1914.

80 W. S. Percy

81 The Bushman's Bride

1912

PC: Spencer's Pictures.

This three-act drama with ninety-one scenes, telling 'a virile tale of pluck and peril in the wilds of Australia's Bush', screened at the Lyric Theatre, Melbourne, for a season commencing on 13 May 1912.

82 A Silent Witness

1912 FRANKLYN BARRETT

PC: West's Pictures. SC: Sydney Stirling. PH: Franklyn Barrett. 2400 ft.
CAST: Cyril Mackay, Irby Marshall, Charles Lawrence, Sydney Stirling, Leonard Willey, George Bryant, Loris Brown.

Franklyn Barrett claimed (in *Theatre*, 1 January 1917) that this detective drama was the first production in which he had 'a free hand'. It screened in Adelaide at West's Olympia Theatre on 22 May 1912.

83 Won on the Post

1912 ALFRED ROLFE

PC: Australian Photo-Play Company.

This racing drama, with scenes of the Randwick racecourse and 'the true Australian bush', was screened at Hoyts St George's Hall on 1 June 1912.

84 The Wreck of the Dunbar, or The Yeoman's Wedding

1912 GASTON MERVALE (?)

PC: Universal Films. 3500 ft.
CAST: Louise Carbasse.

Set in Australia's early colonial days, the film told the story of an Englishman who is the sole survivor of a shipwreck on the Australian coast. The story was based on a play that had been popular in Australia since the 1880s, and included a climax of 'Awful Realism', with a shipwreck staged near the Sydney Heads. The film was released at the Victoria Theatre, Sydney, on 10 June 1912.

Universal Films (unrelated to the American company) was formed in Sydney in May 1912 with J. S. (John Stephen) McCullagh as its managing director. The company took over the assets of Australian Life Biograph, and announced the intention of producing further local films, as well as distributing imported products. *The Wreck of the Dunbar* was the only film completed.

85 Whose Was the Hand?

1912 ALFRED ROLFE

PC: Australian Photo-Play Company. PH: A. O. Segerberg. 3000 ft.
CAST: Charles Villiers, Stanley Walpole.

This detective drama in three acts depicts the use of 'the finger-print system' to catch a criminal after another man is wrongfully accused of murder. Among the highlights were a 'great fire, with the firemen at work, a sensational fall from an eight-storey building, and numerous other exciting scenes' (*Referee*, 29 May 1912). It screened at the Lyric Theatre, Prahran, in Melbourne on 4 July 1912.

86 Moira, or The Mystery of the Bush

1912 ALFRED ROLFE

PC: Australian Photo-Play Company. PH: A. O. Segerberg. 3000 ft.
CAST: Charles Villiers.

'A story of Australian bush life that will appeal to young and old alike', screened in Sydney at the American Picture Palace on 15 October 1912.

87 The Ticket of Leave Man

1912 GASTON MERVALE

PC: Australian Life Biograph Company. 4100 ft.
CAST: Louise Carbasse.

The last production of the Australian Life Biograph Company is today as obscure as most of the company's earlier work. The story was briefly outlined in advertisements as 'the reformation of a man after he has served a term in prison, and the success that attends his efforts to do right' (*Sydney Morning Herald*, 5 May 1913). Although it was made before May 1912 (when the company closed down), no screenings are recorded until 7 November 1912, when it opened at King's Picture Theatre, Perth.

88 The Midnight Wedding

1912 RAYMOND LONGFORD

PC: Spencer's Pictures. SC: Raymond Longford. From the play by Walter Howard. PH: Ernest Higgins. 3000 ft.
CAST: Augustus Neville (Paul Valmar), Lottie Lyell (Princess Astrea), D. L. Dalziel (Captain Rudolph Von Scarsbruck), George Parke (Lieutenant Prince Eugene), Fred Twitcham (Crown Prince of Savonia), Jack Goodall (Father Gerard), J. Barry (Reverend A. Cette), Nellie Kemberman (Stephanie), Arthur Smith (Dr Eitel), Victor Loydell (Sergeant Max), Tim Howard (Corporal Otto), Tom Leonard (Private Bobo), Dorothy Judge (Kathie), Harry Saville (innkeeper), Robert Henry (Major Donelli), and Arno, Mr Spencer's dapple grey horse.

88 *The Midnight Wedding* Augustus Neville and Lottie Lyell on the right

This costume melodrama of middle-European palace intrigue, based on a much-performed play, furnished 'all the ingredients of the yarn in a pictorial salad' (*Bulletin*, 2 January 1913). The setting was the city of Strelitz, the capital of Savonia. In a small chapel at midnight, a mysterious ceremony takes place: an unknown and blindfolded officer has been recruited by a priest to exchange marriage vows with the beautiful Princess Astrea in order to save her from an impossible dilemma. Her brother has insisted that she must either marry the evil Captain Von Scarsbruck or enter a nunnery. The compliant officer who saves her by becoming her nominal husband is Paul Valmar, a lieutenant in the Hussars, who is later revealed to be of royal blood and thus an appropriate match for the princess. In revenge for losing the princess's hand, Von Scarsbruck attempts to ruin Astrea's reputation by invading her chamber late one night. Valmar intervenes and challenges him to a duel. Astrea tries to stop their fighting, but Valmar is wounded. The princess disguises herself as an officer to reach the room where he is recuperating and is discovered there by the crown prince, to whom she confesses that Valmar is her husband. Later, Valmar recovers from his wounds and again crosses swords with Von Scarsbruck, this time emerging the victor. Astrea and Valmar are now reunited in a second wedding ceremony, this time a grand and festive occasion.

The film was the first to be shot at Spencer's new £8000 studio at Rushcutters Bay in Sydney, and sets and costumes were prepared 'on a most elaborate scale'. The cast was largely provided by Clarke and Meynell's theatrical troupe, which had enjoyed great success with the play on the Australian stage. Longford had appeared in stage productions in the role of Von Scarsbruck, but his place was taken in the film by D. L. Dalziel. Lottie Lyell had also acted in the play and 'had been the life of the piece'; she re-created the same role of the princess in the film.

A British production with the same title (but with a quite different story) was released in Sydney in April and prompted Spencer to publish a warning to exhibitors that his film was the only genuine reproduction of the play. Spencer's film opened at the Lyceum Theatre, Sydney, on 7 December 1912, and seems to have been successful, for there were frequent revivals.

88 Spencer's studio at Rushcutters Bay

88 Drying racks at Spencer's studio

89 Call of the Bush

1912

PC: The Gaumont Agency. 2100 ft.
CAST: Charles Woods (the sundowner).

Advertisements offered a formula synopsis: 'The Squatter's Son—A Welcome Home—The Shepherd's Daughter—Bosun, the Dog Hero—Attacked by Blacks—The Last Cartridge—A Foul Revenge—Wrongly Accused—Sundowner to the Rescue—Great Court Scene' (*Sun*, 8 December 1912).

Announcements were made in the trade press that the film had been 'taken in its entirety' by the Gaumont company of Australia (*Referee*, 4 December 1912), and it presumably represented a new, but short-lived, venture into production by this distribution agency. It opened unobtrusively at the Enmore Theatre, Sydney, on 12 December 1912, with an accompanying lecture delivered by Charles Woods, who himself appeared in the film.

90 The Life Story of John Lee, or The Man they could not Hang

1912 ROBERT SCOTT

P, SC: Phillip Lytton. PH: Herbert Finlay. 4 reels.
CAST: Mervyn Barrington (John Lee), Edna Phillips (Kate), Robert Scott, Robert Henry, Fred Cope.

In 1885 an Englishman, John Lee, was found guilty of the murder of his benefactress and sentenced to be hanged. Whether because of divine intervention or because of faulty carpentry, the gallows failed to open at the moment of execution. Three attempts were made to hang him and each failed, at which point his sentence was commuted to life imprisonment. After serving twenty-three years, he was released from prison and allowed to rejoin his wife and mother. Later, a dying woman confessed to the murder and Lee's name was finally cleared.

This story, with its supernatural overtones of a benign force at work in the universe, and its ample opportunity for heart-rending sentiment, became by far the most extraordinary 'sleeper' of Australian film history. The story was supposedly based on fact, but the film probably owed its direct inspiration to a stage play first performed in Australia by Phillip Lytton (real name Charles Phillips) in February 1912. The film was made towards the end of 1912, after the cameraman, Herbert Finlay, left the Australian Photo-Play Company. The producer, Phillip Lytton, was a theatrical entrepreneur of some stature in Sydney, and he employed a young actor, Robert Scott, to direct the film. Scott had appeared already in several (unidentified) films for W. J. Lincoln, and later became a film exhibitor in Queensland in the 1920s. According to Scott, the film cost less than £300, and was shot in a tiny studio in North Sydney: 'It was really only a room, fitted out like a photographer's room' (*RCE*, p.246). He described the result as 'crude' and *Smith's Weekly*, 8 January 1921, recalled it as 'about the worst ever'. Despondent about its commercial prospects, Lytton shelved the film without release, and later passed it on to a former employee, Arthur W. Sterry, reportedly as a 'present' for his long service (*Everyones*, 4 March 1925).

It is unclear when Sterry and his partner, Frederick Haldane, began to show the film, but probably they began in country towns in New South Wales in 1914. Late in 1917 they gave it its first capital city season, at the Alhambra Theatre, Sydney, commencing on 10 September. Repeated screenings followed in Sydney and other state capitals, and profitable business was also done in New Zealand and England. *Everyones*, 4 March 1925, estimated that the film had earned a total of £50 000 before 1921 when Sterry and Haldane rejuvenated their main source of income by remaking the film and embarking on a new series of Australian and New Zealand tours.

For a decade of their lives Sterry and Haldane worked virtually full-time on the promotion and exhibition of the film, branching off in 1918 to make a film version of a back-blocks farce, *The Waybacks*. Either Sterry or Haldane accompanied *The Life Story of John Lee* wherever it was shown, giving a passionate lecture from the stage during the screening; they often simulated the voices of the characters and claimed to be presenting the first 'Speaking Moving Pictures'. The reason for the film's success, though, remains an enigma; the melodramatic tale of crime and punishment was sugar-coated with a tone of reverence befitting the illustration of a miracle, and probably in this way it appealed both to the prurient and the pious in the community, while the emotion-charged performances on stage and screen ensured that neither group was disappointed. Sterry retained an interest in the story for many years more, and acted in a third film version in 1934, under the direction of Raymond Longford.

91 The Opium Runners

1913

PC: The Gaumont Agency. 2400 ft.

The second and apparently last feature production in Australia by Gaumont, shot in Sydney and offered to the trade in February 1913.

92 A Melbourne Mystery

1913

CAST: John Gavin.

This three-act drama screened at Hoyts St George's Hall, Melbourne, from 12 May 1913. In *Everyones*, 9 May 1923, John Gavin mentioned it in passing as a sea story in which he acted 'with Mrs Sculthorpe's son'.

93 Australia Calls

1913 RAYMOND LONGFORD

PC: Spencer's Pictures. STORY: C. A. Jeffries, John Barr. PH: Ernest Higgins, Tasman Higgins, Arthur Higgins. 4000 ft.

CAST: Lottie Lyell (Beatrice Evans), Frank Phillips (Evans), Alfred O'Shea, George Wilkins, William E. Hart (aviator), Andrew Warr (Asian commander), and Arno, Mr Spencer's dapple grey horse.

The story, by two of the *Bulletin*'s regular contributors, vigorously expressed that magazine's xenophobia, and was a warning to apathetic Australians to beware the Yellow Peril. The film begins with scenes of Australians at play—at the beach, at the race-track, and at the football—and over each scene is superimposed a looming vision of a menacing Asiatic invader. On an outback station, Beatrice Evans has rejected a jealous suitor in favour of the hero when news arrives of the Asian attack on Australia's shores. The station hands rush to enlist, and even the Aborigines among them turn upon the local Chinese, with a comic scene showing one of the Aborigines 'hammering' a Chinese cook. On one farm a Peace Society man refuses the call to arms and tears down the proclamation posted on his land. He is later seen protesting with the invader, 'probably about arbitration', and being mercilessly killed. In Sydney, the Australian army gathers and parades through the streets, encouraged by much cheering from the crowds. The city is attacked and a fierce battle ensues; buildings are set on fire and the Asian invader takes over the Mint, the Treasury building and the wireless telegraphy station. Meanwhile the rejected suitor turns traitor and agrees to act as a guide for the Asians in return for money and the girl. Beatrice is captured but is rescued from the Asian camp by the aviator William E. Hart (flying the only plane then in Sydney). Soon the Asian tide is turned and as peace is restored the young lovers are reunited.

The film was a complex production, shot on and off over a year, and involving contributions from each of the three Higgins brothers.

A model of Sydney was built in Spencer's studio at Rushcutters Bay, and cardboard planes, flying down on wires and bombing Sydney landmarks, were used to simulate the Asian attack. Physical assistance was also given by the Defence Department, and to avoid embarrassment to the government's relations with the Japanese, the nationality of the 'yellow peril' was not specified; the invaders were simply called 'Mongolians'. Extras to play the enemy were recruited from Sydney's Chinese community. The white cast included Alfred O'Shea, who later became one of Australia's most prominent operatic tenors.

The film opened at Spencer's Lyceum Theatre, Sydney, on 19 July 1913, with patriotic songs accompanying each screening. Large audiences gave it 'a noisy welcome' during its month-long season, but despite the public enthusiasm, a few critics were unusually frank in attacking the film's technique, if not its theme. *Theatre*, 1 August 1913, found the burning of Sydney to be 'too palpably a fake' and the continuity of the final scenes to be erratic, with the aviator Hart escaping 'hundreds of armed invaders' who had plenty of time to shoot him down before his aeroplane got away. The sudden disappearance of the enemy hordes at the end also detracted from what was nevertheless 'a most effective appeal to the popular mind in the matter of defence'. Similar criticisms were made by a casual contributor to the *Bulletin*, 9 October 1913, who found that the film erred 'on the side of over-subtlety'. For example, the fight between the Aborigines and the Chinese lacked impact because their faces and hence their identities were never clearly revealed. 'Finally, the uniforms are so much alike that half the time . . . an audience is afraid to applaud in a battle scene for fear of cheering the enemy.' If these comments suggest an unusually slapdash production by Longford,

93 C. A. Jeffries and John Barr, authors of *Australia Calls*

they do at the same time reveal how closely he was able to mirror the militant and jingoistic atmosphere just before the outbreak of war. The Chinese later won grudging respect from Australians when they served as allies during the war, but Longford's racist outburst vividly expressed feelings that lay not far beneath the surface of Australian society for many years.

94 A Blue Gum Romance

1913 FRANKLYN BARRETT

PC: Fraser Film Release and Photographic Company.
SC, PH: Franklyn Barrett.
CAST: Tien Hogue (heroine), Tom Middleton (hero), Douglas Lotherington (Aboriginal chief).

The first narrative film produced by the Fraser Film Release and Photographic Company was set in the timber industry area near Gosford on the central New South Wales coast. The action included a corroboree, with Aborigines played by white boys from Gosford. Interiors were shot in the back yard of a house in Sydney, with a large cheesecloth tent spread over the set to diffuse the light. The film was completed by July 1913, when a negative was sent to England, but the only recorded screening was not until 20 September at the Snowden Theatre, Melbourne.

The Fraser film company was formed late in 1912 by two brothers, Archie and Colin Fraser, and operated both as a film exchange and a production house. Financial support was received from Giuseppe Borsalino, an Italian businessman who, besides his fame for hats, was an investor in Italian film production and saw the Fraser film company as an outlet for his films. In addition to importing films from Italy, England and other countries, the Frasers intended to produce their own local material, despite the difficulties of an increasingly closed exhibition market, dominated by the combine. They first commissioned Franklyn Barrett to make a documentary, *Whale-hunting in Jervis Bay*, which was released with some success in Melbourne in January 1913.

94 Colin (*l*) and Archie Fraser

A Blue Gum Romance began a series of narrative films produced sporadically during the next five years until the company's demise in 1918. Although one of their productions, *The Silence of Dean Maitland* (1914), was a major commercial success, pressure from the combine seems to have caused a severe reduction in their production programme, and possibly also affected their survival as a distributor, although their reliance on European sources of supply made them vulnerable to the decline of production there during the war.

95 The Life of a Jackeroo

1913 FRANKLYN BARRETT

PC: Fraser Film Release and Photographic Company.
SC: J. H. Wainwright. PH: Franklyn Barrett.
CAST: Tom Middleton (the Englishman), Tien Hogue (the squatter's daughter), Ruth Wainwright (the actress).

Made immediately after *A Blue Gum Romance*, *The Life of a Jackeroo* used not only the same locations (around Gosford, N.S.W.) and much the same cast, but also some of the same incidents, including an Aboriginal corroboree. The *Bulletin*, 31 July 1913, found that the main difference between the two was that the second had 'more horse' and a stronger plot: 'the story carries its main ballast along a well-grooved track, but makes occasional excursions into new surroundings'. The main character was a young Englishman who leaves an ambitious actress in England to seek colonial experience in the backblocks. The 'new chum' makes good, and falls in love with the daughter of a wealthy squatter. Love runs smoothly until the actress arrives unexpectedly and finds an ally in a villainous overseer on the station. Some local Aborigines are roused to make a raid on the squatter's homestead and the English jackeroo is captured. A daring ride by the heroine and a loyal Aboriginal save his life. The film was screened at Waddington's Grand Theatre, Sydney, on 28 July 1913.

96 The Bondage of the Bush

1913 CHARLES WOODS

PC: Woods' Australian Films. P, SC: Charles Woods. PH: Bert Ive. 4000 ft.

CAST: D. R. Rivenall (Dan Romer), Charles Woods (Gee-Bung), Wilton Power (Wilfred Granger), Jeff Williams (James Bramley), Alfred Bristow (Parson Bramley), Gertrude Darley (Mona Bramley), E. W. Newman, H. Ward, H. N. Gannan, E. L. Betts, and J. Darley (fishermen), G. Filmer (Sergeant Jones), J. Hamilton (Trooper Wallace).

With all of the most familiar ingredients of bush melodramas, this feature directed by the comedian Charles Woods offered the following highlights: 'The great race—a leap for life—horse and man precipitated to raging torrents below—fight with the waters—the dash for liberty—the struggle on the cliffs—the black boy's revenge' (*Sun*, 12 November 1916). Woods himself played Gee-Bung, the 'faithful black boy' of the hero, Dan Romer, a boundary rider. The film screened at the Victoria Theatre, Sydney, on 18 August 1913 and toured widely through suburban and country areas.

97 Pommy Arrives in Australia

1913 RAYMOND LONGFORD

PC: Fraser Film Release and Photographic Company. SC: Raymond Longford. PH: Franklyn Barrett.

CAST: Tom Cosgrove, Lottie Lyell, Tien Hogue, Helen Fergus.

Longford's first comedy exploited one of the popular themes of Australian humour on both stage and screen, the problems faced by 'new chums' from England in adjusting to Australian life. The good-natured immigrant of this film is enticed by a charming trio of Australian 'tomboys' into 'a host of ludicrous situations'. The film opened at Waddington's Grand Theatre, Sydney, on 18 August 1913 for a routine three-day season.

98 The Sick Stockrider*

1913 W. J. LINCOLN

PC: Lincoln-Cass Films. From the poem by Adam Lindsay Gordon. PH: Maurice Bertel. 1200 ft.

CAST: George Bryant (the stockrider), Godfrey Cass (his mate), Roy Redgrave, Tom Cannam.

The film, which survives today in virtually complete form, was based unwaveringly on Adam Lindsay Gordon's famous ballad, first published in the year of his death, 1870. Verses of the poem appear one by one, separated by illustrative tableaux. Many of the visual interpolations are portions of the same long take, showing the stockman lying beside a campfire, gasping his last. A little variety is offered with his grim memories of his mates and their deaths, one from alcohol, another gored by a bull (to represent which an actor turns a somersault over the horns of a quite passive animal), and another accidentally drowned. It is economical and primitive filmed theatre; the interiors are undisguised canvas backdrops, which vibrate with the movements of the actors, and the action is totally reliant on the inter-titles (or an off-screen lecturer, often Roy Redgrave) to overcome the barrier of silence.

It opened in Melbourne on 18 August 1913 at the Royal Pictures, Prahran, and at Hoyts St George's Hall. The *Bulletin*, 9 October 1913, was moved by the admirable sentiments that had prompted the film-makers to embark on the filming of local literature, and remarked that Gordon's poem was 'a sure draw on the bills, but not the easiest of themes for picture treatment'. The most effective moment for the *Bulletin* was the closing image, after the stockrider's death: the children 'frisking' beside the grave, while his lonely mate awkwardly tosses down some ragged flowers in an off-handed gesture that movingly masks his deeply felt grief.

98 *The Sick Stockrider*

The Sick Stockrider was the first product of a new Melbourne 'film factory', Lincoln-Cass Films, formed in July 1913 and based at a studio in the Melbourne suburb of Elsternwick. The managing director of the company was H. Dean Stewart; W. J. Lincoln and Godfrey Cass were employed as the principal film-makers, with Charles Wheeler as stage manager and Maurice Bertel as cinematographer. A regular troupe of performers appeared in each production, and the films varied widely, giving the actors ample opportunity to display their range. The films completed before the company's closure in October included most of the subjects then in popular vogue in the theatre and cinema: gold-mining, the convict days and upper-class decadence, as well as this initial exercise in bush sentiment.

The failure of the company was attributed by Dean Stewart directly to 'the pernicious system of Australasian Films, Ltd., in binding the showmen to take their full programme from them' (*Theatre*, 1 December 1914), and Lincoln-Cass Films were added to the list of victims of Australasian's monopolistic drive. Their studio was later sold to J. C. Williamson Ltd for a new film venture in 1915.

The Lincoln-Cass photographer, Maurice Bertel, was one of the most competent in the industry. Born in France in 1871, he came to Australia in 1890 and learnt his trade with local film companies. In 1907, when Pathé Frères established a laboratory and film production service in Melbourne, he was appointed to supervise their weekly newsreel, the Pathé Gazette, and scenic films under contract to the Australian government. When Pathé's local operation merged with Australasian Films in 1913, Bertel worked on their newsreel for some months before joining Lincoln-Cass. He subsequently worked on the films produced by J. C. Williamson, and when that venture also failed he joined Herschell's in Melbourne as technical adviser to their production service, and remained there, sponsoring many other cameramen and film technicians, until his death in May 1930.

99 Moondyne

1913 W. J. LINCOLN

PC: Lincoln-Cass Films. From the novel by John Boyle O'Reilly. PH: Maurice Bertel.

CAST: George Bryant (Joe Moondyne), Roy Redgrave (Isaac Bowman), Godfrey Cass (Te Mana Roa).

Joe Moondyne is a convict in Western Australia assigned as a labourer to a sadistic settler, Isaac Bowman. Joe escapes and takes refuge with a tribe of Aborigines who tell him about a secret mountain of gold. When he is later recaptured by Bowman, Joe lures him into the bush with the promise of taking him to the gold. The king of the Aborigines, Te Mana Roa, shows them the mine, but later Bowman seizes an opportunity to knock down the king and load his horses with gold. In his haste to get away Bowman loses his way and eventually perishes in the desert, leaving Joe at peace with his Aboriginal friends.

The film was shot in and around Melbourne, and on 1 September 1913 it opened there at Hoyts St George's Hall and at Royal Pictures, Prahran.

99 *Moondyne* George Bryant (*second from right*)

99 *Moondyne* George Bryant (*r*)

99 *Moondyne* George Bryant (*l*), Godfrey Cass

99 *Moondyne* George Bryant (*kneeling*)

100 The Remittance Man

1913 W. J. LINCOLN

PC: Lincoln-Cass Films. PH: Maurice Bertel.
CAST: Roy Redgrave, Godfrey Cass, George Bryant.

This four-act melodrama about a thief's reformation was filmed in Melbourne and screened simultaneously at Hoyts St George's Hall and the Lyric Theatre, Prahran, for a short season commencing on 15 September 1913.

101 Transported

1913 W. J. LINCOLN

PC: Lincoln-Cass Films. PH: Maurice Bertel. 2500 ft.
CAST: Roy Redgrave, Godfrey Cass, George Bryant.

Another in the series of low-budget productions by the Lincoln-Cass company, this convict melodrama received its only major release in Melbourne, simultaneously at Hoyts St George's Hall and at the Lyric Theatre, Prahran, on 29 September 1913. The complex plot begins in England where the squire arranges for a local village girl, Jessie Grey, to marry her true love, Leonard Lincoln. A rejected suitor, Harold Hawk, maddened by drink and disappointment, tries to force her to consent to marriage with him, and she wounds him with a gun. Hawk is arrested and sentenced to life imprisonment in Australia. Years later, Leonard and Jessie, now happily married, go to Australia to seek their fortune on the goldfields. Hawk learns of their arrival and escapes from custody, determined to have revenge. He breaks into Jessie's house and tries to take her away by force, but she is rescued by the timely arrival of Leonard.

101 *Transported*

102 The Road to Ruin

1913 W. J. LINCOLN

PC: Lincoln-Cass Films. PH: Maurice Bertel. 2700 ft.
CAST: Roy Redgrave, Godfrey Cass, George Bryant, Tom Cannam, Beryl Bryant, Ward Lyons, Charles Wheeler, Marcus St John, John Brunton, Marion Willis.

This moral tale offered 'a true vignette of life as it is lived in the great social swim of our capital cities. It discloses the luxury of life, the temptations of the weak, the craving for notoriety, the unscrupulousness of the speculator, the homes of the wealthy and the complex conditions that surround humanity in the race for wealth and position' (*Age*, 11 October 1913). The story was set against the background of numerous Melbourne landmarks, including the cafés of Collins Street, the Caulfield races, and the banks, clubs and theatres of the city centre. The film opened at Hoyts St George's Hall and the Lyric Theatre, Prahran, on 13 October 1913.

101 *Transported*

103 The Reprieve

1913 W. J. LINCOLN

PC: Lincoln-Cass Films. PH: Maurice Bertel. 2500 ft.
CAST: Roy Redgrave, Beryl Bryant, George Bryant, Godfrey Cass.

A simple morality tale, contrasting the working classes with high society, the film began with events leading to the death of an adulterous woman at the hands of her jealous husband. The man, a worker, Richard Gannon, is arrested and sentenced to death, but the judge recommends mercy and asks the Home Secretary for a reprieve. The Secretary, a cold and stubborn man, refuses, but when he mistakenly comes to believe that his own wife is unfaithful, he realizes how easy it might have been for him to kill her in his fury. Chastened by the realization, he grants a reprieve for Gannon and resolves to show his wife more affection.

The film opened at Hoyts St George's Hall, Melbourne, on 3 November 1913.

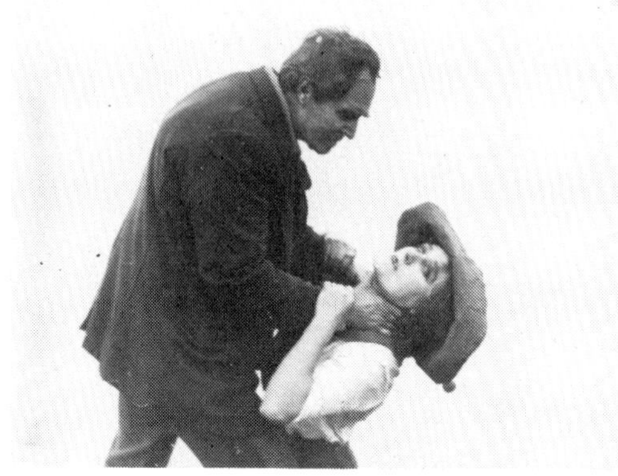

103 *The Reprieve*

104 The Crisis

1913 W. J. LINCOLN

PC: Lincoln-Cass Films. PH: Maurice Bertel. 3000 ft.
CAST: Roy Redgrave, George Bryant, Tom Cannam, Beryl Bryant, Kathleen Lindgren (child).

This story of 'a great temptation' was inspired by a painting, 'The Crisis', by an English artist, Frank Dicksee. The happy home life of a simple fisherman, John Owen, his wife, Nellie, and their child is disrupted by a ruthless philanderer, Frank, who determines to lure the beautiful Nellie away from her husband. He convinces Nellie that John is unfaithful and, emotionally stunned, she deserts her home and child and joins Frank in the city. There she is forced to assist him in 'plucking pigeons' (extracting money from the careless rich) in high society, but she is gradually overcome by guilt and a longing for her old family life. After a violent confrontation with Frank, she escapes back to her home and arrives just in time to provide the mother's love that is needed to save her child from a severe illness, and she is happily reunited with her forgiving husband.

The film opened at Hoyts St George's Hall, Melbourne, on 8 December 1913.

105 The Wreck

1913 W. J. LINCOLN

PC: Lincoln-Cass Films. From the poem 'From the Wreck' by Adam Lindsay Gordon.

Gordon's poem was a ballad telling the story of a frantic ride for help by a farmhand who has witnessed a shipwreck. A film version by the Lincoln-Cass team was made late in 1913 along with their other work in Melbourne, but there is no evidence of a public screening before 21 June 1915, when it was presented at the Strand Kinema de Luxe, Sydney.

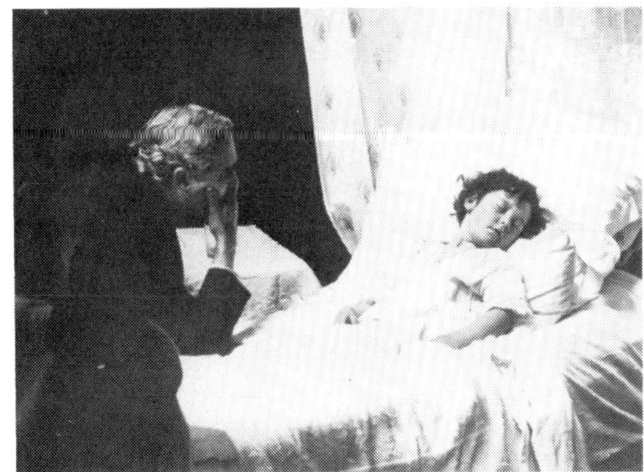

104 *The Crisis*

104 'The Crisis', the painting by Frank Dicksee that inspired the film by W. J. Lincoln

106 Sea Dogs of Australia

1913 MARTYN KEITH (?)

PC: Western Pacific Feature Films. P, SC: J. S. McCullagh. 2500 ft.
CAST: Eric Howell (Lieutenant Verner), Dave Smith (himself), Charles Villiers.

When the hard-drinking Lieutenant Verner of the Australian navy loses his fortune at gambling, an unscrupulous spy, Herman Markoff, tries to blackmail him into stealing the plans for a new explosive developed by his fellow officer and friend, Lieutenant Sidney. Verner is caught in the act of stealing the formula and is discharged in disgrace from the navy. Succumbing to the grip of alcohol, Verner throws in his lot with Markoff and tries to kidnap Sidney, but the attempt is foiled by the timely intervention of Dave Smith, the Australian champion boxer. Verner later lures Sidney into a trap by expressing remorse for his past misdeeds, and after torturing him succeeds in securing the formula. The crazed Verner decides to use the explosive to blow up HMAS *Australia*, but Sidney manages to escape from captivity, and with the aid of the telephone and a fast car he catches Markoff and kills him. Verner, however, eludes him and reaches a mysterious cruiser waiting outside Sydney Heads. Sidney alerts *Australia*, her guns soon destroy the cruiser and Verner perishes with the stolen plans.

The film was previewed to the trade early in December 1913, but the first recorded screening was not until 12 August 1914 at the Wondergraph Theatre, Adelaide. It was withdrawn soon afterwards by order of Commonwealth defence authorities, probably because of the threat to security caused by the footage taken on board *Australia*.

107 'Neath Austral Skies

1913 RAYMOND LONGFORD

PC: Commonwealth Film Producing Company. P: A. C. Tinsdale (?). SC: Raymond Longford. 4500 ft.
CAST: Lottie Lyell (Eileen Delmont), Robert Henry (Colonel Delmont), George Parke (Eric Delmont), Martyn Keith (Captain Frank Hollis), Charles Villiers (Gidgee Dan), Mervyn Barrington (Snowy, boundary rider), Walter Warr (Ah Lum, cook), T. Archer (Monaro Jack, stockman), Frank Phillips (Superintendent of Police), Jeff Williams (station agent).

This drama in 'five colossal acts' about life in the wilds of the Queensland bush, was the only major film produced by the Commonwealth Film Producing Company of Sydney. It opened on 22 December 1913 at the Lyric Theatre, Melbourne, as a supporting feature, and received few other screenings.

The story began, like so many of its contemporaries, in upper-class England and proceeded to the Australian outback. To protect the name of his fiancée's family, Captain Frank Hollis accepts the blame for a theft actually committed by the girl's brother, Eric Delmont. He leaves for Australia and there joins the New South Wales Mounted Police. Back in England, Eric is mortally wounded in a drunken brawl and confesses to his crime. Frank's fiancée, Eileen, and her father set sail for Australia to search for Frank and restore him to their family. They buy a cattle property, and call for a trooper to investigate the theft of some of their stock. Unknown to them, the trooper who responds to their call is none other than Frank, but on his way he is captured by the gang of thieves. With her men, Eileen rides out to rescue the trooper, and arrives at the very moment when the gang throws him into a river to drown. While her men tackle the gang, Eileen grips a knife between her teeth and plunges into the river to save the drowning trooper. To her dismay and delight she realizes that she has rescued none other than her wronged lover, and the dramatic moment of recognition brings the story to a happy conclusion.

The Commonwealth Film Producing Company followed *'Neath Austral Skies* with a short 2000-foot drama, *The Swagman's Story*, made early in 1914 by Raymond Longford, with Lottie Lyell as a country girl who becomes a member of city high society and rejects her unsophisticated parents from the bush. Probably intended as a cheap programme filler, it was previewed to the trade on 2 March 1914.

Part 2:

1914-1918

Australian feature films between 1914 and 1918 reflected sharp changes in popular attitudes to the war in Europe. Enthusiasm to participate in Australia's first major conflict as an independent nation was shown in *The Hero of the Dardanelles* (1915), in which the hero eagerly departed for active service, farewelled by proud parents and friends. Eagerness to prove Australia's loyalty to the British was shown in *The Martyrdom of Nurse Cavell* (1916), in which much was made of the fact that Australians were the first in the world to express outrage against the treatment of the British nurse by the Germans. A spate of films about Gallipoli and the destruction of the German raider *Emden* celebrated the first tangible proof of Australian fighting capability. But eventually the horrible realities of war struck home. By May 1916 a war-weary critic attacked *The Joan of Arc of Loos* for its childish enthusiasm for war as though it were a game, and soon war subjects virtually disappeared as a source of entertainment. In 1917 John Gavin tried to repeat the commercial success of his Nurse Cavell film with *The Murder of Captain Fryatt*, another outcry against the savagery of the Germans, but the film found no audience. The war was too real for romanticizing, and the domestic conscription issue too heated. In 1918 Snowy Baker was obliged to advertise *The Enemy Within* as 'Not a war film'.

With the waning of war stories, a wave of comedies reached the screen, finding a huge public appetite for escapist farce. The upsurge in comedy began with four films by Beaumont Smith about a backblocks family, the Hayseeds, and these were followed by other bucolic comedies about similar rustic types. The Hayseeds series represented the first major attempt at screen comedy in Australia; previously comedy had only occasionally spilled over from the stage to the screen, with minor shorts such as *Charlie at the Sydney Show* (1916), starring Ern Vockler, one of many Chaplin imitators on the local stage. But the usual reliance of comedy on words seemed to have discouraged Australian film-makers

From *Theatre*, 1 January 1915

The moving-picture combine asked the Minister for Customs that no duty be placed on cinematograph films on the ground that there was no local industry to protect.

M.P. COMBINE: Lord, I have killed my competitor! Surely this will entitle me to a privileged place in heaven.

from entering this field, until Beaumont Smith ventured forth in 1917 with verbal humour embodied in frequent and lengthy intertitles.

Other subjects explored in Australian films during the war tended to be tried and tested stage successes, such as *The Rebel* (1915), *The Monk and the Woman* (1917) and a series of filmed plays by the J. C. Williamson theatrical company. Raymond Longford and W. J. Lincoln made forays into a romanticized past—*Mutiny of the Bounty* (1916) and *The Life's Romance of Adam Lindsay Gordon* (1916)—but neither these nor the war films displayed any sign of a serious or deeply felt self-image. On the contrary, the heroes of many war films, including *The Hero of the Dardanelles*, were in spirit members of the British upper classes. It seemed that with the suppression by censorship of the bushranger hero in 1912, no distinctive Australian hero had yet emerged to replace him on the screen.

Throughout the war the production industry continued to adjust to the new power of Australasian Films and Union Theatres over distribution and exhibition. Events surrounding the production of *The Shepherd of the Southern Cross* and *The Silence of Dean Maitland* in 1914 confirmed the ability of the combine to limit the production goals of film-makers. Cozens Spencer tried hard to lead Australasian into world-class production with *The Shepherd of the Southern Cross*, but found himself out-voted in the combine's boardroom. Although he soon withdrew completely from film activity, he believed that there was no doubt that Australasian would one day come to heed his advice. When even modestly conceived local films could attract larger audiences than some imported 'specials', Spencer could not understand why Australasian refused to profit from the clear audience preference. He wrote: 'If pictures were made here all our showmen would have to include them in their programmes. People would not patronise their shows unless they did.' (*Theatre*, 1 January 1915)

Australasian's main distribution rival, the Fraser Film Release and Photographic Company, relied heavily on films from Europe, but the war quickly disrupted world-wide production patterns and the Frasers never recovered from their loss of European supplies. In 1914 they embarked on the production of 'specials' to boost their trade, employing Raymond Longford as their director. He was at the top of his form, and the company's first major film, *The Silence of Dean Maitland*, was a powerful drama to which audiences responded enthusiastically. But Longford's relationship with the Fraser brothers ended in a bitter legal wrangle, in which Longford alleged that Australasian Films had forced the Frasers to cancel their production programme by threatening a general trade embargo. According to Longford, Australasian had the power to manipulate almost the entire exhibition market and sought to stop production by rivals for no other reason than the blind pursuit of power. Longford's charges were never proved, but they were widely believed among film-makers, who regarded Australasian Films and Union Theatres as crucial factors in the success or failure of any production. After 1914, directors like Longford and Franklyn Barrett devoted much of their energy to a search for ways around the combine, or even of working with it if it could be persuaded to release their films on acceptable terms.

Despite these adverse circumstances, feature production continued at a consistent though reduced rate, fragmented among small-scale operations. The more enduring of the wartime production companies included J. C. Williamson Ltd, the powerful theatrical firm, which in 1915-16 made film versions of the most popular plays in its repertoire (for example, *Within the Law*, 1916 and *Officer 666*, 1916) in a bid to ward off the threat of American films of the same plays. Another major producer emerged in 1917—Beaumont Smith, a showman who for many years had displayed a keen awareness of exploitable gimmicks in the theatre, and who turned to cinema to make a series of commercially successful low-budget 'quickies' over the next decade.

Australasian Films ventured into feature production when it suited the company's commercial purposes, but they were quick to withdraw from the financial uncertainties of production as soon as those purposes were realized; their role in film-making was essentially passive. A specific incentive arose in 1915, with a request from the Australian government to make recruiting films, including the narrative feature, *The Hero of the Dardanelles* (1915). Perhaps partly to ingratiate itself with a government that was considering a heavy import duty on film, Australasian made a public display of offering its full co-operation. But although the film was profitable, the combine did not continue long with feature production. Throughout the war it limited its output to newsreels, 'scenics' and novelty items, and leased to other film-makers the large production resources it had inherited from Spencer.

During the war years, Hollywood gained ascendancy in world production, and the growing status of American cinema was reflected in the sharp upsurge of traffic to and from the U.S.A. of film industry people seeking broader experience or new careers. Australian actors had traditionally sought overseas experience within the Empire, especially in South Africa and England, but now the shift to Hollywood was unmistakable. Large numbers of talented or ambitious Australians left the local industry for varying degrees of fame and fortune in the U.S.A., among them Louise Carbasse (later Louise Lovely), Annette Kellerman (a swimmer, who did not make a feature film in Australia but became an important Hollywood star), John Gavin, Sylvia Breamer, Snub Pollard, Enid Bennett, Billy Bevan, Arthur Shirley, Clyde Cook and many more who left gaps in the Australian industry that were hard to fill.

At this time, too, film began to be accepted

more widely in the community and to outgrow its status as a predominantly working-class entertainment. During the war, the government recognized the value of film in promoting recruitment and morale, and it became a valued medium for news. In June 1917 the Australian government sent an official cinematographer, Frank Hurley, to the war zone specifically to record the Australian war effort (previously Australia had depended for news film on the services of British war correspondents). In December 1911 the Commonwealth government had appointed its first staff cinematographer, A. J. Campbell, to make films to promote Australian goods and resources and to record state occasions, but he was dismissed in May 1913 for alleged inefficiency and for striving for 'artistic' effects. The government tried again and its new appointee, Bert Ive, remained as the chief Commonwealth cinematographer for twenty-three years. The government's awareness of the power of film to form opinion was also displayed in the work of the newspaper cartoonist Harry Julius, whom the government hired to make a series of brief animated propaganda films—one of the earliest examples of animation in Australia. These 'war cartoons' were crudely executed—Julius was filmed drawing with chalk on a dark background—but they became popular novelty items in commercial programmes.

Film was also becoming more accessible in a technical sense: there were many competent technicians (over sixty cameramen had applied for the job of government cinematographer in 1913) and the medium was open for use by organizations and individuals who could afford it. In 1918 wealthier sections of Sydney and Melbourne society began to display some interest; various charity organizations, led by upper-class society figures, organized the making of films to assist them with fund-raising, and semi-amateurs like A. C. Tinsdale, who relied on the wealthy for patronage, began to move into production.

The period was characterized by diversification in the uses to which film was put, and in the people making use of it, largely under the stimulus of the war. The number of feature films produced locally was greatly reduced, but the leading film-makers gained in sophistication of style and content and were sufficiently promising to create a public demand for more, a demand that grew in strength through the next decade, the creative peak of Australian silent film.

108 The Shepherd of the Southern Cross

1914 ALEXANDER BUTLER

PC: Australasian Films. P: Stanley Twist. SC: Nell Shipman. PH: Ernest Higgins.

CAST: Arthur Shirley (Devon Collins), Vera Pearce (Lady Helen Reynolds), Roland Conway (Ralph Hughes), Clare Stephenson (nurse), Tien Hogue, Shirley Huxley, P. J. Noonan, Mrs George Lauri.

This drama of the Australian bush opens in London where Lady Helen Reynolds is forced to choose one of two cousins to be her husband in order to inherit a large fortune. One of them is the unscrupulous Ralph Hughes, who contrives to discredit the other, Devon Collins, and succeeds to the extent that Devon leaves England for Australia to become a shepherd. Ralph marries Lady Helen, but when he too comes to Australia, his plans are undone and Helen and Devon are happily reunited.

The formula story was written by an American, Nell Shipman, an actress and a prolific author of Hollywood screenplays, and later one of the few women producers in the U.S.A. Her screenplay, originally entitled *The Shepherdess of the Southern Cross*, was brought to Australia by Stanley Twist, an American hired by Cozens Spencer to supervise the operations of the studio at Rushcutters Bay. Twist arrived in Sydney in January 1914, and was preceded in December 1913 by Alexander Butler, a leading British director whom Spencer had hired to make the first of a series of major productions for the world market. Butler had been to Australia before to produce comic opera for J. C. Williamson, and had then established a firm reputation in British cinema as a director of features for the Barker company. His work in Australia was regarded with some scepticism by local film-makers used to making films much faster and far more cheaply. Longford later criticized Butler for taking as long as eighteen weeks to complete shooting. According to Longford (*RCE*, p.152), some effort was made to achieve realistic effects (including the use of two tons of fuller's earth to simulate a dust storm), but the film was a total failure commercially, returning scarcely a hundred pounds to the production company. A review in *Theatre*, 1 July 1914, expressed reservations about the performance of Vera Pearce ('she does not appear to be able to get into her face the least expression'), but other cast members were more adequate, especially Roland Conway as the villain: 'his facial expressions in his terrified, dying moments are vividly realistic'. Despite her unimpressive screen debut, Vera Pearce continued with a long stage career in Australian musical comedy and revue, and in 1917 made a more noteworthy screen appearance as the tragic heroine of *The Martyrdom of Nurse Cavell*. In 1921 she went to England and readily found leading roles in stage musicals and as principal boy in pantomimes.

The film opened simultaneously at Spencer's Lyceum, Sydney, and at the Majestic Theatre, Melbourne, on 13 June 1914. Publicity stressed spectacular views of flocks of sheep and outback scenery as the main attraction. It was eclipsed, however, by Longford's film of *The Silence of Dean Maitland*, released in Sydney on the same day, and starring the same romantic lead, Arthur Shirley. Spencer's grand schemes for the production of world-class films were immediately thwarted by his fellow company directors who lacked his enthusiasm for production. The making of feature films was abandoned, and by December 1914 Butler had returned to England and resumed his work in British studios. An embittered Spencer soon resigned from the company bearing his name and dissociated himself thereafter from the film trade he had done so much to promote.

109 The Silence of Dean Maitland

1914 RAYMOND LONGFORD

PC: Fraser Film Release and Photographic Company. SC: Lewis Scott. From the novel by Maxwell Gray. PH: Tasman Higgins. ART D: Jack Ricketts, E. Bedford. 3500 ft.

CAST: Harry Thomas (Reverend Cyril Maitland), Charles Keegan (Cyril's father), Nellie Kemberman (Cyril's mother), Gwil Adams (Lilian, Cyril's sister), Arthur Shirley (Doctor Henry Everard), Lottie Lyell (Marion, Henry's sister), James Martin (Ben Lee), Ada Clyde (Mrs Lee), Nellie Brooks (Alma Lee), Charles Villiers (Judkins), Little Tuppeny (Everard Maitland), Little Rebe Grey (Marion Maitland), Jack Goodall.

A shrewd mixture of religion and sex, *The Silence of Dean Maitland* had been a major success on the Australian stage for many years, and the film followed the play closely. Somewhere in rural England a highly respected dean lives with a guilty secret: while in deacon's orders he had been seduced by a young girl, and when assailed by the girl's outraged father, had struggled with him and killed him. Compounding his sins, the young Maitland had indulged his selfish pride and allowed his best friend to be arrested for the murder and sentenced to twenty years' imprisonment. When his friend is finally released, a broken, middle-aged man, he comes to worship in Dean Maitland's church. The shock of his appearance drives the dean to confess his guilt publicly in a sermon, after which he collapses and dies, his conscience clear at last.

After a long search for a suitable location to represent the English setting, Longford staged much of the action in the grounds and buildings of the Gladesville Mental Asylum in Sydney. The £400 production was released at the Palace Theatre, Sydney, on 13 June 1914 to large audiences. Its presentation was unusually elaborate: musical accompaniment was provided by a grand organ and chimes, with a children's choir of fifty voices; as the drama rose to the climax of the dean's last sermon, Longford's camera moved into a close-up of

109 *The Silence of Dean Maitland* Harry Thomas

his face, and an actor stepped onto the stage to deliver the sermon in synchronization with the Dean's lips. Audiences responded enthusiastically as the emotional rhetoric boomed forth: 'The three darkest blots upon the soul of man—IMPURITY, BLOODSHED, TREACHERY—have stained my soul . . . I declare before God and man, I repent.'

In May 1914 Longford had signed a two-year contract with the Fraser brothers under which he was to receive a salary of £1000 a year to produce for them a continuous stream of films, as many as twelve each year. *The Silence of Dean Maitland* was the first in the series, but before the second could be commenced, the Frasers cancelled the contract, claiming that Australasian Films had threatened them with a trade boycott if they continued to produce 'star' features. Longford promptly took an action for damages against Henry Gee of Australasian, and allegations were made by Longford and others in court that Gee had used the threat of withdrawing film supply from any theatre that showed Fraser's production. Gee was allegedly determined to establish a monopoly control over sources of film within Australia and had no intention of seeing major production projects get off the ground (*Theatre*, 1 December 1914). Although Fraser's film did attract healthy returns wherever it was shown, its release was severely hampered by Australasian's actions, and its potential earnings were far from realized. Longford lost his case against Gee (primarily because his contract had not been with Gee in the first place) and he left the Frasers to search for financial backing elsewhere. Before leaving, he completed two short films, the first an adaptation of a narrative poem by Victor Hugo, *We'll Take her Children in amongst our own* (released on 1 February 1915 in Sydney), and a comedy, *Ma Hogan's New Boarder* , starring the Chaplin impersonator Ern Vockler (released on 1 July 1915). After Longford's departure, the Frasers continued to make films only sporadically and abandoned the idea of continuous production.

The Silence of Dean Maitland was re-filmed in 1933 by Cinesound (ironically a subsidiary of Australasian Films), again with enormous popular support.

110 A Long, Long Way to Tipperary

1914 GEORGE DEAN

PC: Higgins Brothers. P: Ernest Higgins.
CAST: Adele Inman.

Molly Malone is an Irish colleen in love with Paddy O'Reilly. Despite her entreaties to stay, Paddy goes off to England to better himself. In London he enlists in the British army, and is sent to the front. Meanwhile, a rival for Molly's hand, Mick, tries to woo her, but she rejects him. Mick swears vengeance on Paddy, and Molly has a nightmare in which the men fight. 'The rose leaf' tells her,

110 *A Long, Long Way to Tipperary*

110 *A Long, Long Way to Tipperary* Superimposition of Molly reading a letter and imagining the fate of her lover

however, that Paddy is safe, and when he returns a hero, they are joyfully married.

This Irish romance based on the popular wartime song was one of several films produced by the Higgins brothers in Sydney in the early years of the war. The other films were short documentaries and compilation films, including *Australia's Response to the Empire's Call* (1914). This isolated venture into fiction was a severe disappointment to them. In an attempt to reach mass audiences, they placed it with Australasian Films for distribution, and after a première at the Lyceum Theatre, Sydney, on 16 November 1914, numerous screenings were held in Melbourne and the suburbs of both cities. They found difficulty, however, in extracting what they regarded as fair payment from Australasian for the screenings (see *Theatre*, 1 March 1915). A further problem arose in December 1914 when the Frasers announced their intention to release a British film by Maurice Elvey with a similar title and almost identical plot. Higgins sought an injunction against them to stop their release of the film, but the result of the action is not known. Certainly the enthusiasm of the Higgins brothers for further feature films was dampened by the experience.

111 The Day

1914 ALFRED ROLFE

PC: Fraser Film Release and Photographic Company. SC: Johnson Weir. From the poem by Henry Chappell.

Alfred Rolfe joined the Frasers after Raymond Longford's departure from the company, and directed at least two films for them, *The Day* and *The Sunny South* (1915). The patriotic war theme of *The Day*, exposing the brutality of the Germans in Europe, drew its inspiration from a widely read poem, said to have been written by an English railway porter, Henry Chappell. The screen adaptation was prepared by the actor Johnson Weir, who also lent his 'elocutionary services' to exhibitors by reciting the poem during screenings. Produced and distributed by the Frasers, the film opened at the Stadium, Sydney, on 23 November 1914 for a three-day season.

111 *The Day*

112 The Sunny South, or The Whirlwind of Fate

1915 ALFRED ROLFE

PC: Fraser Film Release and Photographic Company. From the play by George Darrell. 3000 ft. CAST: Charles Villiers.

The second feature made by Rolfe for the Fraser company was based on a perennial stage favourite, *The Sunny South*, written by the actor George Darrell. The play, a comedy-drama of early Australia and the gold-diggings, was filmed by Rolfe on location at French's Forest on the outskirts of Sydney. The production was released quietly at Waddington's Globe Theatre, Sydney, on 1 February 1915 as part of an all-Australian programme with two short films made by the same company: Longford's *We'll Take her Children in amongst our own* and a 2000-foot comedy, *The Unknown*, directed by J. E. Mathews and starring two popular professional boxers, Peter Felix and 'Porky' Kearns.

113 My Partner

1915

5 acts

This obscure production of unknown authorship screened with little publicity at the Hub Theatre in the Sydney suburb of Newtown for a season commencing on 10 April 1915. The film had been shot on location in the Blue Mountains near Sydney, and used as its basis an American play that had been performed on the Sydney stage in February 1912 by the William Anderson troupe. The story followed the fortunes of Joe and Ned, two mates on the Californian goldfields. Both fall in love with Mary Brandon and quarrel bitterly. Later, when Joe relents and comes to forgive Ned, he finds that Ned has been murdered and that he is the prime suspect. Eventually Joe manages to clear himself of the murder charge, and to protect Mary's name declares that he is the father of her child and that they have been secretly married. Her father accepts him as son-in-law and insists on another marriage ceremony, after which Joe finds that Mary has loved him all along.

114 The Rebel

1915 J. E. MATHEWS

PC: Mathews Photo-Play Company. SC: J. E. Mathews. From the story by James Bernard Fagan.
PH: A. O. Segerberg. ART D: J. S. Mann. 5 reels.
CAST: Allen Doone (Jack Blake), Edna Keeley (Eileen McDermott), Frank Cullinane (Squire McDermott), Onslow Edgeworth (Captain Armstrong).

This 'stirring story of Ireland's struggle for freedom' had been performed with considerable success on the Australian stage since November 1913 by the tenor and comedian Allen Doone, who specialized in Irish romantic dramas. Outdoor settings and the freedom of the camera allowed the action of the play to be considerably expanded; 'Galloping troopers, exciting battle scenes, Irish jaunting cars, dancing on the green, feasting, riding and love-making' all contributed to the 'vigor, grace and excitement' of the film (*Sun*, 27 June 1915). The tale of love, jealousy and patriotism followed the fortunes of a rebel leader, Jack Blake, who is arrested and thrown into jail by a vindictive Englishman, Captain Armstrong. With the aid of his loved one, Eileen, Jack escapes and kills Armstrong in a duel. Together Jack and Eileen board a schooner and sail away to a more peaceful future in France.

Locations to represent Ireland were found close to Sydney and the film was shot in six weeks in April and May 1915, aided no doubt by the cast's familiarity with their parts on stage. Some difficulty was experienced in finding a release for the film, as Doone wrote in a letter to the press: 'I have not been able to get a satisfactory offer from any of the theatre proprietors for the Rights of exhibiting the picture, there seemingly being a prejudice against films "Made in Australia".' (*Daily Telegraph*, 5 June 1915) He was finally rescued by Spencer, who agreed to screen it for a week at the Lyceum Theatre, Sydney, from 26 June 1915.

The director, J. E. (John) Mathews, was an American who claimed experience in Hollywood studios. After making a comedy short, *The Unknown*, for the Fraser brothers, he directed *The Rebel* and opened an acting school in Sydney. Mathews's next film was a two-reel semi-documentary about the boxer Les Darcy, *The Heart of a Champion* (1915), but his plans for continued production soon failed. After one more film for the Frasers, *Murphy of Anzac* (1916), he moved to Adelaide, where he directed his final Australian film, *Remorse, a Story of the Red Plague* (1917).

114 Allen Doone

115 The Hero of the Dardanelles**

1915 ALFRED ROLFE

PC: Australasian Films. SC: Phillip Gell, Loris Brown. 4000 (?) ft.
CAST: Guy Hastings (William Brown), Loma Rossmore (Lily Brunton), C. Throoby (Mr Brown), Ruth Wainwright (Mrs Brown), Fred Francis (Gordon Brown).

Early in 1915 Australasian Films embarked on the production of feature films for the first time since 1912 (they had continued to produce 'novelty' items and newsreels). They returned to narrative films with a 2000-foot propaganda message, *Will they Never Come?*, written by two of Australasian's publicity staff, Phillip Gell and Loris Brown, and directed by Alfred Rolfe, with assistance from the Department of Defence. It was a rudimentary recruiting appeal and contrasted the stories of two brothers, one who willingly does his duty and enlists, the other who persists with a reckless life of sport. It was released at the Crystal Palace, Sydney, on 5 April 1915, and proved in such high demand that Australasian promptly set about a second and more substantial film, *The Hero of the Dardanelles.* The writers, director and much of the cast were retained from the earlier film, and again official endorsement and support came from the Department of Defence.

The central incident in *The Hero of the Dardanelles* was the landing of the Anzacs at Gaba Tepe, which was restaged at Tamarama Bay near Sydney just weeks after the actual event. The story presents, as in the earlier film, the careers of two brothers, one who has already enlisted, and another, William, who soon follows his example. The film shows Will being trained and, while on his final leave, persuading his pals in the pub to enlist. His patriotism and enthusiasm for the war is simple and unquestioning, and he is the pride of his wealthy family and sweetheart. They hold a farewell banquet in his honour and he is clearly established as an upper-class hero who will doubtless be good officer material in the

115 *The Hero of the Dardanelles* Guy Hastings bids farewell to his old life of leisure

army. Once his boat leaves for Egypt, the progress of his story is unknown, for the remainder of the film does not exist today.

The surviving scenes from the early part of the film show a fluent narrative style, with a free use of close-ups for dramatic effect. The missing scenes, re-creating the fighting in the Dardanelles, were based closely on reports by Ashmead-Bartlett and drawings and photographs of the landing. Hundreds of troops from the army training camp at Liverpool, N.S.W., were used, and the army also supplied the appropriate explosions and battle effects. Footage depicting the Anzac landing used in later films such as *The Spirit of Gallipoli* (1928) was almost certainly derived from this 1915 production, and if so, reveals an astute choice of location and a skilful management of mass action.

116 *Within Our Gates* Storming the cliffs of Gaba Tepe

Made at a time of intense public enthusiasm for the war, the film seemed to express for many people the romantic heroism of Australia's role in the war. After its première at the Majestic Theatre, Melbourne, on 17 July 1915, it screened widely, accompanied by vigorous applause from the press and endorsement from many political figures.

116 Within Our Gates, or Deeds that Won Gallipoli

1915 FRANK HARVEY

PC: J. C. Williamson Ltd. SC: W. J. Lincoln. PH: Monte Luke. 6 (?) reels.

CAST: Cyril Mackay (Edgar Ferguson), Leslie Victor (Max Huitzell), Frank Harvey (Carl Heine), Dorothy Cumming (Freda Henschell), John Ralston (Andrew Ferguson), Norman Easty (Heinrich Henschell), Raymond Lawrence, Charles Morse, Frank East.

Late in 1914 the theatrical firm of J. C. Williamson grew alarmed at reports of American films being made from plays that were in their current repertoire. Rather than allow the American films to intrude into their territory, 'the Firm' decided to exploit the movie market themselves, and initiated film adaptations of their own stage productions. As a base for these films, they bought the former Lincoln-Cass studio in Melbourne and retained two of the staff—Maurice Bertel as cameraman, and W. J. Lincoln as script-writer. The project was placed initially under the direction of the visiting American stage producer and actor, Fred Niblo, and in the early months of 1915 Niblo made two films, *Get-Rich-Quick Wallingford* and *Officer 666*. In June Niblo returned to America and production continued on a different tack: two films based on original screenplays, rather than on established stage successes, were made with topical war themes—*Within Our Gates* and *For Australia*. Both were released well in advance of the Niblo films, which were held back from the public until early 1916.

Within Our Gates was a story of German intrigue and Australian valour, which, although ostensibly an original screenplay by W. J. Lincoln, owed considerable debt in its depiction of German spy activity to *The Man Who Stayed at Home*, a play performed in Melbourne earlier in 1915. A German spy is blackmailing Max, a German-Australian clerk in the Melbourne War Office, and thereby securing information which he transmits by wireless equipment hidden in his attic. The spy's adopted daughter falls in love with Edgar, the son of the War Minister, and exposes the dealings of her stepfather. Max and Edgar both enlist and meet in the Dardanelles; Edgar is wounded, but Max atones for his earlier treachery by giving his life to save Edgar.

The highlight, as in *The Hero of the Dardanelles* earlier in the year, was the landing of Australian troops in the Dardanelles. The scene was staged at Obelisk Bay near Sydney: 'the realistic acting, and the similarity of the foreshores of a little bay in Sydney harbor to the landing place at Gaba Tepe most successfully dispelled all ideas of fake. To see over a thousand soldiers jumping wildly from boats waist deep in the water, brandishing their guns in the air, scrambling up the rugged hillside, while attacked viciously by apparently real Turks, who held the top of the hill, must have been a startling sight for the peaceable citizens living near Obelisk Bay.' (*Lone Hand*, 1 October 1915) Assistance was received from military authorities and the film carried a frank propaganda message, to alert Australians to 'the Menace at Our Very Doors'. The cast, drawn from J. C. Williamson stock companies, was directed by the London-born actor Frank Harvey, who had come to Australia in 1914. He remained for a long career on the local stage and in radio, and was the principal screen writer and a versatile character actor for Cinesound in the 1930s.

Within Our Gates opened at the Victoria Theatre, Melbourne, on 19 July 1915, and played extended seasons with strong public response.

116 *Within Our Gates* The landing at Gaba Tepe

117 The Loyal Rebel

1915 ALFRED ROLFE

PC: Australasian Films. SC: Arthur Wright. 5 reels.
CAST: Reynolds Denniston (Stanley Gifford), Maisie Carte (Violet Howard), Charles Villiers (Pellew Owen), Percy Walshe (Major Howard), Leslie Victor (Peter Lalor), Jena Williams (Mrs Gifford), Wynn Davies (soldier).

'A Tale of the old days, the gold days, the roaring days of '54, when hearts beat high and hands grasped true' (*Sydney Morning Herald*, 25 September 1915). Against a background of the miners' rebellion at Ballarat in 1854, the film tells the 'blood-red tale' of a young farmer, Stanley Gifford, who leaves his loved one, Violet, and sets out for the goldfields to seek his fortune. Violet's father is involved in the criminal underworld of Sydney, and to silence a blackmailer named Pellew Owen, he is forced to give Pellew his daughter's hand in marriage. Pellew soon tires of marriage and discards Violet, who goes with her father to Ballarat in search of Stanley. Her father dies of exhaustion on the diggings, and Violet is kidnapped by Pellew after she accidentally interrupts his robbery of a bank vault. She is rescued by the police and Pellew is arrested, only to be released soon after as a police spy. The rebellious stirrings of the miners rise to a climax at the Eureka stockade, where Pellew is killed. Although Stanley is wounded, he and Violet manage to escape and at last find happiness together.

The screenplay by the novelist Arthur Wright won the first prize in a scenario competition promoted by Australasian Films early in 1915, and was intended to carry allegorical relevance for the war in its demonstration of the Australian fighting spirit. Filmed on location near Sydney and in the Rushcutters Bay studio, it introduced a well-known stage actor, Reynolds Denniston, in his film dêbut as the hero. It was released as a routine action film by Australasian at the Crystal Palace, Sydney, on 27 September 1915. *Theatre*, 1 October 1915, found the story 'infinitely better' than much of the imported product, and praised the 'faultless' photography. The acting however left much to be desired: Denniston 'is stiff and stodgy as the hero; and as the heroine Maisie Carte is as mechanical and expressionless as a marionette . . . Then there is Leslie Victor, who as Peter Lalor is entirely out of the picture. No man with the face Mr Victor presents on the screen ever led a rebellion, so superfine is it, and for that reason wholly at variance with the rugged strength one instinctively associates with Lalor.'

118 For Australia

1915 MONTE LUKE

PC: J. C. Williamson Ltd. STORY: Martyn Keith. PH: Maurice Bertel. ART D: Rock Phillips. 4000 ft.
CAST: Alma Rock Phillips (Kana), Boyd Irwin (Stanley Lane), Gwen Burroughs (Mrs DeWinter), Charles Villiers (Carl Hoffman), Percy Walshe.

A newspaper reporter discovers a German spy ring in Sydney but is captured and imprisoned on an uncharted island. With the aid of a half-caste Samoan girl, Kana, he manages to escape and smash the Germans' wireless station, but is recaptured and tied to a tree in a crocodile-infested swamp. Kana saves him in the nick of time. Later H.M.A.S. *Sydney* invades the island, and the ringleader of the spies, Carl Hoffman, falls into the swamp, where he is promptly devoured by a crocodile.

Theatre, 1 January 1916, found 'a lot of leakages' in the plot, with its flights of 'weirdly impossible' fancy. Problems arose with the special effects by J. C. Williamson's principal set designer, Rock Phillips: the crocodile that devours the villain was too evidently made of wood, the wireless station of canvas, and a topical glimpse of the notorious German warship *Emden* too evidently a model. The same critic found *Emden* 'as realistic as the Italian warships that cruise along the walls of some of the Sydney fruit shops'. The characterization too was more suited to the conventions of stage melodrama: 'the persecuted hero, the cursing, cigarette-smoking villain, and the shrinking heroine are all there in full strength. Everything smacks of the stage.'

The film opened at Waddington's Grand Theatre, Sydney, on 6 December 1915 but it did not fare well commercially. The director, Monte Luke, was born in 1885 at Geelong, Victoria. He worked extensively in Australian theatre as an actor but gradually developed an interest in still photography. He was appointed official photographer for J. C. Williamson, taking portraits of stage stars and publicity shots of plays in production, and was placed in charge of their film operation in 1915 after Fred Niblo's departure. He directed three features for Williamson before the production programme was abandoned. Luke thereafter ran his own photographic studio and became well known for his portraits of society figures and visiting celebrities. He died in Sydney in 1962.

118 *For Australia* Boyd Irwin and crocodile

118 *For Australia* Alma Rock Phillips

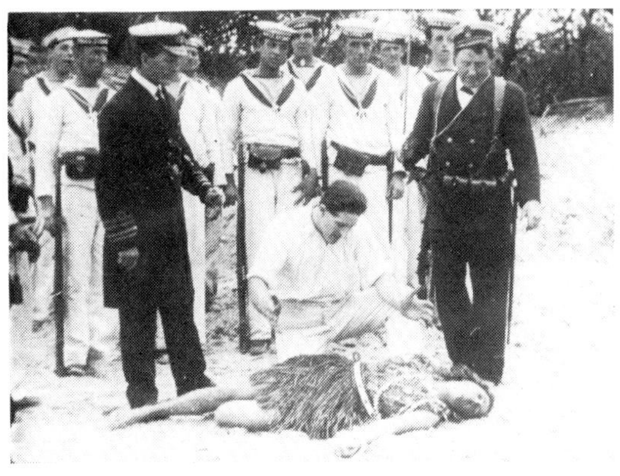

118 *For Australia* Boyd Irwin and Alma Rock Phillips (*c*)

119 How We Beat the Emden

1915 ALFRED ROLFE

PC: Australasian Films.

On 9 November 1914, the German ship *Emden* was destroyed in an engagement at Cocos Island with the Australian ship *Sydney*. Dread of German raiders was transformed immediately into pride and elation over Australia's maturity as a fighting force against such a formidable enemy. Not long after news of *Sydney*'s victory reached Australia, members of the Millions Club in Sydney formed a Cocos Island Syndicate and organized an expedition to make a film about the defeated

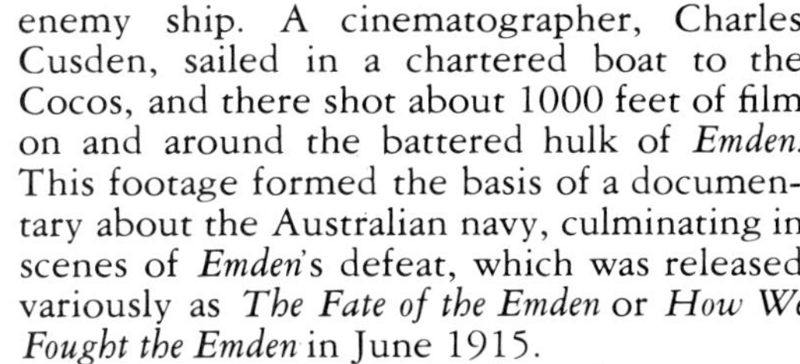

enemy ship. A cinematographer, Charles Cusden, sailed in a chartered boat to the Cocos, and there shot about 1000 feet of film on and around the battered hulk of *Emden*. This footage formed the basis of a documentary about the Australian navy, culminating in scenes of *Emden*'s defeat, which was released variously as *The Fate of the Emden* or *How We Fought the Emden* in June 1915.

Later in the year, Cusden's footage was incorporated into a narrative film produced by Australasian, *How We Beat the Emden*. Made with assistance from the Department of Defence, it told the story of a boy who enrols as a naval cadet and serves on board *Sydney*. Later he returns to tell his mates how the battle with *Emden* had been won: 'As the cadet sits there, surrounded by his companions, his words are illustrated by a succession of views in which are seen the Sydney sighting the Emden, the firing by the Sydney of the first shot, and the manner in which by the shots that follow the German boat was turned into the wreck she became.' (*Theatre*, 1 January 1916) It was released at the Lyceum Theatre, Sydney, on 6 December, and was welcomed by *Theatre* as 'a realistic, convincing story'. An actor, C. Post Mason, took a print with him to Canada early in 1916, and wrote of the reactions of the press in Honolulu on the way over: 'At its conclusion all who had witnessed it declared the film a remarkable piece of photoplay. One can have no conception of the effect of modern high explosives until he has seen the terrible havoc which the Sydney's shots created aboard the famous German commerce raider as shown in this film.' (*Theatre*, 1 May 1916)

119 Charles Cusden photographing the wreck of the *Emden*

120 *A Maori Maid's Love* Lottie Lyell (*c*)

120 A Maori Maid's Love

1916 RAYMOND LONGFORD

PC: Vita Film Corporation. 5 reels.
CAST: Lottie Lyell, Raymond Longford, Kenneth Carlisle.

In 1915, with finance from a Sydney company, the Vita Film Corporation, Longford went to New Zealand to make this undistinguished melodrama. A surveyor named Graham escapes from his selfish, pleasure-seeking wife by going on field duty. He meets a beautiful Maori girl and they become lovers. The girl gives birth to a child and later dies. Graham places his little daughter in the care of Maori Jack. Later, as a grown woman (played by Lottie Lyell), the daughter falls in love with a jackeroo named Jim. After many adventures, Graham is killed by Maori Jack, but his property passes to his daughter and all ends happily.

Shooting began at Rotorua and Auckland in August 1915, with both official and Maori co-operation. As in Australia, Longford experienced difficulties in having his film shown: 'On completion I failed to secure a release owing to the opposition of the Hayward-Fuller organization, which controlled the majority of the New Zealand theatres, and whose interests were allied to those of the [Australian] combine. I returned to Sydney, and the combine refusing a release the picture was given its première at an obscure theatre, the Alhambra, in the Haymarket, Sydney, by its proprietor, Humbert Pugliese.' (***RCE***, p.146)

Distributed by the small Eureka Exchange, it opened at the Alhambra on 10 January 1916. The Sydney *Sun*, 16 January 1916, expressed mixed feelings: 'The story itself . . . is not strong, and is a hackneyed theme at that; the leading man and the leading woman, well as they are acted were not physically suited to the parts; full advantage was not taken of the Maori life, and customs, and the picturesque accompaniments of the Rotorua

121 Muriel Starr

district.' But despite these faults, it was, the *Sun* concluded, 'considerably above the standard of the average imported photoplay'.

121 Within the Law

1916 MONTE LUKE

PC: J. C. Williamson Ltd. SC: W. J. Lincoln. From the play by Bayard Veiller. PH: Maurice Bertel. 4 reels.
CAST: Muriel Starr (Mary Turner).

Mary Turner is a shopgirl wrongly convicted on a charge of theft. She determines to take revenge on Edward Guilder, the powerful businessman who instigated her arrest. After her release from prison she joins another woman in a series of activities that border on criminal blackmail but are always just within the law; their speciality is securing money from wealthy men with threats of breach-of-promise suits. One of Mary's prime targets is Dick Guilder, her enemy's son, but she finds herself falling in love with him. Only after the solving of an underworld killing (for which Dick is framed), and the clearing of her name from the original charge of theft, does Mary change her ways and admit her love for Dick.

Made after Williamson's two war melodramas, *Within the Law* marked a return to the company's original intention of filming the most important plays in their stage repertoire. The leading role was played by an American actress, Muriel Starr, who had come to Australia in 1913 to appear in the stage version of *Within the Law* for Williamson and had immediately became a favourite of the Australian public. The film was shot primarily on the stage of the Theatre Royal, Melbourne, and opened at the Paramount Theatre, Melbourne, on 10 January 1916. *Theatre*, 1 May 1916, noted improvements in the J. C. Williamson production style, with 'better setting of the interior scenes', 'finer acting' and the use of close-ups. Commercial results were poor, although later the play became a recurring favourite of Hollywood producers, with at least four film adaptations, in 1917, 1923 (with Norma Talmadge as Mary Turner), 1930 (under the title of *Paid*, and starring Joan Crawford) and 1939 (with Ruth Hussey).

122 Get-Rich-Quick Wallingford

1916 FRED NIBLO

PC: J. C. Williamson Ltd. SC: Fred Niblo, W. J. Lincoln. From the play by George M. Cohan, based on a story by George Randolph Chester. PH: Maurice Bertel. 4 reels.
CAST: Fred Niblo (J. Rufus Wallingford), Henry Carson Clarke (Blackie), Enid Bennett (Fanny), Eddie Lamb, Pirie Bush, Sydney Stirling.

Get-Rich-Quick Wallingford was the first film in J. C. Williamson's production programme, but one of the last to be released. 'The Firm' had a special interest in American theatre; their founder was American, and both before and after his death in 1913 they brought out many American celebrities to perform in Australian theatres. Among the most notable was Fred Niblo, who, with his wife, Josephine Cohan (sister of the famous writer-actor-composer, George M. Cohan), arrived early in 1912 and remained for over three years, producing and starring in an enormously popular series of plays, including three filmed by Williamson, *Get-Rich-Quick Wallingford*, *Officer 666*, and *Seven Keys to Baldpate*—all written by Niblo's brother-in-law. At first Williamson tried to secure an experienced American director to launch the production programme, but eventually gave Fred Niblo the task. Ironically, given their hesitancy in using him, Niblo later became one of Hollywood's principal silent directors, with major productions including *Blood and Sand* (1922) with Valentino and *Ben-Hur* (1925) with Ramon Novarro.

The first scenario was prepared by Lincoln in a matter of days early in March 1915, and shooting began in mid-April, while Niblo was rehearsing one play in the morning and acting in *Seven Keys to Baldpate* on stage in the evening. After its completion in April, Niblo moved quickly on to a second filmed play, *Officer 666*, which was completed before his departure from Australia in June.

122 *Get-Rich-Quick Wallingford* Fred Niblo (*c*)

122 *Get-Rich-Quick Wallingford* Edith Bennett, Fred Niblo

The film presented a 'potted' version of the play and probably relied heavily on audience familiarity with the plot. The play was a comedy about the American business world: two swindlers, Blackie Daw and J. Rufus Wallingford, arrive in Battlesburg, Iowa, and convince the townsfolk that they are wealthy capitalists in search of a good investment. With the town's money they establish plans for a factory to produce covered carpet tacks and set off a major real estate boom. They are about to skip town with their fortune when they receive a genuine order for an immense supply of tacks. Finding themselves honestly rich, Wallingford and Blackie decide to change their plans, marry local girls and settle down in Battlesburg.

Release was delayed until 31 January 1916 at two Sydney theatres, the Majestic and the Strand, but commercial results were below expectations and contributed towards Williamson's decision late in 1916 to abandon production. The play had more success as a film in Hollywood; it was directed by Frank Borzage for Paramount in 1921, and was profitable enough to inspire the author of the original story, George Randolph Chester, to write and direct a movie sequel in the same year, *The Son of Wallingford*.

The part of Fanny, a stenographer who finally marries Wallingford, was played by Enid Bennett, the understudy to Josephine Cohan on the stage. Enid Bennett went with the Niblos to the U.S.A. in 1915, and after Josephine Cohan's death, married Niblo and became a prominent Hollywood star.

123 The Martyrdom of Nurse Cavell

1916 JOHN GAVIN, C. POST MASON

PC: Australian Famous Feature Company. SC: Agnes Gavin. PH: Lacey Percival. 4000 ft.

CAST: Vera Pearce (Nurse Cavell), Harrington Reynolds (Reverend Thomas Gerard), C. Post Mason (Georges Renard), Percy Walshe (Baron Von Bissell), John Gavin (Captain Von Hoffberg), Charles Villiers (Herr Cries), George Portus (Dr Schultz), Roland Stavely (American Ambassador), James Martin (Monsieur Renard), Robert Floyd (Monsieur Fouchard), George Farrell (disabled soldier), Ethel Bashford (Yvonne Loudet), Clare Stephenson (Madame Renard), Nellie Power (Nurse Marcheau).

On 12 October 1915 an English nurse, Edith Cavell, was executed in Brussels by a German firing squad for allegedly assisting the Belgian resistance movement. News of the German action shocked the world and she became an instant legend in the anti-German propaganda of the Allied countries. Australia was the first to tell her story (or a version of it) on film, and it proved as popular overseas as it did at home, with a world market ripe for an expression of anger against the Germans.

Gavin made his film in three weeks, after reading a newspaper story about Nurse Cavell's death. His wife, Agnes, wrote a scenario literally overnight, and finance for a four-reel film was raised from two of the industry's leaders in distribution, J. D. Williams and the Crick and Jones partnership.

In Gavin's hands, Edith Cavell emerged as a beautiful young 'angel of mercy' tending the war-wounded in a Brussels hospital. In fact Cavell had been a brisk middle-aged lady, but Gavin had no information to help the accuracy of his story. The production was completed early in January 1916. Locations were found in and around Sydney, and as *Theatre*, 1 March 1916, commented, 'Not at any time do the settings of the Belgian war drama . . . suggest any other locality than that of a quiet Sydney suburb.' Interiors were shot at Darlinghurst Gaol and in the Rushcutters Bay studio. Distributed by Australasian Films, the film

opened on 31 January 1916 at the Lyric Theatre, Sydney, and was an immediate commercial success. Gavin's performance as a German cavalry officer was so effective that, according to the *Sun*, 6 February 1916, 'some people even suspect his nationality'.

The film's co-director, the American-born stage actor and singer, C. Post Mason, left Australia in March 1916 to arrange the film's release in North America, and it opened on Broadway in July. It also screened widely in England. Gavin later recalled that for an outlay of a mere £450, the film returned over £25 000: 'You can believe me when I tell you that this picture put several showmen on Easy Street for a long time.' (*Everyones*, 9 May 1923) Gavin subsequently made two comedy shorts, *Charlie at the Sydney Show*, starring the Chaplin impersonator Ern Vockler (released on 20 May 1916 in Sydney), and *An Interrupted Divorce*, with Fred Bluett and Vera Remée, from a scenario by Agnes Gavin (released on 6 August 1916). C. Post Mason meanwhile remained in America and spent some of his profits supervising the production of a three-reel documentary, *The Wonder City of the World—New York by Day and Night* (1916). He fell victim to the influenza epidemic in America, and died on 4 December 1918 in San Francisco.

124 Nurse Cavell [Edith Cavell]

1916 W. J. LINCOLN

P, SC: W. J. Lincoln.
CAST: Margaret Linden (Nurse Cavell), Arthur Styan (Captain Karl), Agnes Keogh (Nita), Stewart Garner (Captain Devereaux).

This rival to John Gavin's *The Martyrdom of Nurse Cavell* was released on 21 February 1916 at a suburban cinema in Melbourne, using a subtitle, 'England's Joan of Arc'. It screened variously as *Nurse Cavell* and *Edith Cavell* in Adelaide and Brisbane in March and seems to have drawn large and responsive audiences. The *Argus*, 21 February 1916, noted that those who had seen it at a private screening were 'unstinting in their praise of the delicacy, restraint, and reverence' of the film. Legal action was taken by Gavin's backers at the time of its Melbourne screening on the grounds that it was an infringement of copyright, and it seems likely that Lincoln was forced to withdraw his film. He used it as a basis, however, for another Cavell story, *La Revanche*, released in April.

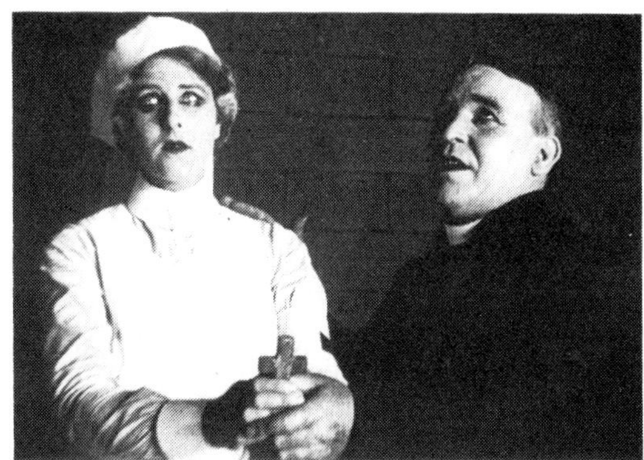

124 *Nurse Cavell* Frame enlargement

124 *Nurse Cavell* Frame enlargement

124 *Nurse Cavell* Frame enlargement

125 Officer 666**

1916 FRED NIBLO

PC: J. C. Williamson Ltd. SC: W. J. Lincoln. From the play by Augustin McHugh, adapted by George M. Cohan. PH: Maurice Bertel. ART D: Rock Phillips. 4 reels.

CAST: Fred Niblo (Travers Gladwin), Enid Bennett (Helen Burton), Marion Marcus Clarke (Mrs Burton), Sydney Stirling (Alfred Wilson), Maurice Dudley (Watkins), Henry Matsumoto (Bateato), Pirie Bush (Whitney Barnes) Edwin Lester (Detective Kearney), George Bryant (Captain Stone), Matee Brown (Sadie), Reine Connelly (Celeste).

In New York, a millionaire, Travers Gladwin, learns of a plot to steal his priceless collection of paintings. In order to observe the operations of the criminals, he pretends to vacate his house for a long trip, but remains in the area disguised as a police constable (number 666). The criminals arrive at his house, led by the gentlemanly Alfred Wilson, who poses as Gladwin, complete with a new valet named Watkins, and a young lady as his fiancée. Gladwin, as the policeman, visits the house and with amusement watches the thieves at work packaging the paintings. When the real police arrive, both Officer 666 and the thief claim to be Gladwin and considerable confusion follows. Gladwin eventually allows the thief to escape in the constable's uniform in order to save the honour of the young girl innocently involved in the crime.

Niblo directed and starred in this comedy immediately after completing *Get-Rich-Quick Wallingford*, and finished it a few days before his return to America in June 1915. Three reels of the film survive today in the National Film Archive and reveal a crude production doggedly faithful to the stage and its New York setting: the camera is merely a passive observer of the stage action (complete with knowing winks of complicity between Gladwin and the audience), and the dialogues, although mute, are retained at length. It opened at the Theatre Royal, Sydney, on 1 April 1916, but like the filmed plays released before it in the J. C. Williamson series, it failed to attract much public attention. Another film of the same play was produced in Hollywood in 1920 by the Goldwyn Corporation.

126 La Revanche

1916 W. J. LINCOLN

P: W. J. Lincoln. SC: W. J. Lincoln, Fred Kehoe.

CAST: Arthur Styan, Agnes Keogh, Stewart Garner.

Following legal action by John Gavin against W. J. Lincoln for their rival films about Nurse Cavell, it seems likely that Lincoln reconstructed his film, added new footage, and released it again as *La Revanche*. Certainly the cast was substantially the same, as was much of the story. The new film was billed as a 'sequel' to *Nurse Cavell* and focused on the revenge sought by her Belgian friends against the German enemy. As the film progresses, other examples of the enemy's inhumanity are detailed: the flogging to death of a man who refuses to salute a German officer, the shooting of an old man who objects to the Germans' treatment of Belgian girls, and the award of an Iron Cross to a German officer who has murdered an innocent woman.

Publicity for the film carried an explicit recruiting message: 'if you turn a deaf ear to your country's call and still STAY AT HOME it may not be long before you find yourself under the domination of these despoilers and barbarians' (*Argus*, 8 April 1916). In addition to the leading players (all established theatre favourites), the film proudly introduced a number of invalided Anzac soldiers in minor roles. It opened at the Britannia Theatre, Melbourne, on 10 April 1916, and at the Town Hall, Adelaide, on 8 July. Perhaps war-weariness or over-familiarity with the Cavell story told against the film, for it was not widely screened and did nothing to revive Lincoln's rapidly declining career.

125 *Officer 666* Foreground left, Enid Bennett, Fred Niblo

127 Murphy of Anzac

1916 J. E. MATHEWS

PC: Fraser Film Release and Photographic Company. 4000 ft.
CAST: Martyn Keith (German spy).

The film was part of the instant myth-making that attended reports from Gallipoli of the exploits of Private Simpson (John Simpson Kirkpatrick), nicknamed 'Murphy' by his mates, an ambulance officer with the A.I.F. who used a donkey to rescue wounded from the firing lines. After saving the lives of over a hundred men, Simpson was killed by a Turkish shell in May 1915 while trying to rescue men from the notorious Shrapnel Gully.

The director, J. E. Mathews, recruited a cast composed largely of returned servicemen and commissioned advice from a Gallipoli veteran, Corporal Robson, who had known Simpson. The film opened simultaneously at Waddington's Globe and Majestic Theatres, Sydney, on 24 April 1916. For *Theatre*, 1 June 1916, it presented 'a glorious figure in an inglorious photoplay', with a sub-plot containing 'the most ridiculous villain that ever smoked a cigarette'.

127 *Murphy of Anzac*

128 The Joan of Arc of Loos

1916 GEORGE WILLOUGHBY

PC: Willoughby's Photo-Plays. SC: Herbert Ford. PH: Franklyn Barrett. ART D: Jack Ricketts. ASST D: Martyn Keith. 5000 ft.
CAST: Jane King (Emilienne Moreau), Jean Robertson (the angel), Clive Farnham (soldier hero), Beatrice Esmond, Arthur Greenaway, Austin Milroy, Harry Halley, Winter Hall, Irve Hayman, Arthur Spence, Fred Knowles.

The town of Loos is taken by the Germans in 1915, but a young peasant girl, Emilienne Moreau, escapes to the Allies and gives them vital information. In the ensuing attempt to re-take the town, Emilienne is inspired by the vision of an angel of war and rallies the retreating Allies back into attack, 'waving a bullet-swept flag and the tricolor of France, and singing the Marseillaise, she turned the tide of battle from the shame of defeat to the glory of victory' (*Australian Variety*, 3 May 1916). For her bravery, Emilienne is awarded a Military Cross, and she becomes the bride of a gallant young soldier who had fought by her side in the battle.

Sets to represent the village were built on Tamarama Beach, Sydney, by Jack Ricketts, an experienced scenic artist from live theatre, and the battle was staged there with 300 extras, including 100 returned soldiers, and many explosives. Other locations to represent the battle area were found in and around Sydney, including an avenue of poplars near Randwick racecourse to suggest the countryside of Flanders. The film opened as a supporting feature at the Glaciarium, Sydney, on 31 April, where it aroused little public or trade attention.

The film initiated a short-lived production programme by George Willoughby. Born in England as George Willoughby Dowse, he travelled back and forth between England and Australia as a theatrical entrepreneur, and in 1912 became managing director of George Marlow's theatrical operations in Sydney. *The Joan of Arc of Loos* was followed within weeks by an adaptation of a popular stage play, *The Woman in the Case*, but neither film was a commercial success and Willoughby abandoned his further projects (which included two South Sea island romances). Critical reaction to Willoughby's first film was discouraging. *Theatre*, 1 May 1916, found it only 'moderately interesting' and criticized the attitude towards war expressed by Emilienne's father, an old war veteran who 'looks forward to war with the eagerness and joy of a child that is about to play with a new toy'. Objection was also taken to the notion that divine intervention, and not courage or skill, had saved the day at Loos. The vision of the armoured angel, however, was one redeeming feature. The part was played by a young Adelaide actress, Jean Robertson, who had acted in Willoughby's stage company, and who appeared 'tall enough to keep one hand up in the clouds, and her off-side foot touching the earth; and in that way to magically do the appearing and disappearing trick at will'. A minor role was played by Winter Hall, who later went on to a prolific career as a character actor in Hollywood in the 1920s.

129 In the Last Stride

1916 MARTYN KEITH

PC: Double A Productions. P: W. S. Jerdan. From the novel by Arthur Wright. 4 reels.
CAST: Alma Rock Phillips, Dave Smith, Les O'Donnell, Dunstan Webb, Charles Villiers, Rock Phillips, Pat McGrath, Harry Jerdan, Percy Walshe.

Dave Smith was the retired heavyweight boxing champion of Australia, and this story took him through various adventures as a sportsman, as a swagman in the bush, and as a fugitive from justice. Opium smuggling and a speedboat chase in Sydney Harbour also formed part of the action. Numerous sporting scenes included a three-round boxing match between Dave and Les O'Donnell, a football match with stars of various Rugby League teams in Sydney, and a climax at Randwick racecourse, where Dave's horse, Sunlocks, on which he has bet his last penny, manages to win the Sydney Cup 'in the last stride'.

The novel by Arthur Wright had sold 30 000 copies and had been serialized in the sporting weekly, the *Referee*, before production of the film began. The Double A ('All Australian') company was formed under the management of W. S. Jerdan, formerly a member of Jerdan's Ltd, pioneer film distributors and photographic equipment suppliers in Sydney in the early years of the century. Another member of the Jerdan family, Harry, appeared in a small role as a bush publican. Other cast members included Dunstan Webb, later to direct several Australian feature films, in two roles, as a black American and as a young Australian squatter. The film opened unobtrusively at the Alhambra Theatre, Sydney, on 1 May 1916.

130 Seven Keys to Baldpate**

1916 MONTE LUKE

PC: J. C. Williamson Ltd. SC: Alex C. Butler. From the play by George M. Cohan. Based on the novel by Earl Derr Biggers. PH: Maurice Bertel. 4 reels.

CAST: Dorothy Brunton (Mary Norton), J. Plumpton Wilson (Peters), Agnes Keogh (Myra Thornhill), Alex C. Butler (Jim Cargan), Gerald Harcourt (Lou Max), Charles Villiers (Thomas Hayden), James Hughes (Jim Kennedy).

The last of J. C. Williamson's filmed plays was based on an American stage success that Williamson had brought to Australia in 1914 with Fred Niblo as star and producer. The play was a 'mystery farce' about a practical joke played on a novelist, William Hallowell Magee, who has bet that he can complete a novel in twenty-four hours. To work on the novel, Magee retires for the night to a lonely mountain resort, taking what he believes is the only key. Throughout the night, however, he is disturbed by a succession of visitors, all with their own key and all apparently involved in a sinister case of political graft and murder. The police finally arrive, and Magee learns that the mysterious visitors are in fact actors hired by his friend to keep him from his work.

Dorothy Brunton was a popular star of Australian musical comedy who later won a following on the British stage as well. Her film début was scarcely distinguished, in the mainly decorative role as the coquettish girlfriend of the novelist. Judging by the three reels of the film preserved today in the National Film Archive, the production was static and graceless, with flimsy canvas sets and lengthy mute dialogues that relied heavily on the audience's familiarity with the play. Monte Luke's evident discomfort in handling film production was confirmed later in the year: after the completion of *Seven Keys to Baldpate*, Williamson sent Luke to Hollywood to study production; after witnessing work on D. W. Griffith's *Intolerance*, he returned, overwhelmed, to recommend that Williamson should abandon production and leave it to the Hollywood experts. 'The Firm' followed his advice and did nothing to revive their film production programme.

Treated with a little imagination by Hollywood directors, the story of *Seven Keys to Baldpate* found ready audience acceptance and was filmed no less than five times by American companies, in 1917, 1925, 1930, 1935 and 1947. The Williamson production, however, created little attention when it was given a suburban release in Sydney, at the Hub Theatre, Newtown, on 24 May 1916.

131 If the Huns Came to Melbourne

1916 GEORGE COATES

PH: Arthur Higgins.

One of several films expressing outrage against German atrocities in Belgium and paranoia about a German invasion of Australia, this low-budget production was not widely shown and was either inadequate dramatically or too grim to attract an audience. Interior scenes were shot in an open-air theatre in Albert Park, Melbourne. Montage effects depicting the horrors of the invasion were devised from enlarged photographs of city buildings; these were mutilated to suggest shell-fire damage, smoke was blown across them during shooting, and then newsreel clips of Germans marching and of Red Cross workers tending the wounded were superimposed over them. The film was premièred in Adelaide, at the Wondergraph Theatre, on 29 May 1916, and opened in Melbourne at the Port Theatre, Port Melbourne, on 5 June.

132 The Woman in the Case

1916 GEORGE WILLOUGHBY

PC: Willoughby's Photo-Plays. P: George Willoughby. From the play by Clyde Fitch. ASST D: Martyn Keith. 5000 ft.

CAST: Jean Robertson (Margaret Rolfe), Loris Bingham (Clare Foster), Fred Knowles (Julian Rolfe), Herbert J. Bentley (Phillip Long), Winter Hall, David Edelsten, Austin Milroy, Clive Farnham.

This old melodrama was revived on the Australian stage with great success by George Willoughby in 1911, and his film version faithfully adhered to the play. As a young man, Julian Rolfe had had an affair with 'a seductive she-devil', Clare Foster, but had later settled down in marriage with a faithful wife, Margaret. Clare however is driven by jealousy to blackmail Julian, but Margaret outwits her and destroys some incriminating letters. Clare becomes desperate and murders Julian's ward, Phillip, leaving evidence to suggest that Julian is the culprit. Julian is arrested and sentenced to death, but Margaret retaliates again by tricking Clare into a confession of guilt. Justice takes its course and Julian is happily reunited with his loving wife.

The cast included Fred Knowles, an English actor who had played in Australia for some time. Soon after completing the film he joined

133 *The Mutiny of the Bounty*

the A.I.F., and was severely injured in France in May 1917; despite an amputated arm and multiple wounds, he returned to the Australian stage and often appeared in vaudeville. *The Woman in the Case* was distributed by a small Sydney company, Eureka Films, and opened at the Alhambra Theatre, Sydney, on 3 July 1916. The *Sun*, 7 May 1916, was critical of the adaptation: 'it is weak because of the inability of the action alone to reveal all that takes place . . . It is impossible to reveal the tricks of dialogue, the shrewd questioning, the piecing together of the admissions by pictorial means.' Further screenings were rare, and Willoughby withdrew from production. At least two other films, both American, were made from the same play, with Pauline Frederick as Margaret in 1916, and by Famous Players-Lasky in 1922 under the title *The Law and the Woman.*

133 The Mutiny of the Bounty

1916 RAYMOND LONGFORD

PC: Crick and Jones. P: Raymond Longford. SC: Raymond Longford, Lottie Lyell (?). PH: Franklyn Barrett, A. O. Segerberg, Charles Newham. 5000 ft.

CAST: George Cross (Captain Bligh), John Storm (George III), D. L. Dalziel (Sir Joseph Banks), Wilton Power (Fletcher Christian), Reginald Collins (Midshipman Heywood), Ernesto Crosetto (Midshipman Hallett), Harry Beaumont (Mr Samuels), Charles Villiers (Burkett), Meta Taupopoki (Otoo), Mere Amohau (Mere), Gwil Adams (Mrs Bligh), Leah Miller (baby), Ada Guilford (Mrs Heywood), Lottie Lyell (Nessy Heywood).

The scenario was a painstaking attempt to re-create the famous mutiny by the crew of the *Bounty* against Captain Bligh. Use was made of records in the Mitchell Library, Sydney, including Bligh's own logbook, and endorsement came from several eminent historians. Care was taken to give an unbiased view of Bligh, and scenes of his tyranny on the *Bounty* were balanced with scenes of his tenderness as a husband and father. Shipboard brutality, the sojourn in Tahiti, and conflicts arising from jealousy over island women, were followed by the mutiny, the flight to Pitcairn and the subsequent life of the mutineers.

Shooting began in April 1916, mainly on location at Rotorua in New Zealand. A few additional scenes were shot on Norfolk Island and in Sydney. Financial backing was received from the distributors, Crick and Jones, in association with J. D. Williams, and the film opened at the Hoyts Theatre in George Street, Sydney, on 2 September. Reviews varied: *Australian Variety*, 6 September 1916, found it 'absolutely the finest production yet manufactured in Australia', but for the *Sun*, 27 August 1916, the 'human interest' was 'weak', and although its details were commendably accurate, it had 'little public appeal'. The film fared well commercially in Australia and New Zealand, and was later re-edited by Lottie Lyell, at the request of Crick and Jones, to prepare it for sale to the British market.

134 The Life's Romance of Adam Lindsay Gordon**

1916 W. J. LINCOLN

PC: Lincoln-Barnes Scenarios. P, SC: W. J. Lincoln, G. H. Barnes. PH: Bert Ive. 5 reels.
CAST: Hugh McCrae (Adam Lindsay Gordon), Alfred Harford (maniac).

This biography of Adam Lindsay Gordon follows his life as 'Hunter, Fighter, Lover, Dreamer, Trooper, Horse Breaker, Steeplechase Rider, POET AND GENTLEMAN' (*Age*, 2 September 1916). From his schooldays in England to his death as a popular but penniless poet, Gordon led a stormy life crammed with incident, and the film presented the most sensational of them, linked by lengthy quotations from his semi-autobiographical verse. In the three reels that survive today, Gordon is seen as a trooper in the Australian bush, where he is given the responsibility of escorting a lunatic to an asylum 200 miles away, and barely survives the assignment. He later resigns from the police force on a point of honour when he refuses to clean the sergeant's boots. The closing scenes, as Gordon falls deeper and deeper into debt and finally resolves to shoot himself, are narrated with more sensitivity than one might expect after the same director's *The Sick Stockrider* (1913); a genuine feeling of tragedy imbues the final tableaux, especially a well-judged long-shot of Gordon's lonely figure standing on an empty shoreline. The story closes with views of a pilgrimage to Gordon's grave in Brighton, Victoria, shot on Sunday 3 September 1916, just one day before the film opened at Hoyts Olympia Theatre, Melbourne.

After working on J. C. Williamson's film programme, Lincoln formed a new company with a theatrical identity from Melbourne, G. H. Barnes, but the venture ran into immediate financial difficulties and only one feature was completed. The leading actor later recounted that on one occasion he and the cameraman were forced to seize the film before they could extract their pay from the company. About this time Lincoln spent some weeks in hospital with alcoholic poisoning. The film was not a great success either with the public or the press, and after Lincoln's death in 1917 it was taken over by the Austral Photoplay company for screenings at their Kookaburra Theatre, Sydney, commencing on 28 October 1918.

134 *The Life's Romance of Adam Lindsay Gordon* Hugh McCrae as Gordon, with his wife, receiving bad news from the bank. Frame enlargement

The star was Hugh McCrae, himself a poet, supposed to have a strong physical resemblance to Gordon. McCrae had acted with Gregan MacMahon's Company on the stage in Melbourne and had spent a year in America trying to find work in the theatre. On his return to Australia he made this sole film appearance, then abandoned acting altogether in favour of professional writing. He soon established himself as a popular wit and essayist.

135 *The Pioneers*

135 The Pioneers

1916 FRANKLYN BARRETT

P: Franklyn Barrett, Leopold A. Nettheim.
SC, PH: Franklyn Barrett. From the novel by Katharine Susannah Prichard. 6 acts.

CAST: Winter Hall (Dan Farrel), Alma Rock Phillips (Deirdre), Lily Rochefort (Mary Cameron), Charles Knight (Donald Cameron), Fred St. Clair (Davey Cameron), Irve Hayman (Thad McNab), Martyn Keith (Steve), Fred Neilson (Fighting Conal), Nell Rose (Jessie).

In 1915 Katharine Susannah Prichard's novel won a £1000 prize in a literary competition conducted by the publishers Hodder and Stoughton. Barrett's film version told the story of two generations in the Australian outback. A convict, Dan Farrel, escapes from Van Diemen's Land and makes his way to a remote settlement where he throws himself on the mercy of a pioneer couple, Mary and Donald Cameron. As years pass the settlement grows, and Dan becomes the local schoolteacher and marries. His wife later dies but he remains in the small township to bring up his daughter, Deirdre. One day a local pub-keeper, McNab, discovers that Dan is an escaped convict, and to buy his silence, Deirdre agrees to marry him. Her sacrifice is in vain, however, for McNab persists in giving his information to the police and Dan is arrested. In a quarrel, Deirdre accidentally kills McNab, and with his evil influence out of the way, Donald Cameron is able to bring about a happy resolution to the family's troubles.

The film was shot early in 1915 near Gosford, N.S.W., and in Barrett's Sydney studio. It was released in Brisbane at the Strand Theatre on 18 October. In Sydney a month later, the *Sun*, 5 November 1916, dealt severely with it, finding it symptomatic of an industry that was 'trying to run before it can walk . . . Photography has been mastered . . . But in acting and accessories and direction it is still away back in the dark ages.' Another film based on the novel was made by Raymond Longford in 1926.

136 Remorse, a Story of the Red Plague

1917 J. E. MATHEWS

PC: Mathews Photo-play Producing Company.
PH: Harry Krischock. 4 reels.
CAST: Cyril Mackay, Mabel Dyson, Ida Gresham, Marie D'Alton, C. R. Stanford, Victor Fitzherbert, Claude Turton.

Even by the time of this production in 1917, sex education and warnings about venereal disease were familiar poses used by the film trade to hint at pornography. Imported films like *Damaged Goods* (1915) were promoted vigorously with a veneer of moral self-righteousness, and earned a great deal of money. *Remorse* was firmly in this tradition, with a grim morality tale offered as a warning against the dangers of loose living. The central character is a naïve country boy who visits the city, where he is led astray and contracts syphilis. Disowned by his father, he becomes a grief-stricken vagabond. One day he meets his former sweetheart, who is now happily married, and he is driven by shame and despair to shoot himself.

The last feature to be directed in Australia by the American J. E. Mathews, *Remorse* was produced in South Australia by his own company, registered in Adelaide in 1916. It opened at the Wondergraph Theatre, Adelaide, on 3 January 1917, and as expected, attracted large audiences. The state's censors regarded the film's moral message as salutory and permitted screenings to be held provided children under sixteen years of age were excluded. In New South Wales the licensing office initially rejected the film as 'objectionable' after an inspector reported in lurid detail on scenes exposing the hero's arms covered with 'syphilitic excrescences' and similar sores on the breasts of a prostitute. This verdict was overruled by the Chief Secretary's Office, and the film was actively distributed in the state by the Co-operative Film Exchange.

137 The Murder of Captain Fryatt

1917 JOHN GAVIN

PC: Australian Famous Feature Company. SC: Agnes Gavin. PH: Franklyn Barrett. ART TITLES: Syd Nicholls. 4 reels.

CAST: Harrington Reynolds (Captain Charles Fryatt), John Gavin (von Kehlen), Olive Proctor (Mrs Fryatt), Percy Walshe, Augustus Neville, Charles Villiers, Miss Roland Watts-Phillips, Mabel Fish (baby).

The story was based on fact: Fryatt was the commander of a merchant ship, which in March 1915 was challenged by a German submarine to surrender. Fryatt refused and rammed his boat into the submarine. He returned to England a hero, but on another voyage in July was captured by the Germans and executed by firing squad.

This emotional 'quickie' followed Gavin's similar exposé of German atrocities in *The Martyrdom of Nurse Cavell* (1916). Both films expressed a vigorous sense of outrage that Gavin clearly felt to be readily marketable at the time. The film begins *after* Fryatt's daring encounter with the submarine and shows the celebration of his heroism in London. The work of the German spies in tracking him down and capturing him provides the main emphasis of the plot; the script introduces the German villain with a title declaring that 'in every hole and corner Lurks England's danger—a menace—that stalks the unwary to their DOOM—THE HUN SPY'.

To avoid censorship problems, Gavin sought a clearance from the New South Wales Chief Secretary in December 1916, in advance of production. Provisional approval was given on 23 December provided that 'the shooting of Captain Fryatt is not actually shown'. Although denied his key dramatic moment, Gavin proceeded rapidly with the production, and by 7 February 1917 was able to submit the film for censorship screening. At the same time, he submitted a scenario that revealed that he had indeed shown only the preparations for the execution, followed by a view of a minister kneeling in prayer beside the corpse. No objections were raised by the censor, and distributed by Gavin himself, the film opened at the Lyric Theatre, Sydney, on 26 February. Gavin's estimation of his audience, however, seems to have been somewhat amiss; although the temper of the film was consistent with his previous popular success, perhaps Fryatt lacked the emotional appeal of the little Nurse Cavell, and war-weariness was beginning to have an effect, for the film did not screen widely and audiences obviously had no enthusiasm for it as entertainment.

138 Beaumont Smith

138 Our Friends, the Hayseeds [The Hayseeds]

1917 BEAUMONT SMITH

PC: Beaumont Smith's Productions. P, SC: Beaumont Smith. PH: Harry Krischock. 5000 ft.

CAST: Roy Redgrave (Dad Hayseed), Walter Cornock (Joe Hayseed), Pearl Hellmrich (Pansy Duggan), Margaret Gordon (Mrs Hayseed), J. Plumpton Wilson (parson), H. H. Wallace (Dan Hayseed), Vera Spaull (Poppy Hayseed), Cecil Haines (Lizzie Hayseed), Jack Radford (Tommie Hayseed), Peter Ward (Peter Hayseed), Tom Cannam (hired hand), Percy Mackay (Mr Duggan), Nan Taylor (Mrs Duggan), Crosbie Ward (Mike Duggan), Fred Carlton (Jack Duggan), Olga Agnew (Mollie Duggan), Gerald Kay Souper (parliamentarian), Esther Mitchell (his wife).

Drawing heavily on the most popular elements of backblocks farce on the stage, especially from *On Our Selection* and *The Waybacks*, this first of seven Hayseeds adventures dealt primarily with the rivalry between the Hayseeds and the Duggans, neighbours on adjoining selections in the bush. Joe Hayseed and Pansy Duggan are keen to be married but a quarrel between Dad Hayseed and Dad Duggan arises when the Hayseeds' cows get into the Duggans' corn, and the young lovers are forbidden to see each other. The quarrel escalates to a brawl between the two families at the boundary fence, which ends in stalemate with both sides too exhausted to continue the fight. It takes the common enemy of a bushfire to bring the families together. Joe and Pansy are wed, and after some time 'a Mystery' is introduced. Dad Hayseed swears that if it is a boy it shall be named after him, Dad Duggan declares likewise, and their quarrel resumes, only to be resolved when the laugh turns against them, for it is not a boy that is born, but twins, both girls.

Beaumont Smith's first feature established the traits that marked most of his future work as producer-director-writer. The film was made so rapidly on its shoestring budget that it was known to contemporaries not as a 'quickie' but as a 'whizzie'. Smith's economical shooting style earned him the trade reputation of 'One-take Beau' or 'That'll Do Beau', and his films always came in on schedule and within budget, come hail, rain or accident. *Our Friends, the Hayseeds* was shot during January, previewed to the trade on 28 February and released commercially on 19 March 1917. The strain of the speed showed; the actors had little opportunity to rehearse, and *Theatre*, 2 April 1917, found the photography 'very indistinct—or blurred'. The dramatic highlight of the bushfire was managed with the aid of stock footage that Smith had secured some years earlier of a fire in the Adelaide hills.

Through his experience as a theatrical entrepreneur, Smith had learnt to treat entertainment as a business and to calculate carefully his audience's susceptibilities. He knew that a few technical rough edges would not affect the box-office, provided that the promotion was right, and none of his films emerged as 'artistic gems', as the contemporary trade press often noted. During 1917 he made four episodes in the Hayseeds series, and each one traded on Smith's knowledge that audiences would respond to the novelty of a local home-grown production. Accordingly, *Our Friends, the Hayseeds* was made on location in Adelaide and promoted in South Australia as the state's own film; and the following Hayseeds films were made variously in Brisbane, Melbourne and Sydney, with similar stress on local appeal in the publicity.

The first Hayseeds film was an instant and outstanding commercial success when it opened at Waddington's Grand Theatre, Sydney, on 19 March. Both publicity and distribution were handled directly by Smith in Sydney, and rights to rural New South Wales and to the other states were sold to other distributors, a practice that Smith usually followed with his subsequent productions.

Smith was born in Adelaide and acquired the 'common touch' as a publicity agent for the William Anderson stage company. He also worked as a journalist on the *Gadfly* with C. J. Dennis, and on the *Critic*, but his greatest strength lay in entrepreneurial work in the theatre. He showed a great flair for novelties and gimmicks, and one of his most successful shows was *Tiny Town*, starring a troupe of midgets whom he brought to Australia in 1911. His work as a film director was prolific but he withdrew from production in the mid-1920s to concentrate on exhibition, with the formation of J. C. Williamson Films, a distribution and exhibition company in which he owned a substantial interest. Throughout his career he moved freely between New Zealand and Australia and promoted all of his productions in both markets. Despite a brief return to production in 1933, he concentrated on exhibition in New Zealand until the early 1940s when he retired to Australia. He died in Sydney in January 1950.

139 Australia's Peril

1917 FRANKLYN BARRETT

P: Franklyn Barrett, Rock Phillips. SC: Franklyn Barrett, J. Brown. PH: Franklyn Barrett. ART D: Rock Phillips. ART TITLES: J. T. Soutar. 5 reels.

CAST: Roland Conway (Jack Rawson), Maie Baird (Marion Oldham), John de Lacey (Frederich Schmidt/Fred Smith), P. G. Sadler (Colonel Oldham), Olga Willard (Joyce), Rock Phillips (Carl Reichardt), Charles Villiers (Wilhelm Heidel), Lily Rochefort (Aunt Lily), Maud Styan (maid), Claude Turton, Charles Beetham.

The story capitalized on popular paranoia about a German spy menace in Australia and the country's vulnerability to attack. Two German cruisers escape to the Pacific and begin to raid the Australian coast. Jack Rawson, a sailor in the merchant marine, is the sole survivor of an attack on his ship by the Germans. He drifts on a raft to an island, which he discovers is an enemy munitions base. He is captured by the Germans, but when he overhears a German radio message about a planned raid on the Australian coast, he makes a desperate bid to escape in a small boat. After weeks of severe privation he is picked up by a ship and taken safely to Sydney. There he is kidnapped by Frederich Schmidt, a German spy posing as an ordinary Australian named Fred Smith, who chloroforms Jack and binds him to a chair in a wooden building, which he then sets on fire. With Schmidt's aid, the German raiding party lands near Sydney and spreads destruction far and wide. Meanwhile Jack is rescued from the fire and is one of the first to volunteer in the struggle to repel the Germans. After a bitter engagement with the Germans, Jack is stranded behind enemy lines and discovers that his fiancée, Marion, is being held captive. He makes his way to her house and finds her being molested by Schmidt. In the ensuing struggle, Marion manages to shoot Schmidt and kill him. News soon comes that the raiders are being driven steadily back to the sea, and Jack and Marion are left free to marry.

Franklyn Barrett collaborated in the production with Rock Phillips, a well-known stage designer for J. C. Williamson's theatrical company. Phillips also acted in the film with his wife, Lily Rochefort. Shooting began early in 1917 with the co-operation of the Commonwealth Defence Department and the New South Wales Recruiting Committee, who recognized the value of the story as a stimulus to their work, and who provided most of the military auxiliaries and background. The film opened at the Theatre Royal, Sydney, on 19 May 1917, but probably because of the war-weariness of the public it failed to attract an audience. Reviews, however, were positive; *Footlighters*, 24 May 1917, found it 'a production de luxe . . . The photography is A1, equal to the best American, the settings of the interiors, (beautiful David Jones furnishings) and the choice of the outdoor locations, are all faultless, and the acting of the artists . . . is splendid.'

Are Our Women Safe from Violation?
Men and Women of Australia, Awake!
DO YOU REALISE YOUR PERIL?
CAN MURDER AND RAPINE BLACKEN THIS SUNNY LAND?
ARE OUR WIVES, SWEETHEARTS, AND LOVED ONES IN DANGER?
THE SUPREME REVELATION OF THE THREE NOBLEST PASSIONS OF A WOMAN'S LIFE—
The Love of a Maid for a Man.
The Love of a Mother for her Child.
The Love of a Woman for her Country.
SEE
Australia's Peril.
The most heart-gripping, pulse-moving Dramatic Spectacle ever seen.
A picture burning with the flaming passion of Home.
Australia's Peril,
Dealing with an imaginary raid on the Australian Coast by the Enemy, and its accompanying horrors. It discloses the grim tragedies that might occur if an enemy invaded our shores.
WAR'S CRUELEST WOUNDS PIERCE THE HEARTS AT HOME.
The Massacre of Inhabitants.
The Ride for Life.
The Fight to a Finish with an Australian girl for the prize.
The Symbol of War—Woeful Womanhood
in
Australia's Peril,
6-Act Cinema Thunderbolt,
TRANSFERRED FROM THEATRE ROYAL,
Showing
ALHAMBRA THEATRE,
TO-MORROW AND ALL THE WEEK.
FRED. BRODRICK

140 The Hayseeds Come to Sydney
[The Hayseeds Come to Town]

1917 BEAUMONT SMITH

PC: Beaumont Smith's Productions. P, SC: Beaumont Smith. PH: A. O. Segerberg. 4000 ft.

CAST: Tal Ordell (Dad Hayseed), Fred MacDonald (Jim Hayseed), Harry McDonna (Cousin Harold), Gladys Leigh (Mrs Hayseed), H. H. Wallace, Jack Lennon, Connie Metters, Vera Spaull, Cecil Haines, Mattie Ive, Beaumont Smith (man on railway station).

Dad takes the family to Sydney for a holiday after he wins the lottery. The film was shot in and around the city in May 1917, with scenes at numerous tourist landmarks, and the result offered 'more scenery than an average travelogue' (*Green Room*, 1 June 1917).

Given the enormous popularity of *Our Friends, the Hayseeds*, Beaumont Smith was able to pre-sell this spin-off to no less than forty Sydney theatres by the end of May. A première was held simultaneously at Waddington's Globe and Majestic Theatres, Sydney, on 9 July. Elsewhere in Australia its title was modified to *The Hayseeds Come to Town*. The *Green Room*, 1 August 1917, wrote in faint praise: 'There is some suggestion of a yarn in it, and one or two of the scenes are surprisingly good . . . Smith has made such an improvement on his first film, in this one, that there is no telling what the next may be.'

The film marked the screen début of an accomplished stage comedian, Fred MacDonald. A frustrated Shakespearian actor, MacDonald became inextricably associated with backblocks farce in 1912, when he joined the stage cast of *On Our Selection* in the role of Dave. He played the same role thereafter for many years on stage and later screen. The character of Jim Hayseed was a close imitation of Dave Rudd and he played the part comfortably in three of Beaumont Smith's productions. He died in Sydney in October 1968.

140 *The Hayseeds come to Sydney*

141 The Monk and the Woman

1917 FRANKLYN BARRETT

PC: Australian Famous Players. P: George Marlow, Harry Musgrove, Franklyn Barrett. From the play by Frederick Melville. ART D: Rock Phillips. 6000 ft.
CAST: Maud Fane (Liane), Percy Marmont (Brother Paul), Harry Plimmer (Prince de Montrale), Monte Luke (the king), Alma Rock Phillips, Hugh Huntley, Charles Beetham, George Young, Mattie Ive (pageboy).

In eighteenth-century France, the evil Prince de Montrale falls in love with the beautiful Liane, but she seeks refuge from him in a monastery. The prince finds her there and commands the abbot to keep her in custody. A young novice, Brother Paul, who has just taken his vow of celibacy, is placed in charge of the prisoner, and falls hopelessly in love with her. When Liane is taken back to the court, the king commands that she must marry de Montrale. A grand wedding ceremony is prepared, but Paul defeats the prince in a duel, steals his cloak and takes his place at the wedding. Vows are exchanged between the monk and the woman before the king discovers the impostor, and Paul is taken away for execution. Meanwhile de Montrale leads a revolt against the king, but Paul helps the king to hold the enemy at bay until loyalists arrive. With the prince vanquished, and Liane out of danger of a forced marriage, Paul renounces the world and returns to his monastery forever.

Marlow had produced the play profitably on the Australian stage after acquiring local rights in 1912. It seems certain that he was prompted into making a belated film version in 1917 by Longford's production of a quite different story with a similar title, *The Church and the Woman*. Legal bluff failed to deter Longford and his backers, and Marlow rushed into production in an attempt to beat Longford's film to the screen. Although Marlow

141 *The Monk and the Woman* Maud Fane, Percy Marmont

won the race by a few days, the quality of his work suffered severely and his box-office was only redeemed by some judiciously timed, and apparently deliberately provoked, controversy with the Catholic community. Marlow had already experienced the force of church protests when he first performed the play in Sydney in December 1912, and it was certainly not without some hope of inflaming a similar controversy that he invited church leaders to a preview and asked them to report on the film. Presumably to avoid conflict with the New South Wales censors, Marlow and his director, Franklyn Barrett, modified the story's ending so that the monk finally renounced his loved one, instead of bravely facing an uncertain future with her in his arms, as in the play. But the Sydney office of the Catholic Federation still found cause for offence throughout the work. The Federation's long report on the film was 'leaked' by Marlow to the daily press, always eager for sensation and scandal. In addition to many specific points (especially the fact of the marriage of the monk to the woman in defiance of his vow of celibacy), the Federation objected to the general tone of the film as a 'vulgar insult to Catholics'. A scene in the monastery showed the monks 'revelling in the gluttony of the table' and generally behaving in an 'offensive travesty on monks and monastic life'; furthermore, the 'weird crosses, variegated dress of the monks, rosary beads used in the oddest fashion, all make the show undignified and ridiculous'. The Federation concluded: 'To set a castellated building in a landscape of eucalyptus scrub and to introduce half a dozen inconspicuous actors in medieval costume, for the purpose of producing a crude, ill-constructed, and wildly improbable melodrama, is no help to Australian art.' (*Sun*, 4 October 1917) Their criticism, however, did not alter the censor's decision that the film was fit for public exhibition without cuts or alterations.

141 *The Monk and the Woman* Harry Plimmer, Maud Fane

Shooting began early in August and within a mere twenty-eight days the film was ready for censor-screening on 6 September. Props and costumes were provided from J. C. Williamson's store, and the film was shot almost entirely indoors on the stage of the Theatre Royal for the low cost of £1000. The cast was led by three British actors then touring Australia—Percy Marmont, Hugh Huntley and the musical comedy star Maud Fane. Marmont and Huntley later went on to long careers in English and American cinema.

The film opened in Sydney at the Lyric and Strand Theatres on 8 October 1917, just one week ahead of Longford's. Commercially, it was highly rewarding, but critical reaction was far from flattering. The *Sun* wrote on 2 September 1917: 'It is not overstating the case to say that the players give the impression of merely walking through their parts . . . Feeling, sentiment, atmosphere, life, are all wanting.'

142 The Church and the Woman

1917 RAYMOND LONGFORD

P: Humbert Pugliese. SC: Raymond Longford. PH: Ernest Higgins. ASST D: Pat McGrath. 7000 ft.

CAST: Lottie Lyell (Eileen Shannon), Boyd Irwin (Doctor Sidney Burton), Harry Roberts (Father Shannon), Percy Walshe (John Shannon), J. P. O'Neill (Mike Feeney), Nada Conrade (Helen Burton), Pat McGrath, Miss Roland Watts-Phillips, George K. Chesterton Bonar.

This drama broached the controversial subjects of mixed marriage between Catholic and Protestant and the responsibility of priests to honour the confidences of the confessional. Eileen Shannon, from a staunch Catholic background, is in love with Doctor Burton, a Protestant. They wish to marry, but her father refuses consent. Later her father is murdered and Burton is arrested and sentenced to death. The real culprit meanwhile confesses his guilt to Eileen's brother, a Catholic priest, but refuses to release him from his confessional obligations. To resolve the dilemma, the priest himself confesses to the murder, and Burton is released. The murderer, however, eventually betrays himself and is duly brought to justice. The priest is released and Eileen and Burton are married, albeit 'behind the altar'.

The production was fraught with litigation. Shooting began in March 1917, and in July George Marlow, who owned rights to *The Monk and The Woman*, issued the first of several legal threats to prevent the release of the film. Marlow's case was weak, since the two dramas bore no relation whatsoever in plot or setting, but both Marlow and Longford doubtless recognized the commercial value of free publicity arising from the legal action. Although Marlow's film reached the screen a few days before Longford's, it gained little advantage by being first, for both films succeeded remarkably well at the box-office.

Locations used in the film included the Sacred Heart Church, Darlinghurst, and the Catholic Riverview College, Sydney, as well as the grounds and interiors of Wentworth House, Vaucluse. A scene depicting a Catholic mass was directed for the Protestant Longford by a deputy, Pat McGrath. The film opened at the Theatre Royal, Sydney, on 13 October 1917.

142 Humbert Pugliese

The trade press generally praised Longford's work: 'Uniformly well-acted, the whole six reels, with a gem of a story . . . Never for a moment is there an unnatural, improbable situation or scene' (*Theatre*, 1 November 1917). The critic in the *Lone Hand*, 1 December 1917, however, was much less kind:

142 *The Church and the Woman* Lottie Lyell

142 *The Church and the Woman* Lottie Lyell, J. P. O'Neill

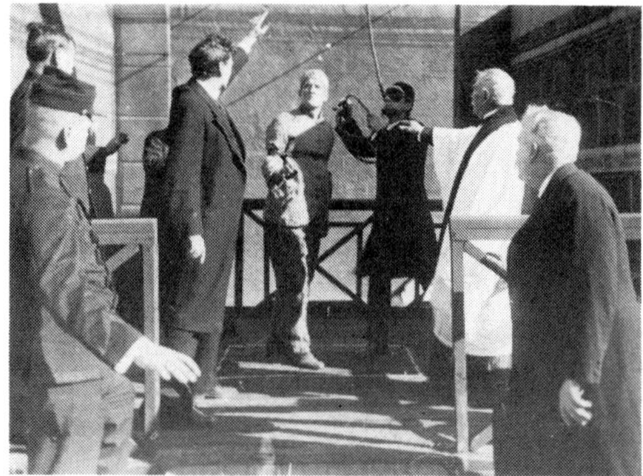

142 *The Church and the Woman* Harry Roberts (*c*), saved from the scaffold

'Australian films are still a whole lot worse than the average incoming pictures . . . The slow action of the picture made many of the scenes tiresomely annoying . . . None of the actors except Harry Roberts displayed either grace, ease or charm.'

In mid-1918, the film figured in another court case, this time relating to the source of the story. Action was brought against the producer, Humbert Pugliese, by the novelist Edward Finn, who claimed that the film had plagiarized a novel he had written in 1888, *A Priest's Secret.* Judgement was passed on 4 July 1918 against Pugliese, and he was barred from further exhibition of the film. It evidently took three years for agreement to be reached between Pugliese and Finn, for the film did not screen in Melbourne until August 1921.

The production was the first of three financed by the Pugliese family. The Italian-born Antonio Pugliese and his wife, Caroline, had been among the first pioneer film exhibitors in Sydney. In 1909 they secured their first major theatre, the Alhambra in the Sydney Haymarket, and presented both vaudeville and film with strong commercial success. Two other theatres were soon added to their group in the Sydney suburbs of Bondi and Leichhardt. Antonio died in 1916, but Caroline continued as treasurer of the family business with her son Humbert as general manager. Like other independent exhibitors, regular film supply was always a problem and they imported many films for their own theatres and provided a city release for many Australian productions. Their own participation in production did not flourish and by 1922 signs of strain were showing; the Alhambra changed hands and was renamed the Melba, and Humbert Pugliese's further career is unknown.

142 *The Church and the Woman* Lottie Lyell and Boyd Irwin are married

143 The Hayseeds' Back-blocks Show

1917 BEAUMONT SMITH

PC: Beaumont Smith's Productions. P, SC: Beaumont Smith. PH: A. O. Segerberg. 4000 ft.

CAST: Tal Ordell (Dad Hayseed), Fred MacDonald (Jim Hayseed), Harry McDonna (Cousin Harold).

Dad and his friends at Stoney Creek decide to hold an agricultural show, and the Governor of Queensland agrees to open it. In preparation, the local brass band painfully starts rehearsing, and the Hayseeds gather together their 'prize pumpkins and poddy calves, [and] all the apples and hen-fruit'. When the day of the show arrives Dad dresses in 'his best boiled shirt and bluchers' and welcomes the guest of honour with a speech and a handshake 'that nearly screws the arm off the governor'. (*Sun*, 28 October 1917) The show is a great success, and after a lively day the governor departs with more exhausting handshaking.

This Brisbane item in the Hayseeds series was released at the Lyric and Grand Theatres, Sydney, on 5 November 1917, while Smith was shooting the next episode in Melbourne. *Theatre*, 1 January 1918, found it 'good wholesome fun—all of it!' and it was another strong commercial success.

144 A Coo-ee from Home

1918 CHARLES WOODS

PC: Woods' Australian Films. SC: Charles Woods. PH: Tasman Higgins. 8000 ft.
CAST: Gertrude Darley (Grace Norwood), Bryce Rowe (Will Morrison), Charles Villiers, Charles Woods.

Will Morrison, a young miner in the Australian bush, falls in love with a wealthy heiress, Grace Norwood, and marries her. A former rival for Grace's hand, Richard Myers, determines to separate the happy couple and claim Grace as his own. He tries to convince Will that Grace is unfaithful, and when that ruse fails, he drugs Will and frames him for murder. Will is arrested and sentenced to death, but a friendly prison chaplain helps him to escape. He joins the crew of a ship, but later at sea he is exposed as a wanted criminal. To escape, he dives into the sea and is attacked by a shark. He manages to kill the shark, but the boat crew give him up for dead. He swims to shore and later reads in a newspaper that Myers has been betrayed by his own henchmen and has been arrested for the murder. Will returns home a free man to his long-waiting wife.

The highlight of this complex tale was the shark fight, which involved genuine danger for the leading actor, Bryce Rowe: after killing the shark as required for the film, he was attacked by another shark and narrowly escaped with his life. According to *Australian Variety*, 11 January 1918, he had to spend two weeks in hospital after the incident. The film was made in and around Sydney by Charles Woods and was distributed by his own company. It opened on 14 January 1918 at the Alhambra Theatre, Sydney. The usually candid critic in *Theatre*, 1 February 1918, praised the film as a melodrama with 'many thrills . . . and some good comedy', and noted the scenic variety of the action, ranging through the New South Wales mining areas and farmlands to the city and the rocky coast.

144 *A Coo-ee from Home* Gertrude Darley

143 *The Hayseeds' Back-blocks Show*

145 The Hayseeds' Melbourne Cup

1918 BEAUMONT SMITH

PC: Beaumont Smith's Productions. P, SC: Beaumont Smith. PH: A. O. Segerberg. 4000 ft.
CAST: Tal Ordell (Dad Hayseed), Fred MacDonald (Jim Hayseed), Harry McDonna (Cousin Harold), Gladys Leigh (Mrs Hayseed), Guy Hastings, Ethel Grist, Mattie Ive.

Dad comes down to Melbourne to enter his horse, Cornstalk, in the Melbourne Cup; his son Jim is the trainer, and his cousin Harold is to be the jockey if he can get his weight down in time. Mum comes too to keep an eye on Dad. In the scenes that follow, Jim falls in love with an actress and learns how to smoke, and Mum has a nightmare in which she sees herself washing the steps of Parliament House. On the day of the big race, Mum wears the latest Stoney Creek fashions to the Flemington racecourse and boils a billy on the lawns for tea. Despite the attempted interference of a crooked bookmaker, Cornstalk wins the race by a clear margin and the Hayseeds return happily to the farm.

This fourth in the Hayseeds series was the last of the 1917-18 group, and Beaumont Smith embarked on a variety of other productions before returning to the Hayseeds in 1923. *The Hayseeds' Melbourne Cup* was filmed entirely in Melbourne in November 1917, and opened at the Star Theatre on 18 January 1918.

146 His Convict Bride

1918 JOHN GAVIN

PC: Australian Famous Feature Company. SC: Agnes Gavin. PH: Lacey Percival. ART TITLES: Syd Nicholls. 6 reels.
CAST: Ethel Bashford (Bess Shelgrove), John Gavin (Jack Warren), Charles Villiers (Adam Wilson), Frank Hawthorne, Claude Turton, Fred Cope, Syd Everett, Walter Vincent, Ray Harris, C. Howard, D. L. Dalziel, Randal Woodhouse, Ruth Wainwright, Rose Rooney, Flo Smith, Miss Roland Watts-Phillips, Baby Edie Taylor, David Edelsten.

England, 1813: Bess Shelgrove rejects a suitor, Adam Wilson, who works as a bank clerk. In revenge, Adam steals money from the bank and frames Bess for the crime. She is arrested and transported for life to Botany Bay. There she is assigned as a servant to Mrs Renshay, a snobbish society leader, whose dishonourable son has driven a previous maidservant to suicide. Bess tries to escape, and after three weeks alone in the bush she meets 'her destiny', in the form of an adventurer, Jack Warren, whom she marries. Later Bess is recognized by Mrs Renshay and is arrested. Jack, meanwhile, encounters Adam Wilson and forces him to confess that he framed Bess. She is released from prison and happily reunited with Jack and her baby daughter.

146 *His Convict Bride* A trade advertisement before the title was changed

The story was a re-working of themes from Gavin's own convict melodramas of 1911. A working title, *For the Term of her Natural Life*, was abandoned shortly before release under the threat of legal action by the daughter of Marcus Clarke, author of *For the Term of his Natural Life*. Shooting began in September 1917, in and around Sydney. While staging a scene in the bush near Penrith, Gavin's horse backed over a forty-foot cliff; Gavin (a formidable 18-stone figure) broke his fall on a tree and was rescued with block and tackle, but his horse had to be destroyed. Distributed by Gavin himself, the film opened at the Lyric Theatre, Sydney, on 4 February 1918. *Theatre*, 1 March 1918, commented that it 'goes down well with a lot in the audience. But to me it's a distressingly poor advertisement for Australian-made pictures.'

Gavin and his wife Agnes left Australia later in 1918 to further their careers in Hollywood; Gavin acted extensively there in Westerns and as a 'straight man' in comedies with Harold Lloyd, Snub Pollard and others. He returned to Australia permanently in 1925, but directed only one more feature, *Trooper O'Brien* (1928).

146 *His Convict Bride* John Gavin, Ethel Bashford

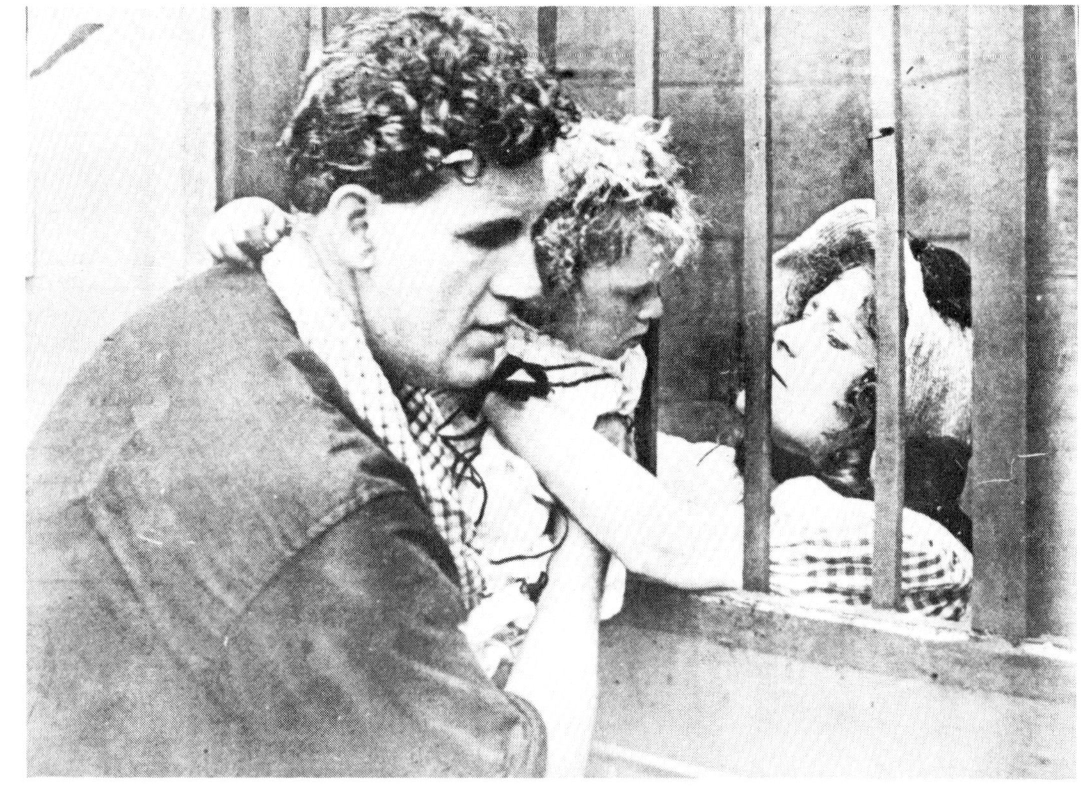

147 The Laugh on Dad

1918 A. C. TINSDALE

PC: Austral Photoplay Company. SC: A. C. Tinsdale. 4 reels.

CAST: Netta Lawson (Jean Forrest), Johnson Weir (John Forrest), May Morton (May), Mrs Tinsdale (Mrs Dumpling), Jules Olaff (Arthur Elliott), Alwyn West (Jim), Olaf Jensen (Ralph Bond), Charles Clarke.

John Forrest, commonly known as Dad, is an ostrich-farmer who delights in crude practical jokes. His daughter, Jean, wants to marry Ralph Bond, but Dad opposes the match. He devises an elaborate joke whereby a farm-hand will dress as Jean and go through the marriage ceremony with Ralph. Jean, however, learns of the plot and successfully turns the laugh against Dad by appearing at the wedding herself.

The Laugh on Dad was the first major production by Austral Photoplay, a company registered in Melbourne in November 1913. The man behind the company was A. C. (Arthur Charles) Tinsdale, a film importer and entrepreneur who acted as Australian agent for several American stage artists and small film production companies. Tinsdale's production plans were set back by the war and by difficulties in raising finance. He personally kept the company going, however, and shot some footage in Ballarat for a feature, *Women and Gold*, but it was never completed. In 1917 Tinsdale transferred the registration of the company to Sydney and set out to raise capital for *The Laugh on Dad* by a novel means of public subscription. Two-shilling shares were offered to the public; every holder of one hundred shares (worth £10) was entitled to receive free 'motion picture tuition' and to take part as an actor in one of the company's films. The cast of the comedy feature was led by a professional stage actor, Johnson Weir, but the supporting players were amateur. Even with most of the cast actually paying to appear in the film, production costs rose to £1000. Most exterior scenes were shot on an ostrich farm at South Head, Sydney, and

147 *The Laugh on Dad* Johnson Weir

interiors in Tinsdale's studio in North Sydney. The film was premiered before an invited (and paying) audience of shareholders and friends at the King's Hall, Sydney, on 2 March 1918. Commercial screenings were arranged only with difficulty and the first recorded season did not begin until 28 July 1919 in Brisbane.

After the Sydney preview, on 10 March 1918 the *Sun* attacked the film as a 'vulgar' comedy redolent of the 'crude humour which prevailed 30 years ago, in certain music halls of English industrial towns'. Undeterred, the company continued to make several more films on the same financial basis, including a short sequel, *Dad Becomes a Grandad* (1918). The company also released *Through Australian Wilds* (1918) by the adventurer Francis Birtles, and purchased the negatives of films made by the Australian Film Syndicate in 1911-12. In 1923 Tinsdale went to England and Europe to try to sell his films, and remained there to produce *Gallipoli*, a compilation of British war newsreels, released in Sydney in July 1928.

148 *The Enemy Within* One of Snowy Baker's stunts, leaping from one moving car to another

148 The Enemy Within*

1918 ROLAND STAVELY

P: Franklyn Barrett (?), Roland Stavely. SC: Roland Stavely. PH: Franklyn Barrett. ART D: Rock Phillips. Approx. 5500 ft.

CAST: Reg L. 'Snowy' Baker (Jack Airlie), John Faulkner (Henry Brasels), Lily Molloy (Myee Drew), Nellie Calvin (Claire Lerode), Billy Ryan (Bill Warne), Sandy McVea (Jimmy Cook), Lily Rochefort (Mrs Drew), Gerald Harcourt (Glassop), Marjory Donovan (the child), David Edelsten, William O'Brien, Frank Baker.

Jack Airlie is a secret service agent called in to crack a ring of foreign agents involved in treason and civil violence in Australia. Jack's sweetheart, Myee, is kidnapped by the villains, but after a long chase, Jack is able to trap the enemy and rescue Myee.

The film identifies the enemy with low-class slum agitators who openly preach sabotage in the Sydney Domain, and who resemble the popular conception of the International Workers of the World movement, then the subject of much hostility in Australia because of their opposition to the war. The ringleaders of the subversive workers are identified as members of Sydney's high society, operating from a luxurious mansion at Palm Beach. The main purpose of the film however was not to express concern about subversion in Australia, although it does incidentally reflect current paranoia; rather it was a *Boy's Own* adventure designed to display the heroic feats and daring stunt-work of one of Australia's most popular sportsmen, Reg L. 'Snowy' Baker. During the course of the film he performs several amazing leaps in pursuit of the enemy, from horse to horse, and from a rooftop to a moving wagon. He also dives eighty feet into a bay to rescue the heroine from the tide, and soundly defeats a pack of hoodlums in hand-to-hand fighting.

Shooting began in December 1917 under the direction of a J. C. Williamson stage producer, Roland Stavely. The supporting cast

148 *The Enemy Within* John Faulkner (*r, with pipe*), as the wealthy ringleader of working-class subversives

COMPANY

included several of Baker's fellow sportsmen, including the Aboriginal boxer, Sandy McVea, as Baker's right-hand man. The film was released by a small independent exchange, Quality Features, at the Strand Theatre, Sydney, on 11 March 1918, with advertisements assuring a war-weary public that it was 'not a war picture'. Commercial results were so strong that Baker moved quickly on to another feature, *The Lure of the Bush* (1918). Critics, however, had many reservations about the plot, and the *Sun*, 10 March 1918, speculated about the villain's reason for kidnapping the heroine: he 'is prompted by neither sentiment nor passion, nor revenge. One suspects that the author makes him do it merely to give [Baker] a chance of enacting a sensational rescue.'

Christened Reginal Leslie, but universally known as Snowy, Baker was born in Sydney in February 1884. While in his teens, he began to display remarkable prowess in a wide variety of sports, winning a New South Wales swimming championship and playing in the Australian rugby team against England. He also distinguished himself at boxing, cricket, rowing, athletics, water polo and diving. In 1908 he boxed in the Olympic Games in London and only narrowly lost a gold medal. Soon after, he established a health and fitness studio in Sydney and joined the John Wren company, Stadiums Limited. His entry into film was eagerly awaited by a curious press and public, and the commercial success of his first two features in 1918 provided a solid basis on which he built a major production enterprise. In 1919 he went into partnership with E. J. and Dan Carroll and imported American crew to produce films for the international market. Three outdoor action movies were completed before he accepted work in Hollywood and starred there in several Westerns. He remained in California and became manager of a country club, where film stars were given training in horsemanship and stunt-work. He died in Los Angeles on 2 December 1953.

149 *The Woman Suffers* Connie Martyn with the children, Doris Wadham and Harry Goodfellow

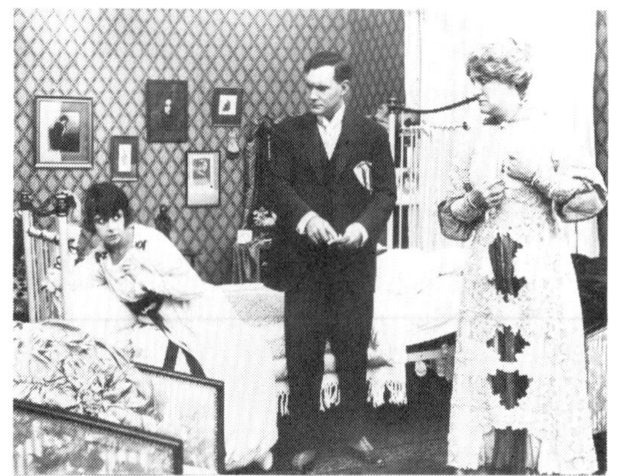

149 *The Woman Suffers* Lottie Lyell, Roland Conway, Connie Martyn (*r*)

149 The Woman Suffers

1918 RAYMOND LONGFORD

PC: Southern Cross Feature Film Company.
SC: Raymond Longford. PH: Arthur Higgins. 8000 ft.
CAST: Lottie Lyell (Marjory Manton), Boyd Irwin (Phillip Masters), Roland Conway (Ralph Manton), Connie Martyn (Marion Masters), Paul Baxter (little Phillip), C. R. Stanford (John Stockdale), Ida Gresham (Mrs Stockdale), Evelyn Black (Joan Stockdale), Charles H. Francis (Stephen Manton), Laurence Dunbar (doctor), Tom Woodville (boundary rider), Joe Martar (overseer), Harry Beaumont (swagman), Herbert Walsh (clergyman), Marjorie Morton, Harry Goodfellow, Doris Wadham, Brian Lawrence, Walter Miller, Winnie Pritchard and Phyllis Wadham (children).

'The woman suffers . . . while the man goes free.' To illustrate this tragic irony, the story takes the concept of primitive justice—an eye for an eye and a tooth for a tooth—and extends it to a sister for a sister. Ralph Manton discovers that his sister, Marjory, has been seduced and, swearing vengeance, he demands to be told the name of the man. Faithful to her lover, she refuses, but later Ralph discovers his identity and goes to confront him. The tables are then turned, for the man is none other than Phillip Masters, whose sister had been seduced by Ralph years before. Phillip reveals that he had seduced Marjory in calculated revenge for the ruin of his own sister and his family name.

The first production of a new South Australian company, *The Woman Suffers* opened with viceregal patronage at the Theatre Royal, Adelaide, on 23 March 1918. The local press praised the 'flawless' photography of the South Australian backgrounds, and especially the outback scenes with their 'strong colours of sunset [and] the pell-mell of wild cattle trailing their dust amid the big spaces'. (*Register,* 25 March 1918). It also opened strongly in Sydney at the Lyric Theatre on 26 August, and *Australian Variety*, 30 August 1918, enjoyed the 'rather spicy theme' and commended it as 'one of the best things ever done by local producers'. It was proceeding

well commercially when, in October, the New South Wales Chief Secretary placed a ban upon further screenings in that state. No reasons were given, even though the ruling was a direct contradiction of the government's written approval for screenings to proceed, given to Longford in July. Despite questions in the state parliament, the ban persisted and Longford became convinced that the combine had brought pressure to bear on the government to suppress the local product (*RCE*, pp. 152-3). The Sydney labour paper, the *Worker*, 31 October 1918, also hinted at sinister motives: 'One cannot help feeling that there is something more in this business than meets the eye . . . this much is certain, that while locally-produced films are being hampered and stopped, the Yankee Trust is getting a greater hold than ever on the country.' *Australian Variety*, 8 November 1918, vigorously opposed the ban as 'a damn piece of absurdity' and 'a scandalous affair', but to no avail: the bureaucracy retained an implacable silence on the matter. Screenings continued, meanwhile, in other states, and the production company was able to proceed with further films, including Longford's masterpiece, *The Sentimental Bloke* (1919).

150 Yachts and Hearts, or The Opium Smugglers

1918 CHARLES BYERS COATES

PC: Antipodes Films. PH: G. L. Gouday. PM: Melville Stevenson. 5 reels.
CAST: Beryl Clifton (Ella Deane), Chris Olsen (Maurice Dean), Arthur Spence (detective), Clare St. Clair (Mrs Friedman), Billie Monckton (crippled boy), Edith Clarke, Vera Chamberlain, Melville Stevenson, Dorothy and Lola Campbell, David Edelsten, Marjorie Sargeant.

Made soon after the completion of their Burke and Wills film (released later in the year), Coates and Gouday turned to a contemporary setting with a detective story based loosely on a recent opium-smuggling case in Sydney. The smuggling yarn was elaborated with a car chase ending in a spectacular crash, a yacht race on Sydney Harbour and a display of forty bathing beauties. A cabaret owned by the villain was a special novelty, for when warning was given of a police raid, it could be rapidly transformed into a church, much to the confusion of the police.

Shot in January 1918, the film was released on 25 March at the Piccadilly Theatre, Sydney, as a supporting feature. It does not seem to have made an impression on either the press or the public, and the company, Antipodes, became inactive.

151 The Waybacks**

1918 ARTHUR W. STERRY

PC: Koala Films. P: Humbert Pugliese. From the play by Phillip Lytton, based on the novels by Henry Fletcher. PH: Ernest Higgins. 7000 ft.
CAST: Vincent White (Dads Wayback), Gladys Leigh (Mums Wayback), Lucy Adair (Tilly), Louis Machilaton (Jabez), Rose Rooney (Frances Holmes), Harry Hodson (Dan Robins), William Turner (Charley Lyons), George Hewlitt (Nigel Kelvin), Lance Vane (Jack Hinds).

The Waybacks had become popular in 1902 with the publication of the first of several novels by Henry Fletcher. A play based on the family's doings was written by Phillip Lytton and first produced in October 1915 in Sydney. Although less enduring commercially and less well received by critics than *On Our Selection*, Lytton's play was nevertheless a strong commercial property in a popular idiom, and this film version was made hard on the heels of Beaumont Smith's success with the Hayseeds series.

The film followed the play closely and presented the exploits of the family both in the bush and on a visit to Sydney. In the city, Dads and his son Jabez befriend a group of Bondi bathing beauties while Mums visits a fortune teller who is good enough at his trade to perceive Dads' game and give him away. The overall tone however was not aggressively farcical, and *Australian Variety*, 17 May 1918, spoke of a certain 'melancholic touch' in the bush scenes, and found that Ernest Higgins's photography of the bush was 'worthy of reproduction in any art gallery'.

Finance was provided by Humbert Pugliese who distributed the film from his Alhambra Theatre in Sydney. Scenes were shot near Windsor, N.S.W., and in Sydney. An animated trademark for Koala Films was drawn by Harry Julius, showing a koala playing with gum leaves and then waddling off screen. The cast included two members of Lytton's original stage production (Gladys Leigh and Harry Hodson). The director himself, Arthur W. Sterry, had acted in the original stage production as the comic yokel, Charley Lyons, and had toured in the play as late as a revival season in Sydney in November 1917. Billed as 'Australia's Sweetest Comedy', the film opened at the Sydney Town Hall on 18 May 1918 and was an instant hit. The continued popularity of the film, and indeed of most films in the genre of backblocks farce, prompted many revivals: it was taken on tour through rural New South Wales in 1922 by Charles Hardy (himself a film director), and was later distributed by F. A. Hughes, who updated its title to *The Waybacks of 1925*. Sterry planned another film along the same lines, to be called *The Cornstalks*, but there is no evidence that it was ever completed.

152 His Only Chance

1918 DICK SHORTLAND

PC: J. C. Williamson Ltd. SC: Captain N. C. P. Conant. PH: Amalgamated Pictures.
CAST: Captain N. C. P. Conant (German spy), Mrs Cass (adventuress), Sir Henry Parker (father), Jack Cannot (bookmaker), Clyde Cook (punter), Maie Baird (dancer).

The Australian Red Cross was active throughout the war devising a variety of fund-raising projects to support the war effort. In 1918 they added film to a range of concerts, balls and other public entertainments. Committees were set up in Sydney and Melbourne to organize two film productions; honorary producers were found (Australasian Films in Sydney and J. C. Williamson in Melbourne), and local society figures were recruited for the cast. The films were presented almost simultaneously in the two cities: *His Only Chance* screened with vice-regal patronage at Tait's Auditorium, Melbourne, on 23 May 1918, and the New South Wales film, *Cupid Camouflaged*, opened a week later in Sydney.

The story of *His Only Chance* was simple and familiar: the playboy son of a wealthy family enlists in the army where he learns to be a 'man' and is decorated for bravery. Some professional players took minor parts, including an athletic vaudeville comedian, Clyde Cook, who soon left for success on the London stage and in Hollywood slapstick comedy. One of Cook's stage specialities was 'eccentric dancing' in partnership with Maie Baird, and a highlight of the film was their performance in a night club scene.

153 Cupid Camouflaged

1918 ALFRED ROLFE

PC: Australasian Films. PH: Lacey Percival. 4 reels.
CAST: Mrs T. H. Kelly (Mrs Manners), Rosamund Lumsdaine (Rosita Manners), Madge Hardy (Althea Gardner), Captain Saltmarshe, A.D.C. (Tony Martin), J. B. N. Osborne (Valentine Loring), John Maude (Charles Leslie), Leslie Victor (loafer), Mrs Venour Nathan and Mr Sydney Yates (dancers), Louis de Groen and his band.

Early in 1918 the New South Wales branch of the Australian Red Cross formed a 'motion picture producing committee' to make a film to aid their fund-raising for the war. The film was produced for them in an honorary capacity by Australasian Films, and a number of Sydney's 'society people' and charity workers appeared in the cast, including over 200 in garden party and ball sequences.

The story, set in pre-war Sydney, depicts the budding romance between Rosita and Tony and their subsequent engagement on a picnic at Port Hacking. Rosita's ambitious mother would prefer to see her daughter married to Valentine Loring, whom she believes to be a member of the British nobility. The lovers elope and a furious car chase ensues, but the young couple manage to escape their pursuers. Mrs Manners then decides to have Loring for herself and extracts a proposal of marriage from him. Only later does she discover that he is not from nobility, but is a mere dress designer with social pretensions.

The film was presented as the highlight of a special charity evening at the Theatre Royal, Sydney, on 31 May 1918, and screened at the King's Cross Theatre during the following week.

154 Satan in Sydney

1918 BEAUMONT SMITH

PC: Beaumont Smith's Productions. P, SC: Beaumont Smith. 6 reels.
CAST: Elsie Prince (Anna Maxwell), George Edwards (Will Wayburn), Charles Villiers (Karl Kroner), Zoe Angas, Ruth Wainwright, Gladys Leigh, Percy Walshe, Eileen Dawn, Edward Jenner, D. L. Dalziel, Gerald Harcourt, Mick Tracey.

An honest country girl, Anna Maxwell, is the victim of a scheming German choirmaster who compromises her reputation and succeeds in persuading her narrow-minded parents to drive her from their home. Anna drifts to Sydney, and when war breaks out, she goes to the Front as a nurse. The German meanwhile opens a gambling hall and opium den in a sleazy part of Sydney, and uses women to entice soldiers there to encourage them to desert from the army. Eventually the German is brought to justice and Anna finds happiness with her true love.

A marked change from Smith's customary Hayseeds farce, this sensationalist melodrama was made in Sydney and scheduled for release at the Lyric Theatre on 15 July 1918. Perhaps Smith anticipated censorship troubles and intended to maximize the clash by staging his encounter with the police in public; but deliberately or not, he neglected to seek a clearance to screen the film before the season began. Attracted by lurid advertisements in the morning's press, the police stopped the screening after the first 11 a.m. session. The District Licensing Inspector, J. Fullerton, viewed the film and found it generally salacious and violent. In addition, scenes were shown in 'a Chinese grog shop with a number of our Australian troops in a drunken condition and women smoking cigarettes . . . This portion of the film is very offensive to Chinese, who are our allies, and it would have a serious effect on recruiting if shown in Country Towns.' Two days later, the newly created Film Censorship Board in the New South Wales Chief Secretary's department overruled Inspector Fullerton's decision and released the film uncut, on the proviso that if the Chinese community approached the government about it, then steps might be taken to reassess the film. The season resumed at the Lyric Theatre on 22 July, but now a minor film had become famous: advertising stridently exploited the temporary ban on the film, and the press devoted much space to speculation about the censor's actions. The trade papers reported that suddenly 6000 people a day were crowding into the Lyric and the film became a 'knockout' box-office hit.

Racist attitudes towards the Chinese (equating them with vices such as prostitution, gambling and drug peddling) were explicit in the film's advertising, although not unusually blatant for the time. The main concern of Australian officialdom was not the racism itself but that the Chinese deserved fair treatment now that they were Australia's ally in the war. The Chinese community quickly objected to the slur against them, not in the film itself, but in the publicity. A merchant, William Yinson Lee, spoke for the community in Sydney and protested about the lobby display at the Lyric, the posters on hoardings around the city and the design of newspaper advertisements. According to Lee, the publicity inferred that the Chinese were the Satan of the title, and that it tended 'to hold the peaceful Chinese community up to ridicule'. Although the jurisdiction of the censors did not extend to publicity materials, they did formally request the Lyric management to remove the posters and to avoid using them in future. These requests were willingly met by exhibitors who had already profited greatly from the censorship confusion.

Censorship apart, the press had mixed reactions to the film. A critic in the *Lone Hand*, 2 September 1918, condemned it as 'a poor production with a drab plot of the penny novelette type . . . The cast is exceedingly weak'; but *Australian Variety*, 26 June 1918, found it 'a pleasant change from the run of war dramas we've been accustomed to lately'.

155 Just Peggy

1918 J. A. LIPMAN

PC: Mia Films. P, SC: J. A. Lipman. 6 reels.
CAST: Sara Allgood (Peggy), Harry Thomas (Peter Wallace), Nellie Phillips (Helen Raymond), Rigby C. Tearle (theatrical manager), Gerald Henson (Frank Leighton), Lily Rochefort, Tralie Nicholson, Fred Ward, Percy Walshe, Vincent White, Aileen Campbell, Monica Dick, Mona Scully, Marjorie Henry, Roma Highes, T. M. Lloyd, T. Moran.

A humpbacked musician, Peter Wallace, marries a blind girl, Helen Raymond. On the birth of their child, Helen regains her sight and is appalled at Peter's deformity. She violently rejects him and runs away. Fearing that the child is also deformed, she abandons it at a convent. The little girl is raised there, known as 'just Peggy', and grows into young womanhood. Instead of her father's deformity, she inherits his musical skills, and a family reunion occurs by coincidence at an opera performance in which Helen is a singer, Peggy is a violinist, and her father the last-minute substitute as orchestra leader.

Publicity stated that 'strange as it may seem to the audience, [the story] is based on an actual occurrence in America'. The incident was drawn to the attention of the director, J. A. Lipman, by the Australian cartoonist and film animator Harry Julius, while both were in America on business. Lipman subsequently developed the screenplay as a vehicle for Sara Allgood, an Irish stage actress from the Abbey Theatre, Dublin, who had come to Australia in 1916 to star in a play, *Peg o' My Heart*. Lipman built a small outdoor studio (80 feet by 60 feet) at Seaforth, near Sydney, and shot the film there and on near-by locations early in 1918 under the emblem of Mia ('Made in Australia') Films.

Just Peggy opened in Sydney at the Theatre Royal on 10 August 1918 and made healthy profits. Distribution was handled by one of Lipman's own companies, Quality Features. Reviews reflected substantial weaknesses in the film as entertainment: the *Sun*, 4 August

155 Sara Allgood

1918, said that the story was 'not told coherently', and the reviewer commented with sarcasm on such logical flaws as the failure of the blind girl to realize that her husband was hunchbacked. *Theatre*, 1 August 1918, also criticized the performance of the star: 'Unfortunately Miss Allgood isn't on the screen the success she is on the stage . . . For one thing she's too heavy—matronly would perhaps be the truer word—for the ingenuous, girlish role.'

Lipman was involved with both the stage and screen, mainly as a businessman, but also occasionally as an actor. He was born in 1882 in Adelaide and while a young man became active as a producer and actor in local theatre, and later in the eastern states, often using the stage name of Rigby C. Tearle (under which name he appears in *Just Peggy*). A colourful extrovert, he had a flair for the wheeling and dealing of the film trade, and moved through a rapid succession of companies and agencies throughout the 1920s and 1930s. He frequently travelled abroad and was one of the pioneers of the exploitation of British features in Australia. Despite the commercial success of *Just Peggy*, he did not return to production again until the 1930s with *The Man they could not Hang* (1934) and *Mystery Island* (1937).

156 *Algie's Romance* Boyd Irwin (*l*), Leonard Doogood

156 Algie's Romance

1918 LEONARD DOOGOOD

PC: South Australian Feature Film Company.
P, SC: Leonard Doogood. 3500 ft.
CAST: Leonard Doogood (Algie), Boyd Irwin, May and June Henry.

Leonard Doogood was an English vaudeville comedian and one of many Chaplin impersonators on the stage at this time. He personally financed, directed and distributed this comedy film while touring in Australia. It was shot in South Australia, with locations on the large cattle station of Sir Arthur Downer, and with technical facilities provided by Southern Cross Feature Films.

The plot was based on the standard convention of the English 'new chum' in quest of colonial experience. Algie was more naïve than most, and arrived at the outback railway station in formal morning attire—top hat, gloves and spats. Many jokes are played on Algie in the bush, but he is redeemed by his skill as a marksman and by his romantic success with one of the beautiful twins on the station.

The film was previewed in Adelaide in May but not released in Sydney until 2 September 1918, when it opened as a supporting feature at the Piccadilly Theatre. *Australian Variety*, 10 May 1918, found it 'brimful of genuine, clean, natural humor', but trade interest was desultory, and it was never widely screened. A second Doogood production (*Dinkum Oil*, based on a novel by a South Australian, Frederick J. Mills) reached an advanced stage of preparation, but was eventually abandoned.

157 A Romance of the Burke and Wills Expedition of 1860**

1918 CHARLES BYERS COATES

PC: Antipodes Films/Austral Photoplay Company. PH: G. L. Gouday, Franklyn Barrett, A. O. Segerberg, Walter Sully. 6 reels.
CAST: Charles Clarke (Robert O'Hara Burke), George Patterson (William Wills), Chris Olsen (John King), G. Gould (W. Grey), Bias Kotes (William Brahe), David Edelsten (Mayor of Melbourne), Vera Chamberlain (Mina Doyle), Ona Landers (Stella McDonald), Madame Carbasse (Mrs Doyle), Melville Stevenson (Dost Mahommed), Astor Lewis (Bridget), Yvonne Blight (maid), Dorothy Beer and Evelyn Hooper (Mina's sisters), Clare St. Clair and Ida Hooper (horsewomen), Dorothy Ashton (Mayor's daughter), Netta Lawson, Josephine Ryan.

157 *A Romance of the Burke and Wills Expedition of 1860* Charles Clarke (*l*), and 'Bias Kotes' (*c*)—the director, Byers Coates—as a villain who tries to disrupt the expedition

This 'Romance of Bravery and Blunder' is told by Mina Doyle to her young sisters, long after the ill-fated Burke and Wills expedition has taken place. The story of the expedition, with the death of Burke and Wills in their attempt to cross Australia from Melbourne to the Gulf of Carpentaria, is alleviated in its grim tragedy by a 'pretty strain of romance'.

A new company, Antipodes Films, formed by Charles Byers Coates and George Louis Gouday, announced the completion of a three-reel film about Burke and Wills in November 1917. Early in 1918 Coates was reported to have spent a further month in central Australia securing footage to expand the film. It was previewed to the trade in May 1918, but was subsequently restructured and retitled, presumably by the Austral Photoplay Company, which in June 1918 submitted the film for censorship. This new version was released quietly under Austral's kookaburra emblem at Tait's Auditorium, Melbourne, on 7 September.

Of passing interest in the cast was Madame Carbasse, the French mother of Louise Lovely, herself a prominent stage actress and society figure in Sydney. Coates and Gouday, who both claimed years of film experience in England and France, made only one more film, *Yachts and Hearts*, released in advance of the Burke and Wills film.

158 The Lure of the Bush

1918 CLAUDE FLEMMING

PC: Snowy Baker Films. SC: Jack North. PH: Franklyn Barrett. 6 reels.
CAST: Reg L. 'Snowy' Baker (Hugh Mostyn), Rita Tress (Trixie Stanley), Claude Flemming (overseer), John Faulkner, Colin Bell, Joan Baker (rider), Margaret Baker (stenographer), Baby McQuade (rider).

The screenplay by Jack North (pseudonym for a well-known Sydney journalist, Percy Reay) was the prize-winner in a competition conducted by the *Bulletin*, and told the story of a boy from a pioneering family in the outback of Australia. The boy is sent to England for an education and returns years later as 'an English dude', complete with monocle, plus-fours, and a riding crop in his hand. Anxious to re-learn the ways of bush life, he gets a job as a jackeroo. When the station hands discover that he believes that bushrangers still roam in the bush, they play a joke on him by staging a mock hold-up, only to find that he trounces them all single-handed. In later scenes he continues to astound the sceptical station hands with his athletic prowess: he breaks in the wildest brumby on the station, wins a boxing match with the biggest shearer (played by a professional boxer, Colin Bell), displays his skill at swimming and diving, and joins the men in a kangaroo hunt. He also competes successfully with the overseer for the hand of the manager's daughter.

The rugged, virile hero, the setting on the rolling plains of central New South Wales, the roughriding and the kangaroo hunt, all carried strong appeal for Australian audiences, and the film reportedly grossed £20 000 for an outlay of £1500 on the production. Distribution was handled for Snowy Baker's company by E. J. Carroll, and the film opened in Sydney at the Globe Theatre on 30 September 1918. Promotion exploited the outback spirit of the film, with, for example, a theatre lobby display of bush foliage with caged bush birds, including kookaburras. Reviews were positive. The heroine, played by a Sydney 'society girl', Rita Tress, was a true Australian heroine, with an impressive horse-riding ability and confidence in the bush to match her beauty and to make her a worthy partner for the manly hero. *Theatre*, 1 October 1918, praised her performance and commented that 'the athletic feats in which the characters figure appear to emanate naturally from the story . . . there are some great views of mobs of cattle and horses and flocks of sheep, and the many birds and animals snapped include a mob of some hundreds of kangaroos . . . Six reels in a truly Australian bush setting, with plenty of thrills and not a dull moment, must be the verdict of all who see the picture.'

Claude Flemming took a print of the film to England in 1920, to seek British distribution under the title of *Australian Justice* or 'something similar'. It was also substantially revamped for the American market: the intertitles were completely replaced, and interior scenes were reshot at the Jesse L. Lasky studio while Baker was visiting Hollywood.

SNOWY BAKER

in his newest drama that is full of typical Australian recklessness

"The Lure of the Bush"

with RITA TRESS, Australia's Sunset Girl

THE GIRL'S FIGHT AND THRILLING RESCUE FROM THE MAN SHE LOATHED

Most contemporary sources credit Claude Flemming as director, although Franklyn Barrett, the film's photographer, later consistently claimed to have been director. Flemming was an Australian-born actor who moved freely between the Australian, British and American stages. He began in 1903 playing Shakespeare in George Rignold's company in Sydney, but soon came to specialize in musical comedy. He also acted in several films in London and Hollywood including Maurice Tourneur's *Trilby* (1917). He returned to Australia early in 1918 and after *The Lure of the Bush* he directed *£500 Reward* in the same year. He continued to travel widely and act in both film and theatre, and in the early years of talkies he worked as a voice coach in Hollywood. In 1933 he returned again to Australia to work for Efftee Films, Melbourne, where he completed *Dear Old London*, one of several travelogues that he personally directed and narrated. His last stage performance in Australia was in a three-year season of the musical comedy *Annie Get Your Gun* (from July 1947) in which he played Buffalo Bill. He died in Sydney on 23 March 1952, aged 68.

159 Scars of Love [Should Children Suffer]

1918 WALTER S. McCOLL [McCALL?]

PC: Austral Photoplay Company. SC: Walter S. McColl. 5 reels.
CAST: Walter S. McColl, Mary McVean.

The story 'shows how the sins of the fathers are visited upon the children in a way that is quite unexpected, leaving two young lives hopelessly blighted' (*Australian Variety*, 18 October 1918). The climax was set on the battlefields of war-torn Europe, where the heroine, a Red Cross nurse, and the hero, an Anzac soldier, both give their lives for their country.

Little is known about the film-makers; like others who worked under the kookaburra symbol of the Austral Photoplay Company, they were probably wealthy amateur enthusiasts. The film screened at the company's Kookaburra Theatre, Sydney, for a week commencing on 21 October 1918. It was not a success, and in mid-1919 an attempt was made to re-release it under a new title, *Should Children Suffer*, but no screenings under this title have been traced.

160 What Happened to Jean

1918 HERBERT WALSH

P: Trench Comforts Fund Committee. SC: Keith Yelland. PH: Harry Krischock. 5000 ft.
CAST: Edith Crowe (Jean), Mrs Ernest Good (Mrs de Tafford), Price Weir (Colonel de Tafford), Herbert Walsh (Reg Stanton), James Anderson (Dad Smith), Ethelwyn Robin (Mum Smith), Janet Ward (Stella), Rita Crowe (maid), Victor Fitzherbert (Ashbourne), Roth Martin (George), Hartley Williams (Jasper), Harold Rivaz (Jabez), Darcy Kelway (Bertie).

Like other wartime fund-raising films sponsored by patriotic and charity groups, this South Australian film for the Trench Comforts Fund was intended only for local audiences. Recognition of the familiar, whether scenic highlights or social figures in the cast, was essential to its appeal, and audiences responded with much applause and laughter at seeing their own city and friends on the screen. In films such as these, no great work was expected from the largely amateur cast and honorary crew; the *Bulletin*, 14 November 1918, wrote that 'the alleged plot is just awful'. Jean is a country girl who loves reading 'penny dreadfuls' and who naïvely sets out to see the world. Arriving in Adelaide she survives an encounter with the villainous Ashbourne, and wins a car in a competition conducted by the Trench Comforts Fund. After several motoring escapades, she meets Mrs de Tafford, a wealthy Adelaide socialite, who still grieves for a long-lost daughter. She adopts Jean as her own, and moving now in high society, Jean attends a garden party at Government House and is sent to a fashionable boarding school to complete her education. In school she learns 'the art of pillow fighting and cigarettes' but emerges as 'a worthy scion of the de Tafford household'. One day information comes to light that reveals her to be, in fact, the lost daughter of the de Tafford family.

The film was screened for three nights at the Adelaide Town Hall, from 7 November 1918, and each screening was a crowded social occasion. One participant later recalled that £2000 was raised in that short time for the charity.

159 *Scars of Love* Mary McVean

161 £500 Reward

1918 CLAUDE FLEMMING

P: Barry Lupino, Claude Flemming. SC: Claude Flemming. PH: Lacey Percival. 5 reels.
CAST: Claude Flemming (Jack), Renée Adorée (Irene), John Faulkner (the captain), Lorna Ambler, David Edelsten.

The heroine is kidnapped in Canada by a villainous sea captain and is taken to sea on his sailing ship. In a typhoon, the boat is wrecked on the Queensland coast, where the girl is rescued by the hero.

The Canadian scenes were staged in the snows of Mount Kosciusko, and heavy seas (presumably to represent the typhoon) were shot from a tugboat on Sydney Harbour. Scenes were also taken at Bermagui on the south coast of New South Wales, and on board a six-masted American sailing ship then visiting Sydney. Interiors were staged in Australasian's Rushcutters Bay studio.

Flemming had constant trouble with the title of the film. A working title of *Wanted for—* was discarded in favour of the hardly more inspired *£500 Reward*, under which it was released on 18 November 1918 at the Globe Theatre, Sydney. This first season was none too successful, and in 1920, while Flemming was in England, his agent attempted on no less than six separate occasions to gain permission from the New South Wales censorship authorities to re-register the film under a more exploitable title. His first proposal, *The Lure of a Woman* (March 1920), was refused as being 'unnecessarily suggestive'; it was, incidentally, close to the title of an American film (*The Lure of Women*) in which Flemming had acted in 1915. A second title, *Primal Passions* (22 March), was also rejected, again for suggestiveness unwarranted by the film's action. *When Men Desire* (1 May), *The Auction of Virtue* (22 June), *The Reckless Lover* (31 August) and finally *A Romance of Two Worlds* (21 October), were also rejected in turn. The New South Wales Chief Secretary's office communicated little to Flemming's agent other than rejection, but internal memoranda indicate that, apart from the undue sensationalism of the titles (although worse were used on many imported American films at the time), the government was afraid that the tactic of title-changing might become endemic and confuse the work of censorship.

Renée Adorée made her screen debut as the heroine. This French actress and dancer had been appearing for several months in Sydney with a touring dance act, and was hired by Flemming to play in the film. She later went to the U.S.A. and became a contract player for M.G.M. in two major films by King Vidor, *The Big Parade* (1925) and *La Bohème* (1926).

Part 3:

1919–1929

Australian feature films in the 1920s showed a growing refinement of production technique and sophistication of subject matter. Both Longford and Barrett produced their finest works, among them several enduring classics of Australian cinema. Bush themes were prominent, among them hillbilly farces, romantic melodramas in the outback and local variations on American Westerns. Barrett's *A Girl of the Bush* (1921) and Longford's *On Our Selection* (1920) established high standards of 'documentary realism' in their portrait of the hardships of bush life, with naturalistic acting and settings that set them far ahead of most of their Australian contemporaries. A desire for unadorned 'realism' extended to the films with urban settings, dominated by Longford's *The Sentimental Bloke* (1919), which offered the public a homely and unsensational representation of city life after the dislocations of war. The inspiration for both city and bush films began to diversify, with adaptations not only from plays but also from novels and poems, and a growing number of stories written directly for the screen, among them *A Girl of the Bush*, *Sunshine Sally* (1922), *The Dinkum Bloke* (1923) and *The Kid Stakes* (1927).

Although their work demonstrated maturity and self-confidence, neither Longford nor Barrett found it easy to make a living from production. Both moved through a succession of small and unstable companies seeking continuity of work. Barrett withdrew in 1922 and became a salaried exhibitor, but Longford continued to fight, aided by his partner, Lottie Lyell, until her death in 1925. The only major producer to establish a stable commercial operation was Beaumont Smith, who used his special gift for publicity to create such public interest in his films that the combine was generally eager to show them, although not always on favourable terms.

Australasian Films and Union Theatres remained the focus of most producers' hopes; effective exhibition depended to a large extent on the combine, and it controlled substantial production resources, which it had inherited from Cozens Spencer. Australasian itself made a renewed investment in feature production in 1925, partly because of the imminent government inquiry into the industry and partly because of the company's weakening position in acquiring overseas films as American branch offices gradually took over the business they had once conducted through the combine. The revival of production also owed a lot to Stuart Frank Doyle, whose rise in the executive hierarchy of Australasian Films and Union Theatres brought an element of extravagance and flamboyance to the companies. Lured by the glamour and power of production as he had witnessed it abroad, Doyle saw himself in the role of Hollywood-style studio head. He loved grand flourishes—as his personal design for the ornate interior of the State Theatre in Sydney indicated—and his influence on Australasian's new commitment to production was evident, not only in 1925, but again in 1932 when he established Cinesound Productions.

Australasian's production programme suffered from bad luck and bad judgement. Its most expensive film, *For the Term of his Natural Life*, was completed in 1927 for world markets, but in 1928, before the film had had time to reach American audiences, talkies began to sweep the world. The company abandoned production in 1928 in the face of technological change in the industry and the financial problems caused by the failure overseas of its films. Heavy funding required elsewhere in the combine for theatre construction also contributed to the decision to withdraw.

The decade after the war saw the first flourishing of the Hollywood publicity and distribution machines and the virtually complete take-over of Australian screens. It soon became a recurrent charge that the Americans had suppressed Australian production, but the Americans did no more than maintain a position that had already been established by Australian businessmen after 1912. Indeed the Americans broke the overwhelming monopoly of Australasian Films, and by the end of the 1920s the combine was matched by a multiplicity of strong distribution companies. An exhibition rival, Hoyts Theatres (American-controlled after 1930), also emerged; it broke the monopoly of Union Theatres, and established a duopoly that existed to the end of the 1960s.

Agents for American production and distribution houses had begun to appear in Australia during the First World War, and by the early 1920s most of the major Hollywood studios had branches in each Australian state. Their decision to open their own offices inevitably weakened Australasian's power as a distributor, driving the company to seek new sources of supply, especially from England. The American companies had no interest in Australian production, since their function was to serve their head offices, and their Australian branches were generally staffed by men who had little freedom to initiate local projects. One of the exceptions was Hercules McIntyre, an Australian exhibitor and publicist who, in 1919, signed a contract with Universal Pictures to run their Australian operations. The generous terms of McIntyre's contract, and his personal energy, made him one of the major patrons of Australian production for several decades, especially in the 1930s and 1940s. He undertook the promotion and distribution of numerous Australian features and became a financial backer of productions by Charles Chauvel.

American companies did not venture into large-scale theatre ownership in Australia during the 1920s, but the possibility that they might was a constant and powerful incentive for Union Theatres and Hoyts to co-operate with them, even to the extent of building new theatres to accommodate American films: the State and Capitol Theatres in Sydney were built by Union Theatres, and the Regent Theatres in Sydney and Melbourne by Hoyts. Eventually, in 1930, a controlling interest in Hoyts was purchased by the American producer-distributor, Fox Film Corporation.

Some producers reacted to the dominance of Hollywood by hiring American cast and crew in the belief that their expertise would guarantee commercial success. E. J. and Dan Carroll, in partnership with the actor-athlete Snowy Baker, invested heavily in production, and brought out to Australia a Hollywood director, writer, actors and technicians. The venture failed when the Carrolls found that Hollywood production methods were too expensive for them, and that the blessings of Hollywood did nothing to ease local distribution problems or to attract the general public.

The aura of glamour with which the Hollywood publicists surrounded production served as an active lure to many people to become involved in production themselves. The relative cheapness and accessibility of equipment and technicians meant that film was not yet exclusively the preserve of big business, and during the decade a growing number of wealthy amateurs, social clubs, child prodigies and even a gangster (Squizzy Taylor, in a short film, *Riding to Win*, made in Melbourne in 1923) dabbled vicariously in the romance of the movie industry. One producer, P. J. Ramster, based much of his operation on an appeal to wealthy members of Sydney society, and to young men and women attracted by the promise of stardom. Film schools, some of them dubious operations, offered star-struck Australians a chance to reach fame and fortune, and many Australians went to Hollywood to work as extras and await their chance for a film career.

The effect of Hollywood on the language and morals of Australian society became an issue of concern to many in the community during the 1920s, and their protests augmented the demand for more Australian content on the screen. In 1925 the Commonwealth government began to release a series of some fifty short films (most around 600 feet) under the general title of *Know Your Own Country*. Produced by the government cinematographic unit under the direction of Bert Ive, the series was designed to inform Australians about their nation's industries and resources, and it was widely screened by the commercial trade. The government also used film extensively in England and other countries to promote Australian trade and immigration. For the British Empire Exhibition of 1924-25, the government prepared a number of documentary and semi-fictional films as part of the campaign to publicize Australia; a feature film by Longford, *Australia Calls* (1923), was prominent among them.

Agitation for an official inquiry into the film industry had grown sufficiently by 1927 for the Commonwealth government to create a Royal Commission to investigate the structure and practices of the industry, and the suitability of existing legislation relating to film censorship, taxation, import duties and film quotas. Only one state at that time, Victoria, had legislated for a film quota, obliging theatres to show at least 1000 feet of Australian film in each programme. The quota was, however, easily filled by a news gazette or a travel film, and it did little to promote production. From June 1927 to February 1928 the Royal Commission, chaired by Walter Marks, M.H.R., interviewed some 250 witnesses from the film trade around Australia and from the general public. Its report was completed in March 1928; it recommended, among other things, that feature production should be supported by cash awards for films of merit in an annual competition, and more importantly, that a quota should be established for feature films made in Australia and from other Empire countries. The quota legislation was never passed, partly because of legal doubts about the Commonwealth's authority to act in that area, and partly because of a reluctance to challenge the economic power of either the Australian theatre companies or the American distributors. The minor incentive of prizes eventually came into being in 1930, a year when barely any candidates were available (only the third prize was awarded), and after one more competition, in 1935, they were abandoned.

Although its main recommendations came to nothing, the Royal Commission provided a strong indirect incentive to production, and in anticipation of government action, 1928 became the most productive year for Australian feature films in a decade. Production soon ceased, however, because of the technological and financial barriers of sound, and because the hopes vested in the Royal Commission were seen to have been misplaced. In 1929 feature production fell to its lowest ebb since 1909, and the decade ended with the industry poised in uncertainty.

162 Australia's Own**

1919 J. E. WARD

P, SC, PH: J. E. Ward.
CAST: Nellie Romer, Garry Gordon.

J. E. (Jack) Ward worked as a sketch artist on the staff of the *Sydney Morning Herald* for eleven years, and as a lithographer and vaudeville performer, before devoting his career in 1915 to travelling in Papua. He began to make film records of his travels, and shot many thousands of feet covering the life and customs of Papuan people. At the suggestion of the entrepreneur Dan Carroll, he decided to exploit his footage commercially by adding a dramatic narrative. In mid-1918, with an Australian actress, Nellie Romer, and an actor, Garry Gordon, he staged a simple romantic story in the Yule Island area near Port Moresby. Unexpectedly, the footage was impounded by the territory administration after Catholic missionaries complained about Ward's activities. Appeals and investigations were made, and eventually, when officials were satisfied that the film would not prejudice relations with the native population, it was returned to Ward. The narrative scenes were subsequently interwoven with documentary footage, under a title that referred to the New Guinea territory, formerly a German possession and now 'Australia's own'. Billed as an exotic adventure movie, with special hand-coloured wildlife segments, it opened at the Globe Theatre, Sydney, on 20 January 1919.

Subsequent screenings were rare and lacked publicity, and commercial results could hardly have been impressive. Undeterred, Ward persisted with production, recycling much of his earlier footage to make new documentaries, including *The Quest for the Blue Bird of Paradise*, a seven-reel film completed around 1923 and probably containing acted scenes from *Australia's Own*, and *Death Devils in a Papuan Paradise*, released in Sydney in October 1924. He departed briefly from his New Guinea subjects in 1925 to direct an urban comedy, *Those Terrible Twins*.

163 *Desert Gold*

163 Desert Gold

1919 BEAUMONT SMITH

PC: Beaumont Smith's Productions. P, SC: Beaumont Smith. PH: Lacey Percival. 6 reels.
CAST: Bryce Rowe, Marie Ney, John Cosgrove, Gerald Harcourt, Gilbert Emery, Desert Gold.

This formula horse-racing story, about gangsters trying to nobble the favourite, was primarily an excuse for racing scenes featuring the successful mare, Desert Gold. The film covered all areas of the racing world, from stud farms and training stables to the betting clubs and Randwick race-track in Sydney. In addition Beaumont Smith provided some fast-paced melodrama—a race between a car and a train, a fight on horseback in the desert and another on the brink of Echo Point in the Blue Mountains, and a climactic aeroplane flight.

Scenes were shot on location in and around Sydney and at the airforce base at Richmond. The desert scenes were staged on sand dunes at Botany Bay. Distributed by E. J. Carroll, the film was booked widely by Union Theatres, but release was delayed by an influenza epidemic. It opened in Brisbane at the Strand Theatre on 24 March 1919, but did not appear in Sydney until exhibition conditions had returned to normal in September. In all theatres the film attracted large audiences, and *Theatre*, 1 November 1919, commended it as offering 'no lack of action' and 'some good race scenes and views of the Blue Mountains'.

164 Does the Jazz Lead to Destruction?

1919

CAST: Ethel Bennetto, George Irving

This comedy about the jazz craze featured several dances, including 'the Walking Waltz', 'the Tickle-Toe' and 'the Whirly-Whirly'. The story involved a family of 'wowsers', who wrote messages to the public in the film's press advertisements. The head of the family, Mr McWowse, wrote in response to the film's title: 'Oh, it's terrible! It leads straight to destruction. Somebody told me it did. And I can assure you that neither Mrs McWowse nor myself will be seen at these terrible doings.' (*Sun*, 3 August 1919) But within a week he had managed to taste the jazz and recanted: 'I, Egbert McWowse, hereby declare . . . I shall no longer wowse, but will Jazz my way to destruction if I want to. And I don't give a dash what the congregation says.'

The film was screened as part of a special jazz week at the Globe Theatre, Sydney, commencing on 4 August 1919. It was later confused in some sources with another jazz comedy, *Why Jessie* (or sometimes *Mabel*) *Learned to Jazz*, directed in 1919 by Frederick Ward for Australasian Films, with a cast including Olga Willard, Beatrice Sherlock and Jack Kirby. It seems likely, however, that this attempt by Australasian to return to feature production was abandoned.

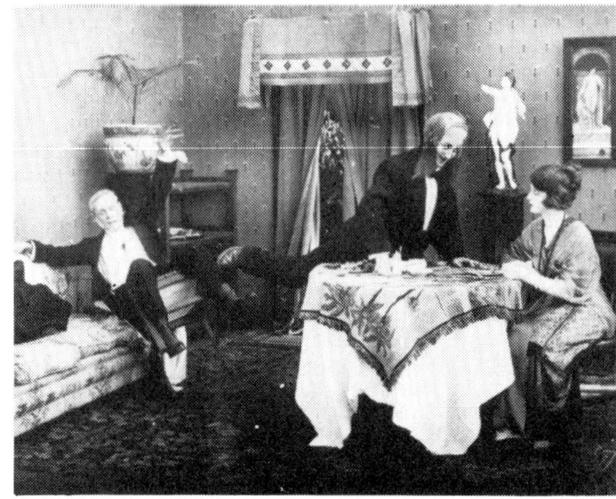

165 *Barry Butts In* Barry Lupino (*c*), Agnes Dobson

165 Barry Butts In

1919 BEAUMONT SMITH

PC: Beaumont Smith's Productions. ASST D: Charles Villiers. 5 reels.
CAST: Barry Lupino (Barry), John Cosgrove, Agnes Dobson, Ernest Stebbing.

Barry, a simple country boy who works in a grocery store, falls in love with a beautiful young dancer in a touring pantomime show. Unknown to Barry, the girl is the granddaughter of Barry's uncle, a wealthy man who had years ago disowned the girl's mother because she had married an actor. The old man sends for his several nephews in order to choose a suitable heir to his fortune, and Barry innocently arrives in Sydney to be subjected to many indignities as his cousins try to disgrace him in the old man's eyes. They underestimate him, however, and he finally wins both the fortune and the old man's granddaughter.

The star was a visiting British vaudeville comedian who incorporated many of his stage routines into the film. His approach was probably a mistake, for *Picture Show*, 6 November 1919, commented that Lupino seemed 'quite oblivious to the fact that [his stunts] have all been done many times in pictures'. The pace of Smith's direction redeemed the show somewhat, and the highlight was a slapstick chase down a city street in Sydney, involving cars, a scooter and a hansom cab.

To promote the production, Smith and Lupino devised a competition with cash prizes for the best suggestion of a title for the film. It was publicized in each state as a film without a title, and the public was invited to see the show and submit suggestions. A prize was never awarded, and a temporary working title of *Barry Butts In* remained with the film, as had probably been intended in the first place. The gimmick worked well, for the film drew large crowds after its opening at the Pavilion Theatre, Brisbane, on 9 August 1919.

166 The Sentimental Bloke*

1919 RAYMOND LONGFORD

PC: Southern Cross Feature Film Company.
P, SC: Raymond Longford. From the verse narrative, *The Songs of a Sentimental Bloke*, by C. J. Dennis. PH: Arthur Higgins. ASST D: Arthur Cross, Clyde Marsh. 6700 ft.
CAST: Arthur Tauchert (Bill, the Bloke), Lottie Lyell (Doreen), Gilbert Emery (Ginger Mick), Stanley Robinson (the Bloke's friend), Harry Young (the Stror 'at Coot), Margaret Reid (Doreen's mother), Charles Keegan (the parson), William Coulter (Uncle Jim), Helen Fergus (nurse), C. J. Dennis (himself).

C. J. Dennis's verse narrative was published in Sydney in 1915. Its colloquial language and casual approach to romantic sentiments appealed strongly to the Australian market, and it sold outstandingly well. By 1918, when Longford won the backing of the South Australian company, Southern Cross Feature Films, for a screen adaptation, the characters of the Bloke, Doreen and Ginger Mick were already widely known. Dennis had set his story in Melbourne, but Longford turned the Bloke into a larrikin from Woolloomooloo in Sydney. He decides to reform after a spell in jail for 'stoushing Johns' during a police raid on an illegal two-up game. He sees his 'ideal tart' in the market and learns that her name is Doreen. A friend arranges an introduction, and the romance begins. The Bloke's jealousy of a more sophisticated rival, the 'Stror 'at Coot', causes a temporary rift, but a reunion follows and Doreen and the Bloke are married. With reluctance, the Bloke forsakes his drinking mate, Ginger Mick, and becomes a faithful husband. One day an ageing uncle offers him a chance to manage his orchard in the country and he willingly accepts. His happiness with Doreen is completed with the birth of a child, and the Bloke promises to work his hands 'to the bone' for his wife and heir. And so, 'livin' and lovin' . . . life mooches on'.

Perhaps more so than Dennis, Longford and Lyell expressed genuine affection for the life-style of the characters and showed no sign of regarding them as either figures of fun or as sociological phenomena. The harmony that the film achieved between the characters and their milieu was carefully nurtured by Longford and Lyell. Cast and crew steeped themselves in the subject: 'They talked Woolloomoolese by day, and slept at night with a book of the verses under their pillows.' Longford also encouraged his performers to appear spontaneous, and scenes that might have provided scope for broad caricature were directed with a disciplined understatement. For instance, the first visit of the Bloke to his prospective mother-in-law's house was an invitation for a display of jokes about etiquette and old ladies, but it emerges as a tender encounter between three credible people enjoying simple pleasures. Dennis's verse in the intertitles makes the obvious jokes and seems too harsh for the warmth generated by the scene. The supporting characters are also refreshingly free of caricature: Uncle Jim looks like a figure from backblocks farce, with his bushy beard and his shabby clothes, but he emerges as a generous and mellow character, approaching his old age with wisdom and without self-pity. The

166 *The Sentimental Bloke* Gilbert Emery, Arthur Tauchert

166 *The Sentimental Bloke* Arthur Tauchert, Lottie Lyell

homely naturalism of the film is enhanced by the 'plainness' of the leading performers: Arthur Tauchert and Lottie Lyell look like ordinary people, not movie stars. With these elements Longford's film became a gentle expression of love—between the characters, and between the film-makers and their subject.

Most of the film was shot on location in the 'Loo itself, with the orchard scenes at Hornsby Valley near Sydney, and interiors staged on open-air sets at Wonderland City, Bondi. A few shots of sunsets and sunrises for the intertitles were taken in Adelaide, the home of the production company. In common with other Sydney film-makers, Longford and Lyell received no co-operation from Sydney local government and other authorities, and had to resort to subterfuge to work their way around official obstruction. The police raid on the two-up game, for example, posed a problem because of a ban on the use of police uniforms and a refusal to allow film-makers to shoot scenes in the city's jails; eventually Longford won the co-operation of Commonwealth dockside officials, who agreed to appear as the policemen and to allow an old watch-house at Woolloomooloo to be used as a jail. Permission was refused even for the brief scene of the Bloke sitting on a park bench in the Botanical Gardens, and Longford shot it in open defiance of the official ruling.

The £2000 production was under way by mid-1918, and a print was ready for private screening in Adelaide in November. Release was delayed by the refusal of Australasian Films to screen it in the Union Theatres chain, but the film was eventually seen by the Queensland entrepreneur and exhibitor, E. J. Carroll, who recognized its potential and undertook to distribute it in Australia and overseas. Its release was carefully publicized and it opened triumphantly to full houses at the Melbourne Town Hall on 4 October 1919. The Sydney release followed on 18 October at the Theatre Royal, where it ran for an unusually long three-week season. Its popularity did not diminish as the months passed, and it appeared regularly in cinemas around Australia.

E. J. Carroll secured wide distribution for it in Britain, where, he stated, it earned 'a great deal of money'. English reviews were as favourable as Australian, and the London trade paper, *Bioscope*, 23 September 1920, perceptively wrote: 'Acted quietly and naturally by players who perfectly embody the types they represent, the film has extraordinary charm. By its rich, shrewd humor and its simple humanity, it will certainly make as powerful an appeal to every class of audience as the famous British film-classic, "My Old Dutch", with which it has been aptly compared.'

America was another matter, and attempts to release it there were futile; the intertitles were partly rewritten in American slang, and much money and effort was spent on promotion and previews, but it failed to win a release. In Australia, meanwhile, the production company capitalized on the local popularity by filming a sequel, *Ginger Mick* (1920),

166 *The Sentimental Bloke* W. J. Coulter (*l*), Lottie Lyell, Arthur Tauchert

THE ARRIVAL OF UNCLE JIM
A CHERUB TOGGED IN SUN-BURN AN' A BEARD—
AN' DUDS THAT SHOUTED "AYSEED!" FER A MILE

and Carroll sponsored a stage production of *The Sentimental Bloke* in 1922, written by Dennis and produced by Bert Bailey, with Walter Cornoch as the Bloke and Tal Ordell as Ginger Mick.

The fortuitous survival of a single nitrate print enabled the film to be preserved in the National Film Archive in the 1950s. Its subsequent rediscovery by film societies and other groups brought Longford some belated recognition in his old age. The film is internationally regarded as a classic, and interest in it is such that, in Australia alone, non-theatrical film libraries have dozens of prints in constant circulation.

Longford once referred to Arthur Tauchert as 'the most lovable larrikin that ever lived'. Tauchert knew the Bloke's territory well. He was born in Sydney on 11 August 1881 and grew up in the inner suburbs. After a number of labouring jobs, he drifted into workers' 'smoko' performances and vaudeville. He toured the Sydney suburban and Newcastle vaudeville circuits as a comic singer, then joined the permanent company at Harry Clay's Gaiety Theatre, Sydney, and worked there for several years as a comedian and blackface artist in minstrel shows. He progressed to the Fuller circuit and joined shows touring widely around Australia and New Zealand. He was working on a freelance basis in suburban vaudeville when Longford and Lyell discovered him. He had previously acted in only one film, a comedy short, *Charlie at the Sydney Show*, directed by John Gavin in 1916. After the release of *The Sentimental Bloke*, the public closely indentified him with the part, and he often appeared on stage reading verses by C. J. Dennis. The identification was strengthened by two further films, *Ginger Mick* (1920) and *The Dinkum Bloke* (1923). His later film roles were less impressive, and he died on 27 November 1933 after a long illness.

167 Maggie Moore

167 **Struck Oil**

1919 FRANKLYN BARRETT

PC: Australian Art Productions. P: Humbert Pugliese. From the play by Sam Smith and Clay Greene. PH: Ernest Higgins. 7 reels.

CAST: Maggie Moore (Lizzie Stofel), Harry Roberts (John Stofel), Percy Walshe (Deacon Skinner), Boyd Irwin, David Edelsten.

Early in the 1870s, J. C. Williamson, then acting on the stage in America, took a theatrical sketch, *The Dead, or Five Years Away*, by a miner, Sam Smith, and commissioned an actor, Clay Greene, to rewrite it under the title of *Struck Oil*. In 1874 Williamson and his wife, a Californian actress, Maggie Moore, came to Australia to begin their long association with Australian theatre. *Struck Oil* opened in Melbourne at the Theatre Royal on 1 August 1874 and quickly became the most popular play in the Williamson repertoire. Maggie Moore was constantly applauded for her vibrant performance in the play, mingling pathos with an irrepressible sense of humour, and she became one of the best known and best loved personalities of Australian theatre. Although a versatile actress, singer and dancer, she became inseparable from her part in *Struck Oil*; as the *Lone Hand*, 2 September 1918, commented, 'to consider one without the other would be an impossibility'. In 1894 she left Williamson and formed her own theatrical company; she defeated legal action by Williamson to prevent her using *Struck Oil* in her repertoire, and in 1899 they were divorced. In 1902 she married Harry Roberts, an American actor, and he became her business and acting partner in several revivals of the play. She died in America in March 1926 at the age of 75.

The play was a melodrama with plenty of sentiment and comic relief. Maggie Moore played Lizzie, the ebullient daughter of John Stofel, a gentle Dutch shoemaker who has settled in America. John goes off to fight in the Civil War in the place of a cowardly deacon, who gives him in return the title deed of a farm. John returns from the war, wounded and insane. When oil is discovered on the farm, the deacon tries to resume the property and leases the ground to an oil company. One day, however, John regains his memory and finds the title deed, which he had hidden. The deacon is confronted with the evidence and is forced to concede that the Stofels own the wealth of the oilfield.

When Maggie Moore made her only screen appearance in the Pugliese adaptation of the play, she was well into her sixties. She remained, however, the perfect trouper, and graciously acknowledged the physical effects of time. *Theatre,* 1 November 1919, reported: 'in years and physique she has long been outside the requirements of a girl-role. Realising this her admirers accept her accordingly—not for what at the moment she is but for the wonderful favorite she so long has been. Almost at the outset Miss Moore herself sets the audience at ease on this point by turning her stoutness to comedy account. "You can't", she says to her lover, Boyd Irwin, in one of their spooning interludes, "get round me with one arm. Take two!" '

The film was shot in Sydney in August and September 1919 and released by the Puglieses at the Sydney Town Hall on 20 October. Commercially the film was unexceptional, suggesting the extent to which the Pugliese enterprise suffered from lack of access to major city theatres in Sydney and Melbourne. At the same time, their judgement may have been wrong: Maggie Moore's popularity belonged to an earlier generation, and a silent film record of the play, probably shot in haste on a shoe-string, promised to be little but a sad reminder of the star's former glory.

168 The Face at the Window

1919 CHARLES VILLIERS

PC: D. B. O'Connor Feature Films. P: D. B. O'Connor. SC: Gertrude Lockwood. From the play by F. Brooke Warren. PH: Lacey Percival. ASST D: Gerald Harcourt. 5 reels.

CAST: D. B. O'Connor (Lucio Delgrado, 'Le Loup'), Agnes Dobson (Marie de Brison), Claude Turton (Paul Gouffet), Gerald Harcourt (Lucien Cortier), Collet Dobson (M. de Brison), Charles Villiers (Barbelon), Percy Walshe (Dr Le Blanc), Lulu Vincent (Mother Pinau), Syd Everett (Bartel), Millie Carlton (maid), Charles Beetham (Prefect of Police), D. L. Dalziel (Detective Drummond), Gilbert Emery (caretaker of bank).

The story of the master criminal 'Le Loup' is tinged with the spirit of *Fantomas*: in the criminal underworld and the apache dens of Paris, a battle of wits rages between the police and Le Loup, a cunning thief and murderer who hides his identity behind a hideous mask and announces himself to each new victim with a frightening wolf-like howl. When he murders an important banker, M. de Brison, his flamboyant exploits become a sensation in Parisian society. A detective, Paul Gouffet, is also murdered, but with the aid of an electrical device invented by a mad doctor, the detective is temporarily revived from the dead and

168 *The Face at the Window*

168 A studio set for *The Face at the Window*

his hand writes the name of Le Loup's real identity. The police promptly challenge Le Loup and he is shot while trying to escape.

What the film lacked in the sound of Le Loup's howls, it clearly made up for in spirited action. The tone was one of light-hearted spoof, and advertisements reported 'roars of hilarious merriment' at each screening. The film was staged in the Rushcutters Bay studio in March and April 1919, under the direction of Charles Villiers, an actor who had spent much of the previous decade playing villains. A scene in which a policeman is stabbed twice by Le Loup drew the attention of the New South Wales censors, but after one of the two blows was deleted the film was passed for public screening, and it opened at the Australian Picture Palace, Sydney, on 8 November 1919. Large crowds led to an extension of the season, and it continued to find ready commercial success in the suburbs and interstate. The play had long been a popular melodrama on the British and Australian stage, and at least three British film versions were made. One, in 1920, caused some confusion with the Australian version, and prompted threats of legal action by the distributor of the British film, who claimed that the British producer alone owned copyright.

A short-lived Sydney journal, improbably called *Real Life in the City and Country*, gave a long and detailed review of this 'good old melodrama' on 13 November 1919: the story had been 'filmatised with the suspense capitally sustained. Not once does interest in the action flag.' The producer, David B. O'Connor, was an Australian theatrical entrepreneur who had made his name as an 'operatic actor' with J. C. Williamson; he seemed to excel in both of his new roles, revealing an astute commercial judgement in his choice of subject and capturing a 'wholly adequate saturnine colour' in his performance. He did not, however, persist with film production, and remained in the live theatre business. A new screen actress, Agnes Dobson, made her debut in the film, although her second film, *Barry Butts In*, was released a few months earlier. Born in 1904, the daughter of a veteran Shakespearian actor, Collet Dobson (who appeared in the film as her screen father), she had acted in many leading stage roles as a child before turning to the cinema. The *Real Life* critic found her a 'very charming' new performer, and she continued to develop an intensely active career in live theatre, both as an actress and as a playwright, with occasional film appearances in the 1920s. She later worked in radio as a writer and actress, and for many years appeared in the ABC radio series, *The Village Glee Club*, as the popular old eccentric, Mrs Sharpshot.

168 *The Face at the Window*

169 *The Man from Kangaroo* Snowy Baker as the parson who provokes the anger of his parishioners by teaching children how to box

169 *The Man from Kangaroo* Wilfred Lucas, Brownie Vernon

169 The Man from Kangaroo*

1920 WILFRED LUCAS

PC: Carroll-Baker Australian Productions. P: E. J. Carroll, Reg L. 'Snowy' Baker. SC: Bess Meredyth. PH: Robert V. Doerrer. ART TITLES: Syd Nicholls. ASST D: John K. Wells, Charles Villiers. 6 reels.

CAST: Reg L. 'Snowy' Baker (John Harland), Brownie Vernon (Muriel Hammond), Charles Villiers (Martin Giles), Walter Vincent (Ezra Peters), Wilfred Lucas (Red Jack Braggan), Malcolm MacKellar (foreman), David Edelsten.

John Harland is a pugilist turned parson who is posted to the town of Kalmaroo, where a gang of thugs has driven the church out of the area. Harland defies the gang by holding a service in the town hall but it is disrupted by threats of violence. In defeat, Harland seeks a job as a station hand and discovers that his sweetheart, Muriel, owns a neighbouring property and that her overseer is none other than Red Jack Braggan, the leader of the gang. Red Jack kidnaps Muriel but after many fights and chases she is rescued by Harland and the town is rid of its rowdy element.

As in Baker's previous films, the main emphasis was on athletic action and stunt-work in the Fairbanks style. Fantastic leaps had been an obligatory element in the now forbidden bushranger genre, and the advertising for Baker's film promised to outdo the tradition with 'Thunderbolt's memorable leap to evade the Troopers [paling] into insignificance' alongside Baker's efforts. The film was shot on location at Kangaroo Valley to the south of Sydney, and at Gunnedah to the north. Production costs were aggravated by the severe drought conditions in New South Wales, which necessitated special fodder shipments for the unit's horses. Interiors were staged at the Theatre Royal, Sydney, pending the preparation of E. J. Carroll's own studio at Waverley.

The film marked the start of Baker's brief but productive partnership with E. J. Carroll. While in Hollywood in 1918 to reshoot scenes for *The Lure of the Bush*, Baker undertook a study of American production methods and, with Carroll, arranged for a team of Americans to come to Australia to launch the Baker-Carroll production programme. Leading the American troupe was the husband and wife team of Wilfred Lucas and Bess Meredyth. Lucas had acted in numerous Hollywood films including many directed by D. W. Griffith, and had directed several minor films himself, including *The Romance of Tarzan* (1918). Bess Meredyth was a professional screen-writer who had worked on most of Lucas's own productions. With them in Australia was an American actress, Brownie Vernon, who had been under contract to Universal and had starred in several B-movies. They also brought an experienced cinematographer, Robert Doerrer, and a production assistant, John K. Wells. The Americans arrived in September 1919 and speedily began work on the first production. Location shooting was completed by late October, and the second production, *The Shadow of Lightning Ridge*, followed immediately. *The Man from Kangaroo* was released by Carroll with considerable ballyhoo at the Lyceum and Lyric Theatres, Sydney, on 24 January 1920. The commercial results were strikingly good, but the *Sydney Mail*, 4 February 1920, found the whole production 'steeped in Americanisms', and the *Sun* reported on 25 January 1920 that Baker had 'considerable headway' to make as an actor. In November 1921 it was released in a re-edited version in America under the title of *The Better Man*.

Carroll-Baker Australian Productions was formed in 1919 with capital of £25 000. The subscribers were the brothers E. J. and Dan Carroll, Snowy Baker, and the Adelaide company, Southern Cross Feature Films. The Carroll brothers had been active in various areas of show business since 1906. E. J. (Edward John) Carroll was born in Queensland on 28 June 1868, and Dan exactly twenty years later. They based most of their early careers in Queensland, screening films in open-air theatres in summer and running skating rinks in provincial towns in winter. As

169 *The Man from Kangaroo* Snowy Baker (*right foreground*)

entrepreneurs they were bold and efficient, and their name carried a certain guarantee of professionalism. They arranged Australian tours by a number of major performers and groups, including the Sistine Choir in 1922 and the violinist Fritz Kreisler in 1925. They also brought British and American plays to Australia during the 1910s and were shareholders in Spencer's film studio at Rushcutters Bay. In 1919 they handled Australian and overseas sales of *The Sentimental Bloke* and moved quickly to consolidate its success by setting up their own production enterprise with Snowy Baker. The old colonial mansion of Palmerston in the Sydney suburb of Waverley was bought and adapted into a studio, and for a while two units—Baker's and Longford's—worked simultaneously. The venture did not prove financially viable and in 1923, after *The Blue Mountains Mystery*, the Carrolls quit production completely and the studio was turned into a block of flats. Thereafter the Carrolls concentrated their efforts on exhibition; in 1924 they were involved in the building of the Prince Edward Theatre, Sydney, and in the development of a chain of theatres in Queensland under the direction of a company known after 1923 as Birch, Carroll & Coyle Ltd. E. J. Carroll had suffered ill health for a decade before his death in Sydney on 28 July 1931. Dan remained a distinguished member of the exhibition trade for many more years, and died in Sydney on 11 August 1959.

170 **Ginger Mick**

1920 RAYMOND LONGFORD

PC: Southern Cross Feature Film Company. SC: Lottie Lyell (?), Raymond Longford. From the verse narrative, *The Moods of Ginger Mick*, by C. J. Dennis. PH: Arthur Higgins. 5500 ft.

CAST: Gilbert Emery (Ginger Mick), Arthur Tauchert (the Bloke), Lottie Lyell (Doreen), Jack Tauchert (Bill), Queenie Cross (Rose), George Hartspur (Keith).

This sequel to *The Sentimental Bloke* was made by the same production team with the same principal players. Several years have passed, and the Bloke has settled down on his farm with Doreen, where he takes sly delight in teaching his young son, Bill, the art of 'stoush'. Ginger Mick's life, on the other hand, is one of hardship, drinking and trouble with the police. Eventually Mick falls in love with Rose, takes a job as a 'rabbit-o', and works hard until he overcomes his cynicism about war profiteers and enlists in the army. The tale is then told episodically, as Mick's letters reach the Bloke: he tells of the nightmare of Gallipoli, and of his initial hostility, then friendship, with another soldier, Keith, who 'wore perjammers an' cleaned 'is teeth'. Later the Bloke and Doreen learn that Mick has been killed on the hills of Sari Bair, and the film ends with an understated but deeply felt tribute from the Bloke.

From its première at the Melbourne Town Hall on 2 February 1920, *Ginger Mick* found instant popularity, and in 1922 it was sold profitably to England. *The Sentimental Bloke* had revealed Longford's strength in directing everyday, homely sentiment, and *Ginger Mick* followed closely in its footsteps. Reviews generally welcomed it as an enjoyable extension of the earlier film, although it did perhaps overstress the C. J. Dennis vernacular in the titles, for the *Sun*, 7 March 1920, found that 'the amount of reading entailed is prodigious' so that the film came close to resembling 'simply illustrated verse'.

170 *Ginger Mick* Gilbert Emery

171 The Kelly Gang*

1920 HARRY SOUTHWELL

PC: Southwell Screen Plays. P, SC: Harry Southwell. PH: Charles Herschell. ASST D: P. Gatwood. 7500 ft.
CAST: Godfrey Cass (Ned Kelly), V. Upton Brown (Dan Kelly), Horace Crawford (Joe Byrne), Jack McGowan (Steve Hart), Robert Inman (Aaron Sherritt), Thomas Sinclair (Sergeant Kennedy), Harry Southwell (Sergeant Steele), Cyril Mackay (Constable McIntyre), Adele Inman (Kate Kelly), Maud Appleton (Mrs Kelly), Frank Tomlin (Constable Scanlon).

Harry Southwell was a Welsh-born actor and writer who spent several years in America before coming to Australia in mid-1919 with his Australian wife. In 1917-18 he had adapted numerous short stories by O. Henry into scenarios for a series of two-reelers produced by Broadway Star Features in America. This screen-writing experience tended to be represented by Southwell in Australia as experience in production and direction, and he was quickly able to impress enough businessmen to gain backing for a local production company. With a koala as his trademark, and promoting himself extensively as 'the Welsh Wizard', he announced plans for five Australian features and for the construction of a studio in Sydney. The first production was *The Kelly Gang*, a subject with a supposedly ready-made audience and ample scope for cheaply staged outdoor action. Shooting began late in 1919 using a temporary outdoor studio in the Melbourne suburb of Coburg. Southwell's inexperience in production is clearly evident in the footage that survives today in the National Film Archive: the sets are grotesquely under-dressed and are exposed to the full glare of sunlight, with heavy shadows across the roofless studio interiors. Other scenes were shot in the countryside on the outskirts of Melbourne. The production was almost naïvely ambitious and took an unusually long two hours to project. The burning of the Glenrowan Hotel was staged both at a real hotel near Melbourne and in the Coburg studio, where the set was burnt down. The cast included several

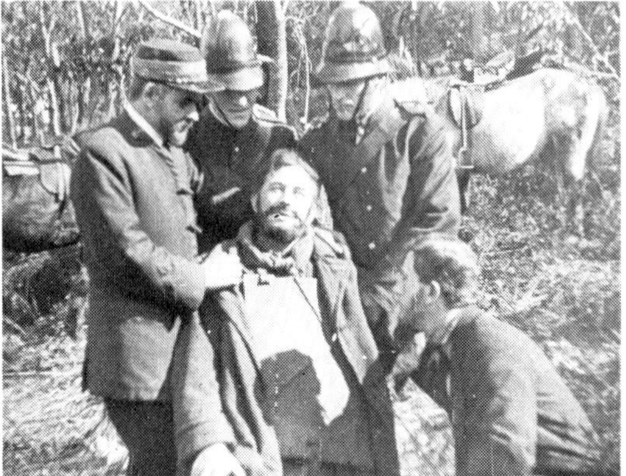

171 *The Kelly Gang* Godfrey Cass. Frame enlargement

experienced stage and screen actors, including three members of the Inman family—Robert, his wife, Maud Appleton, and their daughter, Adele.

For reasons unknown, the film escaped the standing opposition of the New South Wales censors to bushranging stories and opened without delay at the Lyric Theatre, Sydney, on 21 February 1920. Although the Lyric was a minor cinema, it did specialize in action movies, and commercial results seem to have been good enough to warrant a transfer to two other theatres in the following week. The *Picture Show*, 1 April 1920, expressed regret that Southwell had chosen 'the exploits of notorious bushrangers as the subject of his first Australian film. A criminal record can only have a limited appeal as entertainment, and . . . the producer's experience and ability would have been better seen through a different medium.' Such moral objections were probably anticipated by Southwell, for the film carried a laborious warning against the temptations of outlawry, and the message was presumably explicit enough to mollify the censors.

After his next film, *The Hordern Mystery* (1920), Southwell's plans for continuous production unexpectedly collapsed. He attempted to set up another company, Southwell's Ideal Productions, in mid-1921, but this also failed, and early in 1922 he ran for cover with a low budget re-make of the Kelly story, *When the Kellys Were Out*. Southwell turned to Kelly twice again in his career (in 1934 and 1947) but at no stage did the story help him out of trouble. He remained throughout the rest of his life on the shadowy fringes of Australian production, except for a period spent in Europe after 1923, where he made a biblical drama, *David* (1924), and *Le Juif Polonais* (1925), a story that he later refilmed in Australia as *The Burgomeister* (1935).

172 The Shadow of Lightning Ridge

1920 WILFRED LUCAS

PC: Carroll-Baker Australian Productions. P: E. J. Carroll, Reg L. 'Snowy' Baker. SC: Bess Meredyth. PH: Robert V. Doerrer. ASST D: John K. Wells. 7 reels.
CAST: Reg L. 'Snowy' Baker (the Shadow), Brownie Vernon (Dorothy Harden), Bernice Vere (Portuguese Annie), Wilfred Lucas (Sir Edward Marriott), David Edelsten, Boomerang.

A young Australian in England for a university education learns that his mother has been wronged by a powerful Australian squatter, Sir Edward Marriott. Seeking revenge, he returns to Australia and becomes a bushranger, known as 'the Shadow', preying only on Sir Edward's property. One day the Shadow is forced to rescue Sir Edward's young fiancée, Dorothy, from the hands of genuine outlaws, and he falls in love with her. Later, a ring on the Shadow's finger reveals that he is actually the heir to Sir Edward's land, and he is welcomed into the family and wins Dorothy as his bride.

The story included many of Baker's obligatory stunts, including a leap from a horse onto a moving train, and a horseback leap from a cliff through the roof of a hut forty feet below. But otherwise, the content was 'almost pure Yankee . . . The entire population of the country town "tote guns" and wear cowboy hats. A foreigner, seeing this film, would picture Australia as a sort of Bill Hart's back-yard.' (*Smith's Weekly*, 1 May 1920)

The production followed closely on the completion of the first Carroll-Baker film, *The Man from Kangaroo* and was handled by the same American production team. After Baker, the main Australian player was a J. C. Williamson actress, Bernice Vere, as a pub-keeper's daughter who helps the Shadow escape from a police ambush. The film was shot on location in the bush near Sydney and in Carroll's new Palmerston studio at Waverley. Shooting was completed by February 1920, when the director, Wilfred Lucas, and his wife, Bess Meredyth, returned briefly to America to acquire new equipment and staff for the studio. They arrived back in Australia in June for the third of the Carroll-Baker series, *The Jackeroo of Coolabong*.

The Shadow of Lightning Ridge was released by Carroll at the Melbourne Town Hall on 3 April 1920. American release followed late in 1921, in a substantially cut and retitled version.

173 *The Breaking of the Drought* Marie La Varre, Rawdon Blandford

173 The Breaking of the Drought*

1920 FRANKLYN BARRETT

PC: Golden Wattle Film Syndicate. P: Franklyn Barrett. SC: Jack North, Franklyn Barrett. From the play by Bland Holt. PH: Franklyn Barrett. ART D: Rock Phillips. 6 reels.

CAST: Trilby Clark (Marjorie Galloway), Dunstan Webb (Tom Wattleby), Charles Beetham (Jo Galloway), Marie La Varre (Olive Lorette), John Faulkner (Varsy Lyddleton), Rawdon Blandford (Gilbert Galloway), Nan Taylor (Mrs Galloway), Arthur Albert (Walter Flour), Ethel Henry (Molly Henderson).

When the outback station of Wallaby is gripped by drought, the proud old owner, Jo Galloway, can do nothing to prevent the repossession of his land by the bank. In poverty, he moves to the city with his wife and daughter to stay with his son, Gilbert, only to learn that Gilbert has long been embezzling family funds to lead a life of luxury and decadence. Many melodramatic events follow, including a murder and a suicide, before the family can return, reunited, to the station, and the rain starts to fall once more.

Bland Holt, one of the grand old men of Australian theatre, renowned for lavishly produced melodramas, wrote *The Breaking of the Drought* in 1902 as a topical drama about a severe drought that then crippled the country. In 1919 another drought gripped Australia and the time was ripe for a revival of the story. Shooting began in December 1919 at Narrabri and Moree in the far outback of New South Wales, where the ravages of the drought provided Barrett with grim sequences showing trees cut down for cattle fodder, crows feeding off dead livestock, and miles of scorched earth. Indoor scenes were staged in a temporary studio at the Theatre Royal, Sydney. A brief interlude (missing from the only existing copy of the film in the National Film Archive) was provided by a water ballet and diving display by a group of 'water-nymphs', staged amid idyllic surroundings in the National Park near Sydney; many of the nymphs were later disqualified from the Amateur Swimming Association for taking part in the film.

By the time the film opened at the Strand Theatre, Melbourne, on 19 June 1920, the drought had genuinely broken. Its memory however was still vivid, and the *Sun*, 27 June 1920, recommended it to city dwellers who know of country conditions only from newspapers. Other critics were hostile, and *Theatre*, 1 July 1920, wrote: 'the plot, being that of a play so many years ago, is hopelessly old-fashioned [and] the acting, generally, is weak'.

Barrett had intended to contrast the drought scenes with more prosperous rural conditions and to pay tribute to the indomitable spirit of the Australian farmer, but the power of his drought footage unwittingly prompted the tightening of Commonwealth censorship laws affecting the export of Australian films. The censorship issue arose in New South Wales when a state parliamentarian, Mr Wearne, witnessed the filming of the drought scenes and promptly asked in Parliament on 16 December whether the government was aware of a film being made 'with the intention of showing across the seas the disastrous position of this State'. An investigation was made by the Chief Secretary's office, and on 20 January 1920 Mr Wearne was assured that new Commonwealth legislation, proclaimed on 20 December 1919, would prevent the export of the film if the Minister for Customs deemed it to be 'harmful to the Commonwealth'. The legislation completed the censorship cycle: what was bad outside was kept out, and what was bad inside was kept in.

174 On Our Selection*

1920 RAYMOND LONGFORD

P: E. J. Carroll. SC: Raymond Longford. From the stories by Steele Rudd. PH: Arthur Higgins. ART TITLES: Syd Nicholls. 6890 ft.

CAST: Percy Walshe (Dad Rudd), Beatrice Esmond (Mrs Rudd), Tal Ordell (Dave), Arthur Greenaway (Sandy Taylor), Evelyn Johnson (Kate), Fred Coleman (Dan), Charlotte Beaumont (Sarah), Arthur Wilson (Joe), Olga Willard (Nell), Nellie Bisell (Mrs Anderson), Carmen Coleman (Lily White), David Edelsten (parson), Ted Andrews.

From its opening dedication to the 'pioneers of Australia . . . and to you particularly Good Old Dad', Longford's film set out to be an affectionate and personal portrait of life in the Australian bush—not the life of the big stations and powerful squatters, but the daily toil of the small selector who struggled to make a living from his few acres, reliant not on capital but on his own wit and physical labour. The Rudds had become the archetypal bush family for most Australians after the publication in 1895 of the first story by 'Steele Rudd' (Arthur Hoey Davis) in the *Bulletin*. In 1912 a stage adaptation of *On Our Selection* was performed by the Bert Bailey and Edmund Duggan company and quickly established itself as a perennial favourite of Australian audiences. The play added a melodramatic plot involving rival lovers and murder, and transformed the Rudd family into entertaining caricatures of the book's original characters. Longford, however, repudiated the stage version and went back to Steele Rudd's original text. In publicizing his film, he criticized the 'ridicule' to which the play had subjected the bush pioneers, which left audiences with the impression 'that our backblocks are populated with a race of unsophisticated idiots'; the sense of humour with which bush people had faced hardships 'has too often been converted into clumsy clowning of the "slapstick" variety' (*Picture Show*, 1 April 1920).

Longford's film retained the episodic structure of Steele Rudd's stories and was relatively free of artificial plot devices. Mrs Rudd and the younger of her six children go to join Dad and their eldest son, Dave, on the family's selection, where Dad and Dave have made a clearing and built a slab and bark hut. The family gradually adjusts to bush life and everyone helps to till the field with borrowed hoes and to harvest and husk the first crop of corn. With the first sale they are able to buy a horse and plough, and the farm progresses rapidly until set back by a severe year-long drought and a bushfire. Later, romance develops between the Rudds' eldest daughter, Kate, and a neighbour, Sandy Nelson, and the film ends with the celebration of Kate's wedding, and with the handing over to the Rudds of the deeds to the selection.

174 *On Our Selection* Frame enlargement

To give as much authenticity as possible to life on the selection, Longford cast several non-professional actors in supporting roles: Arthur Wilson, who played the mischievous young son, Joe, was found as a street-corner newspaper boy in Sydney, and a character missing from the abridged version of the film preserved in the National Film Archive, Cranky Jack, was played by an uncredited but 'well-known identity' of the Sydney waterfront. Make-up and costumes for the professional players were carefully conceived to give the impression that the characters actually lived and worked in their clothes, and Longford encouraged his whole cast to act spontaneously and free from studied mannerisms. He wrote in *Picture Show*, 1 April 1921: 'I'm making an Australian picture, and I want the people in it to be real Australians. Now, your average Australian is about the most casual person under the sun; so if I put the players through their parts over and over again, worrying them, striving to perfect them, they might do good work, but they wouldn't look like Australians. They'd merely be actors, perfectly conscious that they were acting. My way is to let them know the action I want and allow them to go right ahead with it. For a picture like "On Our Selection", in which it is absolutely necessary that the characters look natural, I think that's the best course.'

Percy Walshe, a stage actor for over thirty years, gave a thoroughly physical performance as Dad, a thin, wiry and self-reliant man, far more credible as a farm labourer than Bert Bailey in Ken Hall's 1932 film version of the play. Tal Ordell as Dave was also a remarkable departure from the witless clown of the play—still gullible, clumsy and comical, but at the same time a hard worker dedicated to the selection's well-being and to the family.

In 1919 E. J. Carroll bought the film rights to *On Our Selection* from Arthur Hoey Davis for £500, equal to the entire budget of some films a few years earlier. According to Longford (*RCE*, p.146), E. J. Carroll originally appointed his imported American director, Wilfred Lucas, to handle the production, but displaying 'a modesty unheard of in his kind', Lucas withdrew because he felt he 'could not do justice to a subject so intrinsically local'. Longford's usual production collaborator, Lottie Lyell, was ill and unable to work on the film, and Longford proceeded on his own, shooting the film in a picnic-like atmosphere

174 *On Our Selection* The arrival at the new home. Frame enlargement

on location at Baulkham Hills near Sydney. Two huts were built there for interior and exterior scenes, and later the company travelled west to Leeton for grimly authentic drought scenes. The bushfire scene was also staged near Leeton with a fire lit by the co-operative townspeople.

Carroll arranged for release through Union Theatres and, heralded by extensive publicity, the film opened at West's Olympia Theatre, Brisbane, on 24 July 1920, and at the Crystal Palace and Lyric Theatres, Sydney, on 7 August. It quickly became the commercial success that Carroll had anticipated, and he moved on at once to a sequel, ***Rudd's New Selection*** (1921), again directed by Longford. Contemporary reviews were mixed, and some critics were clearly bewildered by the painstaking realism and the rejection of conventional plot. *Smith's Weekly*, 7 August 1920, for example, complained: 'The ugliness of bush life is presented without the saving grace of kindliness and good nature . . . This "holding the mirror up to nature" needs discretion.' A critic in *Theatre*, 2 August 1920, however, saw more merit in the work: 'it is a play without a plot—and is quite interesting enough without one . . . [the cast] are all to be commended for life-like studies of their respective characters, while the Dave of Tal Ordell is—well, it IS Dave. We can think of no higher praise . . . The film throughout is just good, unadulterated Australian.'

175 The Man from Snowy River

1920 BEAUMONT SMITH, JOHN K. WELLS

PC: Beaumont Smith's Productions. P, SC: Beaumont Smith. From poems by A. B. Paterson. PH: Al Burne, Lacey Percival. 5500 ft.

CAST: Cyril Mackay (Jim Conroy), Stella Southern (Kitty Carewe), Tal Ordell (Stingey Smith), Hedda Barr (Helen Ross), John Cosgrove (Saltbush Bill), Robert MacKinnon (Dick Smith), John Faulkner (John Carewe), Charles Beetham (Bill Conroy), Dunstan Webb (Ryan), Nan Taylor (Mrs Potts), James Coleman (Trooper Scott), Con Berthal (cook).

Although nominally based on 'Banjo' Paterson's verse, the film offered little but familiar plot situations and stock characters. A country boy, Jim Conroy, drifts back to the bush after an unhappy time in the city. He finds work with a crooked squatter, Stingey Smith, and falls in love with Kitty Carewe, a girl from the neighbouring station. Kitty's father is impressed by Jim's horsemanship and invites him to train the station's finest thoroughbred, Swagman, in the hope that it will win enough prize money to save the station from financial ruin. A jealous station hand plots with Stingey Smith to interfere with the race so that Smith can take over the Carewe station at his own price, but Jim discovers the plot in time and rides Swagman to an easy victory. The celebrations are interrupted only by a temporary misunderstanding between Jim and Kitty when an old flame unexpectedly arrives from the city. Later Smith frames Jim for a theft, but evidence is found in time to incriminate Smith himself, and Jim is left free to marry Kitty.

Beaumont Smith had bought the screen rights to all of Paterson's works and had spent two years preparing a scenario, using the best known of Paterson's titles and cramming into it characters (in name at least) from various works, including a jolly swagman, Saltbush Bill, and the spirited squatter's daughter, Kitty Carewe. Late in 1919, Smith surprisingly announced that he intended to produce this ostensibly very Australian material in Hollywood, partly because of the greater technical expertise available there, and partly in the hope of gaining access to the American market. According to his plan, a few scenes with essential local references would be shot in Australia and then inserted into footage shot in Hollywood with American stars and Californian gum trees. Smith departed for America in November but his plans came to nothing and within six months he was back in Sydney ready to shoot the film entirely in Australia. He brought back instead from America a feature-length documentary about Hollywood and its stars, *A Journey through Filmland*, which he released through Union Theatres in Sydney in February 1921.

Although he failed to shoot the film in America, Smith was able to draw on American talent in Sydney; he hired John K. Wells, then assistant to Wilfred Lucas on the Snowy Baker features, to co-direct the film with him and cast Hedda Barr, an American actress then visiting Australia, as a city vamp. Shooting began in mid-1920 on location at Mulgoa, Wallacia and Luddenham in the Blue Mountains. As usual, Smith handled distribution himself, and the film opened at West's Olympia Theatre, Brisbane, on 28 August 1920. Local reviews were generally polite but an English trade paper, *Kine Weekly*, 21 September 1921, found it 'a very mediocre affair'; the climactic race scene 'quite fails in its effect', largely because it was impossible to identify the horses. 'The scenario is very loosely constructed and contains little dramatic material. . . . The acting throughout bears the impress of amateurism and lifeless direction.'

Although her début in this film was unremarkable, Stella Southern enjoyed a brief but well publicized career as a local star. Discovered by Beaumont Smith as a shop-girl, she starred in several films for Smith and Franklyn Barrett over the next two years. In October 1921 she married a New Zealand director, Harrington Reynolds, and starred in his production, *The Birth of New Zealand*, released in Auckland in February 1922. Her subsequent screen appearances were few and minor.

A.B (Banjo) PATERSON'S
Great Australian Classic
The Man from Snowy River

It is a Beaumont Smith Production!

It makes you proud that you are an Australian

Capacity Houses everywhere of delighted picture lovers

176 Robbery Under Arms*

1920 KENNETH BRAMPTON

PC: Pacific Photo Plays. SC: Kenneth Brampton. From the novel by Rolf Boldrewood. PH: Lacey Percival. ART TITLES: Syd Nicholls, Will Cathcart. 5200 ft.

CAST: Kenneth Brampton (Captain Starlight), S. A. Fitzgerald (Ben Marsden), Roland Conway (Dick Marsden), Cliff Pyatt (Jim Marsden), Roy Redgrave (Dan Moran), William Pearson (Sir Frederick Moranger), Stuart MacRae (Inspector Goring), Wilton Power (George Storefield), Jackie Anderson (Warrigal), H. D. Wise (Mr Knightley), Tien Hogue (Aileen Marsden), Nan Taylor (Mrs Marsden), Phyllis Ruthven (Grace Storefield), Hilda Dorrington (Kate Morrison), Vera Archer (Jennie Morrison), Austral Nichol (Mrs Knightley), Betty Crook (Miss Falkland), Sybil Shirley, Charles Chauvel.

The New South Wales censorship authorities had prevented at least two attempts to make film versions of the Rolf Boldrewood novel, even though stage versions continued to appear regularly in theatrical repertoires. In 1916 the Crick and Jones partnership sought permission from the censors to make a film of the novel under Raymond Longford's direction, but after discussions between Crick and the authorities the project was abandoned. In 1918 a similar attempt was made by Alfred Rolfe, who had directed the last version in 1911, under the title *Captain Starlight, Gentleman of the Road.* Rolfe, too, failed to gain permission, and this time the reasoning of the censor was recorded on official files (Chief Secretary of New South Wales, Letters Received, no. 18/45262, A.O., ref. 5/8006, Archives Authority of New South Wales, Sydney):

> I fail to see that any good or useful object will be served by re-producing on a moving picture film the bad old days; they are gone, let us hope forever. The book itself, as we all know, might be styled as one of our few Australian Classics, nor could any reasonable objection be raised to the spoken play, in which case an audience is composed almost exclusively of adults; in the moving picture proposition we are immediately

176 *Robbery Under Arms* Kenneth Brampton. Frame enlargement

faced with an entirely different set of circumstances—here the audiences are comprised largely of women, young children, and impressionable boys. One thing is certain, the story of Starlight on the screen would be neither edifying nor educational.

Censorship records relating to the 1920 production by Kenneth Brampton are not available, but clearly the producers approached their subject with caution, and laboriously stressed the moral lesson of the story in a stream of titles at both the beginning and end of the film. Brampton's scenario takes the two Marsden brothers through their adventures with the gentlemanly bushranger, Captain Starlight, their romance with local girls, their life on the goldfields and their eventual capture by the police after Starlight is shot. The brothers spend a long term in prison, and emerge to start a new life with their patiently waiting sweethearts. If the censors thought that Brampton's adaptation would carry a salutary message they were mistaken, as *Theatre*, 1 December 1920, noted: the story 'is simply eaten by the average juvenile, to whom Starlight will be a hero—while youth remains'.

Brampton staged the film in strikingly beautiful locations at Braidwood and in the Araluen Valley near Canberra, a location used decades later for the British production of *Ned Kelly* (1970). Distribution was handled by Beaumont Smith, and the film opened at the Strand Theatre, Melbourne, on 2 October 1920 and in Sydney a month later. *Theatre* was unimpressed: 'It has plenty of action; but the titling is poor; and, unlike Boldrewood's book, the interest never grips.' Commercial results from the film seen to have been fairly solid, but Brampton, an experienced stage and screen actor, did not direct another film for two years. In passing, it is worth noting that the supporting cast included the young Charles Chauvel in an unidentified bit part; Chauvel at this time was working around the Sydney studios attending to horses and assisting with mechanical chores.

177 The Jackeroo of Coolabong

1920 WILFRED LUCAS

PC: Carroll-Baker Australian Productions. P: E. J. Carroll, Reg L. 'Snowy' Baker. SC: Bess Meredyth. ED: Dudley Blanchard. ASST D: Bert Glennon. 5000 ft.

CAST: Reg L. 'Snowy' Baker (Brian O'Farrell), Kathleen Key (Edith MacDonald), Wilfred Lucas (John MacDonald), Bernice Vere, Arthur Tauchert, Arthur Greenaway.

Snowy Baker's last film in Australia revived the main plot device of his earlier film, *The Lure of the Bush* (1918). He plays an English 'new chum', complete with spats and monocle, who arrives on a cattle station and takes a job as a jackeroo. The station hands make fun of him and call him 'dearie', but his prowess at riding and boxing convinces them that his 'sartorial resplendency [is] only the covering of a dinkum man'. The station manager, MacDonald, takes the jackeroo to Sydney, where his daughter works as 'a ministering angel' among the destitute in the slums. The girl is held by a gang of criminals, but with his sharp wits and ready fists the jackeroo is able to rescue her.

Alongside Baker's familiar leaps, boxing and stunt-riding, the film was highlighted (as was *The Lure of the Bush*) by a large-scale kangaroo hunt. During the filming of the hunt, an extra, Nellie Park, suffered fatal injuries when she fell from her horse. Other scenes included an encounter with 'wild' Aborigines, from whom the hero escapes by swimming away underwater. Baker's films were never popular with Sydney's critics, and *Theatre*, 1 November 1920, was especially severe with the latest, finding the story 'weak and improbable' and the hero looking old enough to be the heroine's father. But as with the earlier films, it found a large and uncritical audience when E. J. Carroll released it through the Union Theatres chain, beginning at the Crystal Palace and Lyric Theatre, Sydney, on 16 October 1920. It was released in America a year later, renamed *The Fighting Breed*, in a substantially re-edited version, and possibly with some scenes reshot.

In June the American Wilfred Lucas had returned from a brief visit to Hollywood and embarked quickly on this, the third of his Australian features, again with a largely American staff. Work did not proceed happily; Carroll reportedly began to object to the expensive methods of the Americans, and eventually terminated their engagement. Lucas and Bess Meredyth left Australia before the film was released and took Baker with them, leaving Raymond Longford in charge of Carroll's Palmerston studio. Lucas and Meredyth resumed their careers in the mainstream of Hollywood production. Baker had no difficulty finding starring roles in outdoor adventure movies during the early 1920s, and established himself as a colourful figure in Hollywood society.

177 *The Jackeroo of Coolabong* From the left, Bernice Vere, Snowy Baker, Arthur Tauchert

178 The Hordern Mystery*

1920 HARRY SOUTHWELL

PC: Southwell Screen Plays. P: Harry Southwell. SC: Miss M. F. Gatwood. From the novel by Edward Finn. PH: Tasman Higgins. ART D: Austin Fay. 5600 ft.

CAST: Claude Turton (Gilbert Hordern), Flo Little (Midge Hordern), Floris St George (Laura Yellaboyce), Godfrey Cass (Dan Yellaboyce), Thomas Sinclair (Peter Mull), Beatrice Hamilton (Mrs Mull), David Edelsten.

This complex Jekyll-and-Hyde story concerns a money-hungry man, Gilbert Hordern, who pretends to be his own evil twin brother so that he can evade his doting wife and marry a millionaire's daughter. He succeeds in his plan but is driven by a guilty conscience to confess to his fraudulent behaviour. He is about to be arrested for bigamy when he wakes up and realizes that his evil doings were just a nightmare. Chastened by the dream, he vows never to allow money to ruin his life and, counting his blessings, he clasps his wife and child close to his breast.

Southwell's second Australian feature was shot in Sydney's wealthier suburbs in mid-1920 under the working title of *The Golden Flame*. It premièred at the Shell Theatre, Sydney, on 23 October 1920 but attracted little attention. The normally uncritical *Picture Show*, 1 November 1920, attacked it as 'lamentably reminiscent of the poor acting and jumbled plot of pictures in days long gone'.

179 'Possum Paddock**

1921 CHARLES VILLIERS, KATE HOWARDE

P: Kate Howarde. From the play by Kate Howarde. PH: Lacey Percival. 6500 ft.

CAST: John Cosgrove (Andrew McQuade), James Martin (Dan Martin), Leslie Adrien (Nancy McQuade), Jack Kirby (Hugh Bracken).

'Possum Paddock began as a stage production, written and produced by Kate Howarde, one of Australia's few female theatrical entrepreneurs. A backblocks farce closely related to Dad and Dave, it shared the genre's commercial success when it opened at the Theatre Royal, Sydney, on 6 September 1919. Late in 1920, Kate Howarde hired the actor Charles Villiers to assist her in preparing a film adaptation. Many of the stage cast were retained for the film. Since the play had opened, John Cosgrove had played the central character, Andrew McQuade, a burly and bearded man of the land who has fought his way through years of drought and hardship and now faces ruin because of a bank loan he cannot repay. Reluctantly he decides to sell a fifty-acre field known as 'Possum Paddock. One of his daughters, Nancy, is being courted by a young gentleman, Hugh Bracken, who sells his car to pay off the old man's debts, just in time to prevent the sale of the land to a greedy neighbour, Dan Martin. McQuade later learns what Martin had known all along, that a railway line is to go through the paddock and that the land is worth a fortune.

The film opened on 29 January 1921 at the Lyric Theatre, Sydney, after the New South Wales censors demanded a cut in a sub-plot about an unmarried mother, specifically a scene in which she imagines herself desperately throwing her baby into the river. Although the Lyric was not the best of Sydney's theatres, commercial results seem to have been strong and the film was frequently revived, especially in rural areas. The *Sun*, 30 January 1921, found it 'likable', its only major fault being excessive length; otherwise the bush atmosphere, from 'the 'possums to the bad roads [is] well maintained'.

179 Kate Howarde

Kate Howarde (her full name was Kate Howarde Black) made no other films after *'Possum Paddock*, but the play, like the film, remained in demand throughout the 1920s, in both Australia and New Zealand. As an entrepreneur, she had begun to manage her own touring theatrical company while still in her teens, working first in country towns, and later throughout Australia, New Zealand and South Africa. She was also a prolific author of plays, songs and vaudeville acts, but her most popular achievement by far was *'Possum Paddock*. She died on 18 February 1939 at the age of 70. Her daughter, Leslie Adrien (sometimes billed as Lesley Adrienne), often acted in her plays and took the central female part in the film.

179 *'Possum Paddock* John Cosgrove (*l*), Leslie Adrien (*r*)

180 Silks and Saddles*

1921 JOHN K. WELLS

PC: Commonwealth Pictures. P, SC, ED: John K. Wells. STORY: John Cosgrove. PH: Al Burne. PROPS: James Coleman. ART TITLES: Syd Nicholls. ASST ED: Robert Bates. ASST D: Robert MacKinnon. 5500 ft.

CAST: Brownie Vernon (Roberta 'Bobbie' Morton), Robert MacKinnon (Richard Morton Jnr), John Cosgrove (Dennis O'Hara), John Faulkner (Richard Morton Snr), Tal Ordell (Phillip Droone), Evelyn Johnson (Myra Fane), Raymond Lawrence (Jeffrey Manners), Gerald Harcourt (Toby Makin), Tommy Denman (Dingo), Kennaquhair.

Silks and Saddles is firmly within the genre of racecourse melodrama. On the prosperous stud farm of Kangarooie, the squatter's daughter, Bobbie, is torn between rival suitors, and her weak-willed brother is embroiled with a high society vamp and racketeers. After much complex criminal activity in the stables before the big race, the heroine herself rides her horse to victory. A more off-beat element is introduced in one of Bobbie's suitors, a fat squatter who tries to win her affection by forcing himself to lose weight and by giving her pleasure jaunts in his private plane.

The film was the sole production of Commonwealth Pictures, a Sydney company formed in October 1920 with Eric Griffin as

180 *Silks and Saddles* John Faulkner (*l*), Brownie Vernon (*r*)

managing director. To direct the film, the company hired a young American, John K. Wells, who had come to Australia with Wilfred Lucas to work as assistant director on the Carroll-Baker productions. He worked also as associate director with Beaumont Smith on *The Man from Snowy River* (1921). Previously in Hollywood he had worked as an actor and producer in the Universal studios, and had co-produced three independent features starring Sessue Hayakawa.

He directed *Silks and Saddles* on location in and around Sydney, including the Randwick race-track, and on the Macarthur-Onslow estate at Camden, using the current racing champion of the day, Kennaquhair, as the principal horse. Interiors were shot in the Palmerston studios, Sydney, which Commonwealth leased from the Carroll brothers. Shooting was completed late in 1920 for a cost of nearly £6000. Distribution was handled by the Carrolls, and the film opened simultaneously at two Sydney theatres, the Strand and the Lyric, on 5 March 1921. *Theatre*, 1 March 1921 commented: 'The sporting story is not strikingly original . . . But the interest is well sustained, and the scenes at Randwick are capitally produced and very exciting.' The film survives today in its entirety, following reconstruction of the shrunken negative by the National Film Archive in 1977. Several of the performances emerge forcefully and give charm to a technically smooth production. Tal Ordell plays an especially oily villain, and John Cosgrove (author of the film's story) provides pleasant comic relief as the overweight suitor. The American actress, Brownie Vernon, dominates all of her scenes as a graceful and good-humoured heroine, and she provides a more coquettish version than usual of the distinctively Australian heroine who can handle horses and even a two-up game with the station hands, yet emerge demure and dainty when the social occasion arises. She will clearly make both a good mate (as 'Bobbie') and a good wife (as 'Roberta') for the manly overseer when he finally wins her hand.

Commercial returns in Australia were good, and sales were arranged in England and in the U.S.A. (where it was retitled *Queen of the Turf* and the setting changed to Virginia). Despite its profitability and technical competence, the businessmen behind the company were not interested in other ventures. Wells attempted to gain fresh backing for further production, but failed, and in September 1921 he entered Australian vaudeville with a musical act in a Tivoli variety show. In March 1923 he departed abruptly to America, and his subsequent career is unknown.

181 The Betrayer

1921 BEAUMONT SMITH

PC: Beaumont Smith's Productions. P, SC: Beaumont Smith. PH: Lacey Percival. 5500 ft.

CAST: Stella Southern (Iwa), Cyril Mackay (Stephen Manners), John Cosgrove (John Barris), Marie D'Alton (Mrs Manners), Mita (Hauraki), Bernice Vere (Eleanor Barris), Maggie Papakura, Herbert Lee, Raymond Hatton, Dunstan Webb.

The Betrayer belongs to the genre of inter-racial romance, with a wealthy Australian land-owner, Stephen Manners, falling helplessly in love with a part-Maori girl, Iwa. Manners mistakenly believes Iwa to be his daughter from an affair that he had had twenty years earlier with a Maori woman, who had later died. Reluctantly, he tries to turn his feelings of love into more appropriate fatherly sentiments. The truth about her birth is hidden from him by an old Maori chieftain and by a vampish socialite from Sydney who wishes to win him away from Iwa. After many dramatic moments Stephen learns the truth, and Iwa becomes his happy bride.

Smith's film went further than most American films in the genre: usually inter-racial love affairs ended in tragedy, but in *The Betrayer* there is little evidence of social stigma attached to the proposed marriage of Stephen and Iwa, perhaps because her appearance was entirely European. Beyond the central romance the plot is thick with complex manoeuvres and alliances, and depends heavily on secrets, coincidences and last-minute revelations. The settings range widely, from the New Zealand hot springs and mountain scenery at Rotorua, to the Australian outback, the surf at Coogee, and a fashionable ballroom at Sydney's Wentworth Hotel.

The film was shot and previewed under the title *Our Bit o' the World*, but was renamed *The Betrayer* shortly before release because the first title had seemed to indicate a travelogue. It was the first of Smith's productions to straddle the two markets of Australia and

181 *The Betrayer* Stella Southern, Cyril Mackay

New Zealand, although he had been active for some years in selling films and stage shows in both countries. Distributed by Smith himself, it opened at the Hoyts Theatre, Melbourne, on 19 March 1921 and screened widely and profitably throughout Australia and New Zealand. Local critics generally had little to say apart from formula phrases of encouragement. In 1922 Smith re-edited the film for the British market, adding a racecourse scene and a chase between a car and train, probably taken from his 1919 production, *Desert Gold*; he also changed the title again, to *The Maid of Maoriland*. He took a print with him to London in May 1922, but no information about a British release has been traced.

182 A Girl of the Bush*

1921 FRANKLYN BARRETT

PC: Barrett's Australian Productions. P, SC, PH: Franklyn Barrett. ART TITLES: Fred Brodrick. 6000 ft.

CAST: Vera James (Lorna Denver), Jack Martin (Tom Wilson), Herbert Linden (Oswald Keane), Stella Southern (Grace Girton), James Martin (John Burns), Sam Warr (Sing Lee), Emma Shea (Looe Toy), D. L. Dalziel (James Keane), Gerald Harcourt (Reg Howard), Olga Broughton (Mary Burns), Mick Huntsdale (Bill Tresle), Tom Cosgrove (Bill's mate).

Lorna Denver is manager of the wealthy Kangaroo Flat sheep station. Rivalry for her hand in marriage arises between the dissolute Oswald and a dashing young surveyor, Tom Wilson. Lorna gives shelter to a baby that has survived an attack by Aborigines on white settlers, and Tom is led to believe that the baby is actually her own. Hurt by Tom's assumption about the child, Lorna spurns him. Later Oswald is murdered and Tom is arrested and put on trial. At the last moment the Chinese cook on the station reveals that Oswald had been murdered not by Tom, but by the father of a woman wronged by Oswald (in fact the dead mother of the baby found by

182 *A Girl of the Bush* Vera James

Lorna). Tom realizes the truth about the baby and is happily reconciled with Lorna.

Although based on an original screenplay, the film is firmly in the squatter's-daughter tradition: the heroine rides and works as the equal of the men, yet at other times displays a more conventional form of screen femininity, for example, bathing demurely in the nude in a bush pool (actually wearing a flesh-coloured bathing costume). Comic relief, too, comes from a time-honoured source, the parodying of the central love interest by the 'low life' of the station, in this case not Aborigines but Chinese, with a Chinese laundrymaid (played by a white actress) pursued relentlessly by the cook, an old man repeatedly abused by the station hands as a 'damned yeller streak of misery'.

Yet, for all its familiar characters and devices, *A Girl of the Bush* has a distinctive spirit of 'documentary realism'. Picturesque scenes of station activity—sheep shearing, horse breaking and the muster—are interpolated throughout the film, and carry far more punch than the plot mechanics. Similarly, a two-up game and a police raid, filmed in the back streets of Sydney, are full of vigour and immediacy lacking in the studio interiors. Most contemporary reviewers seemed to respond to the freshness of the outdoor scenes and the naturalism of the performances on location; *Theatre*, 2 May 1921, commented on the 'grand scenes of Australian life' and the 'quiet, well-bred charm' of Vera James, and *Everyones*, 4 May 1921, praised the 'wonderful setting and tip-top photography'.

The film was the first of three that Barrett made for his own company, formed in 1920 with the Sydney solicitor, Barry Kenward. The company had plans for the intensive production of four features a year, but in May 1922 the Sydney office closed, and Barrett withdrew entirely from production. Shooting for *A Girl of the Bush* began in October 1920 at the Fremantle Station near Bathurst, N.S.W., and on locations further outback. It opened on 26 March 1921 at West's Olympia Theatre, Brisbane, and screened widely in Australia and New Zealand.

182 *A Girl of the Bush* Herbert Linden, Vera James

The star, Vera James, was born in New Zealand in 1892 and came to Australia to seek a film career in 1919. After several stage plays, she was recruited by Barrett for two films, *A Girl of the Bush* and *Know Thy Child* (1921). She then went to Hollywood and won a leading role in a B-western, *McGuire of the Mounted* (1923), but suffered the disappointment of seeing her major role in *Bavu* (1923) removed in post-production changes. Several bit parts and stage shows as a dancer followed, but in 1929 she returned to Australia and withdrew entirely from show business.

183 Rudd's New Selection

1921 RAYMOND LONGFORD

P: E. J. Carroll. SC: Raymond Longford. From the stories by Steele Rudd. PH: Arthur Higgins. 6000 ft.
CAST: J. P. O'Neill (Dad Rudd), Ada Clyde (Mum), Tal Ordell (Dave), Lottie Lyell (Nell), Charlotte Beaumont (Sarah), Louis Fors (Joe), Billy Williams (Jack Regan), Ernest T. Hearne (Jim Regan), Dick Varley (storekeeper), Clyde Marsh (Trooper Brady), May Renne (Lily), William Coulter (Grogan), Ada St Claire (Mrs Banks), Meadow Peel (Matilda), Anne Parsons (Mrs McFluster), Gilbert Emery (Mr Dandelion), Harrie and Ernie Ranier (the twins), Harry Halley.

183 *Rudd's New Selection* Lottie Lyell, J. P. O'Neill

Longford's second Dad and Dave film opens with Dave's marriage and traces the pattern of daily life on his new selection. A sister, Nell, is introduced into the film family as a representative of a more sophisticated life-style, and her romantic involvement with two likely suitors provides a melodramatic counter-balance to the comedy. One of the major comic episodes introduces Mr Dandelion, a local killjoy and prohibitionist candidate for parliament (the character is played, in a choice piece of casting against type, by Gilbert Emery). A visit by Dandelion and his prohibitionist supporters to the Rudd homestead ends in chaotic good cheer when Joe laces their tea with rum.

Shooting began late in 1920 and continued over a long period well into 1921. Locations for the farm scenes were found in the Megalong Valley in the Blue Mountains, and interiors were shot in the Carrolls' studio at Waverley. Distributed by the Carrolls, it opened simultaneously at the Strand and Lyric Theatres, Sydney, on 28 May 1921, and proved a solid commercial success. Reviews were uniformly favourable. The *Sun*, 29 May 1921, found it 'an advance on previous efforts. Photography and titling are first-rate, story interest and atmosphere are well-maintained, and the general standard of production is high.' Longford's eye for detail emerges in his 'admirable selection of types' in the cast, and throughout he gives special attention to comedy 'to relieve the sterner business of life'. Horsemanship was also emphasized, with Lottie Lyell's horseback skills being matched by a screen newcomer, Ernest T. Hearne, an ex-soldier from Queensland with roughriding experience.

184 The Guyra Ghost Mystery

1921 JOHN COSGROVE

PC: Cosgrove and Regan. SC: John Cosgrove. PH: A. J. Moulton.
CAST: John Cosgrove (Sherlock Doyle), Nellie Regan, the Bowen family.

In April 1921 the townspeople of Guyra, near Armidale in north-eastern New South Wales, were disturbed by reports of a ghost terrorizing a family in an isolated house on the outskirts of the town. For several weeks, windows in William Bowen's house were broken by stones, rocks thudded onto his roof, and his family was kept awake by a mysterious knocking on the walls. Even when police and volunteers stood guard around the house, the stone-throwing continued. Eventually one of the Bowen children confessed that on several occasions she had thrown stones onto the roof to frighten her little sister. Although the police officially dismissed the affair on the basis of this confession, some doubts still remained; the child was barely capable of causing all of the disturbances, and the implication persisted that the Bowens had been the victims of a practical joker.

John Cosgrove's film of the events at Guyra was the only one completed of several rival projects initiated soon after the story captured the attention of the popular press around Australia. With the support of a local Guyra exhibitor (whose business had suffered a severe decline during the period of the ghost rumours), Cosgrove scraped together a hasty scenario and went to Guyra to photograph the scene of the disturbance. After much persuasion, the Bowens themselves agreed to appear in the film, and Mr Bowen was seen shooting his rifle at a ghostly apparition created by trick photography. Cosgrove himself played the role of Sherlock Doyle, in parody of a Mr Moors, a friend of Sir Arthur Conan Doyle with an interest in psychic phenomena, who visited Guyra in the midst of the crisis to try to solve the mystery.

The film opened on 25 June 1921 to a special three-day season at Wirth's Hippodrome, Sydney. The screenings were not widely advertised and were not commercially successful; on 11 November 1922 *Smith's Weekly* noted that Cosgrove had shot the film in three days and that it had spent most of the subsequent time 'on the shelf'. This undistinguished quickie was Cosgrove's only venture into production, although he wrote several scenarios, including *Silks and Saddles* (1921) and *Sunshine Sally* (1922), and acted in these and many other films. A hearty eighteen-stone figure, he worked for some thirty-five years on the Australian stage, both as actor and manager. When he died in Sydney on 11 August 1925 at the age of 58, *Everyones* (12 August) described him as 'a thorough Bohemian, and in parts a sterling actor'.

185 Mated in the Wilds

1921 P. J. RAMSTER

PC: P. J. Ramster Photoplays. PH: Reg Fuz. 5000 ft.
CAST: Elsa Granger (Elsa Hope), Anthony Aroney [Rooney?] (Montgomery Lyle), Fred Oppey (Justin Strong), Maud de Grange, William Shepherd, Lydia Rich, David Edelsten, Louis Witts, Albert Germain, S. P. Woodford, Phillip Raftus, Kathleen Ramster, Winifred Law, Dorothy Shepherd, Nancy Simpson.

A young sportswoman, Elsa Hope, has two rival lovers—a gallant flying ace, Justin Strong, and a mustachioed foreigner, Montgomery Lyle. Justin and Monty depart by motorcycle on a surveying trip, and Monty leaves his rival stranded in the desert to die. Back in Sydney, he tells a touching story of Justin's death at the hand of wild Aborigines and renews his pursuit of Elsa's affections. Elsa insists on seeing Justin's grave, and soon Monty, Elsa and her mother are riding together on motorcycles into the outback. Monty quickly reveals himself to be 'a real cave-man in his methods of love'; he ties Mrs Hope to a tree and is about to carry Elsa away with him when the girl produces a gun and Monty is left 'to grind his teeth in defeat'. Elsa and her mother soon discover Justin in the care of kindly Aborigines, and the future happiness of the young lovers is assured.

P. J. (Percy John) Ramster opened an acting school in Sydney in 1918, promising to give roles in his own films to the students. His recruits included many from Sydney's high society, only a few of whom graduated to professional acting careers. Elsa Granger, the star of several Ramster productions, had acted briefly on the Sydney stage before joining Ramster, and in 1922 sought work in Hollywood, without success. William Shepherd, another of Ramster's trainees, later became a highly proficient film editor and worked on numerous features.

P. J. Ramster ventured into production energetically but, hampered by ineffective distribution and exhibition, his work became increasingly sporadic, until he ceased production altogether in 1928 after *The Russell Affair*. *Mated in the Wilds* was his first feature, and because the cast was unpaid and could work only on weekends, it took a year to complete. Locations were used in and around Sydney, with much celebration of fashionable society and with motorcycles replacing the customary horses in the bush scenes. The film opened commercially at the Shell Theatre, Sydney, on 13 August, but attracted little attention from either the public or the press.

In addition to features, Ramster produced a number of short comedies and dramas, including *High Heels* (1918), a one-reel drama with Fred Oppey and Elsa Granger; a comedy, *Should Girls Kiss Soldiers?* (1918), the first of several Ramster films titled with rhetorical questions; *Jasamine Freckel's Love Affair* (1921), an imitation of Mack Sennett's 'bathing beauty' comedies, starring Nancy Simpson; *The Tale of a Shirt* (1922), a two-reel comedy starring the story's author, Charles Russell, about a man who learns on a holiday that he is not as old as he thought; and *Cattiva Evasione* (or *A Naughty Elopement*), a comedy made in 1923 ostensibly for Sydney's Italian community, with a story by a local Italian actor, Angelo Zommo. None made much visible commercial or critical impact.

186 While the Billy Boils

1921 BEAUMONT SMITH

PC: Beaumont Smith's Productions. P, SC: Beaumont Smith. From the stories of Henry Lawson. ASST D: Phil K. Walsh. 5800 ft.
CAST: Tal Ordell (Bob Brothers), John Cosgrove (One-eyed Bogan), Robert MacKinnon (Dick Webb), Ernest T. Hearne (Steelman), Gilbert Emery (Smithy), J. P. O'Neill (Tom Mitchell), Charles Beetham (Tom Wall), Alf Scarlett (bank manager), Elsie McCormack (Ruth), Loma Lantaur (Tessie Brand), Rita Aslin (Mrs Stiffner), May Renne (Mrs Brighten), James Ward (Old Tallyho), Charles Villiers (Andy Regan), Henry Lawson (himself).

Beaumont Smith bought the stage rights to Henry Lawson's works in 1915, and devised a loosely linked array of his better-known characters in a play produced on the Sydney stage in September 1916. Although the play was only a modest commercial success, Smith proceeded to buy the screen rights from Lawson's publisher and to adapt the play into the second of his 'serious' feature productions (the first had been another literary adaptation, *The Man from Snowy River*, in 1920).

Smith's reliance on formula plot devices dominated even this film with its rich source material. The central character is Bob Brothers, a philosophical bushman who had quarrelled with his father ten years earlier, and had left home and changed his name. With his true identity concealed, he returns one day to his father's station, and takes a job there, eventually becoming the union representative among the station hands. He finds that his young brother, Dick, is involved with a scheming adventuress, Tessie, who is blackmailing him into stealing money for her. Bob nobly takes the blame for the theft to protect his brother, and further complications arise when Dick and Bob both fall in love with another, more honourable woman, Ruth. Bob tries to forget his unrequited love for Ruth by trekking further outback; he loses himself in the desert and is found near death by an Afghan camel-driver. Back at the station, he is further blamed for an attempted bank robbery, and several fights and chases take place before his name is cleared and he is reunited with the family, with Ruth as his bride.

Perhaps the film's major distinction was its brief prologue, in which Henry Lawson himself appeared (although at the time he was seriously ill) in his popular image as a bushman, narrating the story beside the campfire. With characteristically thorough pre-planning, vigorous publicity, and hard physical work, Beaumont Smith shot and edited the film in little more than a month, in July-August 1921, using locations at the country town of Windsor, N.S.W. Smith was assisted by Phil K. Walsh, a young entrepreneur who later directed two features of his own, *Around the Boree Log* (1925) and *The Birth of White Australia* (1928).

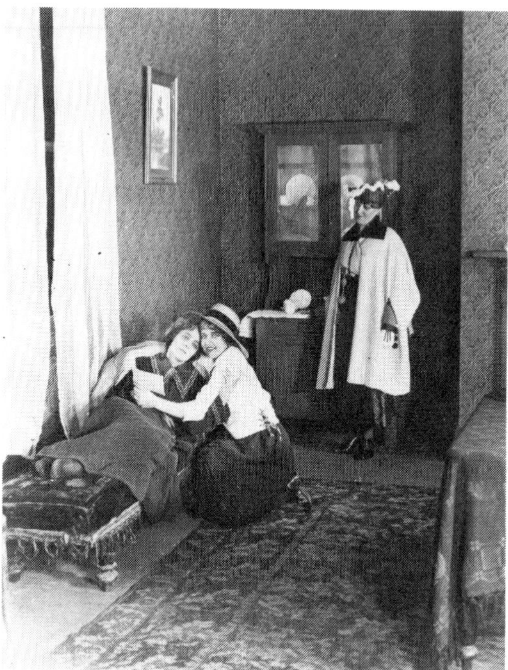

187 *Know Thy Child* Vera James (*l*), Lotus Thompson (*c*)

Distributed by Smith himself, the film opened in Sydney at the Grand and Lyric Theatres on 17 September 1921. It screened widely around Australia and New Zealand over the next few months, with every indication of solid commercial success.

187 Know Thy Child

1921 FRANKLYN BARRETT

PC: Barrett's Australian Productions. P, PH: Franklyn Barrett. SC: Elsie M. Cummins. 6 reels

CAST: Roland Conway (Ray Standford), Nada Conrade (Dorothy Graham), Lotus Thompson (Eileen Baker), Vera James (Sadie McClure), Gerald Harcourt (Geoffrey Dexter), Lily Rochefort.

Know Thy Child was a 'problem drama', nominally exploring a case of social injustice, but actually revelling in sex and scandal. A young commercial traveller, Ray Stanford, seduces a country girl, Sadie McClure, but forgets about her when he returns to the city. In Sydney he marries Dorothy Graham, the daughter of his employer, and eventually becomes the head of the firm. By a trick of fate, his own illegitimate daughter becomes his personal secretary and 'unpleasant complications' follow. His wife is meanwhile active as a social worker, pressuring the government 'to declare as bigamous all marriages contracted by persons, who at the time, were morally pledged to others'. The problem is resolved when the mother of Ray's illegitimate daughter dies and the girl is adopted by Ray and Dorothy as their own.

Although the New South Wales censors found the film 'free from objectionable matter', and the state governor publicly endorsed it as 'astonishingly good', the seal of respectability was somewhat outweighed by sensationalistic publicity: 'Visualise a man, happily married and enjoying the goods of life. Then into his Eden comes Eve to cool his affection for his wife—to take his love from her. And Eve was—HIS OWN DAUGHTER!' (*Sun*, 9 October 1921). Some critics responded with formula phrases of encouragement for the local product, but the *Sun* spoke out strongly against 'the repellent twist' in the plot and the fact that the film would arouse the anger of moralists at a time when politicians and public were beginning to demand films about Australian life to counter-balance the influence of Hollywood; despite such demands, Australian producers seemed to prefer to handle 'age-old' stories that belong 'to no age or country'.

The film was the second to bear the trademark of Barrett's own company. Exteriors were shot in Sydney and at Berowra Waters, north of the city, with interiors at the Rushcutters Bay studio. Distributed by Barrett himself, the film opened at the Lyceum Theatre, Sydney, on 8 October 1921, and made little impact commercially.

The role of the illegitimate daughter introduced Lotus Thompson to the screen. A vivacious comedienne and a striking beauty, she appeared in several Australian features and in February 1924 departed for Hollywood. Within months she made news by throwing acid over her legs and disfiguring them; some claimed it was a desperate publicity stunt, and others that she was driven to it as a protest against the refusal of casting directors to give her acting roles, and for offering her work only as the 'double' for the legs of less well-endowed stars. Whatever the reason, her career continued for several years, with leading roles in several B-grade Westerns and a major supporting role in Cecil B. DeMille's *Madam Satan* (1930).

188 Retribution

1921 ARMAND LIONELLO

PC: Astrolat Film Company. SC: Thorene Adair.
CAST: Thorene Adair (Arabelle Redmond).

This Brisbane production portrayed the efforts of a female detective to crack a crime ring operating in the city and in the sapphire mines of Anakie.

The film opened at Union Theatres' Pavilion, Brisbane, on 22 October 1921, with good results as a local novelty. Although usually a vigorous supporter of Australian production, *Theatre*, 1 December 1921, found little to commend the film: 'Even the photography was bad; and in the perfect photographic air of Queensland, almost genius was required to get that result. With mechanical technique—story, acting, and production so remarkable for stupidity—this picture stands alone.' According to the magazine's correspondent, the production had arisen from the Modern School of Cinema Acting opened in Brisbane by 'Professor Armand Lionello, late of the Cines Film Producing Company, Rome'. Pupils were promised training to reach 'the highest degree of perfection in cinema acting', in consideration of which they were asked to sign a bond not to act for any other company for two and a half years from the date of entrance to the school. The magazine ended its report by proposing legislation to control such exploitation of 'picture-struck girls'.

189 The Blue Mountains Mystery

1921 RAYMOND LONGFORD, LOTTIE LYELL

PC: Southern Cross Feature Film Company. P: E. J. and Dan Carroll. SC: Lottie Lyell. From the novel, *The Mount Marunga Mystery*, by Harrison Owen. PH: Arthur Higgins. 6000 ft.
CAST: Marjorie Osborne (Mrs Tracey), John Faulkner (Henry Tracey/Stephen Rodder), Vivian Edwards (Hector Blunt), Bernice Vere (Pauline Tracey), Billy Williams (Richard Maxim), Redmond Barry (detective), John de Lacey (Captain Banks), Ivy Shilling (dancer).

This story of 'the sunlight and shadows of Australian society' begins with the discovery of a corpse in a fashionable hotel near Katoomba in the Blue Mountains. The murdered man was a wealthy businessman, Henry Tracey, and among the suspects are his ward, Pauline, and one of her admirers, Hector Blunt. Attempts to solve the mystery are complicated by the evil doings of Mrs Tracey and by Pauline's habit of sleep-walking. Eventually the supposedly dead Henry Tracey reappears and announces that he had been kidnapped and that his corpse was in fact the body of Stephen Rodder, a ne'er-do-well who had such a striking resemblance to Tracey that even Mrs Tracey had been deceived.

The last of Longford's films to be handled by the Carrolls, this was a 'society drama', quite distinct from *The Sentimental Bloke* (1919) and the Dad and Dave films; apart from a few scenes at the Carrolls' Palmerston studio in Sydney, most of the film was shot on location in the wealthy holiday resort of Katoomba, in the opulent Carrington Hotel and the near-by Hydro Majestic. The leading part of Mrs Tracey was played by Marjorie Osborne, better known in society as Mrs Henry Hill Osborne, a fashion consultant to the Sydney store of Farmer's and wife of a wealthy land-owner. After the completion of the film (her first), she went to Hollywood to further her career, but with no apparent success; she was divorced by her husband soon after her departure.

Longford was joined in the production by Lottie Lyell, and although she had often assisted him in the past, *The Blue Mountains Mystery* was the first film in which she was formally credited as co-director. The film took an unusually long time to complete, perhaps because of the efforts of Longford and Lyell to make the most of their location settings. *Smith's Weekly*, 12 November 1921, found it to be the 'most elaborate Australian picture to date' with 'magnificent scenic effects'. The total cost of the film was less than £4000 and the Carrolls did well commercially when it opened at the Lyceum Theatre, Sydney, on 5 November 1921. Release was also arranged in England and America.

Some months after the film was released, the Carrolls withdrew from production to concentrate on the more stable exhibition trade. Longford and Lyell quickly formed a new company to produce films under their own names, and returned for their first venture to familiar homely sentiments with *The Dinkum Bloke* (1922).

190 The Life Story of John Lee, or The Man they could not Hang*

1921 ARTHUR W. STERRY

PC: Sterry and Haldane. SC: Arthur W. Sterry. PH: Tasman Higgins. 6 reels.
CAST: Rose Rooney (Kate), David Edelsten (the judge).

Arthur W. Sterry and Frederick Haldane had earned a fortune with the 1912 film of *The Life Story of John Lee.* In 1921 they sought to rejuvenate their means of livelihood by making a new expanded version, including scenes of Lee's happy childhood to sweeten the grim events ahead. The story of Lee's arrest for a murder he did not commit, and the 'miracle' of the gallows that failed to open for his execution, offered no surprises for the audience by this time. The attraction, however, was the intensity of the emotion in both the film and the accompanying 'oration', usually performed by Sterry or Haldane. Piety was heavily stressed: characters often paused for prayer, and the film ended with Lee's small child thanking God for saving her father. Lee himself emerged from jail to pray for those sinners whose perjured evidence had placed him there: 'May those responsible obtain more mercy than they have shown to me. May they at last be finally forgiven.' The crude sentimentality of the scenes of motherly love and self-sacrifice, and the studied cuteness of the children, are thickly evident in the film preserved today in the National Film Archive, and date the film far more than its crude technical standard. Contemporary reviews had little positive to say. *Everyones*, 28 December 1921, said of it: 'Giving [it] the benefit of everything favourable that can be said [of Australian production], there is no comparison, as regards quality or story, with other current releases.' Clearly the trade had little idea why the film should prove so popular.

189 Shooting *The Blue Mountains Mystery*. Raymond Longford in hat and waistcoat, Lottie Lyell beside him

190 *The Life Story of John Lee*

As with the earlier version, Sterry and Haldane travelled with the film in rural areas and in New Zealand before bringing it to capital city theatres in Australia. On 24 December 1921 it opened at the Grand Theatre, Sydney, to catch the Christmas holiday trade, and continued for an exceptional three-week season, attracting an estimated 36 000 people. The commercial success continued well into 1923 before signs of screenings in Australia gradually disappeared. In 1934 the story still carried enough reputation for Raymond Longford to try to salvage his career by making a talkie version, and Sterry was cast in a leading role. Again, despite a film of very doubtful quality, box-office records were easily broken.

191 The Gentleman Bushranger

1921 BEAUMONT SMITH

PC: Beaumont Smith's Productions. P, SC: Beaumont Smith. From the short story, 'A Stripe for Trooper Casey', by Roderic Quinn. 6000 ft.
CAST: Dot McConville (Kitty Anson), Ernest T. Hearne (Richard Lavender), John Cosgrove (Ah Wom Bat), Tal Ordell (Peter Dargin), Nada Conrade, Monica Mack, J. P. O'Neill, Robert MacKinnon, Fred Phillips, Fred Twitcham, Arthur Cross, John M. Walsh, Freddie Tauchert, Alf Scarlett, John Boland, T. Kiley, Fred Coleman, E. J. Kelly, Claude Terry (Superintendent of Police), Fred Read (coach driver).

The bushranger of this film is not a double-dyed villain but merely a victim of circumstance. Richard Lavender is a handsome young British emigrant falsely accused of murdering the ship's captain on the voyage to Australia. With the aid of a 'black boy', Lavender escapes into the bush, where he becomes a gold prospector. He is discovered by Kitty Anson, whom he had met on board the ship and who now runs a near-by selection. She joins Lavender in a successful gold-mining operation, and their life is happy until the villainous Peter Dargin, who had originally accused Lavender of the murder, learns of his whereabouts and frames him for several bushranging crimes. After many adventures, Dargin is brought to justice and the lovers are left in peace.

Comedy was provided by a plump Chinese cook, Ah Wom Bat (played by an unlikely John Cosgrove), complete with flowing gown and buck teeth, who is involved with Dargin in smuggling stolen gold to Sydney. Further comic relief appeared with a touring theatrical company that presents a farcical version of *East Lynne* in the mining town. It is probable that this *East Lynne* segment was 'borrowed' from a short comedy directed by John Cosgrove in 1917, *An East Lynne Fiasco*, in which Cosgrove had starred with Will Gilbert.

This safe variation of the forbidden bushranging genre was shot with Smith's characteristic haste in four weeks in October 1921.

191 *The Gentleman Bushranger* Tal Ordell (*l*), Ernest T. Hearne

Two and a half weeks were spent on location at Bowral and Berrima, N.S.W., where Smith's pace was not deterred by almost unrelieved bad weather. Interiors were shot in Sydney at the Rushcutters Bay studio. The leading lady, in the tradition of Australian outback heroines, was played by a champion equestrienne, Dot McConville.

Distributed by Smith himself in both Australia and New Zealand, the film was 'tried out' at Bowral and Mittagong on 26 December 1921 and premiered in Auckland, New Zealand, on 3 February 1922. It opened in Sydney at the Crystal Palace on 4 March, and proved to be another of Smith's profitable ventures. Reviews, however, betrayed his slapdash methods, and *Smith's Weekly*, 1 April 1922, commented on several anachronisms: despite the setting of 1857, 'one of the heroines flashes upon the screen garbed in the latest riding-habit from Temptation Row, [and] the Chief of Police wears the silver braid upon the peak of his cap, introduced a couple of years ago'.

192 Circumstance

1922 LAWSON HARRIS

PC: Austral Super Films. P: Lawson Harris. SC: Lawson Harris, Yvonne Pavis. PH: Arthur Higgins. PROPS: Jack Miller. 5 reels.

CAST: Yvonne Pavis, Carlton Max, Cane Arthur, Lawson Harris, David Edelsten, Gordon Collingridge.

The story imposed a 'severe strain on the spectator's credulity' (*Theatre*, 1 August 1922). A contemporary urban drama set in Sydney, it told the story of a young woman who is seduced and deserted by a ne'er-do-well and faces a life of poverty as a social outcast. She is rescued by a wealthy novelist, who proposes to write a story about her life, and she becomes the darling of his household. The novelist's cousin returns from the war and asks the girl to marry him, only learning at the wedding hour that she is the same girl he had seduced and forgotten in the wilder days of his youth.

192 Lawson Harris

Austral Super Films was formed by two Americans, Lawson Harris and Yvonne Pavis. Harris, the managing director, was a young all-rounder from Hollywood who came to Australia in 1920 to assist Arthur Shirley with the ill-fated production of *The Throwback*. His partner, Yvonne Pavis, had begun acting in Hollywood in 1910 with the Vitagraph company. She later played both *ingénue* and character roles with other studios under the name of Marie Pavis. Early in 1922 she arrived in Sydney to join Harris, who had left Shirley's enterprise and opened an acting school in partnership with Vera Remée. The production company was formed soon after, and three low-budget features followed in quick succession. The first, *Circumstance*, cost less than £800 and earned a tidy profit after its release at the Haymarket Theatre, Sydney, on 3 June 1922. Distribution was handled directly by the Sydney office of the company.

193 The Triumph of Love

1922 P. J. RAMSTER

PC: P. J. Ramster Photoplays. PH: Jack Bruce, E. R. Jeffree.

CAST: Jack Chalmers, Coo-ee Knight.

Ramster's second feature was shot quickly in April 1922 in the wake of publicity surrounding a daring rescue at Coogee beach, Sydney, by a lifesaver, Jack Chalmers. On 4 February, Chalmers had risked his life to rescue a young man from the jaws of a shark, and although the victim had died soon after, Chalmers was awarded a medal for his bravery.

Soldiers of the Cross

Famous Lasky Film Service Limited
Presents
A LONGFORD-LYELL AUSTRALIAN PRODUCTION
Made in Australia
The "DINKUM BLOKE"
With Arthur Tauchert
A Paramount Picture

GIVE HIM YOUR FIRST VOTE FOR FUN!
Cinesound re-presents
BERT BAILEY
WITH THE INIMITABLE RUDD FAMILY
in
DAD X RUDD M.P.
with
FRED McDONALD · ALEC KELLAWAY
YVONNE EAST · GRANT TAYLOR
BARBARA WEEKS · CONNIE MARTYN
FRANK HARVEY
Produced & Directed by KEN G. HALL
BEF
FOR GENERAL EXHIBITION

194 *A Rough Passage*

Ramster cast Chalmers as the star of a South Sea island romance, in which four men and a young woman are marooned after a shipwreck and a struggle ensues between the men to claim the woman. Interiors were shot at the Palmerston studio, Waverley, which E. J. Carroll had sold to two young newsreel cameramen, Jack Bruce and E. R. Jeffree. The film opened at the Empress Theatre, Sydney, on 24 June 1922, but as usual, Ramster's work was not widely shown and aroused minimal public interest.

194 A Rough Passage

1922 FRANKLYN BARRETT

PC: Barrett's Australian Productions. P, PH: Franklyn Barrett. From the novel by Arthur Wright. 6000 ft.

CAST: Stella Southern (Doiya Reylen), Hayford Hobbs (Larry Larand), Elsa Granger (Belle Delair), Arthur Albert ('Poverty Point'), Gilbert Emery (Jiggy Javitts), Alma Rock Phillips, Robert MacKinnon, David Edelsten, Sybil Shirley, Billy Ryan.

Barrett's last feature was an undistinguished race-track melodrama that showed obvious signs of haste and carelessness. Based on a novel by Arthur Wright published in 1920, it told the story of Larry Larand, a returned soldier down on his luck, who finds work at a training stable in Sydney. With his comic offsider, an unemployed actor nicknamed 'Poverty Point', Larry learns that the stable is not managed on strictly honourable lines. Among the victims of the stable's crooked dealings is none other than Larry's sweetheart, Doiya, whose horse has been stolen by the villains.

Everyones, 26 July 1922, was scarcely impressed by the tale: 'too much use is made of allegedly humorous interpolations. Working along melodramatic lines, the continuity promises well, but breaks away into the meaningless at times.' The part of the ex-soldier was played by an English actor, Hayford Hobbs. After touring Australia some ten years earlier with Oscar Asche's theatrical company, he had acted in several British films and returned to Australia late in 1921, where he was engaged by Barrett. Later in 1922 he left for Hollywood, where he acted in minor roles for several years. The film was shot in the first months of 1922 and distributed by Barrett himself. It opened simultaneously at two Sydney theatres, the Rialto and the Majestic, on 22 July 1922. *Theatre*, 1 August 1922, reported that it drew 'big houses', but it does not seem to have been promoted actively or screened widely. The production company closed down and Barrett's career as a feature director came to an end.

195 A Daughter of Australia

1922 LAWSON HARRIS

PC: Austral Super Films. P: Lawson Harris. SC: Dulcie Deamer, Albert Goldie. PH: Arthur Higgins. PROPS: Jack Miller. 7000 ft.

CAST: Lawson Harris (Hugh Ranleigh), Yvonne Pavis (Barbara Fullerton), Charles Beetham (Mr Fullerton), Gilbert Emery (Jimmy), J. P. O'Neill (Irishman), Lillian Tate, Diana Templeton, Dorothy Hawtree, Charles Villiers.

The plot follows familiar lines: a young Englishman, falsely accused of murder, eludes the police by emigrating to Australia. There he finds work on a cattle station and befriends the squatter's daughter, Barbara, whom he had previously met in England. Being an honourable youth, he cannot propose marriage while the murder charge hangs over him, but after several melodramatic incidents the way is cleared for a happy ending.

Like Austral Super's first production, *Circumstance* (1922), *A Daughter of Australia* was shot speedily in the open to keep overhead costs to a minimum. Locations in Sydney included the Ascot racecourse and the Easter Agricultural Show. Other scenes were shot on the Dalkeith Station near Mudgee. Although local producers frequently experienced difficulty in gaining official permission to stage scenes in public places, the American film-makers of *A Daughter of Australia* readily

195 *A Daughter of Australia* Lawson Harris confers with Gilbert Emery

obtained help from the authorities, and the police even permitted the staging of a gunfight in Martin Place in the midst of Sydney's rush hour, which caused considerable confusion; two extras on horseback were injured.

Distributed by Austral Super, the film played an unusually long season of four weeks at the Apollo Theatre, Sydney, commencing on 2 September 1922. Critics were not impressed, and although *Everyones*, 6 September 1922, found the work of the cast 'first class', the story was 'somewhat unconvincing at times'.

196 East Lynne

1922 CHARLES HARDY

P: Charles Hardy. From the novel by Mrs Henry Wood. PH: Ernest Higgins. 6 reels.
CAST: Ethel Jerdan, Don McAlpine

The novel by Mrs Henry Wood, first published in 1861, had become the archetypal Victorian melodrama and a perennial favourite of stage and screen producers, with at least seven American film versions and five more in England. The story offered much scope for heart-rending emotion: Isobel Vane is seduced away from her happy marriage by a black-hearted villain, Sir Francis Levison, who convinces her that her husband, Richard, is unfaithful. Later she is abandoned by Sir Francis and she returns home in disguise, only to find that Richard has assumed her to be dead and has remarried. Posing as a nurse, she saves the life of one of her own children, but falls seriously ill. On her deathbed she is recognized by Richard, who solemnly keeps her shame a secret.

This sole feature financed and directed by Charles Hardy was an attempt to update *East Lynne* to a modern setting. The cast was led by Ethel Jerdan, a young Australian who had already played a few bit parts in Hollywood. Shooting on locations in Vaucluse, Sydney, and in a studio at the Showground was completed in the early months of 1922, but release was delayed until 18 November, when it opened simultaneously at two minor Sydney theatres, the Melba and the Apollo, as a supporting feature. *Everyones*, 29 November 1922, reported it as a total commercial failure, one of the 'biggest flivvers' in the history of the unfortunate theatres. Commercial results had not been helped by the release of a well-publicized American version of the same story earlier in the year.

Charles Hardy had acted in several early but unidentified Australian films shot by Johnson and Gibson in Melbourne, and had worked extensively as a travelling exhibitor. He later joined J. C. Williamson as an actor, and moved from the stage to film production in 1922. After the failure of *East Lynne* he entered the film distribution trade as Victorian manager for the American company, Selznick Pictures, and became Australian manager in 1926.

197 Sunshine Sally**

1922 LAWSON HARRIS

PC: Austral Super Films. P: Lawson Harris, Yvonne Pavis. SC: John Cosgrove. PH: Arthur Higgins. ASST D: Clyde Marsh. 5000 ft.
CAST: Yvonne Pavis (Sal), Joy Revelle (Tottie Faye), John Cosgrove (Spud Murphy), Dinks Patterson (Skinny Smith), Mrs Hutton (Katie Smith), J. P. O'Neill (Bill Smith), Sheila Moore (Mrs Constance Stanton), Lionel Lunn (Basil Stanton), Mervyn Barrington (James Stanton), Maude Ranier (Salvation Army woman).

The story crosscuts between the narrow streets and shanties of Woolloomooloo and the spacious gardens and wealthy houses of Potts Point as the lives of four typical citizens of the 'Loo gradually become entangled with a rich and respectable family. Sal and her friend Tottie are sacked from their jobs in a laundry, but their spirits improve on a picnic with their larrikin friends, Skinny Smith and Spud Murphy. Skinny and Spud are rivals for Sal's affections but she is not interested in either of their proposals of marriage. One day

197 *Sunshine Sally* John Cosgrove (*l*), J. P. O'Neill, Yvonne Pavis

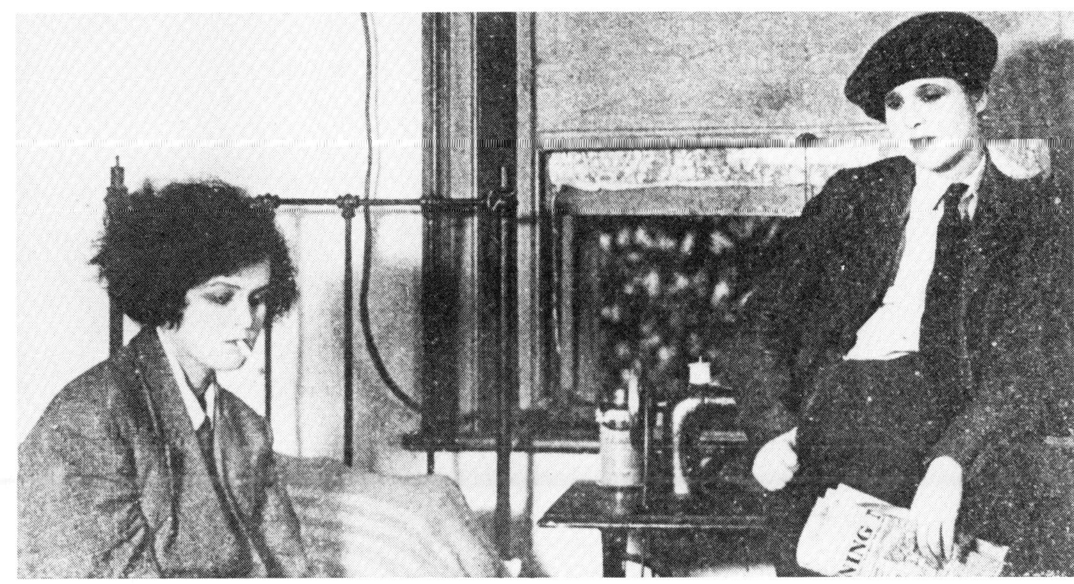

197 ***Sunshine Sally*** Joy Revelle (*l*), Yvonne Pavis

she is rescued from the surf at Coogee by a bronzed lifesaver, Basil Stanton, and is taken to his wealthy Potts Point home to recuperate. Despite the social gap between them, they fall in love and are married. Meanwhile, Spud and Skinny are thrown in jail for drunkenness and emerge reformed men: Spud marries Tottie, and Skinny is taken in tow by a Salvation Army lass.

Although owing much to *The Sentimental Bloke* (1919), *Sunshine Sally* offered a charming portrait of life in the 'Loo, with a rich variety of affectionate incident and detail: the work of Spud and Skinny as hawkers, with a horse that imitates Skinny's habit of crossing his legs whenever he pauses for a chat; the boat-ride and the games on the picnic; Spud and Skinny's drunken delirium at the time of their arrest; and the comical attempts of Sal to learn etiquette in the Stanton home. Much of the film is preserved today in the National Film Archive and it is clearly a work of confident professionalism, offering a perceptive portrait of a distinctively Australian lifestyle. The American star, Yvonne Pavis, and her American director, Lawson Harris, had not only sympathy and clarity of vision but also the ability to express themselves effectively on film, creating credible characters and capturing thoroughly colloquial dialogue in the intertitles.

The film was shot in October and November 1922 under the title of *Winnie of Woolloomooloo*, with the vaudeville comedian Dinks Patterson making his film debut as Skinny. Some studio interiors were shot late at night because of John Cosgrove's commitment to appear on stage in *Cairo* each day at a city theatre. Yvonne Pavis boasted with justifiable pride that she and Harris had succeeded in persuading the authorities to allow them to shoot scenes inside the Long Bay Gaol, the first time film-producers had been given such a privilege. Distributed directly by the production company, the film opened at the Haymarket Theatre, Sydney, on 16 December 1922, but the theatre was not the most suitable, and the publicity was insufficient to make the film a commercial success. In the last week of December, Yvonne Pavis left Sydney to arrange distribution of her films in the U.S.A. Although she announced an intention to return and establish a production company of her own, she remained in America and was joined there by Lawson Harris. They soon married in Los Angeles, but were divorced by 1925. Their subsequent involvement in American production was never more than marginal, for example in B-grade Westerns such as *Law or Loyalty*, which Harris directed in 1926.

198 The Lust for Gold

1922 ROY DARLING

PC: Olympic Films.
CAST: Dorothy Hawtree, Gilbert Emery, Charles Villiers.

Little is known about this melodrama. According to the director's evidence before the 1927 Royal Commission into the film industry, he invested £400 of his own capital towards the total production cost of £900 and lost it all. Union Theatres failed to take up the film and it was given an unrewarding première season at a minor independent theatre, the Shell, in Sydney, some time in 1922.

Born in England, Roy Darling acted in several films in South Africa and made a feature length documentary, *Beasts in the Jungle* (*c.*1918), in India. He came to Australia early in 1922. Despite the failure of *The Lust for Gold*, he persevered with a second feature, *Daughter of the East* (1924), but the results were scarcely better. He then established his own distribution company, Blue Bird Films, but allegedly because of pressure from the combine, the company was soon wound up. During the rest of his career he worked primarily on documentaries and commercials, and was involved also in theatre management in Sydney. In 1947 he attempted to set up another feature production, *Intimate Stranger*, and although he directed a few scenes, the film was never completed. He died in Sydney in 1956.

199 The Dinkum Bloke

1923 RAYMOND LONGFORD

PC: Longford-Lyell Australian Productions.
SC: Raymond Longford, Lottie Lyell. PH: Lacey Percival.
ASST D: Lottie Lyell. 7248 ft.
CAST: Arthur Tauchert (Bill Garvin), Lottie Lyell (Nell Garvin), Beryl Gow (Peggy Garvin aged 7), Lotus Thompson (Peggy Garvin aged 17), Jack Raymond (John Gilder), Rene Sandeman (Mrs Gilder), Cecil Scott (Geoffrey Gilder), Dorothy Daye (Joy Gilder).

The formation of the Longford-Lyell production company with capital of £50 000 was announced in May 1922, a bad time in the industry, for in the same month Franklyn Barrett's company was closing its Sydney office. In their first film, Longford and Lyell made a valiant attempt to repeat the success they had had with *The Sentimental Bloke* (1919), and their script aimed at a similar degree of simplicity and homeliness.

Bill Garvin, a Sydney dock-worker, is happy in his Woolloomooloo home with his loving, hard-working wife, Nell, and their little daughter, Peggy. Nell falls ill, however, and dies after an operation. Her last wish is that Peggy should be brought up to be a lady. Bill sells the little home in order to place Peggy in an expensive convent school, but soon finds he must work after hours as a street-singer to pay for the fees. Ten years pass and Peggy, now grown into a lovely young woman, spends a vacation on a Queensland property with a school-friend, Joy Gilder. Joy's brother, Geoffrey, falls in love with Peggy and Geoffrey's parents approve of their engagement. A dinner is planned at the Gilders' city home at Potts Point, and Bill is invited. He buys a second-hand ill-fitting dinner suit and studies a book on etiquette, but he is not a social success at

199 *The Dinkum Bloke* Beryl Gow, Arthur Tauchert, Lottie Lyell (*r*)

the dinner party, and he leaves ashamed of his poor showing and Peggy's evident embarrassment. The crisis worsens when the Gilders discover Bill singing on a street corner. Peggy breaks off the engagement and returns to the convent, where, despite Geoffrey's pleas, she determines to remain. Bill is aghast at the unhappiness he has caused, but finds inspiration in a story-book, *The Prince and the Beggar Maid*, which he had once given to Peggy years ago. He confronts the Gilders and tells them that Peggy is not his daughter at all but that her parents were 'swell English people' and that she was adopted by the Garvins when her mother died and her father returned to England. The Gilders gladly believe the story, and Bill visits Nell's grave to announce that her wishes have been carried out. Peggy, now accepted as a lady, is married to Geoffrey.

Longford used the studio of Australasian Films, as well as their cameraman and laboratory, in the hope that this would encourage Australasian to distribute the film. Of the film's £4800 production cost, £2100 was paid to Australasian. Other costs were kept to a minimum by shooting most of the film on locations in the streets of Sydney and Woolloomooloo. However, even after a highly successful trade screening in Sydney in December, Australasian refused to handle the film. Not until seven months later did it secure its release through Paramount Pictures, with a première at Hoyts Theatre De Luxe, Sydney, on 2 June 1923. In less than sixteen months the film returned nearly £6000 to the producers, and before the end of 1923 Gaumont paid £2300 for distribution rights in Britain, where it was released as *A Gentleman in Mufti* in February 1924.

Reviews were unanimous in their praise. The *Evening News*, 14 December 1922, described it as 'a very sincere record of the spirit of Sydney city life', and the British trade paper, *Bioscope*, 15 November 1923, concurred: 'The charm of the picture lies in its intense sincerity . . . The plot is conventional and, on analysis, not too convincing, but it is presented with such perfectly natural feeling, and such a wealth of good humour, that it will strike a responsive chord in the heart of even the most sophisticated audiences.' Despite this praiseworthy début, Longford's backers were reluctant to continue with production. By June 1924 the company was in liquidation, but Longford and Lyell continued in partnership, in a new but similarly named company, Longford-Lyell Productions.

200 The Dingo

1923 KENNETH BRAMPTON

PC: British-Australasian Photoplays. SC: Kenneth Brampton, Phyllis Coughlan. PH: Lacey Percival. ART D: Edward Lyon. 6 reels.

CAST: George Edwards (Harry Selby), Phyllis Coughlan (Audrey Onslow), William Coulter (Oily Allen), Sybil Shirley, Godfrey Cass, Gordon Collingridge, Charles Beetham, Fred Twitcham, Jackie Anderson, Lena Edwards, James Bendrodt, Peggy Dawes.

A drunken ne'er-do-well from the city, Harry Selby (nicknamed 'the dingo'), ensnares a country girl in marriage, although knowing that her affections lie elsewhere. She later gives birth to a daughter but dies when she learns that Harry has been arrested on a murder charge. His death sentence is commuted to life imprisonment and after eighteen years in jail he emerges to find that his daughter has been adopted by his former rival, a country doctor. Harry overcomes his hatred for the doctor, and seeing his love for the girl, refrains from revealing that he is her real father. The film ends happily with the marriage of his daughter to a worthy young man.

Most of the film was shot on location near Mudgee, N.S.W., in October 1922. The cast included the director's wife, Phyllis Coughlan, who was a professional Sydney journalist and collaborator on the screenplay. A ballroom scene interpolated into the plot featured a prize-winning dance duo, James Bendrodt and Peggy Dawes. Distribution was undertaken by a new but short-lived firm, Duncan and Jones, and the film premièred at the Lyric Theatre, Sydney, on 23 June 1923. Although not a commercial success, and destined to screen only in minor theatres, it was given some encouragement by *Everyones*, 27 June 1923: 'Although dealing with a somewhat sordid type of characters, the story is not devoid of a great amount of interest . . . The one outstanding feature . . . is the fine character interpretation given by George Edwards.'

201 The Twins

1923 LESLIE McCALLUM

PC: Blue Gum Company, for the Charity Moving Picture Society. SC: Ray Whiting. PH: Leslie McCallum. ASST D: Aubrey Gibson.

CAST: Ray Whiting and Jim Paxton (the twins), Cath McMicking (heroine), Aubrey Gibson (villain), Doreen Gale (vamp), Jim Doods (Horace Hothouse), Keith McHarg, Billy Begg, Norman Carlyon.

This farce-melodrama was produced by a Melbourne cinematographer, Leslie McCallum, with amateur actors and crew. The story contrasted the backblocks with the social whirl of the city, and characters included 'a female vampire' who kills herself after 'a life of intrigue, wickedness, and cigarettes'. The film was intended to raise funds for various charities, including the Melbourne Women's Hospital. Support was received from the popular Carlyon's ballroom at St Kilda; a member of the Carlyon family appeared in the film, and at the ballroom on 19 June 1923 a 'Twins' ball was held. Sections of the film were also screened there to promote the première at the Melbourne Town Hall on 28 June. The film apparently served its purpose well, and press reports indicated that 'a considerable sum' was raised from 'a large and appreciative audience'.

200 *The Dingo*

202 Townies and Hayseeds

1923 BEAUMONT SMITH

PC: Beaumont Smith's Productions. P, SC: Beaumont Smith. PH: Arthur Higgins. 5000 ft.

CAST: George Edwards (Pa Townie), J. P. O'Neill (Dad Hayseed), Pinky Weatherley (Mum Hayseed), Ada St Claire (Ma Townie), Lotus Thompson (Adelaide Townie), W. J. Newman (Choom), Gordon Collingridge (George Fisher), Ena Aldworth, J. Rayner, Freddie Tauchert, Gwen Gamble, Matthew Gamble, Jim Coleman, Gloria Lloyd Weatherley, Jack Tauchert, Harold Parkes.

Beaumont Smith's new episode in the Hayseeds series was a pastiche of situations used in his earlier films. As in *The Hayseeds Come to Sydney* (1917), the comedy derived mainly from city-country contrasts, with Pa Townie taking his family into the country for a holiday and then inviting the Hayseeds to the city. A romantic triangle added a loose link to the episodes, with one of Townie's daughters (named Adelaide because she is so 'cultured') being courted both by a returned soldier and a 'pommy new chum'.

In addition to the familiar characters of the Hayseeds and the new chum, the film offered broad satire of city-dwellers. Pa Townie was conceived as 'a typical Sydney native; one of the sort that reads the "Sydney Morning Herald", belongs to the Millions Club, plays golf, goes to the office at 9.30, comes home punctually at five (and never tarries by the wayside), and goes to the Town Hall Organ Recitals'. His children were patriotically named after each state capital: Sydney, Melbourne, Adelaide, Brissy, Perth and Hobart.

The film offered one of Smith's most remarkable feats of production expediency, for it was written, produced and sold within the space of five weeks. Shooting began early in May 1923 on locations in and near Sydney, and a month later a print was assembled and shown to the trade. Within minutes of the preview, Stuart Doyle of Union Theatres offered to screen the film throughout New South Wales. The rights to the other states and to New Zealand were also promptly sold.

Made to be laughed at!

"Any chance of a job on your Bally ranch, old top?"

TOWNIES and HAYSEEDS

Lavishly promoted, it opened simultaneously at the Lyceum and Lyric Theatres, Sydney, on 7 July. For the Melbourne release, Smith reconstructed the film, replacing Sydney references with Melbourne equivalents. New scenes and titles were shot only a few days before the Melbourne opening at the Melba Theatre on 13 August. The public welcomed it as enthusiastically as the trade had anticipated, and Smith moved quickly on to another Hayseeds comedy. *Everyones*, 11 July 1923, acknowledged its commercial value, but indicated that it was a true Smith production, with its humour 'due more to the cleverly written sub-titles than to most of the actual episodes themselves'.

203 When the Kellys Were Out**

1923 HARRY SOUTHWELL

P, SC: Harry Southwell. PH: Tasman Higgins. 8 reels.

CAST: Godfrey Cass (Ned Kelly), Rose Rooney (Kate Kelly), Harry Southwell (Aaron Sherritt), Charles Villiers (Dan Kelly), William Ellison (Steve Hart), Allan Douglas (Joe Byrne), Fred Twitcham (Constable McIntyre), Syd Everett (Sergeant Steele), Mervyn Barrington (Sergeant Kennedy), W. Ryan (Fitzpatrick), Don McAlpine (Scanlan), D. Sweeney (Lonergan), Rita Aslin (Mrs Kelly), Dunstan Webb (Superintendent Nicolson), Beatrice Hamilton (Mrs Byrne), David Edelsten (the judge).

Southwell's second adaptation of the Kelly story appeared only two years after the first. The cast was entirely new except for Godfrey Cass, once more in the role of Ned. Southwell himself again appeared, but this time as the traitor Aaron Sherritt. The film was made in Sydney and on location in the Burragorang Valley, and shooting was completed by late September 1922.

Although Southwell's first Kelly film screened unhindered by the New South Wales censors, this new version was promptly banned in October 1922. The first commercial screening was not until 9 July 1923 at a minor Melbourne theatre, the Star. Despite lengthy warnings in the film about the dangers of following the Kellys' example, it had a marked capacity to arouse audience sympathy for the outlaws, a fact of which the censors were doubtless fully aware. In Adelaide, the *Advertiser*, 18 September 1923, commented that 'there was no doubt as to the popularity of the picture'; the anger of the Kellys at insults given to their sister by the police 'won them the sympathy of the audience', and the

Kellys' murder of Aaron Sherritt received 'numerous signs of approval'. Soon after the completion of the film, Southwell departed for England, and in August 1924 it was shown to the British trade. Scathing criticism was received from one reviewer (reported in *Everyones*, 8 October 1924) for its lack of historical accuracy—the exaggerated claims of the number of police killed by the Kellys, the 'incorrect' police uniforms, the representation of the large Jerilderie Hotel as 'a small shanty', and the reshuffling of the actual chronology of events. Less informed members of the British trade, however, accepted the film more kindly as 'an undoubtedly good showman's proposition . . . [The] fights are realistic, and the hard riding with which the picture is interspersed is far above the average Western in its genuine horsemanship.' The film was shortened to six reels for the British market, and it seems likely that the fragments held by the National Film Archive of Australia are part of the British version, released as *The True Story of the Kelly Gang*.

204 Should a Doctor Tell?

1923 P. J. RAMSTER

PC: P. J. Ramster Photoplays. P, SC: P. J. Ramster. PH: Jack Bruce, E. R. Jeffree.
CAST: Fred Oppey (Dr Stirling Worth), Thelma Newling, Verna Haines, Anne Parsons, Teddy Austin (Bennie the cripple).

Inspired by a contemporary controversy about the rights of doctors to withhold information about their patients, Ramster's film was promoted with the same prurient exuberance that other film-makers had brought to social problems in *Remorse* (1917) and *Know Thy Child* (1921). The story was unabashed Victorian melodrama, complete with a reprobate count, an innocent woman and a little crippled child. Dr Mather, an advocate of compulsory medical examinations for both sexes before marriage, consents to the marriage of his daughter, Dorothy, to Count Delvo, on condition that he can present a clean bill of health. The count reluctantly agrees, and because of his past dissipation, is found to be infected with venereal disease. His doctor, Stirling Worth, advises him to postpone the wedding, but the count refuses and insists that Worth remain silent. Worth, however, is himself in love with Dorothy and is haunted by a vision of a crippled child, who represents the inevitable consequence of the marriage. On the very day of the wedding, Dr Worth overcomes his professional scruples and dramatically denounces the count. In a fury, the count shoots the doctor, who falls mortally wounded into Dorothy's arms. The police arrest the count and he receives his just deserts.

The film was made for less than £1000 and included, as usual in Ramster's productions, many recruits from Sydney's high society and graduates from his acting school. The New South Wales censors commended the film for its 'good moral lesson' and for the 'decorum' with which it depicted the iniquitous life of the count; the scenes relating to venereal disease were also treated with 'becoming restraint, the allusions . . . being easy to follow'. Released on 18 August 1923 at the Rialto Theatre, Sydney, it was screened widely interstate and was possibly the most commercially successful of Ramster's films.

205 Australia Calls

1923 RAYMOND LONGFORD

PC: Commonwealth Immigration Office/British Empire Exhibition Commission. SC: Lottie Lyell. PH: Arthur Higgins. ASST D: Fred Twitcham. 4000 ft.
CAST: Ernest Idiens.

To supplement the huge display of Australian produce and resources at the British Empire Exhibition in London in 1924, the Australian government prepared a number of films for continuous screening in the Australian Pavilion. Among the films were two by Raymond Longford depicting Australian industry and society, *Australia Calls* (not to be confused with his film of the same title in 1913) and *An Australian by Marriage*. Originally Longford was commissioned to make four films, each of 4000 feet, and each costing £1500, to be funded jointly by the Exhibition Commission and the Commonwealth Immigration Office. However, when bad weather caused delays in the production of the first two films, the government handed the remaining projects over to the official government cinematographer, Bert Ive.

Australia Calls, narrating 'the experiences in New South Wales of a successful immigrant', was a semi-documentary, with the chosen 'new Australian', a farmer, Ernest Idiens, re-enacting events from his own life. Shooting began in March 1923 at the country town of Harden, N.S.W., and the film was completed by June, some six weeks behind schedule. The second film, *An Australian by Marriage* was made immediately afterwards, but very little is known about it. In September, ministerial approval was given for the theatrical release of the films within Australia, and *Australia Calls* opened on 24 November as a supporting feature at the Rialto Theatre, Sydney, advertised as a 'story of grit and industry in this land of promise'. It is doubtful whether many Australians saw it then or later, but next year in London, between June and October, the official film screenings were consistently well-attended, attracting a large proportion of the 14 million people who passed through the Australian pavilion during the exhibition.

206 Prehistoric Hayseeds

1923 BEAUMONT SMITH

PC: Beaumont Smith's Productions. P, SC: Beaumont Smith. PH: Lacey Percival. 5000 ft.
CAST: Hector St Clair (Wup), Lotus Thompson (the Golden Girl), Gordon Collingridge (Owen Osborne), J. P. O'Neill (Dad Hayseed), Kathleen Mack (Mrs Wup), Roy Wilson (Beetle Brows), Pinky Weatherley (Mum Hayseed), Nina Dacre (Tessie Worth), Dunstan Webb (Terry).

A university student, Owen Osborne, investigates claims that a prehistoric race still lives in the Australian outback. With the aid of the Hayseeds, he finds the sole surviving family of the lost tribe, the Wups, living in a cave and wearing clothes made of rabbit-skin. Romance instantly flourishes between Owen and the Wups' daughter, the 'Golden Girl'. Hanging a 'To Let' sign over the cave entrance, the Wups go with the Hayseeds to discover city life, and much comic confusion follows. One of the prehistorics, Beetle Brows, helps a gang of crooks to steal diamonds from the cave and to kidnap the Golden Girl. She is eventually rescued by Owen and the crooks are arrested. A cheerful celebration follows at the Artists' Ball, enjoyed by both the Wups and the Hayseeds.

The central comic notion of stone-age characters thrown into a modern world was familiar from Hollywood and British comedies, among them Buster Keaton's much-publicized *Three Ages*, released in America early in September 1923, which probably provided Smith with his direct inspiration. The film was shot in October 1923, partly on location at Port Hacking. Scenes in the Sydney streets aroused much public attention with the unexpected appearance of cavemen in rabbit-skin costumes. In the past, Australian producers had often fallen foul of administrative red-tape in using public buildings for location shooting, but with this production Smith seems to have suffered more than most: one official barred the use of the Randwick racecourse when he realized that the film-makers were staging anything but racing scenes. The Sydney Town Clerk also forbad the use of the Town Hall for the sequence of the Artists' Ball, and at the last moment Smith was forced to reassemble his sets in the Rushcutters Bay studio. Despite these problems, Smith completed the film with characteristic speed, and it was ready for censorship screening on 7 November. The New South Wales censors insisted on the deletion of a political joke, expressed in an intertitle, referring to the former Prime Minister, William Morris Hughes, and his alleged acceptance of £25 000 from improper sources. As with *Townies and Hayseeds* earlier in the year, Smith was able to dispose of the state and New Zealand rights with ease, and it opened at the Globe Theatre, Sydney, on 24 November for a two-week season. The results, however, fell below expectations and Smith did not return to the backblocks genre until his talkie version of *The Hayseeds* in 1934.

206 *Prehistoric Hayseeds* Hector St Clair (*l*), Lotus Thompson, Kathleen Mack (women in foreground), Gordon Collingridge (*r*)

207 The Digger Earl**

1924 BEAUMONT SMITH

PC: Beaumont Smith's Productions. P, SC: Beaumont Smith. TECHNICAL D: Fred Coleman. PH: Lacey Percival. FURNISHINGS: M. O'Callaghan. ASST D: Dunstan Webb, Gordon Smith.
CAST: Arthur Tauchert (Bill Jones), Gordon Collingridge (the Earl of Margate), Lotus Thompson (Betty Roberts), Heather Jones (Winnie), Doris Gilham (the Duchess of Margate), Dunstan Webb (Captain Halliday), Robert Purdie (Mr Halliday), Reg Wykeham (Brigadier-General), J. P. O'Neill.

Although the wartime trenches and city settings for this comedy were far from Smith's usual Hayseeds territory, his characters were again based on broad national stereotypes. The comedy arose primarily from the idea of placing 'the sentimental bloke' amongst the British aristocracy. Bill Jones is a typical Aussie who sets off for the war in Europe, promising to return a hero to his girlfriend Winnie. The end of the war, however, finds him penniless and stranded in London. He joins the crew of a boat bound for Australia, and on board meets the Earl of Margate, a 'fairly democratic fellow' in search of adventure 'down under'. Hoping to avoid publicity, the Earl persuades Bill to take his place, while he acts as his valet. When the boat reaches Sydney, many comic and romantic complications arise as Bill tries to efface his natural self and rise to Australian expectations of the British nobility. Eventually all is happily resolved and Bill is reunited with his beloved Winnie.

Shooting began in January 1924 at the Rushcutters Bay studio and on locations around Sydney. Newsreel footage was used for the re-creation of wartime Australia, and scenes of trench warfare on the Front were staged on military training grounds at Liverpool, near Sydney. Part of the first reel exists today in the National Film Archive, Canberra, and reveals a dull film with austere sets and heavily stressed performances. The film opened on 12 April at two Sydney theatres, the Lyceum and the new Lyric Wintergarden.

207 *The Digger Earl* Arthur Tauchert

A stage prologue at the Lyceum included a personal appearance by Tauchert and a song composed by Emmanuel Aarons, with lyrics by Beaumont Smith, 'Australia Means Heaven to Me'.

208 Dope

1924 DUNSTAN WEBB

PC: Australasian Picture Productions. SC: Con Drew. PH: Lacey Percival.
CAST: Gordon Collingridge (Tom Searle), Lorraine Esmond (Mildred Murnin), Monica Mack, Robert Purdie, Charles Villiers, Jack Raymond, William Newman, J. N. Tait.

Hugh Murnin is a wealthy and trusted citizen of Sydney, but in his past lies a dissolute life as a pearler on Thursday Island and a drunken brawl in which he believes he killed a man. One of his former drinking mates, Slick Harvey, finds Murnin and blackmails him. Harvey also tries to force his attentions on Murnin's daughter, Mildred, but her fiancé, Tom Searle, curtails his evil doings by exposing him as the leader of a gang of opium smugglers. Harvey is arrested and it is revealed that he, not Murnin, killed the man on Thursday Island. Murnin is relieved of a ghost from his past and the young lovers are happily married.

The story, by a Sydney sports journalist and novelist, Con Drew, was produced by Australasian Picture Productions (quite distinct from Australasian Films) under the working title *The Trail of the Twang.* Shooting was completed in April 1923, but it was not released until 26 July 1924, when it opened as a poorly advertised support at the Lyric Wintergarden Theatre, Sydney. The *Bulletin,* 31 July 1924, commented that the story 'is little better than a sensational front-page scoop in a yellow newspaper, and there is a lot wanting on the technical side'.

209 Joe

1924 BEAUMONT SMITH

PC: Beaumont Smith's Productions. P, SC: Beaumont Smith. From the story collections, *Joe Wilson* and *Joe Wilson's Mates,* by Henry Lawson. PH: Lacey Percival. 5000(?) ft.
CAST: Arthur Tauchert (Joe Wilson), Marie Lorraine (Barbara), Constance Graham (Mary Wilson), Gordon Collingridge, Fernande Butler, Hal Scott, Dunstan Webb.

The plot was based only nominally on Lawson, and owed more to characters and a city-country contrast familiar from Beaumont Smith's slapstick farces. Despite the title, the emphasis seems to have been on women, and the advertising compared the 'gaily dressed' women who 'dance and revel' in the city, with 'their weary, worn, overworked sisters [who] slave in the Bush' (*Everyones,* 13 August 1924). Joe Wilson is a farm hand who marries Mary, a housekeeper for an old squatter named Black, and takes up a selection to begin his own farm. Harry, Black's son, falls in love with Mary's sister, Barbara, but she refuses to join him in his dissipated life in the city. As the film progresses, Harry learns to mend his ways, and becomes a fitting husband for Barbara. The highlights of the action include a high society ball in the city, and a fierce bushfire, which nearly destroys Joe's little homestead.

Shooting began in mid-June 1924 on location in the Burragorang Valley near Sydney, and with interiors at the Rushcutters Bay studio of Australasian Films. The bushfire was described by the New South Wales censor as 'a wonderful fake of cinematic art by means of smoke-screens and imitation fires'. But if care was taken with technical effects, shooting on location was conducted with Smith's usual notorious speed. The grand ball was shot at the Ambassador's Dance Palais in one long, hectic day; according to *Everyones,* 16 July 1924, Smith completed fifty-seven separate 'scenes' in fourteen hours. Distributed directly by Smith's own company, the film was screened widely through the Union Theatres

209 *Joe* Connie Graham, Arthur Tauchert

circuit, commencing with the Lyceum and Lyric Wintergarden Theatres, Sydney, on 23 August 1924.

Joe received more favourable critical comment than most of Smith's work, and the *Bulletin*, 28 August 1924, praised it as his best film yet, 'a faithful reflection of the spirit of the pioneers who battle in the open spaces, with a broad vein of humor running through it'. The cast introduced Marie Lorraine (stage name of Isobel McDonagh), who was soon to enter production herself in 1925, with her sisters, Phyllis and Paulette.

210 Daughter of the East [The Boy of the Dardanelles]

1924 ROY DARLING

PC: Blue Bird Films. P, SC, ART D: Adam Tavlaridi. PH: Tasman Higgins.

CAST: Dorothy Hawtree, Paul Eden, Catherine Tearle, Charles Villiers, Adam Tavlaridi.

The film was written and financed by a Greek café proprietor, Adam Tavlaridi, who wished to make a film showing the positive contribution of the Greek people to the British war effort. The story's young hero is Harry Wharton, born of English parents in Turkey. Just before the outbreak of war he falls in love with an orphaned Armenian girl, Marian, even though he is formally engaged to an Englishwoman. A powerful Turkish pasha also loves Marian and kidnaps her. Wharton tries to rescue her but is captured as a prisoner of war at the moment when war is declared between Britain and Turkey. Eventually he escapes and, disguised as a Greek, makes his way to join the Australians at Anzac Cove. After the war, Wharton tries to find Marian and learns that her mind has been affected by the trials of the war. His appearance brings back memories to her of their happy pre-war days, and seeing how much Wharton and Marian love each other, his stoic English fiancée gives him his freedom.

Roy Darling's reconstruction of the war was attempted at a time when other Australian film-makers were studiously avoiding war themes, in the belief that the war was too close and too bitter to attract an audience. The film was produced in and around Sydney in mid-1923, with battle scenes staged in the sand hills of Maroubra. Under the title of *The Boy of the Dardanelles* it was given a trade preview in October, but reactions were evidently discouraging enough to prevent release for a full year. It finally appeared under a new title, *Daughter of the East*, at the Globe Theatre, Sydney, on 4 October 1924. Press comments were unflattering and the film was not widely shown.

211 Fisher's Ghost

1924 RAYMOND LONGFORD

PC: Longford-Lyell Productions. ASSOC P: Charles Perry. SC: Raymond Longford. PH: Arthur Higgins. 5000 ft.

CAST: Robert Purdie (George Worrall), Fred Twitcham (Fisher), Lorraine Esmond, Percy Walshe, William Ryan, Ted Ayr, William Coulter, Charles Keegan, Ruby Dellew, Ada St Claire, Charlotte Beaumont, Ike Beck, Joe Seaton, Nellie Weldon.

In 1826, in Campbelltown, N.S.W., a settler named Farley is accosted late one night by an apparition. The ghost claims to be the spirit of Frederick Fisher, in search of vengeance for his murder at the hands of George Worrall. The ghost leads Farley along a creek bank to a spot where Fisher's body is later recovered from the water. Ghost or no ghost, Farley's experience leads to the arrest, trial and execution of Worrall.

The Longford-Lyell team were joined in their new production venture by Charles Perry, and the modest sum of £1000 was spent on the film. Location scenes were shot at Campbelltown, and the film was completed in August 1924. Longford experienced difficulty in finding an adequate release, and alleged in evidence before the Royal Commission in 1927 that Stuart Doyle of Union Theatres had rejected the film because it was too gruesome for the public, even though the censors had found nothing objectionable in it (*RCE*, p.147). Eventually Longford accepted unfavourable terms from Hoyts and premièred the film at their Theatre De Luxe, Sydney, on 4 October. Audience reaction vindicated Longford's judgement: the tale drew audiences in large numbers and Hoyts announced record takings. Despite such response, distribution problems persisted, and the film was not released in Perth until March 1926. *Everyones*, 8 October 1924, recommended Longford's work to exhibitors: 'There was not a great deal of story to work upon, but the producer has certainly made out a worth-while one, and he has not descended to exaggeration to accomplish this.'

212 The Price

1924 DUNSTAN WEBB

PC: Australian National Films P, SC: Mary Mallon.

CAST: James Alexander, Muriel Copeland, Doris Brooks, Eddie Hamilton (jockey), Bert Ralton and his Havana Band, Jimmy McMahon.

Tom Howard's wealthy parents want him to follow a banking career, but after quarrelling with his father, Tom leaves home to become a jockey. Fortune is against him and he is soon penniless. When he finally decides to return home, he reads in a newspaper that his father and mother have been killed in a motor accident. Ashamed to appear now and claim the inheritance due to him, he buys an old horse and works for a living as a cab-driver in Sydney. After many hardships he is found in hospital by his sister. She persuades him to return home and he is happily reconciled with his former girlfriend.

The film is notable mainly as a rare production by a woman. Mary Mallon formed her own company, Australian National Films, and spent less than £1000 on the first production. Her funds must have been limited, as *Everyones*, 29 October 1924, reported: 'the ending comes somewhat abruptly, due, we are given to understand, by force of circumstances (mainly financial)'. Shooting began early in 1924 with a largely amateur cast under Dunstan Webb's guidance, and it was ready for censor-screening on 2 September. *Everyones* recommended the film to the trade as 'a creditable story, ably re-told [with] many masterly touches of realism', and found 'a big element of box-office value' in its racing scenes. It opened at the Piccadilly Theatre, Sydney, on 18 October and, although not distributed by a major exchange, it reportedly made a modest profit over its low cost.

212 *The Price*

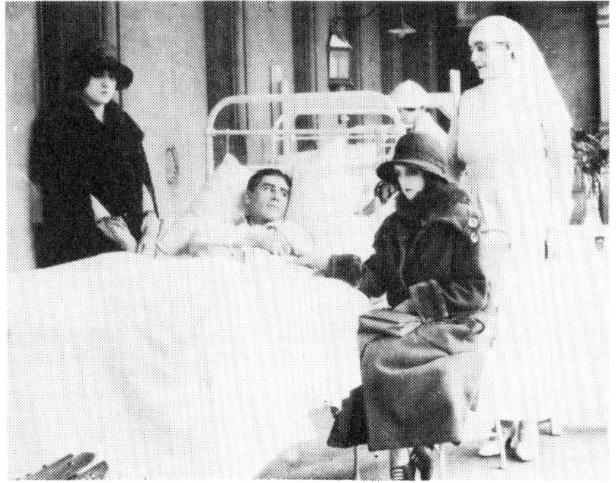

213 The Rev. Dell's Secret

1924 P. J. RAMSTER

PC: P. J. Ramster Photoplays. P, SC: P. J. Ramster. PH: Jack Fletcher. 6000 ft.

CAST: Rex Simpson (David Dell), Thelma Newling (Joyce), William Shepherd, Lyn Salter, Joy Wood.

In this complex melodrama of religion and sex, a zealous missioner in the city underworld strives to save the soul of a young girl who is forced by her evil guardian to dance in a sleazy cabaret. The clergyman is blinded in a fight to defend her, but later has the satisfaction of knowing that she has risen to stardom as a ballerina.

Like Ramster's earlier films, *The Rev. Dell's Secret* was made with an amateur cast drawn largely from his own acting school in Sydney, and cost less than £1000. Commercial release was desultory; distributed by Ramster himself, it opened at the Empress and Piccadilly Theatres, Sydney, on 1 November 1924.

214 How McDougall Topped the Score

1924 V. UPTON BROWN

PC: Pacific Screen Plays. SC: V. Upton Brown. From the poem by Thomas E. Spencer. 5 reels.
CAST: Leslie Gordon (McDougall), Ida Gresham (Mrs McDougall), Dorothy May (Mary McDougall), Wesley Barry (McDougall Jnr), Frank Blandford (Johnstone), William Ralston (Brady), Joy Thompson, Pincher.

A bush cricket match is won by an old Scottish batsman who hits the ball to the boundary, where his sheepdog seizes it. The dog runs away with the ball, with the opposing team in hot pursuit, and the old man has plenty of time to make enough runs to win.

Essentially a one-joke story, already familiar to Australians as a bush ballad, *How McDougall Topped the Score* was not promising material for a five-reel feature, even when padded out with a romantic sub-plot involving the Scotsman's daughter. The scenario and direction were handled by a Victorian actor and exhibitor, V. Upton Brown, and the film was shot for about £800 in the Melbourne suburb of Ashburton and on location in the Dandenong ranges. It premièred at the Grand Theatre, Adelaide, on 10 November 1924, to coincide with the first match between the South Australian cricket team and a visiting English eleven. No further major screenings have been traced.

215 Hullo Marmaduke

1924 BEAUMONT SMITH

PC: Beaumont Smith's Productions. P, SC: Beaumont Smith. 6000 ft.
CAST: Claude Dampier (Marmaduke), Mayne Lynton (Mike Morton), Constance Graham (Mary Morton), Lucille Lisle (Margie), Jimmy Taylor (Huggett), Grafton Williams (Squid Squires), William Coulter, Fernande Butler, Cyril Northcote, Loretta May, J. P. O'Neill, Pinky Weatherley.

Marmaduke is an English 'silly ass', complete with monocle, top hat and cane, an infectious toothy grin, and an appalling naïvety. Claude Dampier had played the character for many years on the vaudeville stage and his first film offered little more than 'the pouring of fresh water over old tea-leaves' (*Bulletin*, 20 November 1924). After his arrival in Australia, Marmaduke goes prospecting in the goldfields where a long-suffering barmaid, on her deathbed, entrusts him with the care of her young daughter. When Marmaduke makes a lucky gold strike, he sends the girl to school in Sydney. There she falls into evil hands and Marmaduke saves her life in a daring rescue from a sinking boat. He later sees her happily married to a wealthy suitor.

The main novelty of the film was the footage, at the climax, of the sinking of HMAS *Australia*. The battleship had been ordered for destruction under the terms of the treaty entered into by the Australian government at the Washington disarmament conference, and was sunk outside Sydney Heads in April 1924. Footage was also taken of HMAS *Pioneer* at the naval base in Sydney, to represent *Australia* before she was sunk.

Interiors were staged in Australasian's studio at Rushcutters Bay, and further shipboard scenes on the liner *Osterley*. Shooting was completed early in October 1924. Wasting no time, Beaumont Smith arranged screenings through Union Theatres, and it opened on 15 November at the Lyceum and Lyric Wintergarden Theatres, Sydney. Stimulated by active promotion, the film proved highly popular, and Smith and Dampier promptly embarked on another 'silly ass' comedy, *The Adventures of Algy* (1925).

216 The Mystery of a Hansom Cab

1925 ARTHUR SHIRLEY

PC: Pyramid Pictures. P, SC: Arthur Shirley. From the novel by Fergus Hume. PH: Lacey Percival. 10 000 (12 000?) ft.
CAST: Arthur Shirley (Brian Fitzgerald), Grace Glover (Madge), Roland Stavely (detective), Cora Warner (Mother Guttersnipe), Isa Crossley (Sal Rawlin), Godfrey Cass, Vera Remée, Isa Millett, Sydney Stirling, Carlton Stuart, Leslie Woods, Frank Barnes, Arthur Orbell, Charles Vincent, John Bruce, Billie Sim.

Arthur Shirley was an ambitious and, judging by his frequent involvement in litigation, aggressive individualist. The rapid rise of his acting career and the praise of contemporary critics suggest a competent acting talent, but after a taste of Hollywood his main interest turned towards production, where his career eventually foundered through bad luck and misjudgement. Born in Hobart, he began acting on the stage as a youth in a Melbourne production of *Sweet Nell of Old Drury* with Nellie Stewart. He subsequently toured with a William Anderson company and played in Sydney with George Marlow and Beaumont Smith. He also won leading roles in two films released in 1914, *The Silence of Dean Maitland* and *The Shepherd of the Southern Cross*. Soon after these films, he left for Hollywood, where he worked for Kalem and Universal, taking prominent roles in several features, including *The Fall of a Nation* (1916) and *Modern Love* (1918). He returned to Australia in April 1920 with plans to establish a major production enterprise in Sydney. Displaying a talent for self-publicity (promoting himself as 'the Big Australian'), Shirley set up temporary studio headquarters in Rose Bay, and began his first ill-fated production, a South Seas romance, *The Throwback*. Shooting began late in 1920, but was beleaguered by law suits and financial problems, and was never completed.

Shirley quickly recovered from the costly fiasco of *The Throwback*, and after acting in several plays (including a production of *The Sentimental Bloke* in Sydney in January 1923),

THEY LAUGHED AT HIM!
Thought him a Goat, a Mug, a Fool, a Simp, a Silly Ass, but—
HE WAS A MAN!

BEAUMONT SMITH
Greets you with a cheery six reel Comedy Drama
"HULLO MARMADUKE"
Featuring
CLAUDE DAMPIER

216 Arthur Shirley

he tried again to realize his production ambitions. Late in 1923 he formed a new production syndicate in Melbourne and purchased the screen rights to Fergus Hume's novel, *The Mystery of a Hansom Cab* (already filmed in 1911). His new company, Pyramid, was soundly backed by leading Melbourne businessmen, including Gilbert M. Johnson, a solicitor with several show business investments in theatres and dance halls. Shooting began in February 1924, with locations in Melbourne and interiors in Sydney at the Rushcutters Bay studio. The cast was led by Shirley himself as the chief suspect in the case, and Grace Glover as his fiancée, Madge. Grace Glover later played the lead in Frank Hurley's *The Jungle Woman* (1926) under her real name of Grace Savieri. The unusually lengthy production was ready for censor-screening in December, and with distribution by a Sydney entrepreneur, Alec Hellmrich, it opened at the Crystal Palace, Sydney, on 7 February 1925. Promotion was sustained and intensive, and the film proved to be a major commercial success, enabling Shirley to embark on another film, *The Sealed Room* (1926).

217 Painted Daughters**

1925 F. STUART-WHYTE

PC: Australasian Films. A Master Picture. PH: Lacey Percival. 6000(?) ft

CAST: Zara Clinton (Mary Elliott), Nina Devitt (Maryon Fielding), Billie Sim (Rita Railton), Marie Lorraine (Evelyn Shaw), Loretta May (Sheila Kay), Fernande Butler (Nina Walcott), Lucille Lisle (Olive Lennox), Peggy Pryde (wardrobe mistress), Belle Bates ('Salvation' Nell), Phyllis Du Barry (Saharab), Rawdon Blandford (Courtland Nixon), Martin Walker (Warren Fielding), William O'Hanlon (Ernest Glenning), Compton Coutts (Harry Selby), Billy Ryan (Eric Thurston), Herbert Walton (Harry Gratton), Grafton Williams (Edward Thayne), Roland Conway (Charles Daley), Louis Witts (Peter Flynn), S. Hackett (Flash).

Painted Daughters was the first in the series of Master Pictures produced by Australasian Films and released through Union Theatres. It marked the start of a determined attempt by the companies to establish continuous production of world-class feature films. The initial project was entrusted to a Scotsman, F. Stuart-Whyte, who had spent some fifteen years in the U.S.A. as a stage producer of comedies and pantomime. He had also been marginally involved in film in Hollywood, and had served as an assistant producer on several films with Douglas Fairbanks.

Stuart-Whyte arrived in Sydney in November 1924 and explained to *Everyones*, 19 November 1924, the policy of Australasian's new production programme: it is 'more the manufacturing of pictures in Australia, than the manufacturing of Australian pictures . . . I propose to construct bright, snappy amusing productions, such as find favor in all parts of the world, and prepare them in an Australian setting. While I am not going to eliminate the Australian atmosphere from my pictures, it must not obtrude.' The result was a studied accumulation of fashionable elements from American productions (elaborate jazz parties and pool-side gatherings of bathing beauties) and a careful avoidance of some of the recurring elements in local production. The formula was welcomed by the *Sun*, 24 May 1925, for whom it 'proved that an artistic Australian picture can be produced without at least one ugly phrase of Australian slang'.

217 The Rushcutters Bay studio of Australasian Films

With publicity promising 'a glorious whirl of perfect girl', *Painted Daughters* emerged as a romantic melodrama about high society and the 'flapper' generation. To the *Sydney Morning Herald*, 25 May 1925, it typified many local productions where more attention was paid to technical competence than to scenarios: 'For without some sort of dramatic interest, be it only primitive melodrama, their most painstaking film plays must become tedious.' It told the story of Mary Elliott and Courtland Nixon, dancing partners in the stage show, *Floradora.* Mary forsakes Courtland and marries a wealthy admirer, who soon goes bankrupt and suicides, leaving her to raise a little daughter, Maryon. Following in her mother's footsteps, Maryon eventually finds success in a theatrical career. One day, a press agent, Ernest Glenning, decides to gather together the original cast of *Floradora* for a charity performance, and Mary again meets Courtland. After the show they are both injured in an apartment building fire, and from their hospital beds, by telephone, they arrange their wedding to coincide with that of Maryon and Ernest.

The film displayed considerable sophistication of treatment, especially in the luxurious jazz-age sets and the fashionable costumes of the women. The photography of Lacey Percival also displayed a high degree of skill and inventiveness, from the trick photography of the opening titles (with Father Time painting the lips of the star) to an impression of an alcoholic's attack of DTs (with doves flying out of a doorway), and the climactic fire sequence involving some convincing superimposition effects.

Shooting began early in 1925 at Australasian's studio at Rushcutters Bay, Sydney. The cast included many tyros, and Stuart-Whyte explained that he was 'inclined to pick types from the general public who will be suitable to the screen'. Accordingly he selected several applicants from a nation-wide 'Screen Test' that had been conducted in 1924 by Louise Lovely as a publicity gimmick for Union Theatres. One of the newcomers was Phyllis Du Barry, who went on to work in Hollywood through the 1930s as Phyllis Barry. Completed for less than £4000, *Painted Daughters* opened at the Lyceum and Lyric Wintergarden Theatres, Sydney, on 23 May 1925, with commercial success. Stuart-Whyte remained in Australia to commence work on the second Union Master production, *Sunrise* (completed in 1926 by Raymond Longford), before departing to the West Indies, apparently for another film.

The renewal of feature film production by Australasian after years of inactivity owed much to the personal initiative of Stuart Frank Doyle, then a managing director of both Union Theatres and Australasian Films. Doyle had had long experience in the film industry, particularly in publicity and theatre management. He started as a magician in touring variety shows, but found the life too precarious and joined a legal firm in Sydney. From there he was employed by J. D. Williams as treasurer of his theatre operations, and when Williams amalgamated his interests with Australasian and Union Theatres, Doyle also joined the new organization and gradually moved up to a dominant position in the executive. With his fellow company directors, including W. A. Gibson and Gordon Balcombe, Doyle committed Australasian to a huge production programme in 1925, developing a new studio at Bondi, used after *Painted Daughters* as a substitute for the old Rushcutters Bay studio. Over £100 000 was spent on equipment and on a series of feature productions between 1925 and 1928. In 1932 Doyle again renewed feature film production with the foundation of Cinesound Productions. In 1937 he retired from the film industry and helped to pioneer the establishment of commercial radio in Australia, and later worked extensively in the aircraft manufacturing business. He died in Sydney in October 1945 at the age of 58.

217 *Painted Daughters* Phyllis Du Barry (*l*), Marie Lorraine (*top*)

217 Stuart F. Doyle

218 The Adventures of Algy*

1925 BEAUMONT SMITH

PC: Beaumont Smith's Productions. P, SC: Beaumont Smith. PH: Lacey Percival, Frank Stewart, Syd Taylor, Charles Barton. 6500 ft.

CAST: Claude Dampier (Algernon Allison), Bathie Stuart (Kiwi McGill), Eric Harrison (Murray Watson), Billie Carlyle (Mollie Moore), George Chalmers (John McGill), Lester Brown (stage manager), Eric Yates, Beaumont Smith, Hilda Attenboro, Verna Blain.

Algy is a direct successor to the English 'silly ass' played by Claude Dampier in *Hullo Marmaduke* (1924). Algy is tricked by a dastardly cousin into inheriting a barren stretch of land in New Zealand instead of a rich sheep station. He falls in love with a neighbour, Kiwi McGill, and later meets her again in Sydney, where she is dancing in a stage show to raise money to help her impoverished father.

Jedda

Outback
Have a drink, mate?
Have a fight, mate?
Have a taste of dust and sweat, mate?
There's nothing else out here.
NLT PRODUCTIONS and GROUP W FILMS presents
DONALD PLEASENCE · GARY BOND · CHIPS RAFFERTY · SYLVIA KAY in
"wake in fright"
Produced by GEORGE WILLOUGHBY Associate Producer MAURICE SINGER Directed by TED KOTCHEFF
Music by JOHN SCOTT Screenplay by EVAN JONES Based on the novel 'WAKE IN FRIGHT' by KENNETH COOK
Executive Producers HOWARD G. BARNES and BILL HARMON
United Artists
SUITABLE ONLY FOR ADULTS

The Aborigine
and the girl
30,000 years apart
...together
WALKABOUT
Just about the most different film you'll ever see
WALKABOUT starring JENNY AGUTTER · LUCIEN JOHN
DAVID GUMPILIL

STONE
TAKE THE TRIP
R

218 *The Adventures of Algy* Claude Dampier. Frame enlargement

218 *The Adventures of Algy* Claude Dampier arrives in New Zealand. Frame enlargement

When he returns to New Zealand, Algy strikes oil on his property; both he and the McGills become rich and Algy and Kiwi are married.

The film, most of which survives today, reveals a heavy reliance on titles to propel the insubstantial plot along, and frequently the images are little more than illustrations for the printed text. The story is padded out to feature length by a tour of New Zealand's scenic highlights, and by two dance sequences, one in a Maori village and another on the stage of a Sydney theatre. The star of both dance items was a young New Zealand actress, Bathie Stuart, making her first feature film appearance.

The New Zealand scenes were shot during the first months of 1925, followed by shooting in Sydney. Smith submitted the film for censor-screening in mid-June, and it opened strongly at the Lyceum and Lyric Wintergarden Theatres, Sydney, on 20 June.

219 The Bushwhackers

1925 RAYMOND LONGFORD

PC: Longford-Lyell Productions. ASSOC P: Charles Perry. SC: Raymond Longford, Lottie Lyell. PH: Arthur Higgins. ASST D: Fred Twitcham.

CAST: Eddie O'Reilly (Bill Lawson), Stella Southern (Bill's wife), Rawdon Blandford (Kenneth Hillyard), Beryl Gow (Bill's daughter), George Chalmers.

The Bushwhackers was a familiar, romantic tale in familiar settings. Sydney's fashionable homes, the Burragorang Valley and Wollondilly River provided the locales for a script loosely based on the theme of Tennyson's 'Enoch Arden'. Bill Lawson and his English-born mate, Kenneth Hillyard, share many adventures in the bush. One day Bill falls over a cliff at the head of a remote creek, and after a fruitless search by Hillyard, is given up for dead. Time passes, and after much wandering, Bill returns to Sydney to find his wife married to Hillyard, who has meanwhile inherited a fortune from his family in England. Seeing that his wife and daughter are happy in the care of a good man who surrounds them with comfort and luxury, Bill refrains from intruding on their happiness, and returns to his lonely life in the bush.

Eddie O'Reilly, a building worker and sometime boxer at the Sydney Stadium, was selected by Longford for the leading role, and a scene in which he trounces a wayside bully enabled him to demonstrate his boxing skill. In a deal unusual for an Australian film, Australasian bought the film outright from Longford and Lyell for a sum that approximated to the actual cost of production. After a viceregal preview in Sydney on 7 May 1925, it opened commercially at the Lyceum and Lyric Wintergarden Theatres on 25 July.

Reviews varied widely. *Everyones*, 29 July 1925, commented on the 'wonderful outdoor photography' and found it 'one of the better class of local productions', but the *Sydney Morning Herald*, 8 May 1925, found the scenery the only asset: 'The story simply meanders onward, without complication and without any very definite aim . . . Those who appear before the camera make little pretense of acting, beyond a little buffoonery.'

220 Those Terrible Twins

1925 J. E. WARD

PC: J. E. Ward Productions.

CAST: Ray Griffen (Ginger Meggs), Billy Canstell (Bluey), Kitty Willoby (Susan Meggs).

This slapstick comedy was filmed on location in the back streets of Sydney during a sojourn in Australia by the Papuan adventurer, J. E. Ward. It marked a radical change from his previous jungle travelogues, and featured that epitome of Australian urban boyhood, Ginger Meggs, a character made famous in comic-strip form. Although Ward announced his intentions to depict 'typical' Australian boys, the *Sydney Morning Herald*, 13 May 1925, commented that the film was 'plainly modelled on the pictures that came pouring into our midst from America . . . There are pie-slinging episodes, bathing beauties, crooks who raid jewellers' shops, and scenes in which undergarments play a prominent part.' It was accepted for distribution by First National, and opened as a supporting feature at the Haymarket Theatre, Sydney, on 25 July 1925.

221 Around the Boree Log*

1925 PHIL K. WALSH

PC: Phil K. Walsh Productions. SC: Phil K. Walsh. From the poems by John O'Brien. PH: Lacey Percival. ASST D: Clyde Marsh. 7100 ft.
CAST: anonymous.

This 'picturization' of poems by John O'Brien (nom de plume of a Catholic priest, Father Patrick Joseph Hartigan) is constructed as a sentimental journey through Australian bush society in the 1870s. The film opens with an invitation to 'walk out into God's fresh air and under his blue sky and to drink in the beauty and harmony shown in the homely surroundings of everyday countrylife'. A priest (presumably intended to be Father Hartigan himself) reads from the book of poems and recollects his earlier life in the country. He remembers children clustering in excitement around a travelling hawker and eyeing the toys wistfully while their mother buys them hats. He remembers his first school, a shaky old slab hut, where the children are preparing for an inspection by the bishop. A tender childhood romance is also recalled, and later the wedding of the girl to another man. The film ends with scenes of the priest's life today—the great cathedrals, the modern church schools, and a light-hearted picnic on St Patrick's Day.

With its cheerful faith in education and progress, its pride in Australia, and its Catholic sentiments, the film had a mixed reaction from the commercial trade. Many exhibitors refused to screen it. One distributor explained: 'The film appealed more particularly to the Irish section of the community, and on that account some of the showmen took exception to it, thinking that it was Roman Catholic propaganda. We had testimonials, even from Protestant ministers, praising the picture, and showing there was nothing whatever in the nature of Roman Catholic propaganda in it, but, nevertheless, we had great difficulty in booking it in the suburbs.' (*RCE*, p.23)

The film was shot entirely in the New South Wales bush, with the Wollondilly River area near Goulburn as the main location. Shooting began early in 1925, using local people in the cast, and it opened for a two-week season at the Crystal Palace, Sydney, on 25 September 1925.

Little is known about the director; his only other recorded involvement in feature film production was *While the Billy Boils* (1921), in which he served as assistant to Beaumont Smith, and *The Birth of White Australia*, which he directed in 1928.

222 Jewelled Nights**

1925 LOUISE LOVELY, WILTON WELCH

PC: Louise Lovely Productions. P: Wilton Welch. SC, ED: Louise Lovely, Wilton Welch. Based on the novel by Marie Bjelke-Petersen. PH: Tasman Higgins, Walter Sully. 10 000 ft.
CAST: Louise Lovely (Elaine Fleetwood), Gordon Collingridge (Larry Salarno), Godfrey Cass (Tiger Sam), Arthur Styan (Cranky Ned), Grafton Williams (Red Roof), John Dobbie (Tiny Tim), Charles Brown (Gus), Harry Halley (wowser), Leslie Woods (Robert Milton), Robert Morgan (Sir John Fleetwood), Clifford Miller (Richard Fleetwood), George Bryant (Dr Mason), Reg Leslie (Frank Reid), Frank Dunn (Dr Hughes), Katrina Barry (Lady Fleetwood), Lucille de Rago (Netta), Joy Law (Nora Foster), Jean Foulis (Yvette).

Louise Lovely returned from Hollywood in 1923 with her husband Wilton Welch, after nearly a decade in the successful pursuit of stardom. She began a long series of stage appearances around Australia, including a 'screen test' competition for Union Theatres, in exploitation of the mystique and glamour surrounding her Hollywood experience. During 1924 she developed the idea for a group of films based on novels by Marie Bjelke-Petersen about north-west Tasmania, and her first choice was *Jewelled Nights*. She formed her own production company and won backing from E. J. Carroll and other Melbourne businessmen, including some already involved in Arthur Shirley's Pyramid Pictures.

The plot of *Jewelled Nights* was not promising. After her father's death, a young socialite, Elaine Fleetwood, promises to marry a man she does not love, but dramatically deserts him during the wedding ceremony. She cuts her hair and, disguised as a boy, goes prospecting in the rugged north-west of Tasmania. There she meets a handsome miner, who, after many adventures, guesses her true sex. He saves her from a villainous rival and they are eventually married.

Actively promoting their work throughout production, Louise Lovely and Wilton Welch approached the film as they had learnt in Hollywood, making few concessions for local conditions. Australian film-makers at this time generally avoided complex studio work in favour of location shooting, and Australian studios lacked facilities to match the sophistication of those in Hollywood. Undeterred, they improvised a studio, first in the skating rink of the Glaciarium in Melbourne and later in Wirth's Circus building, the Olympia. A series of elaborate sets were built, including the interior of a cathedral, but the most extraordinary studio exercise, quite unlike anything attempted before in Australia, was the staging indoors of a fierce storm in a Tasmanian rain-forest. Truckloads of earth, shrubs and trees were installed in the studio, the local fire brigade played hoses on the ceiling, and an aeroplane engine mounted on a truck created the wind. Other scenes were shot in the palatial homes of Melbourne, at the Flemington racecourse (for a scene of the Melbourne Cup) and on location in the Tasmanian forests. The total production cost rose to over £8000, of which £3000 alone was spent on preparing the studio.

Distributed by the relatively new company of Hellmrich and Conrad, the film opened at the Hoyts Theatre De Luxe, Melbourne, on 24 October 1925. Although aided by numerous personal appearances by the star, the film did not come up to expectations; by the end of 1927 only £5000 had been returned to the producers and in the face of government and public indifference about a local industry,

222 *Jewelled Nights* Gordon Collingridge, Louise Lovely

Louise Lovely abandoned her plans for further production. She later divorced Welch, and in 1928 married an exhibitor, Bert Cowen and eventually settled in Hobart.

Not all of the expense lavished on the film was evident in the finished product; no critic was roused to comment on the studio rain-forest, and *Everyones*, 10 March 1926, found the views of the Tasmanian bush so like the scenery within thirty miles of Melbourne that they wondered why the producers had bothered to go there. The primary weakness was the plot, which impressed no-one. The *Sydney Morning Herald*, 8 March 1926, found that the central plot device of the girl's disguise as a boy totally lacked conviction: 'to play the part of "Dick" Fleetwood, Miss Lovely plasters her fair hair close on to her head [but] both her make-up and her gestures as "Dick" are precisely those she uses as "Elaine".'

223 The Moth of Moonbi**

1926 CHARLES CHAUVEL

PC: Australian Film Productions. SC: Charles Chauvel. From the novel, *The Wild Moth*, by Mabel Forrest. PH: Al Burne. ASST D: Edward Lyon. 9000 ft.

CAST: Marsden Hassall (Tom Resoult), Doris Ashwin (Dell Ferris), Arthur Tauchert (Jack Bronson), Charles O'Mara (Ferris), Michael Dwyer (Rodger Down), Colleen Richards (Margery Daw), Billie Stokes (Josephine), Jack Reed (Bill Devine), Darla Townend (Little Dell), Edward Lyon (Martin Brooks), Charles Chauvel (Aboriginal stockman).

Charles Chauvel's first feature was a modest romantic adventure about an innocent young country girl drawn to the bright lights of the city. The girl is a fiery tomboy, Dell Ferris, who is taken in hand in the city by a 'butterfly girl', Margery Daw, who is eager to help Dell spend her money in high society revelling. Dell later returns poorer but wiser to Moonbi, and after adventures with cattle rustlers, she marries her faithful friend and admirer, the head stockman, Tom.

Chauvel was born on 7 October 1897 in the country town of Warwick in south-west Queensland, and he often returned to the area as a location for his films. As a youth he studied art in Sydney and took acting lessons in spare time. With characteristic determination he managed to secure work as production assistant (primarily responsible for the horses) on several local features. He went to California, where he survived for two years writing articles about Australia and finding odd jobs in Hollywood studios. He returned to Queensland in 1923 fired with plans to make his own films.

His first scenario, *The Moth of Moonbi*, was based on a newly published novel by a Queensland author, Mabel Forrest. For his cast, he chose Doris Ashwin, an actress with limited professional experience on the Brisbane stage, and an amateur actor, Marsden Hassall (who later married Doris Ashwin), as the English jackeroo who loves 'the moth'. Chauvel himself played a small part in black-face as an Aboriginal stockman. The main technician was Al Burne, a cameraman on leave from his position as photographer for the Queensland government. Interiors were shot in an improvised studio at the rear of a guest house in the centre of Brisbane, but most of the film was shot on location in the bush outside the city. Despite mid-winter weather, Chauvel also took his small unit into the mountains west of Brisbane and camped in rough conditions, using pack horses in the absence of roads, and taking sheep to supply fresh meat.

The £4400 production was released in Brisbane at the Wintergarden Theatre on 25 January 1926 with promotion supervised by Chauvel. Already, in his first film, Chauvel's characteristics as a director were apparent: his desire to tell stories that used emphatically Australian backgrounds, and to film those backgrounds even on difficult locations, rather than recreate them in a studio; his willingness to experiment with new acting talent in leading roles; and a marked degree of self-reliance, handling production, direction, writing and promotion himself. During the next thirty years, he made only eight more features, but none were routine productions. His sound films usually strove for a grand epic sweep, and indicated his strong romantic vision, which elevated the ordinary life of Australians to the heroic. After gaining technical skill during the 1930s, he matured as a director with *Forty Thousand Horsemen* (1940) and emerged after the war as the only local director of any note to persevere with production in the repressive context of growing foreign control of Australian cinemas. He maintained this struggle until his death on 11 November 1959.

223 *The Moth of Moonbi* Doris Ashwin

224 The Tenth Straw*

1926 ROBERT G. McANDERSON

PC: Pacific Films. PH: Claud C. Carter. 6 reels.
CAST: Peggy Paul (Marie Lowe), Ernest Lauri (Bruce Lowe), James Cornell (Matthew Marr), Jack Fisher (Richard Groves), Syd Everett (Bully Carey), Robert Ball (Tiddley Harris), Robert G. McAnderson (Major Orville).

The central figure in this convict melodrama is Bruce Lowe, 'an aristocrat by birth and a black sheep from choice', who is transported from England to Australia for a crime he did not commit. A malicious officer, Matthew Marr, poses as a friend of Lowe's to gain access to the wealth and affections of his sister, Marie. Later Lowe escapes from prison and takes to the bush. A happy ending is reached after Marr is dramatically denounced by a fellow officer, and Lowe is restored to freedom.

The film, most of which survives today, was screened for a week at the Empress Theatre, Sydney, commencing on 27 March 1926, but it aroused little public interest. Little is known of the director or his cast (all presumably amateur, with the exception of Ernest Lauri, a vaudeville and stage actor known as 'the Singing Anzac'). The story owed much to *For the Term of his Natural Life* (refilmed soon after by Australasian Films). The only twist of any note was an episode involving a rich goldfield discovered by Aborigines, for which real Aborigines were employed in the cast.

225 Sydney's Darlings

1926 THOMAS MARINATO

PC: Beacon Light Productions. P: Thomas Marinato. SC, TITLES: J. Scott Bithell. PH: Ernest Scutna.
CAST: Doris Harrison, Jim McCoy, Will Kay, Charles Chapman, John Walker, Thomas Marinato.

This comedy-drama about yachting had a story that the *Sydney Morning Herald*, 15 March 1926, found 'so slight as to be hardly worth mentioning'. The central incident was a yachting race on Sydney Harbour in which the hero's place is taken by his girlfriend after he is injured in a car accident. She takes his yacht to victory.

Made largely by sporting enthusiasts and amateur film-makers (led by 'the youngest producer in Australia', Thomas Marinato), the film was shot in mid-1925 and screened at a suburban theatre in Sydney in March 1926. The *Sydney Morning Herald* searched 'in vain for those little touches which distinguish art from mere day-labour', and even the yachting scenes resembled those that appeared 'from week to week in the topical gazettes'. The film had few screenings and Marinato did not appear again in production until *My First Big Ship* (1932), a documentary about the pilot service on Sydney Harbour.

226 Peter Vernon's Silence

1926 RAYMOND LONGFORD

PC: Longford-Lyell Productions. PH: Arthur Higgins. 5830 ft.

CAST: Rawdon Blandford (Peter Vernon), Walter Hunt (Philip Kingston), Loretta May (Marie), Rene Sandeman, Iris Webster, Beryl Gow, John Faulkner, George Chalmers, Billy Ryan, Victor Davy, Annie Permain.

The last of the Longford-Lyell productions before Lyell's death in December 1925 was an uninspired melodrama about a man's loyalty to his mate. After his mother dies, Peter Vernon is adopted by a squatter who has a young son of his own, Philip. The boys grow up together in the bush, and fall in love with the same girl, Marie. Philip is the favoured suitor, but he has moral lapses, which are discovered by Marie's father. The father forbids the marriage, and in a fit of rage Philip kills the old man. Peter draws suspicion away from his friend by fleeing on horseback, and he is pursued for many days by police and a blacktracker. The chase continues into desolate snow country (filmed near Kiandra in the Snowy Mountains). Peter is caught, arrested and sentenced to prison. On his release, Peter returns to his old home in time to hear Philip make a deathbed confession to the murder. Peter finds happiness at long last in the love of the girl he has always adored.

226 Rawdon Blandford in *Peter Vernon's Silence*

Everyones, 3 November 1926, found the plot 'very weak and unconvincing' and found little to praise other than 'some very excellent photography'. Distributed by Paramount, the film was premièred in Hobart on 12 April 1926, but by the time it reached Sydney on 30 October it was relegated to the rank of supporting feature.

227 Should a Girl Propose?

1926 P. J. RAMSTER

PC: P. J. Ramster Photoplays. P, SC: P. J. Ramster. PH: Jack Fletcher. 4000 ft.

CAST: Cecil Pawley (Ellis Swift), Thelma Newling (Esma), Rex Simpson, Joy Wood, Norma Wood.

This Ramster quickie employed several players from his acting school, and like his other films, had little to offer the commercial trade. The film light-heartedly explored the foibles of fashionable Sydney society, using a simple plot formula of pretty girl, poor hero and rich unscrupulous villain. Into this frame was poured a wealth of melodramatic and farcical incident, including a male suitor in drag, disguised as the heroine, a runaway car, and the rescue of the heroine by rope from the surf and rocks at Bondi. Ramster's image of the idle rich can be gathered from the *Sydney Morning Herald*, 1 April 1926: 'Mr. Ramster has based his story on American models. He opens with the familiar bathing party scene, with couples gaily jazzing in their swimming costumes round the pool . . . one is plunged into fancy dress, dancing indoors, and scenes on the moonlit terrace, where "modern" girls puff their cigarettes and nonchalantly flirt.' Distributed by a new company, Greater Imperial Films, it opened as a supporting feature at the Piccadilly Theatre, Sydney, on 24 April 1926.

MR. EXHIBITOR—What you have been waiting for!

A 100 per cent AUSTRALIAN PICTURE

AND WHAT A TITLE!!

"SHOULD A GIRL PROPOSE?"

The modern Girl jazzes, smokes, indulges in athletes, enters law and politics, and, in short, does most things a man does, and in most things does better.

WHY SHOULD SHE NOT PROPOSE?

Premiere Australian Release at

PICCADILLY THEATRE

SAT., APRIL 24th

228 The Jungle Woman*

1926 FRANK HURLEY

PC: Stoll Picture Productions. P, SC, PH: Frank Hurley. ED, ASST D: W. G. Saunders. ASST PH: Walter Sully. 6070 ft.

CAST: Eric Bransby Williams (Martin South), Grace Savieri (Hurana), Jameson Thomas (Stephen Mardyke), Lillian Douglas (Eleanor), W. G. Saunders (Peter Mack).

Frank Hurley (1885-1962) was firmly established by 1925 as Australia's most famous photographer. An artist interested less in expressing human experiences than the grandeur of nature and the romance of exotic lands, his work was known to Australians through books, newspaper features and documentary films. His journeys began in December 1911 when he joined Mawson's expedition to Antarctica as official photographer; his stills of the expedition were published widely around the world, and a 4000-foot documentary, *Home of the Blizzard*, was released in 1913.

Another explorer, Francis Birtles, engaged Hurley to travel with him through the tropical north of Australia, the outcome of which was another feature-length documentary, *Into Australia's Unknown.* By the time of its release in January 1915, Hurley was again in Antarctica, this time with a British expedition led by Ernest Shackleton, and it was on this harrowing two-year trip that Hurley took his most famous photographs and films, depicting the destruction of the ship *Endurance* in pack-ice and the crew's long struggle for survival through a polar winter. The footage was released as *In the Grip of Polar Ice* in 1917, and again in 1933, as *Endurance.* In June 1917 he accepted a position with the Australian Imperial Forces as the first official photographer of the Australian war effort. Here Hurley produced some striking 'epic' photography, and perfected his technique of 'combination printing', intensifying the realism of battle photographs by superimposing several negatives together. The war was followed by aeroplane flights with the Australian pioneer aviator Ross Smith, culminating in a highly successful film, *The Ross Smith Flight*, released in mid-1920.

228 Frank Hurley

At this point in his career, Hurley became interested in Papua. In December 1920 he left Australia to record the work of Anglican missions in Papua and to make a 'travelogue entertainment'. The result was *Pearls and Savages*, a documentary released in Sydney in December 1921, with Hurley lecturing from the stage as the film was screened. A lecture and film tour of Australia followed, and another major trip to Papua to secure additional footage. The expanded film, *With the Headhunters in Papua*, was released in Sydney in October 1923, and Hurley travelled widely in Australia and England with the film, acting as both entrepreneur and lecturer. An attempt to broach the American market failed, and Hurley lost many thousands of pounds before becoming convinced that lecture-film packages were impossible for the conditions of the American film trade. He decided to make films in Papua with a narrative interest to hold together the documentary footage so that they could be released in America without the presence of a lecturer. He approached the Australian-born magnate of the British film industry, Sir Oswald Stoll, and won his backing for a major production venture; Stoll provided £10 000 and several of his studio's stars and technicians to go with Hurley to Papua to produce two feature films 'back to back'. The British crew joined Hurley in Sydney in August 1925 and the party set off for Thursday Island, where the first of the films, *The Hound of the Deep*, was shot. The second film (although the first to be released) was *The Jungle Woman.* Hurley had made arrangements to shoot the film in Papua, but at the last moment he was refused permission by the Australian government to work there, on the grounds that 'it would be harmful to show whites and blacks together' in the same film. Unable to spend time fighting what *Everyones*, 27 January 1926, called 'Bumbledom gone riot', Hurley altered his plans, and took his party by open boat across 200 miles of sea to Merauke in Dutch New Guinea. The entire film, including interiors, was shot on location there under difficult physical conditions.

Hurley intended to give new meaning to the South Seas romance. Publicity for *The Jungle Woman* clearly stated his attitude: in the film 'one finds none of the stock studies of drunken beachcombers, brutal planters, placid missionaries, or ill-treated native girls, who turn out to be long-lost society beauties, with millionaire fathers. Instead . . . Hurley takes one direct to the New Guinea he knows, and the natives he understands' (*Everyones*, 19 May 1926). The film as it exists today certainly has many striking scenic effects and

interesting ethnographic details, but the plot is dominant and reveals Hurley's naïvety about human relationships. The story offers a standard screen villain, thin and unshaven, with the sinister name of Mardyke, who joins the dashing young hero, Martin South, on an expedition into the wilds of New Guinea in search of gold and adventure. After a head-hunter attack, Mardyke leaves Martin for dead and returns to white civilization to pursue the hand of Martin's fiancée, Eleanor. Meanwhile, Martin is nursed back to health by a native girl, Hurana, who falls in love with him. Hurana tries to win his affections by helping him to escape from a horde of angry natives, but she is later bitten by a snake and dies. Martin arrives back in time to rescue Eleanor from Mardyke's clutches.

Hurley was supported in the venture by a production administrator from Stoll's office, J. Elder, and by a Stoll actor and assistant director, W. G. Saunders. The star was a rising young British actor, Eric Bransby Williams, son of a well-known character actor. The rest of the small white cast was British, with the exception of the jungle woman herself, played by a Sydney actress, Grace Savieri. The film was edited in Sydney and opened simultaneously at the Lyceum and Haymarket Theatres, Sydney, on 22 May 1926. Commercial results in Australia and later in Britain repaid Stoll's total investment, and the earnings from the second film were clear profit.

After two more trips to Antarctica with Mawson, during which *Siege of the South* (1931) was filmed, Hurley remained in Australia during the 1930s to become the dominant figure in Australian documentary. He also worked as director of photography on several features for Cinesound. During the Second World War he served again as official photographer with the Australian forces in the Middle East until 1943, and remained there until 1946 making films for the British Ministry of Information. After his return to Australia he worked primarily on still photography and book publication. He died in Sydney on 16 January 1962.

228 *The Jungle Woman*

229 The Pioneers

1926 RAYMOND LONGFORD

PC: Australasian Films. A Master Picture. SC: Lottie Lyell. From the novel by Katharine Susannah Prichard. PH: Arthur Higgins. 8000 ft.

CAST: Virginia Beresford, William Thornton, Augustus Neville, George Chalmers, W. Dummitt, Robert Purdie, 'Big' Bill Wilson.

In September 1925 Longford accepted an appointment as director of productions and supervisor of the new Bondi studio by his old enemy, the combine of Australasian Films and Union Theatres. After completing Stuart-Whyte's unfinished *Sunrise* (released later in 1926), he directed two features, *The Pioneers* and *Hills of Hate*, before his alliance with Australasian broke down in renewed bitterness, with Longford accusing Australasian of attempting to discredit and subvert film production in Australia (see, e.g., *RCE*, p.149).

The Pioneers was the second screen adaptation of Katharine Susannah Prichard's novel (the first had been in 1916). The story of the hopes and trials of a Scottish settler and his wife (played by William Thornton and Virginia Beresford) in the Gippsland bush was potential material for a powerful epic adventure, but no critic seemed pleased with the film. It developed slowly for most of its two hours, then ended with a spate of rapid melodramatic happenings that seemed only to confuse the audience. The *Sydney Morning Herald*, 7 June 1926, commented: 'If only "The Pioneers" could be wound up about half-way or two-thirds of the way through, so as to obviate all this trite melodrama, which has been put in obviously as a sop to the populace, it would stand as a landmark in the history of Australian motion pictures'; for, apart from the plot, the film achieved an image of the bush as a place of 'wild yet homely charm [with] open-hearted people, instead of conjuring it up as the abode of bad men and "wild western" heroics.'

Longford himself suggested that the film's uneven quality was due to the fact that the cast had been chosen against his will and that Australasian had expected too much for their small financial outlay (*RCE*, p.147). Location shooting near Gosford began in January 1926, and interiors were shot at Australasian's Bondi studio. The film was released as a prestigious main feature at the Lyceum and Haymarket Theatres, Sydney, on 5 June, and seems to have been moderately successful with the public.

230 The Sealed Room

1926 ARTHUR SHIRLEY

PC: Pyramid Pictures. P, SC: Arthur Shirley. PH: Lacey Percival. ASST D: Clyde Marsh. 7000 ft.

CAST: Arthur Shirley (Paul Craig), Grace Glover (Angela Scardon), George Bryant (Carlo Gelmini), Nellie Ferguson, Cora Warner, Leslie Woods, Cecil Scott, Carlton Stuart, Eric Harrison, Muriel Veck, John Bruce, Harry Halley, Walter Bentley.

This original story by Arthur Shirley, according to the *Sydney Morning Herald*, 5 July 1926, was 'blood-and-thunder of the solid old-fashioned type'. A blind man, Paul Craig, inadvertently uncovers a plot by a gang of anarchists, led by an Italian, to overthrow the monarchy in a country called Ruvania. Later, Paul regains his sight and marries Angela, the sister of one of the gang's murder victims. Angela had lost her memory with the shock of her brother's death, but nevertheless she is able to help Paul bring the culprits to justice and save Ruvania from political turmoil.

Shooting began in May 1925 at Australasian's Rushcutters Bay studio and on location in the Blue Mountains. Release was delayed for unknown reasons until 3 July 1926, when it opened simultaneously at the Lyceum and

Empress Theatres, Sydney. Distribution was undertaken by the production company, and Union Theatres accepted the film for circuit release, but it fell far below the achievements of Shirley's previous film, *The Mystery of a Hansom Cab* (1925). Shirley announced a third project, simply called *1840*, based on a novel by J. H. M. Abbott, *Castle Vane*, but no shooting took place. He went instead to London, and after failing to find a release for his films there, tried to launch a new production enterprise in Rhodesia. After this project also failed, he returned to Australia in mid-1934 and announced new plans for feature production, but again none reached fruition. He lived in Sydney until his death in 1967.

231 Tall Timber

1926 DUNSTAN WEBB

PC: Australasian Films. A Master Picture. STORY: Dunstan Webb. TITLES: Jim Donald. PH: Lacey Percival. 7000 ft.

CAST: Eden Landeryou (Jack Maxwell), Billie Sim (Betty Manning), George Willoughby (John Maxwell Snr), Claude Holland (Dick Desmond), 'Big' Bill Wilson (Steve Black), Jimmy McMahon (Jimmy Manning), Charles Beetham (Desmond Fox), Dan Gallagher (Dan), Nellie Ferguson (Mrs Manning), Ray Watson (Agnes Esdale), J. P. O'Neill (sundowner), Bill Murray (burglar).

Jack Maxwell throws a wild jazz party, which is raided by the police, and he is disowned by his father for causing a scandal. In search of a job, he goes north to visit a friend, Dick Desmond, who owns a timber mill. He takes a job there and falls in love with Betty, the daughter of a timber worker. Jealous of Jack's affair with Betty, and resentful of his interference in the mill, the foreman, Steve Black, tries to kill Jack, and a violent fight ensues on the swaying trucks of a runaway logging train. Eventually a wizened old sundowner arrives at the camp, and shoots Steve in revenge for his seduction many years earlier of the sundowner's wife; the old man is also able to reveal that Steve had long been blackmailing Dick's father for a murder, of which he can now be proved innocent. The sundowner disappears with the dawn, leaving the mill in peace and happiness.

231 *Tall Timber* Billie Sim, Eden Landeryou

The timber scenes were filmed on location at Langley Vale in the New South Wales north coast forests. Light relief was provided by a (silent) banjo solo by the leading actor, Eden Landeryou, known off-screen as a musician and band-leader in Sydney. The film also gave a brief taste of stardom to Billie Sim, a young actress from New Zealand who had previously worked on stage and as a bit-player in several films.

Titles for the film were written by a Sydney journalist, Jim Donald, and apparently attempted to achieve some degree of colloquial flavour, for the *Sydney Morning Herald*, 23 August 1926, commented that the film-makers have 'striven to give Australian atmosphere by loading [the captions] with slang, so that the effect is not only exaggerated, but at times positively displeasing'.

Shooting, which began in December 1925, involved some hardship for the unit, which spent several weeks camped in rugged bush locations. The £3000 production opened at the Lyceum and Lyric Wintergarden Theatres, Sydney, on 21 August 1926. *Everyones*, 25 August, noted that the film 'received the biggest round of applause from a full house we have yet heard given to a locally produced picture'. It was one of the first Australian films to be released in Britain under the Empire quota legislation, passed by the British parliament in 1927.

232 Sunrise

1926 F. STUART-WHYTE, RAYMOND LONGFORD

PC: Australasian Films. A Master Picture. SC: Mollie Mead, Martyn Keith. PH: Charles Ellis, Len Roos. 6000 ft.

CAST: Phyllis Du Barry (Hope Stuart), Robert Travers (George Willis), Zara Clinton (Elsa Willis), Harry Hodson (Old Ben), Dunstan Webb (Arthur Greerson), Dick Thornton.

After the death of his faithless wife in a rock-fall, George Willis seeks solitude in the bush. Some time later he rescues a girl, Hope Stuart, from a flood and tends to her injuries in his cabin. When she is well enough, he brings her back to her father and learns that a former enemy, Greerson, has accused him of murder. Greerson, however, is injured in a mining accident and when George rescues him, Greerson admits that he had lied. George is again a free man and returns to his life as a recluse in the mountains. Hope determinedly sets off to join him there.

Much of *Sunrise* was shot on location in the Blue Mountains, with interiors at the Australasian studio at Bondi. The film was begun by F. Stuart-Whyte, but during shooting he left Australia abruptly for reasons that are still unclear. Longford completed the film as his first assignment after being employed by Australasian Films. It was released as a supporting feature at the Lyric Wintergarden, Sydney, on 16 October 1926.

233 The Hound of the Deep*

1926 FRANK HURLEY

PC: Stoll Picture Productions. P, SC, PH: Frank Hurley. ASST D: W. G. Saunders. ASST PH: Walter Sully. 4 950 ft.
CAST: Jameson Thomas ('Black' Darley), Eric Bransby Williams (John Strong), W. G. Saunders ('Cockeye' Jones), Lillian Douglas (Marjorie Jones).

To inherit his late uncle's fortune, a London playboy, John Strong, must find a pearl in the waters off Thursday Island. His efforts are disrupted by tropical disease and by a rival's attempts to murder him. Eventually John finds his pearl, foils the villain's schemes and finds happiness with the daughter of an island trader.

The Hound of the Deep was the second film released in the two-film package made by Frank Hurley for the British company, Stoll Picture Productions. It employed much the same cast and crew as *The Jungle Woman* (released in May 1926) and was shot on location on Thursday Island, with islanders in minor acting roles. Again, Hurley's strength lay in documentary footage, with ample displays of the island's scenery and of pearling fleets at work. The plot, however, revealed Hurley's adherence to emotionally naïve formulas, as the *Bulletin*, 11 November 1926, commented: the attractions of the 'dinkum' setting 'are subordinated to a hackneyed plot and a made-to-order drama, provided by the ancient stage device of a preposterous will'. Distributed by J. C. Williamson Films, it opened at the Lyceum and Haymarket Theatres, Sydney, on 6 November 1926. British release followed in February 1927 under the title *Pearl of the South Seas.*

234 Greenhide**

1926 CHARLES CHAUVEL

PC: Australian Film Productions. SC: Charles Chauvel. PH: Al Burne. TITLES: Frank White. ASST D: Edward Lyon. 8000 ft.
CAST: Elsie Sylvaney (Margery Paton), Bruce Gordon (Greenhide Gavin), Jules Murray-Prior (Slab Rawlins), Irma Dearden (Polly Andrews), Gerald Barlow (Sam Paton), Frank Thorn (Tom Mullins), Joe Mackaway (Phil Mackin), Alfred Greenup (Bill Mullins), Nell Kerwin, George Barrett.

In Chauvel's first feature, *The Moth of Moonbi* (1926), a country girl had tasted life in the city. In *Greenhide* the story was reversed. Margery Paton is a wilful high-society girl, first seen strumming a mandolin and munching chocolates, enjoying a constant whirl of poolside parties, charleston and jazz. Out of boredom she contrives to visit her father's cattle station in the rugged outback. There, Margery hopes, she might 'be loved by a real man—a cave man' and perhaps even be 'sheiked by a real live Bushranger'. The manager of the station is 'Greenhide' Gavin, a man with an awesome reputation for severity and toughness, who objects strenuously to Margery's presence on the station, especially

234 *Greenhide* Irma Dearden (*r*)

when her 'silk stockings and aptitude for showing off her dimpled knees very nearly demoralise the cow-punching cockies'. In Margery, however, Gavin has met a will equal to his own, and after several adventures involving a gang of ruthless cattle duffers, they fall happily in love.

Characteristically, Chauvel travelled far to find locations for the film and took care to stress them prominently both in the action and his promotion of the film. Most location scenes were shot in May 1926 in the Dawson Valley, some hundred miles out of Brisbane, where the unit camped for five weeks. Interiors were shot in a compact studio erected at the rear of a boarding house (where the unit lived) in the centre of Brisbane. The cast was led by Elsie Sylvaney (born Elsie Wilcox in 1898), a young actress from the Brisbane stage, who became engaged to Chauvel during production and married him in June the next year; as Elsa Chauvel, she collaborated with him in film production thereafter.

On 20 November 1926 the £3800 production opened at His Majesty's Theatre, Brisbane, where capacity crowds were attracted by the promise of seeing their own state on the screen. Chauvel's publicity campaign included a special 'Greenhide Ball', a bathing beauty screen contest (with the screen 'tests' shown on the same programme with *Greenhide*), and personal appearances by Elsie Sylvaney. Despite the success of the première, Chauvel found it difficult to persuade country exhibitors to screen the film; he and Elsie took the film by car around Queensland, persuading cinema managers to put aside their normal American programme, and promoting the film themselves with stage appearances.

In 1928 the Chauvels departed for Hollywood with prints of their two films, but found that talkies were now starting to dominate the film trade. After a year they returned to Australia, and Charles worked as a cinema manager in Melbourne before moving back to Queensland to prepare the script for his first talkie, *In the Wake of the Bounty* (1933).

235 Those who Love

1926 P. J. RAMSTER, PAULETTE McDONAGH

PC: MCD Productions. P, SC: Paulette McDonagh. PH: Jack Fletcher. ART D, PM: Phyllis McDonagh. 6000 ft.

CAST: Marie Lorraine (Lola Quayle), William Carter (Barry Manton), Robert Purdie (Sir James Manton), Sylvia Newland (Bébé Dorée), George Dean (Parker), Kate Trefle (Lady Manton), 'Big' Bill Wilson (Ace Skinner), Charles Beetham (Austin Mann), Reginald Reeves (Sir Furneaux Reeves), Jackie Williamson (Peter), Nellie Ferguson (nurse), Howard Harris (doctor), Edith Hodgson, Herbert Walton.

Those who Love was the first venture of the McDonagh sisters: Paulette, the director and principal writer; Phyllis (the youngest), business manager, publicist and art director; and the eldest, Isobel, who acted under the stage name of Marie Lorraine. The daughters of a Sydney doctor, the sisters were captivated by Hollywood early in their youth. They spent many hours watching films and analysing them, and eventually decided to try their luck in production. With their independent spirit, the girls were undaunted by a film industry dominated by men and by American interests; Paulette spent several months at P. J. Ramster's acting school to learn what she could, while Isobel established the name of Marie Lorraine in several films for other directors. During their production career from 1926 to 1933, they completed four features and several short documentaries, none of which emulated the aggressively Australian patterns popular with other local producers. Their first two features were sensitive romantic dramas set in an undefined country; the characters were sophisticated, well-bred and wealthy, and conflict was often based on class distinctions and prejudices.

235 Paulette McDonagh

The story of *Those who Love* followed patterns of English melodrama: Barry Manton, the son of a knight, falls in love with a dancer, but his father disapproves of the affair and bribes the woman to leave. Humiliated and hurt, Barry leaves home and becomes a labourer on the docks. In a sleazy cabaret he meets Lola, 'a delicate flower among sordid surroundings', and marries her. Meanwhile, Barry's father has repented and his lawyer pleads with Barry to return home. Thinking that she might prevent him from claiming his inheritance, Lola runs away to set him free. Years pass, and Barry lives alone in a squalid attic, while Lola works as a nurse and cares for her young son Peter. One day Barry is injured and rushed to hospital; Lola recognizes him there and realizes that he has refused wealth and status for her sake. She visits his parents to ask for money for a specialist, and although Sir James at first refuses to see her, his little grandson so beguiles him that the family is soon reunited.

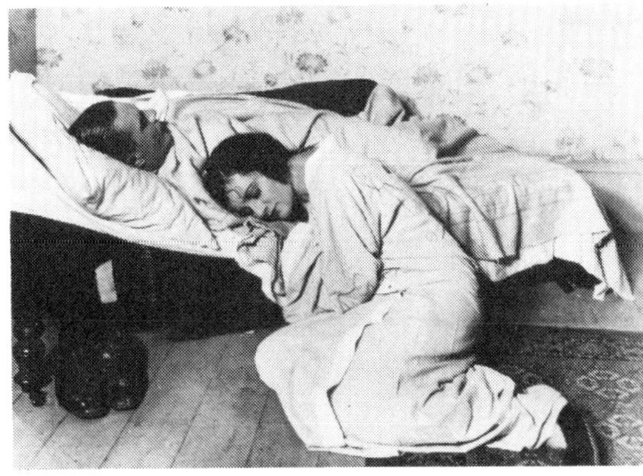

235 *Those Who Love* William Carter, Marie Lorraine

235 *Those Who Love* Jackie Williamson (*l*), Robert Purdie

Uncertain of their ability, the sisters hired a more experienced director, P. J. Ramster, to direct the film, but found that his work did not meet their demands. Paulette progressively assumed responsibility for the production, and Ramster was relegated to the position of 'technical director'. Like all of their films, *Those who Love* was planned and budgeted with careful attention to detail; a tight shooting schedule of ten days was firmly adhered to, and publicity was vigorous and effective. Much attention was given to the dressing of sets, so that although their film was cheap (less than £1000), it looked expensive and authentic. Financed with family funds, the film was shot almost entirely in the McDonagh residence, the historic Drummoyne House; only the cabaret scene was shot in Australasian's Bondi studio.

After a viceregal preview in September 1926, the film was taken for distribution by J. C. Williamson Films, and a public première was held in Newcastle on 22 November 1926, followed by a Sydney release on 11 December at the Haymarket Theatre. Commercial results were strong and served to finance the sisters' next production, *The Far Paradise* (1928).

235 *Those Who Love* Marie Lorraine

236 Hills of Hate

1926 RAYMOND LONGFORD

PC: Australasian Films. A Master Picture. ASSOC P: Victor Longford. SC: E. V. Timms, based on his own novel. PH: Arthur Higgins. ASST D: Fred Twitcham. 6000 ft.

CAST: Dorothy Gordon (Ellen Ridgeway), Gordon Collingridge (Jim Blake), 'Big' Bill Wilson (Black Joe Cummins), Clifford Toone (Jim Blake Snr), Kathleen Wilson (Peggy Blake), Stanley Lonsdale (Stanley Ridgeway), William Thornton, Charlton Stratton, Tom Dalton, Kevin Gallagher, Eric Paton, Joe Laurie, Allie Ryan, Rita Olive.

This action movie, filmed largely on location near Gloucester, N.S.W., was based on a story by the budding novelist E. V. Timms. It depicted a feud between two outback families, spanning a period of thirty years and ending after the war with the uniting of the two families in a marriage between the younger generation.

Shooting began in March 1926 and lasted about five weeks, with Longford's son Victor as associate producer. The cast included Dorothy Gordon in her first Australian screen role; she had spent several years in Hollywood and returned to Sydney to work in films variously as actress, scenarist and art director.

236 *Hills of Hate* Dorothy Gordon, 'Big' Bill Wilson

236 *Hills of Hate* Dorothy Gordon, Gordon Collingridge

She later became better known as a radio commentator and newspaper columnist under the name of Andrea.

The film opened quietly at the Lyric Wintergarden, Sydney, on 27 November 1926.

237 Down Under

1927 HARRY SOUTHWELL

PC: Anglo-Australian Films. PH: Lacey Percival, Cliff Thomas.
CAST: Harry Southwell (Walter Nobbage), Nancy Mills.

Down Under was the first and only production in a series proposed by Anglo-Australian Films for the British and Australian markets. Financed by Perth businessmen, the films were intended to be 'typically Western Australian' in spirit, and according to trade announcements, were guaranteed distribution in England and Europe. Southwell clearly promised local investors more than he could provide, for no record has been found of commercial screenings in either Australia or London.

The film followed an Australian vagabond, Walter Nobbage, through a series of adventures that a local critic described as 'clean and wholesome' (*West Australian*, 24 March 1927). The highlights seemed standard: a trotting race meeting, a cattle muster and an Aboriginal corroboree. Outback scenes were shot late in 1926 and the film was privately previewed in Perth on 22 March 1927.

238 The Kid Stakes*

1927 TAL ORDELL

PC: Ordell-Coyle Productions. P: Tal Ordell, Virgil Coyle. SC: Tal Ordell. Based on comic strip characters created by Syd Nicholls. PH: Arthur Higgins. 5000 ft.
CAST: 'Pop' Ordell (Fatty Finn), Charles Roberts (Tiny King), Ray Salmon (Jimmy Kelly), Frank Boyd (Bruiser Murphy), Edward Stevens (Shooey Shugg), Billy Ireland ('Seasy), Stanley Funnelle (Headlights Hogan), Gwenda Hemus (Betty Briggs), Leonard Durell (Constable Claffey), Joyce Hazeldine (Kitty Kelly), Jimmy Taylor (Horatio John Wart), Eileen Alexander (Madeline Twirt), Tom Cannam (Mr Twirt), David Lidstone (Master Algie Snoops), Evelyn Rawle (Molly Kelly), Tal Ordell (race commentator), Syd Nicholls (himself).

Fatty Finn is the leader of a group of scruffy, irrepressible Woolloomooloo children. They enter Fatty's pet goat, Hector, in a derby but a rival gang, led by Bruiser Murphy, sets Hector loose on the morning of the race. After a series of adventures, Fatty finds the runaway goat and persuades a friendly aviator to fly him to the race-track in time for the main event.

Although it was scarcely recognized as such at the time, *The Kid Stakes* stands clearly today as one of the major films of Australia's silent period. It owed incidental ideas to the *Our Gang* series and to Chaplin's *The Kid* (1920), but the story remained a faithful adaptation of the *Fatty Finn* comic strip drawn by Syd Nicholls for the *Sunday News* in Sydney (which he continued to draw almost until his death in June 1977). Nicholls was both a prolific cartoonist and the designer of art titles for many Australian silent films; he appeared in person in the opening scene of *The Kid Stakes,* drawing a sketch of Fatty, which magically comes to life. The film's success is due

238 *The Kid Stakes* 'Pop' Ordell watches while Syd Nicholls draws. Frame enlargement

in large part to the simple childlike humour of the titles and to the spontaneity of the performances (especially from Ordell's six-year-old son Robin— or 'Pop'—in the main role of Fatty). The freshness of the film also owes much to its outdoor locations in the Woolloomooloo streets and in the palatial Potts Point home of the theatrical entrepreneur Hugh Ward. Goat races were prohibited in New South Wales, but a race sequence was staged in January 1927 in Rockhampton, Queensland, with the enthusiastic support of the local citizens.

The £4000 production was first screened in Brisbane at the Wintergarden Theatre on 9 June 1927, and although it was modestly profitable, the press and the trade tended to dismiss it as a children's film. Following its initial release, it was cut to form comedy shorts, and the goat race was sent abroad in news magazines.

Tal Ordell (real name, William Ordell Raymond Buntine) directed only this one feature. His roles on stage and screen were numerous, and in 1921 he directed a two-reel comedy, *Cows and Cuddles.* He also contributed verse and short stories to the *Bulletin* and wrote a three-act play, *Kangaroo Flat,* produced in Sydney in March 1926. During the 1930s he

238 *The Kid Stakes* The Woolloomooloo children inspect a stranger (*l*) from wealthy Potts Point. Frame enlargement

acted extensively in radio and wrote many broadcast items, including bush yarns, children's stories and a long-running serial, *Wattletown,* in which he acted with his son, Robin. In the late 1930s Robin became known as 2GB's 'baby radio announcer'. He was killed in the airforce during the war. Tal Ordell died in 1948.

239 For the Term of his Natural Life*

1927 NORMAN DAWN

PC: Australasian Films. A Union Master World Picture. P, SC: Norman Dawn. From the novel by Marcus Clarke. TITLES: Norman Dawn, Gayne Dexter. PRINCIPAL PH: Len Roos, William Trerise, Bert Cross. ADDITIONAL PH: Norman Dawn, William Carty, Joe Stafford, Harry Lloyd. ED: Katherine Dawn, Mona Donaldson, Norman Dawn. ART D: Norman Dawn, Dorothy Gordon. SET CONSTRUCTION: James Coleman. STUDIO MANAGER: Frank Marden. ASST D: Claude Turton, William Reed. 10 000 ft.

CAST: George Fisher (Rufus Dawes/John Rex), Eva Novak (Sylvia Vickers), Dunstan Webb (Maurice Frere), Jessica Harcourt (Sarah Purfoy), Arthur McLaglen (Gabbett), Katherine Dawn (Mrs Vickers), Gerald Kay Souper (Major Vickers), Marion Marcus Clarke (Lady Devine), Arthur Tauchert (Warder Troke), Beryl Gow (Sylvia Vickers as a child), Compton Coutts (Reverend Meekin), Mayne Lynton (Reverend North), Carlton Stuart (Commandant Burgess), William O'Hanlon (the Crow), Arthur Greenaway (Lord Bellasis), Edward Howell (Kirkpatrick), Fred Twitcham (Surgeon Pine), Charles Weatherly (Captain Blunt), Steve Murphy (Jemmy Vetch), Claude Turton (convict), Jimmy McMahon (convict boy), Hartney Arthur (convict boy), William Thornton (aide-de-camp).

For the Term of his Natural Life stands as a landmark in the history of the production industry, although in narrative terms it offered nothing new. The story was well known to Australians and had been filmed twice before, in 1908 and in 1911 (as *The Life of Rufus Dawes*), and the new film made no attempt to modify the mid-Victorian devices of the plot for a modern generation. To protect his family's reputation, a young aristocrat accepts responsibility for a murder he did not commit, and under the name of Rufus Dawes is transported for life to the convict settlement of Van Diemen's Land. The bulk of the story follows his life of hardship as a convict and his unrequited love for Sylvia, the daughter of a prison governor. Coincidences form the principal means of plot advancement, from Sylvia's amnesia, which tragically denies her the love of Rufus Dawes, to the revelation of an exact double for Dawes, an evil man who escapes from the colony to take

239 Shooting *For the Term of his Natural Life*. George Fisher holding Eva Novak in the coracle. Note three-piece orchestra on left

Dawes's place in his ancestral home. One of the few major changes in the film was the cautious softening of the ending: the book ended with the tragic reunion of Dawes and Sylvia at the moment of their death in a storm at sea; the film, however, ended ambiguously with the lovers united and alive, but adrift on a raft in the open ocean.

Although a faithful reproduction of the novel's plot, the film lacked its Dickensian passion in exposing the horrors of the convict system. The strongest element of horror relates instead, rather gratuitously, to the cannibalistic habits of the convict escapee, Gabbett, who appears made-up like a Lon Chaney monster. The film relies primarily on spectacle as its main asset and comes to resemble the more sterile extreme of the Hollywood epic genre with cardboard characters parading through picturesque scenery and expensive sets.

Initially, Raymond Longford was assigned to direct a £15 000 production starring Frank Harvey, but he acceded to a request by Australasian to stand down to allow an American director to take his place, with the intention of so ensuring an American release. Longford was promised continuity of work on other productions in return for his sacrifice, but in an incident that confirmed his paranoia about the combine, Australasian allowed his contract to expire without renewal (***RCE***, p.147).

Norman Dawn was a technician with an overriding interest in photographic special effects, which he had learnt during twenty years in Hollywood as a cameraman and minor feature film director. He arrived in Australia early in 1926 to make a series of scenic shorts, and after talks with William Gibson of Australasian Films was offered the job of producing and directing *For the Term of his Natural Life* on an expanded scale.

As news about the production spread, a wave of public opposition arose because it threatened to expose the 'shameful' origins of white settlement in Australia. Questions were asked in the Commonwealth parliament to see what provisions existed to prevent the export of any 'objectionable' film, and even the trade paper, *Everyones*, 14 July 1926, published an editorial protesting against 'those who are seeking to make capital out of the drab and sordid days of Australia'. Because a genuine possibility existed that censorship powers could be exercised to prevent the film's export, Australasian embarked on a defensive publicity campaign, and the film emerged with an opening title that stressed that the story 'is purely a work of fiction' and that, in reminding us of a 'sordid phase of Man's social life [it provides] inspiring evidence of progress and the ultimate millenium'.

The Americans in the cast—Eva Novak, George Fisher, Steve Murphy and Katherine Dawn (the director's wife)—had arrived in Sydney by early August 1926. Shooting began immediately, and a flood of publicity reached the daily papers and the magazines, for Hollywood had now arrived in Australia to make the most expensive film ever attempted in the land. The publicity created euphoria in the production industry, and prophecies for the future well-being of the industry abounded; everyone, even Longford, seemed convinced that employing Americans to make films in Australia was a sure way of gaining access to the eldorado of the American market.

The budget was originally set at £40 000 (at a time when some local film-makers were completing features for less than £2000), but as work progressed the cost rose steadily to nearer £50 000. If the film lacked historical accuracy, it certainly aimed at geographical authenticity, and locations ranged widely through Tasmania and New South Wales. A few scenes in the Bondi studio in mid-August were followed by a month on location in Tasmania, mainly in the ruins of the convict settlement of Port Arthur. There Dawn's technical ingenuity came into its own: complex composite images were created by multiple exposures and an elaborate series of 'glass shots', which allowed Dawn to add roofs to decaying buildings by painting miniature details on glass and positioning them exactly in front of the camera to match the buildings in the distance. No expense was spared: period costumes were borrowed from the Hobart museum and painstakingly duplicated for crowd scenes involving hundreds of soldiers and convicts. In October the unit returned to Sydney, where studio sets had been constructed for the prison interiors.

An old sailing ship, the *Inca,* had also been bought and reconditioned, and was put to sea in Sydney Harbour for the film. Locations used in New South Wales over the next few months included the banks of the Parramatta River near Ryde, where a prison escape scene involving 500 extras was staged at a cost of over £1200 for one day's shooting (with each extra paid at least £1, and six cameras positioned on raised platforms). Other scenes were shot at the old town of Berrima, with its convict-built jail, and at the Wombeyan Caves. Throughout production, a trio of musicians played mood music on the set to help the cast perform with the required intensity.

239 *For the Term of his Natural Life* George Fisher (*l*), Mayne Lynton

Apart from the four American players, the cast included Arthur McLaglen, a boxer and vaudeville performer then working in Australia, who had acted in several British films and later became better known as the brother of Victor McLaglen. A minor part was taken by Marion Marcus Clarke, the daughter of the novelist, but the most publicized Australian player was Jessica Harcourt, a Sydney mannequin with limited experience as a singer and dancer in stage shows for J. C. Williamson. The film's principal cameraman, Len Roos, was an American who had first visited Australia in 1924 to make travelogues for the Fox Film Corporation. He remained in Australia after the completion of *For the Term of his Natural Life* to join other local producers on various minor projects, including a series of one-reel comedies known as *The Adventures of Dot.*

239 *For the Term of his Natural Life*

For the Term of his Natural Life was premièred in Newcastle at the Theatre Royal on 20 June 1927, and opened in Sydney five days later at the Crystal Palace, where it ran for an unprecedented eleven weeks. Its immediate success on the local market was assured, but its value in revival seasons and, more importantly, its value overseas, was gravely undermined by the arrival of talkies on the world market in 1928. Despite Australasian's confidence about an American release, the film made no appearance there until June 1929, when a minor release was arranged in New York. Australasian lost heavily in the venture—not just on the production but also in the costs of the studio renovation at Bondi.

Dawn remained in Australia until September 1927 to see the film launched on its commercial run, and to shoot the second of Australasian's large-scale international productions, *The Adorable Outcast* (1928). He returned to Hollywood and worked on several minor Westerns before coming back to Australia to make a talkie, *Showgirl's Luck* (1931).

240 **Environment***

1927 GERALD M. HAYLE

PC: Advance Films. P: Vaughan C. Marshall. SC: Gerald M. Hayle. PH: Tasman Higgins. 6000 feet.

CAST: Beth Darvall (Mary Garval), Hal Percy (James Denison), Colin Campbell (Arthur Huston), Alf Scarlett (James Masterton), Arthur Bruce (James Garval), Jim Joyce (Wilfred Garval), Dorothy May (Mrs Huston), Max Sorelle (Mr Eltham), Kitty Mostyn (Mrs Eltham), Viva Vawden (Mrs Harrop), Charles Brown (Henry Harrop), George Gilbert (Hal Hawkins), Edward Landor (Abe Halstein), Phyllis Best (Biddy O'Rooke).

Mary is a young girl forced by poverty to pose for a painting of a lightly draped female figure, which the artist calls 'L'Environnement'. She is courted by the artist's suave associate, Arthur, but when she learns that he is married, she runs in panic from his advances. She takes refuge on a farm and falls in love with Jim, a very proper young farmer who loudly denigrates the dissipation of modern woman. Mary and Jim are eventually married, but Arthur plans revenge on the girl who once rejected him. He hires an evil Jewish friend to spy on them and sends them the painting of 'L'Environnement' as a wedding present. Recognizing Mary as the model, Jim's love suddenly turns to hate, but after she sheds many tears he decides to forgive her and begins to destroy the painting. As he does so, he finds a lost will in the frame, which reveals Mary to be the heiress to a large fortune. Thereafter Mary and Jim live happily together in wealth and luxury.

Produced for about £4000, *Environment* was shot in the first months of 1927 on locations in and around Melbourne. The producer-promoter, Vaughan C. Marshall, took pains to woo the wealthier sectors of Melbourne society, not only to find an audience but also to attract investment for further productions. He hired the Palace Theatre ('The House Exquisite'), Melbourne, for two weeks commencing on 23 July 1927, and surrounded the season with an aura of 'high culture' and nationalism (although the film itself contained very little that was specifically Australian).

The attempt cannot have been entirely successful: the film was scarcely seen outside Victoria, and Marshall produced only one more feature, *Caught in the Net* (1928), before withdrawing from production. He had a long career in Melbourne as an exhibitor, and after dabbling in production he returned to exhibition and distribution for the rest of his career. His director on *Environment*, Gerald M. Hayle, had made industrial and advertising films in Melbourne for several years, but after this first feature he left Marshall's staff to direct *The Rushing Tide* (1927) for Koala Films.

241 The Rushing Tide

1927 GERALD M. HAYLE

PC: Koala Films. P, SC: Gerald M. Hayle. PH: Tasman Higgins. 6500 feet.

CAST: Beth Darvall (Ruth Jeffries), Norman Lee (Harold Wilson), Iris Roderick (Mrs Morrison), Godfrey Cass (Howard Morrison), Eardley Turner (Jeffries), Dora Mostyn, Edwin Lester, Barry Lock, Brian Ewart, W. Lane Bayliff.

Harold Wilson inherits a map showing the location of a secret hoard of diamonds. With Howard Morrison and his wife, he sets out to find the jewels. Their search takes them to a lonely stretch of coast where they meet Ruth Jeffries and her father, a fugitive from the police. Morrison steals the diamonds, kills Jeffries, and sets his wife and Wilson adrift in an open boat. Mrs Morrison dies at sea, but Wilson is rescued by a passing boat. Meanwhile, Morrison forces Ruth to go with him to the city, where he finds that the diamonds are worthless. Wilson returns to rescue Ruth, and they are eventually married.

Shooting began in July 1927 at the time when Hayle's first feature, *Environment*, was being premièred in Melbourne. An old cinema in the Melbourne suburb of Glenhuntly was used as a studio, and location scenes were shot near Portsea. The film was screened privately at the Majestic Theatre, Melbourne, on 19 October 1927, but commercial screenings were rare; it did not open in Sydney until 10 November 1928, when it began a minor season at the Piccadilly Theatre. Hayle confessed at the time: 'I have never had anything to do with the releasing of pictures and I do not understand the marketing conditions' (*RCE*, p. 858). The Melbourne *Sun*, 20 October 1927, reported: 'The story is worked out well, and there are many fine scenic effects among the ti-trees and cliffs of Port Phillip.'

239 *For the Term of his Natural Life* Jessica Harcourt

242 The Man who Forgot

1927 A. R. HARWOOD

P: A. R. Harwood. PH: William Hallam. 5000 ft (?)
CAST: Walter Nicholls (Stephen Jackson), William Hallam (Crazy Dan).

Little is known about Harwood's first film. It was clearly a low-budget melodrama shot outdoors to save studio costs, with one of the leading actors also serving somehow as cameraman. The story ranged widely in location, and included scenes at the Ascot racecourse in Melbourne, a fight on the brink of the Werribee Gorge, scenes of timber-felling in the Dandenong ranges, and a dramatic escape by the hero in an aeroplane, staged at the Essendon aerodrome.

242 A. R. Harwood

During 1927 Harwood, partnered by his leading actors, Nicholls and Hallam, leased Louise Lovely's *Jewelled Nights* (1925) and took it 'on the road' around rural Victoria with their own film as a special 'All Australian' show. No city screenings have been traced.

What Harwood lacked in talent as a director, he made up for in perseverance, usually in the face of formidable shortages of finance and equipment. He spent over thirty years in the film business, producing a string of low-budget quickies in the 1930s and working for many years as an independent exhibitor and publicist. Alexander Roy Harwood (generally known as Dick) was born in 1897 in Melbourne. After the war he worked for an insurance company and was posted to Tahiti where he observed the shooting of Maurice Tourneur's *Never the Twain shall Meet* (1925). Thereafter he was determined to become a producer himself, and on his return to Australia he established ties with the film trade, which led to *The Man who Forgot.* He planned a second film with Nicholls and Hallam, a farce called *Struth*, but the project was abandoned in favour of investment in distribution, and for several years Harwood worked with independent agencies in Melbourne. In 1931 he ventured into production again with *Out of the Shadows*, an attempt to capture the market with the first Australian talkie.

243 The Miner's Daughter

1927 LEO FORBERT

PC: Southern Cross Productions. P: Charles James MacLaren.
CAST: Bert McCarthy.

Little is known about this low-budget quickie shot for £1000 in a temporary studio in St Kilda, Melbourne, and on locations in Sydney and the Victorian mining town of Bendigo. The film, apparently financed by members of Melbourne's Jewish community, starred a champion boxer, Bert McCarthy, in the leading role. The proprietor of Southern Cross Productions, Charles James MacLaren, claimed that he had had twenty years' experience of camerawork in England and America. The supervisor of his production was Leo Forbert, a successful Polish photographer and art director who visited Australia briefly in the late 1920s. The film was completed by December 1927 and was handed to A. R. Harwood for distribution. Harwood later recalled that he was 'never able to do anything with it', although he tried to promote it as 'something different, something away from the usual bush story'. His advertising listed highlights, which included a fight on a crane at a city building site, scenes of a police patrol in action, and a 'thrilling' scene filmed at The Gap, outside Sydney Harbour.

244 The Romance of Runnibede*

1928 SCOTT R. DUNLAP

PC: Phillips Film Productions. P: Frederick Phillips. TITLES: Gayne Dexter. From the novel by Steele Rudd. PH: Len Roos, Cliff Thomas. ED: Cecil Hargraves. ASST D: Eric Wilkinson. 6000 ft.
CAST: Eva Novak (Dorothy Winchester), Gordon Collingridge (Tom Linton), Claude Saunders (Sub-Inspector Dale), Roland Conway (Arthur Winchester), Dunstan Webb (Goondai), Marion Marcus Clarke (Miss Frazer), Virginia Ainsworth (Mrs Conley).

The story was based on only one of the incidents in Steele Rudd's novel, which was published to coincide with the film's release and contained stills from it.

Dorothy Winchester returns from school in Sydney to her family's cattle station, Runnibede, in northern Queensland. She finds two equally likeable men eager for her hand in marriage—Tom Linton, the gauche station manager, and the more sophisticated Sub-Inspector Dale of the Queensland mounted police. Some local Aborigines believe that Dorothy is their 'Great White Queen', returned from the dead, and aroused by an evil witch-doctor, they kidnap her. In the ensuing fight, the rivalry of the men for

Dorothy's love is resolved when one of her suitors gives his life to save her.

Frederick Phillips, an American businessman, formed the production company in Sydney in November 1926, when euphoria over *For the Term of his Natural Life* was at its height, and the time ripe to attract investors. Filming commenced in May, and after some interior scenes in Sydney, the unit moved to the main location, a cattle station near the town of Murgon in south-east Queensland. An American director, Scott R. Dunlap, with an extensive background in B-film production, was hired for the film, but his arrival in Australia was delayed and the initial work was directed by William Reed, the husband of Eva Novak and a major shareholder in the production company. Wallace Worsley, a Hollywood director famous for *The Hunchback of Notre Dame* (1923), was visiting Australia at the time and was hired to serve 'in an advisory capacity'. The enterprise was dogged from the start by ill fortune and entrepreneurial inefficiency. Location shooting was dominated by heated arguments and procrastination, and Dunlap reshot much of the footage already taken by Reed.

It emerged as a Hollywood formula movie, designed for overseas audiences, with maps and explanatory titles about Australian geography that were scarcely necessary for the home market. Some of the action (most notably Dorothy's kidnap by the Aborigines) was well photographed, and Eva Novak's performance was pleasantly restrained, but the film was undermined by the two male leads: Dale is especially colourless and Linton is naïve to the point of absurdity. The Aboriginal 'headhunters' are stock figures from Hollywood African adventures, with a corroboree resembling both a conga and an Indian war dance, with a fiendishly daubed Dunstan Webb appearing as an unintentionally hilarious witch-doctor.

Distributed by Australasian Films, the film opened in Brisbane at the Wintergarden Theatre on 9 January 1928. Despite much expensive publicity, the film failed commercially, and by May a receiver had been appointed for the production company. The film had cost about £12 000 and *Everyones*, 13 May 1928, estimated that only £2000 had been returned to the company. Steele Rudd, who had invested heavily in the film, lost most of his money, and Eva Novak left Australia with over £3000 due to her in salary, although she reportedly received American distribution rights for the film as compensation. It was sold in 1928 as a quota production in England, and although trade reviews were positive, it made little impact.

244 *The Romance of Runnibede* Claude Saunders (*r*)

244 *The Romance of Runnibede* Dunstan Webb (*c*), Eva Novak

245 The Shattered Illusion*

1928 A. G. HARBROW

PC: Victorian Film Productions. SC: A.G. Harbrow. PH: Reg Robinson. ASST D: R. Clark Harrison. 5000 ft (?)

CAST: J. Robertson Aiken (Lewis Alden), Gret Wiseman (Joyce Hilton), Don Winder (John Galway), Mary McDermott (Alice Newton), Jack Hooper (Dr Haynes), A. G. Harbrow (tramp), Alec Sutherland (tramp), Norman Arthur (John Elsworth), Clare Dight (Mrs Elsworth).

A financier, Lewis Alden, who believes himself indispensable to his many business operations, suffers a breakdown and loses his memory. He joins the crew of a ship and is marooned after a storm at sea. The shock of the wreck gives him back his memory, and he is overwhelmed with anxiety about his business affairs. One day he finds a drifting lifeboat and a chest of newspapers. To his dismay he reads that his companies have prospered in his absence, and his illusions of self-importance are shattered. He finds solace in the arms of Joyce, another survivor of the wreck, and after their rescue he goes to live with her in the tropical paradise of her family's plantation in New Guinea.

This scarcely credible plot, with its moral that no man is indispensable except to the woman who loves him, relies heavily on its titles and newspaper inserts for continuity. Interiors were shot during the last half of 1927 in a backyard studio in the Melbourne suburb of Abbotsford, and exteriors were staged on bayside beaches. Victorian Film Productions announced in January 1928 that the film was ready for release, and a few screenings followed in the Melbourne suburbs. The company persevered with two more films, a comedy short, *The Tramp* (1929), and another feature, *Tiger Island* (1930), both directed by Gerald M. Hayle.

246 The Menace**

1928 CYRIL J. SHARPE

PC: Juchau Productions. P: Percy Juchau. SC: Louise Miller (?). PH: Jack Bruce. ASST D: Eric Wilkinson (?), Al True (?).

CAST: David Edelsten (doctor).

The 'menace' is the drug traffic in Sydney. A man finds that his wife is an addict, and sets out to break the ring of drug-pedlars, who include several Chinese.

Percy Juchau, a Sydney businessman, formed a film company in November 1926, employing five Australians with varied experience in Hollywood: Cyril Sharpe, who had worked there as a 'technical director',

Jack Bruce, a camera technician, Al True and Eric Wilkinson, minor staff at Universal, and Louise Miller (Sharpe's wife), formerly of the Lasky studio. The only film completed was *The Menace,* shot late in 1926 and early in 1927 at the Sydney Showground. After directing the film, Sharpe left Juchau's employ and became managing director of Commonwealth Film Laboratories in Sydney, with Jack Bruce as his chief technician.

The film was belatedly previewed in Sydney before a trade audience on 2 February 1928, but no theatrical release followed. The *Sydney Morning Herald,* 3 February 1928, castigated it for its 'unhealthy sensationalism . . . It is not as though the drug traffic were here taken seriously as a social problem—it serves merely as a pretext for very thin and bombastic melodrama.'

247 The Spirit of Gallipoli*

1928 KEITH GATEGOOD, WILLIAM GREEN

P: Keith Gategood, William Green. SC: Hal Carleton. PH: Jack Fletcher. 5000 ft.
CAST: Keith Gategood (Billy Austin), William Green (Jack Thomas), Samuel Harris (William Austin), Gwen Sherwood (Mrs Austin), Marie Miller (Gladys Merton).

A rebellious young Australian reluctantly enters the army and is gradually moulded into a responsible adult. After winning distinction in service, he marries and settles down on a farm.

This simple film-with-a-purpose was made by two young army trainees in Sydney, with a cast of amateurs. Their aim was to promote the value of military training in peacetime, and the only glimpses of war appeared in a dream sequence of the Anzacs fighting at Gallipoli. The film was completed early in 1928 and distribution was arranged in Australia and New Zealand through the Fox Film Corporation. It opened at the Piccadilly Theatre, Sydney, on 17 March but attracted little attention.

248 Trooper O'Brien*

1928 JOHN GAVIN

PC: Australian Artists Company. P: Herbert Finlay. SC: Agnes Gavin. PH: Arthur Higgins. ED: John McGeorge. About 5500 ft.
CAST: Merle Ridgeway (Winnie), Gordon Collingridge (Glen O'Brien), John Gavin (Sergeant O'Brien), Charles Stanford (John Alston), Nellie Ferguson (Mrs Alston), Ernest Lauri (John Alston Jnr), Sybil Atholwood (Mrs Alston Jnr), Jimmy McMahon (Glen O'Brien as a child), Reg Quartley (Moori as a child), Betty Taylor (Winnie as a child), Cis Peachy (Mrs O'Brien), Martin Kelly (Detective Burns), Will Harris (Moori), Violet Elliot ('the budgeree flapper'), Walter Vincent (Reverend Matthews), Carlton Stuart, William Thornton.

Disowned by his wealthy father for marrying without his approval, John Alston departs for the bush and changes his name to Brown. He and his wife are killed in an accident, but their baby daughter, Winnie, is found and adopted by a kindly policeman, Sergeant O'Brien. Years pass, and Winnie becomes engaged to O'Brien's son, Glen, who is following in his father's footsteps by becoming a policeman. One day, young O'Brien attends the scene of a burglary in the Alston family home, and the Alstons later visit him to thank him for his help. Mrs Alston recognizes a locket found by Winnie at the scene of her parents' death, and joyfully realizes that Winnie is her long-lost granddaughter.

The film incorporated two long action sequences 'borrowed' from *The Kelly Gang* and *Robbery Under Arms* (both 1920). The excerpts were introduced, as a digression from the main plot, to illustrate two stories that Sergeant O'Brien tells his children about their Uncle Jim, a trooper who gave his life attempting to rid the land of bushrangers. In addition, a sub-plot followed a romance between Glen O'Brien's Aboriginal friend, Moori, and a black 'flapper' whom he meets in the city; the Aborigines are grotesquely broad comic caricatures, both played by white actors in blackface.

Early in 1926, John Gavin returned to Australia from Hollywood and renewed his old production partnership with the veteran entrepreneur, Herbert Finlay. Gavin and Finlay had not worked together for nearly fifteen years, and the film was Finlay's first feature production since 1912.

Shooting began in July 1926 under the title *The Key of Fate,* and the film was completed and censor-screened in September. The censors requested the deletion of scenes showing the shooting of Sergeant O'Brien's brother by bushrangers, but permitted the rest of the bushranging interludes to remain, presumably impressed by the film's long foreword in praise of the 'noble yet silent' men of the police force. Further alterations were made after censorship, with the addition of scenes depicting police training (filmed with the assistance of the Commissioner of Police), and the change of the title to *Trooper O'Brien.* The total cost came to scarcely more than £1000.

Distributed by Finlay, the film opened on 23 May 1928 at the Australian Picture Palace, Sydney, and astounded the trade by drawing 'continuous record business'. Other screenings followed with equally enthusiastic audiences. Its commercial success came from its reputation among uncritical filmgoers as an action movie about bushrangers, for press reviews were not encouraging. The *Sydney Morning Herald,* 13 April 1928, expressed regret that the producers had struggled against severe physical odds to achieve a fair technical standard and yet had made a film that was 'sadly lacking' in any dramatic insight: 'The story wanders vaguely on; the actors key themselves up to tremendous emotional stress over situations that are not essentially dramatic; and there is no sense of proportion whatever.' Gavin directed no further films, and after acting in *The Adorable Outcast* (1928) he retired from production.

249 The Adorable Outcast**

1928 NORMAN DAWN

PC: Australasian Films. A Union Master World Picture. P, SC: Norman Dawn. From the novel, *Conn of the Coral Seas*, by Beatrice Grimshaw. PH: Arthur Higgins, William Trerise. ED: Mona Donaldson. ART D: James Coleman. PM: Frank Marden. 7300 ft.

CAST: Edith Roberts (Luya), Edmund Burns (Stephen Conn), Walter Long (Fursey), Jessica Harcourt (Diedre Rose), John Gavin (Carberry), Katherine Dawn (Elizabeth), Arthur McLaglen (Iron Devil), Arthur Tauchert (Mack), Fred Twitcham (Sir John Blackberry), Compton Coutts (Pooch), William O'Hanlon (pearler), Claude Turton (pearler), Charles Weatherly, Tom Dalton, Walter Hunt.

Norman Dawn's second feature for Australasian Films was a Pacific island romance about a young adventurer, Stephen Conn, and his love for Luya 'a beautiful untamed little Pagan'. Rumours of a hoard of gold belonging to Stephen arouse the interest of an evil 'blackbirder', Fursey, and his fellow traders in 'native flesh'. When Fursey kidnaps Luya the islanders are aroused to warlike fury and with Stephen they attack Fursey's stronghold in their outrigger canoes. Luya is saved, and when an island chieftain reveals that her parents were white, she and Stephen are happily united.

In April 1927 the crew and Australian cast sailed to Fiji, where they were joined by three American players, Edith Roberts, Edmund Burns and the prolific Hollywood villain, Walter Long. Most of the film was shot on location in the Fiji islands, and late in June the unit returned to Sydney for a few interior scenes in Australasian's Bondi studio. Dawn returned to America in September. After a thorough national publicity campaign, Australasian released the film at the Tivoli Theatre, Brisbane, on 25 June 1928. Although trading was initially strong, it is unlikely that the film covered its high production cost of £35 000 before sound eradicated the market for silent films. In 1929 it was given limited release in America under the title *Black Cargoes of the South Seas*. Coming after £50 000 tied up in *For the Term of his Natural Life* (1927), its cost was more than Australasian could justify for the local market without guarantees of adequate overseas distribution. With their heavy commitments in theatre construction, and uncertainty in the industry over sound, the company decided to abandon feature production.

Reviews were cautious: *Everyones*, 26 December 1928, found the story 'too episodic' but acknowledged the potential box-office appeal of the exotic settings. Trick photography, in which Dawn specialized, was less in evidence than in his earlier Australian film, but a few effects were worked into the film, most notably some startling composite shots for underwater scenes, including a cross-section view of a lagoon, showing turtles (actually in an aquarium) swimming beneath native canoes.

249 *The Adorable Outcast* Edith Roberts (*foreground*)

250 Caught in the Net

1928 VAUGHAN C. MARSHALL

PC: Advance Films. P: Vaughan C. Marshall. PH: Tasman Higgins. 5 reels.

CAST: Zillah Bateman (Phyllis Weston), John Mayer (Jack Stacey), Charles Brown (Robson), Peggy Farr, Viva Vawden, Felix St.H. Jellicoe, Beverley Usher.

Vaughan C. Marshall's second Melbourne production (and the first he directed) was, like *Environment* (1927), preoccupied with high society. The story followed the fashionable theme of a social butterfly ensnared in a net of romance. The girl, Phyllis Weston, is loved by two men, the dashing Jack Stacey, and the unscrupulous Robson. In a yacht race (staged for the film by the St Kilda Yacht Club), Robson tries to foul Jack's boat but fails. Unrelenting, Robson persuades his sister to entice Jack into a compromising situation, but a friend manages to save Jack's name from slander, and Robson is denounced.

Zillah Bateman, a British actress visiting Australia for theatrical engagements, was cast in January 1928 to play the lead in Marshall's film. With a budget estimated at £2000, exteriors were shot at the seaside resort of Portsea, where 'many of Australia's best-known society people' were filmed. It was released as a supporting film at the Haymarket Theatre, Sydney, on 14 July 1928, and in 1929 it was offered as a quota production in England. The British trade paper, *Kine Weekly*, 20 June 1928, dismissed it as suitable only for 'cheap halls': the film was dominated by an 'extremely weak plot and amateurish direction', relieved only by some 'exceptionally good' yacht-racing scenes. Marshall announced plans for other feature films, including a horse-racing drama, but none eventuated.

251 The Far Paradise**

1928 PAULETTE MCDONAGH

PC: MCD Productions. P, SC: Paulette McDonagh. PH: Jack Fletcher. ART D, PM: Phyllis McDonagh. 7000 ft.
CAST: Marie Lorraine (Cherry Carson), Gaston Mervale (James Carson), Arthur McLaglen (Karl Rossi), John Faulkner (Howard Lawton), Paul Longuet (Peter Lawton), Arthur Clarke (Lee Farrar), Harry Halley (Brock).

The story is set in Kirkton, the southern capital of an unnamed country. Unknown to Cherry Carson, her father is deeply involved in crime and is the subject of an investigation by the Attorney-General, Howard Lawton. Cherry falls in love with Lawton's son, Peter, but her father tries to disrupt the affair. Soon after, Carson goes into hiding, taking Cherry with him. A year later, Peter finds her selling flowers in a mountain tourist resort, struggling to support herself and her father, who has taken to drink. After a series of emotional confrontations, Carson dies of a heart attack and Cherry is left free to marry Peter.

Locations were used in the Burragorang Valley, at Penrith (for the tourist resort), and at scenic points and stately homes in Sydney and Melbourne. Interiors were shot in the lavishly decorated home of the McDonagh sisters, Drummoyne House, Sydney, and in the Bondi studio of Australasian Films. Released by British Dominion Films, the £2000 production opened strongly at the Regent Theatre, Sydney, on 14 July 1928. In 1930 it was bought by Universal Pictures for British distribution as an Empire quota production.

Compared with *Those Who Love*, the *Sydney Morning Herald*, 20 June 1928, found the sisters' new romance a marked improvement, revealing 'decision in every detail'. The performance of Marie Lorraine reflected Paulette McDonagh's belief in subdued, 'naturalistic' screen acting; she not only showed 'the utmost confidence in every movement, but she has the power of expressing much feeling with a minimum of outward show'.

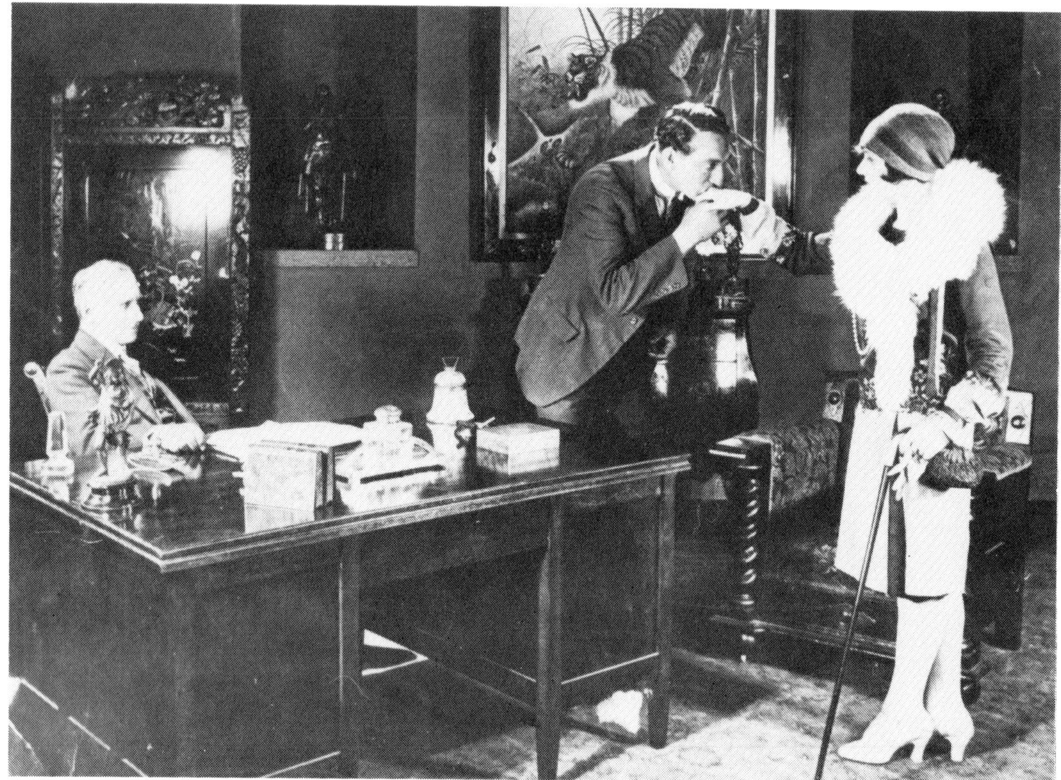

251 *The Far Paradise* Gaston Mervale (*l*), Arthur McLaglen, Marie Lorraine

252 The Grey Glove

1928 DUNSTAN WEBB

STORY: E. V. Timms. TITLES: Gayne Dexter. ED: Mona Donaldson. 5000 ft(?)
CAST: Aubrey Kelner (John Courtney), Val Lassau (Margaret Trent), Phyllis Wheldon (Pauline Hemingway), Charles O'Mara (Inspector Drew), William Thornton (Charlie James), Claude Turton (Simpson), George Ames (Peterson), Carl Francis (Seton Carr), James Alexander (Perry)

An enthusiastic amateur detective, John Courtney, undertakes to catch a mysterious criminal who always leaves a grey glove at the scene of his crimes. After several adventures, including a visit to a Chinese opium den, and a series of murders, John and his fiancée, Margaret, uncover the work of a ruthless foreign spy and manage to capture him.

Based on a newspaper serial by E. V. Timms, *The Grey Glove* was a minor thriller that aroused little trade or press interest. Distributed by J. C. Williamson Films, it was released at the Grand Theatre, Adelaide, on 16 July 1928.

253 The Birth of White Australia**

1928 PHIL K. WALSH

PC: Dominion Films. SC: Phil K. Walsh.
PH: Lacey Percival, Walter Sully. 6000 ft(?).
CAST: Bert Trawley (John Davis), Dot McConville (Mary Davis), Rita Aslin (Miss Dinah Myte), Alice Layton (Madame Sefton), Frank Hardingham (Tom Kendrick), Pietro Sosso (Portuguese Dick), Gamboola.

This panoramic view of Australian racial history, like D. W. Griffith's *The Birth of a Nation* (1915), was intended to portray the genesis of white nationhood. The crucial episode in the gaining of national identity was seen as the stemming of 'the on-rushing tide of Asiatics which threatened the submergence of the white race' in Australia.

The film, which survives today in the National Film Archive, ranges freely back and forth in time, including footage of military parades and views of the national capital and parliament. William Morris Hughes is among the dignitaries seen, making a statement (via intertitles) about the importance of Australia's close links with Britain. Other scenes go back to the origin of white Australia, with the landing of Captain Cook, the work of explorers, and the struggles of early settlers in the bush. The first major test of the young nation comes on the goldfields in the 1850s in Victoria, and above all in the clash between Australian and Chinese miners at Lambing Flat in central New South Wales in 1861. Several violent confrontations at Lambing Flat are depicted, including the attempted murder by Chinese of a white girl after she rebukes them for washing their clothes in the common drinking water. Such clashes persuade the government to introduce legislation to restrict Chinese immigration and the first great blow for white nationhood is struck.

The film was substantially shot on location at Lambing Flat (since renamed Young) and was financed entirely by the townspeople. The director, Phil K. Walsh, formed the production company in February 1927 and raised

253 *The Birth of White Australia*

capital estimated at £3000. Shooting began in September, with a cast largely composed of local Young citizens. Whites were recruited to play Chinese, with stockings over their faces to suggest Mongoloid features, and their grotesque appearance was central to the film's caricature of the Chinese as uncouth barbarians sneaking furtively around their makeshift hovels. The film was privately previewed in Sydney on 24 July 1928, and a public première was held at the Strand Theatre, Young, on 5 September 1928. No commercial screening in Sydney or other state capitals seems to have taken place, and the Young investors lost heavily. Walsh left the town and had no further known association with feature production.

253 *The Birth of White Australia*

254 The Exploits of the Emden**

1928 *Australian sequences:* KEN G. HALL

PC: First National Pictures (Australasia). P, SC, ED: Ken G. Hall. PH: Claud C. Carter, Ray Vaughan. P ASST: Victor Bindley.
CAST: Officers and men of the Royal Australian Navy.

1926 *German original:* LOUIS RALPH

PC: Münchner Lichtspielkunst A.G. (Emelka). SC: R. Werner PH: Ewald Daub, Werner Bohne, Arthur von Schwertführer, Josef Wirsching. ART D: Ludwig Reiber, Botho Höfer. 9000 ft.
CAST: Louis Ralph, Fritz Greiner, Jack Mylong-Münz, Charles Willy Kayser, Maria Minzenti, and former officers and marines of *Emden*, including Kapitänleutnant von Mücke.

This semi-documentary reconstructs *Emden*'s career during the First World War and her final confrontation with HMAS *Sydney* in November 1914. A romantic sub-plot involves a German officer in China who sends for his wife to join him. When war is declared, he is assigned to *Emden*. He meets his wife again by chance when *Emden* takes aboard passengers from the doomed *Diplomat* in the Indian Ocean. The officer is one of the survivors of the final engagement with *Sydney*.

The 9000-foot German film, *Unsere Emden*, made in 1926, was bought for distribution in Australia by First National Pictures, but when prints arrived in 1927, the use of model ships and the casting of heavily Teutonic types to play Australians caused First National some concern. In an attempt to make the film presentable for Australian audiences, John C. Jones, the managing director of First National, assigned his publicity director, Ken G. Hall, to the task of reshooting the sequences dealing with *Emden*'s encounter with *Sydney*. Hall was later to become a major figure in Australian film production (see *On Our Selection*, 1932), but at this time his experience was limited to publicity and exhibition, and he had only handled film physically when re-editing silent films to meet the demands of Australian censorship.

255 *The Russell Affair* Arthur Clarke, Jessica Harcourt

With assistance from a participant in the *Sydney-Emden* engagement, Hall prepared a scenario, which introduced some characteristic touches of broad humour, including a sequence of an Australian sailor on *Sydney* who busily collects his debts before the battle with *Emden* begins. In January 1928, Hall approached the Australian Naval Board in Melbourne, and found its members eager to co-operate because of the potential propaganda value of the film. In March, Hall and two newsreel cameramen, Claud C. Carter and Ray Vaughan, began shooting at Jervis Bay, where *Sydney* was exercising. Naval officers and ratings filled the necessary acting roles. Six thousand feet of film were exposed in one week, and when edited by Hall, increased the length of the German film to over 10 000 feet. After approval from the Naval Board, Hall launched a thorough publicity campaign and the film was released on 21 September 1928 at the Prince Edward Theatre, Sydney, with strong commercial results.

255 The Russell Affair

1928 P. J. RAMSTER

P, SC: Juliette De La Ruze. PH: William Trerise.
CAST: Jessica Harcourt (Ruby Russell), Gaston Mervale (Arthur White), Adrienne Stewart (Juliette Hope), Arthur McLaglen, Fred Twitcham, Arthur Clarke, Robert Purdie, Roy Paine.

In this society melodrama, an artist, Stephen Patrick, falls in love with his young model, a salesgirl, Juliette. But Juliette loves Doctor Lonsdale, who is engaged to a wealthy and beautiful widow, Ruby Russell. Jealous of Juliette, Ruby destroys Patrick's paintings of her, but falls victim to a blackmailer, Arthur White. Juliette meanwhile is charged with the damage to the paintings and is arrested. The ensuing climax 'leaves one a little doubtful and misinformed as to Ruby's fate and the future of Lonsdale and Juliette' (*Sydney Mail*, 10 October 1928).

Juliette De La Ruze was a young woman anxious to make a career in film who invested her own money in the production. Despite her use of experienced staff, the *Sydney Mail* found that 'vagueness . . . in the continuity and general construction of the story' was a liability. After a preview at the Prince Edward Theatre, Sydney, on 4 October 1928, the film seems to have disappeared, although in 1929 it was bought by Fox as a quota film for England.

256 Phyllis Gibbs

256 Odds On

1928 ARTHUR HIGGINS

PC: Arthur Higgins Productions. P, SC: Arthur Higgins. TITLES: Austin Fay. PH: Arthur Higgins, Tasman Higgins. ED: Arthur Higgins, Sheila Moore. 6300 ft.
CAST: Arthur Tauchert (Grafter Jones), Phyllis Gibbs (Betty Grayson), 'Check' Hayes (Sydney Baxter), Stella Southern, Stanley Court, Robert Purdie, John Faulkner, Violet Elliot (the cook), W. H. McLachlan Jnr, Gayne Threlkeld.

This first feature by the veteran cinematographer Arthur Higgins was constructed from familiar plot formulas. A jockey, Sydney Baxter, tries to shield a friend by allowing himself to be suspended for six months for improper riding. Down and out, he joins up with a racecourse urger, Grafter Jones, and sets off to tour country race meetings. Baxter soon finds a job in the stables of a family friend, Mr Grayson, and falls in love with his daughter, Betty. Grayson gives Baxter the chance to ride Brigade, his entry in the local derby, and the horse comes home a clear winner, despite attempts by Baxter's rivals to foil his success.

Odds On was made for £2000 in June 1928 on location at Randwick racecourse, Sydney, and in the Bondi studio of Australasian Films. Distributed by Australasian, it was released at the Haymarket Theatre, Sydney, on 6 October 1928.

257 The Devil's Playground*

1928 VICTOR BINDLEY

PC: Fineart Films Productions. From the lyrics of 'Hell's Highway' by Ashley Durham. TITLES, CONTINUITY: John Bedouin. PH: Jack Bruce, James Grant, Jack Fletcher. ED: J. Stebbing. ART D: Henri Mallard. 8385 ft.

CAST: John R. Allen (Martin Herle), Elza Stenning (Naneena), Petrie Potter ('Bull' Morgan), Terry Short (the mate), John Haddock (Dick Barrington), Richard Alrich (Reverend Andrew Fullerton), 'Dick' Fletcher (Lillian Fullerton), Cyril Callaghan (Chief Trelua), Edna Crofts (Trelua's wife), Stanley Murdoch (Bobby), Vera Campbell (South Coast Sal).

Somewhere in the South Seas, a beautiful island has become notorious for the 'fetish and cannibal rites' of the natives and the 'wild doings' of the white population. 'Bull' Morgan, the owner of the island's liquor store, lusts after a vivacious young white girl known to the islanders as Naneena. One day Naneena falls in love with a visiting airman, Dick Barrington, and they decide to marry. Dick departs, promising to return with his wealthy parents in their steam yacht. Soon after, Naneena is found unconscious on the beach and suffering from amnesia. At the same time, her brother, Bobby, disappears and a wild storm hampers the work of a search party. Later, the native chief, Trelua, leads an insurrection against the whites because of the degradation that his people have suffered since the arrival of the white man. In the confusion, Morgan tries to force Naneena to accept him. The shock brings back her memory and she remembers how she had witnessed Morgan murdering her brother. Dick's yacht arrives at the island and is promptly besieged by native war boats, but a British cruiser hears Dick's distress signal and speeds to the rescue. The native rebellion is quelled but not before Trelua kills his chief oppressor, Morgan.

Riddled with clichés of the South Sea island genre, and suffering from some stilted central performances, the film was nevertheless photographed and edited with finesse. Several scenes include dramatically effective cross-cutting between parallel actions such as the hectic search for Bobby in the raging storm and a wild orgy at Morgan's trading station. The battles and fights of the last reels are also staged with an athletic energy that probably expressed the enthusiasm of the amateur cast, and it is not surprising that these scenes attracted the attention of the censors.

The film was produced by a largely amateur group from the north shore of Sydney who had formed the Fineart film club in mid-1927. Their first production, a Pacific island adventure, *Trobriana*, was never released; it probably formed the basis of *The Devil's Playground*. Scenes were shot on beaches near Sydney, and interiors in the Mosman Town Hall. The cast included a teenager, Elza Stenning, who later became well-known in Sydney's 'high society' as Elsa Jacoby. The island rebels were played by Sydney lifeguards in blackface.

In February 1930 the Commonwealth censors objected to a scene in which Naneena was whipped by Morgan, and prevented the export of the film to England, where the producer had arranged a sale to Universal. The censors had no jurisdiction over Australian screenings, and the producers announced their intention to dub the film with sound and enter it in the Commonwealth film competition of 1930. Nothing further, however, seems to have been done, and it disappeared from view.

258 The Kingdom of Twilight

1929 ALEXANDER MACDONALD

PC: Seven Seas Screen Productions. P, SC: Alexander Macdonald. PH: Lacey Percival, Walter Sully. 8360 ft.
CAST: Wendy Osborne (Dorothy Carrington), John Faulkner (Jim Carrington), Rex Arnot (McCrimmon), David Wallace (Reginald Carewe), Len Norman (Tanami), Laurel Macdonald (baby), Herrick Corbett (Puggy Markham), Jean Seton.

The British author and explorer, Alexander Macdonald, had worked for several years in exhibition and distribution in Australia. In 1927 he formed a company in Scotland and made *The Unsleeping Eye,* an adventure shot in Papua by an Australian cameraman, Walter Sully. Despite adverse trade reviews, *The Unsleeping Eye* was a commercial success when released in England in April 1928, and in June, Macdonald returned to Sydney with his Australian-born wife, the actress Wendy Osborne, to make another outdoor action movie. This new film, shot under the title of *Tanami* but released as *The Kingdom of Twilight,* involved much the same cast and crew as his Papuan film, including Rex Arnot, a former lieutenant-commander in the British navy, and a London journalist, D. Given-Smith, acting under the name of David Wallace. Described by Macdonald as a melodrama about the 'troubles and hardships of the Australian pioneers', it was set in the early days of gold-mining. The middle-aged hero, Jim Carrington, with his resourceful daughter, Dorothy, leaves behind a family scandal in England and seeks new fortunes as a gold prospector in northern Australia. He learns of a mountain of gold guarded by a mysterious tribe of Aborigines, but is wounded and captured by the tribe. He is given up for dead by all except Dorothy, who continues to search for him. Eventually she too is captured by the Aborigines, and finds her father alive. They manage to return together to white civilization, where Dorothy is happily reunited with a young gold-miner who loves her.

Scenes were shot at an old mining camp at Chillagoe, inland from Cairns in northern Queensland. A large number of Aborigines appeared in the film, and a special corroboree was staged in the Mungana caves near Chillagoe. Shooting on Queensland locations was completed in September 1928, and the film was released in London in December 1929 by Universal. It was never released in Australia. The British trade paper, *Bioscope,* 22 January 1930, saw little of value in it: the story was 'long drawn out' and 'sadly stereotyped'. As an exercise in exoticism it was also a failure: 'there is no reason why the savages should not be Red Indians, and the film be called a Western, the scenery suggesting the desert of Arizona rather than tropical Queensland'.

Part 4:

1930–1939

Australian feature films made little direct reference to the Depression, except belatedly with a stylized picture of poverty in *The Broken Melody* (1938). A large number of films, however, made oblique references, for example with Dad and Dave in *On Our Selection* (1932), struggling against forces beyond their control (drought, financial debt, evil land-owners). There were also a number of films about the urban 'little man' with his everyday worries about job security, and his fantasies of sudden wealth. These included *Mr Chedworth Steps Out* (1939) and the comedies of George Wallace. Escape from the Depression was offered by musicals, made possible by the advent of sound, and by a series of exotic romances set on idyllic islands or in the tropical north. Few films were overtly nationalistic and there was a trend away from the distinctive Australian bush to an amorphous city life. Even Dad and Dave were progessively urbanized during the decade, and the city in *Dad and Dave Come to Town* (1938) was an anonymous and stereotyped metropolis.

Australian film-makers had for a long time experimented with sound. In 1928 talkies made their first major bid for the world market, and by early 1930 Australian film-makers were attempting to transform their silent films into partial-talkies, usually employing a sound-on-disc system, which was soon outmoded. The first commercially viable sound feature was *Diggers* (1931), made by Efftee with expensive optical sound equipment imported from the U.S.A. Soon after, the construction of an efficient sound apparatus by Arthur Smith in Sydney became the technical basis for the Cinesound studio. Smith's equipment was used on feature films throughout the 1930s and for many years after on newsreels and documentaries.

Early in the decade production began to consolidate in the hands of big business. The higher production costs involved in sound, the increase in technical sophistication demanded by audiences, and continued distribution and exhibition difficulties, led to a reliance on intensively capitalized studios with specialized facilities. For both financial and technical reasons, feature production became inaccessible to the amateurs and the social groups who had been active in the silent era; women, too, virtually disappeared from production, other than as actresses and continuity girls.

Hollywood models became the basis for much of the industry in the 1930s. A studio on Hollywood lines was established by Cinesound Productions in 1932; the company employed its own regular troupe of actors and technicians, it 'discovered' stars and groomed them, and it supported the whole operation with a large-scale publicity machine promoting the name of the studio as well as the personalities employed by it. National Studios attempted to establish a similar studio at Pagewood in Sydney in 1935, with the construction of large production resources and the mustering of international talent and capital. One film, *The Flying Doctor* (1936), was made before the venture failed for lack of competent management and commercial success. Hollywood writers, directors and actors were sought by the industry, and Clarence Badger, Victor Jory, Charles Farrell and Helen Twelvetrees were among those who worked on local films.

Other producers in the 1930s sought to emulate Cinesound's success, but stable financial backing proved elusive. Charles Chauvel imitated Hollywood conventions in *Uncivilised* (1936) in an attempt to reach the American market, but he had yet to reach full maturity as a director. Later, during the Second World War, he achieved a happier balance between overtly Australian subjects and the conventions of Hollywood genres.

Some of the best or most ambitious actors and actresses were lured away to Hollywood, among them Mary Maguire, Cecil Kellaway, Errol Flynn, Shirley Ann Richards and Jocelyn Howarth. In their absence, local producers were forced to rely heavily on radio and the stage for acting talent. Frank Thring, at his Efftee studio in Melbourne, tied his productions closely to the stage, with a series of seven features between 1931 and 1936. Unlike the Hollywood orientation of Hall and Chauvel, Thring conceived of cinema primarily as a means of recording stage productions. Rarely in his films did images dominate words, and rarely were attempts made to modify stage performances, settings or even make-up for the screen. His films depended almost entirely for their commercial appeal on the presence of top-ranking stage stars, including Pat Hanna, George Wallace and Dorothy Brunton.

Sound arrived at a bad time for the industry. The Depression affecting the whole of Australian society was aggravated for the film industry by depressed conditions in the exhibition trade. The construction of luxury cinemas by both Union Theatres and Hoyts contributed to a 'film famine', with a shortage of films for the major city theatres. Stuart Doyle of the Australasian Films-Union Theatres combine (re-formed as Greater Union Theatres in 1931) decided to revive production in the hope of winning local audiences back into his theatres and of helping to satisfy some of the insatiable demand of the exhibition trade for 'specials'. The establishment of Cinesound in 1932 as a subsidiary of Greater Union marked the beginning of Australia's most profitable production venture. Under the management of Ken G. Hall, the studio produced a continuous stream of commercially successful features and provided other producers with experienced technicians, studio space and equipment at its three locations—at Bondi and Rushcutters Bay (the old Spencer studio) in Sydney, and at St Kilda in Melbourne.

Cinesound's first production, *On Our Selection* (1932), was enormously rewarding financially, and production continued throughout the 1930s on a self-supporting basis, with the income from one film providing the finance for the next. Meanwhile Greater Union Theatres remained in severe financial difficulty, and the pressure on Stuart Doyle culminated in July 1937 with his replacement as managing director by a young accountant, Norman Bede Rydge. While Doyle had encouraged production and taken risks to initiate it, Rydge was wary of the large-scale gamble inherent in making feature films. Rydge saw his primary responsibility as the protection of the investments of shareholders, and he regarded the 'bricks and mortar' of theatres as far safer than production. After continuity in production at Cinesound was broken by the war, Rydge saw no need to renew it in 1946, and plans for feature films in post-war years were not supported by the Greater Union executive until the 1970s.

Following the failure of the Commonwealth government to provide effective support for the industry after the 1927 Royal Commission, pressure continued to grow for effective government action to rationalize distribution and exhibition and to help producers. In 1934 the New South Wales government instituted an inquiry into the industry, out of which came legislation for an Australian film quota, a fixed percentage of Australian films that theatres were obliged to show. The quota legislation lacked adequate enforcement measures and within two or three years had virtually lapsed, despite several legislative attempts to strengthen it. The quota did, however, have a strong initial impact on production; in expectation of favourable effects flowing from the Act, new production activities mushroomed in 1934-35. The Act carried a quality clause intended to prevent the emergence of 'quota quickies' on the British pattern; films deemed by a committee to be of insufficient quality could not be registered as Australian productions, and accordingly, no theatre could count them as part of its quota. Failure to register as a quota production meant financial disaster, and several of the new production companies in the mid-1930s did not survive their first film.

The British Quota Act of 1927-28, under which films from Empire countries were given favoured treatment in Britain, had a greater impact on the production industry. Until this legislation was amended early in 1938, Australian producers continued to find ready sales of their films on the British market. The withdrawal of the British quota market in 1938 forced the cessation of production by at least one director, A. R. Harwood, who had relied on obligatory sales to Britain to cover as much as half of the production costs of his low-budget features.

Apart from feature films, the main production achievements of the 1930s were in newsreels, with the emergence of two sound news magazines in creative competition with each other. Cinesound's news magazine, *Cinesound Review*, revived the tradition of the silent *Australasian Gazette*, which had been produced from the earliest days of the combine until 1929. Supervised by Ken G. Hall and produced by an efficient team of technicians and writers, the weekly Cinesound magazine was designed as an entertainment, and its best episodes were witty and fast-moving, with signs of social conscience in editorial statements on some of the news stories. Its rival, *Movietone News*, managed by Harry Grattan Guinness, was an offshoot of American Movietone; like Cinesound, it employed some excellent local cameramen. It survived side by side with *Cinesound Review* until the two newsreels merged in October 1970.

Documentary production in Australia in the 1930s saw little of the excitement then transforming non-fiction film in England, where John Grierson had founded a new documentary school with film-makers like Harry Watt, Alberto Cavalcanti, Basil Wright and Humphrey Jennings. Frank Hurley remained the dominant Australian documentary film-maker, pursuing his own idiosyncratic style, apparently oblivious of Grierson's philosophies. Hurley's nature portraits became a model for many local film-makers who tried to emulate his high technical standards and grand romantic manner. Cinesound effectively exploited Hurley's personal popularity in Australia by setting him up as a one-man documentary unit in their Sydney studio, making short industrial films for government and private sponsors, such as *Treasures of Katoomba* (1934) and *A Nation is Built* (1937).

Commonwealth government production was relegated during the decade to a small unit in Melbourne; operating with only the most basic technical resources, much of the unit's work was narrowly functional and allowed little scope for film-makers with new ideas about the medium. Exceptions did, however, occasionally appear, and in 1934, Lacey Percival made for the government one of the finest of all Australian documentaries, *Among the Hardwoods*, a brief survey of the timber industry in Western Australia, making use of the natural sounds of the bush in place of conventional commentary and music, and capturing a series of striking images of light and shade in the forest.

Through the 1930s, then, the production industry underwent profound changes, not only technologically with the introduction of sound, but also in its structure, with a growing dependence on studio bases and large capital investment. The failure of the National Studios venture demonstrated that capital and hardware alone did not guarantee commercial viability. Ken Hall's contrasting success at Cinesound showed both an astute business sense and a philosophy of showmanship that stressed the responsibility of the film-maker to the paying audience. The readiness with which each Cinesound feature became a commercial success deceived many ambitious producers and susceptible investors, who were lured into feature production without really understanding the basis for Cinesound's success, and none managed to emulate it on the same scale, with or without the support of major distributors or exhibitors.

259 Tiger Island

1930 GERALD M. HAYLE

PC: Victorian Film Productions. SC: Gerald M. Hayle.
CAST: Beth Darvall, John Barry, Godfrey Cass, Charles Brown.

Shot during 1929 as a silent film, when talkies were rapidly dominating the trade, *Tiger Island* was doomed to early oblivion. The only known screening was in March 1930 in a small city theatre in Melbourne. A critic in the *Bulletin*, 26 March 1930, dealt severely with it: if it 'were five times better acted and five times better photographed, it would still be entirely negligible. It is the most actionless film ever conceived.'

According to the *Bulletin*, the plot followed an 'old man and his beautiful daughter [who] are lured to an island on the Victorian coast with the promise of a share in a deceased person's estate. The father finds that the fortune was made by dope-running, the snow being dropped from passing steamers. The old man is induced to join in the nefarious trade, and after a series of vicissitudes, during which the villain pursues the girl, the hero pursues the villain, and the detectives pursue the lot, the dope-runner is unmasked, papa exonerated and the lover gets his bit of skirt.'

260 The Cheaters*

1930 PAULETTE MCDONAGH

PC: McDonagh Productions. SC: Paulette McDonagh. PH: Jack Fletcher. ART D: Phyllis McDonagh. 6000 ft.
CAST: Marie Lorraine (Paula Marsh), Arthur Greenaway (Bill Marsh), John Faulkner (John Travers), Josef Bambach (Lee Travers), Nellie McNiven (Mrs Hugh Nash), Elaine de Chair (Louise Nash), Frank Hawthorne (Keith Manion), Leal Douglas (the Lady), Stanley Court (Jules Severie), Reg Quartley (Jan).

An embezzler, Bill Marsh, swears vengeance on a businessman, John Travers, who has turned him in to the police. Twenty years pass, and Marsh emerges from jail and establishes himself as the head of a powerful crime empire, with his daughter, Paula, serving as bait to attract wealthy victims. Paula falls in love with Lee Travers, the adopted son of Marsh's old enemy, and begins to have doubts about her life of crime. Only after a series of tragic incidents is she set free to marry Lee and to start life anew.

Although completed as a silent film early in 1929, *The Cheaters* was so long delayed in the McDonaghs' search for a release that they attempted to improve its commercial chances by adapting it into a partial talkie. Additional scenes were filmed in March 1930 in Melbourne, using a sound-on-disc system. The

260 *The Cheaters* Marie Lorraine and Josef Bambach in one of the talkie scenes

260 *The Cheaters* Marie Lorraine

260 *The Cheaters* Arthur Greenaway

talkie scenes, none of which remain in the surviving copy of the film, included a fancy-dress party sequence and a romantic interlude in which Paula at the piano sings a song to Lee. A musicians' union, nervous about the implications of talkies, caused further delays by temporarily preventing its members from recording music for the film, but by May it was ready for entry in the first Commonwealth film competition, where it failed to win a prize. On 1 June it was shown at the Roxy Theatre, Parramatta, to a large invited audience of press and trade representatives, but few commercial screenings followed, partly because of the poor quality of the sound reproduction.

Today, *The Cheaters* stands up well as a vivid crime melodrama. Occasional details of set design and plot are redolent of German expressionist cinema, especially Fritz Lang's *Dr Mabuse der Spieler* (1922); Marsh's crime empire, like Mabuse's, is an unseen force pervading society, and his headquarters are complete with scientific warning devices and secret vaults. Elsewhere, a careful use of close-ups of hands and eyes effectively stresses dramatic highlights, and a striking reverse tracking shot marks the moment when at last Marsh faces his sworn enemy, Travers. Such scenes clearly indicate the sisters' unusual sensitivity to the expressive range of the camera and their awareness of careful scenario construction as a key to emotionally powerful cinema.

261 **Fellers**

1930 ARTHUR HIGGINS, AUSTIN FAY

PC: Artaus Productions. SC: Ashley Durham. PH: Tasman Higgins. M: Barney Cuthbert. SONG: 'Boy of Mine', sung by Grace Quine. SD: Vic Myers. 8000 ft.
CAST: Arthur Tauchert (Roughie), Jean Duncan, Les Coney, Arthur Clarke, Joan Milton, Grace Quine, Arthur Greenaway, Peggy Pryde.

The story, about three mates in the Australian Light Horse in Palestine during the war, was seen by the *Sydney Mail*, 27 August 1930, as 'a hotch-potch of absurd coincidences'. According to a synopsis in *Everyones*, 27 August 1930, one of the trio had gone to the war 'for excitement; another because he thought he had killed a man in a fight over a girl; a third because he thought his girl no longer cared for him. The second is killed, and to save heartbreak for the girl back at home, the third exchanges identification discs, and has himself reported dead, only to learn that his own girl really loves him.' After the Armistice, however, the complications are resolved and the film ends with a reunion of the lovers.

The last reel of the film was synchronized with a few minutes of dialogue and a song, which *Everyones* dismissed as 'in no way important; moreover the recording is irregular. At one moment the voices come over excellently, only to blur a few moments later.' The rest of the film was silent, with a recorded music score as accompaniment, and even that failed to impress: 'the music is far too turbulent, providing for the most commonplace scene a background of such vivid emotions as would be in place only at a grand opera climax' (*Sydney Morning Herald*, 25 August 1930).

Although its soundtrack and story left much to be desired, considerable pains were taken to make the film visually spectacular. Action set in the Palestine desert was staged in sandhills near Sydney; newsreel footage of the actual desert campaigns was interpolated;

261 *Fellers* Arthur Clarke (*l, rear*), Arthur Tauchert (*r, front*)

261 *Fellers* Location scene in the Sydney sand dunes

and the film-makers travelled to western New South Wales to shoot vistas of long camel trains. The advertisements promised the sight of '4600 horses' and '3000 camels', as well as a human cast of several hundred.

The silent sequences were directed by Arthur Higgins, and the talkie sequence by Austin Fay. In May 1930 the film was awarded the third and only prize of £1500 in the Commonwealth film competition. Prizes were awarded on a points system, and Higgins and Fay claimed that their film had been given enough points to warrant the second prize of £2500. Fay announced his intention to sue for the second prize, but the Commonwealth government did not alter its decision.

Higgins hired the Theatre Royal, Sydney, for a two-week season of *Fellers*, commencing on 23 August 1930, but reviews and commercial results were poor.

262 Spur of the Moment*

1931 A. R. HARWOOD

PC: A. R. Harwood Talkie Productions. SC: A. R. Harwood. STORY: Betty Davies. PH: Leslie McCallum, Ed Wintle. ART D: Vic French. SD: J. Watson Gunner, Frank King. 50 mins (?)

CAST: James Alexander (Anthony Iredale), William Green (Inspector Perry), Guy Hastings (Chief of C.I.B.), Darcy Kelway (Joe), Syd Hollister (Alf), Fred Patey (Pop), Charles Bradley (Rutherford), William Ralston (Burton), Norman Balmer (Noble), Russell Cramer (Detective), Herb Moylan (Clerk of Courts), Denis Gerity (lawyer), Beatrice Touzeau (Claire Rutherford), Kath Neil (Mrs Burton), Virginia Parma (cigarette girl), Beryl Swindells (child), Andre Marcelle (Rutherford's secretary), Helene Best (Iredale's secretary), Arthur Hill (bell boy), the Royal Singers.

Early in 1931 Harwood attempted to beat Efftee to the screen with Australia's first talkie. A five reel 'society' romance, *Out of the Shadows*, was shot in Melbourne using a makeshift sound-on-disc recording system. The only set of wax discs, however, buckled in a heat wave before the film could be shown, and the whole enterprise foundered. Undeterred, Harwood secured new financial backing from a Melbourne businessman and converted an old factory in West Melbourne into a sound studio. A crude sound-on-film system was devised, and two features, *Spur of the Moment* and *Isle of Intrigue*, were rushed into production in mid-1931 using the same crew and substantially the same cast.

Spur of the Moment was a static indoors melodrama based on a story by a young Melbourne writer, Betty Davies. As Betty Roland she had written a much-praised play, *The Touch of Silk* (1928), and later became a prolific writer for radio as well as the author of numerous novels and plays. Her story begins when late one night a wealthy socialite, Claire Rutherford, impulsively visits her former lover, Tony Iredale, now a successful lawyer. Next day they are placed in an embarrassing position when Tony is arrested for the murder of a bookmaker the night before. Although Claire can prove his innocence, Tony remains silent to protect her from scandal. Eventually a detective manages to trap the killer during a re-enactment of the crime.

The film was immediately followed by *Isle of Intrigue*, and the two were released at the Palace Theatre, Melbourne, on 26 September 1931, just two weeks ahead of Efftee's first talkie, *Diggers*. The programme had modest commercial success, and after a short season at the Palace, screened widely in rural areas; the films were bought by a British distributor as Empire quota productions. Harwood beat Efftee to the screen, as was his goal, but he soon realized that his equipment could not compete, and he joined them as a publicist and sales manager before entering production on his own again in 1934 with *Secret of the Skies*.

263 Isle of Intrigue

1931 A. R. HARWOOD

PC: A. R. Harwood Talkie Productions. SC: A. R. Harwood. PH: Leslie McCallum, Ed Wintle. ART D: Vic French. SD: J. Watson Gunner, Frank King. 50 mins (?)

CAST: Dorothy Stanward, James Alexander, Helene Best, Darcy Kelway.

The setting of *Isle of Intrigue* was a South Pacific island: 'The pearling schooners of a trading firm are being robbed by a mysterious pirate. The son of the owner of the firm is sent to the island to discover the identity of the robber, and he does so after various complications which include a little romance and some excitement.' (*Argus*, 28 September 1931)

It was released in tandem with *Spur of the Moment*, and the *Australasian*, 3 October 1931, found it the better of the two: it was less dependent on dialogue, its 'atmosphere is correct, and [it] has considerable histrionic and scenic value'.

264 Diggers*

1931 F. W. THRING

PC: Efftee Film Productions. SC: Pat Hanna, Eric Donaldson. DEDICATION VERSES: C. J. Dennis. PH: Arthur Higgins. ART D: W. R. Coleman. SD: D. J. Bloomberg. 61 mins.

CAST: Pat Hanna (Chic Williams), George Moon (Joe Mulga), Edmund Warrington (Fatty), Cecil Scott (Bluey), Norman French (medical officer), Guy Hastings (Quarter-Master Sergeant), John Henry (a 'Tommy'), Joe Valli (McTavish), Rutland Beckett (S.M., hospital), Harry McClelland (Sergeant-Major Blood), Royce Milton (C.O.), Donovan Joynt (Platoon Commander), A. F. Becker (estaminet proprietor), John Cameron (padre), Nell Fleming (Liz), Mabel Gibson (sister), Leal Douglas (Matron), Patricia Minchin (nurse), Eugenie Prescott (mademoiselle).

Diggers was the first feature from the Melbourne enterprise of Efftee Film Productions, established by Frank W. Thring. The screenplay was prepared by Pat Hanna from three sketches used in his popular *Diggers* stage show. The sketches featured two Australian 'cobbers' serving in the A.I.F. in France in 1918: the lanky, phlegmatic Chic (played by Hanna himself) and his short and resourceful friend, Joe. As Hanna originally conceived the film, the first comic episode presented the two friends in their attempt to steal rum from a British army store.

In the next, more serious episode, they relax in a French *estaminet* while a fellow digger romances with the waitress. Finally, the diggers are in hospital, ingeniously feigning illness to stay away from active duty. The three episodes were linked together as long flashbacks within the frame of a diggers' reunion dinner some twelve years later.

In editing the film, Thring substantially restructured Hanna's work: he began the film with the hospital sequence, followed it with the rum episode, and ended with the sombre sequence in the *estaminet*. Hanna believed in finishing his shows with a laugh and was opposed to Thring's reconstruction; to avoid similar interference on future films, he formed his own company and directed his own films thereafter.

George Patrick Hanna was a versatile cartoonist, writer and entertainer born in New Zealand in 1888. He saw active service on the Western Front and in 1918 was put in charge of the entertainment and recreation corps of the New Zealand army of occupation in Germany. There his theatrical career began when he merged two army concert parties into the basis for a comedy troupe, the Diggers. After demobilization, the Diggers began a long and successful stage career, touring repeatedly around Australia and New Zealand. In addition, Hanna developed a reputation for humorous monologues and songs on radio and record. He died in England in 1973 at the age of 85.

Produced for £9000 in Thring's studio in His Majesty's Theatre, Melbourne, the film was more mobile and technically ingenious than some of Thring's later productions, despite a static microphone, which severely limited the movements of the actors. Distributed by Fox, the film opened at the Plaza Theatre, Melbourne, on 6 November 1931, but failed to draw an audience. Later, in some country centres, it unexpectedly broke box-office records, and it was re-released in Melbourne later in the year with far more active interest from the public. In 1933 it was released by Universal in England.

In its initial Melbourne release, *Diggers* was supported by Efftee shorts including *A Co-respondent's Course*, a short romantic drama directed by E. A. Dietrich-Derrick, and starring Donalda Warne and John D'Arcy. In later seasons, this featurette was replaced by *The Haunted Barn*, another short story jointly directed for Efftee by Dietrich-Derrick (camera) and Gregan McMahon (dialogue), which aroused some notoriety when it was temporarily banned by the censors for its alleged horror content.

Thring was born in Wentworth, N.S.W., in 1883. After working as a conjurer in variety shows and as a touring film exhibitor, he rapidly established a leading place in the Melbourne film trade. In 1924 he merged his

264 F. W. Thring

theatre interests with Hoyts, making that chain one of the two major theatre groups in Australia. He served as managing director of Hoyts until September 1930 when he unexpectedly resigned and sold his controlling interest to an American company, the Fox Film Corporation. At the same time he announced his plans to launch a major film production programme in Melbourne, deriving the studio's name of Efftee from his own initials. In preparation he leased the fire-damaged His Majesty's Theatre from J. C. Williamson and converted it into a talkie studio. R.C.A. sound equipment arrived from the U.S.A. early in 1931 and the studio was officially opened in June. Over the next five years Efftee produced seven features and numerous shorts, as well as several stage productions, of which the most notable was *Collits' Inn* (1934), a musical with Gladys Moncrieff. Thring also invested in commercial radio, and was a founder of station 3XY in Melbourne.

In mid-1934 the Efftee studio moved to an improved site, the Wattle Path Dance Palais, in the Melbourne suburb of St Kilda. Always a strong advocate of government support for the film industry, Thring moved the studio again in January 1936 because of the failure of the Commonwealth government to enact quota legislation. Wattle Path was closed and the company moved to the new Mastercraft Studios in Sydney, where Thring hoped to enjoy the protection of the New South Wales quota laws. Before the first Sydney production could begin, however, Thring died, on 1 July 1936 at the age of 53, and the work of Efftee came to a halt. It became evident that Thring had spent his personal fortune on Efftee and had lost an estimated £57 000 in the few short years of its existence. His son, Frank, later became a popular character actor in Australian theatre and appeared in many films, both at home and overseas.

265 Showgirl's Luck**

1931 NORMAN DAWN

PC: Australian Talkies. SC: Martyn Keith. PH: Norman Dawn, Jack Fletcher, Walter Sully. ED: Norman Dawn. ART D: James Coleman. SONGS: Jack O'Hagan, Ormond Bulmers. CHOREOG: Meg Pendrick. ASST D: Fred Bluett. SD: C. S. Pratt, William Marshall. 55 mins.

CAST: Susan Denis (Peggy Morton), Arthur Tauchert (Hap), Arthur Clarke (Barry), Fred Bluett (Hollis), Sadie Bedford (Mona), Paul Longuet (Dud), George Saunders (Uncle George), Peggy Pryde, George Lloyd, Les Coney, Des Tooley, the Loretto Brothers.

The director, Norman Dawn, wrote that *Showgirl's Luck* 'followed the accepted formula of the typical American musical of the period. . . It had the usual simple straight line plot upon which was hung as many musical numbers as could be worked in' (N. Dawn

264 Pat Hanna

notebook, NFA). The heroine is Peggy Morton (played by Dawn's wife, Katherine, under the stage name of Susan Denis), who works as the star of a touring tent show in rural Queensland. She is offered the lead in the first Australian talkie, being made in Sydney, but a rival, Mona Blake, tells her that the offer has been withdrawn and Mona goes to the Blue Mountains film location in her stead. Meanwhile Peggy's tent show closes and she finds a job by posing as a Swedish maid. By chance she is employed at the same hotel being used by the film company, and she soon learns of Mona's deception. Mona's husband attempts to abduct Peggy, but an actor, Barry, beats off the kidnappers. As the company prepares for the first scenes of the talkie, Peggy appears, and Mona departs in disgrace, leaving Peggy to stardom and the attentions of Barry.

Norman Dawn, the American director of *For the Term of his Natural Life* (1927) and *The Adorable Outcast* (1928), returned to Australia in October 1929 with plans for an Australian talkie using a sound-on-disc system of recording. His equipment was first installed at the Lapstone Hill Hotel in the Blue Mountains, and later at the Sydney Showground. With a working title of *Talkie Mad*, shooting began in May 1930, and the film was ready for trade screening in January 1931. By this time, developments in sound had outmoded the disc system, and Dawn attempted to transfer the sound to an optical track. Beyond experimenting with sound, the film also made use of sophisticated optical effects, in which Dawn had long specialized. For example, the opening shot of the burlesque tent show in the bush involved two exposures, the first of a tent show in Balmain, Sydney, with the wires and chimneys matted out of the scene, and the second of mountains and trees in the Blue Mountains as a background. In another scene Dawn used a similar technique to suggest the heroine's queasiness after smoking a cigar: her eyes were made to 'pop out and come forward till they wander all over the screen'.

Early in December the trade press reported the première of the film at the Lawson Theatre in Redfern, Sydney, followed by a week-long season at the Arcadia Theatre, Sydney, the home of Dawn's company, Australian Talkies. Trade comments were poor both at home and in England, where it was released in mid-1933 by Universal. Its commercial failure and the scarcity of capital in the Depression forced Dawn to abandon hopes of further production in Australia. Late in 1931, after travelling extensively in the inland, he returned to Hollywood and directed several more features, including *Tundra* (1936), *Orphans of the North* (1940) and *Two Lost Worlds* (1950). He died in Los Angeles in 1975 at the age of 88.

265 *Showgirl's Luck* 'The Swaggy Chorus'

266 The Sentimental Bloke*

1932 F. W. THRING

PC: Efftee Film Productions. SC: C. J. Dennis, from his poems *The Songs of a Sentimental Bloke.* PH: Arthur Higgins. ART D: W. R. Coleman. SD R: Alan Mill. 92 mins.

CAST: Cecil Scott (the Bloke), Ray Fisher (Doreen), Tal Ordell (Ginger Mick), Athol Tier (Artie), Edna Morecombe (Effie), Keith Desmond (Uncle), Dora Mostyn (Ma), William Carroll (The Stror 'At Coot), Leslie Gordon ('Erb), Katie Towers, William Ralston, Barney Egan.

In adapting his own verse for the screen, C. J. Dennis retained the basic story of a larrikin's reformation through his love for an ordinary working girl. Fragments from the verse appeared in titles superimposed over action or over drawings by Hal Gye that had originally been published with the poems in 1915. Dialogues were rewritten by Dennis in prose and laden with up-dated colloquialisms. Although the language was handled with care, the staging was, as so often in Efftee productions, scarcely adequate: dialogues were presented in static camera set-ups, and the cast tended to play with theatrical emphasis and posturing, often falling into broad caricature. The contrast with the naturalism and relatively fluid movement of Longford's version was marked.

Distributed through Universal, the film opened in Melbourne at the Hoyts Theatre De Luxe on 26 March 1932. Box-office returns were generally strong, and it was one of the few Efftee films to recover its production costs.

Although most critics were either polite or evasive about the quality of the film, the *Sydney Mail*, 15 June 1932, criticized both the choice of subject and the treatment: the Bloke belonged to another era and in 1932 was nothing but 'a fabulous figure of pre-war days, slightly vulgar and ostentatiously common . . . the players [perform] with an obvious spirit of burlesque. Practically every part is heavily over-played and emphasised.'

266 *The Sentimental Bloke* Tal Ordell (*l*), Cecil Scott

267 Ken G. Hall

267 On Our Selection*

1932 KEN G. HALL

PC: Cinesound Productions. P: Bert Bailey. SC: Bert Bailey, Ken G. Hall. Based on the works of Steele Rudd. PH: Walter Sully. ED: George Malcolm. PM: Jack Souter. SD: Arthur Smith, Clive Cross. TECHNICAL SUP: Bert Cross. 99 mins.

CAST: Bert Bailey (Dad Rudd), Fred MacDonald (Dave), Alfreda Bevan (Mum), John McGowan (Maloney), Molly Raynor (Kate), Dick Fair (Sandy), John Warwick (Jim Carey), Billy Driscoll (Uncle), Lilias Adeson (Lil), Len Budrick (Old Carey), Bobbie Beaumont (Sarah), Ossie Wenban (Joe), Fred Kerry (Cranky Jack), Dorothy Dunkley (Mrs White), Fred Browne (Billy Bearup), Arthur Dodds (parson).

Based not on Steele Rudd's stories but on the stage play by Bert Bailey and Edmund Duggan, Ken Hall's film differed markedly from Raymond Longford's version of 1920. The play had first been performed in 1912 and had since appeared almost continuously in Australia and New Zealand, and had reached England in 1920. Although twenty years old by 1932, the play still had a direct appeal for Depression audiences, and Ken Hall exploited it to the full, stressing the characters' ability to fight back against adversity.

A few episodes from the original Steele Rudd stories were transmitted to the film by way of the Bailey and Duggan play, and converted into broad backblocks farce—among them the day when Cranky Jack looks in a mirror, swears he sees his father there and runs amok, and the visit of the parson when the family is on hard times and there is no flour to make scones. In addition, the play gave the film a melodramatic plot involving rival lovers, a black-hearted villain, murder and a last-minute confession. This plot served not only to link the comic episodes, but to give Dad his greatest moment of emotion, with a powerful rallying cry against his enemies, which carried special force in the context of the Depression: 'For years I've faced and fought the fires, the floods and the droughts of this country. I came here and I cut a hole in the bush when I hadn't enough money to buy a billy can with, or a shirt to put on me back. I worked hard and honest, living on dry bread, harrowing me bit of wheat in with the brambles. But I never lost heart for one single moment. The cattle had perished and died before me very eyes, but . . . me spirit was never broken.' The rhetoric and the mechanics of the plot were perhaps alien to Rudd's original stories, and certainly to the naturalism of Longford's film, but they made

267 *On Our Selection* From the left, Fred MacDonald, Bert Bailey, Mollie Raynor, John McGowan

a strong combination with enormous appeal for the broad mass of Australians.

The film was shot in a small 'sound stage', 30 feet by 20 feet, built in the centre of a skating rink at Bondi Junction, Sydney. The building was used every evening for skating, and production facilities were decidedly makeshift. Although recording equipment had been developed by a young Tasmanian radio engineer, Arthur Smith, and had been tested on several short films, such as *That's Cricket* and *Thar She Blows*, it was not until the night before shooting began on location that a mobile sound unit was finally coaxed into operation. Shooting took three months in mid-1931, with location scenes primarily on the Nepean River near Castlereagh. Responsibility for the production lay with Ken G. Hall, personal assistant to Stuart Doyle, the managing director of Greater Union. Hall's previous production experience was slight; he was more thoroughly trained in publicity, journalism and theatre management; but he learnt quickly with the aid of Bert Bailey's theatrical experience, and the technical guidance of Bert Cross, the engineer in charge of the Australasian Films laboratory.

Despite his inexperience and the difficulties of the production, Hall forcefully displayed the traits that came to characterize all of his work: his taste for broad farce, his sophisticated visual sense, which enabled him to construct his films on familiar Hollywood models (already in this film cutting freely between a variety of camera set-ups, and making fluid use of close-ups, long shots and camera movements), and above all his constant attention to the expectations of his future audience. *On Our Selection* opens with a 'Bushland Symphony' of amplified bird song, so that audiences might enjoy the novelty of *hearing* the bush for the first time in the cinema. The sequence was greeted with cheers, and the press recorded that audiences remained vocally responsive through the rest of the film. The *Sydney Morning Herald*, 15 August 1932, praised the editing, which 'makes the movement of the play rapid and exhilarating', and concluded that 'in vitality, in picturesqueness, in originality, and, above all, in the superb beauty of its camera-work, the film can stand comparison with the finest products of Hollywood or Elstree'.

Publicity for the film was intensely nationalistic: 'Australia's first great National screen effort [is] as enduring as Australia itself because the roots dig deep down into the very fibres of our National existence.' Yet criticism was directed at the film because of its grotesque image of Australia, and Creswell O'Reilly, the chief film censor, later declared that it could have been considered 'prejudicial to the interest and reputation of Australia' (*Film Weekly*, 14 April 1938). Despite such opposition, the film was an enormous box-office success, equalled in its time by few productions, local or overseas. Distributed, like all of the later Cinesound productions, by British Empire Films (B.E.F.), a sister subsidiary within the Greater Union complex, *On*

Our Selection opened on 12 August 1932 with an extraordinary six-week season at the Capitol Theatre, Sydney (normally a weekly-change house), where it broke all house records. Similar exceptional seasons were held throughout Australia, and revivals of the film continued into the 1970s. Stuart Doyle reported to the 1934 New South Wales film inquiry that by December 1933 *On Our Selection* had earned over £46 000 in Australia and New Zealand alone. It had cost only £6000 to make. Under the title of *Down on the Farm*, it was released in England by Universal Pictures, but it failed to interest the English public and Doyle expected less than £2000 from the British release.

In June 1932, shortly before the film's release, Stuart Doyle established Cinesound Productions as a formally independent company within the framework of Greater Union. The commercial record of the film ensured both continuation of production and the position of Ken Hall as general manager of the company's studios and as director of production.

Hall was born on 22 February 1901 in Sydney, and after working as a cadet reporter on the *Evening News*, he joined the film industry in 1917 as an assistant in the publicity department of Union Theatres. His rise in the organization was rapid: by the age of 21 he had worked as manager of the Lyceum Theatre, Sydney, and was appointed publicity director for the entire Union Theatres complex. In 1924 he joined the publicity department of First National Pictures in Sydney, and he visited Hollywood in 1925. He had a chance to taste production in 1928 when he reconstructed a German feature for Australian release as *The Exploits of the Emden*. In 1929 he returned to Union Theatres to supervise the publicity campaign for the opening of the State Theatre in Sydney, and was subsequently appointed personal assistant to Stuart Doyle, and then manager of Cinesound. He worked there from 1932 until he resigned in 1956 to accept a position as chief executive in Frank Packer's Television Corporation, operating the Nine network. He retired in 1968, and his autobiography, *Directed by Ken G. Hall*, was published in 1977.

267 *On Our Selection* Romantic interlude

Throughout his career, Hall was guided by a conscious philosophy of showmanship, seeing himself as an entertainer with a responsibility to give his audience their money's worth of amusement or excitement, and never to offend or cheat them. At worst this philosophy meant that some of his screenplays (*Tall Timbers*, for example) strained to include 'something for everyone', but at best it meant that his films were fast-moving and exuberant. As a producer, Hall expressed a strong sense of responsibility to his staff in the context of a vulnerable industry in the Depression, and he placed great emphasis on the importance of continuity of employment for his technical crew. Accordingly he only made films that he regarded as having broad mass appeal, and that did not cost more than they could safely recover on the home market. His formula for popular success included several basic rules: that the film's title should be simple and easily remembered; that the climax should be strong, regardless of what came before, since it was the end of the film that audiences remembered most clearly (several of Hall's features were initiated with ideas for a climax, around which the writers then built a story); and above all, active publicity from the very start of production. In summing up his own philosophy of film, he once said, 'if that's what the audience wants, they have a right to get it', and like many of his contemporaries, he held the sincere belief that the highest goal of production was to serve the audience, humbly, self-effacingly, and untiringly.

268 His Royal Highness*

1932 F. W. THRING

PC: Efftee Film Productions. STORY: George Wallace. ADAPTATION: C. J. Dennis. PH: Arthur Higgins. ART D: W. R. Coleman. M: Alaric Howitt, George Wallace. BALLETS: Jennie Brennan. SD: Alan Mill. 84 mins.

CAST: George Wallace (Tommy Dodds/King of Betonia), Byrl Walkley (Yoiben), Frank Tarrant (Hozzan), Donalda Warne (Babette), Lou Vernon (Torano), Marshall Crosby (Alfam), John Fernside (Giuseppe), Nell Taylor (Molly), John Dobbie (Jim), Clem Milton (Prime Minister), Edwin Brett (Asher Marmaduke), Mona Barlee, Cecil Scott, Billy Maloney, Dan Thomas, William Ralston, Charles O'Mara, Norman Shepherd, Nellie Mortyne, Darcy Kelway, Field Fisher, Bill Innes.

A stagehand, Tommy Dodds, dreams that he has been made king of the land of Betonia. Royalty does not alter Tommy's Australian character, and he scandalizes the court by gambling with the footmen and insisting that his courtiers wear roller skates. Eventually the rightful heir to the throne is discovered and Tommy is forcibly removed from the palace, whereupon he wakes up.

This 'burlesque operetta' impressed critics and audiences alike with its music and sets. The *Argus*, 31 October 1932, found that 'Tommy's vision of Royal splendour provides an elaborate and lavish spectacular display'. The budget of £19 000 included £7000 alone for the basic set of the Betonian palace, for which an extension was made to the studio floor at His Majesty's Theatre in Melbourne. The camerawork and acting, however, bore the hallmarks of Efftee's other productions, and the introductory scenes with Tommy talking and singing to his friends outside the theatre were especially heavy-handed.

Production began in February 1932, and Universal released the film on 1 October at the Regent Theatre, Brisbane. Thring also succeeded in selling the film to Universal in England, where it was widely screened under the title of *His Loyal Highness.*

The film marked George Wallace's début in feature films. He had been an outstanding vaudeville entertainer since 1919 when he appeared as Onkus in the comedy team of 'Dinks and Onkus'. His half-mast trousers, checked shirt and battered hat became his irreplaceable costume both on stage and film, and he became renowned for his acrobatic comic dances and slapstick routines, including a remarkable trick of falling onto his left ear. *His Royal Highness* had been the title of one of his stage revues during the 1920s, and Frank Thring did little to modify his stage routines for the camera: even Wallace's make-up remained heavily theatrical. Not until he came under the tighter control of Ken G. Hall at Cinesound in *Let George Do It* (1938) did Wallace adapt his style for the screen. Although his films were always popular, Wallace remained primarily a stage performer throughout his career; he died in 1960 at the age of 66.

His usual screen partner, John Dobbie, was born in Sydney and worked in American vaudeville for several years before returning to Australia in the mid-1920s, when he took a small part in *Jewelled Nights* (1925). With his giant physique and deep booming voice, he became a familiar figure in comedy on the local stage and screen, and for some time he appeared with J. C. Williamson's Comic Opera Company. He later worked in commercial radio in Brisbane, where he died in 1952.

269 Diggers in Blighty*

1933 PAT HANNA

PC: Pat Hanna Productions. ASSOC D: Raymond Longford. SC: Pat Hanna. ASSOC WRITERS: Wilfred King, Edmund Warrington, Bert Reid. PH: Arthur Higgins. ART D: W. R. Coleman. SD: Alan Mill. 72 mins.

CAST: Pat Hanna (Chic Williams), Joe Valli (Joe McTavish), George Moon (Joe Mulga), Norman French (Sir Guy Gough), John D'Arcy (Captain Jack Fisher), Prudence Irving (Alison Dennett), Thelma Scott (Judy Fisher), Edwin Brett (the Colonel), Nellie Mortyne (Aunt Martha), Isa Crossley (the Sister), Raymond Longford (Von Schieling), Guy Hastings (quartermaster sergeant), Field Fisher (Muddles), George Randall (Colonel Mason), Alfred Frith (a 'Tommie'), Reg Wykeham (W.O. Pay Corps), Sylvia Sterling (French adventuress).

After his unhappy experience with Thring in the production of *Diggers* (1931), Hanna set up a separate firm and hired the Efftee studio to make his own films. *Diggers in Blighty* was again based on sketches used in the Diggers stage show. While serving in France in 1918, Chic and Joe abscond with rum from the quartermaster's store. Later they unwittingly help British Intelligence to pass false battle plans to a German spy and are rewarded with ten days' leave in England. There they rendezvous in a stately home in Essex and find their uncouth manners at odds with the proper behaviour of the English.

A pair of romantic sub-plots involving the diggers' upper-class friends are resolved happily in the final scenes, and the film ends with the diggers enthusiastically broaching a large keg of home-brewed beer.

With a cast largely drawn from the Diggers stage company, the film was shot over a six-week period, commencing early in October 1932. Although less static than *Diggers*, the action remained slow-moving and laborious, with studio scenes relieved only by a few newsreel shots of the war and stock footage of London's tourist highlights. Sound reproduction was also poor, and one critic complained of the 'Niagara of noise' coming from the screen. The *Sydney Morning Herald*, 10 April 1933, found the humour swamped by three

268 *His Royal Highness* George Wallace at rear

269 *Diggers in Blighty* Pat Hanna

269 *Diggers in Blighty* Norman French (*l*), Raymond Longford (*r*)

major faults: the 'torrent of shouting and noise' on the soundtrack; the lack of adequate direction for the cast, especially 'the energetic "registering" of emotion' by the women; and the 'exceedingly weak' continuity of the story.

The film was released by Universal on a double bill with Efftee's *Harmony Row* at the Hoyts Theatre De Luxe in Melbourne, on 11 February 1933.

269 *Diggers in Blighty* The three comic diggers (*at right*), Pat Hanna (*l*), George Moon (*c*) and Joe Valli

270 **Harmony Row***

1933 F. W. THRING

PC: Efftee Film Productions. STORY: George Wallace. PH: Arthur Higgins. ART D: W. R. Coleman. SD: Alan Mill. 78 mins.

CAST: George Wallace (Constable Dreadnought), Phyllis Baker (Molly), Marshall Crosby (the sergeant), John Dobbie (Slogger Lee), Willie Kerr (Leonard), Bill Innes (Detective Brooks), Edwin Brett (the father), Norman Shepherd (the butler), Norman French (the husband), Bebe Scott (the wife), Gertrude Boswell (the housekeeper), Leonard Stephens (the Ferret), Dan Thomas, Nell Fleming, Nell Crane, Elza Stenning, Thelma Scott, Dorothy Weeks, Johnny Marks, Campbell Copelin.

George joins the police force and is assigned to Harmony Row, a notorious haunt of thugs and criminals. On the beat he makes many friends, including Molly, a pretty street musician, and Leonard, a precocious boy soprano who works with Molly. After many adventures, George is persuaded to fight Slogger Lee, the biggest troublemaker in Harmony Row, in a boxing tournament. In the ring Georges loses badly to Slogger until, suddenly reassured of Molly's friendship, he proceeds to knock out not only Slogger but also the referee and several members of the audience. He finally stands triumphant amid the chaos with Molly in his arms.

The £11 000 production was highlighted by its climactic boxing match, where Wallace performed before a live audience and displayed some nimble slapstick antics. It also introduced a young child 'discovery' from Wagga Wagga, Willie Kerr. Kerr had his own act on stage and next appeared in Cinesound's *The Silence of Dean Maitland* (1934); later, as Bill Kerr, he played numerous Australian characters in British radio, theatre and films, including the radio series *Hancock's Half Hour*.

Distributed by Universal, *Harmony Row* was usually screened as a support to *Diggers in Blighty*, and shared that film's relative popularity following their joint première in Melbourne at the Hoyts Theatre De Luxe on 11 February 1933.

The full version of the film, as first released in Australia, included a long 'haunted house' sequence, in which George tries to unravel a mystery in an upper class suburban mansion. A shorter sequence was later shot to replace this episode and to bridge the gap in the plot; in this new sequence, George mistakes a high society gentleman for a thief and tries to apprehend him. Campbell Copelin played the gentleman, but received no credit in the film's titles.

271 *In the Wake of the Bounty* Errol Flynn (*r*)

271 *In the Wake of the Bounty* Tahitian idyll

271 In the Wake of the Bounty*

1933 CHARLES CHAUVEL

PC: Expeditionary Films. SC: Charles Chauvel. PH: Tasman Higgins. ED: William Shepherd. MD: Lionel Hart. SD: Arthur Smith, Clive Cross. 66 mins.

CAST: Mayne Lynton (Lieutenant Bligh), Errol Flynn (Fletcher Christian), Victor Gouriet (Michael Byrne, the blind fiddler), John Warwick (Midshipman Young).

Chauvel's first talkie was a boldly devised entertainment merging documentary footage and dramatic historical reconstruction. The film re-enacts the mutiny led by Fletcher Christian in 1789 against the master of the *Bounty*, William Bligh, and depicts the fate of the mutineers on Tahiti and remote Pitcairn Island. At the same time it provides a unique and spectacular record of the life of the isolated community on Pitcairn in 1932, where most of the inhabitants are descendants of the *Bounty* mutineers.

The film was the first of a projected series of travel adventures to be made by Chauvel for a Sydney company, Expeditionary Films. In March 1932, Chauvel, with his wife, Elsa, and the cameraman, Tasman Higgins, sailed to Pitcairn to shoot the documentary section of the film. The perils and hardships faced during shooting were recounted by Chauvel in serialized stories in the Australian press and in a book published to coincide with the film's release. One scene was shot in a cave at the base of a bleak 700-foot cliff facing the roaring surf and accessible only by ropes; others were shot in whaleboats, braving the dangerous seas around the island. After three months of isolation, the film-makers joined a passing boat and sailed to Tahiti, where a further two months were spent shooting documentary footage.

On return to Sydney in September, the unedited footage was confiscated by the Customs Department and viewed by the censors. Cuts were requested in scenes of bare-breasted Tahitian dancers, and Chauvel responded with a characteristically public protest. Eventually he succeeded in having the footage released to him uncut, subject to a censorship review after the completion of the film.

For the historical sequences, Chauvel used the remainder of his small budget of £6500 to build several austere sets at the Cinesound studio, Bondi. The cast included the young Errol Flynn, but his expressionless performance gave little indication of his future flair for playing romantic adventurers.

When the film was finally resubmitted to the censors, controversy over the dancing scenes was renewed, aggravated by the censors' objection to a flogging sequence on the decks of the *Bounty*. After another appeal by Chauvel, a compromise version was agreed upon, and the film was released, enhanced by the free publicity.

In releasing the film, Chauvel established his long association with Herc McIntyre, the managing director of the Australian branch of the American company, Universal Pictures. McIntyre remained a constant supporter of Chauvel's work, both as a distributor and later as a financial backer. Universal released the film at the Prince Edward Theatre, Sydney, on 15 March 1933, with strong promotion and endorsement from education authorities.

In 1935 M.G.M. bought American rights to the film and re-edited it to form two short travelogues, *Pitcairn Island Today* (1935) and *Primitive Pitcairn* (1936), used as promotional aids for the studio's own production of *Mutiny on the Bounty* (1935), directed by Frank Lloyd, with Clark Gable as Fletcher Christian.

272 The Squatter's Daughter*

1933 KEN G. HALL

PC: Cinesound Productions. Presented by Stuart F. Doyle. P: Ken G. Hall. SC: Gayne Dexter, E. V. Timms. Based on the play by Bert Bailey and Edmund Duggan. PH: Frank Hurley, George Malcolm. ED: George Malcolm, William Shepherd. ART D: Fred Finlay. M: Frank Chapple, Tom King. PM: John Warwick. SD: Arthur Smith. DIALOGUE D: George Cross. TECHNICAL SUP: Bert Cross. 104 mins.

CAST: Jocelyn Howarth (Joan Enderby), Grant Lyndsay (Wayne Ridgeway), John Warwick (Clive Sherrington), Fred MacDonald (shearer), W. Lane Bayliff ('Old Ironbark'), Dorothy Dunkley (Miss Ramsbottom), Owen Ainley (Jimmy), Kathleen Esler (Zena), Claude Turton (Jebal Zim), George Lloyd (shearer), Katie Towers (Poppy), Will Gilbert, George Cross, Les Warton, Victor Knight, Bidgee.

For his second feature production, Ken Hall retained little but the title of an old play by Bailey and Duggan, which had been more faithfully filmed in 1910. Instead of the now taboo subject of bushrangers, Hall's film focused on the rivalry between two sheep stations, one managed by a strong-willed woman, Joan Enderby, and the other by a weak-willed enemy, Clive Sherrington. Joan finds support in the struggle from a mysterious stranger, Wayne Ridgeway. After several violent deaths, unexpected disclosures, and a desperate fight for life in the midst of a raging bushfire, it becomes apparent that Sherrington is merely the son of a station hand and that Wayne is the true heir to the Sherrington estate. He and Joan marry and unite the two stations in harmony.

Ken Hall believed in providing light relief in his dramas and the film introduced some of his most effective comedy sequences. One sub-plot involves a trio of disaster-prone shearers, one of whom unintentionally charms a snake with his bagpipes and is amorously pursued by the deceptively genteel housekeeper at Enderby, Miss Ramsbottom.

Shooting began in January 1933 with a schedule of twelve weeks and a budget of £16 000, more than twice that of *On Our Selection.* Locations were used at Wallacia, near Penrith, and the Tamworth station of Goonoo Goonoo. Interior scenes, including an elaborate party complete with bathing beauties, ballroom dancing and a novelty band of Aboriginal gumleaf players, were staged in Cinesound's Bondi studio. The hero was played by Dick Fair, who had also taken the romantic lead in *On Our Selection*, but this time with his name altered to Grant Lyndsay. Jocelyn Howarth made her film début as the heroine. After one further film for Cinesound, she sought work in America under the name of Constance Worth. Her career there was far from happy, although it began well when R.K.O. gave her a starring role in *China Passage* (1937). After that, however, she found only small roles in numerous B-films, and she died in America in 1963.

272 *The Squatter's Daughter* Grant Lyndsay, Jocelyn Howarth

As in *On Our Selection*, strong nationalistic sentiment pervaded the film, with Elgar's 'Land of Hope and Glory' behind the titles, and several florid speeches about the heritage of the pioneers. Hurley's photography of the outback captured some vistas of impressive grandeur (especially in the opening scenes of a sheep muster), and a prefatory message from Prime Minister Lyons congratulated the producers for their depiction of pastoral resources. But the highlight of the film was the climactic bushfire sequence, for which an explosive and dangerous fire of nitrate film and diesel oil was built in the bush around the actors, close enough to set the camera blimp on fire during a tracking shot, and to give a genuine sense of hysteria to the acting. Tinted amber, these scenes of roaring flame carried 'an admirable amount of dramatic tension' (*Sydney Mail*, 4 October 1933), and today remain possibly the most exciting and extravagantly daring of the action climaxes staged by the Cinesound team.

Billed as a 'Mighty Epic of Australia's Great Open Spaces', and premièred on 29 September 1933 with the full force of Cinesound's energetic promotions team, the film was a marked financial success. It introduced a new (although short-lived) policy of all-Australian programmes at Sydney's Civic Theatre (formerly the Haymarket), and it ran for ten weeks, with long seasons in other capitals. By 1935 it had grossed over £25 000 in Australia and New Zealand, and had been sold for £7000 to M.G.M. in England. The English version (cut by 15 minutes and retitled *Down Under*) was, however, given a very lukewarm reception by the London critics and film trade.

273 Two Minutes Silence

1933 PAULETTE McDONAGH

PC: McDonagh Productions. Based on the play by Leslie Haylen. PH: James Grant. ART D: Phyllis McDonagh. SD: Jack Bruce. 75 mins.

CAST: Marie Lorraine (Denise), Campbell Copelin (Pierre), Leo Franklyn (Private Simpson), Frank Leighton (Captain Lessups), Ethel Gabriel (Mrs Trott), Victor Gouriet (Corporal Smith), Frank Bradley (General Gresham), Leonard Stephens (James), Eva Moss (Miss Tremlitt), Peggy Pryde (Mrs Breen), Arthur Greenaway (curé), Frank Hawthorne (Reverend Thomas), Bert Barton (Toby), Katie Towers (nun), Fred Kerry (flower seller), Hope Suttor, Dorothy Dunkley.

273 *Two Minutes Silence* Campbell Copelin, Marie Lorraine

The play by Leslie Haylen (an Australian journalist, later a federal parliamentarian) had been first performed in Sydney in 1930. It was a bleak anti-war statement set in London, some years after the war. It is Armistice Day, and four people from different social strata are gathered in the drawing-room of General Gresham; as Big Ben strikes eleven, the characters think back to their bitter experiences of war. The charlady, Mrs Trott, relives the day when she heard that her son had been killed in action. The general recalls an error of judgement he made at the front that caused the death of his men. A French girl, Denise, who is governess to the general's grandchildren, remembers the return of her lover, Pierre, from the front. Pierre came back a military hero, but lacked the courage to accept Denise and the child she had borne after sacrificing herself to a German officer. Finally, the general's butler remembers the time after the war when he had lived a beggar's life on the Thames embankment and had seen the suicide of another ex-soldier.

Always insistent on naturalistic acting, Paulette McDonagh fought hard to break down the grand theatrical manner in the performances of her cast of professional stage actors. As a result, the *Sydney Mail*, 7 February 1934, found that 'in every scene the acting is better than [the] drama deserves', and especially praised the 'warm humanity' of Ethel Gabriel's portrait of the cockney charlady, and the 'humour and vitality' of Leo Franklyn as a comic 'Tommy' soldier. Although shot late in 1932 in a studio in the Sydney Showground, the film struck difficulties in finding an adequate release, and it was not until 18 October 1933 that it was premièred before an audience of parliamentarians at the Capitol Theatre, Canberra. Distributed by Universal, it finally opened at the Civic Theatre, Sydney, on 2 February 1934, and attracted strong support from some members of the public and the press. *Smith's Weekly*, 10 February 1934, was especially enthusiastic and found 'the treatment . . . surprisingly free from banality' and the whole film 'a powerful and convincing story, intelligently directed and capable of challenging comparison with world-standards'. It was, however, the last of the McDonaghs' films, for the production team soon broke up as Isobel (Marie Lorraine) went to London to marry, and Phyllis accepted a position as a journalist with a New Zealand newspaper. Paulette died in Sydney in September 1978, and Phyllis a few weeks later in October.

274 **Waltzing Matilda***

1933 PAT HANNA

PC: Pat Hanna Productions. ASSOC D: Raymond Longford. SC: Pat Hanna. ASSOC WRITERS: John P. McLeod, George Breston. PH: Arthur Higgins. ART D: W. R. Coleman. SD: Alan Stuart. 77 mins.

CAST: Pat Hanna (Chic Williams), Joe Valli (Joe McTavish), Field Fisher (Albert), Norman French (James Brown), Dorothy Parnham (Dorothy), Joan Lang, Coral Browne, Nellie Mortyne, Jos Ambler, Dora Mostyn, Bill Innes.

Wrongly believing that they have injured a policeman in a drunken fight, Chic Williams and his friend James Brown evade a private detective who is following them, and set off for the bush. In fact, the detective wants only to inform James that he has inherited a fortune. Chic and James find work at Banjaroo station as drovers and James falls in love with the station-owner's daughter. When the detective arrives and tells James of his good fortune, the young lovers announce their engagement, and Chic sets off alone again with his swag on his back.

Pat Hanna's character of Chic Williams had been a rowdy prankster in the army in his earlier films; now, in the Depression, he is a figure of pathos, often poor, drinking heavily and drifting from job to job. His friends have all found their niche by the end of the film: James in marriage to a wealthy young woman, and his ex-army friend, Joe McTavish, as overseer on the sheep station. Chic is left to tramp on to new horizons, accompanied only by the laugh of a kookaburra and a chorus of 'Waltzing Matilda'.

Like Hanna's previous films, *Waltzing Matilda* was studio-bound and slow, and was little helped by a big 'production number'—a ballroom sequence with 200 extras and a dance band playing an unlikely up-tempo version of the title song. Shot in mid-1933 in the Efftee studio in Melbourne, the film was released by Universal at Hoyts Theatre De Luxe, Melbourne, on 2 December and ran for a meagre two-week season. It had better seasons in some country areas, but Hanna did not return to production.

274 *Waltzing Matilda* Pat Hanna (*l*) and Norman French (*r*) with morning hangovers

275 The Hayseeds*

1933 BEAUMONT SMITH

PC: J. C. Williamson Picture Productions. P, SC: Beaumont Smith. ASSOC D: Raymond Longford. PH: Tasman Higgins. ED: Frank Coffey. ART D: James Coleman. M: Alf Lawrence, Frank Chapple. BALLETS: Richard White. PM: Jack Gibbes. SD: Clive Cross. 98 mins.

CAST: Cecil Kellaway (Dad Hayseed), Katie Towers (Mum Hayseed), Tal Ordell (Joe), Phyllis Steadman (Polly), Stan Tolhurst (Sam), Bryan Kellaway (Billy), Molly Raynor (Pansy Regan), Kenneth Brampton (Mr Townleigh), Leal Douglas (Mrs Townleigh), Shirley Dale (Mary Townleigh), John Moore (Henry Westcott), Arthur Clarke (John Manners), Vincent Pantin (Lord Mornington), the J. C. Williamson Chorus (singing hikers), the Richard White Girls, Jimmy Coates and his Orchestra.

Mary Townleigh hurts her ankle while hiking in the bush, and the Hayseed family invite her to stay in their house until she is better. She befriends a mysterious young prospector, John Manners, and later, at the Townleigh's invitation, the Hayseeds and John visit Sydney. Their holiday is disrupted when John is accused of being a fugitive from justice. After several adventures he is proven innocent and is reunited with Mary; together they sail for England to be married and to live on his wealthy family estate.

Following the enormous popularity of *On Our Selection* (1932), Beaumont Smith decided to update his silent comedy family, the Hayseeds. In addition to the starchy, sophisticated young lovers, with their stage-English accents, Smith introduced several songs and a troupe of musical hikers who performed a precision ballet in conscious imitation of Busby Berkeley. Dad Hayseed was also given numerous rhetorical lines in praise of 'dear old Australia', and Smith decorated the film with frequent visual reference to the flora and fauna of the bush.

When shooting began in Sydney in August 1933 at Cinesound's studio at Rushcutters Bay, trade announcements named Raymond Longford as director, but he was soon displaced by Smith himself. Released by B.E.F., the film opened at the Civic Theatre, Sydney, on 8 December 1933, and quickly vindicated Smith's formula of crude farce and sentimental nationalism. The film was a major holiday attraction in many theatres and made an easy profit over its low cost (estimated at £4500).

275 *The Hayseeds* Cecil Kellaway. Frame enlargement

Cecil Kellaway, who made his first screen appearance in *The Hayseeds,* was experienced in comedy and character roles on the Australian stage. Born in South Africa in 1891, he came to Australia in 1918 and quickly established his reputation as a performer of considerable range and depth. His performance in *The Hayseeds,* however, was derivative of Bert Bailey, and revealed none of the skilful timing and subtlety of characterization that he brought to his later screen roles in Cinesound's *It Isn't Done* (1937) and especially *Mr Chedworth Steps Out* (1939). In 1937 he went to Hollywood and became a valued character actor in many films over the next three decades. He died in America in 1973.

276 A Ticket In Tatts*

1934 F. W. THRING

PC: Efftee Film Productions. STORY: George Wallace, John P. McLeod. PH: Arthur Higgins. ED: W. Albrecht. ART D: W. R. Coleman. SD: Alan Mill. 88 mins.

CAST: George Wallace (George), Frank Harvey (Brian Winters), Campbell Copelin (Harvey Walls), Thelma Scott (Dorothy Fleming), Harold Meade (Mr Fleming), Marshall Crosby (Mr Summers), Nick Morton (Nick), Guy Hastings (Mr Coyle), Norman Shepherd (a crook), Stan Ray (a stablehand), John Dobbie (a stablehand), Darcy Kelway (a farmer), Dan Thomas (a crook), Noel Boyd (Harvey's secretary), Joyce Turner (Marjorie), Marie La Varre (Mrs Doyle), Dora Mostyn (Mrs Carter), Alec Walker (Peters), Frank Crowther (Slade), Royce Milton (head waiter), the Efftee Ballet.

George is a disaster-prone stablehand with a whistle that can make the Cup favourite, Hotspur, run faster. After foiling several attempts by gangsters to drug the horse, George manages to whistle at the right time to help Hotspur win the Cup. As a counterpoint to this anecdote, the film devotes much time to a high-society romance involving a girl who has undertaken to marry an ageing suitor if his horse defeats Hotspur in the Cup. George's timely whistle not only helps the horse to win the race, but also saves the girl from the embarrassment of honouring a rash promise.

Thring made more effort than usual to take the action away from the studio: location scenes were shot on a stud farm near Melbourne, at the Flemington racecourse, and in the grounds of a palatial Melbourne villa. Frequently, however, Thring interrupted the story with stage-bound vaudeville acts, including a long opening sketch in which George destroys a grocery display while trying to serve customers in a store, and some song and ballet items in a cabaret where George poses as a singing waiter in order to spy on the gangsters. The film was the last that Thring shot in his studio at His Majesty's Theatre, before moving his production base to the former Wattle Path Dance Palais at St Kilda.

Released by Universal, it opened at Hoyts Theatre De Luxe, Melbourne, on 13 January 1934, and screened for six weeks. Thring next embarked on the production of *Sheepmates,* an outback story from a novel by William Hatfield. A cast including Frank Harvey, Claude Flemming, Campbell Copelin and George Wallace was announced, and late in 1934 scenes were shot on a central Australian cattle station, but the film was never completed.

277 Secret of the Skies*

1934 A. R. HARWOOD

PC: Centenary Films. SC: Laurence Brewer. PH: Stan Pentreath. ED: A. R. Harwood. ART D: Reg Smith. M: The Early Victorians. PM: Laurie Strickland. SD: Geoffrey Thompson. 56 mins.
CAST: John D'Arcy (Captain Sinclair), Norman Shepherd (Hal Wayne), Ella Bromley (Anne Walters), Fred Patey (Frederick Holtz), James Dee (Monty Wright), Paul Allsop (Larry Hamilton), Guy Hastings (Detective Palmer), Ada Koradgi (Miss McKenzie), Norman Banks (first announcer), Eddie Balmer (second announcer).

Hal Wayne, a bank robber on the run, hijacks a plane, which crashes in remote mountain territory. The survivors eke out their dwindling supplies, but there is little hope of rescue. Growing desperate, Wayne steals the remaining food and abandons the others to their death. Wandering half-crazed in the forest, he throws away his stolen money and is eventually found by a lone prospector. Back in civilization, he lives tormented by guilt and eventually, after three years, confesses his story to the police.

Made quickly for about £4000, *Secret of the Skies* was shot in July 1933, with several weeks of location work in the ranges at Kinglake near Melbourne, and was completed at the Cinesound studio at St Kilda, Melbourne, using old and makeshift equipment.

The story was based on the actual mystery of the Southern Cloud, a plane that had disappeared three years earlier on a flight from Sydney to Melbourne. This exploitable subject gave the film probably the greatest commercial potential of all of Harwood's films. At a time when interest in Australian production was running high, Universal launched the film with an intensively publicized one-week season at three Sydney theatres over the Easter holidays in April 1934. Box-office results were good, but reviews were poor, and the film received little further exposure.

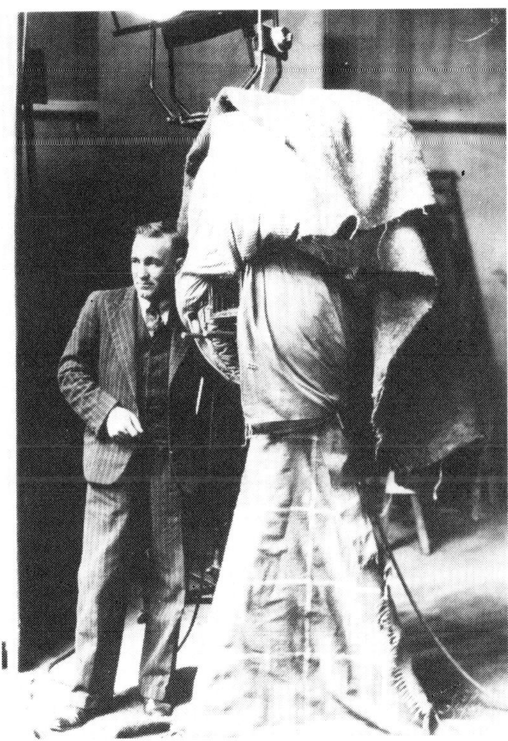

277 Stan Pentreath, with the camera enclosed in its blimp for *Secret of the Skies*

Harwood next ventured into live theatre, with a musical variety show, *Something Different* (1934), and in 1936 he directed a 16 mm feature, *Pearl Lust.* This South Sea island romance, starring Fay Revel and John Bowden, was aimed at the growing home movie market and was not released theatrically.

278 The Silence of Dean Maitland*

1934 KEN G. HALL

PC: Cinesound Productions. Presented by Stuart F. Doyle. P: Ken G. Hall. SC: Gayne Dexter, Edmund Barclay. From the play based on the novel by Maxwell Gray. PH: Frank Hurley. ED: William Shepherd. ART D: Fred Finlay. SPECIAL EFFECTS: George Malcolm. MD: Hamilton Webber. PM: John Warwick. SD: Arthur Smith. DIALOGUE D: George D. Parker. 97 mins.
CAST: John Longden (Dean Maitland), Charlotte Francis (Alma Lee), Jocelyn Howarth (Alma Gray), John Warwick (Henry Everard), John Pickard (Tommy Everard), Patricia Minchin (Marion Everard), Audrey Nicolson (Lillian Maitland), Bill Kerr (Cyril Maitland Jnr), Fred MacDonald (Granfer), George Lloyd (Bill Grove), Claude Turton (Charlie Gray), W. Lane Bayliff (Reverend Maitland Snr), Les Warton (Ben Lee), Leal Douglas (Mrs Lee), Rodney Smith, Douglas Herald, Carlton Stuart.

The story—about a clergyman who denies his responsibility for both the pregnancy of his lover and the death of her father, and then allows his best friend to be imprisoned for twenty years in his stead—was a challenge to any director. Raymond Longford had filmed it in 1914 with notable critical and commercial success, and in 1934 Ken G. Hall attempted a new version, updating the story to a modern setting. He too succeeded remarkably well, for the film was one of Cinesound's most popular productions with both critics and the general public. *Everyones,* 30 May 1934, acknowledged the difficulties of the plot, but reported that Hall had managed to overcome them, 'building his drama strongly, with just the right tempo and smooth-flowing continuity . . . Scene after scene is charged with emotion.'

When the British actor John Longden arrived in a touring theatrical company for J. C. Williamson, he was promptly recruited for the film, along with his stage co-star, Charlotte Francis. Longden had already acted in numerous British features including Hitchcock's *Blackmail* (1930). After the commercial success of *The Silence of Dean Maitland* he remained in Australia for several years

278 *The Silence of Dean Maitland* The sins of the father visited upon the son: Bill Kerr as the blind son of the errant man of the church (John Longden)

working in radio and theatre, as well as making two more films for Cinesound.

With a budget of £10 000, the film was shot at Cinesound's Bondi studio and on locations in Sydney and near Camden. Shortly before it was due for release, the censors demanded cuts in an opening scene where Alma swims on a deserted beach and in the crucial scene where she seduces the rather willing clergyman. Aware of the value of such free publicity, Cinesound mounted a loud public appeal against the cuts and received much press comment in the film's favour. The censor finally lifted his demand for cuts in the love scene, but a brief shot in which Alma's towel slips while she is changing out of her bathing costume was removed.

To make an all-Australian unit programme, Hall produced a low-cost supporting film, *Cinesound Varieties*, a 48-minute collection of musical and comedy items on a nautical theme, starring Fred Bluett and other vaudeville artists. The programme was premièred in May 1934 at the Strand Theatre, Hobart, and attracted large crowds there and elsewhere in Australia. Early in 1935 it was released in England by R.K.O. in a slightly abridged form, and again earned healthy returns.

279 The Man They Could Not Hang*

1934 RAYMOND LONGFORD

PC: Invicta Productions. PROD SUP: Rigby C. Tearle [J. A. Lipman]. SC: Lorrie Webb. From a 'dramatization' by Rigby C. Tearle. PH: George Malcolm, George Heath. ED: George Malcolm, William Shepherd, Terry Banks. ART D: James Coleman. SD: Roy Blanche. 78 mins.

CAST: Ronald Roberts (John Lee), Arthur W. Sterry (John Lee Snr), Ethel Bashford (Mrs Lee), Olive Sinclair (Miss Keyse), Patricia Minchin (Eliza Parrish), Ethel Gabriel (Jane Allen), Claire Barnes (Kate Farmer), Sam Stern (Bertrand), Les Warton (Ted Meeks), George Doran (Captain Giles), Leo Starke (Captain Hill), Nugent Harrington (Tim Sanders), Bobbie Beaumont (Polly Sanders), W. Newton Carroll (Ned Sawkins), Herbert Stallard (prison chaplain), Alf Scarlett (constable), George Randall (Frank Carter), Victor Fitzherbert (prison governor), Walter Dyer (comptroller), Carlton Stuart (Doctor Cann).

Longford's last feature as director told the well-worn story of the convicted murderer John Lee, for whom the gallows failed to open, and elaborated it with a sub-plot about smuggling and secret service agents. The resulting screenplay hinted at much but resolved little, as the *Sydney Morning Herald*, 4 June 1934, commented: 'A long time is occupied in leading up to something but those who are not already familiar with John Lee's story will be at a loss to know what.' *Everyones*, 6 June 1934, found only the performance of Ronald Roberts to be remotely effective; otherwise, 'stilted lines emerge from the players' lips as if recited by children at the annual Sunday School cantata'. *Everyones* also noted that, in reaction to the film, audiences 'tittered audibly', and by the end 'were openly and loudly barracking'.

A production company, Invicta, was formed by J. A. Lipman, who supervised Longford's work as director and took credit under his old stage name of Rigby C. Tearle. The part of Lee's father was played by Arthur W. Sterry, who had made the 1921 film version of the same story. Lipman leased Cinesound's studio at Rushcutters Bay, and with a Cinesound crew, began shooting in March 1934. The production was quickly assembled and set for release through B.E.F. at the Civic Theatre, Sydney, early in June. A few days before the première six hurried cuts were made at the demand of the New South Wales police. All of the scenes deleted were considered by the police to be offensive to their reputation (even though the story was set in England), and despite an outraged reaction from the trade press deploring the action of 'the grotesquely over-pampered' police force, the cuts remained. To the surprise of the trade, the story of John Lee was still able to command a strong public following, especially in country areas, and it was moderately profitable.

280 When the Kellys Rode*

1934 HARRY SOUTHWELL

PC: Imperial Feature Films. SC: Harry Southwell. PH: Tasman Higgins. SD: Clive Cross. 79 mins.

CAST: Hay Simpson (Ned Kelly), John Appleton (Dan Kelly), Norman Wait (Joe Byrne), Robert Inglis (Steve Hart), George Randall (Sergeant Steel), Regina Somerville (Kate Kelly), Kathleen Hamilton, June Middleton, Lorraine Smith, Vashti Wallace, Charles Villiers, Billie Dean, George Doran, Stan Tolhurst, George Lees, Victor Wallen, Louis Grant, Keith Clune, Hugh Raynor, Walter Vincent, Victor Morcom, Howard Carr (David), Bertie Wright (Goliath).

Harry Southwell's third version of the Kelly story was filmed on location in the Megalong Valley in the Blue Mountains, and in Cinesound's studio at Rushcutters Bay. A Cinesound crew was hired by Southwell to shoot the film and assemble it under his supervision. Shot rapidly and with minimal planning, the film had little to recommend it. A critic in the *Argus*, 15 October 1934, found it 'unedifying, unconvincing, and often laughable . . . The actors speak like children at a school recitation night, and the camera waits until the recitation ends.'

The film was released in New Zealand in August 1934 and in Melbourne in October. It would soon have disappeared into oblivion had not the New South Wales police department reimposed the state's old ban on bushranging films. Although it could be openly shown in other states, it remained banned in New South Wales for more than a decade. In June 1948 two showmen, Oscar Shaft and Vic Hobler, resurrected the film and, through B.E.F., presented it at the Capitol Theatre, Sydney. To the surprise of the trade it attracted large crowds, and *Film Weekly*, 8 July 1948, reported that it seemed to be bad enough to serve as 'hilarious first-half entertainment'.

281 Clara Gibbings*

1934 F. W. THRING

PC: Efftee Film Productions. ASSOC D, SC: Frank Harvey. From the play by Aimée and Phillip Stuart. PH: Arthur Higgins. ART D: W. R. Coleman, Franklin Hughes. SD: Alan Mill. 81 mins.

CAST: Dorothy Brunton (Clara Gibbings), Campbell Copelin (Errol Kerr), Harvey Adams (Justin Kerr), Noel Boyd (Yolande Probyn), Harold Meade (Earl of Drumoor), Byrl Walkley (Lady Drumoor), Marshall Crosby (Tudor), Russell Scott (Gallagher), Guy Hastings (Ted).

Clara Gibbings is the proprietress of a London pub who discovers that she is the legitimate but abandoned daughter of the Earl of Drumoor. She launches herself into high society but soon grows disillusioned with the morals and fashions of the aristocracy and decides to return to the 'fresh air' of her own class. A young aristocrat, Errol, has meanwhile learnt to respect Clara's principles and to see his own decadent life in perspective. Impulsively he proposes marriage, and they depart for Australia, presumably to a land where class differences can be forever reconciled.

The play had been presented live by Efftee at the Garrick Theatre, Melbourne, in August 1933, with Ruby May in the title role. The film version, shot early in 1934, remained very much a photographed stage play. The *Argus*, 15 October 1934, commented that the action moved 'with the stiffness and rigidity of a guardsman on parade. This is in no sense the

281 *Clara Gibbings* Dorothy Brunton. Frame enlargement

fault of the cast. [Dorothy Brunton plays] with spirit and understanding [and] Mr Campbell Copelin gives a smooth and competent performance as the hero.'

Released by Universal at the Mayfair Theatre, Melbourne, on 13 October 1934, the film relied on Dorothy Brunton as a drawcard. She had been a star of musical comedy in Australia during the First World War and later in England, and Thring intended her name to carry the film both in the home market and abroad. However, after a three week season at the Mayfair, the film virtually disappeared, despite the award of third prize in the Commonwealth government's film competition in the following year.

282 Strike Me Lucky*

1934 KEN G. HALL

PC: Cinesound Productions. SC: Victor Roberts, George D. Parker. PH: Frank Hurley, George Heath. ED: William Shepherd. ART D: Fred Finlay. ANIMATION: Will Cathcart. M: Hamilton Webber. LYRICS: Victor Roberts. BALLETS: Leon Kellaway, Richard White. ASST D: John Warwick. SD: Arthur Smith, Clive Cross. DIALOGUE D: George Parker. 87 mins.

CAST: Roy Rene (Mo), Yvonne Banvard (Kate), Lorraine Smith (Margot Burnett), John D'Arcy (Larry McCormack), Eric Masters (Al Baloney), Alex McKinnon (Donald), Dan Agar (Major Burnett), Baby Pamela Bevan (Miriam Burnett), Molly Raynor (Bates), Bert Le Blanc (Lowenstein), Les Warton (Bull), Harry Burgess (Mike), Fred Kerry (castaway), Marie D'Alton (Mrs Huckleberry), Arthur Dodds, Charles Wheeler, Jack O'Malley, Charles Keegan, Nellie Small, Eva Sheedy.

Roy Rene appeared in only one feature film, despite his enormous following on stage and radio as Mo McCackie, the leering Jewish clown who parodied and outraged middle-class conventions. Ken Hall's film preserved Mo's most obvious characteristics—his grotesquely exaggerated Jewishness, his sputtering delivery of mildly blue jokes, and his heavy touches of pathos—but the film failed to fulfil its promise. As *Everyones*, 21 November 1934, commented, the film 'will leave a wake of disappointment and disillusionment. For, except on a few occasions, Mo is not funny; and between the genuine laughs lie lengthy gaps of tedium'. Roy Rene himself attributed the dullness of the film to his own inexperience in the film medium: 'I found it too hard trying to be funny to no one. You need the stimulus of the audience, when you've been used to one . . . in the studio no one is allowed to laugh at you, and believe me, you certainly get no reaction from a camera' (R. Rene, *Mo's Memoirs*, Melbourne 1945). Although Rene's contract with Cinesound foreshadowed other films, none followed, and he returned to work in theatre and radio until his death in 1954.

The plot was complex, centring on Mo's friendship with a small girl whom he finds dancing in the streets. Although she claims to

282 *Strike Me Lucky* Roy Rene and Baby Pamela Bevan in a pose derived from Chaplin's *The Kid*, with caricatures of Ken G. Hall and Frank Hurley on the right

be an orphan, the child is in fact the runaway daughter of wealthy parents who are offering a handsome reward for her return. Gangsters try to kidnap the girl, a search is made for a lost gold mine (an episode inspired by Lasseter's stories), and Mo meets a tribe of wild Aborigines, before he finally wins happiness for himself and his friends. Elsewhere in the film a character impersonates Mae West (using the name of June East), a sentimental romance blossoms for a fashionable young couple, and a ballet of 150 dancers performs periodically in Busby Berkeley formations.

Vic Roberts, who had written gags for Rene on the stage, worked with the Cinesound writers to prepare the script, and under a working title of *Swastikas for Luck*, the film began a seven-week production schedule in June 1934 at Cinesound's Bondi studio. The budget was a modest £9000, of which Rene received a reported £70 a week, then a generous salary for a film actor in Australia.

Strike Me Lucky became the only blot on Cinesound's commercial record: of its seventeen features, it was the only one that failed to make a clear profit in the first few years of its release, although it did eventually break even. Rene's risqué humour was a departure from Cinesound's usual formula of family entertainment; furthermore, the film was refused registration under the quality clause of the New South Wales quota act. For other films rejection as a quota production meant financial disaster; Cinesound, however, was protected to some extent by its sister companies in the Greater Union group (the Greater Union theatre chain and the distributor, B.E.F.), and through them *Strike Me Lucky* received the best opportunities to prove itself commercially. It was released at the Capitol Theatre, Sydney, on 16 November 1934 and at first drew large crowds, but these quickly dwindled as the quality of the film became known. Universal released the film in England late in 1935 in a substantially shortened version, but it attracted little attention.

283 Splendid Fellows*

1934 BEAUMONT SMITH

PC: J. C. Williamson Picture Productions. P, SC: Beaumont Smith. ASSOC D: Raymond Longford. PH: George Malcolm. ED: Frank Coffey. ART D: Leo Davis. PM: Jack Gibbes. SD: Roy Blanche. DIALOGUE D: Kenneth Brampton. TECHNICAL D: Victor Bindley. 84 mins.

CAST: Frank Leighton (the Hon. Hubert Montmorency Ralston), Leo Franklyn (Thompson), Frank Bradley (Jim McBride), Eric Colman (Reverend Arthur Stanhope), Isabelle Mahon (Eileen McBride), Peggy Ross (Mrs McBride), Bill Stewart (Teddy Lawson), Andrew Higginson (Lord Ralston), Madge Aubrey (Mrs Brogan), Charles Zoli (Signor Spigoni), Sir Charles Kingsford Smith (himself).

283 *Splendid Fellows* From the left, Frank Bradley, Peggy Ross, Isabelle Mahon, Eric Colman

Montmorency Ralston is a 'typical' Englishman, complete with monocle, plus-fours and a valet. He sails for Australia after an argument with his father, and in a Sydney two-up parlour befriends a 'typical' Australian, Jim McBride. On the McBride's outback station he meets the famous 'flying padre', the Reverend Stanhope, who uses a light plane to tour his parish. Monty manages to persuade his father to buy a new plane for the padre and enters it in the Centenary Air Race from London to Melbourne. While the race is in progress, Stanhope's old plane crashes in remote country and Monty gives up his chance to win the race by flying to his rescue.

Sub-plots included a formula romance in which Jim McBride's daughter, Eileen, coyly cuddles a koala and promises to marry Monty if he wins the air race. A preposterous series of coincidences also told the story of a blind prospector who joins the padre on the flight in which his plane crashes; he regains his sight in the impact of the crash and immediately recognizes the landmarks of a long-lost goldfield (another reference to Lasseter's lost reef).

Despite the sub-plots, *Splendid Fellows* was a considerable improvement over *The Hayseeds* (1933), with naturalistic central performances, subdued portraits of the farmfolk, and relatively sophisticated production technique. Beaumont Smith and his team of co-directors managed to stretch their tiny £5000 budget to include many potentially strong box-office attractions: the cast introduced Eric Colman, the much-publicized brother of Ronald; Sir Charles Kingsford Smith made a personal appearance in flying scenes, shot with the co-operation of his own airways company and the Aero Club of New South Wales; and actual footage was incorporated from the Centenary Air Race and celebrations in Melbourne.

The trade press congratulated the film for its 'red-hot topical theme', but the formula failed to work. When B.E.F. released it at the Lyceum, Sydney, in November 1934, its receipts were not encouraging. Possibly the title was wrong: a New Zealand exhibitor later promoted the film with the sub-title *The Hayseeds at the Melbourne Centenary*, and reported 'tremendous' business. The general failure of the film spelt the end of production for Beaumont Smith, and until his death in 1950 he worked exclusively in exhibition and publicity.

284 The Streets of London*

1934 F. W. THRING

PC: Efftee Film Productions. PH: Arthur Higgins. ART D: W. R. Coleman. SD: Alan Mill. 85 mins.

CAST: Frank Harvey (Badger), Ethel Newman (Mrs Fairweather), Leonard Stephens (Paul Fairweather), Phyllis Baker (Lucy), Guy Hastings (Gideon Bloodgood), Campbell Copelin (Hon. Mark Levingstone), Noel Boyd (Aleda), Ashton Jarry (Edwards), Frank Bradley (Captain Fairweather), George Blunt (Puffy), Beatrice Esmonde (Mrs Puffy), Darcy Kelway (Don Puffy).

This well-worn Victorian melodrama was produced by Efftee on the stage at the Garrick Theatre, Melbourne, from 11 November 1933. The film was little more than a photographic record of the stage production, complete with theatre curtains and glimpses of modern-day theatre audiences. It was rejected for registration under the quality clause of the New South Wales quota act, and no public screenings are recorded.

285 Grandad Rudd*

1935 KEN G. HALL

PC: Cinesound Productions. P: Bert Bailey, Ken G. Hall. SC: Victor Roberts, George D. Parker. From the play by Bert Bailey, adapted from the stories by Steele Rudd. PH: Frank Hurley, George Heath. ED: William Shepherd. ART D: Fred Finlay. PM: Jack Souter. ASST D: John Warwick. SD: Arthur Smith, Clive Cross. 90 mins.

CAST: Bert Bailey (Grandad Rudd), Fred MacDonald (Dave), George Lloyd (Dan), William McGowan (Joe), Kathleen Hamilton (Madge), Lilias Adeson (Lil), Les Warton (Regan), Elaine Hamill (Betty), John Cameron (Tom Dalley), John D'Arcy (Henry Cook), Molly Raynor (Amelia Banks), Bill Stewart (Banks), Marie D'Alton (Mrs Banks), Marguerite Adele (Shirley Sanderson), George Blackwood (school-master), Ambrose Foster (young Dave), Peggy Yeoman (Mum), Percy Danby.

With this, the first of three spin-offs from *On Our Selection*, Hall began a gradual modification of the original Dad and Dave humour. The Rudds were transformed into prosperous farmers, and several newcomers appeared in their family to give the film greater dramatic variety. One of them, a sophisticated grand-

285 *Grandad Rudd* George Lloyd as Dan

daughter, Betty, is the centre of a melodramatic sub-plot in which she is almost seduced into marriage by a suave young bigamist. The main foil to Grandad is no longer Dave but another son, Dan, 'a blear-eyed, blear-nosed gentleman, with a drooping black moustache and the expression of a sad blowfly'. The many episodes of slapstick include a bizarre country cricket match, the pursuit of a runaway tractor, and a Band of Hope meeting, which Grandad breaks up when he gets drunk. The softening of the rustic caricatures was perhaps at the expense of their energy and warmth, and the film's emphasis on Grandad's overbearing and parsimonious nature seemed to destroy much of the sympathy that he had once drawn from the audience. His pioneering spirit and his sudden bursts of good humour were almost entirely lacking.

The film was shot quickly, in October-November 1934, with exteriors at Camden, where Frank Hurley contributed some striking rural panoramas. Despite the uneasiness of critics over the script, the film attracted large crowds during its simultaneous première seasons in Perth and Hobart in February 1935, and it gave Cinesound a comfortable profit over its £15 000 outlay. Late in 1935, Universal released the film in England under the title of *Ruling the Roost.*

286 Heritage*

1935 CHARLES CHAUVEL

PC: Expeditionary Films. SC: Charles Chauvel. PH: Tasman Higgins, Arthur Higgins. ED: Lola Lindsay. ART D: James Coleman. M: Harry Jacobs. P ASST: Ann Wynn [Elsa Chauvel]. ASST D: Chick Arnold. SD: Alan Mill. 94 mins.

CAST: Frank Harvey (Governor Phillip), Franklyn Bennett (James Morrison/Frank Morrison), Margot Rhys (Jane Judd), Peggy Maguire (Biddy O'Shea/Biddy Parry), Harold Meade (Frank Parry), Joe Valli ('Short'), Norman French (Governor Macquarie), Ann Wynn (Mrs Macquarie), Leonard Stephens (Greenway), Austin Milroy (Major Ross), Victor Fitzherbert (William Charles Wentworth), Gertrude Boswell (Mrs Judd), Dora Mostyn (Mother Carey), Godfrey Cass (Harding), Florence Esmond (Mrs Boggs), Victor Gouriet (artist), Field Fisher (Gerald Cracknell), Rita Pauncefort (Mrs Cobbold), David Ware ('Long'), Kendrick Hudson (Morrison Jnr).

Chauvel's love for epic themes flourished in this cavalcade of Australian history. Against a background of early colonial politics, Chauvel traced the life and loves of James Morrison, a hard-living man of action with a formidable reputation for drinking and romancing. On one of his trips to Sydney he dallies with a fiery Irish girl, Biddy O'Shea, but soon heads off to the frontier, where he claims a farmer's daughter as his bride. Some time later he sees an attack by wild Aborigines on a lonely farmhouse and discovers Biddy, now a settler's wife and a mother, dying from wounds. James persuades his wife to raise Biddy's child as their own. Time passes, years become decades, and now in the 1930s, James's des-

286 James Coleman (*r*) with his model of early Sydney for *Heritage*

286 *Heritage* Mary Maguire (*l*)

cendant, Frank Morrison, is struggling with the same determination to maintain his hold on a rugged outback station. A young Australian girl, Biddy's namesake, flies out to his property (she is an expert aviatrix) and convinces him that she would be a suitable mate in his rigorous frontier life. Finally, in a rousing family celebration, they praise the achievements and vision of their forefathers and promise to continue in their footsteps.

Although, as one critic noted, the film lacked nothing 'in epic inspiration', Chauvel's grandiose ideas were somewhat undermined by his limited budget of £24 000, and by the hurried casting of an ineffectual actor from the amateur stage, Franklyn Bennett, in the crucial roles of James and Frank Morrison. Sets and models of early Sydney were constructed in Efftee's Wattle Path studio in Melbourne, and Chauvel characteristically travelled far to find the right outdoor locations for other scenes. Near Copmanhurst in the north-east of New South Wales he filmed the pioneers trekking westwards into new territory; he staged the Aboriginal attack near Canungra in the southern Queensland mountains, where he later shot *Sons of Matthew* (1949); and scenes of the first Sydney settlements were shot on inlets near Sydney itself.

Shooting extended over nearly six months from April 1934. The logistic problems were considerable, involving hundreds of extras, all of whom needed costumes, and the handling of wildlife, including bullocks, inside the studio. As with *In the Wake of the Bounty* (1933), Chauvel wrote a book to accompany the release of the film, this time a historical novel based on his own screenplay. Again, too, he sought new talent for the leading roles: although his experiment with Franklyn Bennett failed, he was more successful in his choice of a 16-year-old Brisbane girl, Peggy Maguire, to play Biddy. Her performance was praised by the press, and after changing her name to Mary Maguire, and appearing in *The Flying Doctor* (1936), she departed for London and appeared in several British and American B-films over the next decade.

In March 1935 *Heritage* won the first prize of £2500 in the Commonwealth government's film competition. Aided further by a vigorous press campaign and endorsement from education authorities, the film was released at the Lyceum Theatre, Sydney, on 13 April.

Although Australian reviewers co-operated with politely congratulatory notices, the film failed to make a profit in the home market. Columbia bought British rights under the impetus of the Empire quota legislation, but trade reviews there gave it a mixed reception and it was not financially successful. American release did not follow until 1941 when a small distributor, Variety Films, bought the rights for $300. Learning from the experience, Chauvel's backers, Expeditionary Films, turned to story material with wider international appeal for their next production, *Uncivilised* (1936).

287 The Burgomeister [Hypnotised]

1935 HARRY SOUTHWELL

PC: Film Players Corporation. P: Harry Southwell. ASSOC D: Gabriel Toyne. SC, LYRICS: Denzil Batchelor. From the adaptation by Leopold Lewis of the play *Le Juif Polonais* by Erckmann-Chatrian. PH: George Heath. ED: William Shepherd. ART D: James Coleman, Rupert Kathner. MD: Isador Goodman. PM: Ben Lewin. ASST D: George Rayner. SD: Clive Cross. 56 mins. (?)

CAST: Harry Southwell (Mathias), Muriel Meredith (Catherine), Janet Johnson (Annette), Ross Vernon (Christian), Stan Tolhurst (the Polish Jew), Gabriel Toyne (Fritz), Harold Meade (Father Walter), Bertie Wright (Heinrich), Leslie Victor (Hans), Lily Molloy (Sozel), Judy Eccles (Baby Annette), Paul Furness (hypnotist), James Toohey (witness), June Munro (Marie), Alf Scarlett, Reginald Riddell.

The old stage melodrama *The Bells* was first filmed in Australia in 1911 by W. J. Lincoln. In 1925, while in Belgium, Harry Southwell filmed another version under the title of the original Erckmann-Chatrian play, *Le Juif Polonais*, and back in Australia in 1935 he again turned to the play for a new film venture.

In April 1935 Southwell formed a production company, Film Players Corporation, with a distinguished list of directors, including Sir John Butters, a director of Associated Newspapers Ltd, W. J. Bradley, K.C., and George H. Rayner, who was described as being 'prominent in society circles', and who worked on the production as assistant director. With a budget of £10 000, shooting began at Cinesound's Bondi studio early in June 1935. The basic set was described by *Everyones*, 12 June 1935, as 'the largest set the plant has housed since it has been a sound studio. With a depth of more than 100 feet, the entire ground-floor of an old Continental inn has been designed by Jim Coleman, so that action can commence in the courtyard outside, proceed through the huge public room, into the living-room at the back, and then to the old-fashioned kitchen at the side.' Mountains of snow for these scenes were made from a mixture of salt and cornflakes, but other winter scenes were shot on location at Mount Kosciusko.

An advertisement in *Everyones*, 25 September 1935, carried the name of R.K.O.-Radio as distributor for the film and billed it as 'The First Australian Quota Picture!' However, under the quality clause of the new New South Wales quota act it was refused registration, and following a private preview on 29 September it was withdrawn from distribution. Later, a re-edited version with the title *Hypnotised* was distributed by Scott Films, and it may have been screened in some country centres. In 1937 the film appeared in England under yet another title, *Flames of Conscience*.

In his somewhat bitter survey of the Australian film industry, *Let's Make a Movie* (Sydney 1945), Rupert Kathner told the sad tale of *The Burgomeister*'s preview: after the screening 'there was an unearthly silence. Lady So and So turned to Sir Whatsisname, who nudged the eminent K.C., who, after swallowing hard, silently thanked his lucky stars that he only had a few hundreds invested in it and not thousands like a lot of others who were seated about him'.

288 Thoroughbred*

1936 KEN G. HALL

PC: Cinesound Productions. Presented by Stuart F. Doyle. P: Ken G. Hall. SC: Edmond Seward. PH: George Heath. ED: William Shepherd. ART D: Fred Finlay, J. Alan Kenyon. MD: Hamilton Webber. PM: Jack Souter, Harry Strachan. ASST D: Ronald Whelan. SD: Clive Cross. 89 mins.

CAST: Helen Twelvetrees (Joan), Frank Leighton (Tommy Dawson), John Longden (Bill Peel), Nellie Barnes (Judy Cross), Elaine Hamill (Linda), Ronald Whelan (Genna), Les Warton (Grafter), Harold Meade (Sir Russell Peel), Nellie Ferguson (Ma Dawson), George Lloyd (Sleepyfeet), Lynton Moore (Hops Warton), John D'Arcy (Jack Dent), Alf Stanton (Midget Martin), Jack Settle (Honest Herman), Pearl Hellmrich (Mrs Dinwiddle), Edmond Seward (Mr Terry), Paul Marcus (Frenchman), Don McNiven, Ruth Craven.

After *Grandad Rudd* (1935) Cinesound closed for six months while Hall visited Hollywood to buy new equipment and study new techniques. His most important purchase was a rear-projection unit which enabled him to stage action in the studio in front of moving backgrounds. The technique saved the expense of moving entire production units into remote locations and it transformed the studio's method of operation. The system was extensively used in *Thoroughbred* and in every Cinesound feature thereafter.

While in Hollywood, Hall also engaged a writer and actress to come to Australia to work on *Thoroughbred*. The young writer, Edmond Seward (who claimed experience with Disney), drew his idea for the climax of the film from Frank Capra's racing comedy, *Broadway Bill* (1934).

The heroine of the story was a Canadian, Joan, the adopted daughter of Ma Dawson, a horse-trainer and breeder now on hard times. Acting on her belief that 'legs don't make a race horse, it's blood', Joan buys an emaciated and unwanted thoroughbred colt named Stormalong. With Ma's son, Tommy, she restores the horse to health and it soon begins to win race after race. Eventually Stormalong becomes a favourite for the Melbourne Cup and attracts the attention of an international

288 *Thoroughbred* Ronald Whelan (*l*) as the arch-villain

gambling syndicate who try to dope the horse and kill it in a stable fire. During the running of the Cup, Stormalong is shot by a sniper but manages to win before collapsing and dying. Tommy, who had been kidnapped by the gangsters, helps to capture the men responsible for the horse's death, and he and Joan decide to marry.

The story was elaborated with numerous sub-plots, with comic relief supplied by the stable hands, and much discussion about thoroughbred people and thoroughbred horses between Joan and her aristocratic neighbour, Bill Peel. Theories of pure breeding are accepted by Joan for horses, but she staunchly rejects the notion that racial purity is beneficial for humans. The blue-blooded Peels and the racing aristocracy are quietly satirized, mainly through Tommy's attempt to emulate their fashions, and the film expressly favours the more homely and spontaneous life-style of battlers like the Dawsons who come from 'a long line of crocks'.

The Hollywood star, Helen Twelvetrees, had been important in the silent era, but by 1935 her popularity had passed its peak and her films were mainly B-productions. Carefully organized publicity, however, won her an enthusiastic welcome in Australia, and public interest in the film was widespread

288 Filming the Melbourne Cup for *Thoroughbred*

288 *Thoroughbred* Frank Leighton, Helen Twelvetrees

both before her arrival in December 1935 and during her stay. The £20 000 production was premièred by B.E.F. at the Mayfair Theatre, Sydney, in May 1936, and box-office success followed throughout Australia. English release was hampered by censorship troubles over alleged cruelty to animals: the British censor ordered cuts in several scenes, including a stable fire sequence, despite Hall's protests that the fire had been filmed with rear-projection and that the horses had never been exposed to flames. It was eventually released in London in July but failed to arouse much interest in the trade.

289 The Flying Doctor*

1936 MILES MANDER

PC: National Productions/Gaumont-British Picture Corporation. SC: J. O. C. Orton, Miles Mander. From the novel by Robert Waldron. PH: Derick Williams. CAM OP: Errol Hinds, Mel Nichols, John Howes. CAM ASST: Damien Parer. ED: J. O. C. Orton, R. Maslyn Williams, Edna Turner. ART D: Richard Ridgway. SET CONSTRUCTION: James Coleman. M: Willy Redstone, Alf J. Lawrence. PM: T. D. Connochie, W. H. Durrant. ASST D: Mervyn Scales, Roy Sebastian, Bert Fontanella. SD: Leslie Fry, Denis Box. 92 mins.

CAST: Charles Farrell (Sandy Nelson), Mary Maguire (Jenny Rutherford), James Raglan (Dr John Vaughan), Joe Valli (Dodger Green), Margaret Vyner (Betty Webb), Eric Colman (Geoffrey Webb), Tom Lurich (Blotch Burns), Maudie Edwards (Phyllis), Katie Towers (Sarah O'Toole), Phillip Lytton (Dr Gordon Rutherford), Andrew Beresford (John Rutherford), Jack Clarke (Pop Snitzler), Phil Smith (Barman Joe), Donald Bradman (himself), Frank Coughlan and the Trocadero Orchestra.

This episodic melodrama focuses less on the flying doctor of the title than on Sandy, a cocky adventurer in the outback. On his wedding night Sandy is smitten by wanderlust and deserts his young bride, Jenny. He finds work in Sydney as a painter on the new Harbour Bridge and eventually befriends a doctor, John Vaughan, who is unhappily in love with a married woman. Vaughan later decides to leave the turmoil of his life in Sydney, and accepts a post as flying doctor in the outback. After serving a prison sentence for his part in a brawl at a cricket match, Sandy also heads for the outback and manages to strike a rich gold vein. He enjoys a new life of wealth but one day is shot in a bar-room fight and loses his sight. His life is further disrupted when he learns that Vaughan has married and that his bride is none other than Jenny. Sandy realizes that she is truly in love with the doctor and decides to take his own life rather than cause her any further unhappiness. He leaves his fortune to the Aerial Medical Service.

The Flying Doctor was an ambitious and well-publicized international production with an American star and technical and financial support from the Gaumont-British company. It marked the first venture of a local company, National Productions, under the general

289 *The Flying Doctor* Charles Farrell (*c*), Joe Valli with suitcase

management of Frederick Daniell, a promoter closely involved with radio and newspaper companies in Sydney. The directors of the company formed an impressive group of business and society leaders and included Sir Hugh Denison, Sir Samuel Walder and Sir James Murdoch. The company was tied closely (through an interlocking directorate) with National Studios, which had built and opened the large studio complex at Pagewood in Sydney, first used for feature production by Chauvel for *Uncivilised* (released later in 1936).

Under its agreement with Gaumont-British, National Productions was provided with a British director (the veteran character actor and comedy director, Miles Mander), a writer (J. O. C. Orton), photographer (Derick Williams), unit manager (T. D. Connochie) and sound recordist (Leslie Fry). Another British photographer who worked on the film, Errol Hinds, came to Sydney under two years' contract to National Studios as head of the camera department. The English crew arrived in November 1935 but shooting did not commence until late in January. Several weeks were lost because of bad weather, and work was still in progress at the end of March when Mander left for Hollywood, leaving Orton to supervise the completion of the film.

The final cost was officially announced to be £35 000, but trade gossip suggested figures of around £45 000, more than twice the budget of a Cinesound feature at that time.

With distribution through Twentieth Century-Fox, the film was premièred with much ballyhoo in Brisbane on 21 August 1936 but earnings were only moderate. To the *Sydney Morning Herald*, 23 September 1936, the film's main failing was its story: 'Instead of selecting and developing some definite dramatic subject, it sprawls and rambles all over the place; and the real conflict does not develop until five minutes before the end. Even then, it is over-sentimental and unconvincing.' Overseas release, too, presented many disappointments; despite the opposition of their Australian partners, Gaumont-British cut the film by some 25 minutes and planned to release it as only a supporting feature. However, Gaumont-British soon withdrew from distribution and complex negotiations were undertaken to transfer the film to a new agency. Finally in September 1937 General Film Distributors released the film but it fared poorly. It was never released in the U.S.A., despite the presence of the American star. National Productions ceased operations, but some of its principals retained interest in occasional later ventures.

290 **Uncivilised***

1936 CHARLES CHAUVEL

PC: Expeditionary Films. SC: Charles Chauvel, E. V. Timms. PH: Tasman Higgins. ED: Frank Coffey, Mona Donaldson. ART D: James Coleman. SPECIAL EFFECTS: George Malcolm. M: Lindley Evans. CHOREOG: Richard White. ASST D: Frank Coffey, Ann Wynn [Elsa Chauvel]. 82 mins.

CAST: Dennis Hoey (Mara), Margot Rhys (Beatrice Lynn), Ashton Jarry (Akbar Jhan), Kenneth Brampton (Trask), Marcelle Marnay (Sondra), Edward Howell (Vitchi), Victor Fitzherbert (Hemingway), John Fernside (Captain), Edward Sylveni (Salter), Norman Rutledge, Don McNiven and Carl Francis (troopers), Frank Dwyer (Blum), Rita Aslin (Nardin), Jessica Malone (secretary).

A successful high-society authoress, Beatrice Lynn, travels into the wilds of northern Australia to investigate the story of a primitive Aboriginal tribe ruled by a white king, Mara. On the way she is kidnapped by an Afghan trader who takes her far into the land where the strange song of the white chieftain echoes through the jungle. Mara buys Beatrice from the Afghan and tries to win her love. After many adventures, including opium smuggling and a battle with an Aboriginal killer, Beatrice grows to love Mara and decides to remain with him in his jungle domain.

This action adventure, with its network of sub-plots, was a conscious attempt by Chauvel to break into the American market. Although it exploited Chauvel's beloved Queensland locations, the film had no readily identifiable Australian content, and its deserts and jungles were standard comic-book settings. Even the Aborigines were converted into stock figures of jungle melodrama with sinister, highly choreographed dances and rituals. For the first and only time in his films, Chauvel cast a non-Australian in the leading role; after searching in vain for a suitable Australian, he selected the British singer and character actor, Dennis Hoey. Hoey's name had virtually no box-office appeal (although he had acted in numerous films), but the presence of an experienced overseas actor added greatly to the glamour and local commercial respectability of the film. Physically, too, Hoey

290 *Uncivilised* Dennis Hoey, Margot Rhys and Aborigines from Palm Island

looked right for the part of an Australian Tarzan, and two song sequences were added to the film to display his strong baritone voice.

Late in 1935 shooting began with six weeks on coastal locations in northern Queensland and on Palm Island, where a native village was constructed especially for the film. Interiors were shot in the newly opened National Studios at Pagewood. There a replica of the Palm Island village was built and twenty Palm Island Aborigines were brought to Sydney to act in the studio scenes.

Completed for about £20 000, the film was released through Universal in September 1936 at the Embassy Theatre, Sydney. Chauvel was again aided by much free publicity when the Commonwealth censor took objection to two scenes, one a nude swim by Margot Rhys in a jungle pool, and the other the strangling of an Aboriginal killer. Although the film was finally permitted to screen intact within Australia, the censor insisted on cuts before export.

In November 1936 Chauvel went to America to study production methods for seven months at the Universal studios in Hollywood, and managed to secure a sale of *Uncivilised* to a small distributor, Box Office Attractions. Although the film was shown in hundreds of American cinemas and earned a healthy revenue for the American buyer, Expeditionary received little benefit from it. Discouraged by the difficulty of arranging effective deals with American distributors, the businessmen backing Expeditionary decided to cease production and released Chauvel to allow him to raise finance elsewhere for his next feature, *Forty Thousand Horsemen* (1940).

291 **White Death***

1936 EDWIN G. BOWEN

PC: Barrier Reef Films. P: Edwin G. Bowen. SC: Frank Harvey. PH: H. C. Anderson, Arthur Higgins. ED: Edwin G. Bowen, William Carty. ART D: James Coleman. M: Isadore Goodman. SONG: 'Moonlight on the Barrier' by J. E. Morhardt. ASST D: Roy Sebastian. SD: Arthur Smith. 81 mins.

CAST: Zane Grey (himself), Alfred Frith (Newton Smith), Nola Warren (Nola Murchison), John Weston (John Lollard), Harold Colonna (David Murchison), James Coleman (Professor Lollard), Peter Williams (boatman), Frank Big Belt (guard).

Late in 1935, Zane Grey, the prolific author of Western adventures, came to Australia on a deep-sea fishing expedition, which was closely followed in the press and on radio. The first feature film in which he had ever acted was a quickie, apparently designed to exploit the awe with which the Australian public regarded his visit.

Grey had brought with him three American photographers to record his fishing trip, including H. C. Anderson, who co-directed the photography on the feature. Grey's general manager, Edwin G. Bowen, was assigned director of the film; it was his first production, although he claimed to have 'grown up' in Hollywood. A sound technician, equipment and full studio and laboratory facilities were hired from Cinesound, and even a Cinesound writer, Frank Harvey, was engaged to provide Grey with a story-line.

In the story Grey figured as himself, in a quest for a great white shark. In his travels, he visits an island in the Great Barrier Reef where he meets a half-crazed missionary whose son and wife were taken by a shark known to the local Aborigines as 'White Death'. Eventually Grey manages to land the shark and rid the island of its monster.

291 *White Death* Alfred Frith

A comic sub-plot parodied Grey's problems in Australia with the Royal Society for the Prevention of Cruelty to Animals: this organization had done much to embarrass Grey with criticism of his fishing exploits, and he gained vengeance through the character of Newton Smith, a member of the Society for the Protection of Fish. Smith became the butt of many jokes, from an encounter with a temperamental camel to his capture by wild Aborigines. The role was played in Buster Keaton style by an experienced stage comedian, Alfred Frith, who was virtually the only professional actor engaged on the film.

In May 1936 the production crew departed for Hayman Island in the Barrier Reef for nearly three months of location shooting. Few expenses were spared: a diving bell for underwater photography was built to Grey's specifications, and Aboriginal extras were brought from Palm Island (some of them already with film experience in Chauvel's *Uncivilised*). White sharks proved elusive throughout the shooting period and the props

master, Jim Coleman, made one out of wood and canvas to meet the demands of the plot. Additional scenes were shot later at Cinesound's Bondi studio, and Grey returned in mid-August to America.

With distribution through B.E.F., the film was premièred in October at Moruya and Bateman's Bay on the New South Wales south coast, where Grey had been based for much of his time in Australia. In November it opened in Sydney at the Mayfair and early in 1937 was released by M.G.M. in England. Although it was initially successful at the box-office, critical reactions were poor indeed; the *Sydney Morning Herald*, 9 November 1936, dismissed it as 'a rambling and rather ramshackle film . . . almost bare of dramatic action'.

292 Orphan of the Wilderness*

1936 KEN G. HALL

PC: Cinesound Productions. P: Ken G. Hall. SC: Edmond Seward. From the story, *Wilderness Orphan*, by Dorothy Cottrell. PH: George Heath. ED: William Shepherd. ART D: J. Alan Kenyon. MD: Hamilton Webber. PM: Jack Souter. ASST D: Ronald Whelan. SD: Clive Cross. 85 mins.

CAST: Brian Abbot (Tom Henton), Gwen Munro (Margot), Ethel Saker (Mrs Henton), Harry Abdy (Shorty McGee), Ronald Whelan (Mel), Joe Valli (Andrew McMeeker), Sylvia Kellaway (Jill), June Munro (June), Edna Montgomery (Nell), Claude Turton (Dan), Arthur Cornell (circus watchman), Leo Cracknell (Otto Ambergres), Sid Knowles (Beller), Jack Souter (grocer), Victor Fitzherbert and Jack Solomons (seconds), Captain A. C. Stevens (Burke), George Scott (the Strong Man), Dick Ryan (the kid).

Chut is a baby kangaroo whose mother is killed by hunters. After wandering through the bush, he comes across a homestead where he is befriended by the owner, Tom Henton. Years later, Tom places Chut in a travelling circus managed by the sadistic Shorty McGee.

292 The studio bushland setting for *Orphan of the Wilderness*

292 *Orphan of the Wilderness* Gwen Munro turns on Harry Abdy after learning that he has been mistreating the circus animals

Tom's girlfriend, Margot, is a performer in the circus and she promises to see that Chut is properly cared for. McGee trains Chut to box, and Chut's circus act becomes famous around the country. Only later do Margot and Tom discover that McGee has been whipping Chut into obedience. One day Chut fights back against McGee and escapes into the bush, hotly pursued by men with rifles and dogs. Tom's station hands ride to the rescue, and after a brawl between the two parties, Chut returns safely to Tom's care.

Originally planned as a 50-minute B-film to support *Thoroughbred*, the script was expanded shortly before production began to include 'love interest' in an attempt to broaden its commercial appeal. The £12 000 production commenced in May 1936 with location work in the Burragorang Valley and Camden, followed by some of the most ambitious studio work ever attempted by an Australian company. Under the direction of J. Alan Kenyon, a bushland setting, 140 feet by 70 feet, was reproduced inside the studio at Bondi; eucalypt trees, ferns, shrubs and grasses were replanted in the studio around a waterfall and bush pool. A score of animals—kangaroos, an emu, koalas, a snake and a bullfrog—were moved inside. Problems of filming the animals were plentiful: most were sensitive to the studio's lights, and the kangaroos, after settling in, were difficult to prompt into action. The result, however, was an introductory twelve-minute sequence that stands today as one of Cinesound's best. The *Sydney Morning Herald*, 21 December 1936, found the opening pastorale 'extraordinarily beautiful . . . The tender, lyrical images flow across the screen, graced by exquisite photography and pleasant music, in a way which recalls the soothing beauty of the silent screen.'

Off-screen, Chut was a partially trained kangaroo owned by Harry Abdy, who had travelled extensively in Australia and the U.S.A. with a boxing kangaroo act. After his film appearance, Chut became so popular that, as Hall later recalled, every kangaroo became 'Chut' to child audiences, in much the same way that Skippy, the bush kangaroo, rose to fame in the late 1960s. Chut dolls were sold in chain stores, the story was serialized in children's magazines, and Chut made numerous personal appearances in theatres and shopping centres. The film also introduced one of Cinesound's most promising players, Gwen Munro. A former model, she had won the Australian section of an international beauty contest, which gave her a small part in a Hollywood movie, *The Search for Beauty* (1934). After several stage roles in the U.S.A., she returned to Australia and appeared with a J. C. Williamson theatrical company, before being recruited by Cinesound.

Opening at the Lyceum Theatre, Sydney, in December 1936, the film went on to play to large school holiday crowds in every state. It became a firm favourite in children's matinees and was voted the best Australian film of 1936 by the newly formed Film Critics' Guild of Australia. In the U.S.A. it was retitled *Wild Innocence* and opened at the Belmont Theatre, New York, on 10 November 1938, where it attracted some encouraging notices from the press. In England, the film was banned for alleged cruelty to animals, even though in Australia the Royal Society for the Prevention of Cruelty to Animals and the New South Wales Department of Education had endorsed the film. Eventually, in 1938, a version severely cut to 69 minutes was released by Pathé.

293 Rangle River*

1936 CLARENCE BADGER

PC: National Studios/Columbia Pictures. STORY: Zane Grey. ADAPTATION: Charles and Elsa Chauvel. PH: Errol Hinds. CAM ASST: Damien Parer. ED: Frank Coffey, Mona Donaldson. ART D: Harry Whiting. M: Alfred Lawrence. PM: Bert Fontanella. ASST D: George Hughes. SD: Denis Box. 86 mins.

CAST: Victor Jory (Dick Drake), Margaret Dare (Marion Hastings), Robert Coote (Reggie Mannister), Cecil Perry (Donald Lawton), George Bryant (Dan Hastings), Rita Pauncefort (Aunt Abbie), Leo Cracknell (Barbwire), Georgie Sterling (Minna), Stewart McColl (Black).

This Australian Western, complete with a hero's comic sidekick called 'Barbwire' and a scene of campfire vocal harmonizing, centres on the rivalry between neighbouring cattle stations. On one side is a patriarchal cattleman, Dan Hastings, and his rugged young manager, Dick Drake; on the other, Donald Lawton, a suave and ruthless villain. When Lawton blocks off the Rangle River (which flows through both stations), Dan's property is left without water. Dick, followed by Dan's daughter, Marion, travels up the dry river-bed to investigate, but Lawton dynamites his dam and traps Marion in the flood. After rescuing Marion (with a fine display of acrobatics), Dick confronts Lawton and they fight a fierce duel with stockwhips. Lawton is soundly defeated, and later Dick nervously confesses his love for Marion. As the lovers walk across the landscape at the end, it is Marion who carries the stockwhip.

This second attempt by the National group to produce films for the international market was made in equal partnership with the Australian branch of Columbia Pictures. As with *The Flying Doctor*, the director, principal technicians and players were imported. The story had been written by Zane Grey during his recent visit to Australia and revised by Charles and Elsa Chauvel; a critic in the *Sydney Morning Herald*, 21 December 1936, found their script both 'intelligent and intelligible', qualities that he considered rare in local productions. The veteran American director, Clarence Badger, was brought from Hollywood in June 1936, along with the actor Victor Jory. With a budget of some £20 000, shooting commenced in mid-July on location near Gloucester and in the Burragorang Valley.

Released with considerable ceremony by Columbia at the Plaza Theatre, Sydney, in December 1936, the film ran for five satisfactory weeks and did well elsewhere in Australia. Shortened by about five minutes, it opened in England early in 1937, again distributed by Columbia. Most of the cuts were caused by the British censor's objections to the violence, particularly in the climactic stockwhip fight. Release in America was delayed until 1939, when an independent distributor, J. H. Hoffberg, issued it under the title of *Men with Whips*.

Although today it seems a routine action movie, in 1936 even the cautious *Sydney Morning Herald* declared that it was 'decidedly the best film that has been produced in Australia so far'. Jory was praised as a convincing hero, but the scene-stealer was Robert Coote as a comic 'new chum', Reggie. Coote, who had been cast in the film while touring on the Australian stage, soon went on to Hollywood and appeared there in numerous 'silly ass' roles. After *Rangle River*, Clarence Badger remained in Sydney and retired from production. Apart from *That Certain Something* (1941), he made no further films. He died in Sydney in June 1964 at the age of 84.

294 It Isn't Done*

1937 KEN G. HALL

PC: Cinesound Productions. Presented by Stuart F. Doyle. P: Ken G. Hall. SC: Frank Harvey, Carl Dudley. STORY: Cecil Kellaway. PH: George Heath. ED: William Shepherd. ART D: Eric Thompson, J. Alan Kenyon. MD: Hamilton Webber. PM: Jack Souter, Harry Strachan. ASST D: Ronald Whelan. SD: Clive Cross. 90 mins.

CAST: Cecil Kellaway (Hubert Blaydon), Shirley Ann Richards (Patricia Blaydon), John Longden (Peter Ashton), Frank Harvey (Lord Denvee), Nellie Ferguson (Mrs Blaydon), Harvey Adams (Jarms), Campbell Copelin (Ronald Dudley), Bobbie Hunt (Lady Denvee), Leslie Victor (Potter), Harold Meade (Lord Addersley), Rita Pauncefort (Mrs Dudley), Douglas Channell (Harry Blaydon), Sylvia Kellaway (Elsie Blaydon), Hilda Dorrington (Mrs Ashton), Ronald Whelan (Perroni), Les Warton (swaggie), Frank Dunn (Mr King), William Edgley (doctor).

Hubert Blaydon, a humble Australian farmer, unexpectedly inherits an old baronial estate, and goes to England with his wife and daughter to take possession of it. Suddenly placed among the English upper class, Hubert finds that his casual manners are not entirely acceptable, despite the attempts of the family butler to explain what is and isn't 'done'. Hubert's daughter, Patricia, falls in love with Peter Ashton, an impoverished young writer. When legal difficulties arise over the estate, Hubert contrives evidence to prove that Peter is in fact the rightful heir to the estate. Patricia and Peter are married, and Hubert and his wife return to Australia where they know they will be happier.

The production of a story set in England was facilitated by Cinesound's rear-projection equipment, which enabled action to be staged in the Bondi studio in front of Engiish backgrounds. The backgrounds, filmed for Cinesound by British International Pictures, were supplemented by sets designed by Eric Thompson, who had just returned to Australia after several years' experience with M.G.M. in Hollywood. Exteriors for the Australian scenes were shot in Sydney and at Camden, and shooting was completed in late

294 *It Isn't Done* Shirley Ann Richards, Cecil Kellaway

November 1936 after a compact six-week schedule.

After an intensive national publicity campaign by the distributors, B.E.F., *It Isn't Done* was premièred in February 1937 at the Wintergarden, Brisbane, and was an instant box-office success. In England it was shortened to 77 minutes and released by M.G.M. early in 1938.

The *Sydney Morning Herald*, 8 March 1937, welcomed it as 'one of the most workmanlike and skilful efforts which have so far emerged from the Cinesound studios . . . By looking toward England frankly, and sometimes a trifle crudely, from the Australian point of view, the film is doing something really significant in the development of a national consciousness.' Kellaway, as the farmer, was far removed from the backblocks farce of the Hayseeds, and *Everyones*, 10 March 1937, noted his 'sincere portrayal, characterised by a wit and genialness'.

Soon after the film was completed, Cinesound suffered a brief exodus of personnel; John Longden returned to England after four years in Australia, and Cecil Kellaway and the American writer, Carl Dudley, left for Hollywood. A new career began, however, for Cinesound's most publicized 'discovery', Shirley Ann Richards. Born in 1918 in Sydney, she had done only a little amateur acting before being given solid dramatic training at Cinesound's 'Talent School' by Frank Harvey and George Parker. She was cast in a leading role in *It Isn't Done* and was subsequently placed under a two-year contract by Cinesound. She remained to appear in four of the studio's features and one wartime featurette, *100,000 Cobbers* (1942). When Cinesound abandoned feature production for the war she went to Hollywood, where her name was changed to Ann Richards to avoid confusion with the actress Anne Shirley. She first appeared there in a short narrative film for M.G.M., *The Woman in the House* (1942), and went on to many features, including King Vidor's *An American Romance* (1944). In the early 1950s she retired from films, and in 1971 published a book of poetry, *The Grieving Senses.*

295 Mystery Island*

1937 J. A. LIPMAN

PC: Commonwealth Film Laboratories. P SUP: Jack Bruce. P, PH: George Malcolm. SC: Harry Lauder 2nd. STORY: Captain T. D. Bairnsfather. ED: Arthur Hansen. MD: Rex Shaw. SONG: 'Mystery Isle', lyrics and music by Frank Coughlan. SD: Mervyn Murphy. 56 mins.

CAST: Brian Abbot (Morris Carthew), Jean Laidley (Audrey Challoner), W. Lane Bayliff (Captain Druce), William Carroll (Chief Officer Vowels), George Doran (Reverend Abel), Desmond Hay (Packer), Mollie Kerwin (Miss Fortescue), Moncrieff Macallum (Green), Douglas MacKinnon (cook), Edward Druitt (Seabright).

Two women and eight men are shipwrecked on a South Pacific island. Among them is a murderer, but his identity is known only to the ship's captain, who has lost his memory.

The story was filmed almost entirely on one of the Admiralty Islets, close to Lord Howe Island. A production unit of twenty sailed from Sydney in September 1936 for a month's work on the islet, taking several tons of equipment and props. Shooting involved many hardships and accidents, including the loss in rough seas of 2000 feet of exposed film, which had to be reshot. Tragedy struck early in October when two members of the cast, Brian Abbot and Leslie Hay-Simpson (who acted under the name of Desmond Hay), attempted to return to Sydney in a sixteen-foot open boat and were never seen again.

After the return from Lord Howe Island, the film was completed in the studio of Commonwealth Film Laboratories, Sydney, where the shipwreck was staged with models. Distributed by Paramount, it opened on 6 March 1937 at the Prince Edward Theatre, Sydney, as a supporting feature. Critics found the unusual location to be the film's primary asset, although some attention was drawn to the pleasant theme song, sung in the film by Brian Abbot and Jean Laidley (known in Sydney's theatre circles as Jean Mort).

The film's principal backer was Jack Bruce, then managing director of Commonwealth Film Laboratories and an important figure in the development of laboratory services in Australia. He had worked extensively as a newsreel and feature photographer in Sydney after the First World War, and in the 1920s had spent several years in Hollywood as a camera technician. He returned to Australia to join Commonwealth Film Laboratories at its formation in 1927, and in 1935 was a key figure with Raymond Longford and others in an unsuccessful attempt to open a new Sydney studio, the Mastercraft Film Corporation.

296 **Phantom Gold***

1937 RUPERT KATHNER

PC: Kathner-Tolhurst Australian Productions.
P, SC, PH: Rupert Kathner. ASSOC P: Stan Tolhurst.
ED: Cecil Blackman. M: Rex Shaw. SD: Mervyn Murphy.
64 mins.

CAST: Stan Tolhurst (Harry Lasseter), Bryce Russell (Paul Johns), Captain W. L. Pittendrigh (himself), Bob Buck (himself), Old Warts (himself), Reg King (S. J. Hamre). NARRATOR: Captain A. C. Stevens.

In May 1936 an expedition led by a Sydney businessman, H. V. Foy, set out to investigate the lost gold reef discovered by Harry Lasseter in central Australia. Foy took with him two young film-makers, Rupert Kathner and Stan Tolhurst, to record the trip. On the way the party met several people who had known Lasseter, among them the bushman, Bob Buck, who had found and buried his body in 1930, and Old Warts, an Aboriginal who had befriended him. Kathner and Tolhurst formed the idea of reconstructing scenes of Lasseter's last attempt to rediscover the reef in 1930, and Tolhurst himself acted the part of the lone prospector. After three months in central Australia, the party returned to Sydney, where additional scenes were shot. These included a re-enactment by Captain W. L. Pittendrigh of the incident in which he and his co-pilot S. J. Hamre had flown in search of Lasseter and had been forced by fuel shortage to land in the desert, where they suffered severe hardship for three weeks before being rescued.

Apart from an opening interview with Foy, none of the film had synchronized dialogue; it was accompanied throughout by a commentary by a Sydney radio personality, Captain A. C. Stevens. The film was rejected under the quality clause of the New South Wales quota act and failed to attract a major distributor. Kathner himself arranged a few screenings in country towns such as Woy Woy and Gosford, N.S.W., in mid-1937, and on 24 September it opened at the Cameo Theatre, Sydney, as a supporting feature. After four days, however, it was withdrawn following legal action by the publishing firm, Angus and Robertson, who alleged that the film was an infringement of the copyright on *Lasseter's Last Ride*, a book by Ion Idriess, which they had published in 1931. The case was never contested in court, but Foy complied by barring any further screenings of the film.

Kathner was a sketch artist who began working in set design in local film studios in the early 1930s. Before *Phantom Gold* he tried in vain to find backing for a feature based on a story by Stan Tolhurst, *Falling for Fame*, 'depicting the phonies who came from overseas and wasted the [film] industry's money'. A similar jaundiced view of the industry was expressed in his book, *Let's Make a Movie*, published in Sydney in 1945. Altogether he completed five features and several shorts, none of which recovered its cost. He died in Cairns on 31 March 1954, aged 50.

Stan Tolhurst had worked as a 'specialty dancer' on stage before joining the casual staff at Cinesound where he was used to 'cod' newsreels (adding humour to otherwise routine items). As a character actor he appeared in numerous films over the next few decades, and was valued by Ken G. Hall as a comic drunk in films such as *Let George Do It* (1938). In 1938 he collaborated with George Hughes and the young cameraman, Damien Parer, on a short-lived but much-praised series of 'film poems', *This Place Australia*, illustrating verse by Henry Lawson and A. B. Paterson.

297 *Tall Timbers* Comic relief with Letty Craydon (*l*), Joe Valli (*c*), George Lloyd

297 J. Alan Kenyon with the model forest during the shooting of *Tall Timbers*

297 *Tall Timbers* Frank Leighton knocks out a labour agitator

297 Tall Timbers*

1937 KEN G. HALL

PC: Cinesound Productions. P: Ken G. Hall. SC: Frank Harvey. STORY: Frank Hurley. PH: George Heath. ED: William Shepherd. ART D: Eric Thompson. SPECIAL EFFECTS: J. Alan Kenyon. MD: Lindley Evans. PM: Jack Souter, Harry Strachan. ASST D: Ronald Whelan. SD: Clive Cross. 89 mins.

CAST: Frank Leighton (Jim Thornton), Shirley Ann Richards (Joan Burbridge), Campbell Copelin (Charles Blake), Frank Harvey (Darley), Harvey Adams (Stephen Burbridge), Aileen Britton (Claire Darley), Ronald Whelan (Ludwig Rich), Joe Valli (Scotty), George Lloyd (Bill), Letty Craydon (Rosanna), W. Lane Bayliff (Gavan), Peter Dunstan (Robbie).

A young forestry graduate, Jim Thornton, is involved in a race between timber companies to fill a major contract. Jim joins the crew of a genial timber baron, Burbridge, and foils attempts by a rival, Blake, to sabotage their work. Jim and Burbridge plan a 'timber drive', partly cutting through trees on a slope and then dynamiting the trees at the top of the ridge, so that the trees along the whole hillside collapse in chain reaction. One of Blake's henchmen traps Jim and Burbridge's adopted daughter, Joan, in the path of the timber drive but, as the trees crash around them, they manage to escape. The drive is a success and Burbridge wins the contract. Meanwhile, a chance conversation has revealed that Jim is Burbridge's long-lost son, and he is married to Joan in a grand wedding ceremony.

J. Alan Kenyon's special effects were the highlight of the film. Two attempts were made in January 1937 to stage timber drives on a twenty-acre slope near Gloucester, N.S.W.; six cameras were strategically placed along the slope to cover the event, but on both occasions the drives failed to work. Kenyon finally made a model of the timber slope and a drive was staged in miniature, with close-up shots intercut from the abortive real-life drives. Spectacle elsewhere in the film, including an opening scene of a surf rescue at Palm Beach, and the dynamiting of a railway bridge, helped to compensate for a novelettish plot and florid dialogue. Comic relief was provided by Joe Valli as a Scottish timber-train driver amorously pursued by a shrill-voiced maid at the Burbridges' country house.

The popularity of the £18 000 production maintained Cinesound's record of commercial success: the première at the Tivoli Theatre, Brisbane, in August 1937 reputedly broke records established by *On Our Selection* (1932). In January 1938 it was released in England by Paramount at the Plaza Theatre, in London's West End.

298 The Avenger*

1937 A. R. HARWOOD

PC: New Era Film Productions. SC: Bert Hollis. PH: Arthur Higgins, Tasman Higgins. ART D: Tom McNiven. M: Frank Chapple. MD: Rex Shaw. PM: Neville Bletcher. ASST D: Don McNiven. SD: Mervyn Murphy. 55 mins.

CAST: Douglas Stuart (Terry Druton), John Fernside (Max Hart), Karen Greyson (Della, the maid), Marcia Melville (Gwen), Marshall Crosby (Detective Sergeant O'Neill), George Lloyd (Happy Evans), Raymond Longford (Warren), Pat Twohill (solicitor), Jim Max (gardener), Albert Callanan (publican), Reg King (carrier), Jack Couver (Dick), Val Atkinson (actor), Fay Revel (barmaid), Winnie Edgerton (Mrs Thompson), Rae Maurice (Mrs Pitman), Jeanne Battye (Jean), Mardy Harwood (detective), 'Tich' Irvine (drunk), Midge Harwood.

A reformed thief marries a wealthy socialite but is bedevilled by a former accomplice who tries to frame him for murder.

This static and rather confusing melodrama was produced by a Melbourne company but shot in Sydney, largely in the National Studios, Pagewood, in October and November 1937. Assembled with great rapidity, it was ready for a trade preview in Sydney on 17 December. Distribution was arranged through a small Sydney exchange, Atlas Films, but although it was registered as a New South Wales quota production, no release followed in major centres. Early in 1938, British rights were purchased by Columbia for a sum amounting to nearly half of the production cost.

299 Lovers and Luggers*

1937 KEN G. HALL

PC: Cinesound Productions. P: Ken G. Hall. SC: Frank Harvey. STORY: Edmund Barclay. From the novel by Gurney Slade. PH: George Heath, Frank Hurley. ED: William Shepherd. ART D: Eric Thompson. SPECIAL EFFECTS: J. Alan Kenyon. MD: Hamilton Webber. PIANIST: Paul Schramm. PM: Jack Souter, Harry Strachan. ASST D: Ronald Whelan. SD: Clive Cross. 99 mins.

CAST: Lloyd Hughes (Daubenny Carshott), Shirley Ann Richards (Lorna Quidley), Sidney Wheeler (Captain Quidley), James Raglan (Craig Henderson), Elaine Hamill (Stella Raff), Frank Harvey (Carshott's manager), Ronald Whelan (Mendoza), Alec Kellaway (McTavish), Leslie Victor (Dormer), Campbell Copelin (Archie), Charlie Chan (Kishimuni), Marcelle Marnay (Lotus), Horace Cleary (China Tom), Claude Turton (Charlie Quong), Bobbie Hunt (Lady Winter), Paul Furness (Professor of Psychology), Charles Zoli (Carshott's valet).

Daubenny Carshott is a celebrated London pianist infatuated with an ambitious socialite, Stella Raff. She insists that he prove himself a man by bringing her a pearl with his own hands from the waters off Thursday Island. Blinded by passion, Daubenny travels to the island, where he befriends Craig Henderson, who later turns out to be another of Stella's lovers on a similar mission. He soon begins to enjoy the simple island life and is attracted to Lorna, an unaffected (white) island girl. Daubenny starts to dive for pearls and eventually finds one big enough to satisfy Stella, but has to fight to keep it from the clutches of rivals. Stella, meanwhile, visits the island and Daubenny and Craig plot together to repay her for her double-dealing, leaving Daubenny free for a happy ending with Lorna.

Lloyd Hughes had been a prominent star in the silent days of Hollywood, but by the mid-1930s was working mainly in B-movies. He arrived in Sydney in July 1937 and was welcomed with all of the ceremony and fanfare that Cinesound could muster. Shooting began later in the same month with an eight-week schedule and a budget of £24 000. Earlier in the year Frank Hurley had gone to Thursday Island to shoot scenic

299 *Lovers and Luggers* Shirley Ann Richards

299 *Lovers and Luggers* Island 'low-life', with Ronald Whelan (*l*), and Claude Turton as the Chinese barkeeper

interludes and backgrounds for the rear-projection unit. These were then merged in a large set, occupying the entire studio, with bungalows and palm trees to give the illusion of an island village. For the underwater scenes, a huge tank with glass portholes was built in the studio, but the Sydney water supply proved too dirty; efforts to purify the water failed and the underwater sets were rebuilt in the North Sydney Olympic Pool where a filter plant had been installed.

The story's wealth of island eccentrics provided good opportunity for character actors, and several new members were introduced to the regular Cinesound troupe. Sidney Wheeler, a stage and radio actor promoted by Cinesound as 'Australia's Wallace Beery', played a rascally sea captain with a spirit of mischievous good humour. Alec Kellaway, brother of Cecil, played the first of many character roles for Ken Hall, and provided the film's main comic relief as a Scottish drunkard.

On 31 December 1937 B.E.F. presented a simultaneous première in Brisbane and Hobart, and the film quickly became one of Cinesound's most profitable ventures. It was bought for what was claimed to be a record price by Paramount for the English market, and in 1940 it was released in the U.S.A. as *Vengeance of the Deep*. Locally, the film was generously reviewed; the *Bulletin*, 29 December 1937, found that the acting and technical work made it an 'almost incredibly better film than the narrative outline might seem to permit', and the *Sydney Morning Herald*, 28 February 1938, declared 'without qualification that Australia has definitely "arrived" as a film-producing country with vast possibilities'. Ken Hall's 'astute' direction created both an exciting air of authenticity in the diving scenes and a tropical atmosphere that 'creates a thrill of pride'.

300 The Broken Melody*

1938 KEN G. HALL

PC: Cinesound Features. P: Ken G. Hall. SC: Frank Harvey. From the novel by F.J. Thwaites. PH: George Heath. ED: William Shepherd. ART D: Eric Thompson. SPECIAL EFFECTS: J. Alan Kenyon. OPERETTA SCENES, VIOLIN THEME: Alfred Hill. INCIDENTAL M: Horace Keats. MD: Hamilton Webber. PM: Jack Souter, Harry Strachan. ASST D: Ronald Whelan. SD: Clive Cross. 89 mins.

CAST: Lloyd Hughes (John Ainsworth), Diana Du Cane (Ann Brady), Frank Harvey (Jules de Latanac), Rosalind Kennerdale (Madame Le Lange), Alec Kellaway (Joe Larkin), Harry Abdy (Sam Harris), Rita Pauncefort (Bella), Harold Meade (Michael Ainsworth), June Munro (Nibs Ainsworth), Ronald Whelan (Bullman), Lionello Cecil (the tenor), Letty Craydon (maid), Marshall Crosby (rowing trainer), Gough Whitlam (man in nightclub).

After a nightclub brawl, John Ainsworth is sent down from university and rejected by his father. Unemployed and penniless in the depths of the Depression, he drifts about Sydney, and one nights saves an impoverished girl, Ann, from suicide. She comes to share a cave-dwelling with him on the foreshores of Sydney Harbour. Inspired by her, John begins to play his violin again and eventually progresses from the street corner to a cabaret. There he comes under the patronage of a French entrepreneur, who sends him to England, where he soon finds fame as a com-

300 *The Broken Melody* Victims of the Depression, Lloyd Hughes and Diana Du Cane

poser and conductor. Some time later, John returns to Australia as the conductor of a touring company performing his own opera. When the fiery soprano refuses to sing, her local understudy is rushed on stage and John recognizes her as Ann. The opera is a huge success and John is happily reunited with Ann and forgiven by his father.

The story was so freely adapted from F.J. Thwaites's novel that it can be considered an original work. In sharp contrast to Hall's routine of action and farce, the film was a prestige production with both 'high drama' in the tale of two lovers caught in the grip of the Depression, and 'high culture' in the lengthy climactic performance of the operetta. At the same time, Hall played safe by peppering the film with his customary touches of light comic relief and moments of deliberate sentimentality (including a death-bed reunion between John and his dying father).

Although the story failed to impress the critics, the music did, and the long operetta sequence, especially composed for the film by Alfred Hill, was applauded: the British trade paper, *Today's Cinema,* 29 March 1938, found it 'really commendably staged [and] one of the most promising things that [has] come out of Australia in the film line so far'.

Shot in October and November 1937, the film was released by B.E.F. at the Embassy Theatre, Sydney, on 17 June 1938. Carefully promoted, it made an easy profit and late in 1938 was released in England by R.K.O. under the title, *The Vagabond Violinist* (to avoid confusion with a 1934 British crime melodrama also called *The Broken Melody*).

301 Let George Do It*

1938 KEN G. HALL

PC: Cinesound Productions. P: Ken G. Hall. SC: George Wallace, Frank Harvey. STORY: Hal Carleton. PH: George Heath. ED: William Shepherd. ART D: Eric Thompson. SPECIAL EFFECTS: J. Alan Kenyon. MD: Hamilton Webber, Maurie Gilman. PM: Jack Souter, Harry Strachan. ASST D: Ronald Whelan. SD: Clive Cross. 79 mins.

CAST: George Wallace (Joe Blake), Letty Craydon (Clara), Joe Valli (Happy Morgan), Alec Kellaway (Mysto the Great), Gwen Munro (Molly), George Lloyd (Unk), Harry Abdy (Elmer Zilch), Neil Carlton (John Randall), Leal Douglas (Mrs Burp), Jack Settle (stage manager), Millie Doris (Madame Montez), Sid Doody (poultry farmer), Lou Vernon (Martini), Butt and Berrigan (Dean and Donovan), Charles Lawrence (solicitor), Stan Tolhurst (drunk), Dud Cantrell's Vocal Trio (vocalists), Pat Noonan (Patsy), Frank Perrin (Monty), Dan Agar (chemist).

301 George Wallace

Unemployed and frustrated in love, Joe gets drunk and decides to commit suicide. He offers to leave his few possessions to a gangster, Zilch, if Zilch will arrange a painless death. Next day Joe thinks better of the offer, especially when he learns that he has become the heir to a large fortune. Zilch, however, insists on holding to his part of the deal, and in order to get the inheritance, tries to kidnap Joe. A wild speedboat chase across Sydney Harbour ensues before Joe's possession of the money is ensured.

Let George Do It was the first of two comedies that George Wallace made with Cinesound. With relatively tight direction from Ken Hall and a scenario written specifically for the screen, he performed with far greater energy and a more apparent sense of humour than in his earlier films for Efftee. Dominating the action was the climactic speedboat chase, a rapidly edited sequence making extensive use of the studio's rear-projection equipment, and smoothly switching between location action and studio set-ups. A water ballet, choreographed by Jan Kowsky (the stage name of Leon Kellaway, a brother of Cecil), was shot at some expense but was largely deleted for the sake of the film's pace, and only a vestige remains at the end of the speedboat sequence.

Shot in February and March 1938, the £21 000 production was released by B.E.F. simultaneously in Hobart and Brisbane on 17 June 1938, and attracted large crowds. Early in 1940 an abridged version titled *In the Nick of Time* was released in England by A.B.F.D., and the title *Let George Do It* was used there instead for a George Formby feature released in the same year.

302 Show Business

1938 A.R. HARWOOD

PC: New Era Film Productions. P: A.R. Harwood. SC, M: Frank Chapple. ADDITIONAL DIALOGUE: Alex Rosenblum. PH: Arthur Higgins. PM: Neville Bletcher. ASST D: Chick Arnold. SD: Mervyn Murphy. 90 mins.

CAST: Bert Matthews (Cogs), Joyce Hunt (Nina Bellamy), Fred Tupper (Fred Hamilton), Chick Arnold (Red), Bonnie Dunn (tap dancer), Barbara James (singer), Betty Matear (Jean), Jimmy McMahon (Wally Winter), John Barrington (Bill Winter), Guy Hastings (Sir James Winter), Douglas Stuart (Benson), Fay Astor (Elsie), Charmaine Ross (Joan), Paul Leon (Jackson), Jimmy Coates and his band, the Pathé Duncan Ballet.

Two brothers, Bill and Wally Winter, become infatuated with a scheming gold- digger, Nina Bellamy, who persuades them to ask Sir James, their wealthy father, for £10 000, so that Bill can produce a professional stage show, and Wally a movie, both to star herself. Sir James discovers the truth about Nina and gives the money to his sons on condition that they leave town in secret for one month to write their shows, and that they use only newly-discovered talent in their casts. Bill visits a country town where a local group is rehearsing an amateur floor show; impressed by their work, he buys their show and brings it to the city where it opens with great success. Meanwhile Wally meets a girl from a local film exchange, and together they plan to re-release an old Australian feature film with a comic commentary. Furious at being ignored, Nina tries to disrupt a preview of the film, but it too is a huge success. Undeterred, Nina tries to blackmail Sir James but is finally exposed as a fraud and is turned away penniless.

Shooting on Harwood's longest and most expensive film (budgeted at £8000) began late in April 1938, using the Cinesound studio at St Kilda, Melbourne. The studio was found to be too small and the technical facilities too poor for a musical comedy, and early in May the entire unit was shipped to Sydney to complete the film at the National Studios, Pagewood. The finished film was passed as a New South Wales quota production, but after a preview in Melbourne on 7 August 1938 it failed to find a major city release. Scattered screenings in independent theatres in suburban and country areas were arranged by Atlas Films, but New Era Films was soon wound up and Harwood dropped out of production and worked as a suburban cinema manager in Melbourne, as an insurance broker and real estate agent, until 1952, when he made *Night Club,* a partial remake of *Show Business.*

301 George Wallace's famous fall onto his left ear: from a rehearsal for *Let George Do It*, with Letty Craydon (*l*), and Alec Kellaway (*r*) in the role that was eventually played by Joe Valli

303 *Typhoon Treasure* Utan, Joe Valli

303 Typhoon Treasure* [The Perils of Pakema Reef]

1938 NOEL MONKMAN

PC: Commonwealth Film Laboratories SC: John P. McLeod. PH: George Malcolm, Harry Malcolm. UNDERWATER PH: Bruce A. Cummings. ART D: Harry Whiting. PM: R. L. Wilkinson. SD: Beresford Hallett, James E. Place. CONTINUITY: Kitty Gelhor. 89 mins.

CAST: Campbell Copelin (Alan Richards), Gwen Munro (Jean Roberts), Joe Valli (Scotty Macleod), Douglas Herald (Buck Thompson), Kenneth Brampton (Alfred Webb), Norman French (patrol officer), Utan (Utan), Marshall Crosby, Moncrieff Macallum, Ossie Wenban, Douglas Channell, Benjamin Brown.

Dedicated to 'the Spirit of Adventure', Noel Monkman's first feature was a lively yarn told with a minimum of dialogue and a maximum of action and scenic novelty. The story follows the adventures of Alan Richards, the sole survivor of a pearling lugger wrecked on Pakema Reef during a typhoon. Richards sets out to retrieve the pearls lost in the wreck, taking a treacherous route through dense jungle inhabited by savage headhunters.

Apart from the opening shipwreck in which a very obvious model is tossed about in a tank, most of the film was staged on location, with the Great Barrier Reef and the Queensland coast standing in for the New Guinea islands where the story is nominally set. Underwater and island scenes were filmed on Green Island off the coast from Cairns. Location shooting began in June 1937, and by December the few studio scenes were completed in the Commonwealth Film Laboratories' studio at the Sydney Showground. Musical accompaniment was collated from popular classics including Tchaikovsky's *Swan Lake.*

The film was released by United Artists in September 1938 with a première season at the St James Theatre, Brisbane. Despite good press notices it was given only a meagre run of one week as a supporting feature in Sydney in October. A slightly abridged version was released in England in 1943. In the early

303 *Typhoon Treasure* Douglas Herald, Gwen Munro

1950s, rights were bought by the film's photographer, George Malcolm, who reduced it to about 40 minutes and retitled it *The Perils of Pakema Reef,* primarily for screening in newsreel theatrettes.

By 1937 Noel Monkman had established a firm reputation for his educational 'nature study' films. Two series, the *Monkman Marvelogues* and one on the Barrier Reef, had been produced by Australian Educational Films, a company that Monkman had founded with F. W. Thring in Melbourne. The script of *Typhoon Treasure* had once been the property of Efftee Film Productions and credit was taken by the Efftee writer, John P. McLeod. As in all of his work, Monkman was assisted by his wife, credited under her maiden name of Kitty Gelhor.

304 Dad and Dave Come to Town*

1938 KEN G. HALL

PC: Cinesound Productions. P: Ken G. Hall SC: Frank Harvey, Bert Bailey. STORY: Ken G. Hall. PH: George Heath. ED: William Shepherd. MONTAGE EFFECTS: John Kingsford Smith. ART D: Eric Thompson. SPECIAL EFFECTS: J. Alan Kenyon. MD: Hamilton Webber, Maurie Gilman. PM: Jack Souter, Harry Strachan. ASST D: Ronald Whelan. SD: Clive Cross. 97 mins.

CAST: Bert Bailey (Dad Rudd), Shirley Ann Richards (Jill), Fred MacDonald (Dave), Billy Rayes (Jim Bradley), Alec Kellaway (Entwistle), Sidney Wheeler (Pierre), Connie Martyn (Mum), Ossie Wenban (Joe), Valerie Scanlan (Sarah), Muriel Ford (Myrtle), Leila Steppe (Sonia), Marshall Crosby (Ryan Snr), Peter Finch (Bill Ryan), Cecil Perry (Rawlings), Billy Stewart (Bob Thompson), Marie D'Alton (Miss Quince), Leslie Victor (Brown), George Lloyd, Jack Settle, Sid Doody and Cyril Northcote (bailiffs), Raymond Longford (policeman).

The third in Cinesound's Dad and Dave series had virtually nothing in common with Steele Rudd's stories and was based instead on one of Ken Hall's favourite comic formulas of the 'fish out of water'. The Rudd family tree, always mutable in the Cinesound series, was modified by the addition of Jill, a sophisticated adult daughter, and by the removal of Dave from his marriage bonds. Also, because Hall believed that the rural setting was exhausted after the popularity of Dad and Dave on radio and in the two earlier films, he moved the main location of the plot to a bustling modern city (unnamed to avoid Sydney-Melbourne rivalries).

Dad unexpectedly inherits a women's fashion store in the city, and the family moves there to take charge. They find it hard to adapt; Dad still rises at dawn (feeding time for the fowls) and a modern bathroom causes complete confusion. Entwistle, an effeminate floor-walker at the shop, helps the Rudds to foil a plot by a rival firm to put the store out of business. In the process Dad becomes renowned as 'the farmer dress-maker' and stages a giant fashion show, which is a huge success. With the business saved, Dad returns to the farm and leaves the store in the hands of his daughter, Jill.

304 *Dad and Dave Come to Town* Connie Martyn, Bert Bailey

With a budget of £23 000, the film was shot in mid-1938 at Cinesound's Bondi studio and on location at Camden. The highlight was the fashion show (complete with a ballet and rear-projected backgrounds), conceived by Hall and designed jointly by the costumier Mavis Ripper with Eric Thompson and J. Alan Kenyon. The film also introduced Peter Finch in the small part of a gangling yokel in love with Sarah Rudd. Born in London in 1916, Finch had come to Australia at the age of twelve. His acting career began in vaudeville and in George Sorlie's touring tent show in New South Wales and Queensland. He quickly progressed to radio drama and the Sydney stage, and made his first film appearance in *The Magic Shoes* (1935), an unreleased children's short directed by Claude Flemming. His later film roles in Australia were character parts and varied widely, from the yokel in *Dad and Dave Come to Town* to a Nazi spy in *The Power and the Glory* (1941), a sensitive English-born soldier in *The Rats of Tobruk* (1944) and a dissolute drunkard in *A Son is Born* (1946). Finch was also a leading figure in the progressive Mercury Theatre in Sydney, a radio producer for the A.B.C., and an assistant director on two documentaries made in Arnhem Land by George Heath. In Septem-

304 *Dad and Dave Come to Town* Valerie Scanlan, Peter Finch

ber 1948, after playing a brief but effective role in *Eureka Stockade,* he went to London and quickly established himself there as a major international star. He died in the U.S.A. in January 1977, and in March 1977 was posthumously awarded an Academy Award for his performance in *Network* (1976).

Dad and Dave Come to Town was first released by B.E.F. on 30 September at the Capitol Theatre, Sydney, where it ran for three weeks despite the Capitol's normal weekly change of programme. Early in 1939 a version shortened to 78 minutes was given a West End release in London under the title *The Rudd Family Goes to Town.* Unlike the earlier Dad and Dave films, it proved quite popular in England, probably because of its more sophisticated comedy, and it received over 1800 bookings in British theatres, claimed at the time to be a record for an Australian production.

305 Below the Surface

1938 RUPERT KATHNER

PC: Australian Cinema Entertainments. SC: Rupert Kathner. STORY: Stan Tolhurst. PH: Tasman Higgins. ED, ASST D: Stan Tolhurst. ART D: Rupert Kathner, Stan Tolhurst. PM: George Hughes. About 55 mins.
CAST: Phyllis Reilly, Neil Carlton, Stan Tolhurst, Jimmy McMahon, Lawrence Taylor, Reg King.

Two miners compete for an important coal contract. One of them threatens violence and uses sabotage in an attempt to ruin the opposition but eventually fails.

Shooting began in November 1937 with locations at Cronulla and in the Newcastle coal-mining area. Studio scenes, including the interior of the mine (a large set constructed by Kathner and Tolhurst themselves), were filmed at National Studios, Pagewood. By February 1938 shooting had been completed and an early release was promised. The film, however, failed to win registration as a New South Wales quota production, and its financial backer, a prominent music house in Sydney, decided to withhold it from public screening.

306 Mr Chedworth Steps Out*

1939 KEN G. HALL

PC: Cinesound Productions. P: Ken G. Hall. SC: Frank Harvey. Based on a novel by Francis Morton Howard. PH: George Heath. ED: William Shepherd. ART D: Eric Thompson. SPECIAL EFFECTS: J. Alan Kenyon. MD: Hamilton Webber. PM: Jack Souter, Harry Strachan. ASST D: Ronald Whelan. SD: Clive Cross. 92 mins.
CAST: Cecil Kellaway (George Chedworth), James Raglan (Brian Carford), Joan Deering (Gwen Chedworth), Rita Pauncefort (Mrs Chedworth), Jean Hatton (Susie Chedworth), Peter Finch (Arthur Chedworth), Rodney Jacobs (Fred Chedworth), Sidney Wheeler (Leon Fencott), Ronald Whelan (Benny), Leslie Victor (Leslie), Cecil Perry (MacGuire), Charmaine Ross (Ada Fencott), Harvey Adams (Mason), Ben Lewin (Welch), Barrett Lennard (Perse Faulkiner), Field Fisher (bailiff), Letty Craydon (Mrs Blundell), Les Warton (Sol Barnes), Phil Smith (estate agent).

306 *Mr Chedworth Steps Out* Australia's Deanna Durbin, Jean Hatton. Hamilton Webber conducts the orchestra

This family entertainment takes place 'behind the front door of Mr and Mrs Average Man'. Chedworth, a mild-mannered clerk, is underpaid and abused by everyone: his wife nags at him for lacking enterprise, and his son takes advantage of his gentle nature by borrowing money to pay for gambling debts. When his employers are forced to reduce staff, Chedworth is demoted and becomes caretaker of an old warehouse. He despairs of his financial situation but one day finds a bag of money, which, unknown to him, is counterfeit. He starts to take a new interest in life and soon wins a fortune from an accidental racing bet and from some apparently worthless goldmining shares sold to him by crooks. Quietly he starts to change his ways and moves his family to a larger house, where his wife revels in their new material wealth. The counterfeiters kidnap him but he is saved by a Treasury official who has been investigating the source of his money; the gang leaders are arrested and Chedworth surrenders the counterfeit hoard but retains his legitimate fortune and his new self-confidence.

Through its comedy the film presents a bleak portrait of suburban conditions and aspirations in the 1930s. The opening scenes

306 *Mr Chedworth Steps Out* Harvey Adams gives notice to his faithful old employee, Cecil Kellaway

establish Chedworth as a victim of both economic and social exploitation, and he is by far the most convincing of all the 'little men' and underdogs in Hall's films. Although the depiction of his private rebellion is blunted occasionally by the intrusion of melodramatic plot devices, the part of Chedworth is played by Cecil Kellaway with a pathos and a genial sense of humour that give the film a strong and endearing centre. The film's satire of snobbery and social pretension is also taken further than elsewhere in Hall's work, with an incisive and sometimes bitter parody of the *nouveaux riches.*

The role of Chedworth was written specifically for Kellaway, who interrupted his Hollywood contract with R.K.O. to return briefly to Australia at Cinesound's expense. The film also began a brief screen career for Jean Hatton, a teenage soprano whom Cinesound billed as 'Australia's Deanna Durbin'. Produced in October and November 1938 for about £21 000, the film was released in April 1938 and made a comfortable profit. It was released in England late in 1939.

307 **Gone to the Dogs***

1939 KEN G. HALL

PC: Cinesound Features. P: Ken G. Hall. SC: George Wallace, Frank Harvey, Frank Coffey. PH: George Heath. ED: William Shepherd. ART D: Eric Thompson. SPECIAL EFFECTS: J. Alan Kenyon. MD: Henry Krips. SONGS: 'We'll Build a Little Home', lyrics and music by George Wallace; 'Gone to the Dogs', lyrics by Harry Allen, music by Henry Krips. PM: Jack Souter, Harry Strachan. ASST D: Ronald Whelan. SD: Clive Cross. 83 mins.

CAST: George Wallace (George), Lois Green (Jean MacAllister), John Dobbie (Henry Applegate), John Fleeting (Jimmy Alderson), Ronald Whelan (Willard), Alec Kellaway (Mad Jack), Letty Craydon (Mrs MacAllister), Kathleen Esler (Irene Inchcape), Howard Craven (Ted Inchcape), Harold Meade (Mr Inchcape), Lou Vernon (Doctor Sundermann), George Lloyd (Quin), Harry Abdy (Hogg), Reginald Collins (Benson), Jack Settle (head keeper), Stephen Doo (Sing Lo), Hughie (Aloysius, the dog).

George is a disaster-prone attendant at the zoo. One day he accidentally discovers a substance that accelerates motion, and tests it on a prize greyhound, which runs faster than ever before. A gang of crooks, whose hide-out is disguised as a haunted house, kidnap George's dog and plan to substitute their own dog in an important race. George and his friends, however, manage to foil the crooks and their dog wins the race.

Hall followed the pattern of *Let George Do It* (1938), introducing a romantic sub-plot and several songs, dances and self-contained comedy routines. Among the highlights are the chorus and ballet for the catchy title song, performed in the yard of the greyhound kennels; George's trip through the haunted house; and an opening slapstick scene in the zoo where he tangles with an angry gorilla.

The £20 000 production was premièred by B.E.F. at the Tivoli Theatre, Brisbane, in August 1939, and made a clear profit. It was released in England by Renown, late in 1940, in a version shortened by some twenty minutes.

307 *Gone to the Dogs* A musical climax, with George Wallace, Lois Green

307 *Gone to the Dogs* George Wallace (*l*), John Dobbie and Lois Green

307 *Gone to the Dogs* Lou Vernon, as the German scientist who leads the gang of villains

308 Come Up Smiling* [Ants In His Pants]

1939 WILLIAM FRESHMAN

PC: Cinesound Features. P: Ken G. Hall. SC: William Freshman. STORY: John Addison Chandler [Ken G. Hall]. PH: George Heath. ED: William Shepherd. ART D: Eric Thompson. SPECIAL EFFECTS: J. Alan Kenyon. MD: Henry Krips. SONGS: 'That's the Way to Handle Your Man', lyrics by Bob Geraghty, Ronald Whelan; 'Poor Little Sheep', lyrics by Will Mahoney, Ronald Whelan, music by Bob Geraghty, Henry Krips; 'Come Up Smiling', lyrics by Harry Allen, music by Henry Krips. PM: Jack Souter, Harry Strachan. ASST D: Ronald Whelan. SD: Clive Cross. 77 mins.

CAST: Will Mahoney (Barney O'Hara), Shirley Ann Richards (Eve Cameron), Jean Hatton (Pat), Evie Hayes (Kitty Katkin), Sidney Wheeler (Worthington Howard), Alec Kellaway ('The Killer'), Guy Hastings (Colonel Cameron), John Fleeting (John Wynyard), Ronald Whelan (Max), Harry Abdy (Charley), Lou Vernon (Signor Rudolpho), Harold Meade (Sir James Hall), Charles Zoli (Rudolpho's valet), Bob Geraghty (pressman), Jack Dunleavy (referee), George Lloyd and Chips Rafferty (men in the crowd).

Barney O'Hara and his young daughter, Pat, have a sideshow act in a touring carnival. One day Pat is invited to sing at a party given by a wealthy land-owner but her voice fails her. A specialist tells Barney that an operation is needed to save her voice. To raise the hospital fee he reluctantly agrees to fight a boxer known as 'The Killer' and goes into training with the aid of a sympathetic dancer, Kitty Katkin. On the day of the fight, ants are slipped into Barney's boxing shorts and, bitten into a raging fury, he soundly defeats 'The Killer' and wins the prize-money needed for Pat's operation.

Come Up Smiling was the only Cinesound feature not directed by Ken Hall. The task was entrusted to an actor, William Freshman, while Hall supervised the production and prepared work on the studio's next feature, *Dad Rudd, M.P.* (1940). Hall had also written the original story for the film, using his occasional pseudonym John Addison Chandler. Freshman had been born in Australia but had developed his career as a 'beauty actor' in numerous British films, starring as a romantic

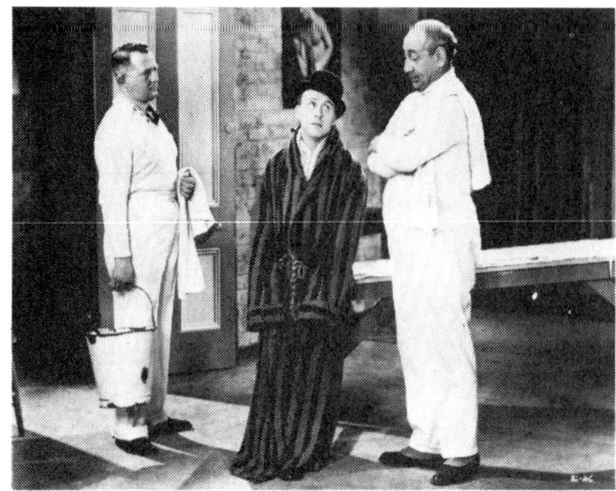

308 *Come Up Smiling* Will Mahoney (*c*), Sidney Wheeler (*r*)

hero in films such as *Eileen of the Trees* (1928) and *A Broken Romance* (1929). Early in 1939 Cinesound brought him from England, along with his wife, who, as Lydia Hayward, had been a prolific writer of film scenarios in England. Despite the change in director and writer, the *Sydney Morning Herald*, 1 January 1940, found the film 'an average Cinesound sample', suggesting both the thoroughness of Hall's supervision and the consistency of the Cinesound production team.

Will Mahoney was an American vaudeville comedian who toured Australia in 1938 with his wife, Evie Hayes, and manager, Bob Geraghty. In January 1939 Hall signed all three of them to work on the film and they stayed mainly in Australia for the rest of their careers. Several song and dance routines in the film gave Mahoney ample scope to display his skill at precision tap-dancing (he was renowned for his stage act of dancing on a xylophone) and his lively, irreverent comedy style.

With a budget of about £22 000, the film was shot in Cinesound's Bondi studio, and at the Sydney Showground for carnival exteriors. It was premièred by B.E.F. at the Strand Theatre, Hobart, on 3 November 1939, but did not attract good business. Hall promptly renamed it *Ants in His Pants* and added a comic song to explain the new title. In this new version it fared much better at the Capitol Theatre, Sydney, where it opened immediately after Christmas. Late in 1940 a version shortened to 65 minutes was released in England under the original title.

309 Seven Little Australians*

1939 ARTHUR GREVILLE COLLINS

PC: O.B. Pictures. SC: Patrick V. Ryan. From the novel by Ethel Turner. PH, ED: George Malcolm. ART D: Harry J. Weston, Mamie Marks. M: Nellie Weatherill. MD: Gabriel Joffe. PM: R. L. Wilkinson. ASST D: Harry Lauder 2nd. SD: Beresford Hallett. 63 mins.

CAST: Charles McCallum (Captain Woolcot), Patricia McDonald (Esther), Sandra Jaques (Meg), Robert Gray (Pip), Mary McGowan (Judy), Janet Gleeson (Nell), Ronald Rousel (Bunty), Nancy Gleeson (Baby), Donald Tall (the General), Harold Meade (Colonel Bryant), Nan Taylor (Mrs Bryant), John Wiltshire (Gillet), John Fernside (doctor), Edna Montgomery (Aldith), Howard Craven (Andrew), Letty Craydon (Martha), George Doran (groom), Nesta Tait (Bridget), Carl Francis (Fred Hassel), Connie Martyn (Mary Hassel), Nellie Lamport (school teacher), Mary Swan (Marion), Jean Hart (Betty), Margaret Rousel (Doris), Richard Dowse (Major Martin), Norman Wait (Mr Hill), Eve Wynne (Mrs Hill).

Ethel Turner's popular novel, first published in 1894, was updated to the 1930s for this crudely made and rambling film. The seven children of the title live with their tyrannical father, Captain Woolcot, and their stepmother, Esther. Try as they may, the children can never please their father, and after several misadventures, the oldest girl, Judy, is sent away to boarding school. Later, Judy runs away from school and falls ill. When she is found by her father, he allows her to go for a holiday in the country to recuperate. The other children accompany her and for a time they are happy. One day a branch falls from a tree and Judy is killed. Her death makes the captain aware of how he has mistreated the children, and as the months pass he learns how to relax and enjoy life with his family.

Shooting began early in August 1939 and was completed quickly within a month. Country scenes were shot on location at Camden, but most scenes were staged in the studios of Commonwealth Film Laboratories, Sydney. Distributed by Universal, the film opened shortly before Christmas at the Lyceum Theatre, Sydney, but did not fare well, commercially or critically.

O.B. Pictures, a Sydney company headed by a businessman, Edward H. O'Brien, had planned more films but none followed, and the director, Arthur Collins, did not make another feature until 1947 when he began *Strong is the Seed*. Collins had worked extensively on stage and screen in both England and America, and in the mid-1930s had directed several B-features in Hollywood including three released in 1936: *The Widow from Monte Carlo*, *Nobody's Fool* and *Thank you, Jeeves!*

Part 5:

1940-1945

Production activity during the war focused on newsreels and propaganda films made under contract to government departments. At Cinesound, feature films were formally abandoned in June 1940 for the duration of the war; staff was laid off and only a small, compact unit remained under Ken G. Hall's direction. Elsewhere, too, production resources were turned almost entirely to the preparation of propaganda and news services. The recruitment of technicians and actors to the armed services, and a crippling shortage of raw film stock (since film and explosives used some of the same materials), made feature production extremely difficult. Supplies of raw stock were limited both by government import controls and by scarcity on the international market, and often there was only enough to supply the two local newsreels.

Just before the war, the New South Wales government had legislated its first effective measure of support for feature film production. An amendment to the state's quota legislation made it possible for the government to guarantee the bank overdraft of companies to the extent of £15 000 for each production. Four films were scheduled in the initial group of guarantees, approved in January 1940 by the state parliament—Cinesound's *Dad Rudd, M.P.*, Chauvel's *Forty Thousand Horsemen*, and two from Argosy Films. No further guarantees followed, and the war displaced feature production from government priorities. The few features of the period were dominated by Chauvel's major breakthrough in *Forty Thousand Horsemen.* Shown widely around the world as a tribute to the Australian fighting spirit, Chauvel's film not only helped to boost morale and recruitment in Australia but also gave the Australian 'digger' an international identity as an irrepressible and effective fighter. Pat Hanna's self-effacing comic characters in the Diggers stage show in the 1920s and in his films in the early 1930s were replaced by Chauvel's grand vision of virile heroism and national pride. His second wartime feature, *The Rats of Tobruk* (1944) perpetuated the image, but with enthusiasm for battle subdued in a bleak realization of the pain and suffering of war.

Ken G. Hall directing Grant Taylor (*l*) and Ron Randell in a wartime propaganda short; Bert Nicholas at the camera

While feature production was all but halted during the war, other branches of the film trade prospered. People flocked to the cinemas for both news and escapist entertainment, and the audience was swelled even more by the arrival after 1942 of thousands of American servicemen. Cinema profits soared, and with them distributor income. For Greater Union Theatres, the war provided such a stimulus to trading that the heavy overdraft carried by the group throughout the 1930s was fully repaid and transformed into a healthy profit; the organization's reports of combined trading results rose from a loss of £11 000 in 1938 to a profit of over £106 000 in 1942. Admissions to Australian cinemas reached a peak of 151 million per year in 1944-45, compared with the later peacetime figure of 133 million in 1947-48. In an industry speech, the head of Hoyts Theatres flippantly remarked that his company and Greater Union should erect a statue in honour of Hitler for what he had done to boost their business.

At the start of the war, no government department had a film unit capable of producing propaganda films in sufficient quantity for massive theatre distribution, and the Commonwealth government depended entirely on the production resources of the private sector. Up to 375 prints were required of some propaganda shorts to achieve saturation coverage of Australian theatres—for example, to allay panic buying of scarce items or to raise funds in war loan drives. To achieve results of this order it was essential that the government have the co-operation of the private trade. The Commonwealth Department of Information was responsible for the official propaganda and news programme, and a National Films Council was set up to advise it, with leading distributor and exhibitor representatives (including Norman Rydge from Greater Union, Bernard Freeman from M.G.M. and Ernest Turnbull from Twentieth Century-Fox). The government also recruited cameramen to serve as official war correspondents on overseas fronts and within Australia, but their work was edited and transformed into a theatrically acceptable form by private companies.

Propaganda films sponsored by the department made few attempts at overt ideological propaganda or to identify national goals or ideals beyond the short-term purpose of each film. Some of the more ambitious films were mini-features—short narrative films designed to make their message through an emotionally engaging drama, often featuring familiar stars such as Bert Bailey, Grant Taylor, Chips Rafferty or Shirley Ann Richards. The government's propaganda needs were often so vaguely defined, both in style and content, that producers were given wide freedom in constructing their own films on a given subject, or even in proposing subjects themselves. Directors like Chauvel and Hall, accustomed to feature production, responded to this creative freedom and to the urgency of the war effort with vigorous and striking work. Only a little of their propaganda work is extant, but from what remains, and from contemporary reports, it seems that both men rose to the occasion. Hall's *100,000 Cobbers* (1942), a three-reel recruiting film, stands among his most polished achievements.

Australian film-makers won great public recognition for their newsreel coverage of the war, from both local and overseas audiences. At the outbreak of the war the Australian government made a decision to channel news footage to the public through the existing newsreel companies, Cinesound and Movietone; footage was offered for sale simultaneously to both companies at a nominal price, and editing and commentaries were prepared independently of each other. Although their original source material was identical, the differences in the two reels were marked: Cinesound tended to devote much more time to footage of the Australian war effort than Movietone, and Cinesound's news magazine tended to carry a greater emotional content than its competitor. A note of dramatic urgency was characteristic of the Cinesound reel during the worst months of the New Guinea campaign, and Hall was determined to arouse Australians from their apathy by expressing his fears for Australia's security with all the force and rhetoric he had learned as a film publicist.

The first official Australian team of war correspondents sent to the Middle East included the brilliant young cameraman, Damien Parer, the writer and editor, Ron Maslyn Williams, the still photographer, George Silk, and a sound technician, Alan Anderson, all of whom were placed under the control of Captain Frank Hurley. Parer soon came to challenge Hurley's fame as a photographer, especially with his spectacular front-line footage of the war in New Guinea, often taken at considerable personal risk. The public also responded to the winning frankness of his personality in newsreel commentaries and radio broadcasts. A deeply committed Catholic, Parer tried to capture on film the moment of truth when men on the front line were most aware of life and death. His determination to record human experience in war was in strong contrast to Hurley's romantic images of battle-scarred landscapes and the machinery of war. In September 1942, Ken Hall brought Parer into the Cinesound studio to film a personal introduction to a newsreel survey of the entire New Guinea action. This particular edition of *Cinesound Review*, subtitled *Kokoda Front Line*, was shown widely in America and England and received Australia's first Academy Award as the best documentary of 1942. Parer soon won offers of work from the American newsreel companies, and in October 1943 he joined Paramount. He was killed in September 1944 filming American front-line action on Peleliu Island.

The propaganda and information carried by the newsreels reached a large audience. In 1941, some 70 per cent of theatres in Australia and New Zealand screened the *Cinesound Review*. The business of specialist newsreel theatrettes boomed during the war: in 1942 there were thirteen such theatrettes, including six in Sydney, showing films to an estimated audience of 60 000 each week. In addition, propaganda films were distributed widely in South-East Asia and the Pacific, wherever the war permitted, and for this purpose a special newsreel compiled from both Cinesound and Movietone was issued regularly in a number of languages.

The years of the war were thus a period of heightened activity for all areas of the industry, even if the number of feature films declined. Of the two major directors, Chauvel managed to complete two features, but for Hall the industry was simply marking time: the war closed with the reputation of his studio enhanced by its public service activities and by its Academy Award. It had also served as the operational base for the film unit of the U.S. Signal Corps after 1942 and had helped the Americans to prepare their regular newsreel for American troops in the South-West Pacific. Hall was buoyant with optimism that feature production would resume without delay after the war, and he had many plans ready for implementation. In May 1944 he wrote: 'It's an extraordinary thing that after nearly five years in the doldrums we find ourselves overwhelmed with opportunity.'

310 Dad Rudd, M.P.*

1940 KEN G. HALL

PC: Cinesound Features. P: Ken G. Hall. SC: Frank Harvey, Bert Bailey. PH: George Heath. ED: William Shepherd. ART D: Eric Thompson. SPECIAL EFFECTS: J. Alan Kenyon. MD: Henry Krips. PM: Jack Souter, Harry Strachan. ASST D: Ronald Whelan. SD: Clive Cross. 83 mins.

CAST: Bert Bailey (Dad Rudd), Connie Martyn (Mum), Yvonne East (Ann Rudd), Fred MacDonald (Dave), Ossie Wenban (Joe), Valerie Scanlan (Sally), Alec Kellaway (Entwistle), Frank Harvey (Henry Webster), Grant Taylor (Jim Webster), Jean Robertson (Mrs Webster), Barbara Weekes (Sybil Vane), Ronald Whelan (Lewis), Letty Craydon (Mrs McGrury), Marshall Crosby (Ryan), Joe Valli (MacTavish), Field Fisher (Jenkins), Billy Stewart (Bloggs), Natalie Raine (Susie), Lorna Westbrook (Minnie), Leo Gordon (Fordham), Chips Rafferty (fireman), Raymond Longford (electoral officer).

A sequel to *On Our Selection* (1932) about Dad's career in politics was proposed as early as 1932. When completed in 1940, the film had almost nothing in common with the original Steele Rudd stories, and resembled instead the sort of small-town family comedy epitomized by Hollywood's Andy Hardy series. Dad Rudd became less a naïve comic figure than a bastion of middle-class morality, and the story turned from the frivolity of the earlier films to an inherently more sober, if rudimentary, allegory on the war in Europe.

Young Jim Webster is in love with Ann Rudd, but their families are at loggerheads. Jim's father is the local member of parliament and is using his influence to prevent improvements to a new dam. Dad Rudd knows that the dam is vital to the welfare of small farmers in the district and decides to fight Webster in the coming elections. On the eve of polling day a fierce storm causes the dam to collapse, proving Dad's criticisms of the design to be correct. Dad is duly elected to parliament and the film ends with his rousing maiden speech, a grand tribute to the little man's struggle to preserve his rights in the face of intimidation from powerful enemies.

Comic interludes scattered through the basically serious plot included a scene with a team of country firefighters who operate with

310 *Dad Rudd, M.P.* From the left, Joe Valli, Bert Bailey, Field Fisher, Connie Martyn

all the efficiency of the Keystone Kops (a scene in which Chips Rafferty appeared, uncredited, as one of the firemen). The film also displayed some of J. Alan Kenyon's most polished special effects, with models and complex matte work to represent the collapse of the dam. But the main strength of the film was Bert Bailey, with a performance that perfectly realized Dad as a 'beaming philosopher' and 'public-spirited tiller of the soil'; as the *Sydney Morning Herald*, 17 June 1940, wrote, Bailey performed 'with the full conviction of a great personality'.

The film was released in June 1940, and became an immediate financial success. Later in the same year it was released in Britain and proved to be one of the most popular Australian productions screened there, receiving over 1400 screenings by mid-1941.

Dad Rudd, M.P. was the last of the Cinesound features; after shooting was completed in February 1940, the studio and crew were leased for three months to Chauvel for *Forty Thousand Horsemen*, but in June, Hall reluctantly announced the cessation of feature production for the duration of the war. Staff was substantially reduced and the few who remained worked only on the production of newsreels and official propaganda. Ironically *Dad Rudd, M.P.* was the first feature to win tangible government encouragement in the form of a State-guaranteed overdraft of £15 000.

Grant Taylor who played the juvenile romantic lead, was soon to become one of Australia's most popular stars in Chauvel's *Forty Thousand Horsemen*. He was born in England in 1917 and came to Australia as a child. His extensive work on the local stage and in radio was aided by a strong and distinctive voice, and his personality led easily to the portrayal of cheerful and solid Australian citizens, at home or at war. Instead of pursuing a Hollywood career, which could readily have been his after *Forty Thousand Horsemen*, he remained in Australia to see the film industry fade away. He later moved to England and worked on the stage and in television, but his British film appearances were never more than slight character parts, such as an overweight London bobby in *Quatermass and the Pit* (1967). He died in England in 1971.

311 Wings of Destiny*

1940 RUPERT KATHNER

PC: Enterprise Film Company. P: Rupert Kathner. SC: Rupert Kathner, Alma Brooks. PH: Arthur Higgins, Joe Stafford, Tasman Higgins. ED: Syd Wood. ART D: Guy Crick. SD: Mervyn Murphy. 68 mins.
CAST: Marshall Crosby (Francis Jamieson), John Fernside (Mark Heinrich), George Lloyd (Monty Martin), Cecil Perry (Arthur Rogers), Johnny Williams (Tommy Ryan), Jimmy McMahon (Jerry Marsden), Reginald King (Mulga Flannigan), Patricia McDonald (Marion Jamieson), Raymond Longford (Peters), Stan Robinson (prospector).

Supposedly based on an actual incident, the film warns of attempts by fifth columnists to secure control of Australia's supplies of wolfram, a mineral needed for the manufacture of munitions. A plane carrying a team who are investigating a wolfram find is sabotaged by a German agent, Mark Heinrich, and is forced down in the central Australian desert. The group survives a threat from hostile Aborigines, but the young pilot is killed when he tries to fly the damaged plane. His friends swear to seek vengeance for his death. When they return to Sydney they find Heinrich has killed the owner of the wolfram field and has kidnapped his daughter. After an armed struggle, the girl is rescued and Heinrich is sentenced to fifteen years' imprisonment.

Slightly less studio-bound than other Kathner quickies, *Wings of Destiny* included location scenes on the Sydney waterfront and in central Australia, with footage of Aboriginal tribal life probably shot originally for *Phantom Gold* (1937). Raymond Longford appears in a small role as an old bushman who drives his truck into the desert to rescue the stranded party.

With distribution by National Films of New South Wales, the film opened at the Capitol Theatre, Sydney, on 13 September 1940 as a supporting feature. Earlier, a slightly different version had been shown to the press, after which some 'atmospheric' scenes at Alice Springs were deleted and a crude courtroom scene added to the end of the film. Although it was one of the few Kathner films to be passed for registration as an Australian quota production, reviews were unfavourable, and Josephine O'Neill, in the *Sunday Telegraph*, 15 September 1940, found herself in 'a dazed condition' after the preview.

312 *Forty Thousand Horsemen* Chips Rafferty (*l*), Grant Taylor

312 Forty Thousand Horsemen*

1940 CHARLES CHAUVEL

PC: Famous Feature Films. P: Charles Chauvel. SC: Charles and Elsa Chauvel. STORY: Charles Chauvel, E. V. Timms. PH: George Heath. ADDITIONAL EXTERIOR PH: Frank Hurley, Tasman Higgins, Bert Nicholas, John Heyer. ED: William Shepherd. ART D: Eric Thompson. SPECIAL EFFECTS, EXTERIOR ART D: J. Alan Kenyon. OPTICAL EFFECTS: Garnett Lowry. M: Lindley Evans. ADDITIONAL M: Willy Redstone, Alfred Hill. DANCES: Gertrud Bodenweiser. PM: Jack Souter. ASST D: Ronald Whelan. LOCATIONAL ASST: George Hughes. SD: Arthur Smith, Clive Cross. STUNT SHOOTING: Lionel Bibby. 101 mins.
CAST: Grant Taylor (Red Gallagher), Betty Bryant (Juliet Rouget), Chips Rafferty (Jim), Pat Twohill (Larry), Harvey Adams (Von Hausen), Eric Reiman (Von Schiller), Joe Valli (Scotty), Albert C. Winn (Sheik Abu), Kenneth Brampton (German officer), John Fleeting (Captain Gordon), Harry Abdy (Paul Rouget), Norman Maxwell (Ismet), Pat Penny (Captain Seidi), Charles Zoli (café proprietor), Claude Turton (Othman), Theo Lianos (Abdul), Roy Mannix (Light Horse Sergeant), Edna Emmett, Vera Kandy, Iris Kennedy and Joy Hart (dancing girls), Michael Pate (Arab).

From its opening, with its title carved in stone and martial music swelling through a medley of national songs, *Forty Thousand Horsemen* attacks its legend-making task with gusto. Intended as 'a message of inspiration for a new generation of soldiers', the film narrated the heroic work of the Anzacs in the Sinai Desert campaign in the First World War. Chauvel's uncle, General Sir Harry Chauvel, had commanded the Australian Light Horse in the deserts of Palestine and the story had long been nurtured by Chauvel as a feature project. The war provided him with the ideal time to realize his plans, and the film expressed his personal tribute to 'the greatest cavalry force of modern times'.

The film follows the exploits of three brave Anzacs in the Light Horse—Red, Larry and their gangling, comic mate, Jim. Irrepressibly

312 *Forty Thousand Horsemen* Three merry Anzacs: (*from left*) Pat Twohill, Grant Taylor, Chips Rafferty

94.

312 *Forty Thousand Horsemen*

proud to be Australian, the trio teach the Arabs in a market-place how to play two-up, and win donkeys, which they boisterously ride into a cabaret. They are settling down for a cheerful time with the dancing girls when the call comes to return to their unit. The film progresses with long scenes of the desert campaigns: the march by the Light Horse to Ogratina, the battle of Romani and the famous charge at Beersheba. At Gaza Larry and Jim are mortally wounded, but Red fights on to victory with the Light Horse. He finally finds true love with a beautiful French girl, Juliet, whom he had first met when she was disguised as an Arab boy and spying on the Germans.

On 1 February 1938, Chauvel filmed part of the Light Horse charge in the sandhills at Cronulla, using a cavalry division that had been organized in Sydney for the New South Wales sesquicentenary celebrations. The charge was filmed in one day (the only time permitted by the sesquicentenary committee) by a four-camera unit, composed of Frank Hurley, Tasman Higgins, Bert Nicholas and John Heyer. The cost of filming the sequence was personally met by Herc McIntyre, managing director of Universal in Australia and a personal friend and supporter of Chauvel's work. McIntyre contributed a total of £5000 towards the entire film, and undertook to distribute it free of distribution charges up to the recovery of production and print costs. He also worked hard, using the cavalry charge as a 'shop window' to attract the rest of the finance, which eventually rose to £32 000. McIntyre gained the support of Charles Munro, managing director of Hoyts Theatres, and the company contributed £10 000, the first occasion on which Hoyts had invested directly in Australian production. The remaining half of the finance was raised through a bank overdraft guaranteed by the New South Wales government in January 1940.

Interiors were shot at the Cinesound studio, Bondi, which Chauvel leased for three months with the full Cinesound crew, following the conclusion of *Dad Rudd, M.P.* Chauvel characteristically began promoting the film intensively even before shooting began in May 1940, and when he advertised for extras to play Arabs 1500 applicants arrived and jammed the streets around the studio. While street scenes (complete with camels) and the cabaret sequence were being shot in the studio, Chauvel used a second unit to build a desert village at Cronulla, including a mosque, markets and date-palms. The battle scenes, including the remainder of the charge at Beersheba, were shot there in July and August with the participation of the First Light Horse (Machine Gun) Regiment.

McIntyre and Hoyts prepared an elaborate première at the Mayfair Theatre, Sydney, on 26 December 1940. In the month before, the film was previewed by government ministers, military officials and other public figures, and glowing tributes began to circulate. The Commonwealth film censor, Creswell O'Reilly, however, demanded three major cuts—shots depicting alleged cruelty to horses during the Beersheba charge, a romantic scene between Red and Juliet in a lonely desert hut, and the display of the dancing girls in the cabaret. O'Reilly's jurisdiction applied only to the export of the film and to the state of Victoria (for which he held a delegated responsibility), and his action threatened to delay the release of the film both in America and in Melbourne. A controversy arose in the daily and trade press just days before the film's Sydney opening. Eventually the Minister for Customs, Eric Harrison, decided to overrule the decision of both O'Reilly and the appeals censor and permit the film to be screened uncut.

With a market so well prepared, the film readily broke box-office records, and its rousing entertainment values established it firmly as an enduring favourite of Australian audiences. It was re-edited and shortened to 89 minutes for the British market and opened in London in August with strong box-office trading. Similar success greeted the film in America when it opened in New York in September. It also screened widely through Asia, and the female star, Betty Bryant, was sent to Singapore for a prestigious South-East Asian première in June 1941.

The nationalistic sentiment glorifying Australian manhood and the Anzacs' achievements in battle clearly hit the right note for 1941. The *Film Weekly*, 2 January 1941, voiced common feelings when it called the film 'a magnificent tribute' to the Australian soldier, and found stirring emotion in every detail—even 'Waltzing Matilda', as sung by the Light Horsemen, 'has never sounded so grand before'. Overseas, more praise awaited the film. The *New York Times*, 15 August 1941, regretted the 'foolish' romantic scenes, but applauded the rest as 'a brawling, boisterous entertainment' with 'the sweat and sound of battle in it. Those earlier Anzacs were men's men, all of them, and when they rode toward battle with a full-throated "Waltzing Mathilde" they were fearful folk—fearful and gay.'

The film gave Grant Taylor his first starring role after his minor part in *Dad Rudd, M.P.* (1940), and also introduced two other young players of exceptional promise. Betty Bryant was a relatively untried actress from radio and repertory theatre, chosen by Chauvel in a widely publicized quest for the perfect woman to match his idealized Anzacs. She acted with a relaxed and thoroughly charming manner, and although a likely prospect for an international career, she retired from acting after this sole feature film and married Maurice Silverstein, a senior M.G.M. sales executive

312 Charles and Elsa Chauvel with Grant Taylor (*r*) during the shooting of *Forty Thousand Horsemen*

whom she had met during her promotional visit to Singapore.

Chips Rafferty also made his first major appearance in the film after two uncredited bit parts for Cinesound. Born in 1909 as John Goffage, Rafferty had worked in numerous outdoor jobs—as drover, opal miner, canecutter and deck hand—before settling into work at a wine cellar in Sydney and trying his hand at acting. In *Forty Thousand Horsemen* and especially in *The Overlanders* (1946), he established a screen persona that remained with him throughout his acting career. For three decades, in numerous films, he played a character that came to be widely regarded as essentially Australian. Few other actors so clearly and consistently became identified with the expression of national characteristics. Although he was usually cast in type, and initially owed much to Pat Hanna's style of comedy, the character was always distinctively his own and he rarely descended to caricature. On and off screen, his heavy drinking and gruff irreverence for authority were balanced by a laconic good humour, sincerity in friendship and a determined optimism. He worked hard to establish an Australian film industry, and in the 1950s devoted enormous energies and personal funds to the Southern International venture. He also acted in many American films and television series, usually in character parts, but always maintained his base in Australia. His sudden death on 28 May 1971 was a shock to many. The *Canberra Times*, 29 May 1971, published an editorial in tribute to his work: 'more than any other Australian actor [he] represented the almost mythical Australian male . . . he brought to life that rare stereotype, the lean, brown, honest, soft-hearted Australian bushman ready to drink, fight, or ride at the lift of a bushy eyebrow, and he did so with joy.'

313 That Certain Something*

1941 CLARENCE BADGER

PC: Argosy Films. P: Frederick Daniell. SC: Clarence Badger. PH: Arthur Higgins. ASST PH: John Howes. ED: Frank Coffey. ART D: William Baker. MD: Willy Redstone. PM: L. W. Watt. ASST D: Alan Mill. SD SUP: Murray Stevenson. SD R: Z. Bryl, Tom Innes. 90 mins.

CAST: Megan Edwards (Patsy O'Connell), Thelma Grigg (Miss Hemingway), Georgie Sterling (Blanche Wright), Lou Vernon (Robert Grimble), Charles Kilburn (Allan Burke), Joe Lawman (Bill Lake), Howard Craven (Jimmie Jones), Ronald Morse (Marcel Du Bois), Leslie Victor (Maurice Appleby), Marshall Crosby, Connie Martyn, Raymond Longford, Ross Vernon, William Beresford, John Byrne, Arundel Nixon.

A famous director, Robert Grimble, comes to Australia to make a film about pioneering women and launches a talent quest to find a girl with 'that certain something' for the starring role. Jimmie Jones tries to persuade Grimble to consider his girlfriend, Patsy, but his efforts irritate the director, who casts her only in a bit part. The main role goes to Miss Hemingway, an ambitious socialite whose tantrums soon disrupt production. Jimmie tricks Miss Hemingway into believing she has been offered a better role in another film and she walks off the job. Grimble is eventually convinced of Patsy's talent and makes her a star.

Clarence Badger came out of retirement in Sydney to direct this undistinguished film for a new company, Argosy, formed by principals formerly involved in National Productions. Badger's basic idea of 'That Certain Something—a Perfect Blending of Heart, Mind and Loveliness, as Mystical and Refreshing as a day in Spring', was clearly an attempt to recapture the success of his Hollywood hit with Clara Bow, *It* (1927). His story also offered a bitter view of the Australian film world, with the director, Grimble, harassed by a committee of uninformed and nervous investors, and struggling with incompetent actors and poseurs seeking to boost their ego and social status.

The film was the first for three years to be shot in the National Studios, Pagewood, which had fallen into disrepair. Like Argosy's next production, *The Power and the Glory*, the film received tangible government support in the form of an overdraft guarantee from the New South Wales government, a contribution for which Frederick Daniell, the general manager of Argosy, had long campaigned.

Distributed by R.K.O., it opened at the Mayfair Theatre, Sydney, on 22 May 1941 with poor results.

314 The Power and the Glory* [The Invaders]

1941 NOEL MONKMAN

PC: Argosy Films. SC: Noel Monkman, Harry Lauder 2nd. STORY: Noel Monkman. PH: Arthur Higgins. AERIAL PH: George Malcolm, Bert Nicholas. ED: Frank Coffey. ART D: Laurence Johnson, William Baker. SPECIAL EFFECTS: W. Goodridge. MD: Henry Krips. PM: L. W. Watt. ASST D: Harry Lauder 2nd. SD: Z. Bryl, L. Nadel. SD RE-R: Alan Mill. 93 mins.

CAST: Katrin Rosselle (Elsa Marnelle), Eric Bush (Ted Jackson), Lou Vernon (Professor Marnelle), Eric Reiman (Von Schweig), Peter Finch (Frank Miller), Sidney Wheeler (His Excellency), Charles Kilburn (John Burton), Joe Valli (Mack), John Fernside (Dr Vass), Max Osbiston (Fight Leader), Beatrice Wenban (Freda), Harry Abdy (Fritz Grubler), Horace Cleary (Wong), Ron Dargin (Bluey), Clement Kennedy (Weary), Raymond Longford (Nazi Admiral), Arnold Riches, Keith Connolly.

A peace-loving Czech scientist, who has unintentionally discovered a poison gas, escapes from the Gestapo to Australia. The government gives him a laboratory where he can continue his work in secrecy and convert his discovery into a motor fuel. Eventually fifth columnists discover his whereabouts and steal his formula. An Australian pilot who has befriended the scientist pursues the enemy's plane and in an aerial dogfight shoots it down. The film ends with an emotional plea by the scientist for the preservation of peace and 'the power and glory which is all mankind's heritage'.

The film's outspoken anti-Nazi sentiments are apparent immediately in an opening title that shrilly warns against 'the primitive beast who . . . would deluge the world in blood'. The Nazis are stock characters of evil incarnate, led by a Gestapo agent played by Eric Reiman in the Von Stroheim manner, complete with shaven scalp, monocle and twisted smile. More subdued, and more disturbing, are the fifth columnists (one played by Peter Finch), who to all appearances are normal Australians, mingling freely with the men in the R.A.A.F. mess-room.

314 Noel Monkman on the set of *The Power and the Glory*

Shooting began in June 1940 at the Pagewood and Figtree studios in Sydney, immediately after the completion of Argosy's first feature, *That Certain Something.* Both films were made possible only by the support of the overdraft guarantee of the New South Wales government.

Distribution was secured through M.G.M., the first time the company had handled an Australian feature. After elaborate promotion it opened at the Mayfair, Sydney, on 4 April 1941, a few weeks earlier than *That Certain Something.* Reviews were encouraging and especially praised the aerial combat scenes staged for the film by the R.A.A.F. at Camden. Although he displayed a promising skill as a director in this and his earlier feature, *Typhoon Treasure* (1938), Monkman seemed to be thoroughly disillusioned with the difficulties of establishing regular feature production and returned to the Great Barrier Reef to concentrate on nature films and underwater and microphotography. He died in May 1969.

In 1952 *The Power and the Glory* was revived by Jimmy Wallace, a vaudeville showman, who renamed it *The Invaders* and toured Queensland with it as part of his show.

315 Racing Luck*

1941 RUPERT KATHNER

PC: Fanfare Films. P: Rupert Kathner. ASSOC P: Alma Brooks. PH: Tasman Higgins. MUSICAL MOODS: Rex Shaw. 66 mins.

CAST: Joe Valli (Darkie), George Lloyd (Bluey), Marshall Crosby (Sir Reginald Franklin), Olga Moore (Sylvia Perry), Keith Wood (Robert Franklin), Connie Martyn (Mrs Perry), Darby Munro (himself), Raymond Longford.

Bluey and Darkie, both veterans of the First World War, save an ailing racehorse from destruction. With potions used on camels in the war, Bluey restores the horse to health and it wins a fortune in prize-money, but in the excitement Darkie suffers a stroke and dies.

A stage-bound mixture of comic patter, Anzac sentiment and clichéd romance, *Racing Luck* had sufficiently good performances by Valli and Lloyd to pass for registration under the New South Wales quota act. Most of the film was shot in mid-1941 in a tiny North Sydney studio. One of the few location scenes was a flashback to a battle, staged in an open field with noisy sound effects but little visible action. Music was compiled from popular classics, especially Tchaikovsky's *1812 Overture.*

Kathner secured a minor release for the film at the Civic Theatre, Sydney, on 21 November 1941, and it was later acquired by B.E.F. for distribution. Kathner's next project, *The Kellys of Tobruk*, was to be a war comedy with Syd Beck and Ossie Wenban, using actual footage from the Tobruk action. Some attempt was made to prepare the film for release early in 1942 before Chauvel's better publicized Tobruk feature, but it seems never to have been completed. Kathner's company, Fanfare, ran into financial difficulty, and his studio was taken over by Supreme Sound System.

316 A Yank in Australia**

1942 ALF GOULDING

PC: Austral-American Productions. SC: Alf Goulding. PH: George Malcolm. SD: Jack Bruce. 65 mins.
CAST: Al Thomas (Headlines Haggerty), Hartney Arthur (Clarence Worthington), Kitty Bluett (Clara Matthews), Jane Conolly (Dolly), Graham Wicker (Horace), Alf Goulding (Japanese spy), Joy Nichols, Frank Bradley, Marie La Varre.

The director, Alf Goulding, was born in Australia but established his career as a comedy director in Hollywood in the 1920s. He returned to Australia after directing Laurel and Hardy in *A Chump at Oxford* (1940), but like Clarence Badger, his Australian work was unimpressive, possibly because he was more comfortable with the silent cinema or because he relied on the support of the Hollywood production system. His sole Australian feature embraced familiar absurdist elements from American farce and was narrated from an American viewpoint. Two rival newspaper editors in New York send writing teams to the South Pacific to find new material; one sends an American, Headlines Haggerty, and a 'silly ass' Englishman, Clarence Worthington (played with a falsetto voice by Hartney Arthur), and the other sends two women. The four reporters meet on board the same ship and are marooned together on the tropical Australian coast after a Japanese submarine sinks their ship. They are rescued by a girl who gives them shelter in a tumbledown shack where she lives with her gruff father and precocious little nephew, Horace. With their Australian friends, the four reporters uncover and foil a plot by the Japanese to invade Australia.

The film was shot in mid-1942 in the Sydney studio of Commonwealth Film Laboratories, with exteriors at Taronga Park Zoo and in the bush near Sydney. A 'world première' was not held until 11 November 1944 at the City Hall in Brisbane. One critic was appalled by the film as a 'nose dive to a new low level in Australian production futility' (*Sunday Mail*, Brisbane, 12 November 1944). Few other Australian screenings took place. Early in 1945 it was given limited release in England as a supporting film, and it was screened later in New York.

316 *A Yank in Australia* Al Thomas (*l*), Hartney Arthur (*r*), and their newspaper boss in New York

317 **The Rats of Tobruk***

1944 CHARLES CHAUVEL

PC: Chamun Productions. P: Charles Chauvel. SC: Charles and Elsa Chauvel. COMMENTARY: Written by Maxwell Dunn. PH: George Heath. ED: Gus Lowry. ART D: Edmund Barrie, Eric Thompson. MD: Lindley Evans. ASSOC MD: Willy Redstone, Charles Mackerras. PM: George Barnes. ASST D: Harry Freeman, Roy Sebastian. SD: Jack Bruce, L. J. Stuart. 95 mins.

CAST: Grant Taylor (Bluey Donkin), Peter Finch (Peter Linton), Chips Rafferty (Milo Trent), Pauline Garrick (Kate Carmody), Mary Gay (Sister Mary Ellis), George Wallace (the Barber of Tobruk), Joe Valli (the Northumberland Fusilier), John Sherwood, Walter Pym, Norman Blackler, Gilbert Ellis, Robert Carlyle, Joe Anderson, Toni Villa (Japanese soldier).

Three men—Bluey, a tough, 'two-fisted' drover; Milo, a laconic dingo-trapper; and Peter, an intellectual English 'new chum'— join the A.I.F. at the outbreak of war. Together they serve in North Africa against Rommel and take part in the defence of Tobruk during the long months of the siege. Peter is killed in action shortly before the end of the siege. Bluey and Milo later serve in New Guinea where Milo too is killed. Bluey returns home alone to the girl who has been waiting for him.

Although, like *Forty Thousand Horsemen* (1940), it was ostensibly a tribute to the Australian fighting spirit, *The Rats of Tobruk* was dominated less by rhetorical patriotism than by a sense of the tragedy and heartbreak of war. George Wallace and Joe Valli appear frequently during the film to improvise some laborious comic relief, but the mood remains set by the three heroes as they soberly face their responsibilities in the war and dream sadly about the women back home. There are few of the boyish pranks and little of the spirit of adventure found in *Forty Thousand Horsemen.*

The Chauvels' task was not easy, to reconstruct a story held dear by the public, and to achieve an acceptable air of authenticity within the severe physical limitations placed on wartime film production. After a year of research and writing, the Chauvels raised finance from Hoyts Theatres, R.K.O.-Radio and Commonwealth Film Laboratories, and secured the co-operation of the army and airforce. Shooting began late in 1943, with the three stars on leave from their service units. A large set representing a war-torn street in Tobruk was built in a field near Camden, and underground firing posts and dugouts were reconstructed in the small studio of Commonwealth Film Laboratories, Sydney. Desert battles were staged at night in the sand dunes at Cronulla. The closing scenes in New Guinea, which brought the story up-to-date in the war, were filmed on location in southern Queensland and in Papua, with additional footage from army cameramen on the front line.

The film was released by R.K.O. on 7 December 1944, with simultaneous premières in Sydney and Melbourne. Although *Film Weekly*, 21 December 1944, commended it as 'solid entertainment . . . for the rank and file', it failed to attract the same popularity as *Forty Thousand Horsemen.* It was released in England in 1949, and in America in 1951.

317 War weariness in *The Rats of Tobruk*. Peter Finch. Frame enlargement

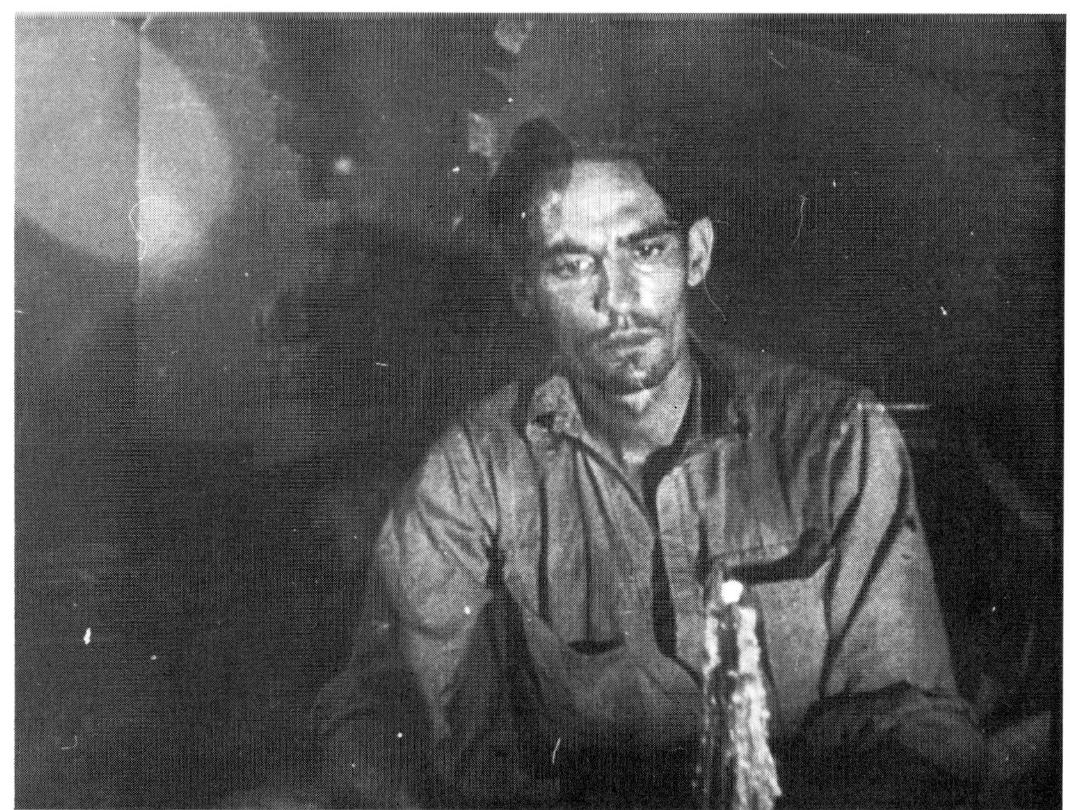

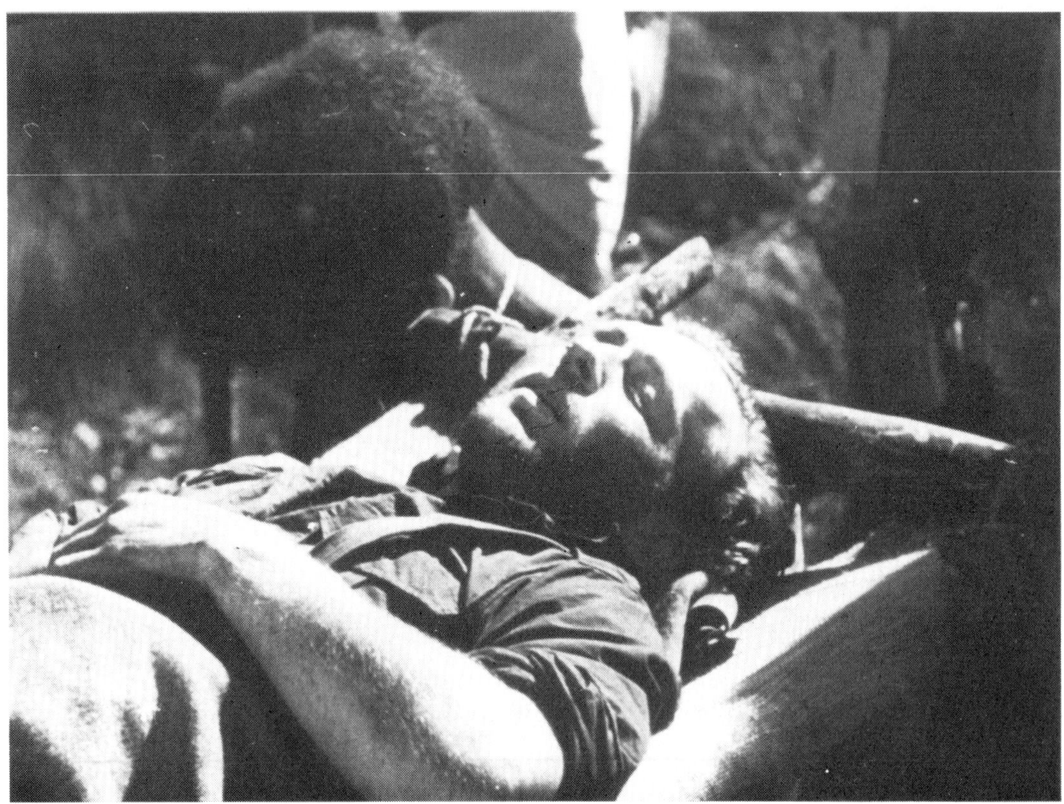

317 *The Rats of Tobruk* Grant Taylor, wounded in action in New Guinea. Frame enlargement

318 Red Sky at Morning [Escape at Dawn]

1944 HARTNEY ARTHUR

PC: Austral-American Productions. SC: Hartney Arthur. From the play *Red Sky at Morning* by Dymphna Cusack. PH: Rupert Kathner, Bob Gould. ED: Alex Ezard, Ross Wood. ART D: Gwen Oatley. SD: Mervyn Murphy.
CAST: Peter Finch (Michael), Jean McAllister (Alicia), John Alden (Captain Farley), Dorothea Dunstan (Emma), Desmond Rolfe (innkeeper), Dorothy Whiteley (innkeeper's wife).

Winter, 1812: Alicia Farley flees from her sadistic husband, a captain in the colonial military corps. A storm forces her to take refuge in an inn at Parramatta, where she attracts the attentions of Michael, an Irish rebel working as an ostler at the inn. Soon Captain Farley discovers Alicia's whereabouts, and attempts to make her return home, but she escapes with Michael to a ship leaving the colony.

Despite wartime shortages and the commercial failure of their first feature, *A Yank in Australia* (1942), Austral-American embarked on an adaptation of a play by the Sydney writer, Dymphna Cusack, first performed in Sydney in 1935. The film's few exteriors were taken in the Windsor and Mulgoa areas, and the interiors were staged at Rupert Kathner's small studio (Fanfare Films) in North Sydney. Shooting was completed with considerable difficulty in mid-1943. In 1944 the film was rejected for registration under the quality clause of the New South Wales quota act, and it received only a few screenings in country theatres. In mid-1948 a version reduced to 48 minutes was screened in England by a small distributor, Carlyle. Later, Gordon Wharton, the principal backer of Austral-American, asked Ray Rushmer, an Australian film distributor, to view the film. Rushmer proposed several changes and these were implemented by a Sydney film-maker, James Pearson. Several scenes were deleted, a new opening was shot at Berrima, N.S.W., and a new ending photographed at sea. Music

318 *Red Sky at Morning* Peter Finch, Jean McAllister

and sound effects were also re-recorded. Re-titled *Escape at Dawn*, and running for about 55 minutes, the film now succeeded in being registered as an Australian quota production and was re-released in England, primarily on the strength of Peter Finch's name. No screening, however, seems to have taken place in Australia.

Reviews of neither version were flattering. The *Monthly Film Bulletin*, June 1948, wrote of the first version: 'This is a thoroughly boring film which has absolutely nothing to justify its production. The story is weak, the settings are extremely monotonous, being almost entirely restricted to the interior of a house, and all the sound effects come from "off stage".'

Born in Tasmania in 1917, Hartney Arthur acted in a small role in *For the Term of his Natural Life* (1927). He later became active on the Sydney stage and in radio as a writer, actor and director, and played one of his customary 'silly ass' roles in *A Yank in Australia*. After a period as an independent film exhibitor in Sydney, he settled in New York as a theatrical and film agent.

319 **Harvest Gold***

1945 MERVYN MURPHY

SPONSOR: Caltex. PC: Supreme Sound System. P: Harold Gray. PH: Arthur Higgins. ED: James Pearson. ART D: Harry Whiting. M: Sydney John Kay. SD: Mervyn Murphy. CONTINUITY: Gwen Oatley. 55 mins.

CAST: Joe Valli (McDougal), Harry Abdy (Johnson), Tal Ordell (Mat), Leal Douglas (Mrs McDougal), Ethel Lang (Mrs Johnson), Maurice Flannery (Mr Harrison), Clifton Penny (shire clerk), Bruce Beeby (Harry Johnson), Grace Lappin (Betty McDougal), Zoe Holland (Zoe), Peter Dunstan (Peter McDougal), Beverley McMahon (Nancy McDougal).

This narrative film, sponsored by the oil company, Caltex, is a skilful blend of 'hard sell' propaganda for the mechanization of farming, and of 'soft sell' publicity for Caltex fuels and lubricants. The story focuses on the conflict between Andy Johnson, a farmer who has taken full advantage of mechanization, and McDougal, a hard-headed Scot who stubbornly refuses to discard his antiquated farming methods. A change is only wrought when a cyclone threatens McDougal's crop: Johnson comes to the rescue with his machines and helps him to complete harvesting in time.

The film is chiefly notable for a fine comic performance by Joe Valli and for its semi-documentary record of the life of a small agricultural community under wartime conditions, with its War Agricultural Committee and Women's Land Army unit. Exteriors were shot in and around Tamworth and Campbelltown, N.S.W., and interiors at Supreme's small North Sydney studio. Raw film stock, then scarce, was made available for the production because of support from the Department of Agriculture. Released on both 35mm and 16mm, the film screened widely in non-commercial outlets in 1945 and after the war.

Harvest Gold was the only feature directed by Mervyn Ross Murphy, one of Australia's foremost technicians and a pioneer in sound recording. In 1935 he opened his own business, Supreme Sound System, initially making

319 Mervyn Murphy, director of *Harvest Gold*

sound equipment and servicing many local productions. In the late 1930s, with cameraman Arthur Higgins, he developed a bi-pack two-colour system called Solarchrome, but Murphy soon left Higgins to establish an identical rival system, Panachrome, which he used in numerous advertising films. After the war Supreme expanded to offer full technical and laboratory facilities to producers, and became one of the major service centres in the industry. These facilities were used by many features, including *The Back of Beyond* (1954), *On the Beach* (1959), *The Sundowners* (1960) and *Journey out of Darkness* (1967), in which Murphy invested heavily. He died suddenly in March 1971 while still intensely active in the industry.

Part 6:

1946-1964

Most of the important feature films in the twenty years after the war were made by British and American companies. For the Americans, Australia was little more than an exotic background for dramas that reflected their own preoccupations and that could mostly have been made in America itself—for example, *Kangaroo* (1952), *Long John Silver* (1954) or *On the Beach* (1959). Many of the American ventures were motivated simply by the need to use capital frozen in Australia by wartime restrictions on dollar exports, and the films reflected no basic commitment to Australia nor any interest in exploring its national character. Most of the film-makers (Lewis Milestone, Stanley Kramer and others) arrived immediately before production began and left immediately afterwards. The British, on the other hand, came with the intention of setting up a permanent unit; although their plans failed, their films reflected curiosity about Australia and a desire to crystallize Australian experiences on the screen for British audiences. In so doing, films like *The Overlanders* (1946) went much further in defining some Australian characteristics and attitudes than Australian film-makers themselves had done. Directors like Harry Watt and Ralph Smart had the advantage of being sympathetic outsiders who could see Australia with a degree of objectivity and place it in the broad perspective of the British Commonwealth.

Among the local producers, Chauvel completed his most ambitious feature, *Sons of Matthew* (1949), an epic tale of man pitted against the elements, imbued with a folksy family life on the frontier that was redolent of John Ford. His final feature, *Jedda* (1955), was a landmark in the portrayal of Aborigines on the screen, with two full-blooded Aborigines in the leading roles and a story that presented Aborigines as people with individual personalities and emotions with which white audiences could identify. In both films, Australian landscapes—the dense forests of south-east Queensland, the central Australian desert—provided spectacular settings for Chauvel's human dramas, and were integral to the attraction his films had for urban and overseas audiences.

Exotic settings—Thursday Island, Tahiti, New Guinea, and central Australia again—were exploited during the 1950s by a more prolific director, Lee Robinson. In collaboration with Chips Rafferty in the company, Southern International, Robinson made a series of films that placed formula comic-strip action in remote locations, but he did not share Chauvel's epic vision of heroic deeds in settings of grandeur. Robinson's work was methodical and unromantic, and he failed to win the same following that Chauvel's films had attracted.

Cecil Holmes was intellectually a more adventurous director, with an overt left-wing political commitment. In his first feature, *Captain Thunderbolt* (1953), he depicted the bushranger as both a folk hero and a victim of class struggle; in his second feature, *Three in One* (1957), he explored Australian attitudes to mateship, presenting two short stories about workers' solidarity and a third that told a consciously 'neo-realist' story of a working-class romance. The Australian marketplace had no room either for Holmes's films or for his politics. He found most of his support in the growing film society movement, among intellectuals, and overseas socialist countries, none of whom could provide an adequate financial basis for his work.

Despite the efforts of a handful of film-makers like Chauvel, Robinson and Holmes, Australian feature films virtually disappeared by the end of the 1950s. The major producer of the 1930s, Cinesound, had never really resumed production after the war; *Smithy* (1946), which they made under contract to an American company, was to have been the precursor of a new international outlook for the studio, but in 1947 Cinesound's parent company (Greater Union) abandoned plans to expand their facilities and to co-produce features with England, and the studio quickly shrank into a small newsreel and documentary operation. New initiatives for feature production were scarce, and even those companies such as Southern International that attempted to come to terms with the newly emerging television market did not endure for long.

The failure of the indigenous feature industry coincided with recession in the Australian economy in the 1950s, and in the film trade in particular with the impact of television in the mid-1950s. Market conditions were much more forbidding for local producers after the war: in the 1930s Greater Union Theatres had been one of the main routes for Australian films to the screen, but in 1947 the chain became almost completely inaccessible to the local product when a controlling interest in the company was sold to the Rank Organisation of England. With Rank concerned primarily to promote its own product on favoured terms, Australian films were simply redundant, and attempts to involve Greater Union in local production ventures won little sympathy.

Producers like Southern International were faced with another problem, inevitable in a failing industry—the shortage of local 'stars' to feature in their work. Not unexpectedly, the industry was unable to offer much to people seeking a career in film, and the post-war years saw a continuing drain of talent. Among the actors to leave were Peter Finch, John McCallum, Ron Randell, Rod Taylor, Michael Pate, Guy Doleman, Charles Tingwell, Grant Taylor and Jeanette Elphick (later Victoria Shaw), who proceeded to establish careers overseas in the British or American industries.

While feature production foundered, documentary production turned in new directions. The dominance of the romantic Hurley school weakened during the war, although Frank Hurley himself continued to make his own idiosyncratic films. His approach was displaced by the influence of John Grierson on both the content and style of documentaries, a decade or more after Grierson had transformed documentary production in England and North America.

Harry Watt, who had made some of the best Grierson films in the 1930s, provided a strong stimulus to local documentary film-makers and to the intellectuals in the film community. A further stimulus to the spread of Grierson's ideas came with the appointment of a former Grierson man, Stanley Hawes, to direct the Australian government's film unit in Sydney. In the early 1930s in England, Grierson had actively promoted the removal of the Hollywood veneer of mysticism and glamour from the cinema and had sought to make films accessible to the man in the street. He organized the making of films about the experiences of the common man (albeit with an occasional paternalistic tone), and films were made available to all areas of society by the development of 16mm film societies, film libraries and film services in schools. In Australia the aspect of Grierson's work that received most attention from the Commonwealth government was the less political second area, the development of non-commercial distribution. Much energy and money were devoted to establishing 16mm lending libraries, at the National Library in Canberra, and in the various state film centres. The use of film as a training tool in education and industry, and as a vehicle for official statements, grew rapidly. But the creative stimulus that Grierson had given the British and Canadian cinemas did not find full expression in Australia. The Australian government maintained a narrow view of the power and function of film, allowing the official film unit little scope for thoughts or emotions that might disturb or provoke any audience. One of the exceptions was *Mike and Stefani* (1952), made by Maslyn Williams under extraordinary circumstances, which remained a rare venture by the government unit into enacted drama and feature-length film.

A number of substantial documentaries were made outside of the government unit and away from the Grierson influence. John Kingsford Smith, who had trained as a self-reliant, all-round technician in Australian studios, made *The Inlanders* (1949). It was a stark and forceful film on the work of the Australian Inland Mission and covered the same territory as *The Back of Beyond* (1954), a more widely shown romantic 'Grierson' film. Elsewhere, the Waterside Workers' Federation in Sydney sponsored a series of rough-hewn films by a small group of dedicated people that expressed far more passion than was possible in government productions. An initial impetus was given by Joris Ivens, who made a clandestine documentary, *Indonesia Calling* (1946), for the Federation to express its solidarity with the Indonesian independence movement. Later, the Federation's film unit, led by Jock Levy, Keith Gow and Norma Disher, spoke out against the Menzies government and explored social problems that the government would rather have forgotten; but their films, such as *The Hungry Miles* (1954) and *Pensions for Veterans*, were not widely shown, for the most effective outlets for 16mm film were controlled by the government and were cautious of left-wing content.

With the loss of the impetus and resources provided by Cinesound for feature film production in the 1930s, the industry lacked a focus in the post-war years. In the Menzies era, public and governmental preoccupation with material well-being and political security made the absence of an Australian film culture a matter of little general concern; the past achievements of the industry were forgotten. For three decades after the start of the war, the public grew accustomed to thinking about film only in terms of the American or British product. Australian distributors and exhibitors lost whatever interest they had once had in Australian production, and most fell into deep pessimism as they confronted competition from television. In this generally negative context, local directors who dared to rock the boat with films of political or moral force were destined to be frustrated, as both Cecil Holmes and Maslyn Williams found. Self-censorship became ingrained in the government film bureaucracy, and conservatism in the commercial trade. The film industry had reached an all-time low, from which it began to recover only in the late 1960s with the decision of the Gorton government to invest money in the arts, including film, and the great increase in public support for the arts provided by the Whitlam government.

320 Smithy

1946 KEN G. HALL

PC: Columbia Pictures. P: N. P. Pery. SC: John Chandler [Ken G. Hall], Alec Coppel. STORY: Ken G. Hall, Max Afford. RESEARCH: Norman Ellison. PH: George Heath. SECOND CAMERAMAN: Bert Nicholas. ED: Terry Banks. ART D: J. Alan Kenyon. SPECIAL EFFECTS: Jack Gardiner. M: Henry Krips. PACIFIC SCORE: Alfred Hill. ASST D: William Shepherd. SD: Arthur Smith, Clive Cross. 119 mins.

CAST: Ron Randell (Sir Charles Kingsford Smith), Muriel Steinbeck (Mary Powell), John Tate (Charles Ulm), Joy Nichols (Kay Sutton), Nan Taylor (Nan Kingsford Smith), John Dunne (Harold Kingsford Smith), Alec Kellaway (Captain Allan Hancock), John Dease (Sir Hubert Wilkins), Marshall Crosby (Arthur Powell), Edward Smith (Beau Sheil), Alan Herbert (Tommy Pethybridge), John Fleeting (Keith Anderson), Joe Valli (Stringer), G. J. Montgomery-Jackson (Warner), Gundy Hill (Lyon), William Morris Hughes, Captain P. G. Taylor and John Stannage (themselves).

This 'bio-pic' about the pioneering Australian aviator, Sir Charles Kingsford Smith, was the last feature made by the Cinesound team. It was not, however, a Cinesound production and was initiated and entirely funded by the American company, Columbia Pictures, using film hire revenue frozen in Australia by government restrictions on the export of capital. The managing director of Columbia's Australian branch was N. P. Pery, a flamboyant American salesman who persuaded his head office in 1943 to approve the production of a film to absorb the company's rapidly accumulating capital. Since the film was intended to exploit an overseas market as well as the Australian, Pery asked Ken Hall for a film about a great Australian known outside his home country. Three were considered: Ned Kelly, Dame Nellie Melba and Kingsford Smith. Kelly was rejected because he had often been filmed before without marked commercial success, and censorship problems were still likely within Australia. Melba was also rejected because of prohibitive expenses involved in staging grand opera and in finding a singer to simulate Melba's voice. Kingsford Smith presented fewer difficulties: with rear-projection Hall could make Smithy's plane fly across any sky, and his death while attempting to set new records was inherently more romantic than Melba's decline into old age and sickness.

320 *Smithy* Ron Randell as Kingsford Smith at the height of his popularity

320 Ken G. Hall (*l*) and William Morris Hughes during the shooting of *Smithy*

Several writers were commissioned to prepare treatments, among them Jesse Lasky Jr, an American stationed at Cinesound with the U.S. Signal Corps; Josephine O'Neill, a Sydney film critic; and the Australian playwrights Alec Coppel (later author of the British comedy *The Captain's Paradise*, 1952) and Max Afford, who finally shared credit with Hall himself (under his occasional pseudonym of John Chandler). Although the characterization of Smithy owed something to Hollywood conventions of heroism, considerable effort was made by Hall to give authenticity to the background. Smithy's old plane, the *Southern Cross*, was resurrected from storage and flown for the film by two of its old pilots, Captain P. G. Taylor and Harry Purvis. Taylor was joined in the cast by John Stannage, a former radio operator with Smithy. The most celebrated addition to the cast was a former Prime Minister of Australia, William Morris Hughes, playing himself as a younger man interviewing Smithy in London.

When finally released in June 1946 at the State Theatre, Sydney, *Smithy* was a major box-office success and carried strong prestige for Cinesound. It had cost £53 000, more than twice the budget of any previous Cinesound feature, and the publicity campaign to launch it was proportionately greater. Much of the publicity centred on two new local stars, Ron Randell and Muriel Steinbeck: both had acted for several years in radio, theatre and war-time propaganda films, and had appeared together in another local feature, *A Son is Born*, made shortly before *Smithy* (although released later). Late in 1946 Randell accepted a Hollywood contract from Columbia and began his long career in American and British films. In mid-1947 Columbia released the film in England under the title *The Southern Cross* and at the same time in America as *Pacific Adventure*.

The credit that *Smithy* brought to Cinesound was short-lived. The company had no share of the profit made by the film and the success did nothing to re-establish the self-supporting pattern of the studio's pre-war activity, where profits from one film had helped to finance the next. It was also soon apparent that Columbia had no intention of fulfilling Pery's promises of further films. In 1947 when Hall visited Hollywood, he met Harry Cohn, the notoriously ruthless head of Columbia. According to Hall, Cohn in no way shared Pery's enthusiasm for production away from the controls of the Hollywood head office, and Hall attributed to Cohn the severe re-editing of *Smithy* in the U.S.A., as though Cohn wished to disguise the fact that the film had been made by Australians; about twenty minutes were deleted and new credits were substituted, which removed Pery's name along with any indication of the film's Australian origin, including acknowledgements to the Sydney Symphony Orchestra and the R.A.A.F.

321 A Son is Born

1946 ERIC PORTER

PC: Eric Porter Studios. P: Eric Porter. STORY: Gloria Bourner. PH: Arthur Higgins. WAR PH: Damien Parer. ED: James Pearson. ART D: Leslie Shearer. M: Sydney John Kay. ASST D: Dudley Porter. SD: Mervyn Murphy. 85 mins.

CAST: Muriel Steinbeck (Laurette Graham), Ron Randell (David Graham), Peter Finch (Paul Graham), John McCallum (John Seldon), Jane Holland (Kay Seldon), Kitty Bluett (Phyllis), Peter Dunstan (David Graham as a boy), Cecil Perry (Tazzy), Clifton Penny (Mr Humphries), Eva Moore (Mrs Humphries), Mayne Lynton (minister), Peter Tate (Dr Roger Grant), Betty Suttor (Vera), Adele Kay (cook).

In 1920 Paul Graham marries Laurette but their marriage soon disintegrates because of Paul's drinking and his affairs with other women. Paul spoils their son, David, and when Laurette eventually walks out, David chooses to stay with his father. Years later, Laurette re-marries, this time John Seldon, a wealthy industrialist and a widower with a teenage daughter, Kay. When Paul is killed in a car accident, David, who has never forgiven his mother for 'deserting' Paul, comes to live with the Seldons. Seeking revenge, David seduces Kay into marriage and deserts her immediately after the ceremony. Later, he serves with the army in New Guinea and through the catharsis of war, his personality changes. He is discovered in a camp hospital by Kay, who is now a nurse, and he promises to make amends to her and the family. The film ends with the title, 'Unto us a son is born.'

321 *A Son is Born* Muriel Steinbeck and John McCallum in the foreground, Ron Randell at rear. Frame enlargement

321 *A Son is Born* Muriel Steinbeck. Frame enlargement

The film was shot in the Supreme Sound System studio in North Sydney early in 1945. The climax set in New Guinea was skilfully composed from Porter's own re-enactment and official footage by Damien Parer. Despite wartime restrictions and a low budget of £10 000, Porter managed to achieve a veneer of sophistication in the sets and costumes; the Seldon mansion was so opulent, in fact, that it came as a 'shock' to the *Monthly Film Bulletin*, December 1946, given the wartime setting of the story. The sophistication helped to compensate for a novelettish plot and a surly central character of unbelievable vindictiveness. Humour was restricted to subdued gossip among the Seldon domestics, and it was in the grimness of the film's mood that the trade expressed most fears about audience reactions. After much hesitation, the distributor, B.E.F., opened the film on 20 September 1946 at the Victory Theatre, Sydney, where it achieved 'solid' results. Although Porter's plans for another feature, *Storm Hill*, were well advanced, he turned instead to develop his more secure business as a producer of sponsored documentaries and commercials.

322 The Overlanders

1946 HARRY WATT

PC: Ealing Studios. P: Michael Balcon. ASSOC P: Ralph Smart. SC: Harry Watt. RESEARCH: Dora Birtles. PH: Osmond Borradaile. CAM OP: Carl Kayser. CAM ASST: Axel Poignant. SUPERVISING ED: Leslie Norman. ED: Inman Hunter. M: John Ireland. PRODUCTION SUP: Jack Rix. UNIT M: Arch Spiers. SD R: Beresford Hallett. SECOND UNIT D: John Heyer. 91 mins.

CAST: Chips Rafferty (Dan McAlpine), John Nugent Hayward (Bill Parsons), Daphne Campbell (Mary Parsons), Jean Blue (Mrs Parsons), Helen Grieve (Helen Parsons), John Fernside (Corky), Peter Pagan (Sinbad), Frank Ransome (Charlie), Stan Tolhurst (Bert), Marshall Crosby (Minister), Clyde Combo (Jacky), Henry Murdoch (Nipper), Edmund Allison and Jock Levy (two-up players).

322 *The Overlanders* Daphne Campbell

Harry Watt came to Australia in February 1944 with a strong record in documentary and feature production. In 1936 he had collaborated with Basil Wright on the documentary landmark, *Night Mail*, and among other highly honoured documentaries, had made *North Sea* (1938) and *Target for Tonight* (1941). His two features, *Nine Men* (1942) and *Fiddlers Three* (1944), had also won considerable attention. In 1943 the Australian government approached the British Ministry of Information to see whether the coverage of the Australian war effort could be improved in British propaganda. Watt was seconded from Ealing, although still on their payroll, and sent to Australia as an official war correspondent and a guest of the Australian government. After six months of research he settled on a story suggested to him by the Commonwealth Food Controller: a gigantic cattle drive that had taken place in 1942 as part of a 'scorched earth' policy in northern Australia to remove food supplies from the reach of the Japanese. Altogether some 85 000 cattle were driven from the north of Western Australia to the Queensland coast, a 2000-mile trek taking nearly two years to complete.

Elements of romance and comedy were woven lightly into Watt's screenplay to provide commercial ballast, but his film was primarily documentary in spirit, with most of its drama arising from the natural hazards of the trek—poison weed, dry bores, boggy creeks, horse-breaking and stampedes. Watt also displayed strong interest in the characters of the men who undertook the drive against such heavy physical odds. His screenplay was a careful assembly of mannerisms, vocabulary and attitudes to characterize the Australian bushman. Chips Rafferty had previously been cast primarily in comic roles, and Watt was the first director to take his screen persona seriously; together Rafferty and Watt succeeded in articulating particular characteristics that, for many observers, expressed the essential qualities of the outback Australian. For the *Sydney Morning Herald*, 30 September 1946, he was 'the Australian Everyman, in speech, action, and character'. Watt matched the male characters with Daphne Campbell, playing a young woman who joins the cattle drive. Instead of treating her as conventional 'romantic relief', Watt transformed her into one of the most vivid of the traditional Australian bush heroines, combining her expert horsemanship and thorough knowledge of her job with a demure and charming manner. Daphne Campbell had never acted before and was working as a nursing orderly when Watt tested her for the role. In addition to moments of moonlit romance on the trail, Watt introduced several scenes specifically to display her considerable riding ability, and photographed them to emphasize her speed and grace in the saddle.

Like many directors from the Grierson documentary school in the 1930s, Watt expressed certain socialist values through his films. His social conscience emerges only in muted form in his later Australian films, but in *The Overlanders* it is clearly if briefly evident in a scene in which Rafferty makes an impassioned protest against the disinheritance of the Aborigines and the 'get rich quick' white exploitation of the Northern Territory's resources. Watt's commitment was more consistently evident off the set, in his contribution to the intellectual life of the Sydney film community. He was, as one local film-maker put it, a 'Pied Piper', providing stimulus for a large group of young would-be directors and actors, including members of the New Theatre in Sydney, the Waterside Workers' Federation Film Unit, and the younger of the government's film staff. Watt's contribution was also important, with Joris Ivens, in the completion of the clandestine political documentary, *Indonesia Calling* (1946), made for the Australian waterside workers, to express their solidarity with the Indonesian independence movement.

To handle the production of *The Overlanders*, Watt brought four staff from London—Rix, Borradaile, Kayser and Hunter—and recruited the rest of his unit and his entire cast in Australia. Several Commonwealth departments supported the production with technical aid and transport because of the substantial propaganda and prestige value inherent in the project. In 1944 Watt had travelled the route of the trek while Dora Birtles researched the subject in government files and public archives. Five hundred cattle were purchased by the film company as a business proposition, marked with the 'Overlanders' brand, and moved to the first location site; after their appearance in the film they were sold at a profit. In April 1945 shooting began in Sydney at the North Head quarantine station, which was disguised as the meat export centre at Wyndham in Western Australia. The unit of some twenty-five people was then flown by the R.A.A.F. to Alice Springs, where they were based in an army camp. After three months, the unit moved north to the Roper River to camp on the Elsey Station for another month. Here one of the major dramatic highlights of the film was staged—the dangerous crossing of the crocodile-infested Roper River. The unit returned to Sydney in mid-September after five months of coping with bulldust, flies, isolation and extremes of temperature. In addition to Watt's main unit, a second camera team led by John Heyer spent several weeks filming the movement of cattle from the air. Editing and sound recording were completed in London, and the total cost was around £40 000.

The world première was organized by B.E.F. at the Lyceum Theatre, Sydney, on 27 September 1946, where it ran for an unprecedented season into February of the following year. Its commercial success in England was equally remarkable, and it became the first Ealing film to receive wide-scale distribution in Europe, especially in eastern European countries. It also screened profitably in the U.S.A. after a New York opening in December. Critical reaction was uniformly enthusiastic; the film won its way onto many 'Best Ten' lists around the world and became a perennial favourite of family audiences in Australia and Britain.

When *The Overlanders* had clearly established itself as a commercial success, Ealing prepared detailed plans for continuous production in Australia at the old Pagewood studio in Sydney. In mid-1947 a co-production deal seemed imminent with Cinesound, but in August Norman Rydge withdrew Cinesound from the venture, and Ealing continued alone. Shooting on the next film, *Eureka Stockade*, began under Watt's direction in November 1947, and early in the next year, the managing director of Ealing, Major Reginald Baker, announced a proposal to spend £25 000 on re-equipping Pagewood. The goal of a permanent Ealing unit in Australia, however, was never realized; another production, *Bitter Springs* (1950) was completed, but the reluctance of either Australian private enterprise or the government to invest in or even partially guarantee the venture forced the eventual abandonment of the continuous production programme. Watt proceeded to Africa where investment was available, and there made two features for Ealing, *Where no Vultures Fly* (1951) and *West of Zanzibar* (1953).

323 **Bush Christmas**

1947 RALPH SMART

PC: Children's Entertainment Films. P, SC: Ralph Smart. PH: George Heath. ED: James Pearson. M: Sydney John Kay. PM: Lloyd Ravenscroft. SD: Eric Williams. 76 mins.

CAST: Chips Rafferty (Long Bill), John Fernside (Jim), Stan Tolhurst (Blue), Helen Grieve (Helen), Nicky Yardley (Snow), Morris Unicomb (John), Michael Yardley (Michael), Neza Saunders (Neza), Pat Penny (father), Thelma Grigg (mother), Clyde Combo (Old Jack), Edmund Allison (policeman). NARRATOR: John McCallum.

A group of bush children carelessly boast to three strangers about their father's valuable mare. The next day the mare is missing, and suspecting the strangers of the theft, the children set off with a young Aboriginal friend, Neza, to try to recover the horse. They are soon lost in the mountains and are reduced to eating grubs and snake. When they discover the horse thieves, the children harass them and steal their food and shoes, but are trapped when they follow the thieves to an old ghost town. However a search party soon arrives, the thieves are arrested and the children return home for a belated Christmas party.

Bush Christmas was the first feature produced by Children's Entertainment Films (later the Children's Film Foundation), an English organization, which, under the auspices of J. Arthur Rank and the direction of Mary Field, screened films to children in hundreds of cinema clubs throughout England on Saturday mornings. Originally planned as a serial, the feature was shot entirely on location in the Blue Mountains and the Burragorang Valley. All work on the film, including the post-synchronization of dialogue and the music score, was completed in Sydney by June 1947, and it was released in the same month to the English cinema clubs, with enthusiastic responses from both children and the press. In Australia it was released during the school holidays, on 19 December, and ran for an eight-week season at the Embassy Theatre, Sydney. Its popularity with children prompted numerous

323 *Bush Christmas* The three comic villains: (*from left*) John Fernside, Chips Rafferty, Stan Tolhurst

re screenings in Australia and Europe as well as the serialization of the story in children's magazines and the publication of the story in book form in several languages.

Mary Field, in her history of the Children's Entertainment Films movement, *Good Company* (London, 1952), suggested several reasons for the film's extraordinary popularity. Children were able to identify easily with the characters, whose ages ranged from six to twelve; the villains were comical rather than frightening; and curiosity was aroused by the setting, the Australian accents, and episodes such as Neza's cheerful eating of a witchetty grub. The film also moved slowly enough for young children to follow, and its slightly fanciful adventure appealed strongly to young imaginations.

The director, Ralph Smart, was born of Australian parents in London in 1908. He entered the English film industry in 1927 and worked extensively as a comedy writer and documentary director. In 1940 he came to Australia and directed short films for the R.A.A.F. and the Department of Information, including *Island Target* (1945). He worked on *The Overlanders* (1946), and after *Bush Christmas* returned to England to direct features for various British companies. He came back to Australia temporarily in 1949 to direct *Bitter Springs*.

324 Always Another Dawn

1947 T. O. McCREADIE

PC: McCreadie Brothers Embassy Pictures. EXEC P: A. K. McCreadie. P: T. O. McCreadie. SC: Zelma Roberts, T. O. McCreadie. PH: Harry Malcolm. ED: Alex Ezard. ART D: Edmund Barrie. SPECIAL EFFECTS: Arthur Hansen. MD: Iris Mason, Hal Saunders. SONG: 'Men of the R.A.N.' by T. O. McCreadie. 'Dawn Concerto' by Wilbur Kentwell. SD: Beresford Hallett, John Heath. 108 mins.

CAST: Charles Tingwell (Terry Regan), Guy Doleman (Warren Melville), Queenie Ashton (Molly Regan), Betty McDowall (Patricia), Douglas Herald (the Commodore), Charles Zoli (Scotty McGrath), Russell Jarrett (Dixie Dean), Max Gibb (Bill Carson), Brian Farmer (Kanga Campbell), William J. Mason (James T. Henderson), Norton Howarth (tanker captain), David Lowe (tanker mate), Glenn Clark (first merchant seaman), Michael Brand (second merchant seaman), Kevin Gunn (postman), Frank Waters (Commander Regan), Terrence Coy (small boy), Lassie (herself), officers and men of the Royal Australian Navy.

324 *Always Another Dawn* Queenie Ashton, Charles Tingwell

During the Second World War Terry Regan enlists in the Australian Navy, inspired by the memory of his father, a naval officer who had died in action in 1916. Terry sees active service in the Mediterranean, and while home on leave, falls in love and promises to marry. Later he is killed when his destroyer engages a Japanese squadron, but a close friend, Warren, survives and resolves to carry on the tradition to which Terry had sacrificed his life.

Always Another Dawn was the first of three features produced by the McCreadie brothers. Tom and his elder brother Alec had formed their production company, Embassy Pictures, in 1940, and had completed several shorts before making a determined entry into feature production. They also had interests in exhibition and distribution, and their work as suburban exhibitors in Sydney extended back to the 1920s. They had also imported several European films for distribution in specialized theatres and had won trade attention in 1946 with a Russian feature, *Memory's Harvest*, which they had re-recorded with English dialogue, the first time that dubbing had been attempted locally. Their production venture eventually foundered in 1950 because of internal disagreements and financial problems.

With their first feature they took pains to achieve a veneer of authenticity, and the naval scenes shot at the Flinders Naval Depot, Sydney, and on board HMAS *Bataan* during exercises, emerged with strong documentary interest. Shooting began in February 1947 with a budget of £30 000 and lasted some six months. Technical services and a studio were provided by Commonwealth Film Laboratories, Sydney. Distributed by Universal, the film opened at the Embassy Theatre, Sydney, on 24 September 1948, but critical opinion was adverse and it ran for only two weeks. Critics drew attention to banal dialogue and the many platitudes about war and tradition, but a boxing match and a passionate piano concerto (played by the dead hero's friend) were seen as some compensation. In 1949, a version shortened to 73 minutes was released in England by Eros Films and in this abridged form it won far kinder comments from the press; the *Monthly Film Bulletin*, June 1949, found it 'quietly moving and sincere'.

325 Eureka Stockade

1949 HARRY WATT

PC: Ealing Studios. P: Michael Balcon. ASSOC P: Leslie Norman. SC: Harry Watt, Walter Greenwood. ADDITIONAL SCENES: Ralph Smart. RESEARCH: Rex Rienits. PH: George Heath. ED: Leslie Norman. ART D: Charles Woolveridge. COSTUMES: Dahl Collings. M: John Greenwood. PRODUCTION EXECUTIVE: Eric Williams. UNIT M: Ronald Whelan. ASST D: Alex Cann, Peter Cuff. SD SUP: Stephen Dalby. SD ED: Mary Habberfield. SECOND UNIT D: Julian Spiro; PH: Harry Gillam. 102 mins.

CAST: Chips Rafferty (Peter Lalor), Jane Barrett (Alicia Dunne), Jack Lambert (Commissioner Rede), Peter Illing (Rafaello Carboni), Gordon Jackson (Tom Kennedy), Ralph Truman (Governor Hotham), Sydney Loder (Vern), John Fernside (sly-grog seller), Grant Taylor (Sergeant-Major Milne), Peter Finch (Humffray), Kevin Brennan (Black), John Fegan (Hayes), Al Thomas (Scobie), Ronald Whelan (Bentley), Dorothy Alison (Mrs Bentley), Reg Wykeham (Dr Moore), Betty Ross (Mary O'Rourke), John Wiltshire (Father Smythe), Nigel Lovell (Captain Wise), Charles Tasman (Governor La Trobe), Mary Ward (Lady Hotham), John Cazabon (Seekamp), Nicky Yardley (schoolboy), Paul Delmar (Ross), Leigh O'Malley (Nelson), Alex Cann (McGill), Jean Blue (Ma McGinty), Marshall Crosby (postmaster), Rex Dawe (auctioneer), Andrina Watton (little girl), Reg Lye (digger).

325 *Eureka Stockade* Chips Rafferty (*standing*)

Harry Watt conceived *Eureka Stockade* as the first of a series of films to be made around the British Commonwealth showing the birth of democracy. A brief prologue made his intention clear: 'The story of the world is the story of man's fight for freedom. In that fight England has her Magna Carta, France her Revolution, America her Declaration of Independence, and Australia, Eureka Stockade.' His grand vision of rebellion on the Ballarat goldfields, however, was not entirely realized in the rest of the film. In an attempt to apply documentary principles to a historical subject, he sought to portray Peter Lalor, not as the charismatic rebel leader that he had generally been painted in popular legend, but as a man of doubts and principles. Watt's pursuit of the greys and mediocrities of historical truth was undermined by compromises during the arduous physical difficulties of the production, and above all by the miscasting of Chips Rafferty in the role of Lalor. The Rank Organisation had placed Rafferty under contract after *The Overlanders* and insisted that Ealing cast him as the star. The part required subtleties that were beyond Rafferty's range as an actor, and although Watt tried to work his way around the problem, he could not entirely avoid a weak centre to his story. The film finally emerged as an offbeat action movie, with its dramatic highlights lying not in statements about independence and freedom, but in violent fight scenes.

Watt had worked in Australia with a small team of historians for some six months researching the events of 1854, and his recreation of daily life in the goldfields was an extraordinary achievement; it contributed most to the film's high cost of around £125 000. The country around Ballarat no longer offered a suitable site, and an alternative location for the film's goldfields was

1946/64 chosen in a valley near Singleton, about 150 miles from Sydney. A complete township was constructed with solid buildings (not simply façades) to withstand the rough action scenes, and the diggings were prepared complete with mineshafts. The fight scenes, with extras and horses provided by the Australian army, produced a number of minor casualties, including two broken ribs and burnt hands for Chips Rafferty.

Shooting was scheduled to start in September 1947 but was delayed for two months by uncertainty over the new British tax on film hire revenue earned by 'foreign' films; eventually Ealing managed to ascertain that *Eureka Stockade* would be deemed a British film for the purposes of the tax, and shooting began on 19 November using cameras and other equipment imported from England. Interiors were shot at Cinesound's Bondi studio and at Pagewood. The Pagewood studio had fallen into a severe state of disrepair during the war years, when it was used as an army store, and the Ealing crew had had to work for several months to re-fit it and build a large set there to represent the Victorian parliament (for a scene eventually cut from the film). Shooting was completed in May and Watt returned to England in August.

The film was released in London on 26 January 1949 at the Gaumont Theatre, and in Australia at the Lyceum Theatre, Sydney, on 7 May 1949. American release followed in December 1950, when it opened in New York in an abridged version retitled *Massacre Hill.*

326 Strong is the Seed [The Farrer Story]

1949 ARTHUR GREVILLE COLLINS

PC: Collins Productions. P: Arthur Greville Collins. SC: Ru Pullen. From a radio play by Helen Bousfield. PH: Ross Wood. ED: William Shepherd. ART D: J. Alan Kenyon. MD: Henry Krips. PM: William McGowan. SD: Beresford Hallett. 80 mins.

CAST: Guy Doleman (William Farrer), Maree Marsden (Nina de Salis), Lloyd Lamble (Dr Guthrie), Queenie Ashton, George Randall, Frank Bradley, Nellie Lamport, Enid Lorrimer, George Willoughby, Ossie Wenban, Eric Wright, Charles Cusperson, Harvey Adams, Rod Gainford, Ben Lewin.

This ill-fated film, a reconstruction of the life of the agricultural scientist, William Farrer, and his work in developing a rust-resistant wheat, was the second and last feature made in Australia by Arthur Greville Collins.

Shooting began in November 1947 with a six-week schedule and a £20 000 budget. After location work near Bathurst, the remaining scenes were shot in a studio at the Sydney Showground. A print was ready for screening in July 1948, and at this point the film began to strike trouble. Originally Collins had intended to release the film as part of the Farrer commemorations in July, but reactions at previews made it clear that changes were needed to made the film acceptable to the public. Plans for the première were scrapped and the film was reconstructed: several scenes were deleted, new scenes were shot, and a new soundtrack and music score recorded. Again, in February 1949, it was ready for release, but Collins failed to find a distributor. In March the production company rented the Majestic Theatre, Adelaide, and presented the film with poor critical and commercial results. Later screenings were restricted to country and suburban theatres.

In 1950 it was sold to a British distributor, Monarch, who shortened it to 58 minutes. A minor Australian distributor, Ray Films, also prepared an abridged version and, retitled *The Farrer Story*, it secured a few bookings in 1952.

Collins attempted to return to production as a member of the board of directors of the Tas-American Television Corporation, registered in Tasmania in 1960. Some £27 000 was spent on a feature, *Port of Escape*, directed by and starring an American actor and magician, John Calvert. The venture ended in a cloud of scandal and litigation, and the film, if completed, was never released.

327 Into the Straight

1949 T. O. McCREADIE

PC: McCreadie Brothers Embassy Pictures. EXEC P: A. K. McCreadie. P: T. O. McCreadie. ASSOC P: John Gray. SC: Zelma Roberts. PH: Harry Malcolm. ED: Alex Ezard, Jack Gardiner. ART D: Edmund Barrie. SPECIAL EFFECTS: Arthur Hansen. M: Wilbur Sampson. SD: Beresford Hallett, John Heath. 82 mins.

CAST: Charles Tingwell (Sam Curzon), Muriel Steinbeck (Laura Curzon), George Randall (W. J. Curzon), Nonnie Peifer (June), James Workman (Hugh Duncan), Shirley Hall (Bunty), Alan White (Paul Duncan), Margo Lee (Zara Marlowe), Charles Zoli, Nan Gunn, Noreen Flannery, Edward Smith, John Alden, Tim McNamara, Snowy Towers, Jack Purtell, George Moore.

The Curzon family is visited on their stud farm by Hugh Duncan, an English horse trainer, and his playboy son, Paul. Both father and son are attracted to June, Curzon's daughter, but when she is crippled in a fall, Paul loses interest in her and she realizes that she really loves his father. Encouraged by Hugh, she struggles to overcome her physical disability, and while confined to her wheelchair, writes a piano concerto. Eventually she learns to walk again. Meanwhile Sam, the weak-willed Curzon son, steals money from his father to pay gambling debts, and allows suspicion for the theft to fall on Paul. The conflict is resolved on the racecourse when a horse secretly trained by Paul wins the Melbourne Cup.

The script included a number of diversions from the main emphasis on racing. Like the McCreadies' first feature, *Always Another Dawn* (1947), the film had an original piano concerto occupying several minutes of screen time. More noteworthy was a fine parody of the Hollywood vamp by Margo Lee as a night-club singer who creates temporary confusion in the lives of the men on the farm. Shooting began in June 1948 with locations on a stud farm at Scone, N.S.W., and interiors were filmed later at the studio of Commonwealth Film Laboratories, Sydney. In October the Victoria Racing Club staged a mock Melbourne Cup meeting at Flemington for the film, and several famous jockeys (including Jack Purtell and George Moore) made brief personal appearances.

With distribution by Universal and publicity supervised by the McCreadies themselves, the film opened in Perth in July 1949 and proved highly successful. Release in Sydney was delayed until January the next year, when it was overshadowed by Chauvel's *Sons of Matthew* (which also featured the young Nonnie Peifer) and received only a mediocre week at the Capitol Theatre.

328 Sons of Matthew

1949 CHARLES CHAUVEL

PC: Greater Union Theatres in association with Universal Pictures. P: Charles Chauvel. ASSOC P: Elsa Chauvel. SC: Charles and Elsa Chauvel, Maxwell Dunn. PH: Bert Nicholas, Carl Kayser. ED: Terry Banks. ART D: George Hurst. M: Henry Krips. PM: Jim Donohoe. ASST D: Alec Kellaway, Julian Savieri. SD: Allyn Barnes, Clive Cross. 107 mins.

CAST: Michael Pate (Shane), Ken Wayne (Barney), Tommy Burns (Luke), John Unicomb (Terry), John Ewart (Mickey), Wendy Gibb (Cathy McAllister), John O'Malley (Matthew O'Riordan), Thelma Scott (Jane O'Riordan), Dorothy Alison (Rose O'Riordan), Diane Proctor (Mary O'Riordan), Tom Collins (young Shane), Max Lemon (young Barney), Rodney Fielder (young Luke), Doug Smith (young Terry), Jimmy White (young Mickey), Marion Dickson (young Rose), Baby Lawson (young Mary), John Fegan (Jack Farrington), Robert Nelson (Angus McAllister), Barbara Armstrong (young Cathy), Laurel Young (Bessie Benson), Nonnie Peifer (Molly Benson), Betty Orme (Selina Benson), John Fleeting (doctor), Carrie Moore (midwife), Alan Poolman (Dan McGregor). NARRATOR: Wilfred Thomas.

Sons of Matthew was an epic story of Australian pioneer life, tracing the story of three generations of settlers in rugged frontier land. Matthew and Jane O'Riordan raise a family of five sturdy sons and two daughters on their farm in the valley of Cullenbenbong. Despite bushfire and drought, they maintain a close and stable family life. As the years pass, the sons begin to seek land of their own. With an old bush hand, Angus McAllister, and his daughter Cathy, the five sons set out to establish a home on the wild Lamington plateau, deep in the mountainous rain forest of southern Queensland. There they fight together against the jungle and the elements, and gradually establish a hold on the land. Rivalry between two of the brothers, Shane and Barney, for Cathy's affections reaches an emotional climax during a cyclone, but the genuine love of Shane for Cathy eventually wins through and the family is united once more.

Queensland was Chauvel's home state and he had long been inspired by the life story of the pioneering O'Reilly family, who had settled in the mountains in the south-east of the state. Bernard O'Reilly had written two books about his family's life—*Green Mountains* (Brisbane, 1940) and *Cullenbenbong* (Brisbane, 1944). In 1945 Chauvel acquired the screen rights to the books and commissioned Maxwell Dunn and the radio writer, Gwen Meredith, to prepare a screenplay about the O'Reillys and the rescue of survivors from the crash of a Stinson aeroplane in the mountains in February 1937. Gradually, however, Chauvel turned towards the characters of the O'Reillys themselves, and by the end of 1946 had settled on his own simple story of pioneers in a spectacular new frontier.

The story of making the film was itself a tale of great perseverance in the face of formidable physical odds. Chauvel's usual financial backer, Herc McIntyre of Universal Pictures, succeeded in persuading Norman Rydge of Greater Union (no great advocate of local production) to join him as a partner in financing the film. A crew was assembled with a core of technicians from Cinesound and early in March 1947 the large unit of about 70 people, including the cast, set off for the main location site near the town of Beaudesert in the heart of the wild mountain terrain.

Their arrival coincided with one of the worst wet seasons on record and the first three months on location saw scarcely three weeks of weather suitable for filming. This major setback to morale and to the shooting schedule was aggravated when work began in earnest and it became clear that the terrain was far more treacherous than had ever been anticipated. For six months the unit worked under very trying conditions, sometimes travelling by pack-horse and foot to reach remote location sites. Changes to the script also provided unexpected extensions to the shooting schedule, and eventually a second camera unit, under the direction of Carl Kayser, was brought on to the location to accelerate the work. The delays caused anxiety to Chauvel's backers and Rydge and McIntyre both travelled up to the location to

328 *Sons of Matthew* Michael Pate nursed by Wendy Gibb, watched by Ken Wayne

inspect progress; Rydge has recounted how he came so close to abandoning the production that he actually tossed a coin to decide whether he would continue to support it.

After six months the unit withdrew from the location to recuperate and to shoot interiors and close-ups in the Cinesound studio at Bondi. After two months in the studio, the unit returned again to Queensland and the struggle resumed for a further five months. In March 1948 they returned to the Bondi studio where technical and financial necessity dictated the reshooting of several scenes in studio sets where sound and camerawork could be properly controlled. Much use was also made at this stage of rear-projection to complete scenes that had proven impracticable on location. Shooting was finally completed some eighteen months after it began, and the Cinesound technicians were released from the production. Altogether about £120 000 was spent on the production and 250 000 feet of film exposed. Long scenes that had taken weeks to film, such as a stampede of wild horses, or the driving of cattle up steep slopes to the plateau, were reduced to brief seconds to keep the final film to manageable length. Chauvel, however, was not satisfied with the rough cut of the film and took a small unit, with Carl Kayser as camera man, into the Blue Mountains to shoot an alternative ending. This final expedition was ultimately unproductive, for opinions generally favoured the original ending and the new footage was discarded.

The arduous months of the production revealed more clearly than ever before Chauvel's passionate urge to risk any cost and hazard in expressing his deeply nationalistic vision of a people in their struggle to conquer the most hostile of terrains. His methods were somewhat vindicated, however, by the emotional power of the film's best scenes and by its commercial success. The action scenes—above all the scenes of the cyclone—are still exciting and spectacular cinema, with genuine physical strain clearly evident in the performances. For the British trade paper, *Kine Weekly*, 26 January 1950, it was a 'lusty tale' with 'full-blooded' characters and 'spectacular battles with the elements'.

The Australian box-office figures were impressive from the start, following a première at two Sydney theatres, the Lyceum and the Victory, on 16 December 1949. But the film had been so expensive that healthy returns were needed from overseas markets to cover costs. Universal prepared the film for the American and British markets by cutting it by nearly 30 minutes, and giving it a new title, *The Rugged O'Riordans.* Released by the Rank Organisation, the American version opened in London on 26 January 1950 and promptly failed. With so much at stake, Norman Rydge immediately sent Gordon Ellis from B.E.F. to London to salvage the film. Ellis worked hard to organize promotional gimmicks and achieved a steady improvement in the British returns. In the U.S.A., too, the film failed to find an audience when it opened at the Park Avenue Theatre, New York, on 5 January and it was taken off after only one

328 Shooting the cyclone sequence for *Sons of Matthew*

week. From subsequent screenings in the U.S.A., however, and from the Australian and British revenue, the film did eventually make a comfortable profit.

Chauvel prided himself on his ability to pick talented new stars, and several acting careers were launched by the film. Michael Pate had been an extra in *Forty Thousand Horsemen* (1940) and had appeared on the stage and in radio. In November 1950 he left for Hollywood and appeared in many American productions; he returned to Australia in the late 1960s to work as an actor and producer in local cinema and television. Dorothy Alison (or Allison as she was initially billed) made a solid career in British features, certainly with more success than Wendy Gibb, who also went to London to further her career soon after completing *Sons of Matthew*. Co-starring with Pate as the O'Riordan brothers were four other screen newcomers: Tommy Burns, a boxing champion with a big local following; and John Unicomb, John Ewart and Ken Wayne, all of whom became professional actors with long careers in Australian stage, radio and, occasionally, cinema.

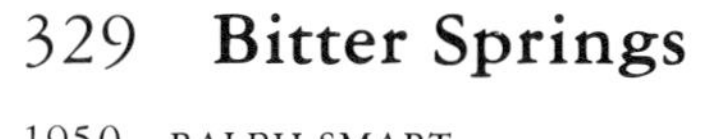

329 Bitter Springs

1950 RALPH SMART

PC: Ealing Studios. P: Michael Balcon. ASSOC P: Leslie Norman. SC: W. P. Lipscomb, Monja Danischewsky. STORY: Ralph Smart. PH: George Heath. CAM OP: Ross Wood. ED: Bernard Gribble. ART D: Charles Woolveridge. M: Vaughan Williams. PRODUCTION EXECUTIVE: Eric Williams. PM: Jack Rix. ASST D: Michael Forlong, David Moore. SD R: Hans Wetzel. SD ED: Mary Habberfield. SD SUP: Stephen Dalby. 86 mins.

CAST: Tommy Trinder (Tommy), Chips Rafferty (Wally King), Gordon Jackson (Mac), Jean Blue (Ma King), Michael Pate (trooper), Charles Tingwell (John King), Nonnie Piper (Emma King), Nicky Yardley (Charlie), Henry Murdoch (Black Jack).

In the early 1900s a pioneer family undertakes a 600-mile trek to the land in outback South Australia that they have bought from the government. When they arrive they clash with an Aboriginal tribe that depends for survival on the waterhole now claimed by the settlers as their own private property. One of the family is speared before a compromise is reached and the Aborigines and settlers agree to work together to establish a profitable sheep station around the waterhole.

As the *Monthly Film Bulletin*, August 1950, noted, the film is 'fundamentally a serious study of the relations of white settlers and aborigines'. Liberal attitudes towards the problem of Aboriginal land rights are expressed by a roving trooper (played by Michael Pate), whose impassioned defence of the Aborigines is in direct conflict with the intolerant views of Wally King, the leader of the white intruders. Only after his son is wounded by the Aborigines does King relent and agree to let the tribe remain on 'his' land. The film ends with a brief glimpse of King and the Aboriginal chief shearing sheep together, but there is little doubt who is master and who is profiting most from the partnership. Despite the unconvincing compromise of the ending, the film's overall sympathy for the plight of dispossessed Aborigines was characteristic of Ealing liberalism in the 1940s, and was more honest than

329 *Bitter Springs* Chips Rafferty (*l*), Tommy Trinder

most Australian film-makers ventured to be at that time.

Many critics tended to overlook the film's serious intentions and looked upon it as an adventure yarn: for C. A. Lejeune in the London *Observer*, 9 July 1950, it was 'utterly simple and unaffected . . . [the film-makers] have clearly enjoyed themselves and managed to convey to the audience every scintilla of that enjoyment'. Others were less drawn by the film's good nature; in an unusually biting review on 26 October 1950 *Film Weekly* commented on the indecisiveness of the script in trying to be fair to both settlers and Aborgines, depicting one side as unpleasantly ruthless and the other as unbelievably naïve and ineffectual.

Location shooting began in the Flinders Ranges in South Australia in May 1949 and was completed in November, nearly two months behind schedule. Two weeks of interior studio scenes followed at Ealing's Pagewood base in Sydney. A world première was held in Adelaide at West's Theatre on 23 June 1950, and the film enjoyed solid local support.

330 The Kangaroo Kid

1950 LESLEY SELANDER

PC: Allied Australian Films. EXEC P: Beau Sheil. P: T. O. McCreadie. ASSOC P: Howard C. Brown. SC: Sherman Lowe. STORY: Anthony Scott Veitch. PH: Russell Harlan, Harry Malcolm. ED: Alex Ezard. MD: Wilbur Sampson. PM: A. K. McCreadie. ASST D: Peter Dimond. SD: Beresford Hallett, John Heath. 72 mins.

CAST: Jock O'Mahoney (Tex Kinnane), Veda Ann Borg (Stella Grey), Guy Doleman (Sergeant Jim Penrose), Martha Hyer (Mary Corbett), Douglas Dumbrille (Vincent Moller), Alec Kellaway (Baldy Muldoon), Alan Gifford (Steve Corbett), Grant Taylor (Phil Romero), Haydee Seldon (Mrs Muldoon), Frank Ransome (Robey), Sheila McGuire, Raymond Bailey, Charles McCallum, Ben Lewin, Clarrie Woodlands.

The last McCreadie brothers' film was written and directed by Americans long experienced in low-budget formula movies. It was a B-western, well-populated with stock characters and stock situations. Tex Kinnane is an American cowboy-detective sent to Australia to find a man responsible for a series of gold robberies in the U.S.A. Tex traces him to the town of Gold Star, where several Americans have settled, any one of whom could be the culprit. Eventually, with the aid of a comic Australian 'cobber', Baldy Muldoon, Tex manages to unmask the villain and round up his gang.

The film was distinguished from its myriad American counterparts only by occasional close-ups of Australian wildlife, and by a few carefully stressed 'exotic' details such as Baldy's cork-rimmed hat or a blacktracker's skill with the boomerang. Financed jointly by American and Australian interests, the production was dominated by Americans in both crew and cast (the only Australians with roles of any substance were Guy Doleman and Alec Kellaway). It was shot so quickly in March 1950 that it was completed under-budget. Locations were used in the old mining town of Sofala, N.S.W., and interiors were shot in the studio of Commonwealth Film Laboratories, Sydney.

Marco Polo Jnr. versus the Red Dragon

Dot and the Kangaroo

Walkabout

Petersen

The Cars that Ate Paris

Between Wars

330 *The Kangaroo Kid* Jock O'Mahoney, Veda Ann Borg

It was released in the U.S.A in September 1950, and *Variety*, 11 October 1950, expressed some interest in the unusual background to an otherwise routine 'oats opera'. In March 1951, B.E.F. released it at the Victory Theatre, Sydney, but it created little excitement.

331 Wherever She Goes

1951 MICHAEL S. GORDON

PC: Faun Film Productions. P, SC: Michael S. Gordon. ADDITIONAL DIALOGUE: Barbara Woodward. From the novel, *Prelude*, by Clare H. Abrahall. PH: George Heath. ED: Brereton Porter. ART D: Charles Woolveridge. M: Grieg's Piano Concerto in A Minor, played by Eileen Joyce with the Philharmonia Orchestra conducted by Ernest Irving; 'Brown Study' composed and played by Sefton Daly; 'Daniel's Air' composed by Clive Douglas. PRODUCTION EXECUTIVE: Eric Williams. ASST D: David Moore. SD R: Hans Wetzel. SD ED: Mary Habberfield. 81 mins.

CAST: Suzanne Parrett (Eileen Joyce), Muriel Steinbeck (Mrs Joyce), Nigel Lovell (Will Joyce), John Wiltshire (Daniel), George Wallace (stage manager), Tim Drysdale (John Joyce), Rex Dawe (Mr James), Syd Chambers, Eileen Joyce (herself).

This film biography of Eileen Joyce, the celebrated Australian pianist, concentrated on her childhood in the Tasmanian bush and the Kalgoorlie goldfields. Opening and closing scenes showed the pianist herself performing at a concert.

The film was one of several planned by independent companies in association with Ealing to keep the studio at Pagewood open between full-scale Ealing productions. The director was an English documentary film-maker, Michael S. Gordon, who arrived in Australia in August 1949 for preparatory work. An eleven-year-old Sydney girl, Suzanne Parrett, was found to play the child prodigy, and an ageing George Wallace was given a small part as a flustered stage manager. Some scenes were shot on location in Kalgoorlie, Western Australia, but most of the film, including some Tasmanian bush scenes, was staged indoors at Pagewood.

On 6 July 1951 the film opened in London at the Rialto Theatre, but it lasted only one week. Critics generally found it a 'harmless' attempt to 'dramatize the undramatic'. B.E.F. released it in Australia with an elaborate première in Hobart on 7 September, but it did not attract large audiences.

331 *Wherever She Goes* Suzanne Parrett

332 The Glenrowan Affair

1951 RUPERT KATHNER

PC: Australian Action Pictures. P, SC: Rupert Kathner. ASSOC P: Alma Brooks. PH: Harry Malcolm (interiors), Rupert Kathner (exteriors). ED: Alex Ezard. ASST D: Bill Crowe. SD R: Beresford Hallett. 70 mins.
CAST: Bob Chitty (Ned Kelly), Albie Henderson (Joe Byrne), Ben Crowe (Dan Kelly), Bill Wright (Steve Hart), John Fernside (Father Gibney), Charles Tasman (Commissioner Nicolson), Charles Webb (Superintendent Hare), Edward Smith (Superintendent Standish), Frank Ransome (Sergeant Steele), Stan Tolhurst (the blacksmith), Beatrice Kay (Kate Kelly), Wendy Roberts (Mrs Skillion), Hunt Angels (Aaron Sherritt), Dora Norris (Mrs Jones), Joe Brennan (the bank manager), Arthur Hemsley (the old man). NARRATOR: Charles Tingwell.

In August 1947, Harry Southwell, the veteran of three earlier films about Ned Kelly, arrived in Benalla, in the heart of 'Kelly country' in central Victoria, to begin work on yet another version of the story. His script, entitled *A Message to Kelly,* had been written by a Melbourne journalist, Keith Manzie, and he hired as his assistant another director of low-budget quickies, Rupert Kathner. A few weeks earlier Kathner had been in Ballarat to try to raise money from local citizens for a film about the poet Adam Lindsay Gordon, but had abandoned the project. Despite the protests of some townsfolk (who wished to escape from the memory of Kelly), Southwell and Kathner managed to establish a company, Benalla Film Productions, and attract substantial local investment. With an initial budget of less than £6000, shooting began in September and about 1000 feet was completed with a local football hero, Bob Chitty, in the role of Ned. In October Southwell departed, apparently after disagreements with Kathner, and Kathner took over responsibility for the production. More disagreements followed, and in November Benalla Film Productions announced their intention to find another director to replace Kathner. Undeterred, Kathner left Benalla and returned in December 1947 with finance from a new company, Australian Action Pictures, to make his own film about Kelly. For a while the town was faced with two rival companies planning to film the same story. Eventually Benalla Film Productions withdrew and Kathner continued to complete his film as *The Glenrowan Affair.* Because the original screenplay by Keith Manzie belonged to Benalla Film Productions, Kathner was forced to write a new script derived largely 'from his own fertile imagination'. Locations were used around Benalla for exterior scenes, and interiors were shot in the new studio of Commonwealth Film Laboratories at Turrella in Sydney. Kathner managed to secure Bob Chitty from the original project to play Ned, but other roles were recast. Kathner himself appeared in a prologue as an artist sketching the landscape in present-day Benalla who recalls the days when Ned Kelly roamed; he reappears later in the film as Aaron Sherritt, using the cryptic stage name of Hunt Angels.

Distributed by B.E.F., the film opened on 17 August 1951 at the Capitol Theatre, Sydney. Reviews were harsh and it received few other screenings. On 3 April 1952 a Victorian première was held, ironically enough at Benalla, where, despite the protests and derision of the audience, some £400 was raised for charity.

A typical review, in the *Sunday Herald,* 19 August 1951, commented that Kathner seemed 'content to assume that this Australian legend has enough appeal in itself to need less than the minimal requirements of filmcraft . . . The script is dreary, the photography more often out-of-focus than in, the editing is unimaginative and the acting petrified.'

333 Mike and Stefani

1952 R. MASLYN WILLIAMS

PC: Film Division, Department of the Interior, for the Department of Immigration. P, SC: R. Maslyn Williams. DIALOGUES: Roland Loewe. PH: Reg Pearse. ED: R. Maslyn Williams, Inman Hunter, Brereton Porter. M: Robert Hughes. SD R: R. Maslyn Williams, Alan Anderson, Kevin Long. 64 mins.
CAST: Mycola, Stefani, Ginga, Ladu, Valerie Paling (themselves). NARRATORS: Martin Royal, Josephine O'Neill.

When war breaks out, a young Ukrainian couple, Mike and Stefani, are taken away to separate German labour camps. With the declaration of peace, Stefani finds herself one of eight million 'displaced persons' in Europe. After months of loneliness and despair, she is reunited with Mike at a refugee camp and for the next two and a half years they remain there, afraid to return to their homeland with its new regime. In 1949, the disbandment of the refugee camps forces them to make a decision and they undertake the long process of seeking resettlement in Australia. An exhaustive medical examination is followed by a gruelling interrogation from an Australian immigration selection officer. They are eventually accepted and join a migrant ship bound for Australia and a new future.

The film had a twofold purpose, to counter criticism within Australia that immigration selection procedures for displaced persons were inadequate and that 'undesirables' were slipping through the net, and to encourage Australians to accept the sudden influx of non-British immigrants in the immediate post-war years. To make the film, Maslyn Williams was sent to Europe in June 1949, accompanied only by an experienced documentary cameraman, Reg Pearse. Their budget was meagre (about £5000) and their equipment limited to what the two men could carry (a 35mm camera with three lenses, a wire recorder for sound, and a few lights). Williams spent several months researching and developing his script. He chose as his main location a camp for Polish and Ukrainian refugees at Leipheim in Bavaria, where the commandant was an Australian woman, a former Melbourne schoolteacher, Valerie Paling. A family was selected and a detailed script prepared that followed their own experiences during and after the war. In order to establish the background of the family, and to convince Australians that the refugees were people with family backgrounds and aspirations much like their own, scenes were added to represent their pre-war life in the Ukraine.

Shooting took place over a two-month period in the winter of 1949-50, primarily at the Leipheim camp and in surrounding areas. Crowd scenes—of refugees in flight along a road and being loaded into a train bound for a labour camp—were staged with the willing co-operation of people in the Leipheim camp. Williams directed the action without rehearsals and rarely with more than one take; participants in the crowd scenes were given a detailed explanation of the narrative and the continuity and encouraged to improvise within this framework. The technique worked well, and the refugees entered into the spirit of the re-enactment, taking pains to find their own costumes and props to improve the authenticity of the film. Williams later intercut the re-enactments with newsreel footage culled from the archives of French and American newsreel companies (including some newsreel scenes shot by Williams and Damien Parer in the Middle East war zone).

333 *Mike and Stefani* Separation during the war. Frame enlargement

The climax of the film, and its most controversial scene, was the selection interview. The interrogation was genuine: it was one of the last scenes to be filmed, and Williams had made it clear since the start of production that the family's part in the film could not guarantee their acceptance by the immigration authorities; he promised only to help them find jobs in Australia if they were accepted. The interview came then at the end of a long film-making schedule and was especially tense, not only for the prospective emigrants and the film-makers, but also for the immigration officer, who had been instructed not to appear too lenient. The result was a harrowing and emotional scene, with Mike on the point of breaking down, and not unexpectedly it created official unease back in Australia.

Following acceptance of Mike and Stefani, Williams and Pearse sailed with them on a migrant ship to Sydney, arriving in June 1950. A few additional shots were taken at the Film Division headquarters at Burwood in Sydney to fill continuity gaps. The voice of Valerie Paling was provided by the Sydney film critic, Josephine O'Neill. An orchestral score was also prepared, based on an emotional Ukrainian folk song that Williams had transcribed while on location in Europe.

Despite Williams's hopes for a full theatre release, the film was never widely shown. The commercial film trade rejected it because of the grim subject and because of its unusual length for a government production. Immigration authorities also reacted against the film for its bleak depiction of the humiliations involved in the selection procedures. Its release was delayed for nearly a year and it was never actively promoted. No attempt was made to distribute it overseas through the

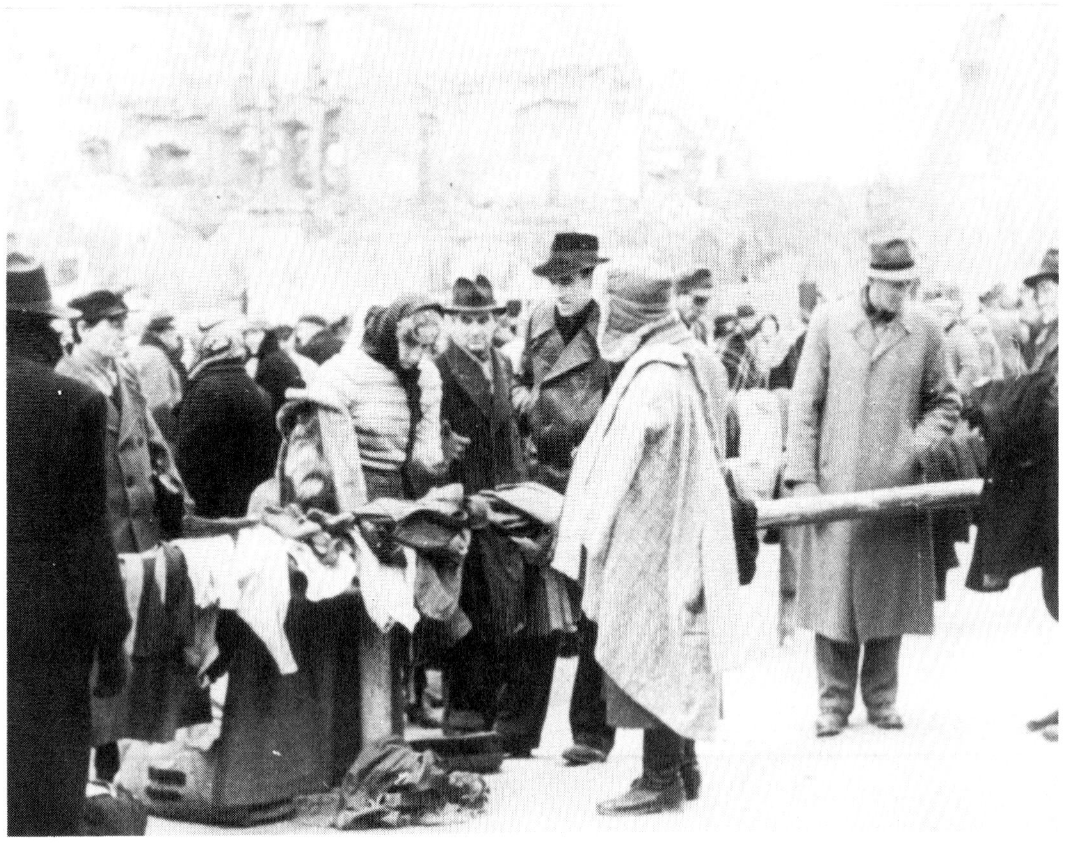

333 *Mike and Stefani* Stefani sells her coat on the black market. Frame enlargement

normal channels for government productions, and within Australia it was largely restricted to non-theatrical screenings and distribution through government film libraries. An entry was arranged in the Jubilee Film Festival in Melbourne in January 1952 where it had its first public screening and won a major prize. A few commercial screenings took place in October 1953 at an independent art cinema in Sydney.

Williams conceived the film as a neo-realist drama, at a time when most Australian film-makers were producing films exclusively in a Hollywood idiom. His familiarity with Rossellini and other Italian neo-realists, and with humanist film-makers such as Robert Flaherty and Jean Renoir, served to enrich the language of the film. Australian critics who managed to see it were impressed; the *Sydney Morning Herald,* 15 October 1953, praised it as 'a respectable and responsible piece of film-making . . . well ahead of the pretentious immaturity of most Australian feature films'.

Williams was primarily a documentary film-maker and *Mike and Stefani* was his only opportunity to make a narrative film of feature length. Born in England in 1911, he was educated mainly in Australia and found work in Sydney as a journalist and radio script-writer. In 1935 he joined the staff of National Studios, where he became closely involved in the technical support work for several features, including *The Flying Doctor* (1936). Self-styled a 'romantic Catholic', he formed a close friendship at this time with another staunch Catholic, the photographer Damien Parer, and after the close of National Studios in 1938, the two found work in the Commonwealth government's film unit in Melbourne. Active service followed in 1940 as a war correspondent with Parer and Frank Hurley in the Middle East, and later as a government journalist in Sydney. Towards the end of the war he became actively involved in the bitter political struggles surrounding the establishment of the National Film Board and the Film Division of the Department of the Interior (later the Commonwealth Film Unit). He took up a post with the new government film operation as senior producer, and was responsible for innumerable documentaries, many of them made in Papua New Guinea by a semi-independent branch of the Film Unit under Williams's own control. Most of his films were strictly functional productions to meet specific government demands, but occasionally films of distinction emerged, such as *New Guinea Patrol* (1958), a journey into spectacular unexplored areas of the western New Guinea highlands, narrated with a strong feeling for the human dimensions of the historic trek. In 1962 he resigned from the Film Unit and began a new career as a writer, completing a rapid succession of books about life in China, South-East Asia and Papua New Guinea.

334 **Kangaroo**

1952 LEWIS MILESTONE

PC: Twentieth Century-Fox. P: Robert Bassler. ASSOC P: Robert F. Snody. SC: Harry Kleiner. STORY: Martin Berkeley. PH: Charles G. Clarke. ED: Nick De Maggio. ART D: Lyle Wheeler, Mark-Lee Kirk. SPECIAL EFFECTS: Fred Sersen. M: Sol Kaplan. MD: Alfred Newman. SD: Eugene Grossman, Harry M. Leonard. 85 mins. Colour.

CAST: Maureen O'Hara (Dell Maguire), Peter Lawford (Richard Connor), Finlay Currie (Michael Maguire), Richard Boone (Gamble), Chips Rafferty (Trooper Leonard), Letty Craydon (Kathleen), Charles Tingwell (Matt), Ronald Whelan (Fenner), John Fegan (Burke), Guy Doleman (gambler), Reginald Collins (ship's officer), Frank Ransome (Burton), Clyde Combo (Aboriginal stockman), Henry Murdoch (blacktracker).

The film is a Western, set in the Australian outback at the turn of the century. An English adventurer, Richard Connor, poses as the long-lost son of an old cattleman, Maguire. Connor's ruthless companion, Gamble, plans to murder the old man so that Connor will inherit the family fortune, but the plan is complicated by Connor's attraction to Maguire's daughter, Dell. During muster on the drought-stricken station, Connor's love for Dell grows, and to allay Maguire's fear of incest, he confesses that he is not his son and that he is wanted by the police in Sydney. Connor and Gamble quarrel and in a fierce stock-whip fight, Gamble is killed. Later, as the drought breaks, Connor gives himself up to the police to stand trial for his misdeeds. Dell promises to wait for him.

Kangaroo was the first of several large-scale American productions shot on location in Australia during the 1950s. As with most of them, an entire Hollywood unit was transported to Australia and only minor technical and acting roles were reserved for Australians. Twentieth Century-Fox spent over £800 000 on the production as a re-investment of their capital reserves that had been frozen in Australia by government restrictions on dollar exports. The first of the crew arrived in July 1950, among them Robert Snody, the associate producer, who handled the huge task of organizing the production. Lewis Milestone, director of *All Quiet on the Western Front* (1930), arrived in August with the script. After absorbing local colour, he attempted to persuade the Hollywood head office to alter the story to something more appropriate to the location, but 'trying to convince them from a distance of ten thousand miles away was hopeless'. As a compromise, Milestone contrived to emphasize the theme of the drought as a background to the story, and an Aboriginal rain-making corroboree became one of the highlights. But despite Milestone's intentions, the film remained predominantly a formula movie; the *New York Times*, 17 May 1952, described it as 'a tedious tale of cupidity and double-dealing that is in the familiar Western groove'.

334 *Kangaroo* Charles Tingwell (*l*), Maureen O'Hara, Chipo Rafferty

Most of the film was shot on location in the Flinders Ranges and near Port Augusta in South Australia, and in the older parts of Sydney. Milestone later said: 'I wanted to concentrate on Sydney's historic landmarks . . . to emphasize the fact that we were actually in Australia: out in the wide open spaces you might as well be in Arizona' (interview in C. Higham and J. Greenberg, *The Celluloid Muse*, Sydney, 1969). During September 1950 preparations began near Port Augusta for the location unit. Just out of the town, a settlement mushroomed, designed to house 150 technicians and officially named Zanuckville (after the head of Twentieth Century-Fox) in an opening ceremony performed by the Premier of South Australia, Thomas Playford. Shooting began in Sydney in early November, using the Pagewood studio as a base, and continued in South Australia until late in February 1951. The Technicolor film stock was processed in the U.S.A.

Each phase of the production was accompanied by an abundance of publicity, especially the arrival of Maureen O'Hara, which became the occasion for many civic receptions and charity functions. The reaction of the Australian media was often one of sceptical amusement at the grand extravagance of the American visitors, but a few were less happy, among them Australian producers whose projects remained unfunded while the Americans gave their mundane script enough money to make thirty or more films by local production standards. The unions too were quick to react to the American 'invasion', and Actors' Equity publicized both an attempt by the Americans to pay lower wages to Aboriginal extras and the refusal of Maureen O'Hara to pay £5 from her salary of £2000 a week to join the Australian union.

Despite the constant flow of publicity, the film failed to capture the imagination of the public, not only in Australia but also abroad. After a brief world première season at the Roxy Theatre, New York, commencing on 16 May 1952, the film opened on 4 June in six Australian centres, all of them promoted as important social occasions in aid of charity. Nowhere, however, did the film attract good business and it is reported to have lost money heavily.

335 Night Club

1952 A. R. HARWOOD

PC: Cambridge Films. P: David Bilcock. SC: A. R. Harwood. PH: Len Heitman. ED: Barbara Baxter. ART D: Bill Slatter. SONG: 'Just for a Time', composed by Geoff Kitchen. BALLET: Olive Wallace. PM: Rudy Unger, Neil Duncan. 55 mins.

CAST: Joey Porter (Nick Arnold), Joff Ellen (Joss), Joan Bilceaux (Nita Fleming), Colin Crane (James Winters), Frank Holbrook (Bill Winters), Marjorie Harwood (Joan McDonald), Alex Roy (Jack Hanson), Ray Jones (compere), Reg Glenny (detective), Johnny Goodwin (cleaner), Barney March, Lloyd Nairn, the Clarence Sisters, the Leonard Boys, the Spencer Trio, the Geoff Kitchen Quintette.

Bill Winters goes to a country town to work quietly on the script for a musical show. There he sees some local variety acts and persuades his wealthy father to present them in a city night club. The show is a success, despite an attempt by a jealous singer to cause disruptions.

Night Club was Harwood's last attempt to re-enter feature production. In retrospect it seems to have been ill-fated from the start. For his subject he chose to remake *Show Business* (or at least one of its twin plots), even though he had failed commercially with the story the first time. Minimal finance of about £7000 was provided entirely by a Melbourne documentary firm, Cambridge Films. Shooting began in July 1952, with Harwood's daughter as the leading *ingénue*, Harwood himself (under his given names of Alex Roy) as a Puckish private detective, and a number of amateur and semi-professional variety artists. For the sake of economy, sound (including the musical items) was recorded 'wild' on a simple wire recorder, and it proved impossible to achieve perfect synchronization in editing.

After private previews at the end of 1952 the film virtually disappeared, although small distributors such as Ray Films occasionally arranged one-night stands in suburban and country theatres over the next few years.

336 Captain Thunderbolt

1953 CECIL HOLMES

PC: Associated T.V. P: John Wiltshire. SC: Creswick Jenkinson. PH: Ross Wood. ED: Margaret Cardin. ART D: Keith Christie. M: Sydney John Kay. PM: Peter Cuff. ASST D: Rod Adamson. SD: Robert Allen. 69 mins.

CAST: Grant Taylor (Fred Ward), Charles Tingwell (Alan Blake), Rosemary Miller (Joan), Harp McGuire (Mannix), John Fegan (Dalton), Jean Blue (Mrs Ward), John Fernside (Colonel), Loretta Boutmy (Maggie), Ronald Whelan (Hogstone), Charles Tasman (Colonial Secretary), Harvey Adams (parliamentarian), Patricia Hill (Belle), John Brunskill (Judge), John Unicomb, Sydney Loder, James Doogle, Frank Bradley, Dennis Glenny, William Collins.

Fred Ward is a gallant adventurer who runs foul of the repressive colonial law. Sentenced to hard labour for horse stealing, he escapes and becomes a bushranger under the name of Captain Thunderbolt. Stealing mainly from

336 *Captain Thunderbolt* Charles Tingwell (*l*), John Fernside

the decadent squattocracy, he quickly becomes a notorious public figure. Under political pressure, the police assign the sadistic Sergeant Mannix to capture him dead or alive. Eventually Mannix traps Thunderbolt but after a long gunfight discovers that he has killed only Thunderbolt's friend, Alan Blake, and that Thunderbolt has escaped. Mannix passes off Blake's body as Thunderbolt's but cannot prevent the growth of a legend that Thunderbolt still roams free in the bush of northern New South Wales.

This eccentric bush Western was a conscious attempt to make Thunderbolt a folk hero and to portray him as a victim of class struggle. The theme was partly expressed through rousing choruses of 'The Wild Colonial Boy' on the soundtrack, and partly through grotesque caricatures of the governing classes, recalling the portraits of class enemies in the films of Eisenstein and other Soviet directors with which Holmes was familiar.

The film was financed entirely by Benjamin Fuller (son of the theatrical entrepreneur, Sir Benjamin Fuller) at the instigation of Colin Scrimgeour, a prominent figure in the history of radio in Australia and New Zealand, who had visions of producing films like *Captain Thunderbolt* for television, years before the television market had properly developed in Australia. With a budget of £15 000 the film was shot in the first months of 1951 on location in the New England area of New South Wales, Thunderbolt's home territory. Holmes made careful use of historic buildings and relics to give authenticity to the background. Interiors were shot in the small studio of Supreme Sound System in North Sydney, and a bush dance was staged in a woolshed at Pyrmont.

Holmes at this time had had no experience of handling actors or of directing narrative cinema. Born on 23 June 1921 in New Zealand, he had worked first as a newsreel editor and later as a documentary director with the New Zealand government film unit, and had been one of the founders of the New Zealand film society movement in the 1940s. In 1949 he came to Australia to direct a documentary, *The Food Machine* (1950), for the Shell Film Unit under John Heyer. He then became involved in Scrimgeour's plans for *Captain Thunderbolt* and found himself thrust into feature production. The cast, especially Grant Taylor, helped him to reduce the script's reliance on dialogue (its author, Creswick Jenkinson, usually wrote for radio), and he found support in technical direction from Margaret Cardin, who had recently arrived from England, where she had worked as an editor in film and television studios.

A preview was held in January 1953, but the Australian trade paid scant attention. Despite their lack of interest, the film went on to earn £30 000 (twice its cost) from overseas sales, especially to Britain, Germany, Canada and the U.S.A. Australian release, through Ray Films, was slow and spasmodic. A première was held near the film's location site at Armidale in June 1955, and in September 1956 it ran in Sydney for a week at the Lyric, a 'blood house' reserved for action movies.

Holmes followed *Captain Thunderbolt* with a documentary for the trade union movement, *Words for Freedom* (1952), and then devoted his energies to a distribution enterprise, New Dawn Films, which specialized in Russian cinema. He was still closely involved with New Dawn in 1955 when a chance arose to direct his second feature, *Three in One* (released in 1957).

337 The Phantom Stockman

1953 LEE ROBINSON

PC: Platypus Productions. P: Chips Rafferty, George Heath. SC: Lee Robinson. PH: George Heath. ED: Gus Lowry. M: William Lovelock; guitar played by Don Andrews. SD: Hans Wetzel, John Heath. 67 mins.

CAST: Chips Rafferty (the Sundowner), Jeanette Elphick (Kim Marsden), Max Osbiston (McLeod), Guy Doleman (Stapleton), Henry Murdoch (Dancer), Bob Darken (Roxey), Joe Scully (the Moth), George Neil, Hawkeye Tim, Bill Gregory, Albert Namatjira (himself).

Convinced that her father has been murdered, young Kim Marsden, the heiress to a cattle station near Alice Springs, sends for the legendary bushman known as 'the Sundowner'. With Dancer, his Aboriginal offsider, the Sundowner finds cattle rustlers at work and trails them to their hide-out. He discovers that they are in league with Stapleton, the owner of the neighbouring station, who has been forcing his attentions on Kim. The rustlers capture the Sundowner, but using a method of mental telepathy known only to Aborigines, he alerts Dancer, who rides to his rescue with the station hands.

Collaboration between Chips Rafferty and Lee Robinson began in January 1952 when both failed to gain permission from the government to raise capital for separate production projects. Rafferty had planned a £120 000 company to produce thirteen three-reel films for world television, and a feature, *The Green Opal*, about immigration problems. At the same time, Lee Robinson, a young director with the Film Division of the Department of the Interior, was seeking to make a series of features beginning with an urban thriller, *Saturday to Monday*, which he had written with the English editor, Inman Hunter. However, under the restrictions on capital that existed at the time, film-making was ruled a non-essential industry and investment over £10 000 prohibited. Robinson later sold his scenario to Ealing, who used it as the basis for *The Siege of Pinchgut* (1959).

337 Albert Namatjira and Lee Robinson during the shooting of *The Phantom Stockman*

337 *The Phantom Stockman* Chips Rafferty

Rafferty and Robinson decided to make a feature together within the £10 000 limit. With a third partner, the photographer George Heath, they formed a company, Platypus Productions, and on a tight schedule began shooting at Alice Springs in July 1952 with enthusiastic co-operation from the townspeople. Interiors were later shot in Sydney.

One of Robinson's many documentaries for the Department of the Interior had been *Namatjira the Painter* (1947) and he added a brief, if scarcely relevant, scene with Namatjira to *The Phantom Stockman.* A cursory romantic sub-plot was also added, with Max Osbiston, a radio actor, and Jeanette Elphick, a Sydney model making her film debut. She later appeared in several American features as Victoria Shaw.

The final cost of the film was £10 800. Within a year, before its Australian release, it had earned more than £23 000 from overseas sales. It was released in America as *Return of the Plainsman* and in Britain as *Cattle Station.* With Australasian distribution through Universal, the film opened in Brisbane in June 1953. Most critics were pleased by the novelty (even for Australians) of the setting, the effective action scenes, and the pleasant background music, provided mainly by a solo guitar. Most, however, found the pace too slow: 'Hopalong Cassidy could probably clean up a dozen mysteries in the time it takes Chips Rafferty to draw wisely upon a cigarette' (*Sunday Herald*, 19 July 1953).

338 King of the Coral Sea

1954 LEE ROBINSON

PC: Southern International. P: Chips Rafferty. ASSOC P: Hugh Molesworth. SC: Chips Rafferty, Lee Robinson. PH: Ross Wood. UNDERWATER PH: Noel Monkman. ED: Alex Ezard. M: Wilbur Sampson. ASST D: Dennis Hill. SD: Hans Wetzel. 85 mins.

CAST: Chips Rafferty (Ted King), Charles Tingwell (Peter Merriman), Ilma Adey (Rusty King), Rod Taylor (Jack Janiero), Lloyd Berrell (Yusep), Reg Lye (Grundy), Charles Peverill (Sergeant Charlie Wright), Frances Chin Soon (Serena), Salapata Sagigi (Salapata), Jack Assam, Charlie Juda.

Ted King, a pearler in the Torres Strait, finds a body floating in the sea which gives him a lead to a racket in illegal immigration. Joined by Peter Merriman, the playboy owner of the pearling company, King investigates the crime and discovers that one of his own men, a half-cast sailor, Yusep, is involved. The racketeers kidnap King's daughter, Rusty, and hold her as hostage, but King and Merriman use aqualung gear and spearguns to surprise the gang in their island hide-out. They rescue Rusty and she is reunited with Merriman, the man she loves.

The second Rafferty-Robinson feature, produced by their new company, Southern International, was far more ambitious than their first, *The Phantom Stockman* (1953). With a budget of £25 000, more than double that of the earlier film, they spent over six weeks on location at Thursday Island, followed by further underwater shooting at Green Island, off the north Queensland coast, completed by November 1953. The world première was held on 17 July at Thursday Island, and mainland release through B.E.F. began on 12 August at the Majestic Theatre, Melbourne. Overseas sales alone were sufficient to recover the production cost, and local box-office results were also encouragingly strong, despite press criticism of the unconvincing characters (especially Rafferty as the rather unlikely father of the heroine) and the slack pace of the action. However, most critics praised the exotic setting and the film's detailed observation of the pearling industry. (Pearling had been the subject of one of Lee Robinson's better documentaries for the Department of the Interior, *The Pearlers*, 1949.)

338 *King of the Coral Sea* Ilma Adey, Chips Rafferty, Rod Taylor (*r*)

339 *The Back of Beyond*

339 The Back of Beyond

1954 JOHN HEYER

PC: Shell Film Unit. P, ED: John Heyer. SC: John Heyer, Janet Heyer, Roland Robinson. DIALOGUES, NARRATION: Douglas Stewart, John Heyer. PH: Ross Wood. M: Sydney John Kay. P ASST: Max Lemon. ASST D: George Hughes. SD: Mervyn Murphy, John Heath. 66 mins.

CAST: Tom Kruse, William Henry Butler, Jack the Dogger, Old Joe the Rainmaker, the Oldfields of Etadinna, Bejah, Malcolm Arkaringa, the people of the Birdsville Track. NARRATOR: Kevin Brennan.

This reconstruction of life on the Birdsville Track follows the daily work of Tom Kruse, an outback representative of the Royal Mail. Each fortnight he drives 300-odd miles through the desert in his old lorry to deliver supplies and mail to the few isolated settlements between Marree and Birdsville in central Australia.

The film offered a tightly structured, romantic view of outback life, with the desert seen not so much as a hostile environment but as a mould that creates resilience and resourcefulness in the people who live there. The film's poetic licence is especially apparent in comparison with *The Inlanders* (1949), a documentary that John Kingsford Smith filmed in the Birdsville area, which presented a much rougher and unadorned portrait of a barren country and its hardened people. As Eric Else wrote in his book, *The Back of Beyond* (London, 1968), Heyer's film is 'probably the last of the great romantic documentaries' in the tradition of the pre-war Grierson films; 'the social ethic of *The Back of Beyond* is that of *Night Mail*'.

In preparation for the £12 000 film, Heyer travelled on the Track with Tom Kruse, then returned to Sydney to write a detailed shooting script. Location shooting, with a unit of about twenty technicians and actors, took six weeks during spring 1952. The unit's five trucks carried supplies and equipment including a wind machine, a dolly for tracking shots and a tower for high angle shots. Guide tracks for the dialogue were recorded on location and professional actors later dubbed in the dialogue in Sydney.

Like other Shell productions, the film was released widely through non-commercial outlets, and Shell estimated that over 750 000 Australians saw it during 1954, the first year of its release. It was televised extensively overseas, and represented Australia at several film festivals, including Edinburgh and Venice, where it won the Grand Prix in 1954.

John Heyer was born in Tasmania in 1916. During the 1930s he worked as an assistant sound engineer and assistant editor for both Efftee and Cinesound. During the war he directed several documentaries and propaganda films, and after working on *The Overlanders* (1946) he was appointed producer with the new Australian National Film Board. He served there until his appointment as producer in charge of the Australian branch of the Shell Film Unit in 1948. In 1956 he became executive producer of films and television for Shell International in London and worked there until 1967, producing and directing a large volume of commercials and documentaries, many of which won awards at film festivals around the world. After 1967 he worked as a consultant and producer for the Australian Broadcasting Commission and made films for Australian commercial television. He also spent three years making a feature-length documentary, *The Reef*, released theatrically in 1979, about the history and resources of the Great Barrier Reef. Through much of his career, Heyer maintained an active interest in the film society movement, and was President of the Sydney Cinema Society from 1944 to 1954.

340 Long John Silver

1954 BYRON HASKIN

PC: Treasure Island Pictures. P: Joseph Kaufman. SC: Martin Rackin. PH: Carl Guthrie. CAM OP: Ross Wood, Carl Kayser. ED: Manuel Del Campo. ART D: William Constable, Charles Woolveridge. M: David Buttolph. PM: Mark Evans. ASST D: Maurie Power, Hans Von Adlerstein. SD R: Hans Wetzel, Alan Allen. 106 mins. Colour. CinemaScope.

CAST: Robert Newton (Long John Silver), Connie Gilchrist (Purity Pinker), Kit Taylor (Jim Hawkins), Lloyd Berrell (Mendoza), Grant Taylor (Patch), Rod Taylor (Israel Hands), Henry Gilbert (Billy Bowlegs), Harvey Adams (Governor Strong), Muriel Steinbeck (Lady Strong), John Brunskill (Old Stingley), Harry Hambleton (Big Eric), Eric Reiman (Trip Fenner), Syd Chambers (Ned Shill), George Simpson-Lyttle (Captain McDougal), Tony Arpino, Al Thomas, Owen Weingott, Don McNiven, Charles McCallum, John Llewellyn, James Workman.

Byron Haskin had first directed Robert Newton in the role of Long John Silver in 1950, in Walt Disney's production of *Treasure Island*. In this sequel, Silver renews his attempts to find a lost pirate treasure. The film opens with Silver biding his time on a Caribbean island, trying to avoid marriage with Purity Pinker, the amorous owner of a waterfront tavern. When he learns that his former shipmate, young Jim Hawkins, has been kidnapped by a pirate chief, Mendoza, Silver contrives to rescue him. Hoping that Jim can help him find the gold, Silver sets sail with the boy to Treasure Island. After further clashes with Mendoza and a violent encounter with Israel Hands, a crazed blind man marooned on the island, Silver and Jim succeed in finding the gold. Later they celebrate their find in Purity's tavern, but now her marital plans are keener than ever, and Silver is soon forced to leave in search of new horizons.

Long John Silver was only one part of an ambitious production programme involving film, television and radio. Led by an independent American producer, Joseph Kaufman, a new company, Treasure Island Pictures, leased the Pagewood studio in Sydney and planned to spend over US$1 000 000 on a

340 *Long John Silver* Robert Newton (*c*)

full-length feature film, 26 half-hour films for a television series, and recorded radio plays. The programme attracted investment from Twentieth Century-Fox in return for distribution rights in Britain and Australia, and production began in May 1954. The feature was shot simultaneously in CinemaScope (using imported cameras) and in regular wide screen format to ensure release through theatres not yet equipped with CinemaScope facilities. Substantially the same crew and cast were used for both the feature and the series, although a second Hollywood director, Lee Sholem, directed many episodes of the television series. Scenes were shot along the coastline near Sydney and in the Jenolan Caves, and large sets representing the pirate ship and a waterfront street in the Caribbean were built in the grounds of Pagewood. Music was recorded at Pagewood by the Sydney Symphony Orchestra under the direction of the Hollywood composer, David Buttolph, but other post-production work was completed by Haskin in London.

The world première was held in Sydney at the Plaza Theatre on 16 December 1954, with publicity aimed at children and stressing the novelty of CinemaScope (introduced to Australian cinemas only a year earlier). Release in the U.S.A. produced disappointing results and further Australian productions by Kaufman were abandoned. Over the next few years episodes from the television series were edited into at least two B-features, *Under the Black Flag* and *South Sea Pirates*, released in England in 1956 and 1957.

Critics were generally unkind to *Long John Silver* for its rambling script, a 'prettified' Jim Hawkins (played by Grant Taylor's son, Kit), and especially the uncontrolled mannerisms of Robert Newton's performance as the roguish old salt. Virtually in self-destructive parody of his earlier roles as a buccaneer, Newton dominated the film with throaty growls and rolling eyes, which the *New York Times*, 7 April 1955, found 'outrageously hammy, to the point of freakishness'.

341 Jedda

1955 CHARLES CHAUVEL

PC: Charles Chauvel Productions. P: Charles Chauvel. DIALOGUE D: Elsa Chauvel. SC: Charles Chauvel, Elsa Chauvel. RESEARCH: Bill Harney. PH: Carl Kayser. ED: Alex Ezard, Jack Gardiner, Pam Bosworth. ART D: Ronald McDonald. ANIMATION: Eric Porter. M: Isadore Goodman. UNIT M: Harry Closter. ASST D: Philip Pike. SD: Arthur Browne. 101 mins. Colour.

CAST: Ngarla Kunoth (Jedda), Robert Tudawali (Marbuck), Betty Suttor (Sarah McMann), Paul Reynall (Joe), George Simpson-Lyttle (Douglas McMann), Tas Fitzer (Peter Wallis), Wason Byers (Felix Romeo), Willie Farrar (little Joe), Margaret Dingle (little Jedda).

On a lonely cattle station in the Northern Territory, a newly born Aboriginal baby is adopted by a white woman, Sarah McMann, in place of her own child who has died. Sarah names the baby Jedda, after a wild bird, and raises her as a white child, forbidding contact with the Aborigines on the station. Years pass, and Jedda, a beautiful teenage girl, is drawn by the mysteries of the Aboriginal people but restrained by her upbringing. One day a powerfully built full-blood Aboriginal, Marbuck, arrives at the station seeking work. Jedda is fascinated by him and one moonlit night is drawn by his song to his campfire. He takes her away as his captive. Dragging the half-willing but frightened girl across the desert, Marbuck returns to his tribal lands, only to find himself rejected by his tribe for breaking their marriage taboos. Pursued by the men from Jedda's station and haunted by the death wish of his own tribe, Marbuck is driven insane and finally falls, with Jedda, over a cliff.

The film falls readily into two halves. The first, detailing Jedda's upbringing and emotional turmoil, concisely presents the dilemma faced by liberal whites in their relations with Aborigines: should they be trained as whites, or allowed to pursue their own culture free of white interference? The dilemma is resolved by Jedda herself, when the call of her blood leads her, bewildered and frightened, into the physical and psychological world of her forefathers. The second half of the film concentrates on the tension of the chase. In this part of the film, the landscapes become a significant part of the entertainment, with a wide variety of central and north Australian geographical features compressed into a highly coloured exotic terrain. *Jedda* was the first feature in colour by an Australian company, and the Chauvels used it to full effect in these exterior sequences.

Chauvel's original inspiration for the film came while he was in the U.S.A. for the re-editing of *Sons of Matthew*, when he became determined to find another story that could only be told in Australia by Australians. His usual backers, Universal, refused to support the project, believing it to be excessively offbeat, and Chauvel proceeded to form his own company and raise finance from businessmen in Sydney. After an extensive and difficult search, the Chauvels selected Robert Tudawali, a full-blood Aboriginal from Melville Island, to play Marbuck, and a shy Arunta girl from an inland mission station, Ngarla Kunoth, to play Jedda. Only three professional actors were used in the cast (Betty Suttor, George Simpson-Lyttle, and Paul Reynell as Jedda's half-caste fiancé on the station). Casting was completed by July 1953 and shooting on location in Central Australia was completed by November. Most scenes were shot on the Coolibah station in the Northern Territory, and others at such geographical landmarks as Standley Chasm and Ormiston Gorge, and in the buffalo and crocodile country around Mary River in the far north. Elaborate arrangements were made for the handling of the sensitive colour film stock in the heat of the desert locations; raw and exposed film was stored in rivers and in caves, and flown periodically under refrigeration to London for processing. An air crash destroyed several thousand feet of negative covering the last scenes in the film, and these were reshot around the Jenolan Caves and in the Blue Mountains. Interior scenes were shot at the Avondale Studios, Turrella, at the end of the year. To facilitate work with the colour laboratory, editing and sound recording were completed in London.

The première was held on 3 January 1955 at the Star Theatre, Darwin, attended by the Aboriginal stars and press representatives from around Australia. With the film's distributor, Columbia, Chauvel mounted a strong publicity campaign, and the film opened at the Lyceum Theatre, Sydney, on 5 May with initially excellent commercial results. Critics at home and later overseas had much praise for the film's visual grandeur and the sincerity of its script. Robert Tudawali attracted attention for his performance, and was praised variously by the press for his 'sheer animal magnificence' and his 'natural "mystery"'. Stardom did not rest easily on Tudawali's shoulders, and after one further film role (*Dust in the Sun*, 1958) he found difficulty in adjusting to life in Darwin and died in 1967. In 1960 Ngarla Kunoth joined a convent in Melbourne, but in 1969 left the order to work in Aboriginal welfare in Victoria.

Jedda was released by British Lion in England in 1956, severely reduced by nearly forty minutes, and appeared in America early in 1957 as *Jedda the Uncivilized.* The Chauvels' next project, an adaptation of *Wards of the Outer March,* from the novel by Kay Glasson Taylor, was abandoned when the British Broadcasting Commission hired them to make a thirteen-part television series, *Walkabout,* in the Northern Territory. The series was completed in 1958, but before any feature film projects could be resumed, Chauvel died on 11 November 1959.

342 Smiley

1956 ANTHONY KIMMINS

PC: London Films. An Alexander Korda presentation. P: Anthony Kimmins. SC: Moore Raymond, Anthony Kimmins. From the novel by Moore Raymond. PH: Edward Scaife. CAM OP: Ross Wood. ED: G. Turney-Smith. ART D: Stan Woolveridge. M: William Alwyn. THEME SONG: sung by Shirley Abicair. PM: Cecil Ford. LOCATION M: Ronald Whelan. ASST D: Jim Donohoe. SD R: Hans Wetzel, Red Law. SD SUP: John Cox. 97 mins. Colour. CinemaScope.

CAST: Colin Petersen (Smiley), Bruce Archer (Joey), Ralph Richardson (Reverend Lambeth), John McCallum (Jim Rankin), Chips Rafferty (Sergeant Flaxman), Jocelyn Hernfield (Miss Workman), Reg Lye (Pa Greevins), Margaret Christensen (Ma Greevins), Charles Tingwell (Mr Stevens), Marion Johns (Mrs Stevens), Gavin Davies (Fred Stevens), Toni Hansen (Jean Holt), William Rees (Mr Johnson), John Fegan (Nobby), Guy Doleman (Bill McVitty), Leonard Thiele (doctor), Letty Craydon (lady at christening).

Smiley is a mischievous barefoot boy who lives in the small country town of Murrumbilla. His family is poor: his father is an alcoholic drover, and his mother an embittered, hard-working woman. Spurred on by the taunts of more privileged school mates, he determines to save enough money to buy a bicycle and become the 'speed king' of the town. He works hard at odd jobs to earn money, but cannot help getting involved in pranks which cost him dearly. Unwittingly, too, he helps the local publican, Rankin, to sell opium to Aborigines who live in a camp near the town. One day Smiley's father steals the boy's savings to pay for gambling debts; Smiley accidentally knocks him out and runs away in panic into the bush where he is bitten by a snake. His life is saved by a swagman, Bill McVitty, and after Rankin is arrested, the townspeople club together to buy Smiley his bicycle.

This enormously popular children's adventure had long been a project of the British producer-director, Anthony Kimmins, and since the war he had made several attempts to set up the production. Finally, in September 1955 he arrived to search for the child stars of the film; after interviewing some 2000 boys he chose a nine-year-old Brisbane boy, Colin Petersen, to play Smiley, and another nine-year-old, Bruce Archer, to play his friend, Joey. The budget of £250 000 was partly provided from Twentieth Century-Fox's accumulation of revenue frozen in Australia by government restrictions on dollar exports. The film was shot entirely in Australia, commencing late in October at the township of Murrumbilla specially built on the grounds of the Camden Park estate. Shooting ended eight weeks later, and post-production work was completed at Pagewood, Sydney. Apart from Ralph Richardson (giving an energetic performance as an eccentric bush parson with a patched cassock and noisy old car), the cast was entirely Australian, with John McCallum returning to the local industry after a successful decade in British cinema.

A few concessions were made to overseas audiences, including details such as Smiley's habit of calling yabbies 'crayfish', and more noticeably, the heavy orchestral score by William Alwyn, which was better suited to an English pastoral comedy. But otherwise Kimmins presented an unusually honest view of the Australian bush, resisting any urge to introduce exotic wildlife or to indulge in tourist photography. Boozing and gambling are openly shown as integral parts of bush life, not only in the threatening character of Smiley's dissipated father, but also in a scene in which the boy sings 'Waltzing Matilda' to a ragged group of drinkers in the local pub. The film also quietly displays the extreme poverty of the town's exploited Aboriginal outcasts. Yet the overwhelming tone is one of affection for Australia, a feeling that some critics sensed in their praise of the film's 'fresh' and 'homespun' story, the 'natural charm' of its performers, and the 'sympathetic' direction.

Released world-wide by Twentieth Century-Fox, the film opened in London on 28 June 1956 and won the immediate favour of the public. Colin Petersen was soon offered

342 *Smiley* Reg Lye (*l*), Colin Petersen

roles in British films, and in 1956 starred in *The Scamp* with another Australian, Dorothy Alison; he later became a drummer in the pop group, the Bee Gees. On 18 October *Smiley* opened at the Regent Theatre, Brisbane, and began a record-breaking box-office career in Australia. Its progress was helped by and reflected in the popularity of a song, 'A Little Boy Called Smiley', composed after the film was completed by a Brisbane musician, Clyde Collins. This new song far outstripped the popularity of the film's own title song, and was used as the musical theme of *Smiley Gets a Gun,* which Kimmins shot in the following year.

343 Walk into Paradise

1956 LEE ROBINSON, MARCEL PAGLIERO

PC: Southern International (Australia)/Discifilm (France). P: Chips Rafferty. SC: Lee Robinson, Chips Rafferty. SC ADAPTATION: Rex Rienits. PH: Carl Kayser. ED: Alex Ezard. M: Georges Auric. PM: George Hughes. SD: Arthur Browne, Don Connolly. CONTINUITY: Joy Cavill. 93 mins. Colour.

CAST: Chips Rafferty (Steve McAllister), Françoise Christophe (Louise Demarcet), Pierre Cressoy (Jeff Clayton), Reg Lye (Ned 'Sharkeye' Kelly) Regimental Sergeant Major Somu (Towalaka), District Officer Fred Kaad, Captain Richard Davis.

This adventure followed the Rafferty-Robinson formula of a comic-strip yarn in an exotic location. In New Guinea a small expedition led by Steve McAllister, a district officer, makes its way towards Paradise Valley, beyond the head of the Sepik River, where Sharkeye Kelly, an Australian adventurer, has discovered oil. In the party are a malaria-stricken crocodile-hunter, Jeff Clayton, and a United Nations doctor, Louise Demarcet. The natives help Steve to prepare an airfield, but tension arises when Louise is attacked by a witchdoctor after she takes blood samples from some sick children. The timely recovery of the children saves the party from massacre.

The film had been in advanced stages of preparation by Southern International when a visiting French producer, Paul-Edmond Decharme, proposed a series of co-productions between the Australians and his French company, Discifilm. The screenplay was altered to accommodate two French stars, and shooting began in New Guinea in June 1955. Robinson as director was assisted by a French dialogue director, Marcel Pagliero, and dialogue scenes were filmed twice, in English and French. Despite the hazards and trials of working in the highlands, shooting fell only three days behind the twelve-week schedule, and the final cost was a modest £65 000. The film was edited in Paris, and under the title of *L'Odyssée du Capitaine Steve* it opened at five theatres in Paris on 28 July 1956, with Pagliero given full credit as director (in the French version only).

343 *Walk into Paradise (From left)* Chips Rafferty, Françoise Christophe, Reg Lye and policemen

On 24 October M.G.M. gave the film a 'splash release' at six Sydney theatres. It was later bought for a fixed sum by Joseph E. Levine for American release, and was retitled *Walk into Hell;* embellished with additional jungle footage, it was screened widely with substantial financial return to Levine.

344 Three in One

1957 CECIL HOLMES

PC: Australian Tradition Films. P: Cecil Holmes. PH: Ross Wood. ED: A. William Copeland. M: Raymond Hanson. PM: Bewick Hack. ASST D: R. G. Bayly, D. B. Hart. SD: Hans Wetzel. INTRODUCED BY: John McCallum. 89 mins.

The film consists of three stories:
Joe Wilson's Mates SC: Rex Rienits. From the short story by Henry Lawson, 'The Union Buries its Dead'.
CAST: Edmund Allison (Tom Stevens), Reg Lye (the swaggie), Alexander Archdale (Firbank), Charles Tasman (the undertaker), Don McNiven (Patrick Rooney), Jerold Wells (Wally), Chris Kempster (Longun), Brian Anderson (Joe), Kenneth Warren (Andy), Evelyn Docker (Maggie), Ben Gabriel (the priest), the Bushwhacker's Band.
The Load of Wood SC: Rex Rienits. From a story by Frank Hardy.
CAST: Jock Levy (Darkie), Leonard Thiele (Ernie), Ossie Wenban (Sniffy), John Armstrong (Chilla), Jim Doone (Joe), Ted Smith (Coulson), Edward Lovell (Tye), Keith Howard (Shea), Eileen Ryan (Mrs Johnson).
The City SC: Ralph Peterson.
CAST: Joan Landor (Kathie), Brian Vicary (Ted), Betty Lucas (Freda), Gordon Glenwright (Alex), Ken Wayne (first cab driver), Stewart Ginn (second cab driver), Alan Trevor (preacher), Pat Martin and Margaret Christensen (customers), John Fernside (vagrant), Alastair Roberts (bodgie).

This trilogy about mateship began as a single story, *The Load of Wood,* written by Frank Hardy, which Hardy himself sponsored. After this short film had been completed, Julian Rose raised finance for two more stories and Holmes tied the three together with introductions by John McCallum. The concept of the film abandoned the Hollywood models usually followed by Australian directors, and in the third story Holmes sought to adapt the spirit of Italian neo-realist cinema to the Australian scene.

The first story, *Joe Wilson's Mates,* is set in the 1890s. Joe Wilson is a stranger in town who dies alone without friends or family. Because he carries a union card, however, the local union members give him the honour of a decent burial. *The Load of Wood* is also about workers' solidarity. During the Depression of the 1930s, a group of unemployed men in a small country town are given relief work on

1946/64

The Adventures of Barry McKenzie

Picnic at Hanging Rock

The Adventures of Barry McKenzie

Caddie

Mad Dog Morgan

The Getting of Wisdom

Eliza Fraser

The Last Wave

the roads, but they still cannot afford to buy enough fuel to keep their families warm. Two of the men steal a truck-load of wood from a rich man's estate, and deliver it to the needy around the town. The final episode, *The City*, is a love story set in modern Sydney. The lovers are a young factory worker and a shop assistant whose plans to marry are frustrated by the high cost of housing. After quarrelling and spending the night wandering separately in the city streets, they realize that their love is more important than money.

Shooting for all three stories was based at the Pagewood studio, Sydney, before and after the production there of *Smiley* in the last half of 1955. Exteriors for the first two stories were shot near Camden, and the 'portrait of a city' at the heart of the third story was shot at night in the streets of Sydney. The effect of the film was uneven: Ralph Peterson's story lacked dramatic tension, but the first two episodes were welcomed by overseas critics. A writer in *Sight and Sound*, Autumn 1956, found the film 'remarkably human and alive', and recorded a remark by a French critic, 'Ça, c'est du cinéma!' *Monthly Film Bulletin*, May 1957, applauded Holmes's work: 'Although an uneven film, *Three in One* is full of energy and promise. An honest and determined attempt to create a national style, it may well be a landmark in the development of the Australian cinema.'

The Australian film trade, however, was not ready to acknowledge the achievement, and it failed to find a full commercial release. The major distributors and exhibitors rejected it, perhaps because of uneasiness about Holmes's left-wing commitment, clearly apparent in the film and also in his involvement in the distribution of Russian films in Australia through New Dawn Films; but at the same time, the trade was inhibited by its commitment to British and American interests. Officially voiced opinions were defensive and denigrated the film and those associated with it: Ron Michaels, the managing director of United Artists in Australia, answered a newspaper criticism of the trade's indifference by asserting that the film had 'little box-office appeal' and that 'any well-produced Australian film, embodying the necessary qualities which appeal to theatre patrons, will readily find both distribution and exhibition outlet' (*Sun*, 15 May 1957).

After screening at the Edinburgh and Karlovy Vary Film Festivals in 1956, the film was sold to several European countries and very profitably to China. It opened almost simultaneously in London and New Zealand in March 1957. Australian screenings were limited to a few independent theatres, and individual episodes of the film were later screened as part of supporting programmes in the major chains. It failed however to recoup more than half of its cost of £28 000, and Australian Tradition Films was liquidated in 1959.

Holmes remained with New Dawn Films for several more years until he began directing documentaries again in the early 1960s. He made several films for the Methodist Church, including *Lotu* (1962) in Papua New Guinea and *Faces in the Sun* (1964) in Central Australia. He moved to Darwin in 1964 and directed a series of ethnographic films for the Australian Institute of Aboriginal Studies as well as several television films on racial themes, both for the Australian Broadcasting Commission and commercial networks. He also worked as a journalist and for some time edited a monthly magazine, *The Territorian*. In the late 1960s he returned to Sydney as a staff director for the Commonwealth Film Unit, and there found an opportunity to direct his third narrative feature, *Gentle Strangers* (1972).

344 *Three in One (The Load of Wood)* Jock Levy (*c*) and Leonard Thiele (*r*) discuss workers' problems during the Depression. Frame enlargement

344 *Three in One (Joe Wilson's Mates)* Reg Lye at Joe's funeral. Frame enlargement

345 The Shiralee

1957 LESLIE NORMAN

PC: Ealing Films. P: Michael Balcon. ASSOC P: Jack Rix. SC: Neil Paterson, Leslie Norman. From the novel by D'Arcy Niland. PH: Paul Beeson. CAM OP: Chic Waterson. ED: Gordon Stone. ART D: Jim Morahan. M: John Addison. SONG sung by Tommy Steele. P SUP: Hal Mason. PM: Norman Priggen, Ralph Hogg. AUSTRALIAN LIAISON: Ronald Whelan. ASST D: Tom Pevsner. SD R: Ray Palmer. SD ED: Alastair McIntyre. SD SUP: Stephen Dalby. 103 mins.

CAST: Peter Finch (Macauley), Dana Wilson (Buster), Elizabeth Sellars (Marge), George Rose (Donny), Rosemary Harris (Lily Parker), Russell Napier (Parker), Niall MacGinnis (Beauty Kelly), Tessie O'Shea (Bella), Sidney James (Luke), Charles Tingwell (Jim Muldoon), Reg Lye (Desmond), Barbara Archer (shop girl), Alec Mango (Papadoulos), John Phillips (doctor), Bruce Beeby (solicitor), Frank Leighton (barman), Guy Doleman (Son O'Neill), Nigel Lovell (O'Hara), Lloyd Berrell, John Cazabon, Mark Daly, Ed Devereaux, Bettina Dickson, Gordon Glenwright, Fred Goddard, Clifford Hunter, Betty McDowall, Henry Murdoch, Frank Raynor, Lou Vernon, David Williams. Chin Yu, Bill Kerr, Ronald Whelan. NARRATOR: Charles Tingwell.

This episodic drama follows the life of a swagman, Macauley, and his 'shiralee' (an Aboriginal word for burden) in the form of his five-year-old daughter, Buster. Mac's road is none too smooth: his neurotic wife in the city is suing him for divorce and her lover sends thugs to beat him up. He also quarrels with an old girlfriend, Lily, whom he had deserted years before when she became pregnant. He tries in vain to leave Buster with friends along the way, but she persists in following him despite his rugged life and gruff manner. Gradually Buster's devotion begins to tame him and draw him closer to the sympathetic Lily, who is waiting for him to return and settle down.

The film was financed jointly by Ealing and the British branch of M.G.M. It was shot in the last months of 1956, partly on location in north-east New South Wales and partly at the M.G.M. studios in London. The cast included many of the Australian actors then working in London, among them Bill Kerr, Frank Leighton (from Cinesound's heyday), and Ed Devereaux. The film was released in London in July 1957 and was given a much-publicized Australian première at the country town of Scone, N.S.W., in August. It opened a few days later at the St James Theatre, Sydney, for a long and successful season.

Monthly Film Bulletin, July 1957, along with many Australian reviewers, admired the 'proud and fiercely independent spirit' of the character portrayed by Peter Finch and found the story 'touchingly observed'. A dissident voice was heard in *Films and Filming*, July 1957, claiming that 'the film cheats in every direction' to make a 'singularly unattractive theme' commercially acceptable: by casting a 'charming and cultured personality like Finch' in the central role; by making the wife 'a complete bitch' in obvious contrast to the loyal girlfriend; and by having Mac's conscience assuaged by nothing more convincing than a timely thrashing.

345 *The Shiralee* Dana Wilson, Peter Finch

346 Robbery Under Arms

1957 JACK LEE

PC: Rank Organisation. P: Joseph Janni. SC: Alexander Baron, W. P. Lipscomb. ADDITIONAL SCENES: Richard Mason. From the novel by Rolf Boldrewood. PH: Harry Waxman. CAM OP: James Bawden. ED: Manuel Del Campo. ART D: Alex Vetchinsky. M: Matyas Seiber. PM: Jack Hanbury. LOCATION M: Ronald Whelan. ASST D: Bert Batt. SD R: Geoffrey Daniels, William Daniels. SD ED: Harry Miller. 104 mins. Colour.

CAST: Peter Finch (Captain Starlight), Ronald Lewis (Dick Marston), Maureen Swanson (Kate Morrison), David McCallum (Jim Marston), Jill Ireland (Jean), Laurence Naismith (Ben), Jean Anderson (Ma), Ursula Finlay (Grace), Laurence Taylor (Burke), Vincent Ball (George), Ewen Solon (trooper), Russell Napier (Mr Green), Max Wagner (Goring), John Cadell (Warrigal), Edna Morris (Aunt), Dudy Nimmo (Eileen), Colin Ballantyne (Runnimal), Stephen Scrutton (auctioneer), Bartlett Mullins (Paddy), Philippa Morgan (child's mother), George Cormack (minister), Robert Reardon (Mr Mullockson), Pat Hagan (Barker), Sergeant Holmes (Mr James), John Hargreaves (clerk), Ivor Bromley (Falkland), Rita Pauncefort (lady in coach), Billy Pepper (blacktracker).

A sound version of Rolf Boldrewood's novel had been planned as early as 1933, when Cinesound bought the rights from Raymond Longford. For many years Ken Hall of Cinesound nursed the project as one of his favourites, and at various times planned to star, first, John Longden, and later, Reginald Denny, as Captain Starlight. Hall's plans never reached fruition, partly because of uncertainty about censorship following the New South Wales ban on another bushranging film, *When the Kellys Rode* (1934). The primary stumbling block, however, was the preparation of a suitable screenplay: Hall commissioned several writers to work on the script but none succeeded in reducing the long, rambling novel to a manageable shape.

The English director, Jack Lee, had earlier visited Australia to film the closing sequences for *A Town Like Alice* (1956), a British film starring Peter Finch, about the occupation of Malaya by the Japanese. Shooting for his version of *Robbery Under Arms* began in January 1957, with two months on location in the Flinders Ranges, South Australia, and near the outback town of Bourke, N.S.W. Two days were spent at the Pagewood studio, Sydney, filming interior scenes with the Australian cast, and in April the unit returned to London to complete both interiors and exteriors at the Pinewood studios.

346 *Robbery Under Arms* David McCallum (*l*), Ronald Lewis

After a world première in London in October, the film was given a joint Australian opening near the actual location sites, at Port Augusta in South Australia, and at Bourke, early in December. Subsequent screenings in the Australian capitals proved popular despite guarded critical comments. The *Sun-Herald*, 15 December 1957, found it 'most uneven' but appreciated the 'largeness of style' with which the outback had been filmed, and the 'purposeful tension' of the closing scenes showing the fate of Starlight's gang.

Lee returned to Australia to live in 1963. He continued to make documentaries, including *From the Tropics to the Snow* (1964), a popular parody of tourist travelogues, which he co-directed with Richard Mason for the Commonwealth Film Unit. In 1976 he was appointed Chairman of the South Australian Film Corporation.

347 The Stowaway

1958 LEE ROBINSON, RALPH HABIB

PC: Discifilm/Silverfilm (France)/Southern International (Australia). P: Lee Robinson, Paul-Edmond Decharme, Robert Dorfmann. ASSOC P: Joy Cavill. SC: Lee Robinson, Joy Cavill. From the novel, *Le Passager clandestin*, by Georges Simenon. PH: Desmond Dickinson. CAM OP: Keith Loone. ED: Stanley Moore, Monique Kirsanoff. PM: George Hughes. SD: Don Connolly. 93 mins. Colour.

CAST: Martine Carol (Colette), Roger Livesey (Major Owens), Serge Reggiani (Mougins), Carl-Heinz Boehm (Jean), Arletty (Gabrielle), Reg Lye (Buddington), James Condon (the purser), Charley Mauu (Taro), Yvon Chabana (Max), Vahinerii Tauhiro (Vahinerii), Doris Fitton, John Martin, Frederic Gray.

René Maréchal, the heir to a large fortune, lives in secret on a tropical island near Tahiti. A group of adventurers compete with one another to find Maréchal and claim a reward offered for locating him. They include Major Owens, a raffish middle-aged Englishman with a phoney military background; Colette, a night-club hostess who had once been Maréchal's mistress; and Mougins, a ruthless criminal. Owens discovers the island on which Maréchal lives, but is murdered by Mougins, who sets out for the island, forcing Colette to come with him. They are overtaken by Jean, who had earlier helped Colette to stow away on the boat to Tahiti, and in the ensuing fight Mougins falls overboard and is killed by a shark. Jean and Colette decide to give up the search for Maréchal and, like him, retire to a quiet life in the islands.

The film was the second of Southern International's co-productions with the French producer, Paul-Edmond Decharme, and they were joined by a third company, Silverfilm, represented by Robert Dorfmann, producer of several notable French films including *Jeux interdits* (1951) and *Gervaise* (1955). *The Stowaway* was shot in the last months of 1957, at a cost of over £250 000. Tahiti and the Society Islands were the locations for most of the shooting, with an island studio and the ship, the *Calédonien*, used for interiors. Like *Walk into Paradise*, dialogue scenes were filmed

347 *The Stowaway* Martine Carol, Serge Reggiani

twice, in French and English, with a French director, Ralph Habib, working in collaboration with Robinson and given full credit as director in the French version of the film. The screenplay was adapted from Simenon's novel by Robinson in collaboration with Joy Cavill, who had been associated with Southern International since its foundation, first as continuity and script-girl and later as production associate.

Under the title of the original novel, *Le Passager clandestin*, the film opened simultaneously at four Paris cinemas on 22 March 1958. *Cahiers du cinéma*, April 1958, noted that the spirit of Simenon's novel, which had been 'the sadness of Tahiti', was completely betrayed. A critic in *Le Monde*, 4 April 1958, wrote that the film treated its few native dances and feasts with discretion, but the background had only superficial relevance to the plot, and the charm of the islands was subverted by the story: 'under the enchanted skies the characters wield guns and fists exactly as in the low dives of Pigalle'. Australian distribution through Universal began in December 1958 with a première in the country town of Dubbo, N.S.W., to open a new theatre there, but the first capital city screening was not until September 1959 at the Tivoli Theatre, Brisbane.

348 Smiley Gets a Gun

1958 ANTHONY KIMMINS

PC: Canberra Films. P: Anthony Kimmins. ASSOC P: Leslie Gilliat. SC: Anthony Kimmins, Rex Rienits. From the novel by Moore Raymond. PH: Edward Scaife. CAM OP: Ross Wood. ED: G. Turney-Smith. ART D: John Hoesli. SPECIAL EFFECTS: Jock Levy, Keith Gow. M: Wilbur Sampson. THEME SONG composed by Clyde Collins. PM: Bewick Hack. ASST D: Jim Donohoe. SD SUP: Hans Wetzel. SD R: William Constable, Lloyd Colman. 90 mins.

CAST: Keith Calvert (Smiley), Bruce Archer (Joey), Sybil Thorndike (Granny McKinley), Chips Rafferty (Sergeant Flaxman), Margaret Christensen (Ma Greevins), Reg Lye (Pa Greevins), Grant Taylor (Stiffy), Leonard Thiele (Mr Scrivens), Guy Doleman (Quirk), Verena Kimmins (Miss MacCowan), Bruce Beeby (Dr Gaspen), Ruth Cracknell (Mrs Gaspen), John Fegan (Tom Graham), Brian Farley (Fred), Janice Dinnen (Jean Holt), Barbara Eather (Elsie), William Rees (Mr Protheroe), Gordon Chater (Reverend Galbraith).

This sequel to *Smiley* (1956) followed a similar story pattern: instead of a bicycle, Smiley desperately wants to have his own rifle. The local policeman promises to give him one if he can stay out of mischief and behave 'responsibly'. In one of many misadventures, he is suspected of stealing a cache of gold and runs away in shame. Later the real thief is caught and Smiley is rewarded with the gun.

The frank but affectionate view of Australia that Kimmins had revealed in *Smiley* was less apparent in this sequel: the direction seemed careless and the script insufficiently developed. Concessions to popular taste weakened elements of conflict present in the original film: Smiley's father was transformed from a dissipated drunkard into a respectable blacksmith; signs of extreme rural poverty and racial discrimination disappeared; and the film relied for local colour on unimaginative devices such as a tame kangaroo, which Smiley now has a pet. Furthermore, Ralph Richardson's genial eccentricities in *Smiley* were replaced by a heavily mannered performance from Sybil Thorndike as Granny, a secretive old lady whom the children regard as a witch.

Because the original Smiley, Colin Petersen, had found work in England, Kimmins was obliged to launch another large-scale search for a child to play the leading role. His choice was a ten-year-old Victorian boy, Keith Calvert, who proved to be a competent actor. Shot in the last months of 1957, the film again used locations at Camden and the post-production services of the Pagewood studio, Sydney. It was released by Twentieth Century-Fox in London in May 1958, and in Australia during the following Christmas holidays, but was far less successful commercially than *Smiley*. A projected third film, *Smiley Wins the Ashes*, was abandoned.

349 Dust in the Sun

1958 LEE ROBINSON

PC: Southern International. P: Chips Rafferty. ASSOC P: Joy Cavill. SC: W. P. Lipscomb, Lee Robinson, Joy Cavill. From the novel, *Justin Bayard*, by Jon Cleary. PH: Carl Kayser. CAM OP: Keith Loone. ED: Stanley Moore. M: Wilbur Sampson. PM: George Hughes. SD: Don Connolly. 86 mins. Colour.

CAST: Jill Adams (Julie Kirkbride), Ken Wayne (Justin Bayard), Maureen Lanagan (Chris Palady), James Forrest (Tad Kirkbride), Robert Tudawali (Emu Foot), Jack Hume (Ned Palady), Henry Murdoch (Spider), Reg Lye (Dirks), Alan Light (Inspector Prichett).

Justin Bayard is a Northern Territory policeman taking an Aboriginal captive, Emu Foot, to Alice Springs to be tried for a tribal killing. When they are attacked by Aborigines, Bayard is wounded and Emu Foot helps him to a remote cattle station. There Bayard is involved in a domestic crisis centring upon Julie, the bored and neurotic wife of the station owner. Acting on impulse, Julie sets Emu Foot free and is later murdered, with evidence pointing to the Aboriginal as the culprit. Emu Foot is killed by tribesmen seeking vengeance for his earlier killing, and Julie's real murderer is uncovered by Bayard on the station.

In May 1956, Rafferty and Robinson bought the old Cinesound studio at Bondi, as a base for their television company, Australian Television Enterprises, but it was first used for shooting the interiors for *Dust in the Sun*.

Exteriors were filmed on location near Alice Springs in October and November. The first draft of the screenplay was written, uncredited, by the British scenarist, W. P. Lipscomb. Jill Adams, an English actress with a background in comedy, was brought out as the star, ostensibly because of a shortage of trained actresses in Australia.

The film was premièred at the Sydney Film Festival in October 1958, but not until August 1960 did Universal release it commercially in Sydney, with a poorly publicized week at the Capitol. Reviews had little to say in favour of the film beyond noting the spectacular Territory landscapes and 'the calm presence' of Robert Tudawali as the Aboriginal captive.

350 The Restless and the Damned

1959 YVES ALLÉGRET

PC: Silverfilm (France)/Australian Television Enterprises (Australia). P: Robert Dorfmann, Lee Robinson. ASSOC P: Paul-Edmond Decharme, Joy Cavill. SC: Réné Wheeler. From the novel, *Manganese*, by Francois Ponthier. PH: Carl Kayser, Henri Persin, Louis Stein, Gilles Bonneau. ED: Albert Jurgenson. ART D: Georges Wakhevitch. M: Henri Crolla, André Hodeir, Ray Ventura. PM: Henri Jaquillard. ASST D: Suzanne Bon, Claude Pinoteau. SD: Louis Hochet. 98 mins. Colour.

CAST: Edmond O'Brien (Buchanan), Richard Basehart (George Rancourt), Andrea Parisy (Dominique), Nicole Berger (Claire), Nigel Lovell (André), Reg Lye (Matthews), Jean Marchat (Uncle Albert), Denise Vernac (Aunt Edwige).

In Tahiti, an ambitious woman, Dominique, promotes the fortunes of her husband, George, by seducing a prospective business partner and by extracting money from George's family to finance his operations. When she learns that George intends to leave her for another woman, she vindictively plans to murder him.

Shooting began late in 1958 on Tahiti and the Tuamotu Islands. The film was another Franco-Australian co-production shot in both French and English versions. Lee Robinson was originally to have directed the English dialogue scenes, but after a few days' work he deferred to the French director, Yves Allégret, who subsequently handled both versions.

It was presented as *L'Ambitieuse* at the Locarno Film Festival in July 1959, and opened simultaneously at three Paris cinemas on 15 October. A *Variety* reporter wrote from Locarno (5 August 1959): 'Yves Allégret's direction is listless. O'Brien, as the boss, and Basehart, as the weak husband, can not do much with their stereotyped roles while Andrea Parisy is incapable of giving animation to [her] complicated character.' The film failed to attract theatrical release in England and the U.S.A., but it was later released to American television by the Desilu organization under the title of *The Climbers*. English language prints were also prepared with the title of *The Dispossessed*.

Because of the financial failure of the Rafferty-Robinson production team (of which Australian Television Enterprises was part), the film was never released in Australia, and it proved to be the last of their feature ventures. Robinson was commissioned in July 1959 by a rock music promoter, Lee Gordon, to make *Rock 'n' Roll*, a feature-length record of an all-star concert at the Sydney Stadium. He subsequently worked in television as a producer and director, and after *They're a Weird Mob* (1965), in which he was administratively involved, he became one of the principals behind Fauna Productions, the company responsible for the highly successful television series, *Skippy*, and in 1969 he directed *The Intruders*, a feature film based on the series.

351 Summer of the Seventeenth Doll

1959 LESLIE NORMAN

PC: Hecht-Hill-Lancaster (Australia). P: Leslie Norman. ASSOC P: Cecil Ford. SC: John Dighton. From the play by Ray Lawler. PH: Paul Beeson. CAM OP: Jeff Seaholme. ED: Gordon Hales. ART D: Jim Morahan. M: Benjamin Frankel. PM: Ronald Whelan. SD R: Alan Allen, Red Law. SD ED: Peter Thornton. 94 mins.

CAST: Ernest Borgnine (Roo), Anne Baxter (Olive), John Mills (Barney), Angela Lansbury (Pearl), Ethel Gabriel (Emma), Vincent Ball (Dowd), Janette Craig (Bubba), Deryck Barnes (Bluey), Frank Wilson (Vince), Al Garcia (Dino), Jessica Noad (Nancy), Al Thomas (Spruiker), Tom Lurich (the Atom Bomber), Dana Wilson (little girl).

In July 1957 the American company, Hecht-Hill-Lancaster, bought the screen rights to Ray Lawler's play for a reported £134 000. Several major changes were made to the play, presumably to improve its commercial potential following lukewarm reactions to the play in America. The changes met with solid opposition in Australia. A geographic shift of location from Carlton to Sydney was seen by the *Sydney Morning Herald*, 3 December 1959, as 'quite alien to the spirit of Lawler's drama'. But the most substantial change was the addition of a positive, optimistic ending, and to the same critic the whole film was angled more towards 'violence and rough jostling' than towards the sentiment at the heart of the play, the passing of a cherished dream.

Roo and Barney are Queensland canecutters who spend the off-season each year in Sydney. For sixteen years Roo has spent the summer with Olive, a barmaid, each year bringing her a kewpie doll as a symbol of their union. In the seventeenth summer, however, things fail to run as smoothly as in the past. Roo has had a bad season and is short of money, and Barney's girl has been married. Olive arranges for a manicurist, Pearl, to move in with Barney, but they are not compatible. Difficulties intensify when Roo's position as head of the canecutting team is taken

351 *Summer of the Seventeenth Doll* Ernest Borgnine (*l*), John Mills

over by a younger man, Dowd, and both Roo and Barney realize they are growing old. Later Barney leaves to work with Dowd, and Roo tries to persuade Olive to settle down with him in marriage. She refuses angrily but in the morning finally accepts.

A new company, Hecht-Hill-Lancaster (Australia) Pty Ltd, was formed to produce the film entirely in Australia using the studios of Pagewood and Artransa. Early announcements about the cast promised Burt Lancaster, Rita Hayworth and James Cagney for the leading roles. Shooting began in December 1958 with location scenes around Sydney to 'open up' the play. For one scene, shot on Sydney Harbour, foreshore residents were asked to leave their lights burning all night to provide a romantic background to the action. Other scenes were shot in Luna Park and on Bondi beach.

With distribution by United Artists, the film was given a world première at the Century Theatre, Sydney, on 2 December 1959.

352 On the Beach

1959 STANLEY KRAMER

PC: Lomitas Productions. P: Stanley Kramer. SC: John Paxton, James Lee Barrett. From the novel by Nevil Shute. PH: Giuseppe Rotunno. CAM OP: Ross Wood. AUTO RACE PH: Daniel Fapp. ED: Frederic Knudtson. ART D: Fernando Carrere. SPECIAL EFFECTS: Lee Zavitz. P DES: Rudolph Sternad. M: Ernest Gold. PM: Clem Beauchamp. ASST D: Ivan Volkman. SD: Hans Wetzel. SD EFFECTS: Walter Elliott. 134 mins.

CAST: Gregory Peck (Dwight Towers), Ava Gardner (Moira Davidson), Fred Astaire (Julian Osborn), Anthony Perkins (Peter Holmes), Donna Anderson (Mary Holmes), John Tate (Admiral Bridie), Lola Brooks (Lieutenant Hosgood), Guy Doleman (Farrel), John Meillon (Swain), Harp McGuire (Sundstrom), Ken Wayne (Benson), Richard Meikle (Davis), Joe McCormick (Ackerman), Lou Vernon (Davidson), Basil Buller-Murphy (Froude), Paddy Moran (port man), Kevin Brennan (Dr Forster), John Casson (Salvation Army captain), Grant Taylor (Morgan), Jim Barrett (Chrysler), Rita Pauncefort (woman at party), Keith Eden (Dr Fletcher), John Royle (senior officer), Frank Gatcliff (radio operator), C. Harding Brown (Dykers), Elwyn Peers (jewellery salesman), Harvey Adams (Sykes), Mayne Lynton (Cadogan), Al Thomas (bartender), Stuart Finch (Jones), Colin Crane (porter).

This cautionary tale about nuclear holocaust was filmed largely on location in and around Melbourne at an estimated cost of US$3 000 000. The film tended to emphasize the romantic sub-plots of Nevil Shute's novel rather than the frightening technical detail that Shute had carefully assembled to give credibility to his theme. Shute later refused to attend the première of the film because of his disagreement with Stanley Kramer's interpretation of the novel.

The time is five years in the future (1964), and Melbourne has not yet succumbed to the drifting radioactive fall-out caused by atomic war in the northern hemisphere. The story follows five people in their preparation for death: Dwight Towers, captain of an American submarine in Melbourne; Peter Holmes, a naval officer, and his wife, Mary; Moira Davidson, a dissipated Australian woman who is regenerated through her love for Towers and comes to accept her fate calmly; and Julian Osborn, a conscience-stricken scientist.

Shooting began in January 1959 with a ten-week schedule and some additional work in America, including the staging of a car-racing sequence. Co-operation was received from the Royal Australian Navy, which lent an aircraft carrier and three submarines, and from the Melbourne City Council, which closed off main thoroughfares for the use of the unit.

With distribution by United Artists, the world première was held simultaneously in seventeen cities, including Melbourne, Moscow and New York, on 17 December 1959. The press loudly acclaimed the film for its 'shattering' impact and echoed its publicity claim to be 'the most important film of our generation'. There were, however, some dissident voices, among them a critic for the *Monthly Film Bulletin,* February 1960, who found little to admire in the film's emotionalism: despite obvious good intentions, 'its humanism is only too plainly of the order that seeks the support of a clamorous music score. The characters remain little more than spokesmen for timid ideas and Salvation Army slogans, their emotions hired from a Hollywood prop-room.'

353 The Siege of Pinchgut

1959 HARRY WATT

PC: Ealing Films. P: Michael Balcon. ASSOC P: Eric Williams. SC: Harry Watt, Jon Cleary. SC CONTRIBUTION: Alexander Baron. STORY: Inman Hunter, Lee Robinson. PH: Gordon Dines. CAM OP: Herbert Smith. ED: Gordon Stone. ART D: Alan Withy. M: Kenneth V. Jones. P SUP: Hal Mason. PM: L. C. Rudkin. ASST D: Michael Birkett, Eric Price. SD R: Cyril Swern. SD ED: Lionel Selwyn. SD SUP: Stephen Dalby. 104 mins.

CAST: Aldo Ray (Matt Kirk), Heather Sears (Ann Fulton), Neil McCallum (Johnny Kirk), Victor Maddern (Bert), Carlo Justini (Luke), Alan Tilvern (Superintendent Hanna), Barbara Mullen (Mrs Fulton), Gerry Duggan (Pat Fulton), Kenneth Warren (Police Commissioner), Grant Taylor (Constable Macey), Deryck Barnes (Sergeant Drake), Richard Vernon (under-secretary), Ewan McDuff (naval captain), Martin Boddey (Brigadier), Max Robertson (motorcycle policeman), John Pusey (small boy), Fred Abbott (constable), Jock Levy (policeman).

Matt Kirk escapes from jail to attract public sympathy for his demand for a re-trial in which he can prove his innocence. With three accomplices he lands on Fort Denison (commonly called Pinchgut), a fortified island in the middle of Sydney Harbour, after their getaway boat breaks down. They hold the caretaker and his family as hostages, and threaten to use a navy gun to fire on a nearby munitions ship and hence blow up the foreshore area, unless Matt is publicly guaranteed his re-trial and a new judge.

The story had originally been written by Lee Robinson and the English editor, Inman Hunter, when they were working together in the government film unit in Sydney. They had attempted to set up their own production of the story in 1950 but had subsequently sold their work to Ealing. Harry Watt altered their original 'thriller' concept to develop the idea of a man fighting to prove his innocence before a corrupt and unsympathetic judicial system. His theme, however, was not fully developed, as *The Times* (London), 24 August 1959, noted: 'the film dithers in its attitude towards justice and officialdom, at one moment criticizing, and the next defending

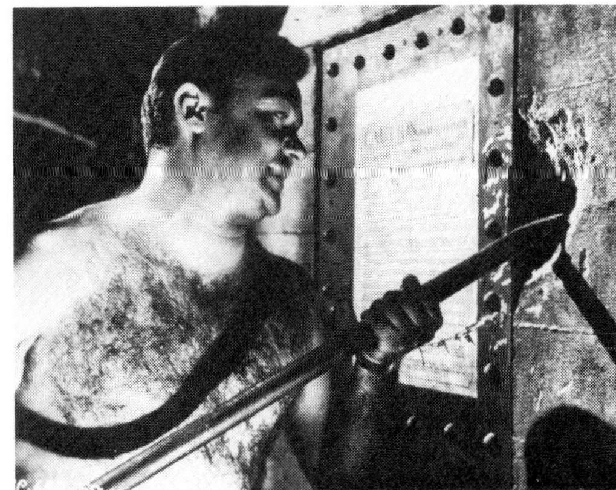

353 *The Siege of Pinchgut* Aldo Ray

them, while the question of Matt's innocence is left in the air'. Watt also intended to present a portrait of 'the modern city and its people' as an integral part of the action, and here he was more successful, with some striking use of locations: *Monthly Film Bulletin,* October 1959, commented that the 'best scenes have a documentary sharpness and a feeling for detail characteristic of Watt's early training and experience'.

Watt returned to Sydney in February 1958 after ten years' absence, and shooting began in November, with substantial co-operation from the police and naval authorities. Equipment was imported from London, and local studio facilities were provided by Southern International. The leading roles were played by imported actors, a fact forced on Watt by the British unions, which he attempted to explain away as an illustration of the 'New Australian' element in Sydney society. The film was a British entry in the Berlin Film Festival in 1959 and it opened in London in August. Distributed in Australia by Warner Brothers, it opened at the Embassy Theatre, Sydney, on 3 March 1960 and attracted little local commercial interest.

The film was the last to carry Ealing's name; after a series of financial difficulties the British company ceased production while *The Siege of Pinchgut* was being prepared for release. Watt next made a children's film for a Danish company, *The Boy who Loved Horses* (1962), then retired from production.

354 Shadow of the Boomerang

1960 DICK ROSS

PC: World Wide Pictures. P: Dick Ross. SC: John Ford, Dick Ross. PH: Mark McDonald, James B. Drought. ED: Irving Berlin. ART D: Dennis Gentle. M: Ralph Carmichael. SONGS: 'Shadow of the Boomerang' by Ken Taylor and Hal Saunders, sung by Jimmy Little; 'Return' by Ralph Carmichael, sung by Georgia Lee. PM: Dennis Atkins, Eugene Anderson Sr. ASST D: Bede Whiteman, Eugene Anderson Jr. SD: Allyn Barnes, John Kean. 98 mins. Colour.

CAST: Georgia Lee (Kathy Prince), Dick Jones (Bob Prince), Jimmy Little (Johnny), Marcia Hathaway (Penny), Ken Frazer (stockman), Keith Buckley (stockman), Vaughan Tracey (Dr Cornell), Hugh Sanders, Maurice Manson, Orville Sherman, the Billy Graham team.

The American evangelist, Billy Graham, had mounted a major crusade in Australia early in 1959. *Shadow of the Boomerang* was a 'Christian Western' designed to show the role played by the crusade in the lives of particular individuals. The story centred on an American brother and sister, Bob and Kathy Prince, who come to Australia to manage a cattle station owned by their father. Bob, unlike his broadminded sister, is prejudiced against Aborigines, but after several adventures Bob hears the Billy Graham message on a radio relay, and overcomes his resentments to become more charitable towards his fellow men.

Apart from a few studio scenes in Hollywood, *Shadow of the Boomerang* was shot on location in New South Wales, mainly near Camden, using the production services of Cinesound. In October 1959, several months after Billy Graham's Australian crusade, the American stars and director arrived in Sydney, and production began in November. The director, Dick Ross, was at that time President of World Wide Pictures, the motion picture arm of the Billy Graham Evangelistic Association. The screenplay was prepared by Ross in collaboration with a Sydney novelist and publicist, John Ford.

354 *Shadow of the Boomerang* Dick Jones carrying the injured Jimmy Little

Georgia Lee, 'the First Lady of Motion Picture Evangelism', and Dick Jones, a stunt rider and television cowboy star, were both active in Hollywood Christian groups and evangelical film production. The Australian supporting cast included the Aboriginal singer, Jimmy Little, in his first film role.

The £75 000 production was given its world première in New York at Madison Square Garden on 9 October 1960. Distributed by M.G.M., it opened as a supporting feature at the Liberty Theatre, Sydney, on 17 August 1961.

355 The Sundowners

1960 FRED ZINNEMANN

PC: Warner Bros Productions. P: Gerry Blattner. SC: Isobel Lennart. From the novel by Jon Cleary. PH: Jack Hildyard. ED: Jack Harris. ART D: Michael Stringer. M: Dimitri Tiomkin. PM: John Palmer. UNIT D: Lex Halliday. ASST D: Peter Bolton, Roy Stevens. SD: David Hildyard. 133 mins. Colour.

CAST: Deborah Kerr (Ida Carmody), Robert Mitchum (Paddy Carmody), Peter Ustinov (Venneker), Glynis Johns (Mrs Firth), Dina Merrill (Jean Halstead), Chips Rafferty (Quinlan), Michael Anderson Jr (Sean Carmody), Lola Brooks (Liz), Wylie Watson (Herb Johnson), John Meillon (Bluey), Ronald Fraser (Ocker), Mervyn Johns (Jack Patchogue), Molly Urquhart (Mrs Bateman), Ewen Solon (Halstead), Ray Barrett (two-up player), Leonard Teale (shearer), John Fegan.

Paddy Carmody is an itinerant farm labourer in the Australian outback. His wife, Ida, and their teenage son, Sean, want him to save money and settle down, but he always manages to elude their pressures. During their travels the family shares many adventures with a jovial Englishman, Venneker: they experience a bushfire, witness Paddy's defeat in a shearing contest, and see their savings gambled away at two-up, the night before Sean rides to victory at a country race meeting. In the end Ida realizes that she cannot change Paddy's love for the free, nomadic life, and the family sets off once again in their wagon.

This American production was filmed on locations ranging from the Snowy Mountains to the semi-desert country near Port Augusta in South Australia. Plans for the film dated back to September 1957, when it was announced that Gary Cooper would take the role of Paddy. Cooper was replaced by Mitchum early in 1959 and shooting began in October. Studio interiors were completed early in 1960 at Elstree, England.

The world première was held on 8 December 1960 at the Radio City Music Hall, New York, and the film was released in Australia as a Christmas attraction at the end of 1961. In

355 *The Sundowners*

Australia, as overseas, the film was popular as family entertainment and received a warm response from critics. The *New York Times*, 9 December 1960, praised the 'romantic, warm-hearted' picture of 'simple, honest people' and found 'a sense of outdoor living and a tingle of open-air adventure' central to the film's appeal.

356 **Bungala Boys**

1961 JIM JEFFREY

PC: Jimar Productions, for the Children's Film Foundation. P: Otto Plaschkes. ASSOC P, ED: Terry Trench. SC: Jim Jeffrey. From the novel, *The New Surf Club*, by Claire Meillon. PH: Carl Kayser. M: Edwin Astley. PM: John Fitzgerald. ASST D: Bill Lambert. 61 mins. Colour.

CAST: Peter Couldwell (Tony), Alan Dearth (Brian), Terry Bentley (Normie), Julie Youatt (Nancy), Ross Vidal (Timmy), Geoffrey Parsons (Buzz), Jon Dennis (Hatch), Max Osbiston (Reg Phelan), Leonard Teale (Sam Taylor), John Sherwood, Margaret Roberts, Jack Armistead, Betty Dyson.

This film was the second made in Australia by the British Children's Film Foundation but failed to win the extraordinary popularity of the first, *Bush Christmas* (1947). In line with a recurring C.F.F. story formula, the film was an illustration of children's initiative in a worthy group effort, with a final reward of community approbation. Brian, a newcomer to Bungala Beach, near Sydney, forms a new surf lifesaving club; after several exciting rescues his club wins first prize in an important surf-boat race. An element of menace is introduced by a gang of delinquents who try in vain to spoil the club's chances of winning the race.

356 *Bungala Boys* Peter Couldwell rescues John Sherwood from the surf

Shot in Australia with local actors and technicians, the film used facilities at the Artransa studios, Sydney. The chief location was Bungan Beach, which Claire Meillon had named Bungala in her original novel, and extensive co-operation was received from lifesaving associations and surf clubs.

The film was released first to the English C.F.F. clubs during the Christmas holidays, 1961-2, and in July 1962 won a prize at the children's film festival in Venice. *Monthly Film Bulletin*, January 1962, found it a 'sturdy if conventional tale' with surf scenes that were 'excitingly photographed in fine Eastman Colour'. In Australia it was released by B.E.F. and screened primarily in children's matinee programmes, after a première organized by the Children's Film Society, Canberra, on 24 April 1964.

357 They Found a Cave

1962 ANDREW STEANE

PC: Visatone Island Pictures. P: Charles E. Wolnizer. ASSOC P: Bertram Wicks. SC: William Eldridge, James Pearson. From the novel by Nan Chauncy. PH: Mervyn Gray. ED: Robert Walker, Alan Harkness. ART D: Robert Ward. M: Peter Sculthorpe; harmonica played by Larry Adler. SD: Lloyd Colman, Charles Cramp. 63 mins. Colour.

CAST: Beryl Meekin (Ma Pinner), Mervyn Wiss (Pa Pinner), Barbara Manning (Aunt Jandie), Anne Davies (Cherry), Christopher Horner (Tas), Michael Nation (Nigel), Michael Woolford (Nippy), Peter Conrad (Brick), Michael Boddy (Sergeant Bentley), Cecily McKinley (Mrs Clancy), Joseph Smith (Bluey).

Four English orphans come to live with their aunt, Jandie, on a farm in the Tasmanian bush. When Jandie goes to hospital, the children are left in the care of the overbearing housekeeper, Ma Pinner, and her sinister husband. The Pinners make the children's lives miserable, but guided by Tas, the Pinners' young foster-son, they run away to live in a cave in the hills. Later they discover that the Pinners plan to steal Jandie's money, but manage to alert the police and foil their plot. When Jandie returns she invites Tas to stay on with the other children.

This Tasmanian feature was the result of a campaign by the Australian Council for Children's Films and Television for locally made children's films on Australian subjects. In 1961 Island Film Services, a Tasmanian company formed by Charles E. Wolnizer, joined Visatone Television in an adaptation of a popular children's novel by the Tasmanian author, Nan Chauncy. Most of the film was shot in the south-east of the state in the summer and autumn of 1961, and interiors were staged at the Elwick Showground in Hobart. Like most of the cast, the director, Andrew Steane, was Tasmanian; he had previously worked extensively with the state's Department of Film Production.

With distribution by Columbia, the film opened at the Odeon Theatre, Hobart, on 20 December 1962, and ran during the school holidays in most states. Although it was not commercially successful, press comments were encouraging: the unusual setting, and a script carefully designed to appeal to children, helped to compensate for stilted acting and a bizarre studio set representing the interior of the cave. The film was later distributed in England by the Children's Film Foundation, and in 1969 world rights were bought by the Australian Council for Children's Films and Television and local distribution efforts renewed.

Part 7:

1965-1977

In the 1970s film-making suddenly boomed after three decades of few local initiatives in feature production. More people began to work professionally in the industry than ever before, making a wider variety of films, and access to the medium by non-professionals was greater than it had ever been. The attitudes of film-makers had also changed: in the 'golden years' of Australian cinema the most successful directors had been guided by their own sense of showmanship, in which their relationship with the local audience was crucial. But by the 1970s television had taken over much of film's mass entertainment function, and most film directors came to their work with a perspective that was not purely local but was related to the movement of cinema world-wide. Film-makers came back from overseas to work in Australia, reversing the tradition of 'talent drain', and a new cosmopolitan atmosphere pervaded the industry.

The revival of feature production in 1969-70 was almost entirely the result of government subsidy and investment. Calls for government assistance went back to the earliest days of the industry when producers first encountered marketing difficulties, and attempts to investigate and assist the industry had been made periodically by state and federal governments, including a Senate Select Committee on Australian production for television; it presented its report (known as the Vincent Report) to Parliament in 1963. The assistance that came at the end of the 1960s was primarily directed towards production, and the long-standing structural problems of distribution and exhibition were left unaltered, although they gradually eased as distribution and exhibition complexes were drawn into production.

In 1969 the Commonwealth government finally responded to pressure from producers and others involved in film and television, and announced a three-part programme of assistance to the industry. The Gorton government promised funds for (i) an investment corporation to assist the financing of feature films and television programmes, (ii) a national film and television school, and (iii) an 'experimental film' fund to facilitate the making of 16mm low-budget films and to encourage new film-makers.

A certain degree of administrative confusion followed as new organizations were established to fulfil Gorton's programme. The Australian Film Development Corporation was created in 1970, and in 1975 re-established with wider powers as the Australian Film Commission. The Commission then became the focal point for the administration of government funds, including responsibility for Film Australia (the former Commonwealth Film Unit). An Experimental Film and Television Fund, administered initially by the Australian Film Institute (a private organization subsidized by the government), also became the direct responsibility of the Film Commission, as part of its Creative Development Branch. Film-makers were also able to receive funds from the Australian Council for the Arts (or the Australia Council, as it became) until the activities of the Council's Film, Radio and Television Board were also transferred to the Commission. The only major new body that continued to function outside of the Commission's control was the Film and Television School, which began operation in 1973 with Jerzy Toeplitz as its foundation director.

State governments also became involved in feature production. In 1972 the Dunstan government established the South Australian Film Corporation to provide investment and facilities for feature films and television series, as well as handling the production of official films for government departments and operating the state's educational film library service. The success of the South Australian model in contributing towards a progressive image for the state, and the major commercial and critical success of its first feature investments (*Sunday Too Far Away*, 1975, *Picnic at Hanging Rock*, 1975, and *Storm Boy*, 1976), soon lured other state governments into the field. State corporations, with powers to invest in feature films, were established in Victoria, New South Wales, Tasmania and Queensland by 1978.

Diversity of sources for feature film funding was improved further by the involvement of commercial distribution and exhibition companies in production ventures. Roadshow Distributors invested heavily in Hexagon Productions, a company that maintained continuity of feature output for four years after the outstanding commercial success of its first production, *Alvin Purple* (1973). The Greater Union Organization also began to support local features with post-production investments in several films, including *Stone* (1974), and their first pre-production investment since *Sons of Matthew* (1949), in *The Man from Hong Kong* (1975). The new commitment of such companies was partly prompted by the same motives that had led Stuart Doyle and others into production in earlier decades: a shortage of product for local theatre chains (especially a factor for Greater Union after 1976); the impact of the economic climate, with inflation in the 1970s forcing theatre expenses up and ticket prices out of the range of family audiences; and the fear of government intervention in exhibition and distribution practices, with an inquiry by the Tariff Board into the industry in 1973. The commercial success of a few pioneering films, among them *Stork* (1971) and *The Adventures of Barry McKenzie* (1972), demonstrated that worthwhile profits could be made from Australian films, and proved yet again that Australian audiences, if given a choice, could show an emphatic preference for local product.

After 1975 the continued effects of inflation and the impact of colour television simultaneously pushed up the expense of production and greatly reduced (by as much as 30 per cent) potential revenue from cinemas. It became increasingly difficult for local producers to rely on the local market to recover costs, and the industry moved towards a reliance on the government not only to provide investment capital but also to carry the burden of the deficit, allowing private investors to recover their capital from a film's first earnings. Taxation concessions for investors were also introduced in 1978.

The new industry found a responsive public at a time of increased nationalism in the early 1970s. An atmosphere of euphoria was encouraged by the Film Commission and others in the promotion of Australian films at home and abroad, especially at market-places like the Cannes Film Festival. Critics who pointed out the emptiness or 'softness' of many of the new films were castigated as betraying a national cause. The euphoria obscured the important fact that the losses of the industry were severe, and that 70 per cent or more of the films were failing to recover their costs. Given this high failure rate, the Australian Film Commission had much to gain by feeding the mass media with publicity that could help to sustain confidence and safeguard the continuity of government funds in the climate of economic cutbacks following the fall of the Whitlam government in 1975.

In re-establishing the industry, lessons that might have been gained from the past were generally neglected. Only a few producers (principally Anthony Buckley and Joan Long) had much awareness of how the Australian industry had once operated. The young people who dominated the industry had grown up since the Second World War, in a period when virtually no Australian films were made, and they had become accustomed to thinking about film only with reference to overseas models. The past of Australian film tended to be scoffed at, without much awareness of what exactly was being repudiated.

There was little conscious continuity, then, with earlier years in the thematic development of Australian film. Many films rifled the past for 'nostalgia', carefully reproducing the material surfaces of earlier periods, but only a few, such as *Between Wars* (1974) and *The Getting of Wisdom* (1977), achieved a sense of historical dynamism and created characters who seemed alive in their exotic period settings. Films with contemporary settings usually had urban backgrounds, and protagonists of a vague cosmopolitan character. Some local film-makers followed overseas models closely to produce films in the style of Chinese kung fu movies (*The Man from Hong Kong*), soft-core sex comedies (*Alvin Purple*), Italian Westerns (*Raw Deal*, 1977), folksy family yarns from the American Deep South (*The Mango Tree*, 1977), and exploitation films emphasizing violence or sex (*The Inn of the Damned*, 1975, or *Fantasm*, 1976).

The most distinctive locally rooted character was the 'ocker', a distant relative of the urban larrikin of *The Sentimental Bloke* and of Pat Hanna and Chips Rafferty, although more extreme in his language and pursuit of sex because of relaxed censorship standards in the 1970s. He appeared frequently in comedies, such as the Barry McKenzie films, as well as in dramas like *Petersen* (1974) and *Don's Party* (1976). A few 35mm films explored more personal or intimate subjects, especially the problems of adolescence, but it was mainly in the low-budget and 16mm films that film-makers were free to explore more rigorously issues of social concern (*27A*, 1974), or questions of spiritual fulfilment (*Solo Flight*, 1975, or *Down the Wind*, 1975).

A sharp contrast developed between big-budget 35mm production and the makers of low-budget films. A few marketing techniques explored in such 16mm productions as *The Naked Bunyip* (1970) and *Stork* (1971) lent ideas to the mainstream industry, and a few film-makers bridged the gap by moving from 16mm to 35mm production, but generally there was little contact between the two areas of production. Most new directors in the mainstream came not from independent 16mm production but from television, and the rise of television drama series in the late 1960s not only provided a pool of trained film-makers but also contributed strongly towards the pressure on the government to revive the feature film industry.

In the 1960s the two main centres of 16mm film activity developed in markedly different directions. In Melbourne, 16mm production centred on a group of film-makers in Carlton, drawing actors and directors from the experimental theatre, La Mama, and influenced strongly by the work of French 'New Wave' directors. Their films tended to be experiments in narrative fiction and contrasted strongly with a heavy stress in Sydney on experiment in abstract forms of cinema. The founders of Ubu Films (which eventually became the Sydney Film-makers Co-operative), especially Albie Thoms, Aggy Read and Dave Perry, drew much of their inspiration not from European commercial cinema but from avant-gardists in European art and theatre, including Marinetti and Artaud, and also experimental film-makers from the American West Coast. Ubu also provided a crucial focus for radical film debate, encouraging a broadened base for the discussion of film as an art form, actively campaigning against film censorship and government attitudes to film, and establishing exhibition channels for 'underground' films, whether politically or aesthetically opposed to the dominant views of Australian society.

In the early 1970s, the availability of government grants for minority films made the 'underground' reliant on government funding agencies; in January 1972 Albie Thoms wrote that 'underground film in Australia is dead' (*The Review*, 22-28 January 1972), in the sense that radical films no longer were made and shown in an atmosphere of clandestine rebellion. Minority groups within the community began to make films as more and more people gained access to the medium. Pioneering women's films, such as *Got At* (1972), produced at La Trobe University, Melbourne, and the work of the Sydney Women's Film Group began to examine sexism in Australian society and other issues of concern to women. Efforts were made to make film and video available to Aborigines and to European migrant groups. The potential of film as an art form also continued to be explored, especially in the work of Arthur and Corinne Cantrill in Melbourne, with an extraordinary series of films about Australian landscapes, a major exploration of the philosophy of the Sydney poet, Harry Hooton, and investigations into perception and the nature of the film medium itself. The Cantrills also contributed persistently to debate about film through their magazine, *Cantrills Filmnotes.*

In documentary film, the Commonwealth Film Unit (or Film Australia) experienced a new wave of enthusiasm after 1970 when young directors, including Peter Weir, Oliver Howes and Brian Hannant, were given opportunities to direct narrative films, beginning with the three-part feature *Three To Go* (1971). The Film Unit, together with the Australian Institute of Aboriginal Studies, assisted the growth of ethnographic film, with the work of Ian Dunlop and Roger Sandall, and later the Americans David and Judith MacDougall in central and northern Australia.

Specialized documentary films were also made for the surfing community by Bob Evans, Paul Witzig and others, and shown profitably by the film-makers themselves on coastal circuits. Occasionally surfing films reached wider audiences: *Morning of the Earth* (1972), by Albert Falzon, with effects by Albie Thoms and music by G. Wayne Thomas, was promoted as psychedelia, and *Crystal Voyager* (1973), by David Elfick, screened widely overseas and was given circuit distribution by Greater Union.

The commercial success of surfing movies was paralleled by other 16mm documentaries made by people outside of the mainstream industry recording travels around remote parts of Australia. These travellers' tales, in the old tradition of Francis Birtles and Frank Hurley, were screened often in makeshift conditions in town halls and disused cinemas in the city and country, usually with the film-maker in attendance, giving an accompanying lecture, selling tickets and operating the projector. Some of these films earned huge profits for their makers, notably *Northern Safari* (1966), by Keith Adams, *Across the Top* (1969), by Malcolm Douglas and David Oldmeadow, and films by the Leyland brothers, including *Wheels Across a Wilderness* (1967) and *Open Boat to Adventure* (1970). Films such as these helped to break down assumptions about exhibition and audiences that had dominated the trade for decades.

By the end of 1977 the energy of the industry had been tempered slightly by the Fraser government's economic cutbacks, and the Whitlam years of 1973-75 looked increasingly like a peak of confidence in the new industry. But although by 1978 the industry was undergoing a more sober appraisal of its direction, the potentials of film-making remained rich and strong. Comparison with any earlier decade of production showed that most of the conditions that earlier film-makers had fought for, especially sympathetic government assistance and access to theatres, had come into existence. The change was not just a superficial one of quantity, but a change of attitude, and the old scepticism of exhibitors about Australian product had been eroded. Only the film-makers were needed to take advantage of these dramatically improved conditions, and as the 1970s drew on, figures like Peter Weir, Phil Noyce and Ken Cameron began to fulfil the promise that the whole industry showed.

358 Clay

1965 GIORGIO MANGIAMELE

P, SC, PH, ED: Giorgio Mangiamele. ASST PH: Ettore Siracusa. SD: Bruce McNaughton. 85 mins.
CAST: Janine Lebedew (Margot), George Dixon (Nick), Chris Tsalikis (Chris), Claude Thomas (father), Robert Clarke (Charles), Sheila Florance (deaf-mute), Lola Russell (Mary), Cole Turnley (businessman).

A fugitive murderer, Nick, finds refuge in the isolated home of a sculptress, Margot. They fall in love, and when Nick is betrayed to the police by a jealous rival, Margot kills herself.

Giorgio Mangiamele began his first 35mm feature in 1964 aided only by a camera assistant and a sound technician. To raise £12 000 for the film he mortgaged his house and devised a co-operative scheme whereby the members of the cast each contributed £200, to be repaid from the film's earnings. With a six-week schedule, shooting began in May 1964, using the artists' colony of Montsalvat near Melbourne as the basic location. The cast was led by a 19-year-old, Janine Lebedew, who had had no previous acting experience. Her voice was dubbed by a Melbourne actress, Sheila Florance, who herself took a small non-speaking role. Background music was improvised by a quartet of university students.

The film attempted to explore the subjective responses of the girl to the fugitive, and through his camerawork Mangiamele created a dreamlike atmosphere that made the development of the story deliberately ambiguous and vague. Early reactions to the experiment were encouraging: in March 1965 the Australian Broadcasting Commission bought television rights for £2600 and in May the Australian Film Institute gave the film two awards for photography. It was also screened at the 1965 Cannes Film Festival. However, when it was premièred at the Sydney and Melbourne Film Festivals in June, the reception was far from sympathetic. A critic in the *Australian*, 19 June 1965, wrote that Mangiamele's 'highly commendable' photography

358 *Clay*

could not obscure 'a truly ludicrous plot and appalling script.' Commercial interest was virtually non-existent, and Mangiamele himself rented the St Kilda Palais, Melbourne, and screened the film there for one week from 25 August 1966. Subsequent screenings were rare.

Born in Italy in 1926, Mangiamele worked in the photographic division of the Rome police force and gained experience there in camerawork and editing. In 1952 he emigrated to Australia and established his own business in Melbourne as a commercial photographer. His first films in 16mm centred on migrant problems: *The Contract* (1953), *The Brothers* (1958) and *The Spag* (1962). In 1963 he made his first 35mm film, *Ninety-Nine Per Cent*, a 45-minute story about an Italian migrant's search for a wife through a marriage bureau.

359 Funny Things Happen Down Under

1965 JOE McCORMICK

PC: Pacific Films. P, PH: Roger Mirams. SC: John Sherman. ED: Lindsay Parker, Raymond Daley. M: Horrie Dargie, arranged by Vern Moore. CHOREOG: Joe Latona. PM: Chris Stewart. P ASST: Leo Clohesy, David Morgan, Jeff Lawton. SD: Jim Davies. 54 mins. Colour.
CAST: Sue Haworth (Teena), Ian Turpie (Lennie), Bruce Barry (Frank), Howard Morrison, Olivia Newton-John, William Hodge, Kurt Beimel, Frank Rich, John Gray, Tanya Binning, and the Terrible Ten: Gary Gray, Rodney Pearlman, Gavan Ellis, Melissa Orr, Beverly Murch, David Morgan, Joanne Mirams, Robert Brockman, Fiona Orr, Robert McKenzie.

This comedy with the Terrible Ten was a sequel to their successful television series, which began in 1965. The Ten, a group of country children from Wallaby Creek, are trying to save their headquarters, an old woolshed, from demolition. Accidentally they discover a formula that makes sheep grow coloured wool, but they have great difficulty convincing adults that their multi-coloured sheep are genuine. Eventually the formula is eaten by the Ten's rainbow-coloured goat, but the story ends happily when, at a Christmas party, the winners of a shearing contest donate their prize-money to save the Ten's woolshed.

The Terrible Ten were the creation of Pacific Films, a New Zealand company that extended its operations to Australia in the mid-1950s. The film was made entirely in Victoria, on location near Melbourne, and in Pacific's studio. A Maori singer, Howard Morrison, was brought to Melbourne to appear as a shearer and to sing several songs. A teenage pop star, Ian Turpie, also sang and acted in the film, as the spoilt son of a station owner. Olivia Newton-John also made her first film appearance, long before reaching fame in the U.S.A. as a singer and actress.

The film was premiered in August 1965 in provincial theatres in New Zealand, and in September it was presented at the Commonwealth Arts Festival in London. Unable to attract a commercial distributor in Australia, Pacific released the film themselves at the Princess Theatre (normally a live theatre) in Melbourne, in December 1966. The company also produced other features in New Zealand, including an allegorical drama, *Runaway* (1965), and a musical with some Australian sequences, *Don't Let It Get You* (1966), both directed by a New Zealander, John O'Shea.

360 They're a Weird Mob

1966 MICHAEL POWELL

PC: Williamson-Powell International Films. P: Michael Powell. ASSOC P: John Pellatt. SC: Richard Imrie [Emeric Pressburger]. From the novel by Nino Culotta [John O'Grady]. PH: Arthur Grant. CAM OP: Keith Loone, Graham Lind, Dennis Hill.
ED: G. Turney-Smith. ART D: Dennis Gentle.
M: Lawrence Leonard, Alan Boustead. SONGS: 'Big Country' and 'In this Man's Country' by Reen Devereaux; 'I Kiss You, You Kiss Me' by Walter Chiari. CRETAN DANCE: Mikis Theodorakis, from *Ill Met by Moonlight*.
P SUP: Lee Robinson. LOCATION M: Jefferson Jackson.
UNIT M: Bruce Bennett. ASST D: Claude Watson.
SD R: Alan Allen. SD ED: Don Saunders, Bill Creed.
TECHNICAL ADVISER: John O'Grady. 112 mins. Colour.

CAST: Walter Chiari (Nino Culotta), Clare Dunne (Kay Kelly), Chips Rafferty (Harry Kelly), Alida Chelli (Giuliana), Ed Devereaux (Joe), Slim de Grey (Pat), John Meillon (Dennis), Charles Little (Jimmy), Anne Haddy (barmaid), Jack Allen (fat man in bar), Red Moore (texture man), Ray Hartley (newsboy), Tony Bonner (lifesaver), Alan Lander (Charlie), Keith Peterson (drunk man on ferry), Muriel Steinbeck (Mrs Kelly), Gloria Dawn (Mrs Chapman), Jeanie Drynan (Betty), Gita Rivera (Maria), Judith Arthy (Dixie), Doreen Warburton (Edie), Barry Creyton (hotel clerk), Graham Kennedy (himself), Robert McDarra (hotel manager), Noel Brophy.

Nino Culotta, an Italian journalist, emigrates to Australia and finds work as a builder's labourer. After initiation into some of the social rituals of his new country, he becomes a firm friend of his Australian workmates. He meets a rich girl, Kay Kelly, and after a stormy romance, they decide to marry. Opposition from Kay's father, an Australian who hates

360 *They're a Weird Mob* Walter Chiari

Italian migrants, is overcome, and Nino and Kay proceed to celebrate with his mates.

A film based on the enormously popular novel by John O'Grady (written under the pseudonym Nino Culotta) had been proposed as early as 1959 by Gregory Peck. It was not made, however, until 1965, when a British-Australian co-production agreement was signed between the British director, Michael Powell, and the Australian theatrical company of J. C. Williamson Ltd. of which John McCallum was managing director. With a budget of $600 000, shooting began on location in Sydney in October 1965. The film was carefully promoted as an 'Australian' production, despite Powell's presence as producer-director, his British director of photography, and a screenplay by his regular collaborator in England, Emeric Pressburger (using the pseudonym Richard Imrie).

The film revealed little sign of the genius evident in Powell's earlier films such as *The Thief of Baghdad* (1939) or *The Red Shoes* (1948). Most of the humour dwelt on the incomprehensibility of Australian slang to the newcomer, and went no further. The relationship between Kay and Nino was 'just a routine women's magazine romance in a new setting' (*Monthly Film Bulletin*, November 1966). But no criticism from the press could erode the novelty for Australians of seeing a home-grown entertainment. After a long 'drought', with no substantial local involvement in Australian feature production for about seven years, the film was eagerly awaited and received much free advance publicity. The film became the focus of a new wave of pressure on the government to provide financial support for the industry. When it was released by B.E.F. at the State Theatre on 19 August 1966, the film instantly drew huge audiences. Long record-breaking seasons in every state contributed rapidly to a gross revenue estimated at $2 000 000 from the home market alone within a year. For British audiences the film was much less relevant and it attracted little attention when it was released in London by Rank in October 1966. Despite the high gross in Australia, the production company failed to cover its costs: McCallum wrote in the *Bulletin*, 13 January 1968, that the producers had received barely $400 000 of the $2 000 000, after exhibitors and the distributor had taken their share and had profited greatly—'a very poor return for the grower of the vegetable'. He deplored the attitude of the theatre chains—'you make it and we'll show it for you'—and pleaded with the trade 'establishment' to show more faith in the commercial value of local product by investing in it. His appeal, and the demonstration of wide public interest in local film, did much to accelerate the steps leading towards government aid for the industry.

361 Pudding Thieves

1967 BRIAN DAVIES

P, SC: Brian Davies. PH: Sasha Trikojus. ED: Peter White. M: George Tibbits, the Wild Cherries, the Loved Ones, Ian Topliss. SD: Lloyd Smith, Lloyd Carrick. 54 mins. 16mm.

CAST: Bernice Murphy, Bill Morgan, George Tibbits, Tina Date, Burt Cooper, Dorothy Bradley, George Dixon, David Kendall, Julien Pringle, Bert Deling, Mandy Boyd, Nick Yardley, Chris Maudson, Peter Nicholls, Sue Ingleton.

Bill and George dabble in pornography to supplement their livelihood as photographers. Business is hard and they desperately need a new girl to pose for them. Bill's girlfriend (the sheltered daughter of a door-to-door evangelist) discovers their clandestine trade and leaves him in disgust. Later Bill betrays George to the police.

Pudding Thieves was the first major achievement of the 'Carlton school': like other films to follow from Carlton directors, it was made entirely outside of the commercial production industry. The film was shot on borrowed 16mm equipment, largely with Davies's own capital and a cast and crew drawn primarily from his circle at the University of Melbourne. Production stretched from 1963 to 1967, and new characters and incidents evolved over the years. Three separate endings were shot before the film was finally allowed to rest. A première was held in Melbourne at the St Kilda Palais on 17 September 1967, and subsequent screenings were held principally on university campuses and among film societies.

Like many of the Carlton films, *Pudding Thieves* was fired by the spirit of the French 'New Wave', and it revealed a variety of conscious styles and intellectual influences from Godard, Chabrol and Truffaut (especially the male friendship theme of *Jules et Jim*), as well as American cinema. Ken Quinnell in the *Sydney Cinema Journal*, Summer 1968, found that the film expressed 'a devotion to cinema' rather than to Davies's 'own ultimate concerns', but it remained 'a rewarding experience: the first Australian film in more than a decade to stand on its own feet'.

361 *Pudding Thieves*

Davies, born in 1938, devoted most of his university career to the Melbourne University Film Society and to editing various magazines, including the short-lived *Film Journal*. He also began making 16mm films, and after several experiments started *Pudding Thieves*. In 1970 he completed *Brake Fluid*, a more tightly structured comedy co-scripted with John Romeril, about a man (played by John Duigan) who has communication problems with the girl he loves. Davies also worked briefly for the Australian Broadcasting Commission in Melbourne, and produced several plays, but subsequently left Melbourne and the film scene to follow a business career in Adelaide.

362 Journey Out of Darkness

1967 JAMES TRAINOR

PC: Australian-American Pictures. P: Frank Brittain. SC: Howard Koch, James Trainor. STORY: James Trainor. PH: Andrew Fraser. CAM OP: Peter Hopwood, David Gribble. ED: Bronwyn Fackerell, James Trainor. M: Bob Young. PM: John Gray. ASST D: Peter Scott. SD R: Lyle Hughes, Rick James. SD ED: Tim Wellburn. 92 mins. Colour.

CAST: Konrad Matthaei (Peterson), Ed Devereaux (Jubbal), Kamahl (prisoner), Ron Morse (Sergeant Miller), Marie Clark (Mrs Miller), Betty Campbell (Jubbal's wife), John Campbell (first child), Don Campbell (second child), Julie Williams (Aboriginal girl), Nukitjilpi (chief), Roy Dadaynga (tribesman), the Arnhem Land Dancers from the Yirrkala Mission.

Central Australia, 1901: a zealous young trooper is sent to arrest an Arunta man responsible for a ritual killing. On the return journey with the captive, the trooper's black-tracker, Jubbal, dies, leaving Peterson to cross the desert alone with his prisoner. Their roles are soon reversed and through the experience Peterson gains a new understanding of Aborigines.

With entirely Australian finance, shooting began in January 1967, making extensive use of central Australian locations. Studio scenes were shot in Sydney at Supreme Sound, whose manager, Mervyn Murphy, had invested in the project. A little-known American actor, Konrad Matthaei, was cast as Peterson, and Kamahl, a popular singer from Ceylon, played the captive. The film was directed by the original creator of the story, James Trainor. Born in Western Australia, Trainor had worked at the Commonwealth Film Unit before settling in the U.S.A., where he became a director of American television documentaries and serials. He collaborated on the screenplay with Howard Koch, a Hollywood writer whose earlier work included *Casablanca* (1942). Despite the liberal message of the plot, the film was curiously anachronistic in its casting of a white actor, Ed Devereaux, in a principal Aboriginal role. This element, more than anything else, dated the film quickly at a time when consciousness of Aboriginal affairs was growing stronger in the Australian community.

362 *Journey out of Darkness* Ed Devereaux

A première, attended by the Governor-General and the Prime Minister, was held in October 1967 at the Center Cinema, Canberra. Subsequent distribution through B.E.F. yielded little revenue, and the film failed to find a market overseas.

363 Time in Summer

1968 LUDWIK DUTKIEWICZ

PC: Arkaba Films. FILM FORM, PH: Ian Davidson. ED: G. Turney-Smith. M: Richard Meale. 64 mins.
CAST: Christina O'Brien (Anne), Peter Ross (her brother), Rory Hume (Shawn), Andrena Gwynn-Jones (Mrs Harper), Gillian Young, Lorraine Irving, Neal Hume, Andrea Adams, Anne Holzner, Ahla de Lazareff, Peter Perry, Susan Tipping, Bill Kay.

This South Australian feature was described by its director as 'a note-book of experiences and thoughts recorded during an Australian summer'. Two stories are interwoven: a young woman experiences her first love affair, while her brother is nearly killed in a car crash and lies semi-conscious with his mind hovering over the events leading up to the crash.

The film was a climax in the career of the photographer, Ian Davidson. Displaying firm control over a wide range of optical effects, he created a timeless, dreamlike setting for the fragmented action, although the fragile poetry of his images was undercut somewhat by stilted dialogue and clumsy direction of the cast. The film was screened at the Berlin Film Festival in 1968, but the commercial trade in Australia showed no interest. A world première season was held on 17 March 1968 at a university theatre during the Adelaide Festival of Arts.

The director, Ludwik Dutkiewicz, was born in 1921 and came to Australia from Poland after the war. He established himself as an abstract painter of some note, and while working in theatre in Adelaide he met Ian Davidson. They first collaborated on *Transfiguration* (1964), a four-minute exploration of Eisenstein's montage principles, with images edited schematically to the music of Bruckner. This experimental short won many awards and led to a more elaborate investigation of the 'metaphysical implications' of sequence structure and image composition in *Time in Summer.*

363 *Time in Summer*

Ian Davidson had worked during the 1950s as a documentary and news photographer, and had collaborated with Stan Ostoja-Kotkowski in a series of short abstract films, including *The Quest of Time* (1955). He later worked again with Ostoja-Kotkowski on a lavish multi-media presentation, *The Oldest Continent—Time Riders* (1970), combining electronic sound and music effects with poetry readings and ballet. After *Time in Summer* he attempted to set up further productions with Dutkiewicz, but they failed to raise the necessary finance.

364 Koya No Toseinin [The Drifting Avenger]

1968 JUNYA SATO

PC: Toei Company. P: Koji Shundo, Wataru Yabe. SC: Yoshihiro Ishimatsu. PH: Ichiro Hoshijima. CAM ASST: David Gribble. ART D: Shinichi Eno. M: Masao Yagi. LIAISON M: Roland Litchfield. LOCATION M: Stanley Moore. PM: Hirokuni Shirahama. ASST D: K. Teranishi. SD: Y. Uchida. STUNTS: Peter Armstrong. 107 mins. Colour. Scope.
CAST: Ken Takakura (Ken Kato), Ken Goodlet (Marvin), Judith Roberts (Rosa), Kevin Cooney (Mike), Ron Lea (Franco), Clive Saxon (Billy), John Sherwood (Carson), Reginald Collins (doctor), Ray Lamont (Sheriff), Mike Dunning (Laker), John Yusef (Duncan), Stan Rogers (Rogers), Tony Allan (Jack), Chuck Kehoe (Ricky), Reg Gorman (Otto), Carlo Manchini (Wayne), Hans Horner (manager), Graham Keating (Wess), Peter Armstrong (cowboy).

The cowboy hero of this Japanese Western is Ken Kato, the son of a Japanese samurai who migrated to California in the mid-1800s. The samurai spirit still lives in Ken, and when his parents are killed by bandits, he swears to take revenge. For three years he rides the West in search of the murderers, and succeeds in killing them all.

Made by one of the major Japanese production companies, and starring one of the most popular of Japanese film stars, *The Drifting Avenger* was a routine action movie, distinguished from others in the mainstream of the Japanese industry by its exotic setting.

364 *Koya no Toseinin*

An entire production unit and two actors (Takakura and an American child actor living in Tokyo, Kevin Cooney) were sent to Australia for the film, and Australian involvement was limited to supporting roles in the cast and to technical servicing (provided by three Sydney companies—Ajax Films, Supreme Sound and Artransa Park Studios). Locations for the American West were found around Tamworth, and shooting took place in May 1968 on a tight three-week schedule, with considerable community support. Interior scenes and the dubbing of Japanese voices for the English-speaking cast were completed in Japan, and in an extraordinarily short time (by Australian standards) the film opened in Tokyo in mid-June. It was never released theatrically in Australia.

365 Moeru Tairiku [Blazing Continent]

1968 SHOGORO NISHIMURA

PC: Nikkatsu Corporation. P: Takiko Mizunoe. SC: Ei Ogawa, Michio Sobu. STORY: Jiro Ikushima. PH: Shohei Ando. ED: Masanori Tsujii. ART D: Yokoo Yoshinaga. M: Keitaro Miho. ASST D: Isao Hayashi. SD R: Koshiro Jimbo. 101 mins. Colour. Scope.

CAST: Tetsuya Watari (Keiichi Isomura), Chieko Matsubara (Saeko Yashiro), Yuka Kumari (Teena), Ken Sanders (Danny), Masumi Okada (Kenneth McVane).

Keiichi Isomura (played by Tetsuya Watari, one of the most popular stars of 'youth' movies in Japan) is a young artist who leaves the pressures of Tokyo for the wide open spaces of Australia. There he falls in love with a Japanese girl, Saeko, but she cannot bring herself to forsake her fiancé, an Australian mining engineer. The dilemma is only resolved by Saeko's suicide, and Isomura returns to Japan with nothing but sad memories of his visit to the 'blazing continent'.

This undistinguished romance by one the principal Japanese production companies was made on location in Sydney, Newcastle and Tamworth. The entirely Japanese crew and cast arrived in August 1968, and even the Australian engineer was played by a Japanese actor. The film was released in Japan in December but was never distributed in Australia.

365 *Moeru Tairiku*

366 *You Can't See 'Round Corners* Ken Shorter (*c*)

366 You Can't See 'round Corners

1969 DAVID CAHILL

PC: Amalgamated Television Services. P: Peter Summerton. LOCATION DIRECTOR, ED, SPECIAL EFFECTS: Jacques De Vigne. SC: Richard Lane. From the novel by Jon Cleary. PH: Graham Lind. CAM OP: Donald Clay. ART D: Bill Wells. M: Tommy Tycho. PM: Geoff Healy. SD: Weston Baker. 98 mins. Colour.

CAST: Ken Shorter (Frankie McCoy), Rowena Wallace (Margie Harris), Carmen Duncan (Myra Neilson), Judith Fisher (Peg Clancy), Lyndall Barbour (Mrs McCoy), Slim de Grey (Mick Patterson), Max Cullen (Peeper), Kevin Leslie (Ern), Goff Vockler (Barney), Lou Vernon (Nugget), John Armstrong (Jack Kelly), Peter Aanensen (Sergeant Quinn), Max Phipps (Keith Grayson), Vincent Gil (Lennie Ryan), Henri Szeps (Peter), Marion Johns (Mrs Harris), John Barnes (Mr Harris), the Atlantics.

Jon Cleary's novel, first published in 1947, was updated for the screen to the 1960s: Frankie McCoy, a 'born loser' from the Sydney suburb of Newtown, is conscripted into the army for the Vietnam war but deserts. In pursuit of easy money he falls into debt to illegal bookmakers at the local pub. Rejected by his girlfriend, Margie, he drifts into a King's Cross discotheque and accidentally kills a girl in an argument. On the run, he returns to Margie, but a gang of hired thugs attacks him, and blinded by blood, he runs into a car and is killed.

The novel was orginally adapted to form a 26-episode television serial, produced in mid-1967 by the Seven network. The film version was produced immediately following the completion of the serial by the same television team, in one of the first local attempts to produce a theatrical spin-off from a television series. Completed for $60 000, the film confined most of its action to studio interiors, with brief outdoor interludes of army training and a tour of Sydney Harbour. Distributed by Universal, it broke records in Perth where the world première was held on 16 January 1969, and moderately successful seasons followed in the eastern states.

367 Age of Consent

1969 MICHAEL POWELL

PC: Nautilus Productions. P: Michael Powell, James Mason. ASSOC P: Michael Pate. SC: Peter Yeldham. From the novel by Norman Lindsay. PH: Hannes Staudinger. CAM OP: John McLean. UNDERWATER PH: Ron Taylor. ED: Anthony Buckley. ART D: Dennis Gentle. PAINTINGS, TITLES: Paul Delprat. M: Peter Sculthorpe. PM: Kevin Powell. ASST D: David Crocker, Hal McElroy. SD R: Paul Ennis, Lloyd Colman. SD ED: Tim Wellburn. 105 mins. Colour.

CAST: James Mason (Bradley Morahan), Helen Mirren (Cora), Jack MacGowran (Nat Kelly), Neva Carr Glyn (Ma Ryan), Andonia Katsaros (Isabel Marley), Michael Boddy (Hendricks), Harold Hopkins (Ted Farrell), Slim de Grey (Cooley), Max Meldrum (TV interviewer), Frank Thring (Godfrey), Clarissa Kaye (Meg), Tommy Hanlon Jnr (Levi-Strauss).

A successful Australian artist, Bradley Morahan, withdraws from the pressures of New York to a secluded Barrier Reef island. In this idyllic setting he finds fresh inspiration in Cora, a shy, nubile girl in her mid-teens who agrees to pose for him. In an argument with Cora's drunken grandmother, the old lady falls and dies, and Morahan helps Cora to deceive the police about her death. The attentions of Morahan begin to stir feelings of love in Cora, and the film ends as she finally manages to open his eyes to see her as more than merely his model.

Michael Powell's second Australian-based feature after *They're a Weird Mob* (1966) was a slightly romanticized adaptation of Norman Lindsay's novel: the artist is a success, not a failure as in the novel; and the Barrier Reef is a more exotic setting than the novel's use of the New South Wales coast. Michael Pate had held the rights to the novel for some years before Powell became interested in the story and, with Pate, assigned Peter Yeldham to prepare a screenplay. A budget of $1 200 000 was provided largely by Columbia Pictures in London and shooting began in March 1968. Apart from a few interiors in the Ajax studios, Sydney, most of the film was made on location in Brisbane and on Dunk Island off the Queensland coast.

The première was held at the Odeon Theatre, Brisbane, on 27 March 1969. Both overseas and local release was handled by Columbia, and the film opened at the Metropole Theatre, London, in November 1969 in a slightly altered version: Peter Sculthorpe's music was replaced with a score written by Stanley Myers, and about six minutes, including an opening art gallery sequence, were cut. The film was welcomed by some critics as a distinct improvement on *They're a Weird Mob*. *The Times*, 13 November 1969, was 'disarmed' by the film's 'extrovert robustness, its elements of very hearty, knockabout humour, its unaffected delight in the Australian scene, its naive, uncomplicated eroticism'.

367 *Age of Consent* Helen Mirren, James Mason

368 Two Thousand Weeks

1969 TIM BURSTALL

PC: Eltham Film Productions/Senior Film Productions. P: Patrick Ryan, David Bilcock Snr. ASSOC P: John B. murray. SC: Tim Burstall, Patrick Ryan. PH: Robin Copping. CAM OP: Harold Koch. ED: David Bilcock Jnr. ART D: Rosemary Ryan. M: Don Burrows. SD R: Russell Hurley. SD MIX: Paul Ennis, Lloyd Colman. 89 mins.

CAST: Mark McManus (Will Gardiner), Jeanie Drynan (Jacky Lewis), Eileen Chapman (Sarah Gardiner), David Turnbull (Noel Oakshot), Michael Duffield (Will's father), Stephen Dattner (Sir George Turnbull), Bruce Anderson (Rex Stapleton), Dominic Ryan (young Will), Nicholas McCallum (young Noel), Anne Charleston (Will's mother), Graeme Blundell (journalist).

By the time he made *Two Thousand Weeks*, Tim Burstall was the strongest hope of many propagandists for a feature film industry in Australia. Born in England on 20 April 1929, he was raised in Australia and educated at Geelong Grammar and the University of Melbourne. In 1960 he wrote and directed his first film, a 45-minute children's story, *The Prize*, which won an award at the Venice Film Festival and instantly established him as a film-maker of artistic promise. He formed Eltham Films with Patrick Ryan and proceeded with a series of short films on the work of Australian artists (Nolan, Perceval, Boyd), followed by a children's television series, *The Adventures of Sebastian the Fox* (1962-63), and another children's story, *Nullarbor Hideout* (1965), made for the Commonwealth Film Unit. Plans for a feature film on Ned Kelly failed to reach fruition. In 1965 he accepted a Harkness fellowship and spent two years in America, working at the Actors' Studio in New York and as an assistant to Martin Ritt on *Hombre* (1967). On his return to Australia he began work with Patrick Ryan on his first feature, *Two Thousand Weeks*. Burstall's wife, Betty, also returned from America inspired by the Greenwich Village theatre, La Mama, to establish an experimental theatre and writers' workshop of the same name in Carlton; the theatre soon proved to be a major stimulus for Australian theatre as well as for some Australian film-makers, including Tim Burstall himself, whose second feature, *Stork* (1971), arose directly from a La Mama production.

368 Tim Burstall

Two Thousand Weeks was a semi-autobiographical film about the isolation and frustration of an artist in the (pre-government subsidy) wasteland of Australian culture. The story presents a subjective view of a crisis in the life of a writer in his early thirties, who calculates that he has two thousand weeks left in his life to fulfil himself. The crisis is both personal and professional: he is faced with a choice between his wife and his mistress, and

371 The Set

1970 FRANK BRITTAIN

PC: Mawson Continental Pictures. P: Frank Brittain. EXEC P: Wilfred Arthur Mawson. PROD CO-ORD, ASST D: Julian Gibsone. EXECUTIVE IN CHARGE OF PRODUCTION: David Hannay. SC: Diane Brittain, Roger Ward. SPECIAL MATERIAL: Ken Johnson. STORY: Roger Ward. PH: Sandor Siro. CAM OP: Calvin Gardiner. ED: Bob Ritchie. ART D: David Furley. M: Sven Libaek. TITLE SONG sung by the Flanagans. SD R: Barry Brown. 102 mins.

CAST: Sean McEuan (Paul Lawrence), Rod Mullinar (Tony Brown), Denis Doonan (Mark Bronoski), Hazel Phillips (Peg Sylvester), Julie Rodgers (Cara), Brenda Senders (Marie Rosefield), Ann Aczel (Leigh Radford), Michael Charnley (John L. Fredricks), Bronwyn Barber (Kim Sylvester), Elsa Jacoby (Baroness Bronoski), Tracey Lee (Theo), Les Berryman, Muriel Hopkins, Hugh Sawkins, Ken Johnson.

'An exposé of high life in upper-crust Sydney', the film had a complex network of sub-plots, most of them dealing with sex. The central story followed the life of Paul, a young artist who is drawn into the amoral world of Sydney's 'arty high society', known as 'the set'. He becomes the homosexual lover of a young student, Tony, but their affair is not happy and Paul attempts suicide. When he recovers, he is reunited by chance with a former girlfriend, Cara, and forgets Tony in a wild poolside party.

The production of *The Set* provided sensational material for the Sunday papers and the daily columnists, but the focus of their attention was not the homosexual theme but the more conventional incidents of the film, particularly a nude bathing sequence featuring Hazel Phillips, a television personality usually associated with afternoon programmes for housewives. Headlines were also made of the return to show business of a flamboyant Sydney socialite, Elsa Jacoby (who had appeared in *The Devil's Playground* in 1928). One columnist, Ron Saw, felt 'the need for a long, hot, soapy bath' after reading the script. Official advertising for the film cultivated the air of scandal and prompted Mike Thornhill in the *Australian*, 28 February 1970, to comment that here was 'Australia's first professional sexploitation movie'.

The pressure of the film's notoriety drew extreme critical reactions when it was released. Colin Bennett in the *Age*, 9 February 1970, commented only that at last his '18-year search for the worst film ever made has ended'. Some, however, saw past the sensationalism to find elements of merit in its unabashed sexuality and open moral stance. Scott Murray, in *Cinema Papers*, 16 February 1970, concluded that it was 'a good film with obvious weaknesses . . . one detects wisdom and sincerity on the director's part, especially in the refusal to exploit or even rationalise, sexual perversion and permissive society'.

The Set was filmed in the first months of 1969 on a low budget, estimated at $60 000. No studio sets were used, and locations were found in private houses on Sydney's north shore and in Paddington. The cast was led by Sean McEuan, a young English-born actor making his film début. Predictably, censorship troubles beset the film: according to the trade press, a dozen cuts were demanded before an export licence could be granted, but on appeal only four words were deleted. It was refused registration as an Australian quota production in New South Wales under the quality clause of the state's quota act.

A world première was held on 4 February 1970 at the new Trak Cinema in the wealthy Melbourne suburb of Toorak. With all its publicity *The Set* attracted some initially strong trading but did not sustain its success, nor was it effectively distributed abroad.

372 Squeeze a Flower

1970 MARC DANIELS

PC: NLT Productions/Group W Films. EXEC P: Bill Harmon, Howard Barnes. P: George Willoughby. SC: Charles Isaacs. PH: Brian West. ED: Stanley Moore. ART D: Dennis Gentle. M: Tommy Leonetti. TITLE SONG: Lyrics by Bobby Troup, composed and sung by Tommy Leonetti. PM: Don Cash. ASST D: Warwick Freeman. SD R: John Appleton. SD ED: Max Lemon. 106 mins. Colour.

CAST: Walter Chiari (Brother George), Jack Albertson (Alfredo Brazzi), Rowena Wallace (June Phillips), Dave Allen (Tim O'Mahoney), Kirrili Nolan (Maria), Alec Kellaway (the Abbot), Michael Laurence (Brother James), Alan Tobin (Brother Peter), Charles McCallum (Brother Sebastian), Harry Lawrence (Vequis), Roger Ward (bosun), Alex Mozart (truck driver), Sandy Harbutt and Amanda Irving (grape pickers), Jeff Ashby (Bert Andrews), Penny Sugg (stewardess), Sue Lloyd (receptionist), Barry Crocker (waiter), Lea Denfield (flower seller), Pat Sullivan (laboratory assistant), Beryl Cheers (housewife), Bobby Limb, Dawn Lake.

An Italian priest, Brother George, is the sole guardian of a secret recipe for a liqueur, Liquore D'Oro, which provides the main source of income for his monastery. To escape pressures on him to reveal the recipe for commercial gain, George travels incognito to Australia, where he finds work in a Hunter Valley vineyard owned by another Italian, Alfredo Brazzi. He begins to produce his special liqueur for Brazzi and sends his share of the profits back to the monastery. After resisting several attempts by Brazzi to discover his secret, George manages to secure favourable terms for marketing it and leaves his friends in Australia to return to the monastery.

This situation comedy was the first in a proposed series of ten features to be made jointly by NLT Productions, a television production company in Sydney, and Group W, a division of the American Westinghouse Broadcasting Company. NLT was supported in the venture by Motion Picture Investments, a company directed by prominent Australian businessmen including Sir Reginald Ansett. Investment was on a major scale and the budget for the first film was $750 000.

372 *Squeeze a Flower* Walter Chiari

As with the second film in the series, *Wake in Fright* (1971), the principal members of the production staff and cast were imported. The director and writer were both veterans of American television series, and the producer, George Willoughby, had produced several other films for Group W in Europe. The main Australian acting part was taken by Rowena Wallace, supported by Alec Kellaway from Cinesound's heyday. Three television personalities, Bobby Limb, Dawn Lake and Barry Crocker, made brief guest appearances during a party sequence.

Studio facilities were provided by Ajax Films, Sydney, and locations included St Patrick's College, Manly, as the Italian monastery, and the Mount Pleasant vineyards in the Hunter Valley. Shooting began in mid-February 1969 and was completed quickly within a month. The film was released by B.E.F. with a première attended by the Prime Minister, John Gorton, at the State Theatre, Sydney, on 12 February 1970, but box-office results were mediocre and critics were unimpressed.

373 Jack and Jill: a postscript

1970 PHILLIP ADAMS, BRIAN ROBINSON

P, SC, PH, ED: Phillip Adams, Brian Robinson. M: Peter Best. SD SUP: Alan Pay. ADDITIONAL SD: Philip Webster. 67 mins. 16mm.

CAST: Anthony Ward (Jack Anderson), Judy Leech (Gillian O'Keefe), Lindsay Howatt (Christopher), Stanley Randall (Stan), Jean Higgs (Mrs Whelan), Phyllis Freeman (Mrs O'Keefe), Alan Higgs (Mr O'Keefe), Gerry Humphries (Gerry), Bob Cornish (television announcer), Gordon Rumph (minister), Sylvia Threlfall (minister's wife), Ray Watts (the singer), Claire Humphries-Hunt (go-go girl). NARRATORS: Rosemary Adams, Jim Berinson.

The long saga of the film's production began in 1964 when Phillip Adams and Brian Robinson devised the script for a series of brief sketches in which nursery rhymes provided ironic commentaries on modern suburbia. These episodes were later merged to form one continuous narrative, depicting, with shades of *The Sentimental Bloke*, the tragicomic clash of two incompatible cultures, as represented by a bikie, Jack, and a kindergarten teacher, Jill. She lives quietly with her Catholic parents and has a mild-mannered boyfriend who takes her to church socials on his motor scooter. Jack rides a fierce, powerful motorbike, lives in squalid surroundings, and expects women to conform to his 'rudimentary moral structure'. The two meet at a church dance, which the bikies gate-crash, and as their relationship develops, they try in vain to involve each other in their own habitual pattern of existence. Jack wants to see *Sexy Follies* but Jill would rather watch Fellini; she takes him to the ballet and he takes her to the wrestling; but she cannot adapt herself to his 'slot-machine culture' and rejects his advances, with tragic results.

In the *Australian*, 30 March 1970, Adams described the five-year film-making marathon as 'an exercise in limitations', both in terms of finance and the technical expertise of the two-man production team. Surviving numerous problems—laboratory accidents, the demolition of chosen location sites, and

373 *Jack and Jill: a Postscript* Anthony Ward, Judy Leech

changes wrought by time on various of the cast members who 'fell in love, went to gaol, got pregnant, committed suicide, divorced and defected'—the film was completed in mid-1969 for a total cost of $10 000. It proceeded to gather numerous prizes, including a silver award in the Australian Film Awards in December 1969 and the second prize in a film competition conducted by the Festival of Perth in February 1970 (first prize ironically going to a solo short film by Brian Robinson, *A Fine Body of Water*). Reviews were also encouraging: Colin Bennett in the *Age*, 6 December 1969, wrote that the film was 'a rough blueprint for a really excellent feature marrying fiction and documentary. Sharply edged, full of refreshing ideas, character sketches and stabbing humor, it comes closer than most to seeing urban Australians as they are.' Despite the awards and the reviews, the film remained on the shelf until Adams and Robinson supplied 35mm prints to Columbia, and it was given general release as a supporting film in a slightly abridged form, opening at the Metro, Bourke Street, Melbourne, on 29 October 1970.

By the time of its release, both Robinson and Adams had moved far beyond being enthusiastic amateurs. Robinson headed the film staff at the Swinburne College of Technology, Melbourne, and had made several short films of his own. Adams had become television critic for the *Australian* and begun a career as a satirical commentator on Australian society and culture. His articles appeared regularly in the *Age*, the *Sydney Morning Herald* and other Australian newspapers, and he also wrote extensively for television, including episodes of the revue *The Mavis Bramston Show*. He was also soon involved in film production on a more substantial scale with *The Naked Bunyip* (1970) and *The Adventures of Barry McKenzie* (1972), and he became a key figure in the development of government support for the film industry. He had earlier been appointed by the Prime Minister, John Gorton, to an advisory committee to assist the government in the drafting of its film policy, and had made an extensive study of the film industries in Eastern and Western Europe and in North America. He subsequently served as foundation chairman of the Film, Radio and Television Board of the Australian Council for the Arts, and also as a foundation member of the Council itself. He was also chairman of the Australian Film Institute, and an adviser to Don Dunstan, the Premier of South Australia, on the establishment of the South Australian Film Corporation. In addition, he maintained a position as partner in a leading advertising agency in Melbourne, and after several years involved in the complex politics of the government arts bureaucracy, returned to feature production with *Don's Party* (1976).

374 Color Me Dead

1970 EDDIE DAVIS

PC: Goldsworthy Productions/Commonwealth United Corporation. EXEC P: Reginald Goldsworthy. P, SC: Eddie Davis. Based on a screenplay by Russell Rouse and Clarence Greene. PH: Mick Bornemann. ED: Warren Adams. ART D: Sid Fort. M: Bob Young. PM: Kit Denton. ASST D: Warwick Freeman. SD: John Appleton. STUNTS: Peter Armstrong. 95 mins. Colour.

CAST: Tom Tryon (Frank Bigelow), Carolyn Jones (Paula Gibson), Rick Jason (Bradley Taylor), Patricia Connolly (Marla Rakubian), Tony Ward (Halliday), Penny Sugg (Miss Foster), Reg Gillam (Eugene Phillips), Margot Reid (Mrs Phillips), Peter Sumner (Stanley Phillips), Michael Laurence (George Reynolds), Sandy Harbutt (Chester), John Dease (doctor), Tom Oliver (doctor), Phil Haldeman.

This thriller revived the plot of *D.O.A.*, a Hollywood film directed in 1950 by Rudolph Maté, about a lawyer who discovers he has been poisoned and has only a week to live. He spends his last days tracking down his own murderer.

The leading players were imported from Hollywood, and Australians filled supporting roles and technical positions under the direction of the American, Eddie Davis. Shooting on the $300 000 production began in September 1968 with locations at Mittagong, Surfers Paradise and Sydney. Australian theatrical release through M.G.M. was cursory. A poorly publicized week, beginning on 5 March 1970, at three Melbourne theatres was scarcely a success. Reviews by the few critics who managed to see it were not enthusiastic and the *Sunday Telegraph*, Sydney, 22 March 1970, noted 'the cardboard characters' and 'inept dialogue'.

375 Nothing Like Experience

1970 PETER CARMODY

PC: Melbourne University Film Society. SC: Peter Carmody. PH: Doug Hobbs, Gary Vaughn, Dave Downey, Kevin Anderson, Norton Bradshaw [Nigel Buesst]. P ASST: Phillip Griffith, Peter Green, Jenny Walsh, Ian McFadyen. PROD CONSULTANT: Kevin Anderson. SD: Lloyd Carrick. HAIRSTYLES: Nigel Buesst. 50 mins. 16mm.

CAST: Bill Garner (the Enthusiast), John Romeril (the Cynic), Martin Phelan (the Schizoid), Tony Rudd and Warren Woolcock (the bikies), Anna Raknes and Jane Washington (the girlfriends), and students and performers including Lindsay Smith, Peter Cummins, Brian Davies, Dave Downey, Chris Wallace-Crabbe, Garrie Hutchinson, Tim Burstall, Nigel Buesst, Rod Parker.

The Second University Arts Festival was held at the University of Melbourne in the May vacation, 1969. Made with finance from the Festival committee, Carmody's part-documentary, part-fiction film observes the reactions to the Festival of 'three basic student types'—the Enthusiast, the Cynic and the Schizoid. Through the three characters, Carmody presents a hectic and often very funny race through the Festival's activities: a performance by the Hungarian String Quartet; a film-maker's seminar at which Tim Burstall and Nigel Buesst speak; the 'Batman Breakfast' in the University Union, where free cereals were provided with screenings of a Batman serial; a plastic environment; poetry readings; dances; and jazz concerts. In addition the film manages to take in set-pieces of narrative in which the three student types are labelled and analysed, and a sequence in which the Enthusiast sleeps with the girlfriend of a bikie and drives off into the distance at the end of the film with bikies in hot pursuit.

The Carlton theatre La Mama provided the three main actors, and the film opened with a long section about student life in a romanticized Carlton, an area of old buildings and Bohemian lifestyle. The film was first screened during Orientation Week, 1970, at the University of Melbourne, and on other university campuses later in the year.

375 *Nothing Like Experience* Rod Parker (*l*), Bill Garner

Born in Melbourne in 1938, Carmody worked for eleven years as a boiler-maker before enrolling at the University of Melbourne and becoming involved in student drama and the work of La Mama. After leaving university he taught in Victorian high schools, and later took a position as lecturer in the history of theatre at the National Institute of Dramatic Art in Sydney.

376 Adam's Woman

1970 PHILIP LEACOCK

PC: SBP Films for Warner Bros-Seven Arts. P: Louis F. Edelman. ASSOC P, P SUP: Arthur M. Broidy. SC: Richard Fielder. STORY: Lowell Barrington. PH: Wilmer C. Butler. ED: Anthony Buckley. ART D: Dennis Gentle. SPECIAL EFFECTS: Milton Rice. M: Bob Young. LYRICS: Kit Denton. ASST D: William Owens. SD R: Paul Ennis. SD ED: Tim Wellburn. 115 mins. Colour. Scope.

CAST: Beau Bridges (Adam Beecher), Jane Merrow (Bess), James Booth (Dyson), Andrew Keir (Sergeant O'Shea), Tracy Reed (the Duchess), Peter O'Shaughnessy (Magistrate Barrett), John Warwick (Lord Croydon), Harry Lawrence (Muir), Katy Wild (Millie), Mark McManus (Nobby), Harold Hopkins (Cosh), Doreen Warburton (Fat Anne), Clarissa Kaye (Matron), Peter Collingwood (Chaplain), John Mills (Sir Philip MacDonald).

In this rambling 'convict Western' set in the 1840s, a young American, Adam Beecher, is transported to Sydney after being wrongfully arrested. His rebellious nature attracts the attention of the governor, Sir Philip MacDonald, who offers him a pardon if he will help to pioneer new land for the growing colony. With the bride of his choice, a fiery Irish woman, Bess, Adam manages to establish a successful farm in the wilderness, despite harassment from bushrangers. Later he helps to build a township near the farm, but opponents of the governor persuade a visiting Crown commissioner, Lord Croydon, to revoke Adam's pardon. Bitterly disappointed, Adam tries to escape from the colony but is arrested; Bess intercedes with the governor, and a full pardon is finally granted.

Although some of the film's colonial officials were modelled on actual people and a few authentic locations were used (including the convict-built court-house and church at Windsor), any sense of historical accuracy was lost in the complex mechanics of the plot. Period feeling was also weakened by the American actor, Beau Bridges, who played Adam in a 1970 idiom, complete with a fashionable drooping moustache, a disrespect for authority and a slick facility with the words and ideals of contemporary youth.

376 *Adam's Woman* Jane Merrow, James Booth (*c*), Beau Bridges (*r*)

Billed as 'Australia's first multi-million dollar co-production', the film was shot entirely in Australia for some $2 500 000, mostly supplied from America. The director, script, photographer and stars were imported, leaving only supporting acting roles and technical positions for Australians. The film was shot late in 1968 and early 1969, mostly on location near Nowra, N.S.W., with studio services provided by Ajax Films, Sydney, where it was edited and recorded. A world première was held in Canberra at the Center Cinema on 19 March 1970, but despite some local box-office success, reactions were poor enough to discourage Warner Brothers from releasing the film widely overseas.

377 Beyond Reason

1970 GIORGIO MANGIAMELE

P, STORY, PH: Giorgio Mangiamele. SC: Oriel Gray, Robert Garlick. DIALOGUE: Robert Garlick. ED: Russell Hurley. M: Enzo Marciano. TITLE SONG: lyrics by Ollie Ven Skevics, music and vocal by Sergio Fochi. PM: John Gauci. ASST D: Ettore Siracusa. SD R: Chris Tsalikis. SD ED: Dennis Wahren. 84 mins. Colour.

CAST: George Dixon (Dr Sullivan), Maggie Copeland (Marion), Ray Fellows (Dr De Groot), Louise Hall (Rita), Ollie Ven Skevics (Richard), John Gauci, Pat Palmer, Robert Henderson, Victor Pandov, Glenda Wynack, Tom Melvold, Joan Hall, Lola Russell, Andrew Gaty.

When atomic warfare breaks out, the staff and patients of a mental hospital take refuge in an underground bunker and are accidentally locked in. The doctors try to organize an orderly existence, but discipline soon disintegrates and the patients, led by a paranoiac, Richard, begin to resist their authority. Believing the sane are responsible for the present chaos, Richard devises a scheme for a new social order in which the sane will play no part. The doctors use tranquillizers to maintain order, but when they are released at last into the outside world the patients rebel and seize control.

After the commercial failure of *Clay* (1965), Mangiamele attempted to improve his chances by using colour stock and professional writers, and by introducing elements of sex and violence into the story. A budget of about $130 000 was raised from private investors and even Mangiamele's camera and recording equipment were sold after shooting to help pay laboratory charges. Shot over three weeks in August 1968, the film was staged primarily in a large underground room at the Royal Melbourne Institute of Technology.

After a long delay, distribution was arranged through Columbia, but screenings were sporadic, badly publicized and financially unrewarding. In Melbourne the film was released simultaneously at two suburban theatres in May 1970, but attracted little attention.

378 Dead Easy

1970 NIGEL BUESST

P, SC, ED: Nigel Buesst. PH: Vince Monton. SD: Lloyd Carrick. 53 mins. Colour. 16mm.

CAST: Peter Carmody (the student), Kurt Beimel (the professor), Anna Raknes (the girlfriend), Peter Cummins and David Carr (two strangers), Martin Phelan (cameraman), Brian Davies and Bruce Spence (two friends), Shirley Carr (woman on stairs), Alan Finney.

A student of criminology is completing a thesis on mass murders committed in Melbourne. With the aid of a visiting German professor, he visits the scenes of historic crimes and using a movie camera and tape recorder they reconstruct the lives of four of the murderers—Frederick Deeming, Norman List, Arnold Sodeman and Edward Leonski. One day the student goes to visit the professor and is in time to see him attacked by two strangers. The professor knifes one of the men and leaps onto a departing train.

Buesst was one of the key figures in the upsurge of 16mm production in Melbourne in the late 1960s. As well as photographing films for other directors, he made several short experiments, including *Fun Radio* (1964) and *The Twentieth* (1966), and in 1969 completed a highly praised documentary about a Melbourne gangster from the 1920s, *The Rise and Fall of Squizzy Taylor. Dead Easy* was a companion film, and it used an ironic narrative context for its four segments of documentary case study. In the cast were two other Carlton directors, Peter Carmody and Brian Davies, and several stage actors who became familiar faces in Melbourne films. Like the small crew, the cast was drawn from among Buesst's friends: 'I suppose it's really just a home movie but I like it that way. We all live around Carlton and spend our evenings playing pool at Johnny's Green Room.' The fictional scenes were shot over one week in January 1970 in Buesst's own flat and on locations in and around Melbourne where the murderers had lived. Buesst himself shot and recorded the documentary segments over a longer period. In June 1970 the film was premièred in Sydney at a weekend of underground films at the Mandala Theatre, Paddington. Later screenings were primarily outside of the commercial film trade, organized through co-operatives and film societies.

Advertising himself as the 'sixth best photographer in Melbourne', Buesst ran a photographic studio in Carlton until 1970, when he began teaching film at the Swinburne College of Technology, Melbourne. Born in 1938, he worked for some years with the Australian Broadcasting Commission and local documentary units before going to London in 1967, where he joined the unit of the *cinéma vérité* director, Alan King. He began work on *The Rise and Fall of Squizzy Taylor* in Melbourne in 1968.

379 Ned Kelly

1970 TONY RICHARDSON

PC: Woodfall. P: Neil Hartley. SC: Tony Richardson, Ian Jones. PH: Gerry Fisher. ED: Charles Rees. ART D: Andrew Sanders. P DES: Jocelyn Herbert. M, LYRICS: Shel Silverstein. SONGS: sung by Waylon Jennings. PM: Gavrick Losey. ASST D: Andrew Grieve. SD: Ian Masters, Peter Keen. 103 mins. Colour.

CAST: Mick Jagger (Ned Kelly), Allen Bickford (Dan Kelly), Geoff Gilmour (Steve Hart), Mark McManus (Joe Byrne), Serge Lazareff (Wild Wright), Peter Sumner (Tom Lloyd), Ken Shorter (Aaron Sherritt), James Elliot (Pat O'Donnell), Clarissa Kaye (Mrs Kelly), Diane Craig (Maggie Kelly), Sue Lloyd (Kate Kelly), Alexi Long (Grace Kelly), Bruce Barry (George King), Janne Wesley (Caitlyn), Ken Goodlet (Nicholson), Nigel Lovell (Standish), Martyn Sanderson (Fitzpatrick), Robert Bruning (Sergeant Steele), John Laws (Kennedy), Liam Reynolds (Lonigan), Lindsay Smith (McIntyre), John Gray (Stratton), Reg Gorman (Bracken), John Hopkins (O'Connor), Peter Whittle (Devine), Anne Harvey (Mrs Devine), Bill Charlton (Richards), Graham Keating (first trooper), Ben Blakeney (tracker), Bill Hunter (Officer), Frank Thring (Judge Barry), Alex Cann (McInnes), Gerry Duggan (Father O'Hea), John Dease (Whitty), Andrew Sanders (Farrell), Jessica Noad (Mrs Scott), Tim Van Rellim and Patrick McCarville (sportsmen), Kamahl (Gloster), Cliff Neate (Living), Brian Nyland (Mackie), Doreen Warburton (Mrs Jones), David Copping (Mr Curnow), Kurt Beimel (Anton Wicks), Jack Allen (Melbourne).

379 *Ned Kelly*

Richardson's Ned Kelly is a legendary folk hero rather than the hell-bent outlaw of earlier Australian films: in a balladic style, the film presents episodes from Kelly's life and links them with song. Kelly emerges as a rebel against an unjust society, and Richardson stresses the social conflict inherent in the legend, between poor Irish Catholics and powerful British colonialists. The casting of a modern-day rebel as Ned was not an entirely successful attempt to develop the heroic theme; as Jan Dawson pointed out in the *Monthly Film Bulletin*, August 1970, Jagger's 'flat delivery and diminutive stature undercut the Kelly legend, without even evoking the Mick Jagger legend in its place'.

Richardson had inherited Kelly from another British director, Karel Reisz, who had long planned to star Albert Finney as Ned and had commissioned several draft screenplays by British playwrights, including David Storey. Richardson eventually wrote his own screenplay in collaboration with Ian Jones, an authority on Kelly and a writer and producer of television police dramas for Crawford Productions in Melbourne. During the long evolution of Richardson's film, rival Kelly projects abounded. At least two Australians, Tim Burstall and Gary Shead, planned to make features on the Kelly legend, and the Italian producer, Dino De Laurentiis proposed a Western, *The Iron Outlaws*, using Australian exteriors and studio interiors in Rome.

With Jagger in Australia and a director who shunned publicity, the film aroused a wide curiosity, and probably no other film made in Australia received so much free coverage in the local media. Citizens of 'Kelly country' in Victoria petitioned parliament to prevent Jagger's entry into Australia, especially since he had been remanded on drug charges in London shortly before his departure for Australia. Not only the petitioners but also a sceptical press wondered at the wisdom of casting 'a puny Pom' as 'our Ned'. The $2 500 000 production by Richardson's own company, Woodfall, began shooting on 12 July 1969 and brought a brief boom of activity and wealth to the main location site around the old country town of Braidwood, N.S.W. Amused locals suddenly found the British visitors offering to buy derelict wooden sheds and paying them to shoot kangaroos and ride horses. Jobs abounded as the main street of the town was covered with dirt, a replica of the Glenrowan Hotel and railway station were built, and extras were recruited for scenes in the township. The bit players also included many leading Australian stage and television actors, eager to gain experience with the British crew, regardless of the pay. Shooting was completed within ten weeks, and the unit returned to England for post-production work.

Released through United Artists, the film opened in London in June 1970 and on 28 July it was given a noisy Australian première at Glenrowan in Victoria's 'Kelly country'. Neither in Australia nor overseas did it attract much critical respect or public favour.

380 Strange Holiday

1970 MENDE BROWN

PC: Mass-Brown Pictures/Artransa Park Films. P, SC: Mende Brown. ASSOC P: Alex Ezard. From the novel *Deux ans en vacance* by Jules Verne. PH: Brendan Brown. CAM OP: Richard Wallace. ED: G. Turney-Smith. ART D: Charles Woolveridge. M: Tommy Tycho. ASST D: Alec Cox. SD R: Gordon Malcolm. SD MIX: Peter Fenton. 75 mins. Colour.

CAST: Jaeme Hamilton (Briant), Mark Healey (Doniphan), Jaime Massang (Moco), Van Alexander (Gordon), Ross Williams (Jacob), Simon Asprey (Iverson), Peter Alexander (Garnett), Michael Berry (Service), Mark Lee (Costar), Larry Crane (Wilcox), Carmen Duncan (castaway nurse), Ben Gabriel, Mark Hertson, Goff Vockler, Tony Allan, Don McNiven, Nigel Lovell.

Ten boys and a dog are shipwrecked on a lush Pacific island. They establish a comfortable life for themselves, aided by a comprehensive range of salvaged equipment. After a storm they discover that another boat has been shipwrecked on the island. They befriend two of the survivors—a kindly nurse and a ship's carpenter—but three other survivors turn out to be cut-throat mutineers prepared to shoot anybody who crosses their path. The children use numerous tricks to drive the mutineers against each other, and eventually destroy them. The carpenter builds a boat and takes the children back to their homeland.

This children's yarn, based nominally on a Jules Verne story, was a low-budget quickie marred by poor performances and frequent continuity lapses. Initiative in the venture was taken by an American company with its eye primarily on the colour television market in the U.S.A. About one-fifth of the budget was provided by the Australian television studio of Artransa Park, in the form of technical and laboratory services. Shooting began in April 1969 in the Artransa studios, Sydney, and on the coast near by, under the direction of Mende Brown, an American long experienced in rapid television work. It was followed immediately by a second feature, *Little Jungle Boy*, and the two films were distributed theatrically by the Seven television network as a unit programme, opening at the Village Cinema, Glenelg, in Adelaide on 28 August 1970. Seasons followed sporadically in other capital cities in 1971 and 1972, and with local theatrical revenue to augment American earnings, both films eventually returned a comfortable profit to their backers.

381 Little Jungle Boy

1970 MENDE BROWN

PC: Mass-Brown Pictures/Artransa Park Films. P, SC: Mende Brown. ASSOC P: Alex Ezard. PH: Brendan Brown. CAM OP: Richard Wallace. ED: Jackie Poynter. M: Laurie Lewis. ASST D: Alec Cox, Dol Haron. SD R: Gordon Malcolm. SD MIX: Peter Fenton. 76 mins. Colour.

CAST: Rahman Rahmin (Momman), Mike Dorsey (Doctor Mike Martin), Niki Huen (Doctor Niki Sung), Michael Pate (the Sultan), Noel Ferrier (Father John), Willie Fennell (Doctor Barney O'Hara), Les Berryman.

Doctors at a research centre somewhere in South-East Asia discover a boy who appears to have grown up with wild animals in the jungle. Attempts by unscrupulous journalists to kidnap the 'nature child' are thwarted, and later the boy helps the doctors to overcome the hostility of a witch-doctor in a remote village, thus enabling them to avert an epidemic of a dangerous disease. Eventually the boy returns to his home in the jungle.

Made immediately after *Strange Holiday* by the American Mass-Brown Corporation and the Australian Artransa Park studios, *Little Jungle Boy* was marginally a better film. Character parts by Willie Fennell as a self-doubting and bumbling medical aide, Noel Ferrier as a paternalistic missionary, and Michael Pate as a humanistic sultan, all provided colourful moments, but their roles were largely incidental to the main action, and the script's sticky sentimentality and verbosity detracted from its potential appeal to young audiences. Much of the film was shot on location in Singapore and Malaysia, with interiors at the Artransa studios in Sydney. It was released theatrically in tandem with *Strange Holiday* by the Seven television network.

382 The Naked Bunyip

1970 JOHN B. MURRAY

PC: Southern Cross Films. EXEC P: Phillip Adams. P: John B. Murray. SC: Ray Taylor, John B. Murray, Phillip Adams. PH: Bruce McNaughton. ED: Brian Kavanagh. SONG: 'Let's make love', music by Janet Laurie, Gerald Lester; lyrics by John Romeril. 136 mins. Colour/b&w. 16mm.

CAST: Graeme Blundell (the market researcher), Gordon Rumph (the computer chief), Barry Humphries (Edna Everage).

A shy and introverted young man is chosen by an advertising agency to conduct a survey on sex in Australia. He is soon adrift in a sea of sexual experience as he investigates homosexuality, transvestites, prostitution, strip clubs, pack-rape, permissive morality, pornography—everything in fact except 'normal' heterosexuality.

Within its fictional framework, the film consisted mainly of interviews, unrehearsed and unscripted, and recorded with direct sound. Interviewees spoke directly to the camera, and questions were later removed from the soundtrack, to encourage intimacy between the audience and the people on the screen. The interviews were conducted with a wide variety of people including Barry Humphries (as Edna Everage), the actress Jacki Weaver, underground film-maker Aggy Read, theatrical entrepreneur Harry M. Miller, the abortion law reformer Dr Bertram Wainer, the pop singer Russell Morris, numerous academics, doctors, moral guardian groups, female impersonators, strippers, prostitutes, homosexuals and bikies.

Adams and Murray decided to make the film after much study of the current industry, especially the fate of *Two Thousand Weeks* (1969) and the extraordinary wave of popularity experienced by 16mm travel documentaries showing in public halls in the suburbs and the country. A light-hearted semi-documentary about sex was chosen as the best means of overcoming the apparent resistance of audiences to fully fictional local products and of winning support for a professional production company. Finance for the $35 000 film was provided largely by Bob Jane, a Melbourne car and tyre dealer, and it was shot on 16mm, a gauge still repudiated at that time by many people in the industry as unfit for professional film making. Both black and white (some of which was later tinted) and imported colour negative stock were used.

Rather than work through an established distributor, Murray decided to exhibit the film himself, leasing theatres directly and handling his own publicity. It was also decided to release the film on 16mm and not to make 35mm blow-ups. Since the exhibition trade had barely ever contemplated 16mm presentation, Murray was obliged to install his own equipment in each hall or cinema he used, and he often projected the film himself or sold tickets at the door. The première was held at the St Kilda Palais, Melbourne, on 12 November 1970, and the calculations behind the film immediately paid dividends: within weeks it was playing simultaneously to full houses in two Melbourne theatres. Murray spent the next two years marketing the film, not only to ensure adequate returns but also 'to research the feasibility of such a plan for the future and as both an alternative and a challenge to the distribution and exhibition monopolies' (letter to the authors, 6 January 1978). The approach of direct exhibition in independent cinemas and halls was followed by other film-makers, including Tim Burstall with *Stork* (1971) and Phillip Adams with his own later productions. The film's profit was also augmented by a sale to commercial television for an unusually high fee, at a time when few independent Australian films were being accepted by the television networks.

Publicity for *The Naked Bunyip* was substantially aided by a censorship controversy that arose before the première screening. The Commonwealth censors had insisted on deletions totalling about five minutes, but the producers refused to cut the film and simply blacked out the offending images and 'bleeped' the sound-track. On the black footage, a caricature of a bunyip was printed, performing a parody of the forbidden action. The censors were even more outraged by a preview that Murray arranged for the press, in which he projected the film uncut, in defiance of the censorship authorities, using lamps on stage to indicate where the cuts had been demanded. The resulting coverage in the media was widespread and contributed substantially to the movement towards reform of film censorship standards.

Murray had gained production experience with the Australian Broadcasting Commission and as an independent director of numerous sponsored documentaries and over a hundred television commercials. He became closely associated with the regeneration of the Australian feature film industry, and apart from his own direct involvement in feature production, he served as President of the Victorian branch of the Producers and Directors Guild of Australia for four years. He resigned in August 1973 to become Executive Director of the Film, Radio and Television Board of the Australia Council, where he was responsible for programmes to stimulate low and medium budget film, television and video activity in Australia. He resigned in June 1975 to take up the first Australian government cultural award in India as part of a cultural exchange agreement between the two countries.

382 *The Naked Bunyip*

383 That Lady from Peking

1970 EDDIE DAVIS

PC: Goldsworthy Productions/Commonwealth United Corporation. EXEC P: Reginald Goldsworthy. P, SC: Eddie Davis. PH: Mick Bornemann. CAM OP: Philip Pike. ED: Anthony Buckley. ART D: Sid Fort. M: Bob Young. SONGS: 'Target for tonight' by Ben Oakland, Jack Elliot; 'Talk to me softly' by Bob Young, Kit Denton; sung by Bobby Rydell. ASST D: Warwick Freeman. STUNTS: Peter Armstrong. 86 mins. Colour.

CAST: Carl Betz (Max Foster), Nancy Kwan (Sue Ten Chan), Bobby Rydell (Buddy Foster), Sid Melton (Benny Segal), Don Reid (Spronsky), Eva von Feilitz (Natalia), Vicki Benet (Tess), Owen Weingott (Barina), Sandy Gore (Marisa Russo), Grahame Rouse (Varitch), Kevin Golsby (the butcher), Penny Sugg (Shirley), John Warwick (Inspector), Susan Jarett (Lydia), Robert Bruning (Karl), Brian Evis (C.I.A. man), Peter Carver (the skipper), Ruth Cracknell (fortune teller), Tom Oliver (coffee shop man), Brian Moll (Father Leonard), Tony Ingersent (Communist guard), Nicki Turner (the maid), Robyn Fong (bellgirl), Jack Thompson (flunky), Peter Armstrong (flunky), Mike Bellinger (second butcher).

A defecting Russian diplomat is murdered in Hong Kong while trying to give his story to a world-famous author, Max Foster. Foster's attempts to find the diplomat's diary bring him to Sydney, with Chinese, Russian and American spies in hot pursuit.

The third and last of Goldsworthy's quickies, intended primarily for American television, was made, like the others, with imported American stars, the same American director-writer and even less specific Australian background. Shooting began in Sydney in July 1969, with Nancy Kwan amusing the local press with her fiery temperament; although given star billing, her role was both brief and marginal to the main plot. Extras to play Chinese guards were recruited from among Asian students in Sydney. Interiors for both the Hong Kong and Australian scenes were shot in Sydney, but in August a few exterior scenes were shot on location in Hong Kong.

The film remained unreleased in Australia until 1975; it was censor-screened in August and, with distribution by Regent, it opened as a support at the Village Twin, Brisbane, on 13 November. With its comic-book action, long nightclub scenes, and an outdated theme (the diary is at issue because it will expose the 'truth' about 'Red' China), the film offered minimal commercial potential and was not widely screened.

384 Sympathy in Summer

1971 ANTONY I. GINNANE

EXEC P: Antony I. Ginnane, Brian B. Davis. ASSOC P: John Caust. SC: Antony I. Ginnane. PH: Nigel Buesst. ED: Elliot Hartley. M: Bill Hood, Beethoven, the Van Winkles. SONG: 'We are none of us perfect', sung by the Van Winkles. SD R: Stephen Vaughan. 88 mins. 16mm.

CAST: Connie Simmons (Anne Benton), Vincent Griffith (Lenny Marshall), Tony Horler (the other man), Robin Wells (the perfect woman), Pam McAlister (Candy), John Caust, Marlene Schulenburg, Leon Boyle.

Antony I. Ginnane, a law student at the University of Melbourne, was 19 when he shot this 16mm feature in 1968. He had been a key figure in the Melbourne University Film Society for a brief and stormy period in 1968 when he produced the only two issues of a montly magazine, *Film Chronicle*. Part of the film's $5000 budget was provided by M.U.F.S. Imbued with the spirit of the French New Wave, Ginnane wrote the script early in 1967 when Godard's *Alphaville* was released in Melbourne, and the concept of the film was modelled on this and other films by Godard, Truffaut and Resnais. The main character is Lenny, a young student whose appearance as an opportunistic womanizer is contradicted by the romantic idealism of his thoughts, which are heard on the soundtrack as a monologue. The film follows Lenny as he recalls his self-destructive relationship with his girlfriend, Anne. The breathless commentary, the 'thought flashes' cut into the action, the vision of Carlton as Bohemian Paris, and the closing moment when Lenny turns to swear at the camera—all clearly indicate the nature of Ginnane's intentions.

Release was delayed until March 1971 when a version cut to about one hour opened at a Melbourne suburban cinema, the Grand, Footscray, followed by screenings around Carlton. By this time Ginnane had helped to establish a small distribution operation in Melbourne, Studio Films, and arranged for the importation of numerous art films (including several by Godard). He re-entered production in 1976 with *Fantasm*.

385 Peter Weir during the shooting of *Three to Go (Michael)*

385 Three To Go

1971 PETER WEIR, BRIAN HANNANT, OLIVER HOWES

PC: Commonwealth Film Unit. P: Gil Brealey. PH: Kerry Brown. ED: Wayne Le Clos. SD: Gordon Wraxall, Julian Ellingworth. 89 mins.

The film consists of three stories:

Michael. D, SC: Peter Weir. M: The Cleves. PM, ASST D: Brian Hannant.

CAST: Matthew Burton (Michael), Grahame Bond (Grahame), Peter Colville (Neville Trantor), Georgina West (Georgina), Betty Lucas (mother), Judy McBurney (Judy).

Judy. D, SC: Brian Hannant. ADDITIONAL DIALOGUE: Bob Ellis. M: Grahame Bond, Rory O'Donoghue.

CAST: Judy Morris (Judy), Serge Lazareff (Mike), Mary Ann Severne (Margaret), Gary Day (David), Penny Ramsey (Heather), Wendy Playfair (mother), Brian Anderson (father), Cliff Neate (Mr Vickery).

Toula. D, SC: Oliver Howes. M: Mozart, edited by James McCarthy.

CAST: Rina Ioannou (Toula), Erica Crowne (Assimina), Andrew Pappas (Stavros), Joe Hasham (John), Gabriel Battikha (Nick), Theo Coulouris (father), Ketty Coulouris (mother), Yaya Laudeas (grandmother).

These three stories on the problems of youth were intended as discussion-starters for community and educational groups. Each story presents a young Australian at a moment of decision about his or her future life-style. No answers are given, but the dilemmas are posed with sympathy for both sides of each problem. In the first story *Michael*, a young man faces a choice between the life represented by his wealthy middle-class parents and the alternative of a permissive pot-smoking group of radicals. In *Judy*, a teenage country girl persists, against the wishes of her parents and boyfriend, with her decision to go to the city in search of a more exciting life. *Toula*, the third story, explores the culture clash between Australian and traditional Greek communities in Sydney, with a young girl from a Greek family trying to reconcile her affection for an Australian boy with the social restraint expected by her parents.

These case studies transcended their functional purpose to become the first major

385 *Three to Go (Michael)*

landmark in the new wave of enthusiasm and energy that swept the Commonwealth Film Unit in the late 1960s. *Michael* opened the trilogy flamboyantly with a film-within-a-film depicting Sydney under siege from young revolutionaries (filmed in the early mornings at Circular Quay with a liberal array of rubble, barricades and smoke), and the scene seemed to be a symbol both of the film's sympathy with the rebelliousness of youth and of the new spirit then felt to be storming the barricades at the Film Unit.

Of the trio, *Michael* was filmed first in 16mm (later blown up to 35mm) late in 1969, and the other two stories were shot on 35mm early in 1970, with *Judy* staged primarily on location in Tamworth, N.S.W. The stories were placed in the hands of promising young talent in the Film Unit, each given his first chance to write and direct a narrative film with professional actors. Under a group title of *Three To Go*, the film won considerable prestige when *Michael* won the seldom-awarded Grand Prix at the Australian Film Awards in November 1970, and critics generally gave high praise to the trio when they were screened together on commercial television in March 1971. Each part was subsequently taken for theatrical distribution by B.E.F. and was screened widely in supporting programmes.

Peter Weir was born on 21 August 1944 in Sydney. His first film, *Count Vim's Last Exercise* (1967), was a 16mm comedy made for the social club of Channel Seven in Sydney, where he was a studio assistant. In the following year he made another 16mm fantasy *The Life and Flight of the Reverend Buckshotte*, and began to direct film sequences for the channel's variety series, *The Mavis Bramston Show*. In 1969 he joined the Commonwealth Film Unit as a production assistant and soon directed a Public Service Board training film, *Stirring the Pool*, from which he progressed to *Michael* and a career as an independent director.

Brian Hannant was born on 13 February 1940 in Brisbane. Working as a teacher in Queensland secondary schools, he taught film-making to pupils and spent his spare time making short films and running the Brisbane film underground. In 1967 he was accepted as a production assistant at the Commonwealth Film Unit and worked in various positions there until he resigned in 1978 to work as a freelance director in South Australia. His other work as director at the Film Unit included Indonesian and Thai episodes in the documentary series *Our Asian Neighbours*, and a feature film, *Flashpoint* (1972).

Oliver Howes was born on 29 March 1940 in England. After graduating in English from the University of Sydney in 1963, he joined the Commonwealth Film Unit as a production assistant. His films there after *Toula* included *Wokabout bilong Tonten* (1974), a feature sponsored by the Papua New Guinea government and filmed in Pidgin with an entirely local cast. He subsequently worked in the Papua New Guinea Office of Information and returned to Film Australia in 1976 to direct the children's feature, *Let the Balloon Go*, and a telemovie, *Say You Want Me* (1977), produced jointly by Film Australia and the Nine network.

386 Nickel Queen

1971 JOHN McCALLUM

PC: Woomera Productions. EXEC P.: Bob Austin, Lee Robinson. P: John McCallum, Joy Cavill. SC: Henry C. James, John McCallum, Joy Cavill. STORY: Henry and Anneke James. PH: John J. Williams. CAM OP: John Seale. ED: Don Saunders. ART D: Bernard Hides. M: Sven Libaek. DANCE NUMBERS: Ossie Sanderson, Raymond Walker. SONGS: 'Go anywhere' and 'Look everyday', composed by Sven Libaek, Adrian Linden, sung by Kerrie Biddell, Terry Kaff. P SUP: Ron Hannam. LOCATION M: Betty Barnard. ASST D: Bill Lambert. SD R: Tony Patterson, Peter Fenton. 89 mins. Colour.

CAST: Googie Withers (Meg Blake), John Laws (Claude Fitzherbert), Alfred Sandor (Ed Benson), Ed Devereaux (Harry Phillips), Peter Gwynne (Andy Kyle), Doreen Warburton (Betsy Benson), Tom Oliver (Roy Olding), Joanna McCallum (Jenny Blake), Ross Thompson (Arthur), Eileen Colocott (Beatrice Whittaker), Maurice Ogden (Ernest Whittaker), Sir David Brand, Charles Court and Arthur Griffith (themselves).

Meg Blake, the widowed proprietress of a pub in a small desert town in Western Australia, hears a rumour that nickel has been found near by and stakes the first claim. A crooked American mining executive, Ed Benson, who had started the rumours to sell shares to gullible investors, thrusts Meg into social prominence in Perth as 'the Nickel Queen'. Meanwhile Claude Fitzherbert, the opportunistic leader of a band of hippies, shaves off his beard and follows Meg into high society and becomes her lover. Eventually Benson is exposed as a fraud, and Meg is left penniless. Fitzherbert deserts Meg and absconds with Benson's grossly overweight wife, in whose name Benson had deposited the proceeds from the swindle. A little wiser, Meg is happily reunited with an old suitor back in her home town.

This comedy, inspired by the mining boom of the late 1960s, held strong local appeal for Western Australians and received enthusiastic community support both during production and after release. Shot in November 1970 primarily on location in Perth and in the tiny mining town of Broad Arrow near Kalgoorlie, the film was peppered with free plugs for companies that helped the production, and hundreds of Western Australians were cast as bit players and extras, among them the Premier of Western Australia, Sir David Brand, and two of his ministers. Finance for the $500 000 production came partly from a Perth syndicate, which included the local television Channel Seven, and partly from Fauna Productions in Sydney.

The original story was co-authored by Henry James, an Australian-born journalist who had worked in England since the 1930s, with occasional screen credits, including *The First of the Few* (1942). The film was McCallum's first as director. Born in Brisbane in 1918, he had acted extensively on the Australian stage and had played the leading role in *A Son is Born* (1946), before spending a successful decade as an actor in England. In the late 1950s he returned to Australia with his wife, the British actress Googie Withers, and became a director, and later managing director, of the theatrical firm of J. C. Williamson Ltd. He was actively involved in the production of *They're a Weird Mob* (1966) and subsequently joined the film and television company, Fauna Productions.

Distributed by B.E.F., *Nickel Queen* was given a rousing world première in Perth on 1 April 1971, and opened commercially the next day at the Piccadilly Theatre for a record-breaking run of six months. In eastern states where the regional appeal was weaker, the film was coolly received by both critics and the public.

387 Demonstrator

1971 WARWICK FREEMAN

PC: Freeman-Fishburn International/Act One Productions. P: James Fishburn, David Brice. SC, PM: Kit Denton. STORY ED: Rae Knight. From the novel by Elizabeth and Don Campbell. PH: John McLean. CAM OP: Keith Lambert. ED: Anthony Buckley. ART D: Sid Fort. M: Bob Young. LYRICS: Ted Ottley. ASST D: David Johnstone. SD R: John Appleton. STUNT CO-ORD: Steven Farrer. 110 mins. Colour.

CAST: Joe James (Joe Slater), Irene Inescort (Marion Slater), Gerry Maguire (Steven Slater), Wendy Lingham (Sarah Wainwright), Kenneth Tsang (Thao Kimalayo), Michael Long (Hugh Prentiss), Harold Hopkins (Malcolm), Elizabeth Hall (Beth), Kerry Dwyer (Robin), Slim de Grey (Prime Minister), John Warwick (Frank Jamison), Stewart Ginn (Superintendent Ackland), Ken Goodlet (Inspector Graham), Redmond Phillips (Sir David Crawford), Alex Cann (Henry Hoffman), Alastair Duncan (Ted Packard), Noel Ferrier (Governor-General), Paul Karo (Charles East), Don Philps (Lloyd), Doreen Warburton (Australian lady), Arnold Christopher (Pakistani), Michael Aitkens (Haler), Joseph Awe (Mr M'waso), David Lu (Japanese delegate), Max Meldrum (TV director), Jon Stephens (Communist student), Peter Cruzado (conference delegate).

The Australian Defence Minister, Joe Slater, has organized an Asian security conference in Canberra. His son, Steven, leads a protest by university students against the conference. Eventually, Steven is beaten and rejected by his father, loses the love of a girlfriend (his father's secretary) to one of the Asian delegates, and sees his peaceful demonstration disrupted by cynical professional agitators.

The film was conceived by its makers as 'apolitical' and most of the characters were from unspecified political groups. The country of the main Asian protagonist (played by the Hong Kong actor, Kenneth Tsang) is ambiguous, and his views, which are supposedly crucial to the conference, are never defined. Instead, the main emphasis is on the 'generation gap' within the Slater family, with a misunderstood youth torn between loyalty to his father and to his political ideals.

Accompanied by much publicity about the producer's wish to re-establish a viable commercial film industry in Australia, *Demonstrator*

387 *Demonstrator* Noel Ferrier and Slim de Grey (*c*)

began shooting in September 1970 on location in Canberra. Most of the film's $300 000 was provided by Canberra businessmen, and the former television director, Warwick Freeman, painstakingly exploited the scenic highlights of the national capital throughout the film. Students from the Australian National University appeared as demonstrators and conference delegates, and the Prime Minister, John Gorton, supported the venture by instructing government departments to assist wherever possible, provided that no direct expenditure was made. With distribution by Columbia, a world première was held in Canberra at the Center Cinema on 8 April 1971. Despite some local commercial success in Canberra, the film was overall a financial and critical failure. Michael Thornhill, in the *Australian*, 17 April 1971, expressed disappointment in the film for its political 'cop-outs', especially after its long promotion as the latest 'saviour' of the Australian film industry.

388 Homesdale

1971 PETER WEIR

P: Richard Brennan, Grahame Bond. SC: Peter Weir, Piers Davies. PH: Anthony Wallis. ED: Wayne Le Clos. M: Grahame Bond, Rory O'Donoghue. ASST D: Brian Hannant. SD R: Ken Hammond. 50 mins. 16 mm.

CAST: Geoff Malone (Mr Malfry), Grahame Bond (Mr Kevin), Kate Fitzpatrick (Miss Greenoak), Barry Donnelly (Mr Vaughn), Doreen Warburton (Mrs Sharpe), James Lear (Mr Levy), James Dellit (manager), Kosta Akon (Chief Robert), Richard Brennan (Robert 1), Peter Weir (Robert 2), Shirley Donald (matron), Phil Noyce (Neville).

Peter Weir's first solo feature, after contributing *Michael* to the anthology *Three To Go* (1970), was a black comedy about a group of ill-assorted people on holiday at the remote Homesdale Hunting Lodge. They include Mr Kevin, a butcher by day and rock singer by night, Mr Vaughn, a neurotic war veteran, and an octogenarian, Mr Levy. All are subjected to discipline by Homesdale's staff and forced to participate in a series of sardonic games about death and murder. The games are devised by Homesdale's manager who proposes that strength to face life can best be found in confrontation with death. Gradually the distinction between games and reality

388 *Homesdale* Kate Fitzpatrick

becomes blurred and the true character of the guests begins to emerge.

The film was shot in March 1971 using Weir's own house in Sydney as the basic location. The total cost, a little over $3000, was partly covered by a grant from the Experimental Film and Television Fund. It premièred at the Sydney Film Festival in June and won the Grand Prix in the Australian Film Awards in November. It was released through the co-operative movement and screened widely in universities, schools, film societies and occasionally special sessions in commercial cinemas. A sale was also made to the Seven television network at a time when very few independent Australian films were being accepted by television.

389 Country Town

1971 PETER MAXWELL

PC: Outback Films/Avargo Productions. P: Fenton Rosewarne. ASSOC P: Gary Gray, Terry McDermott. SC: Barbara Vernon. PH: Bruce McNaughton. CAM OP: David Robinson. ED: Raymond Daley. M: Bruce Clarke. TITLE SONG: lyrics and music by Johnny Young, sung by Bobby Bright. ASST D: Michael McKeag. SD: John Phillips. 106 mins. Colour.

CAST: Terry McDermott (Max Pearson), Gary Gray (David Emerson), Lynette Curran (Rhoda Wilson), Gerry Maguire (Philip Henderson), Sue Parsons (Jean Fowler), Carl Bleazby (Colonel Jim Emerson), Maurie Fields (John Quinney), Carmel Millhouse (Marge Bacon), Brian Anderson (Stan Bacon), Margaret Cruickshank (Doctor Liz), Mark Albiston (Bob Wright), Kirsty Child (Julie), Frank Rich (Georgio Lini), Rosie Sturgess (Anna Maria Lini), Kurt Ludescher (Mr Grossark), Gerda Nicolson (Fiona Davies), Dorothy Bradley (Rose Lang), Moira Carleton (Olive Turner), Stella Lamond (Molly Wilson), Gabrielle Hartley (Maggie Emerson), Telford Jackson (Bert Hammond), Syd Conabere (Ted Atkins), Roy Day (Montgomery), Anne Charleston (Dorothy Atkins), Sheila Florance (old Mrs Bacon), Peter Cummins (first lair), John Lowe (second lair).

This spin-off from the Australian Broadcasting Commission's television serial *Bellbird* was made during the serial's January recess in 1971, and featured most of the regular television cast, although the ABC itself was not formally involved. The serial, appearing four nights a week since its première in August 1967, presented episodes from the daily life of a fictional country town. The film retained the familiar television characters, and involved them in a plot centring on the township's fight against the effects of a severe drought.

The film was devised by two of the serial's regular cast members, Gary Gray and Terry McDermott, who formed a production company, Avargo, with Fenton Rosewarne, an ABC film editor, and Rod Barnett, a chartered accountant. Barbara Vernon, the original writer of the serial, agreed to write a screenplay, and one of the most experienced television directors then working in Australia, Peter Maxwell, was signed to direct. In England Maxwell had worked on many series including *The Buccaneers, William Tell, Danger Man* and *Court Martial.* He had come to Australia in 1961 for the *Whiplash* series, and again in 1968 for *Riptide,* after which he remained to direct numerous episodes of *Skippy* and *Barrier Reef* for Fauna.

With a budget of $70 000 the film was shot on 16 mm with a four-week schedule beginning late in January 1971. The town of Yea in central Victoria served as the main location, but for the drought scenes the crew moved to Wentworth, N.S.W., where shooting was, ironically, dogged by persistent rain. After editing had been completed the newly formed Australian Film Development Corporation provided $15 000 to cover the cost of preparing 35 mm prints.

Handling distribution themselves, Gray and McDermott released the film in rural Victoria and Queensland in mid-1971, with a première in Mildura on 19 June. It did not reach Sydney until April 1973. Reviews from country areas were enthusiastic, and in Melbourne the *Herald,* 9 March 1972, noted the 'authentic ring' of the drought scenes: 'the feel of the film is right . . . a worried family sits despondently on a veranda swatting flies . . . locals gather in the pub and curse "the bloody wool firms" [and] a city reporter dramatising their despair in the press is treated with suitable disdain'.

390 *Walkabout* Jenny Agutter, David Gulpilil

390 Walkabout

1971 NICOLAS ROEG

PC: Max L. Raab-Si Litvinoff Films. EXEC P: Max L. Raab. P: Si Litvinoff. ASSOC P: Anthony J. Hope. SC: Edward Bond. From the novel by James Vance Marshall. PH: Nicolas Roeg. SPECIAL PH: Tony Richmond. ED: Anthony Gibbs, Alan Patillo. P DES: Brian Eatwell. ART D: Terry Gough. M: John Barry. PM: Grahame Jennings. ASST D: Kevin Kavanagh. SD R: Barry Brown. SD RE-R: Gerry Humphreys. 100 mins. Colour.

CAST: Jenny Agutter (girl), Lucien John (brother), David Gulpilil (Aboriginal), John Meillon (father), Peter Carver (no-hoper), John Illingsworth (husband), Barry Donnelly (Australian scientist), Noelene Brown (German scientist), Carlo Manchini (Italian scientist).

Overwhelmed by pressures in the city, a father drives his children into the desert and tries to kill them before shooting himself. The 14-year-old girl and 6-year-old boy wander aimlessly until they meet an Aboriginal boy who is on a solitary walkabout as part of his tribal initiation into manhood. The three become travelling companions and gradually sexual tension grows between the girl and the Aboriginal. When they approach white civilization and the trek nears its end, the Aboriginal dances a night-long courtship dance, but the girl refuses to acknowledge its meaning. In the morning she finds his decorated corpse hanging from a tree. Continuing their journey, the children arrive at a mining town where they find a cool reception from the inhabitants.

An 'epic poem' of an odyssey through a strange land, *Walkabout* painted its characters in broad, mythic terms. The city is a disorienting jangle of noise and pollution and its people faceless and corrupted. The Aboriginal boy, by contrast, is a noble innocent, falling victim to a girl whose freedom to respond to her own natural urges has been limited by her urban upbringing. The otherworldly sounds of a music collage on the sound-track (Stockhausen, Rod Stewart and others), violent colours in the landscapes, and constant visual reference to exotic animal life, reinforce the strangeness of the land through which the children wander. Reactions to the film varied widely: some were made uneasy by the intense romanticism and wilful thematic naïvety, while others applauded it as 'a paean to nature's infinite variety and infinite menace' (*Monthly Film Bulletin*, November 1971) and as 'a modern parable of survival and loss in cinematic blank verse' (*Sydney Morning Herald*, 20 December 1971).

Walkabout was the second feature directed by the British cinematographer, Nicolas Roeg. His first, *Performance* (1970), with Mick Jagger, remained banned in Australia until 1973. Roeg had long planned to film *Walkabout*, but it was not until the British playwright Edward Bond rewrote Roeg's screenplay that the project gained the backing of two American businessmen, Raab and Litvinoff. Their production company was incorporated in Australia, but the budget of over $1 000 000 was raised entirely from American sources. World rights were subsequently sold to Twentieth Century-Fox. Location shooting began in Sydney in August 1969 and the unit later moved to a base at Alice Springs. The leading roles were taken by the teenage British actress, Jenny Agutter, one of Roeg's sons, Lucien John, and David Gulpilil, an Aboriginal from Arnhem Land, born in 1953, who had toured overseas in an Aboriginal dancing troupe before *Walkabout*, and who later appeared in episodes of the television series *Boney* and *Homicide*, as well as several films. *Walkabout* was released by Twentieth Century-Fox in America in June, and in Australia in October, but did not fare well commercially.

391 **Wake in Fright**

1971 TED KOTCHEFF

PC: NLT Productions/Group W Films. EXEC P: Bill Harmon, Howard Barnes. P: George Willoughby. ASSOC P: Maurice Singer. SC: Evan Jones. From the novel by Kenneth Cook. PH: Brian West. CAM OP: John McLean. ED: Anthony Buckley. ART D: Dennis Gentle. M: John Scott. LOCATION M: John Shaw. ASST D: Howard Rubie. SD R: John Appleton. SD ED: Tim Wellburn. 109 mins. Colour.

CAST: Gary Bond (John Grant), Donald Pleasence (Doc Tydon), Chips Rafferty (Jock Crawford), Sylvia Kay (Janette Hynes), Jack Thompson (Dick), Peter Whittle (Joe), Al Thomas (Tim Hynes), John Meillon (Charlie), John Armstrong (Atkins), Slim de Grey (Jarvis), Maggie Dence (receptionist), Norman Erskine (Joe the cook), Buster Fiddess (Charlie Jones), Tex Foote (Stubbs), Owen Moase (first controller), John Dalleen (second controller), Colin Hughes (stockman), Jacko Jackson (van driver), Nancy Knudsen (Robyn), Dawn Lake (Joyce), Harry Lawrence (Higgins), Robert McDarra (Pig Eyes), Carlo Manchini (poker player), Liam Reynolds (miner).

John Grant is an English teacher in an outback school. On his way to the Sydney beaches for a holiday, he stops at a pub in the rough mining town of Bundanyabba, loses his money in a two-up game and finds himself stranded. Gradually he is overwhelmed by the nightmare of life in 'the Yabba', especially the perpetual beery stupor of the iocals and their insistent and claustrophobic 'mateship'. In despair, after participating in a violent kangaroo hunt and being homosexually assaulted by an alcoholic doctor, Grant is driven to shoot himself in attempted suicide. By the time his wound heals his holidays are over, and resigning himself to life in the outback, he returns to his isolated school in the desert.

Wake in Fright was the second and last product of the Australian-American alliance between NLT and Group W. The novel by Kenneth Cook had been published in 1961 and had first been proposed as a film in 1963 by Dirk Bogarde and Joseph Losey. The novelist Morris West later bought the film rights for his own projected production, but again no film emerged. Eventually the rights were bought by NLT and Group W, and with a budget of $800 000, shooting began in January 1970. A month was spent on location in Broken Hill, the town that had originally inspired Cook as the setting for his novel. Interiors were shot in Sydney, mostly at the Ajax studios, Bondi. The director was Ted Kotcheff, a Canadian who had worked in England from the late 1950s producing television plays and occasional feature films, most notably *Two Gentlemen Sharing* (1969).

391 *Wake in Fright* Gary Bond

Early in 1971 United Artists acquired the film for world distribution and on 22 July, under the title of *Outback*, it opened in Paris and ran for a highly successful five month season. In London again it was warmly received by the public and the press when it opened (as *Outback*) at the Pavilion on October 29. In Australia, however, it made less happy progress; although critics were unanimous in their support, publicity was poor and the public stayed away. After mediocre seasons in Brisbane and Sydney, Bill Harmon, one of the film's executive producers, went to the press with criticism of the half-hearted way in which United Artists had promoted the film: in the *Australian*, 23 October 1971, he accused U.A. of 'treating it like nothing ... It almost seems nobody wants anything to succeed here.'

392 And the Word was Made Flesh

1971 DUSAN MAREK

P, SC, PH, ED: Dusan Marek. M: Robert Pendlebury. SD: Robert Pendlebury, Bob Allen. 65 mins. 16mm.
CAST: David Stocker, Christine Pearce, Jan Cernohous, David Tiley, Jo Van Dalen, John Kirk.

This experimental narrative presents a series of surrealist actions: a scientist finds a cocoon from which emerges an ideal woman; she is menaced by two faceless monsters collecting specimens for a museum; and she is hunted by a killer while she and the scientist make love in a sea of sand.

Marek described his theme as a man's attempt to 'retain his inside freedom . . . and not be moulded by the outside'. Throughout the film, time is manipulated freely, often with reverse actions, repetitions and a flow of images designed as 'a musical composition' to be perceived and enjoyed 'instinctively' by the audience without explanations from the film-maker. 'People should be free to experience it without any interference from the filmmaker and from themselves because they destroy their contact by asking questions, they do damage to their perception' (*Cantrills Filmnotes*, October 1971). Made in association with students from Flinders University, Adelaide, and with finance from the Experimental Film and Television Fund, the film was shown in August 1971 during a festival of work by Australian independent film-makers in Sydney, and was released primarily through the co-operative movement.

Marek was born in Czechoslovakia in 1926 and studied art in Prague. He migrated to Australia in 1948 and quickly made a name as a surrealist painter, with one-man exhibitions in Adelaide, Sydney and Port Moresby. Apart from five years in Papua New Guinea (1954-59), he worked primarily in Adelaide until 1973, when he moved to Hobart to lecture in art at the Tasmanian College of Advanced Education. Using film as an extension of his painting, he made several puppet films in the 1950s, and in 1962 made a short animated film, *Adam and Eve*, 'a story of man from creation to the bomb'. This 16mm film won several awards and was shown widely in Australia and abroad. In 1966 he began work on his first feature-length film, *Cobweb on a Parachute*, and although it was shot (on 35mm colour), edited and recorded, release prints were never made because of a disagreement with his backers.

392 *And the Word Was Made Flesh*

393 Bonjour Balwyn

1971 NIGEL BUESST

P: Nigel Buesst. SC: John Romeril, Nigel Buesst, John Duigan. PH: Tom Cowan. ED: Peter Tammer, Nigel Buesst. M: Carrl and Janie Myriad, Mike Deany. SD: Lloyd Carrick. 59 mins. 16mm.

CAST: John Duigan (Kevin Agar), Peter Cummins (TV repairman), John Romeril (Alan), Patricia Condon (secretary), Barbara Stephens (Christine), Reg Newson (theatrical producer), Camilla Rowntree (Rhonda), Marcel Cugola, Jim Nicholas, Alan Finney, Peter Carmody, Geoff Gardner.

Kevin Agar is the idealistic and disorganized editor of *Bolo*, a magazine with limited circulation. The film traces his attempts to stave off the inevitable crash as creditors close in and his personal life goes awry. On the way, the film reveals an affectionate portrait of Melbourne, from the brittle middle-class home of Kevin's parents in Balwyn to the comfortable poverty of the Carlton terrace houses of his friends.

393 *Bonjour Balwyn* John Duigan

The film is rich in incident and benefits from a tight and witty script written partly by the Melbourne playwright John Romeril (who appears as one of Kevin's friends). Especially notable are Kevin's interview with an elderly theatrical producer who is conducting auditions for a nude show; a visit to the Saturday night trotting races where Kevin is pestered by a surly thug to whom he owes money; and above all the fast-paced sequence that closes the film, when Kevin nervously starts to earn a living as a con man, using subterfuge to repossess electrical goods. John Duigan (who later directed his own features) plays Kevin as a truculent 'egomaniac in a jam', but it is Peter Cummins who steals the film in the last few minutes as the seedy television repairman who employs Kevin in his petty criminal activities.

Made cheaply on 16mm with assistance from the Experimental Film and Television Fund, the film was screened at the Melbourne Co-op Cinema in October 1971. Although occasional commercial screenings were successful (for example in Canberra on 29 April 1973), the film was not widely seen outside Melbourne.

394 Stockade

1971 HANS POMERANZ

PC: Spectrum Film Producers. P: Hans Pomeranz. DIRECTOR OF ACTING: Ross McGregor. SC: Kenneth Cook. PH: Oscar Scherl. ED: Ronda MacGregor. M: Michael Caulfield, Jack Grimsley, Max Hynam; words and traditional music arranged by Kenneth Cook and Patricia Cook. SD: Barry Brown. STUNT CO-ORD: Peter Armstrong. 90 mins. Colour. 16mm.

CAST: Michelle Fawdon (Elizabeth Green), Rod Mullinar (Peter Lalor), Graham Corry (George Black), Sue Hollywood (Ma Bentley), Charles Thorne (Captain Thomas), Norman Willison (Johnny), Max Cullen (Rafaello Carboni), Michael Rolfe (Captain Wise).

Stockade began as a musical play detailing, with reasonable historical accuracy, the events at the Eureka Stockade when rebellious miners fought against government regulation of the goldfields in Ballarat in 1854. It was the first play by Kenneth Cook (whose novel, *Wake in Fright*, was already a film), commissioned by the New South Wales Drama Foundation and first performed in March 1971 at the Independent Theatre, Sydney.

The film version closely followed the Independent Theatre production, retaining the play's producer, Ross McGregor, as 'director of acting' and most of the original cast. In May 1971, immediately after the close of the play's Sydney season, shooting began with a very short two-week schedule in the ready-made colonial setting of the Australiana Village, Wilberforce, near Sydney. The production, in 16mm, was aided by two government subsidies, one of $15 000 from the Australian Council for the Arts, and another of $16 000 from the new Australian Film Development Corporation. The total cost was over $90 000.

The film's producer-director, Hans Pomeranz, had come to Australia in 1954 from the Netherlands. After working with the Australian Broadcasting Commission on current affairs programmes, he formed his own company, Spectrum Film Producers, in 1963, and produced numerous sponsored documentaries and television commercials.

394 *Stockade* Max Cullen (*centre l*), Rod Mullinar (*centre r*)

Critics were generally hostile to his first feature; Sylvia Lawson, for example, in the *Australian*, 14 December 1971, wrote that it 'took extraordinarily little advantage of much inherently dramatic history'.

Stockade was of far greater strategic importance in the political struggles of the film industry than it was intrinsically as a film. As the first feature to receive financial aid from the government, it was exposed to much public and political attention. In December 1971, the Liberal M.P. for Ballarat, Dudley Erwin, deplored the use of government money to produce a film with 'immoral content' (referring primarily to the film's brothel scenes) and called for it to be withdrawn from circulation. A far more serious controversy arose over the failure of the film to find a distributor. Kenneth Cook and Hans Pomeranz drew attention to the regulations governing the production and exhibition of films in New South Wales: the state government refused to enforce its old quota for Australian films, but at the same time enforced regulations that prohibited public screenings in unlicensed halls, thereby preventing Australian producers from finding any alternative to the established film exhibition trade. The struggle attracted a great deal of media coverage, and public interest reached a climax when Pomeranz issued a formal demand to the Chief Secretary, Eric Willis, for an inquiry into the New South Wales industry. Their role as 'film-producing David against the Goliaths of the film trade' was weakened, however, when the film was finally released, and the trade was vindicated in its claim that had the film been any good they would have been glad to handle it. Cook and Pomeranz withdrew from the public arena and the issue lapsed. The regulations remained unaltered by the storm, but the public had become more acutely aware of their inconsistencies.

After a preview on 3 December 1971 in Ballarat (on the 117th anniversary of the Stockade incident), Cook and Pomeranz launched the film themselves on 9 December in an independent suburban theatre in Sydney. Further theatrical screenings were rare, but the demand for the film from schools was strong, and it was later shown on television in an abridged form.

395 Stork

1971 TIM BURSTALL

PC: Tim Burstall and Associates/Bilcock and Copping Film Productions. P: Tim Burstall. SC: David Williamson, from his play *The Coming of Stork*. PH: Robin Copping. ED: Edward McQueen-Mason. ART D: Leslie Binns. M: Hans Poulsen. ASST D: Ross Dimsey. SD R: Ron Green. SD RE-R: Alan Allen, Julian Nathan. 90 mins. Colour.

CAST: Bruce Spence (Graham 'Stork' Wallace), Graeme Blundell (Westy), Sean McEuan (Tony), Helmut Bakaitis (Clyde), Jacki Weaver (Anna), Peter Green (clergyman), Madeleine Orr (Stork's mother), Peter Cummins (sculptor), Michael Duffield (judge), Alan Finney (tailor), Robin Copping and David Bilcock Jnr (explorers), Larry Stevens (farmer), Nanette Good (farmer's wife), Kerry Dwyer (nun), Brendan Cassidy (gallery manager), Lynne Flanagan (matron), George Whaley (businessman), Jan Friedl (women's libber), Dennis Miller (university lecturer), Terry Norris (Anna's father), Max Gillies (Uncle Jack), the Captain Matchbox Whoopee band.

Tim Burstall's second feature was a broad comedy about a would-be revolutionary whose height (6 feet 7 inches), hypochondria and sexual hang-ups make him vulnerable to the world. The film episodically follows his 'Walter Mitty' dreams of revolution and his anarchistic encounters with most of the sacred cows of contemporary Australian society: women's liberation, avant-garde art, alternative life-styles, Australian rules football, trade unions, Toorak high society and university education. After being sacked by General Motors-Holden's for doing a strip-tease at work, he descends on the flat of two young 'trendies', Clyde and Tony, who are sharing the same girlfriend, Anna. After disrupting their lives, Stork loses his virginity to Anna and becomes infatuated with her. Later Anna announces that she is pregnant and Clyde decides to marry her. Objecting to the marriage as a sop to suburban moral convention, Stork proceeds to make sure that the wedding is a riot and that he is taken along on the honeymoon.

Williamson's play belonged aggressively to Melbourne, especially to Carlton, and was first performed there in 1970 at Betty Burstall's experimental theatre, La Mama.

395 *Stork* Bruce Spence

The film version, adapted by Williamson himself, was shot in Melbourne in March and April 1971 using 16mm film stock and a small crew of twelve technicians. The total cost was kept to around $70 000, with only $7000 of government subsidy, from the Experimental Film and Television Fund. To attract a viable distribution deal, Burstall and his associates initially released the film themselves at the St Kilda Palais, Melbourne, on 27 December 1971, where it ran for a highly rewarding six-week season. Distribution was subsequently arranged through Roadshow, and the film proceeded to play widely throughout Australia, using 35mm prints blown up from the 16mm original. Reviews were far more positive than for Burstall's first feature, *Two Thousand Weeks* (1969), and Colin Bennett (*Age*, 24 December 1971) gave the film strong support as a 'very funny entertainment—hilariously coarse, unashamedly vulgar'.

The role of Stork was played by the New Zealand actor Bruce Spence, who had come to Australia in the late 1960s and had become an active member of the Australian Performing Group at La Mama and later at the Pram Factory in Melbourne, as both actor and director. His performance, and Jacki Weaver's as Anna, were acknowledged in the 1972 Australian Film Awards, where they shared the Hoyts prize for acting. A $5000 prize from the Australian Film Development Corporation for best narrative feature, and a $1000 prize for best direction, were among several other awards won by the film at the same time.

Advertising played down the film's Australian origin, on the basis of market research findings that Australian films were generally distrusted by the public. Nevertheless, its commercial success was taken widely as a demonstration that low-budget features could be made and sold profitably in Australia. Its significance in providing a lead for other producers, and in stimulating production investment, was equivalent in many ways to the stimulus provided by *On Our Selection* in 1932. For Burstall personally, the film restored his credibility in the commercial trade after the failure of *Two Thousand Weeks*, and in mid-1972 the production company of Hexagon arose directly from his association with Roadshow in the release of *Stork*.

396 Bello Onesto Emigrato Australia Sposerebbe Compaesana Illibata [Girl in Australia]

1971 LUIGI ZAMPA

PC: Documento Film. EXEC P: Fausto Saraceni. P: Gianni Hecht Lucari. SC: Rodolfo Sonego, Luigi Zampa. STORY: Rodolfo Sonego. PH: Aldo Tonti. ED: Mario Morra. ART D: Flavio Mogherini. M: Piero Piccioni. PM: Romano Dandi. UNIT M: John Shaw. SD: Massimo Loffredi, Robert Peck. 114 mins. Colour.

CAST: Alberto Sordi (Amedeo), Claudia Cardinale (Carmella), Riccardo Garrone (Giuseppe), Corrado Olmi, Angelo Infanti, Elli Maclure, Joe Sofia, Betty Lucas, Fred Cullen, Noel Ferrier, Paul Kamsler, Frank Martorella, Roger Cox.

Amedeo is a lonely middle-aged linesman in a small settlement in the desert near Broken Hill. Desperate for a wife, he sends the photo of a handsome friend to an Italian girl, Carmella, and pays for her fare to Australia, hoping that he can entice her into marriage. Carmella has also been deceiving Amedeo: she is not the simple country girl he believes, but a spirited Roman prostitute eager to escape the clutches of her pimp. When she arrives in Australia, Amedeo is overwhelmed by her beauty and cannot bring himself to reveal his true identity. Only after many adventures and misunderstandings on the long journey to Broken Hill do Amedeo and Carmella come to accept each other in their true guise.

Made by Italians for Italians, *Girl in Australia* manages to say far more about the life of migrants in Australia than the hybrid *They're a Weird Mob* (1966). The loneliness of Italian men in Australian working-class society, their reluctance to look for wives among Australian women (who are regarded as too independent), and their self-sacrifice over long periods to save money for an uncertain future happiness, are all themes central to the screenplay of this film. At the same time the film is essentially an assembly-line production with persistent, bland music, and a tendency to belabour the most obvious points. The film also lacked any sense of geographical consistency, and the route followed by Amedeo and Carmella from Sydney to Broken Hill takes them through dense tropical jungle and past Ayers Rock.

Shot in Australia in February and March 1971, and recorded in Italy, the film was released in December 1971 in Rome, and in mid-1972 in Australia with English subtitles. Its Australian distributor, Columbia Pictures, restricted most screenings to Italian cinemas in the major cities, presumably fearing the reaction of Australian audiences to the film's geography and to the anomaly of local actors such as Noel Ferrier speaking fluent Italian.

397 A City's Child

1972 BRIAN KAVANAGH

PC: Kavanagh Productions. P, STORY, ED: Brian Kavanagh. SC: Don Battye. PH: Bruce McNaughton. ART D: Trevor Ling. M: Peter Pinne. PM: Rhonda Finlayson. SD: Wally Shaw. 80 mins. Colour.

CAST: Monica Maughan (the woman), Sean Scully (the man), Moira Carleton (the mother), Vivean Gray (first neighbour), Marguerite Lofthouse (second neighbour), Beverley Heath (shopgirl), Michael Howell (doctor), Roger Scales (man on beach), Donna Drake (girl on beach), Mary Marshall (woman on train).

The problem of loneliness in a large city is explored in this story of an unloved spinster who drifts into a fantasy world after the death of her dominating invalid mother. Living alone in her suburban house, the woman collects dolls, which become central to her fantasies. One day she meets a young man, who may or may not be real. He becomes her lover and lives with her, until one morning she finds he has gone. She returns to her drab existence but is now even closer to her imaginary world.

The director, Brian Kavanagh, had previously directed and edited many industrial documentaries and commercials. For the cast of his first feature he chose Monica Maughan, a Melbourne stage and television actress, and Sean Scully, who had acted as a child in several Walt Disney films, including *The Prince and the Pauper* (1962), and later in Australian television series such as *Bellbird*. The film was shot on 16mm for about $30 000, with financial assistance from the Experimental Film and Television Fund. Two weeks were spent in the small Melbourne studio of Cambridge Films (for the interior of the house), and a further two weeks on locations around the city's suburbs. After completion it attracted an additional investment of $5000 from the Australian Film Development Corporation towards the cost of 35mm prints.

Before releasing the film in Australia, Kavanagh attempted to establish its reputation by entering it in film festivals, including London, Edinburgh and Chicago in 1971, and Sydney in 1972. In the Australian Film Awards for 1971, Monica Maughan won the major acting prize and the film itself a bronze award for its 'gentle exploration of a neglected territory—a mind cut off from love'. Commercial distribution was not easily arranged. After a one-week season at the Lower Melbourne Town Hall from 23 March 1972, the film was virtually unseen until released by B.E.F. at the suburban Roseville Cinema, Sydney, on 23 May 1974. A two-week season there was not successful and few other screenings followed. Distribution was not helped by the refusal of the New South Wales government to register the film as an Australian production under the quality clause of the quota act.

398 Shirley Thompson versus the Aliens

1972 JIM SHARMAN

PC: Kolossal Piktures. P: Jim Sharman. ASSOC P: Matt Carroll. SC: Helmut Bakaitis, Jim Sharman. PH: David Sanderson. ED: Malcolm Smith. ART D: Brian Thomson. M: Ralph Tyrell. SONGS: sung by Jeannie Lewis. ASST D: Meg Stewart, Rex Cramphorn. SD: Ken Hammond. 104 mins. Colour. 16mm.

CAST: Jane Harders (Shirley Thompson), June Collis (Dr Leslie Smith), Tim Elliot (Dr George Talbot), Marion Johns (Rita Thompson), John Llewellyn (Reg Thompson), Marie Nicholas (Narelle Thompson), Helmut Bakaitis (Harold), John Ivkovitch (Bruce), Bruce Gould (Blake), Kate Fitzpatrick (nurse), Alexander Hay (Alien), Ron Haddrick (replica of Prince Philip), Phil Kitamura, Candy Raymond, Julie Rodgers, Georgina West, Max Hess and Sue Moir (gang members).

Dubbed by its director as a 'psychological thriller cum 50's rock musical/science fiction/fantasy movie . . . the only A-grade B-movie loathed by underground, art-house and commercial managements alike', *Shirley Thompson versus the Aliens* was the story of a 'widgie' in the 1950s in Sydney who is visited by aliens from outer space. Shirley and her gang try desperately to convince Australia that the aliens exist, but their message is ignored by the closed minds of the Menzies era. Shirley is assumed to be insane and is committed to an asylum where she repeatedly narrates her story to psychiatrists.

Shot on 16mm for a privately raised sum of $50 000, the film was the first and only product of Kolossal Piktures, formed by Sharman, Carroll, Thomson and Bakaitis to achieve the 'mass production of B-grade movies, serials or anything else away from the treacherous art, underground or worst of all commercial circuits'. Despite a large collection of memorabilia from the rock-and-roll era (including songs by Johnny O'Keefe on the juke-box and a lot of newsreel footage), the film was closer in spirit to the pop culture of the early 1970s, with visual effects drawn from pop art and psychedelia. After a preview at the National Film Theatre in London in March 1972, it screened at the Sydney Film

398 *Shirley Thompson Versus the Aliens* Jane Harders (*l*)

Festival on 6 June and was unobtrusively distributed through the co-operative movement. In 1976 Sharman substantially re-edited it, reducing it to a compact 79 minutes, and in this form it was re-released through the co-operatives and the film lending collection of the National Library.

Born in 1945, Jim Sharman attended the National Institute of Dramatic Art in Sydney and quickly established a reputation as an *enfant terrible* of Australian theatre. He joined the entrepreneur Harry M. Miller, and directed the rock musicals *Hair* and *Jesus Christ Superstar* in Australia and abroad. *Shirley Thompson versus the Aliens* was his first feature film, shot over a three-week period in 1971. In 1975 he directed his second feature, *The Rocky Horror Picture Show*, produced in England for Twentieth Century-Fox, and based on his own highly successful stage show. He returned to Australia to direct his third feature, *Summer of Secrets*, in 1976.

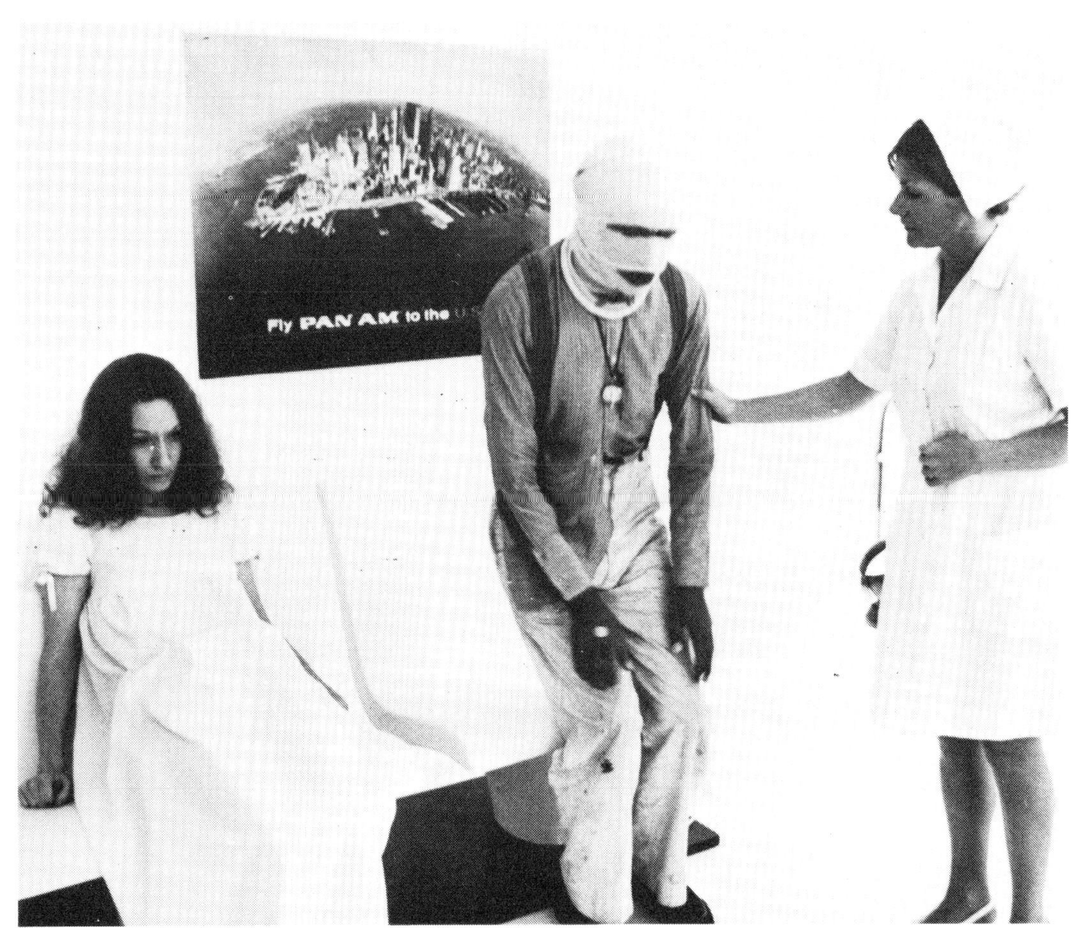

398 *Shirley Thompson Versus the Aliens* Jane Harders (*l*)

399 Private Collection

1972 KEITH SALVAT

PC: Keisal/Bonza Films. P: Keith Salvat. SC: Keith Salvat, Sandy Sharp. PH: David Gribble. ED: G. Turney-Smith. M: Mike Perjanik. LYRICS: Gary Reilly. PM: Matt Carroll. SD: Barry Brown. 92 mins. Colour. 16mm.

CAST: Peter Reynolds (Henry Phillips), Pamela Stephenson (Mary Ann Phillips), Brian Blain (Joseph Tibbsworth), Grahame Bond (Kleptoman), John Paramor (sailor), Noel Ferrier (police inspector), Les Foxcroft (citizen).

This black comedy was the first feature by Keith Salvat, then a 25-year-old film-maker from Sydney. It was shot on 16mm with almost all of its $30 000 budget being provided by the Australian Film Development Corporation. The main characters are rival collectors of bric-à-brac, living in their own private worlds of nostalgia and fantasy. One is married to a woman who seems at first to be little more than a prize object in his collection. Dressing like a 1930s movie star with a Harlow wig, she seems to spend most of her days idly tap-dancing to old records. But her mask-like face is deceptive: she has a secret lover and is privately nurturing ruthless schemes of murder.

The film was shot on location in Sydney in January 1972, and was premièred at the Sydney Film Festival in June. Village Theatres gave it a three-week season at the Australia Twin, Melbourne, commencing on 12 April 1973, but the results were mediocre. Subsequent screenings were primarily in co-operative cinemas.

Keith Salvat came to film from theatre. After studying direction at the National Institute of Dramatic Art in Sydney, he worked as a director with the Melbourne Theatre Company and at La Mama in 1973. Before *Private Collection* he made several 16mm shorts, including *Sacrifice* (1971), a 30-minute horror story that prefigured the black tone of his feature.

400 The Adventures of Barry McKenzie

1972 BRUCE BERESFORD

PC: Longford Productions. P: Phillip Adams. SC: Bruce Beresford, Barry Humphries. Based on the comic strip written by Barry Humphries, drawn by Nicholas Garland. PH: Don McAlpine. CAM OP: Gale Tattersall. ED: John Scott, William Anderson. P DES: John Stoddart. M: Peter Best. SONGS: 'The adventures of Barry McKenzie', lyrics by Peter Best, sung by Smacka Fitzgibbon; 'One-eyed trouser snake', 'Old Pacific sea', lyrics by Barry Humphries; 'When his light shines on me', lyrics by Barry Crocker. PM: Richard Brennan. P ASST: Robert Bentley, Andrea Way, Chris Löfven. SD: Tony Hide. 114 mins. Colour.

CAST: Barry Crocker (Barry McKenzie), Barry Humphries (Aunt Edna/Hoot/Meyer de Lamphrey), Peter Cook (Dominic), Spike Milligan (landlord), Dick Bentley (detective), Dennis Price (Mr Gort), Julie Covington (Blanche), Avice Landon (Mrs Gort), Joan Bakewell (herself), Paul Bertram (Curly), Mary Anne Severne (Lesley), Jonathan Hardy (Groove Courtenay), Jenny Tomasin (Sarah Gort), Chris Malcolm (Sean), Judith Furse (Claude), Maria O'Brien (Caroline Thighs), John Joyce (Maurie Miller), Margo Lloyd (Mrs McKenzie), Brian Tapply (avant-garde composer), John Clarke (underground film-maker), Wilfred Grove (customs officer), William Rushton (man on plane), Bernard Spear (taxi-driver), Jack Watling, Alexander Archdale.

Barry Humphries's comic-strip character first appeared in the British satirical magazine *Private Eye* in 1964. In this film adaptation, Humphries presented a loosely connected series of comic situations deriving from the culture clash between the Australian innocent, 'Bazza' McKenzie, and the English—from a taxi-driver who takes Barry from Heathrow to Earls Court by way of Stonehenge, to the decadent upper classes with their public school fetishes, the swinging scene of pop music promoters and Jesus freaks, and eventually the hallowed halls of BBC television.

The film offered a vigorous parody of the Australian 'ocker': anti-intellectual, xenophobic, obsessed with beer and sex, but never capable of relating positively with women, using a vernacular of prodigious vulgarity and inventiveness, and totally oblivious of anything beyond his own narrow conception of the order of things. The comedy appealed strongly to the 'ocker' element in Australia and the film often prompted rowdy celebrations of Bazza's behaviour; like the backblock farces many decades before, it drew criticism from public-spirited Australians about the damage it would do the the country's image abroad. But at the same time, the film's affectionate parody of the banalities of Australian life, and the name of Barry Humphries, won it broad popular support in Australia, and like *On Our Selection* in 1932, it became a record-breaking commercial success.

The film's importance in crystallizing the image of the Australian 'ocker' was supplemented by its crucial role in boosting the confidence of the production industry and financiers. Budgeted at $250 000, the film was funded in its entirety by the Australian Film Development Corporation, the only time that complete funding was approved for feature films. Shooting began in London in January 1972, with Barry Crocker, an Australian cabaret and television singer, in the leading role. Late in February the unit returned to Australia to complete the few remaining scenes, and encountered union troubles because of the presence of British technicians in the crew. A compromise was reached with the employment of shadow Australian technicians, and shooting was completed in March. Distribution was handled personally by Phillip Adams, and with an R certificate as the reward for its deliberate vulgarity, the film opened at the Capitol Cinema, Melbourne, on 12 October 1972. Its immediate commercial success in Australia enabled the production company to repay most of the government investment within three months of release. It also did very well commercially in London, where it established a record for any Australian film released there.

Bruce Beresford made his first film, *The Devil to Pay*, in 1962, while a student at the University of Sydney. This short 16mm narrative with overtones of *Citizen Kane* traced

400 *The Adventures of Barry McKenzie* Barry Crocker, Paul Bertram

the rise and fall of a master criminal, and at a time when few narrative films of any artistic pretension were being made in Australia, it was seen as a ray of hope by the struggling supporters of an indigenous creative cinema. In 1963 Beresford left Australia for Europe, and in 1964 went to Nigeria to work in the government film unit there and in theatre. In 1966 he was appointed supervisor of the British Film Institute's production board and later film adviser to the Arts Council of Great Britain. He also directed a consistent stream of 16mm films, including a number of documentaries about art and artists. After *The Adventures of Barry McKenzie* he remained in Sydney and made a series of television specials for Reg Grundy Productions, including a dramatized documentary, *The Wreck of the Batavia* (1973).

401 The Office Picnic

1972 TOM COWAN

PC: Child's Play Moving Picture Company. P, SC: Tom Cowan. PH: Michael Edols. ED: Kit Guyatt. M: Don Mori. SD: Peter Cherny, Don Mori. 83 mins.
CAST: John Wood (Clyde), Kate Fitzpatrick (Mara), Philip Deamer (Peter), Gaye Steele (Elly), Patricia Kennedy (Mrs R), Ben Gabriel (Mr Johnson), Max Cullen (Jim O'Casey), Anne Tait, Francis Flannigan, Graham Richards, Alex Grace, Graham Smith, Byron Kennedy, Elaine Smith, Don Jarry, the Eclipse Alley Five.

A group of office workers go on an annual picnic, a sordid and boozy affair that brings none of them closer together. The only couple who do relate to each other are the office juniors, Peter and Elly, whose budding romance is the butt of office jokes. During the course of the picnic Peter and Elly disappear; they fail to appear for work the next day, and attempts by the others to find them fail.

This study of interaction between ill-assorted people in a claustrophobic situation had moments of clear perception, especially in the relationship between Clyde, a frustrated musician who has opted for the security of a bureaucratic career, and Mara, a self-assured typist who remains aloof from the petty office preoccupations and has her eyes firmly set on her own private goals. The film was shot on 35mm with a budget of $30 000, partly provided by the Experimental Film and Television Fund. After a sneak preview at the Trak Cinema, Melbourne, on 17 November, it failed to attract an adequate offer from a commercial distributor, and most subsequent screenings were organized by the director himself.

Tom Cowan started in film as a trainee at the Australian Broadcasting Commission and later joined the Commonwealth Film Unit, where he spent four years working as a cameraman. He left in 1968 to work as a freelance cameraman in Australia and abroad, and shot many shorts and features including the much-praised *Samskara (Funeral Rites)*, directed by T. P. Rama Reddy in India in

401 Tom Cowan

1969, and the first feature directed by Philippe Mora, *Trouble in Molopolis*, shot in London in 1970. In 1974 Cowan shot his own second feature, *Promised Woman*, and his third in India in the following year. This Indian feature, *Wild Wind*, was suppressed for political reasons and was not released in India until mid-1977.

402 Sunstruck

1972 JAMES GILBERT

PC: Immigrant Productions. P: Jack Neary, James Grafton. SC: Stan Mars. ADDITIONAL MATERIAL: James Gilbert, James Grafton, Elwyn Jones. PH: Brian West. ED: Anthony Buckley, Barry Peters. ART D: David Copping. M: Peter Knight. PM: Hal McElroy. SD: Ken Hammond. 92 mins. Colour.

CAST: Harry Secombe (Stanley Evans), Maggie Fitzgibbon (Shirley Marshall), John Meillon (Mick Cassidy), Dawn Lake (Sal Cassidy), Peter Whittle (Pete Marshall), Bobby Limb (Bill), Norman Erskine (Norm), Jack Allen (Banjo), Lorna Wilde (Jennifer Morgan), Roger Cox (Ben), Tommy Mack (Gunboat), John Armstrong (Shiller), Stuart Wagstaff (announcer), Jeff Ashby (Pearson), Max Brouggy (Willie Marshall), Benita Collings (Alice), Charles McCallum (Carter), Dennis Jordan (Steve Cassidy), Donald Houston, Derek Nimmo.

Stanley Evans, a shy immigrant from Wales, is assigned to a one-teacher school in the bush town of Kookaburra Springs. Despite harassment from the children, he forms a school choir, which fares well in a singing competition in Sydney. The choir returns triumphantly to Kookaburra Springs, and with new confidence, Stanley decides to stay in the town and marry.

Sunstruck was inspired by a poster used by the New South Wales government to attract teachers from Britain, in which a figure clad in bathers, academic gown and mortar-board stands on the golden sands of Bondi Beach. The film was designed primarily as a vehicle for the British singer and comedian, Harry Secombe, who had made several trips to Australia for television and stage performances. It was shot in January 1972, largely on location near Parkes, N.S.W. The budget of under $400 000 was raised from English and American sources, with $100 000 from the Australian Film Development Corporation. The director, James Gilbert, came to Australia on leave from BBC television, where he specialized in light entertainment programmes.

A world première was held in Parkes on 18 November 1972. Distributed by B.E.F., it was released at the Rapallo Theatre, Sydney, on 22 December, with mediocre commercial results. Reviews were mixed, but most had some words of praise for John Meillon's performance as the publican at Kookaburra Springs.

402 *Sunstruck* John Meillon

403 *Marco Polo Jnr Versus the Red Dragon*

403 Marco Polo Jnr. versus the Red Dragon

1972 ERIC PORTER

PC: Animation International Inc./Porter Animations. P: Eric Porter. EXEC P, STORY: Sheldon Moldoff. STORYBOARD DIRECTION: Eric Porter, Sheldon Moldoff. SEQUENCE DIRECTION: Cam Ford, Peter Gardiner. STORYBOARD: Al Kouzel, Eli Bauer. ANIMATION: Jerry Grabner, Gairden Cooke, Stan Walker, Richard Jones, Paul McAdam, Ray Nowland, Dick Dunn, Wallace Logue, Yvonne Pearsall, Cynthia Leech, Vivienne Ray, Peter Luschwitz, George Youssef. SPECIAL ANIMATION EFFECTS: Toshio Tsuchiya. SPECIAL OPTICAL EFFECTS: Terry Moesker. CAMERA: Joe Dugonics, John Cumming. MD: Joel Herron. SONGS: 'Awaits my star', 'For the first time', music by Jack Grimsley, Julian Lee, lyrics by Larry Pontius; 'Xanadu', 'Illusions', 'I'll be coming back', music and lyrics by Joel Herron; 'The Red Dragon', 'The Delicate Dinosaur', music by Joel Herron, lyrics by Sheldon Moldoff. 80 mins. Colour.

VOICES: Bobby Rydell (Marco Polo Jnr.), Arnold Stang (the Delicate Dinosaur), Corie Sims (Princess Shining Moon), Kevin Golsby (the Red Dragon), Larry Best (the Guru), Gordon Hammet, Lionel Wilson, Arthur Andersen, Merril E. Joels, Sam Gray.

Australia's first animated feature told the story of an adventurous lad who discovers that he is the seventh son of the seventh son of the original Marco Polo. He sets off for the land of Xanadu to search for the missing half of an old family heirloom, the golden medallion of Khubla Khan, which symbolizes friendship. In Xanadu he finds that the evil Red Dragon has usurped the throne and imprisoned the rightful heir, Princess Shining Moon. Helped by a friendly guru, Marco braves the perils of water, earth and fire, overcomes the threat of a timid monster, the Delicate Dinosaur, and thwarts the Red Dragon by destroying the magic source of his power. The two halves of the magic medallion are reunited and the princess is restored to the throne.

The film was conceived and scripted by an American comic-book artist, Sheldon Moldoff, and co-produced with Eric Porter's animation studio in Sydney. Porter had toyed with animated shorts since the 1930s, and had later expanded to series made under contract to American television. Finance was raised jointly by Moldoff's company, Animation International, and by Porter, with an investment of $60 000 from the Australian Film Development Corporation. Preliminary storyboard work and designs for the characters were contributed by two American animation story men, Al Kouzel and Eli Bauer, but all subsequent production was handled entirely in Australia by Porter's crew. The sound-track was pre-recorded in America, but was revised and edited in Australia as the production developed.

Under Porter's overall supervision, the animation was directed by Cam Ford and Peter Gardiner, two Australians with substantial experience in the animation of television cartoon series. Ford had also worked for several years in Europe and in 1967 had been one of several Australian animators employed on the Beatles' feature, *Yellow Submarine.* Although the final production cost of $650 000 was relatively low, the film was animated more lavishly than most work previously done in Australia and to standards much higher than in conventional television work. Altogether some seventy artists were employed for nearly two years on the film, from mid-1970 until May 1972.

Despite the care taken during production, the film was ill-fated: shortly before its release in Australia in December 1972, an American cartoon special about the original Marco Polo was screened on local television, and Porter's distributor, B.E.F., introduced a clumsy longer title to distinguish the film from the television show. Commercial results were poor. The publication of three books using artwork from the film, and the winning of two major prizes at the 1973 Australian Film Awards, made little difference. The title was changed again, to *The Magic Medallion,* for the film's television release in Australia in 1976. In America, Moldoff failed to attract major exhibition outlets and the film's release there and in Britain was fragmentary.

After completing *Marco Polo Jnr.,* Porter persevered with animation in his own television series, *The Yellow House,* a pastiche of old and new material, but with the commercial failure of *Marco Polo Jnr.* he was forced to close down the animation studio in 1975. Porter continued to concentrate on live-action television commercials, and produced a tele-movie, *Polly Me Love* (released in 1976), a drama set in the early days of Sydney, starring Jacki Weaver and Hugh Keays-Byrne.

404 Flashpoint

1972 BRIAN HANNANT

PC: Film Australia. P: Gil Brealey. SC: Brian Hannant, Harold Lander. PH: Kerry Brown. CAM OP: David Sanderson. ED: Wayne Le Clos. PM: Richard Brennan. ASST D: Hal McElroy. P ASST: Esben Storm, Meg Stewart, Richard Moir. SD: Julian Ellingworth. SECOND UNIT D: Arch Nicholson. 36 mins. Colour. 16 mm.

CAST: Serge Lazareff (David), Wyn Roberts (Foxy), Jan Kingsbury (Vicky), Hu Pryce (Ben), Kevin Leslie (Arthur), Barry Donnelly (Andy), Harry Lawrence (Jimmy), Ben Gabriel (mine manager).

David, a newcomer to a mining town in north-west Australia where men outnumber women fifty to one, finds that the flashpoint in human conflict is set dangerously low. He befriends a veteran worker for the mining company, Foxy, and his sensitive wife, Vicky. Although Foxy is confident and aggressive at work, he is far from secure in his private relationships and resents David's friendship with Vicky. Tension between the two men grows to a violent showdown on the open face of the mine.

Buoyed by the success of *Three To Go* (1970), Film Australia planned to make further drama productions, beginning with a pair of feature films with common characters and common opening scenes. The films, about the separate experiences of a father and son, were intended to explore different aspects of Australian society—the father a tradesman coping with unemployment at middle age, and the son facing the hard facts of life in a tough new job. The film about the father, written by Frank Moorhouse, was eventually abandoned while the other was already being shot in the last months of 1971.

404 *Flashpoint* Hu Pryce (*l*)

Locations were used in the mining company town of Mount Newman in the Pilbara iron ore country in the north of Western Australia. In preparation the director, Brian Hannant, spent several weeks working incognito among the mining crews, and then developed his script, first in an attempted collaboration with Frank Hardy, and subsequently with the British television writer, Harold Lander. During the editing of the film, an entire sub-plot was removed (about David's affair with a kindergarten teacher, played by Kirrily Nolan, which induces Foxy to regard David as 'safe' enough to introduce to his wife) to keep the film within a length considered by Film Australia to be suitable for television. An opening scene of David's arrival in Port Hedland and his decision to take a job in the mining town was also deleted and replaced with a 'teaser' sequence of action from the story's violent climax. The film was distributed widely through non-commercial libraries in Australia, and was shown on commercial television in 1973 and later on television in several European countries.

405 Gentle Strangers

1972 CECIL HOLMES

PC: Film Australia. P: Roland Beckett. SC: Cecil Holmes. SCRIPT ED: Harold Lander. PH: Mick Bornemann, Kerry Brown, Bruce Hillyard, Don McAlpine, David Sanderson. ED: Graham Chase. M: Barry Conyngham. PM: Richard Brennan. P ASST: Phillip Robertson, Greg Tepper, Esben Storm, Meg Stewart. SD: Julian Ellingworth. 58 mins. Colour. 16 mm.

CAST: Yee Choo Koo (Preeyan), Clem Chow (Lawrence), Ric Lay (himself), Eric Lay (himself), Yanti Lay (herself), Jennifer West (Miss Emerson), Lyn Murphy (Mrs Baker).

This 'mini-feature' about the problems faced by Asian students in Australia was made by Cecil Holmes during his three-year period as a staff director with Film Australia. Experiences of culture shock are narrated through the tentative romance of a Chinese boy and a Thai girl who meet in a seedy boarding house in Sydney and through the story of an Indonesian student posted to a rural research centre while his wife and child are left to cope with life in the city.

Holmes spent a year researching and writing the film, and it was shot on 16 mm with a largely non-professional cast. When completed it ran for about 75 minutes, but in a process that Holmes later described as 'insidious self-censorship', Film Australia cut the film by some 20 minutes, reducing episodes of the Chinese boy's involvement in gambling, and removing a sequence in which the Indonesian visits a rural R.S.L. club and experiences direct racial hostility. The film was released through non-commercial film libraries and on commercial television but did not attract theatrical screenings.

405 Cecil Holmes during the shooting of *Gentle Strangers*

406 Night of Fear

1973 TERRY BOURKE

PC: Terryrod Productions. EXEC P: Rod Hay. SC: Terry Bourke. PH: Peter Hendry. ED: Ray Alchin. P DES: Gary Hansen. PM: Cathy Garland. ASST D: Michael Lake. SD ED: Ian Barry. 54 mins. Colour.

CAST: Norman Yemm (the man), Carla Hoogeveen (the woman), Mike Dorsey (the lover), Briony Behets (horse-girl).

Filmed entirely without dialogue, *Night of Fear* was a horror film about the terrorizing and murder of a woman by a crazed hermit after her car crashes on a lonely country road.

Shot quickly on a twelve-day schedule in mid-1972, the film was originally intended as a pilot for a television series called *Fright*. A crew and 35 mm production facilities were provided by the Australian Broadcasting Commission in return for television rights. The budget of \$21 500 included \$13 500 invested by the Australian Film Development Corporation. When the ABC finally rejected the proposal for the series, Bourke and Hay released the pilot as a theatrical feature film, and they attracted enough overseas sales to recoup the production costs even before its release in the home market.

Australian release was delayed by the banning of the film in November 1972 on the grounds of indecency. A month later, with its reputation greatly boosted by the incident, the film was passed uncut on appeal, and it was released profitably as a main feature in independent cinemas and drive-ins, beginning with the Penthouse, Sydney, on 18 March 1973.

Terry Bourke worked as a show business journalist, stuntman and production assistant in Hong Kong for several years in the 1960s. There he directed *Sampan,* his first feature, in 1967-68, using an all-Chinese cast. In 1970 he directed a second feature, *Noon Sunday,* on Guam. After his return to Australia in 1971 he spent many months seeking backing for the *Fright* series, and during this time directed several episodes of *Spyforce* and met the English editor, Rod Hay, who became his partner in feature production.

407 Libido

1973 JOHN B. MURRAY, TIM BURSTALL, FRED SCHEPISI, DAVID BAKER

PC: Producers and Directors Guild of Australia. EXEC P: Christopher Muir, John B. Murray. 118 mins. Colour.

The film consists of four stories:
The Husband. D: John B. Murray. SC: Craig McGregor. PH: Eric Lomas. ED: Tim Lewis. M: Tim Healy, Billy Green. PM: Ross Dimsey. SD R: Lloyd Carrick.
CAST: Elke Neidhardt (Penelope), Bryon Williams (Jonathon), Mark Albiston (Harold).

The Child. D: Tim Burstall. SC: Hal Porter. PH: Robin Copping. CAM OP: Dan Burstall. ED: David Bilcock Jnr. ART D: Leslie Binns. M: Peter Best. ASST D: Ross Dimsey. SD R: John Phillips.
CAST: John Williams (Martin), Jill Forster (mother) Judy Morris (Sybil), Bruce Barry (David), Louise Homfrey, George Fairfax.

The Priest. D: Fred Schepisi. SC: Thomas Keneally. PH: Ian Baker. ED: Brian Kavanagh. ART D: Trevor Ling. M: Bruce Smeaton. P ASST: Graeme Rutherford, Cheryl Gough. SD R: Danny Dyson.
CAST: Robyn Nevin (Sister Caroline), Arthur Dignam (Father Burn), Vivean Gray, Vicki Bray, Valma Pratt, Penne Hackforth-Jones.

The Family Man. D: David Baker. SC: David Williamson. PH: Bruce McNaughton. ED: Edward McQueen-Mason. M: Bruce Smeaton. PM: John Morgan. ASST D: Ross Dimsey. SD R: John Mulligan.
CAST: Jack Thompson (Ken), Max Gillies (Gerald), Debbie Nankervis, Suzanne Brady.

The Husband is a study of an immature university-educated man with limited emotional experience. He fears the domination of his aggressive wife and fabricates a boyish dream world, including a stereotyped sex orgy in which his wife is a submissive and willing participant. *The Child*: In 1912 a young boy is left on the family estate while his father is overseas. Bored and lonely, the boy gradually becomes infatuated with his new governess but is traumatically shocked when he discovers her making love with a local playboy. *The Priest* is the story of the tortured love between a priest and a nun; although it cannot be consummated, the intensity of their love has already driven the priest into a nervous breakdown, and now he tries in vain to persuade the nun to join him in renouncing their vows so that they may marry. *The Family Man*: Ken's wife has just given birth to their third daughter. While she is still in hospital, he joins his mate Gerry in the pub, where they meet two likely women whom they lure to Ken's beach house. As the night progresses Ken and Gerry find that the girls are more difficult to master than they had expected.

The film was derived from a series of workshops conducted in 1971 by the Victorian branch of the Producers and Directors Guild (of which John B. Murray was President) to acquaint writers with the needs of commercial narrative film. As an extension of the workshops, professional writers were invited to prepare short stories on the theme of love. The stories were then adapted and produced by members of the guild under the general supervision of a production committee; four were subsequently linked together to form a portmanteau film for commercial release.

All of the films were shot in and around Melbourne on 16 mm colour negative with an overall budget of about $100 000, including $26 000 from the Australian Council for the Arts. When the production reached fine-cut stage, B.E.F. Distributors advanced $20 000 towards the cost of blow-ups to 35 mm. Publicized vigorously by B.E.F. as a film about 'the erotic drive within us all', it opened on 6 April 1973 at the Rapallo Theatre, Melbourne, and ran for a strong three-month season. It was also taken up by the British distributor, Anglo-E.M.I., and opened in London (with *The Priest* deleted) in mid-1974. Local critics were especially warm in their praise of Burstall's episode. Mike Harris in the *Australian,* 7 April 1973, applauded both his evocation of the Edwardian period and his portrait of a confused child's mind: it 'is a beautiful piece of cinema'. Bob Ellis in *Nation Review,* 19-27 April 1973, found Murray's piece a 'sadly accurate' depiction of the relationship between an attractive woman and a dull man, and found Baker's closing episode a 'sheer delight' in its exploration of 'a cultural

407 *Libido (The Family Man)* Jack Thompson (*l*) and Max Gillies

407 *Libido (The Child)* John Williams

found work again in Australia as a prolific director of television series, including *The Magic Boomerang, Animal Doctor* and *Spyforce.* After his episode in *Libido* he made a grim short story with a colonial bush setting, *Squeaker's Mate,* released belatedly in 1976, and his first feature, *The Great MacArthy* (1975).

class struggle between a well heeled sophisticated alf and a couple of rather naive hash headed womens libbers'.

Of the directors, Murray and Burstall had already made their mark in feature production. Fred Schepisi came from a solid background in advertising; in 1964 he had joined the Victorian branch of Cinesound Productions, and in 1966 had formed his own company, the Film House, to take over Cinesound's operation in that state. He produced and directed innumerable documentaries, public relations films and television commercials in the following years until his first feature, *The Devil's Playground* in 1976.

David Baker was born in Tasmania, and in the early 1950s entered the film industry in England, where he worked in various minor capacities on features and television programmes before returning to Australia in 1957 to devise and produce *Young Seven,* an inventive children's programme appearing daily on Melbourne television. He returned to England in 1961 and produced the current affairs programme, *People and Places,* for Granada television for fifteen months. In 1964 he

408 The Sabbat of the Black Cat

1973 RALPH LAWRENCE MARSDEN

P, SC, PH, ED: Ralph Lawrence Marsden. From a story by Edgar Allan Poe. CAM OP: Adrian Carr. MD: Jan Skot. SD: John Costa, Jim Davies. 80 mins. Colour. 16 mm.
CAST: Ralph Lawrence Marsden (Edward Alden), Barbara Brighton (Virginia Alden), Babylon (Sabbat dancers), Tracey Tombs (Scarlet Lady), David Bingham (tavern keeper), Jim Fitch (Senior Constable).

The film is based on Edgar Allan Poe's story about a man driven to destruction by a black cat, which haunts him after he accidentally witnesses a ritual gathering of witches.

Virtually a one-man production, this 16 mm feature was shot on a part-time basis during 1971 for about $7000 (partly provided by the Experimental Film and Television Fund). Locations included the old gold mining settlement of Maldon, Victoria, and the principal interior scenes were shot in a terrace house in Melbourne. The film was distributed through the co-operative movement, with a première at the Melbourne Co-op Cinema on 10 May 1973.

Marsden was 26 when the film was shot. He had previously been involved for four years in the production of television commercials with Senior Films, Melbourne. Later he worked for the Australian Broadcasting Commission, until 1975, when he went to London to further his career.

409 An Essay on Pornography

1973 CHRISTOPHER CARY

PC: Chase Films. P: James Steiner. ASSOC P: Carroll Holloway. PH: Mike Franklin. ED: Frank Heimans. SD: Ken Hammond. 82 mins. Colour.
CAST: Helen Mason (Helen), Glen Johnston (Glen), Terry Blake (himself), John Fewester, Paul van Sebring, Doctor Twinkle.

An Essay on Pornography was a pseudo-documentary about the thoughts and experiences of people involved in the making of a pornographic film. An aspiring actress, Helen, auditions for a role in the film because no other work is available for her and because she hopes that the part may lead to other acting opportunities.

Originally a 55-minute television report on the pornographic film trade in Australia, the film was programmed by ATN7 for broadcast in Sydney in October 1972 but at the last moment was withdrawn by the channel. The producers, Chase Films, subsequently expanded the film for theatrical release, inserting into the black and white film some colour excerpts from an actual 'blue movie'. This expanded version was released through B.E.F. with considerable commercial success in the 'sexploitation' market, commencing on 1 June 1973 at the Albany Theatre, Melbourne.

Chris Cary was an American television actor and theatre producer who had settled in Sydney; with James Steiner, his American partner in Chase Films, he later made another feature-length film, *Marijuana, Possession and the Law,* documenting his own arrest in January 1973 on charges of possessing and using Indian hemp.

410 Lost in the Bush

1973 PETER DODDS

PC: Audio-Visual Education Centre, Education Department of Victoria. SC, ED: Peter Dodds. STORY: Les Blake. PH: Lee Wright. PROPS: Graeme Mullane. M: Geoff D'Ombran. PRE-P: Ross Campbell. ASST D: Ross Matthews. SD: David Hughes. 64 mins. Colour. 16 mm.
CAST: Gabrielle Bulle (Jane Duff), Colin Freckleton (Isaac Duff), Richard McClelland (Frank Duff), Adrian Crick, Barbara Maroske, Don Mitchell, Bill Tregonning.

In 1864, Jane Duff, aged seven, and her two younger brothers spend nine days lost in the Victorian bush before being found in an advanced state of exhaustion by a search-party led by Aboriginal trackers.

Made for schools by the Victorian government, *Lost in the Bush* was released widely through non-commercial film libraries around Australia. The heroic survival of Jane Duff and her brothers was still a popular legend in the Wimmera area of Victoria where the events had taken place, and a tourist-conscious local community did much to help the production. The director, Peter Dodds, was at the time a 22-year-old cameraman and editor with the Victorian Education Department. Shooting took place in February 1972 on location near the Wimmera town of Horsham, with three Horsham children in the leading roles and many of the local citizens appearing in the search-party scenes. The world première was held in the town on 13 June 1973.

411 Don Quixote

1973 RUDOLF NUREYEV, ROBERT HELPMANN

PC: International Arts/Australian International Finance Corporation/The Australian Ballet Foundation. P: John Hargreaves. ASSOC P: Pat Condon. SC, CHOREOG: Rudolf Nureyev. Based on the ballet by Marius Petipa. PH: Geoffrey Unsworth. ED: Anthony Buckley. ART D: Bill Hutchinson. P DES., COSTUMES: Barry Kay. M: Ludwig Minkus. MD: John Lanchbery. PM: Hal McElroy. ASST D: Bryan Ashbridge, Wallace Potts. SD R: Ken Hammond. SD ED: Bob Hathaway. 111 mins. Colour.

CAST: Robert Helpmann (Don Quixote), Ray Powell (Sancho Panza), Rudolf Nureyev (Basilio), Francis Croese (Lorenzo), Lucette Aldous (Kitri/Dulcinea), Colin Peasley (Gamache), Marilyn Rowe (street dancer/queen of the Dryads), Kelvin Coe (Espada), Gailene Stock and Carolyn Rappel (friends of Kitri), Ronald Bekker, John Meehan, Rex McNeill, Rodney Smith, Joseph Janusaitis and Frederic Werner (matadors), Alan Alder and Paul Saliba (gypsy dancers), Ronald Bekker (gypsy king), Susan Dains (gypsy queen), Julie da Costa and Leigh Rowles (gypsy girls), Patricia Cox (Cupid), Janet Vernon and Gary Norman (leading fandango couple), and dancers of the Australian Ballet.

Nureyev's adaptation of the nineteenth-century Russian ballet by Petipa had been added to the repertoire of the Australian Ballet in 1970. This film version, conceived as an extension of the Ballet's international career, was produced by a private syndicate, which included Sir Robert Helpmann. Finance was raised largely in the U.S.A. Most of the production crew were Australian but their work was supportive to the British director of photography and art director.

The film was shot on a tight four-week schedule to fit in with Nureyev's European engagements. Sets were built in disused aircraft hangars at the Essendon airport, Melbourne, and shooting began on 13 November 1972, with a budget quoted variously as $600 000 and $750 000. A month earlier the musical director of the Australian Ballet, John Lanchbery, and the Melbourne orchestra of the Elizabethan Theatre Trust had recorded the film's sound-track, and the film was shot entirely to the pre-recorded music.

The world première was held on 19 July 1973 during the opening festivities of the Sydney Opera House. World-wide distribution was handled by the Walter Reade Organization in the U.S.A., and exhibition in Australia was mainly in independent cinemas.

412 *Come out Fighting* Michael Karpaney

412 Come Out Fighting

1973 NIGEL BUESST

P: Nigel Buesst. From the play by Harry Martin. PH: Byron Kennedy. ED: Tony Patterson. M: Smetana and others. SD: Lloyd Carrick. 50 mins. Colour. 16mm.

CAST: Michael Karpaney (Al Dawson), Joey Collins (Eddie), Bethany Lee (Susan Parker), Cliff Neate (Stan Harkness), Peter Green (Rocko Garibaldi), Bob Horsfall (Phil Bench), Brian Torrens (Carl Price), Peter Adams (Garry Day), Martin Phelan (student), Harry Williams (Aboriginal drinker), Max Pescud (trainer), Bert Williams (Aboriginal drinker), Kris McQuade ('Sporting World' hostess), John Jacobs (trainer), John Duigan (student).

The film depicts a crisis in the life of an Aboriginal boxer, Al 'The Bomb' Dawson. Unable to reconcile the conflicting demands on his life by his Aboriginal friends, the fight promoters and a group of students campaigning for Aboriginal rights, he rejects them all and gives away his chance to contend for a world title.

Directed with hard colour and harsh sound, and aided by some fine performances (notably from Peter Green as Al's seedy trainer), the film captured some powerful moments, especially a scene in which two drunken Aborigines hurl violent abuse at Al for what they see as his desertion of their life style. Given its budget ($6000) and short length, the film was seen by the *Sydney Morning Herald*, 24 September 1973, as 'a good, strong film which could have been better . . . if only the film-makers had had the time and money'.

Buesst, who had long been a boxing fan, completed the film in February 1973 with the aid of the Experimental Film and Television Fund. Michael Karpaney was himself a trained boxer and the fights seen in the film were actual contests. The film opened profitably at the Pram Factory (a home for experimental live theatre in Melbourne) in July 1973.

413 Avengers of the Reef

1973 CHRIS McCULLUGH

PC: Timon Productions. P: Noel Ferrier. SC: Anne Brooksbank. PH: Peter James. CAM OP: Richard Wallace. ED: Tim Wellburn. M: John Sangster. UNIT M: Esben Storm. SD R: Barry Brown. SD ED: Rod Hay. Colour. 84 mins.

CAST: Simon Drake (Tim Stewart), Biu Rarawa (Sai), Tim Elliot (Kemp), Noel Ferrier (Updike), Gary McDonald (Updike's aide), Dibs Mather (Bill Stewart), Lesie (Chieftain), Judy Morris (airline hostess), Jenny Lee, Richard Lupino, Bob Lee, Eddie Osborne.

This children's adventure, filmed almost entirely in Fiji, was initiated by the actor Noel Ferrier, and jointly financed by him and the Australian Film Development Corporation. A scientist, Bill Stewart, flies to Fiji with his son, Tim, to investigate the appearance of the parasitic Crown of Thorns starfish in the reefs off the islands. Unknown to Stewart, a multinational mining syndicate is deliberately seeding the reefs with the starfish to destroy environmental objections to their mining of the reef area. The syndicate leader, Updike, hires a bumbling professional killer, Kemp, to assassinate Stewart. Although his first attempt fails, both Kemp and Tim think he has succeeded. Tim escapes to an island village but is hotly pursued by Kemp. With a Fijian boy, Sai, Tim has many adventures at sea and in the tropical jungle before Kemp is captured and he is reunited with his father.

Shooting began in Fiji in September 1972 primarily on the island of Taveuni. Shortly before work ended, a major cyclone hit Taveuni and several weeks of delay were caused, sending the film substantially over its low budget of $100 000. The screenplay by Anne Brooksbank expertly made use of local colour, from fire-walking to witchcraft, and she was awarded a prize by the Australian Writers' Guild for her work. The young director, Chris McCullugh (ex-Commonwealth Film Unit), made the most of the picturesque locations and, with a sinister percussive score by John Sangster, the film emerged as a highly competent children's entertainment. It was selected by the Australian Council for Children's Film and Television to screen during the opening festivities of the Sydney Opera House on 21 October 1973. As with many children's films, it gained little critical recognition, and was released unobtrusively by Roadshow.

414 Dalmas

1973 BERT DELING

PC: Apogee Films. SC: Bert Deling. PH: Sasha Trikojus. M: Spectrum. SD: Lloyd Carrick. 103 mins. Colour. 16mm.

CAST: Peter Whittle (Dalmas), Peter Cummins (Plastic Man), Max Gillies (Rojack), John Duigan (film director), Roger Ward (policeman), and Tribe.

Dalmas opens with a statement from Fanon: 'The spectator is either a traitor or a coward.' An ex-cop, Pete Dalmas, is pursuing a drug-runner, Mr Big. He visits another ex-cop, Rojack, now a pathetic drug-addicted cripple surrounded by books and television receivers, and extracts from him a lead to the Plastic Man, an anarchistic drug-pedlar. Dalmas is questioning a girl in a drug centre run by Plastic Man when the police raid the building and Dalmas is beaten up in the fight. Undeterred, he follows Plastic Man to a seaside camp where a group of young hippies are being filmed by an arrogant documentary film-maker. Suddenly, without warning, the fiction collapses: the documentary film-maker and Plastic Man disappear; Dalmas becomes Peter Whittle the actor; and the production crew, including the director, Bert Deling, join the hippy group (Tribe) in a communal exploration of the film medium and of their experiences with drugs. From a fictional, structured treatment of the drug scene, the film turns into an exercise in self-expression by the Tribe, communicating directly to and with the camera, without the medium of Deling as director. As Deling said later: 'First is the half I had some control over . . . Then I become one of 30 people' (*Lumiere*, April 1973).

The film took some four years to complete and cost $20 000, half of which was supplied by the Experimental Film and Television Fund. In November 1973, when political feeling about Australian films was high during the Tariff Board inquiry into the industry, Village Theatres gave the film a season at the Australia Twin Cinema, Melbourne. Other screenings were primarily arranged through film co-operatives.

415 Alvin Purple

1973 TIM BURSTALL

PC: Hexagon Productions. P: Tim Burstall. ASSOC P: Alan Finney. SC: Alan Hopgood. PH: Robin Copping. ED: Edward McQueen-Mason. P DES: Leslie Binns. ART D: Neil Angwin. M: Brian Cadd. PM, ASST D: Hal McElroy. SD R: John Phillips. SD MIX: Peter Fenton. 97 mins. Colour.

CAST: Graeme Blundell (Alvin Purple), Abigail (girl in see-through), Lynette Curran (first sugar girl), Christine Amor (Peggy), Dina Mann (Shirley), Dennis Miller (Mr Horwood), Jill Forster (Mrs Horwood), Fred Parslow (Alvin's father), Valerie Blake (Alvin's mother), Alan Finney (Spike Dooley), Gary Down (Roger Hattam), Elli Maclure (Tina Donovan), Peter Aanensen (Ed Cameron), Jenny Hagen (Agnes Jackson), Kris McQuade (Samantha), Shara Berriman (kinky lady), Stan Monroe (Mrs Warren), Penne Hackforth-Jones (Dr Liz Sort), George Whaley (Dr McBurney), Jacki Weaver (second sugar girl), Eileen Chapman (patient), Jan Friedl (Miss Guernsey), Barbara Taylor (Mrs Phillips), Anne Pendlebury (woman with pin), Danny Webb (newsreader), Noel Ferrier (judge), Jon Finlayson (Liz's lawyer), John Smythe (Alvin's lawyer), Brian Moll (clerk of court), Lynne Flanagan (foreman of jury), Peter Cummins (cab-driver), Debbie Nankervis (girl in blue movie), Elke Neidhardt (woman in blue movie), Les James (leader of angry husbands), Tony Holtham (skydiver jumpmaster), Bill Bennett (Tina's boss), Clare Balmford (first nun), Sally Conabere (second nun), Carole Skinner (Mother Superior), Valma Brown (schoolgirl on bicycle).

This celebration of male wish-fulfilment fantasies told the tale of a naïve young male who finds himself the object of every woman's desires. The story follows him from his schooldays through various jobs as water-bed salesman, sex therapist and eventually convent gardener, always searching for true love but unable to escape or resist the sexual initiatives of the women who pursue him.

Graeme Blundell's deadpan performance presented Alvin as a rather ordinary urban Australian, not a larrikin or a sophisticate, but a quiet type who would just like to settle down if he did not always find himself in circumstances beyond his control. He never really understands why he should be in such demand, and much of the comedy derives from his reaction to each new seduction, whether puzzled, blasé or desperate. Most Australian critics accepted it at face value as an unpretentious sex-comedy; as Sandra Hall in the *Bulletin*, 22 December 1973, wrote: 'It is cheerfully sexist, unashamedly mindless and, in the Carry On manner, leaves no innuendo unexploited . . . it is bountiful in full frontals and happy vulgarity.' With its nudity and simulated sex made palatable for general audiences by the consistently light-hearted tone, it became a runaway commercial hit when it opened just before Christmas 1973 in four state capitals around Australia.

415 *Alvin Purple*

The production company, Hexagon, was established in 1972 by three parties—Roadshow Distributors, Bilcock and Copping, and Tim Burstall and Associates. The budget of little over $200 000 was covered entirely by the Hexagon partners, and the only government involvement was a short-term loan from the Australian Film Development Corporation, which was repaid before the film's release. Its continuing success led to a sequel, *Alvin Rides Again* (1974), and to the Australian Broadcasting Commission's production (without Hexagon) of a controversial television series in 1976. World-wide distribution was handled by Warner Brothers, and it opened in London in mid-1974. By the end of 1977 it had grossed film hire revenue of over $1 600 000, and stood clearly as the most commercially successful of all Australian features released between 1971 and 1977.

416 Moving On

1974 RICHARD MASON

PC: Film Australia. P: Don Murray. SC: Anne Brooksbank, Cliff Green. PH: Dean Semler. ED: Tim Wellburn. ART D: Jim Coffey. M: Richard Connolly. PM: Bruce Moir. ASST D: Brian Hannant. SD R: Tony Hide. 57 mins. Colour. 16mm.

CAST: Ewen Solon (George Collier), Kay Taylor (Elizabeth Collier), Ken Shorter (Alan), Lyndell Rowe (Anne), Carole Yelland (Pauline), Brian Anderson (Ron), Michelle Brooker (Margaret), Jonathan Hardy (Anne's boyfriend), Jeff Ashby (city man in country pub), Bruce Spence (road worker), Roger Ward (stock agent), John Fegan (unemployed grower), Robert McDarra (financier), Betty Crosby, Bill Ayers, Deryck Barnes, Doris Goddard, Hilda Cheney, Ken Goodlet, Jim Conlan, Donald Crosby, Edward Howell, John Larking, Don Philps, John Llewellyn, Richard Meikle, Charles Metcalfe, Brian Wenzel, Dolore Whiteman.

George Collier is a sheep farmer facing hard times: after several seasons of drought and falling wool prices his farm is virtually bankrupt. The film traces his attempts to secure financial aid and eventually to establish a new life in the city.

This government-produced feature was designed partly to help farmers who faced difficult decisions about their future, and partly to encourage urban audiences to be more tolerant of the problems of the rural poor. As the film presents them, the issues are far from clear-cut: George makes decisions rashly, without a full comprehension of how government aid programmes work, and to some extent his financial problems are self-generated; at the same time, city people fail to appreciate the burden of social pressures on country families who move into the new world of the large cities.

The screenplay, with its difficult task of condensing a variety of viewpoints and problems into a compact and economical structure, was awarded a prize by the Australian Writers' Guild as the best feature screenplay of 1973. The film was widely distributed through non-theatrical film libraries in Australia and was screened on commercial television in January 1974.

Richard Mason had had a long career at the Commonwealth Film Unit, and had won many prizes for his work. He wrote and directed numerous documentaries, including *Training Champions* (1957) and *The Jackeroo* (1960), and he co-directed with the British director Jack Lee a popular parody of sponsored travelogues, *From the Tropics to the Snow* (1964). He also produced many films for other directors, including the feature, *Let the Balloon Go* (1976), and was executive producer on three telemovies made in 1977-78 by Film Australia, *A Good Thing Going, Cass* and *Say You Want Me.* He also held a number of positions on industry committees, including five years on the New South Wales executive of the Theatrical and Amusement Employees Association.

417 Matchless

1974 JOHN PAPADOPOULOS

P: John Papadopoulos. SC: Sally Blake. PH: Russell Boyd. ADDITIONAL PH: Wolfgang Kress. ED: Kit Guyatt. M: Charles Pileso. PM: Phil Noyce. ASST D: Graham Shirley. SD R: Rod Pascoe. 55 mins. 16mm.

CAST: Alan Penney (Victor), Denise Otto (Annie), Sally Blake (Cynthia), Marguerite Frewin, Kevin Healey and Henry Heideman (psychiatrists), Bill James and Gwen Baxter (social workers), Erica Hayes (Brunhild), Louis Wishart (Louis), Eddie Selwyn (neighbour), Storry Walton (health inspector).

Three of society's fringe-dwellers—Victor, an ageing alcoholic, Annie, a schizophrenic on the verge of a breakdown, and Cynthia, a dreamy epileptic—live together in an old broken-down house. None of them is capable of standing alone in the outside world, but together they form a stable group, mutually protective and balancing each others' difficulties. The film traces the tragic imbalance caused in their lives by the intrusion of well-meaning authorities.

In 1973 John Papadopoulos, a 26-year-old Vietnam veteran, was accepted as one of the small group of students in the first year of training offered by the new Film and Television School in Sydney. He had previously worked for the Mental Health Authority in Melbourne, and had made several short 16mm films about mental problems, including *Dead End* (1972) about the last minutes in the life of an alcoholic. *Matchless* was shot in spare time during his year at the School, with involvement from some fellow students (Noyce, Shirley and others). The main location was a derelict house in the northern Sydney suburb of Thornleigh. The Experimental Film and Television Fund contributed $6000 towards the total cost of $8800.

The film was screened at the Sydney Filmmakers' Co-op in March 1974, and in August it was entered in the Shiraz Film Festival, Iran, where it won first prize. Prompted by the award, the Australian Broadcasting Commission bought the film for national broadcast later in the year. Critics generally welcomed the film; Colin Bennett in the *Age*, 27 September 1974, found that 'two promising unorthodox talents are at work in this off-beat little film—compassionate but starkly pessimistic'. During 1974, Papadopoulos and his associate writer Sally Blake began preparations for their second 16mm feature, *Jog's Trot*, a 'psycho-surrealist' fantasy with Arthur Dignam, but it was not released until March 1978.

418 **Number 96**

1974 PETER BENARDOS

PC: Cash Harmon Television. P: Bill Harmon. ASSOC P: Ross Hawthorn. SC: David Sale, Johnny Whyte. PH: John McLean. CAM OP: Russell Boyd, Richard Wallace, David Gribble. ED: Alan Lake, Ron Williams. ART D: John Northcote. MD: Tommy Tycho. ASST D: Ian Leigh-Cooper. SD: Barry Brown. SECOND UNIT D: Brian Phillis. SECOND UNIT PH: Peter Hopwood. 113 mins. Colour.

CAST: Johnny Lockwood (Aldo), Philippa Baker (Roma), Gordon McDougall (Les), Sheila Kennelly (Norma), Pat McDonald (Dorrie), Ron Shand (Herb), Bunney Brooke (Flo), Joe Hasham (Don), Tom Oliver (Jack), Rebecca Gilling (Diana), Lynn Rainbow (Sonia), Alistair Smart (Duncan), James Elliot (Alf), Elisabeth Kirkby (Lucy), Jeff Kevin (Arnold), Elaine Lee (Vera), Chard Hayward (Dudley), Bettina Welch (Maggie), Thelma Scott (Claire), Harry Lawrence (Horace), John Orcsik (Simon), James Condon (Nick), Patrick Ward (Tony).

The television serial *Number 96* began in March 1972, playing five nights a week and attracting a huge audience until it ceased production in mid-1977. This theatrical version was made by the producers of the serial and employed the same cast. It also followed the same episodic format of the serial, moving rapidly from farce to melodrama, and exploiting the greater freedom of film censorship to include a heavy emphasis on sex and occasional frontal nudity.

During the course of the film, residents at the apartment building No. 96, are involved in one pack rape, two attempted murders and a fatal car crash. One man tries to drive his wife to suicide so that he can live with the girl next door; an ex-prostitute fears that her past will ruin her planned marriage to an eminent politician; and two homosexuals find each other and become lovers. On a lighter note, Dorrie, the building's resident busybody, finds that, because of a clerical error, she had been unwittingly married years ago to an alcoholic layabout who suddenly arrives to claim his conjugal rights; a fancy-dress party reveals Herb, Dorrie's ageing husband, in a Tarzan suit; and Herb builds a sauna bath in the basement, which produces soot instead of steam.

418 *Number 96* Ron Shand (*l*)

Shot on 16mm in eleven days with a budget 'so low that its producers won't talk about it', the film displayed many signs of haste and economy. The scorn of critics ('a total rip-off', 'it's bloody awful') did little to dissuade the enthusiasm of audiences, especially of children, who constituted the major part of its following. Incredulous critics noted the high level of audience involvement; Mike Harris in the *Australian*, 8 May 1974, wrote: 'I've never been in a cinema before where the audience has applauded when characters made their entrances.'

The film was released during the May school holidays in 1974, and initially attracted enormous crowds. Release in capital cities was organized by the O-Ten television network (which broadcast the serial), while distribution in suburban and country areas was handled by Regent.

419 **27A**

1974 ESBEN STORM

PC: Smart Street Films. P: Haydn Keenan. SC: Esben Storm. PH: Michael Edols. CAM OP: Malcolm Richards. ED: Richard Moir. ART D: Peter Minnett. M: recorder, Winsome Evans; guitar, Michael Norton. P ASST: Nick Ash. ASST D: Peter Gailey. SD R: Laurie Fitzgerald, Peter Cherny. SD ED: John Mutton. TITLES: Chris Noonan, Yoram Gross, Esben Storm. 86 mins. Colour. 16mm.

CAST: Robert McDarra (Bill), Bill Hunter (Cornish), Graham Corry (Peter Newman), T. Richard Moir (Richard), James Kemp (Slats), Kris Olsen (Gloria), Brian Doyle (Lynch), Richard Creaser (Jeremy), Michael Norton (Mark), Haydn Keenan (Jeffrey), Gary McFeeter (Samuel), Tom Farley (Vic), Jim Doherty (suicide), Peter Gailey (co-escapee), Karl Florsheim (German patient), Race Gailey (office boy), Bob Maza (Darkie's mate), Zac Martin (Ernie), Kevin Healey (old acquaintance), Betty Dyson (drunkess), Beth Brookes (singer), Pauline Foxall (pianist), Robert Ewing (public servant), Max Osbiston (Frederick Parsons). NARRATOR: Guy LeClaire.

Bill Donald is a middle-aged metho-drinker sentenced to six weeks in prison for a minor offence. There he volunteers for psychiatric treatment for his alcoholism and is committed to a hospital for the criminally insane, supposedly only for the duration of his prison sentence. He finds, however, that under section 27A of Queensland's mental health act he can be held there until the hospital authorities declare him eligible for release. He clashes repeatedly with a sadistic male nurse, Cornish, and is detained in the hospital because of his 'unco-operative' attitude. Three times he escapes, to drink and to visit his dying wife. Eventually, with the help of a journalist, his case attracts public attention and he is released.

27A is remarkable above all for the central performance of Robert McDarra as Bill Donald. McDarra, who died in December 1975, was himself an alcoholic and had been a professional actor for many years in radio with the Australian Broadcasting Commission, on stage and occasionally in films. With the director, he created a character who is no mere victim of a disease or of a bureaucratic system: he emerges forcefully as a man with no illusions either about himself or about the

419 Robert McDarra (*l*) and Esben Storm during the shooting of *27A*

419 *27A* Robert McDarra

people around him; he can be surly and cynical, but still compassionate towards his fellow-travellers. The screenplay was developed from interviews that Esben Storm conducted early in 1972 with Robert Somerville, whose forcible detention in a Queensland hospital had caused a local controversy in the late 1960s. Storm did not conceive of his film as an exposé of government malpractice; the Queensland mental health act, which had enabled the hospital to detain Somerville, had already been modified to prevent similar incidents from occurring. Rather, his film explored the 'social neurosis' which created the situation: 'the asylum in the film is not a reflection of the people in it, but more a reflection of the society that built it'. Sandra Hall in the *Bulletin*, 27 July 1974, welcomed the film as 'one of the best features so far produced here, adorned with bitter and sometimes funny dialogue [and] rich characterisations'.

The 16mm film was shot on location in March 1973 at a Christian Brothers' psychiatric hospital near Sydney. Following advice from Cecil Holmes, who had helped edit Storm's script, the production was elaborately pre-planned and shooting was relatively trouble-free. The production cost of $40 000 was raised from a syndicate of businessmen and from a grant of $13 000 from the Film and Television School.

Late in 1973 the film figured prominently in the Australian Film Awards and in June 1974 was presented with general critical acclaim at the Sydney Film Festival, but major distributors remained nervous of the film's subject. Eventually it was taken over by a small but effective Melbourne enterprise, Sharmill Films, and was released on 25 July 1974 as the opening attraction at the Playbox Cinema, Melbourne, a new cinema administered by the Australian Film Institute.

Esben Storm and Haydn Keenan were both in their early twenties when the film was made. They had studied film at the Swinburne College of Technology, Melbourne, and in Sydney worked briefly as production assistants at the Commonwealth Film Unit. For their own production company, Smart Street Films, they made several short films including *In His Prime* (1972), directed by Esben Storm, and *Stephanie* (1972), directed by Haydn Keenan, before embarking on *27A*.

420 The Cars that Ate Paris

1974 PETER WEIR

PC: Salt Pan Films/Royce Smeal Film Productions. P: Hal McElroy, Jim McElroy. SC: Peter Weir. STORY: Peter Weir, Keith Gow, Piers Davies. PH: John McLean. CAM OP: Richard Wallace, Peter James, Andrew Fraser. ED: Wayne Le Clos. ART D: David Copping. M: Bruce Smeaton. PM: Pom Oliver. ASST D: Hal McElroy. SD R: Ken Hammond. SD MIX: Peter Fenton. STUNT CO-ORD: Peter Armstrong. 91 mins. Colour. Scope.

CAST: John Meillon (the mayor), Terry Camilleri (Arthur), Kevin Miles (Doctor Midland), Rick Scully (George), Max Gillies (Metcalf), Danny Adcock (policeman), Bruce Spence (Charlie), Kevin Golsby (insurance man), Chris Haywood (Daryl), Peter Armstrong (Gorman), Joe Burrow (Ganger), Edward Howell (Tringham), Max Phipps (Reverend Mulray), Melissa Jaffer (Beth), Tim Robertson (Les), Herbie Nelson (man in house), Charles Metcalfe (Clive Smedley), Deryck Barnes (Al Smedley).

A sardonic exercise in Australian Gothic horror, *The Cars that Ate Paris* introduces an indecisive innocent, Arthur, who is a passenger in a car that crashes on a country road near the lonely town of Paris. Stranded in the town, Arthur gradually realizes that the townspeople make a living from car accidents and deliberately cause them. A climax comes when a fleet of monstrous vehicles, reconstituted from wrecked cars and driven by local delinquents, attack the town and cause widespread destruction. In the conflict, Arthur overcomes his fear of driving and leaves the scene of mayhem behind him.

The film marked a leap for Weir from Commonwealth Film Unit documentaries and his previous 16mm feature, *Homesdale* (1971): made in colour and Scope, by a highly proficient crew experienced in feature production, and conceived with overseas markets in mind, the production was initiated and organized by the McElroy brothers, after a long apprenticeship in administrative positions on numerous feature film and television projects. Most of their budget of $250 000 was raised from the Australian Film Development Corporation, with additional funds and equipment from Royce Smeal Film Productions in Sydney. Shooting began in October 1973, primarily on location at the small town of Sofala, near Bathurst, N.S.W.

420 *The Cars that Ate Paris*

An energetic effort was made to launch the film at the Cannes Festival in May 1974, with a publicity campaign highlighted by the appearance in Cannes of the film's killer car—a Volkswagen covered with deadly spikes. Much publicity was given in Australia to a likely distribution deal with the American Roger Corman, but as months passed it failed to eventuate. Reactions at the Sydney and Melbourne Film Festivals in June were vigorously divided, prefiguring the critical acclaim and commercial failure that occurred when the film opened at the Australian Cinema, Melbourne, on 10 October 1974. Attempts were made to salvage the film commercially by changing distributors (from M.C.A. to B.E.F.) and by changing the advertising campaign from horror movie to art film (in Canberra during the 'Australia 75' arts festival), but neither succeeded. London, too, was a disappointment, with four weeks in a West End cinema, the Rialto, in June 1975, but there, as in Australia, the general critical reaction was some consolation. Many Australian critics welcomed it as a change from 'ocker' comedy and for the sophistication of its narrative method; John Meillon's performance in particular as the sinister mayor of Paris was singled out for praise, and for Mike Harris in the *Australian*, 15 June 1974, the film indicated that, after many 'false dawns . . . the sun has finally come up' for Australian cinema.

421 Stone

1974 SANDY HARBUTT

PC: Hedon Productions. EXEC P: David Hannay. P: Sandy Harbutt. SC: Sandy Harbutt, Michael Robinson. PH: Graham Lind. ED: Ian Barry. ART D: Tim Storrier. M: Billy Green. SD: Cliff Curll, Tim Lloyd. STUNT CO-ORD: Peter Armstrong. 126 mins. Colour.

CAST: Ken Shorter (Stone), Sandy Harbutt (Undertaker), Deryck Barnes (Doctor Townes), Hugh Keays-Byrne (Toad), Roger Ward (Hooks), Vincent Gil (Dr Death), Dewey Hungerford (Septic), James H. Bowles (Stinkfinger), Bindi Williams (Captain Midnight), John Ivkovitch (Zonk), Lex Mitchell (Ballini), Rhod Walker (Chairman), Slim de Grey (Inspector Hannigan), Owen Weingott (Adler), Ray Bennett (Sergeant Larsen), Bill Hunter (barman), Helen Morse (Amanda), Rebecca Gilling (Vanessa), Sue Lloyd (Tart), Ros Talamini (Sunshine), Victoria Anoux (Flossie), Jane Gilling (Eurydice), Eva Ivkovitch (Tiger), Billy Green (69), Michael Robinson (Pinball), Gary McDonald (bike mechanic), Terry Bader (hamburger man), Lachlan Jamieson (disco proprietor), Drew Forsythe, Ros Spiers, Harry Lawrence.

When several members of a motorcycle gang are violently murdered, Stone, an undercover cop, is sent to investigate. Posing as a member of the gang, he finds himself protecting the 'bikies' and at the same time trying to prevent them from taking bloody vengeance on suspected enemies.

The idea for the film originated in 1970 when Harbutt wrote a script for an episode in the television series, *The Long Arm*, in which he was appearing regularly as a detective. The series was abandoned before his story was filmed. Later Harbutt revived the project and won support from the Australian Film Development Corporation, which invested $154 000 in the film. The remainder of the total budget of $195 000 and most of the technical facilities were supplied by Ross Wood Productions, Sydney.

The film was shot late in 1973 in and around Sydney. Interior scenes were shot on location, many of them in an old bikie haunt, the Forth and Clyde Hotel in Balmain, which was restored from dereliction to its former glory for the film. Harbutt himself had long been involved in bike-riding activities, and members of Sydney bike gangs were recruited to play bit parts. Principal cast members included Harbutt's wife, Helen Morse, as Stone's high-society girlfriend, and Hugh Keays-Byrne, formerly of the Royal Shakespeare Company, as one of the gang.

The film emerged as a curious cross between a violent thriller and a sympathetic exploration of the gang's lifestyle. The action scenes (including spectacular stunt work devised and executed by Peter Armstrong) and the heavy rock music were designed especially for young audiences. The Australian censors, however, gave it an R certificate for its violence, thereby cutting it off from a large part of the youth market (those under the age of 18).

The distributors, B.E.F., arranged a world première on 28 June 1974 at the Forum Theatre, Sydney, with guests ranging from amused bikies to government ministers, and with strong promotion it went on to make a profit for the government investment body within eighteen months.

421 *Stone*

421 *Stone*

422 Yackety Yack

1974 DAVE JONES

PC: Acme Films. P, SC, ED: Dave Jones. PH: Gordon Glenn. ASST D: Rod Bishop. P ASST: Ian Armet, Andrew Pecze. SD R: Peter Beilby and Lloyd Carrick. 86 mins. 16mm.

CAST: Dave Jones (Maurice), John Flaus (Steve/himself), Peter Carmody (Zig), Peggy Cole (Caroline), John Cleary (building manager), Jerzy Toeplitz (man in the street), Doug White (Socrates), Rod Nicholls (Kirilov), Andy Miller (Mishima).

Maurice is a would-be film director trying to hold a rational discussion about film with his friends, Steve, Zig and Caroline. They are helpless against his authoritarian power as director, and any of their statements that displease him are edited out of the discussion. The opinion is also sought of the man in the street (played by an unsuspecting Jerzy Toeplitz, just before his appointment as head of the Film and Television School). Three famous suicides (Mishima, Socrates and Kirilov) are staged to provide correlatives for Maurice's own intended suicide, and the increasingly megalomaniacal director murders the camera crew and sound technicians, before forcing Steve and Zig to assist in his suicide.

Openly intended 'to commit as many outrages as possible against standard aesthetic criteria of film', *Yackety Yack* was an aggressive intellectual comedy, peppered with Godardian political and theoretical pronouncements, both by Maurice (in his verbal onslaught) and by the film's 'real' director, Dave Jones (in messages flashed on the screen to enlighten and insult the critics and the audience). By playing the role of Maurice himself, Jones effectively blurs the relationship between the film and 'reality', since at times Maurice is more obviously in control of the film than Jones, instructing the camera to 'keep rolling' and threatening to edit out pieces he doesn't like (which he often does).

Despite its apparently random surface, the film had been carefully rehearsed on video and was fully scripted. It was made while Jones was on the teaching staff of the Media Centre at La Trobe University in Melbourne. An American with an M.A. in film from Stanford University, Jones had made several short films in the U.S.A., had written episodes for Warner Brothers television series, and had come to Australia to lecture in film at La Trobe in 1971. *Yackety Yack* was shot in the evenings over a five-week period in the film studio at the university, and was completed by the end of 1972 with financial aid from the Experimental Film and Television Fund. Jones left Australia soon after, and the film was placed in the Vincent Library for distribution. With an R certificate (because of the strong language and Caroline's persistent nudity, which Maurice demanded for box-office reasons), it opened at the Melbourne Co-op Cinema in mid-September 1974.

Supporting Jones in the cast were Peggy Cole, a student in Jones's classes, John Flaus, probably Australia's most articulate analyst of American film genres, then lecturing with Jones at La Trobe, and Peter Carmody, an important figure in Carlton theatre and himself an occasional film director.

423 Petersen

1974 TIM BURSTALL

PC: Hexagon Productions. P: Tim Burstall. ASSOC P: Alan Finney. SC: David Williamson. PH: Robin Copping. ED: David Bilcock. ART D: Bill Hutchinson. M: Peter Best. SD R: Ken Hammond. SD MIX: Peter Fenton. 107 mins. Colour.

CAST: Jack Thompson (Tony Petersen), Jacki Weaver (Susie Petersen), Wendy Hughes (Trish Kent), Belinda Giblin (Moira), Arthur Dignam (Charles Kent), Charles Tingwell (Reverend Petersen), Helen Morse (Jane), John Ewart (Pete), David Phillips (Heinz), Christine Amor (Annie), Sandy Macgregor (Marg), Joey Hohenfels (Debbie), Amanda Hunt (Carol), George Mallaby (executive), Anne Pendlebury (Peggy), Dina Mann (Robin), Karen Petersen (Teresa), Syd Conabere (Annie's father), Charmain Jacka (Annie's mother), John Orcsik (Walter), Robert Hewitt, Lindsay Smith, Tim Robertson and Graham Matherick (bikies), Moira Farrow (Mrs Blunden), Cliff Ellen and Bill Bennett (bushmen).

423 *Petersen* Jack Thompson

Tony Petersen, an electrical tradesman and former football star, reacts against the values of suburbia (as represented by his beer-swilling and intolerant mates) and enrols at university in the Arts faculty. In this new milieu, he is quickly involved in a public demonstration of love-making as a protest against sexual conventions, a fight with bikies at a party, and an affair with his tutor, Trish Kent, who wants him to give her a child. In all of these activities, Petersen is welcomed for his ingenuous, extroverted manner and his physical aggression, but he ultimately finds himself betrayed when Trish rejects him for a post at Oxford and her husband fails him in the examinations. Hurt and bitter, he violently rapes Trish and returns, defeated, to his work as an electrician.

Intended as an exploration of conflict between university-educated middle-class liberalism and self-made working-class values, the film was seen by Bruce Beresford in *Quadrant*, June 1975, as a revelation of 'the vulnerable under-side of the Ocker image'. The trampling of Petersen's sensibilities by hypocritical academics was expressed mainly in comic terms in the scenes of culture-clash on the campus and especially in the idiomatic dialogues by David Williamson. Numerous scenes of sexual activity, both romantic and comic, and with much frontal nudity, also lightened the tone. Aided by strong performances, especially from Jacki Weaver as Petersen's cosy suburban wife and Wendy Hughes as his ambitious academic lover, the film opened to generally favourable reviews at the Rapallo Theatre, Sydney, on 25 October 1974. The distributor, Roadshow, launched a major promotion of the star, Jack Thompson, and the film attracted solid commercial results throughout Australia. It was released in England late in the following year and, retitled *Jock Petersen*, it received a major U.S. release (using 120 prints) through Avco-Embassy.

424 **Between Wars**

1974 MICHAEL THORNHILL

PC: Edgecliff Films/McElroy and McElroy/T. and M. Films. P: Michael Thornhill. ASSOC P, PM: Hal McElroy. SC: Frank Moorhouse. PH: Russell Boyd. CAM OP: David Gribble. ED: Max Lemon. P DES: Bill Hutchinson. COSTUMES: Marilyn Kippax. M: Adrian Ford. ASST D: Michael Lake. SD R: Ken Hammond. SD MIX: Peter Fenton. 101 mins. Colour.

CAST: Corin Redgrave (Dr Edward Trenbow), Judy Morris (Deborah Trenbow), Günter Meisner (Dr Karl Schneider), Arthur Dignam (Dr Peter Avante), Patricia Leehy (Marguerite), Jone Winchester (Deborah's mother), Brian James (Deborah's father), Reg Gillam (Trenbow's father), Betty Lucas (Trenbow's mother), Neil Fitzpatrick (Lance Backhouse), Martin Vaughan (Dick Turner), John Chance (radio announcer), John Armstrong (barman), Noel Brady (Rodney at 20), Peter Collingwood (judge), Peter Cummins (Colonel Steele), Betty Dyson (Mrs Riley), Stuart Finch (Syme), David Goddard (minister), Ken Goodlet (New Guard major), Reg Gorman (dispensary orderly), Martin Harris (Major Hook), Judy Lynne (officer), Max Meldrum (Reverend Smith), John Morris (superintendent), Rob Steele (vomiting patient), Melissa Jaffer (matron), Graham Corry (asylum director), Robert Quilter (barrister).

Between Wars is a portrait of a man observed at four crisis points during his life. In 1918 Edward Trenbow is a well-intentioned but blundering army doctor treating shell-shocked soldiers from the trenches in Flanders. Later, in the 1920s, while working as a psychiatrist in a Sydney insane asylum, he becomes involved in experiments with Freudian psychiatry and provokes the repressive attention of a Royal Commission. To escape notoriety, he retreats to the country in the 1930s to work as a doctor in a small town, but again finds himself thrust into conflict as the figure-head of a farmers' co-operative in a violent clash with the reactionary New Guard. He withdraws to Sydney and establishes a prosperous psychiatric practice, but soon war is upon him again; a German colleague who had first introduced him to Freudian psychology is interned, and Trenbow fights with the Australia First movement against this and similar injustices, but again to no avail. Bitter, emotionally drained by a turbulent lifetime, and branded as a traitor, he helplessly watches as his son goes off to fight in the war.

424 *Between Wars*

424 *Between Wars* Corin Redgrave (*l*), John Chance

Through Trenbow the film offered an ambitious sketch of the interaction between new ideas and a conservative, parochial establishment. Trenbow is trapped in the middle; as Mike Harris wrote in the *Australian*, 16 November 1974, he is the perfect realization of 'the noble acquiescent: he's hounded by circumstances and events and heroic causes at which he finds himself unwillingly the centre . . . Corin Redgrave [as Trenbow] exudes exactly the right air of an idealist bewildered by what he is championing, and even more by the reactions of those about him.'

424 *Between Wars* Arthur Dignam

Thornhill's first feature arose out of a long friendship and collaboration with the short-story writer and novelist, Frank Moorhouse. They had both been part of a Sydney intellectual and anarchist pub culture (with John Flaus, Ken Quinnell and others), and Thornhill had made one short film, *The American Poet's Visit* (1969) from one of Moorhouse's stories and two others from scripts written by him, *The Girl from the Family of Man* (1970) and *The Machine Gun* (1971). Moorhouse's script for the feature had originated as a project for the Commonwealth Film Unit in the new wave of creative enthusiasm there around 1970. The project was dropped for several years, but with script development funds from the Australian Council for the Arts and the Australian Film Development Corporation, it was later revived and turned into a workable screenplay. Thornhill proceeded to secure a 50 per cent investment in the $320 000 production from the A.F.D.C., and the remaining funds came primarily from a Sydney property developer. Shooting took place in February-March 1974, with interiors staged in the former Cinesound studio at Bondi, and locations including the New South Wales town of Gulgong and the Rippon Lea mansion in Melbourne.

Thornhill approached the marketing of the film with determined independence: avoiding the use of distributors, he made arrangements directly with exhibitors, including Greater Union Theatres, and the film opened simultaneously in Sydney and Canberra on 15 November 1974. Critical support was generous and the film's appeal was strongest to the 'art house' audience, unfortunately too small to return much money to the producers. After its initial release in the major cities it was rarely screened and was eventually placed for distribution in the Vincent Library. Overseas sales were aggressively pursued and in March 1976 it opened in London at the Gate Cinema, but again became more of a critical than a commercial success.

Born in Sydney on 29 March 1941, Thornhill worked for several years as a film critic for the *Australian* and wrote extensively about the politics and economics of the Australian film industry. He also lectured in film at the University of New South Wales while developing his expertise in film production. In addition to his three short narrative films, he made several documentaries for the Commonwealth Film Unit and worked as a freelance film editor in Sydney.

425 Alvin Rides Again

1974 DAVID BILCOCK, ROBIN COPPING

PC: Hexagon Productions. P: Tim Burstall. ASSOC P: Alan Finney. SC: Alan Hopgood. ADDITIONAL SCENES: Tim Burstall, Alan Finney. PH: Robin Copping. ED: Edward McQueen-Mason. ART D: Bill Hutchinson. M: Brian Cadd. PM, ASST D: Ross Dimsey. SD R: Des Bone. 89 mins. Colour.

CAST: Graeme Blundell (Alvin Purple/Balls McGee), Frank Thring (Fingers), Chantal Contouri (Boobs La Touche), Lloyd Cunnington (Mr Dimple), Clare Balmford (Greta), Marcia Essers (second girl), Candy Raymond (Miss Willing), Alan Finney (Spike), Briony Behets (Miss Williams), Maurie Fields (garage proprietor), Abigail (Mae), Debbie Nankervis (Gwen), Dina Mann (Myrtle), Penne Hackforth-Jones (Meredith), Esme Melville (cleaning lady), Nanette Good (butch lady), John-Michael Howson (bellboy), Reg Gorman (bookmaker), Lindsay Edwards (first barracker), Terry Gill (second barracker), Gus Mercurio (Jake), Nat Levison (Harry), Arna-Maria Winchester (Nancy), Kris McQuade (Mandy), Joy Thompson (Cindy), Jeff Ashby (Loopy Schneider), Ross Bova (dwarf), Frank Wilson (house detective), Jon Finlayson (magician), Noel Ferrier (The Hatchet), Brian Cadd and the Bootleg Family.

Alvin's search for a steady job is repeatedly disrupted by the irresistible attraction that he seems to hold for women. When he and his friend Spike help a team of women cricketers win a match they decide to spend their share of the prize-money in a casino. There they become entangled in the world of international crime and Alvin is persuaded to impersonate an American gangster, Balls McGee, whom he happens to resemble and who has just been accidentally killed. Thereafter Alvin has to cope with rival gangsters as well as with the continuing series of eager and passionate women.

This $300 000 sequel to *Alvin Purple* (1973) found only a small part of the original's popularity, but was still a highly profitable venture, grossing film hire of over $600 000 by the end of 1977. Directed jointly by Tim Burstall's photographer, Robin Copping, and his editor, David Bilcock, the film was scarcely a critical success. The *Bulletin*, 4 January 1975, found that the film had moved 'a long way from the Oz innocence that won the first picture its success', and saw no evidence

425 *Alvin Rides Again* Graeme Blundell

that the directors 'knew what they had with the first film'.

With the full force of Roadshow's publicity machine, the world première was held at the Paris Theatre, Brisbane, early in December 1974. Offered as a school holiday attraction, the film, with its frontal nudity and alleged immorality, aroused the ire of local church groups and the state censorship authorities, but the attendant publicity only helped its commercial progress.

426 *Barry McKenzie Holds his Own* Barry Crocker (c)

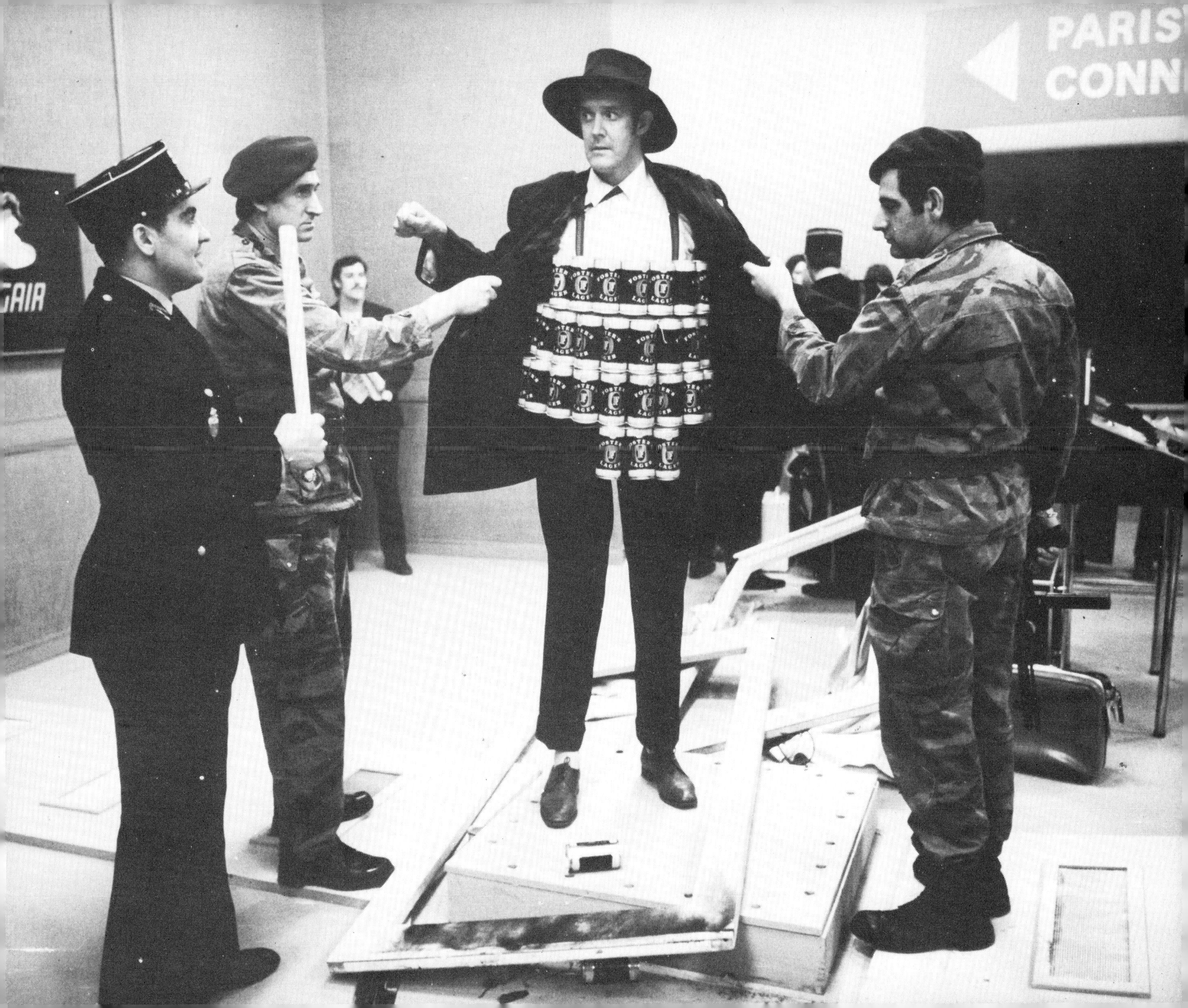
PARIS
CONN
FOSTERS
LAGER

426 Barry McKenzie Holds His Own

1974 BRUCE BERESFORD

PC: Reg Grundy Productions. P: Bruce Beresford. ASSOC P: Jane Scott. SC: Barry Humphries, Bruce Beresford. PH: Don McAlpine. ED SUP: John Scott. ED: William Anderson. ART D: John Stoddard, Alan Casse. M: Peter Best. PM: Drummond Challis, Jean-Pierre Avice, Marie-Claude Sourd. ASST D: Neil Vine-Miller, David Barrow. SD R: Des Bone. SD RE-R: Peter Fenton. 98 mins. Colour. Scope.

CAST: Barry Crocker (Barry McKenzie/Kevin McKenzie), Barry Humphries (Senator Douglas Manton/Edna Everage/Meyer de Lamphrey/offensive buck-toothed Englishman), Donald Pleasence (Count Plasma), Dick Bentley (Col 'The Frog' Lucas), Ed Devereaux (Sir Alec Ferguson), Roy Kinnear (Bishop of Paris), Frank Windsor (police sergeant), Derek Guyler (police constable), Arthur English (Cockney spiv), Desmond Tester (Marcel Escargot), John Le Mesurier (Robert Crowther), Tommy Trinder (Arthur McKenzie), Michael Newman (Foureyes Fenton), Brian Tapply (Sir Nigel Stewart), Clive James (Paddy), Louis Negin (Hugo Cretin), Paul Humpoletz (Modeste Imbecile), Beatrice Aston (Cherylene McKenzie), Don Spencer (quizmaster), Little Nell (Nerida Brealey), Katya Wyeth (Germaine), Merdelle Jordine (Rhonda Cutforth-Jones), Robert Gillespie (Dorothy), Andrew Lodge (Scrotum Baker), Nancy Blair (Clothilde), Chantal Contouri (Zizi), Craig Canning (Tassie), Michael Downey (Skeeter), Lincoln Webb (Ambrose Cutforth-Jones), Meiji Suzuki (kungfu champion), Gough Whitlam (himself), Margaret Whitlam (herself), Tony Rayns.

The second Barry McKenzie film follows his further adventures in London, Paris and Transylvania. His Aunt Edna is mistaken for Queen Elizabeth of England and kidnapped by the Transylvanians in a vain bid to boost their tourist industry. Barry joins forces with his twin brother, the Reverend Kevin (who is in Paris lecturing on 'Christ and the Orgasm'), and a party of officials from Australia House in London, and they invade the Transylvanian castle of the vampire, Count Plasma. The count is vanquished with a cross made from beer cans, and Edna is rescued just in time from an automatic blood-sucking machine. Barry and Edna are repatriated back to Australia and are welcomed at Sydney airport by the Prime Minister, Gough Whitlam, and his wife.

A home movie that Edna takes to Europe was shot at Palm Beach, Sydney, in December 1973, and late in the month, Bruce Beresford flew to London for five weeks of pre-production work. Shooting on the major part of the film began in February. A few studio scenes were staged in London, but most of the film was shot on location in England, Wales and Paris. Work continued rapidly despite attempted disruption by British unions who objected to the Australian cast and crew working on British soil. The finance (approximately $450 000) was entirely Australian, provided by the television entrepreneur Reg Grundy, and it was one of the few Australian features after 1970 to be made without government investment. Apart from Barry Crocker and Barry Humphries, the Australians in the cast were recruited from among expatriates and visitors in London, including Clive James, a literary critic playing the drunkest of Barry's mates, and Ed Devereaux in a delightful portrait of an Australian diplomat dressed perpetually in baggy shorts and long socks.

Distributed by Roadshow, it opened simultaneously in Sydney (at the Ascot) and Melbourne (at the Bryson) on 12 December 1974 and played strongly throughout the holiday period. Following the success of the first film in Britain, the sequel was readily accepted for distribution and it opened well in London in mid-1975.

427 The Love Epidemic

1975 BRIAN TRENCHARD SMITH

PC: Hexagon Productions. EXEC P: Alan Finney, Tim Burstall. P, SC: Brian Trenchard Smith. ASSOC P: Geoff Brown. COMEDY MATERIAL: Michael Laurence. PH: Russell Boyd, Greg Hunter, Stuart Fist, Ross Blake. ED: Ronda MacGregor. SD: Cliff Curll, Bob Hayes, John Franks. 83 mins. Colour.

CAST: Michael Laurence, Ros Spiers, Peter Reynolds, Grant Page, Tim Lynch, John Ewart, Barry Lovett, Jane Lister, Luda Apinys, Ken Doyle, Billy Thorpe and the Aztecs. NARRATOR: Deryck Barnes.

This semi-documentary about venereal disease incorporates clinical case studies and sex health instruction with comic sketches illustrating aspects of the theme. The cast play different roles in each sketch: Peter Reynolds, for example, appears variously as Henry VIII, undergoing a cure for syphilis far worse than the disease, and as a Woody-Allen-inspired character named Gonorrhoea who reminisces with Syphilis over a few cans of beer inside the intestines of their next victim. Interviews with the actor Roger Ward, singer Billy Thorpe, movie stuntman Grant Page and other are scattered through the film.

The documentary scenes, according to *Variety*, 15 January 1975, were 'full of interest, appear to be well researched, and . . . no one could take offense [at them]'; the rest was weakened by 'feeble and predictable comedy sequences which provoke many yawns and little laughter'. The sex education elements were further overshadowed by digressions including a wild party, nude love-making, a pop concert, and a history of VD with a violent reconstruction of the siege of a medieval castle by marauding Vikings.

Shot on 16mm and blown up to 35mm for theatrical release, it was promoted as a 'sexploitation' film and released by Roadshow in theatres catering mainly for the 'raincoat brigade' at the State Theatrette, Sydney, and the Times Theatrette, Melbourne, both on 3 January 1975. Later that month two members of the cast, Luda Apinys and Ken Doyle, sought an injunction to have the film withdrawn on the grounds that they had been engaged to act in an educational film, which had emerged as 'nothing but pornography'. Their action failed and distribution of the film continued.

428 The Firm Man

1975 JOHN DUIGAN

P, SC, M: John Duigan. PH: Sasha Trikojus. ED: Tony Patterson. SD: Lloyd Carrick. GRAPHICS: Lynsey Martin. 100 mins. Colour. 16mm.

CAST: Peter Cummins (Gerald Baxter), Eileen Chapman (Melissa), Bethany Lee (the girl), Peter Carmody (Barry), Dianne Preston (Christie), Sarah Chapman (Sally), Marie Keenan (pub lady), John Preston (Melissa's lover), Max Gillies (managing director), Barry Pittard (George), Larry Stevens (marketing manager), Cliff Ellen (Carl), Alan Finney (Michael), Don Gunner (Representative 306), Kris McQuade (Anne Thropormorphic), C. Jas Mitchell (Speaker), Robert Meldrum and Bruce Spence (messengers), Lindsay Smith (narrator, street theatre), Bill Garner (teacher, street theatre), Howard Parkinson (stripper), John Duigan (diner).

Gerald Baxter, a middle-aged businessman, starts a new job as a highly paid executive in a company known as the Firm. After a meaningless interview with a supervisor who is preoccupied with his vegetable garden, Gerald is introduced to his secretary, Miss Anne Thropomorphic, and finds that his only duties are to collect occasional messages from a mysterious pair of agents. Frustrated and bored, Gerald becomes alienated from his suburban home life and from his wife, who has taken on a lover from the Firm. For a while he befriends a girl who represents an alternative life of freedom and fulfilment, but finally he succumbs to the manipulations of the Firm and accepts his place as a complacent member of the staff.

This fantasy about middle age and mediocrity, big business and alternative society, was an ambitious but undisciplined début by John Duigan. He had previously written and acted in several Melbourne films, most impressively in Nigel Buesst's *Bonjour Balwyn* (1971). He had also worked extensively as writer, director and actor in experimental theatre in Melbourne, and had written a novel, *Badge*, published in Sydney in 1975. *The Firm Man* was shot in Victoria, partly with funds provided by the Australia Council. Its premiere was held on the opening night of the 'Australia 75' festival in Canberra, on 7 March. A month later it began a short season at the Playbox Theatre, Melbourne, but subsequent screenings were rare.

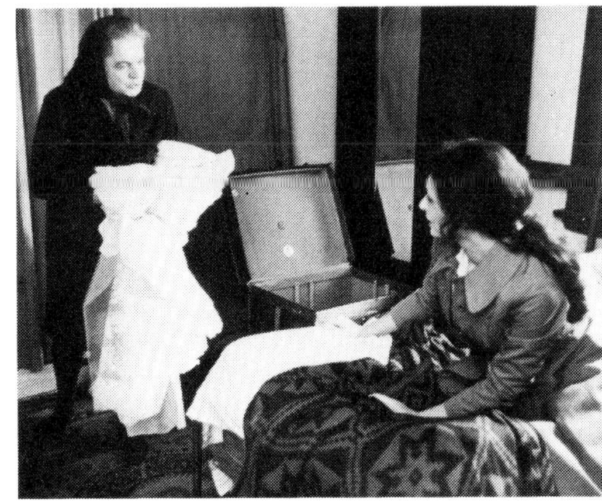

429 *Promised Woman* Yelena Zigon (*r*)

429 Promised Woman

1975 TOM COWAN

PC: B.C. Productions. P: Tom Cowan, Richard Brennan. SC, PH: Tom Cowan. From the play *Throw Away Your Harmonica* by Theo Patrikareas. ED: David Stiven. ART D: Gillian Armstrong. M: Vassili Daramaras. PM: Errol Sullivan. ASST D: Graham Shirley. SD: Laurie Fitzgerald. 84 mins. Colour.

CAST: Yelena Zigon (Antigone), Takis Emmanuel (Manolis), Nikos Gerissimou (Telis), Kate Fitzpatrick (Marge), Darcy Waters (Ken), Carmel Cullen (Helen), George Valaris (Nick), Alex Alexandrou (Basil), Thea Sevastos (Elpitha), Jean-Claude Petit (the lover), Maria Valaris (Cleo), Jim Kaldis (Mr Papadopoulos), Anne Hallinan (girl at front door), John Papadopoulos (himself), Sally Blake (Lulu), Graham Shirley (employment officer), Gillian Armstrong (nurse), John Delacour (trolley attendant), John Nassim (groom at airport), Dorothy Economou (bride at airport).

Antigone, the prospective bride in an arranged marriage, arrives in Sydney from Greece, only to be rejected by her proposed groom, Telis, who had expected a younger woman. Telis's older brother, Manolis, sympathizes with Antigone, but she gradually withdraws into herself, remembering her earlier life and romance in Greece, and longing for control over her own destiny.

Narrated from the viewpoint of a migrant newly arrived in Australia, and exploring the life of the Greek community in Sydney, *Promised Woman* was a welcome change from the customary Australian image of migrants in comedies such as *They're a Weird Mob* (1966) or *Sunstruck* (1972). The film was based on a play by a Greek writer, Theo Patrikareas, who had lived for a time in Australia and whose play had first been performed in Sydney in 1962 by the Hellenic Theatre Company. The supporting cast for the film was assembled locally, including several actors from the Hellenic troupe, but the leads were filled by imported players—Yelena Zigon from Yugoslavia and Takis Emmanuel from Greece, both with substantial acting experience on the stage and screen of their own countries. Both established close ties with Australia; Takis Emmanuel appeared later in a featured role in *Caddie* (1976), and

Yelena Zigon returned in October 1976 to play in *The Picture Show Man* (1977). Like Cowan's *The Office Picnic, Promised Woman* was shot on 35mm for a fraction of the cost of other local features being made at the same time. The total cost was around $80 000, a large proportion of which was provided by the Australian Film Development Corporation. The small crew of fourteen technicians included Gillian Armstrong and Graham Shirley among several recruits from the Film and Television School. Shooting began early in March 1974 and proceeded for three weeks on locations around Sydney and in a boarding house in the suburb of Kirribilli. Early in April, Cowan, Brennan and Yelena Zigon flew to Greece to film her village home life and scenes with her lover, played by Jean-Claude Petit.

A version of the film running 96 minutes premièred at the 'Australia 75' arts festival in Canberra in March 1975. In the following months some scenes were cut and the ending was altered to show Antigone walking alone towards an uncertain future (originally the film had ended with her marriage to Telis). It was not until 3 December 1976 that it opened in Sydney at the Village City Cinema complex where it failed despite the support of critics. Sandra Hall in the *Bulletin*, 11 December 1976, found the atmosphere of the 'grey, terraced landscape of inner Sydney . . . striking, pervasive and totally convincing', but although it was 'supremely well-cast', the film was ultimately flawed by its script, with 'good moments arranged around what is basically a contrived theme'. It was released in Greece in April 1977.

430 The True Story of Eskimo Nell

1975 RICHARD FRANKLIN

PC: Quest Films/Filmways Australasian Distributors. P: Richard Franklin, Ron Baneth. SC: Alan Hopgood, Richard Franklin. PH: Vince Monton. ED: Andrew London. ART D: Josephine Ford. M: Brian May. PM: Sue Farrelly. ASST D: Darryl Sheen. SD R: John Phillips. SD RE-R: Peter Fenton. SECOND UNIT D: Jacques Jean. STUNTS: Graham Matherick. 103 mins. Colour.

CAST: Max Gillies (Dead Eye Dick), Serge Lazareff (Mexico Pete), Paul Vachon (The Alaska Kid), Abigail (Esmerelda), Kris McQuade (Lil), Elli Maclure (Elly), Grahame Bond (Bogger), Max Fairchild (Posthole Jack), Anthony Bazell (Professor Brayshaw), Ernie Bourne (barman), Paddy Madden (the real Eskimo Nell), Victoria Anoux (the dream Eskimo Nell), Elke Neidhardt, Bob Horsfall, Jerry Thomas, Luigi Villani, Kurt Beimel.

430 *The True Story of Eskimo Nell* Max Gillies. Frame enlargement

In the mid-nineteenth century, two drifters wander through the goldfields of Australia—a one-eyed, yarn-spinning voyeur, Dead Eye Dick, and a cowboy womanizer, Mexico Pete. Driven on by Dick's extravagant dreams and by a faded picture postcard, they search obsessively for their ideal woman, the legendary Eskimo Nell, and eventually find her in a mining town hotel.

This adaptation of the bawdy ballad (attributed to the Canadian writer Robert Service) concentrated on Dead Eye Dick as a pathetic and ageing dreamer rather than on Pete's supposed sexual prowess, and the frankest moments of sex lay in a few verses of the ballad read on the soundtrack.

Financed largely by the Australian Film Development Corporation and the Australian distributor, Filmways, the $200 000 production was shot in mid-1974 on location in rural Victoria (including Falls Creek for the snow scenes) and in an improvised studio in the Exhibition Building, Melbourne. After completing the Australian scenes, the director, his cameraman, and the actor Max Gillies, flew to Canada to shoot one day's work in a large bar-room setting that had been built for the Montreal Expo in 1967. A Canadian crew was hired to shoot another sequence, at Sept Isles, Quebec—involving a pursuit on ice-floes, supposedly in the style of D. W. Griffith's *Way Down East* (1920)—but the results were poor and most of the sequence was reshot in Melbourne in close-up.

As release neared, morally vigilant groups such as the Festival of Light claimed that government funds were being used to produce pornography, leading to questions in parliament and to television debates. Most of the protests served, however, to publicize the film and did not delay its release. A more serious threat arose in the form of a British comedy, *Eskimo Nell*, based on the same ballad and produced at about the same time; it was only after long manoeuvring that the Australian release of the British film was delayed until 1976 and its title changed to *The Sexy Saga of Naughty Nell and Big Dick*. The Australian film was later released in England as *Dick Down Under*.

The film was released by Filmways at the Hoyts Cinema Centre, Melbourne, on 27 March 1975, and ran for eight weeks. Critical opinion varied widely, from 'a really high quality pic' (*Variety*, 9 April 1975), to 'the film is simply not worth showing' (*National Times*, 7-12 July 1975). To improve its commercial chances, the director cut some seven minutes after the first Melbourne release (reducing it to 94 minutes), but he was unable to save it from a disastrous Sydney season in June.

Born in Melbourne in 1948, Richard Franklin studied film for two years at the University of South California before returning to work in television, first with the Australian Broadcasting Commission, and later for Crawford Productions in Melbourne, where he directed episodes of the *Homicide* series.

431 Sidecar Racers

1975 EARL BELLAMY

PC: Universal Pictures. P: Richard Irving. SC: Jon Cleary. PH: Paul Onorato. ED: Robert Kimble. M: Tom Scott. PM: Jim Hogan, Warwick Freeman. SD SUP: Les McKenzie. SD R. John Heath. STUNT CO ORD: Everett Creech. STUNTS: Peter Armstrong, Bill Peters. 100 mins. Colour.

CAST: Ben Murphy (Jeff Rayburn), Wendy Hughes (Lynn Carson), John Clayton (Dave Ferguson), John Meillon (Ocker Harvey), John Derum (Pete McAllister), Peter Gwynne (Rick Horton), Serge Lazareff (Stumpy Wilson), Paul Bertram (Bob Horton), Patrick Ward (Tex Wilson), Arna-Maria Winchester (Marlene), Vicki Raymond (Virginia), Kevin Healey (store manager), Brian Anderson (store detective), Brenda Senders (Mrs Horton), Liddy Clark (cashier), Brian Nyland (ambulance man), Loretta Saul (singer), Peter Graves (Carson).

A young American surfer visiting Australia drifts into the world of sidecar motorcycle racing. He forms a close friendship with a dedicated rider and his girlfriend, and the two men form a champion racing team.

The simple formula of the plot, designed to allow a maximum of racing, resembled the sort of teenage sports movie (usually about surfing) that Universal had produced in the 1960s. Although filmed in Australia, the finance was entirely American and key personnel came primarily from the mainstream of American television. Shooting began in March 1974, with race sequences at the Sydney Showground and at the Mount Panorama circuit, Bathurst, during the Easter bike trials. The film had its world première at the Ascot Theatre, Sydney, on 30 April 1975.

432 Sunday Too Far Away

1975 KEN HANNAM

PC: South Australian Film Corporation. P: Gil Brealey, Matt Carroll. SC: John Dingwall. PH: Geoff Burton. CAM OP: Graham Scaife. ED: Rod Adamson. P DES: David Copping. M: Patrick Flynn, arranged by Michael Carlos. PM, ASST D: Malcolm Smith. SD R: Barry Brown. SD ED: Greg Bell. SD MIX: Peter Fenton. STUNTS: Ian Jamieson. 94 mins. Colour.

CAST: Jack Thompson (Foley), Max Cullen (Tim King), Robert Bruning (Tom West), Jerry Thomas (Basher), Peter Cummins (Arthur Black), John Ewart (Ugly), Sean Scully (Beresford), Reg Lye (Old Garth), Graham Smith (Jim the Learner), Laurie Rankin (old station hand), Lisa Peers (Sheila), Philip Ross (Mr Dawson), Gregory Apps (Michael), Doug Lihou (George), Ken Weaver (Quinn), Kurt Jansen (Wentworth), Phyllis Ophel (Ivy), John Charman (Sydney), Ken Shorter (Frankie), Bill O'Dea (station master), Hedley Cullen (Harry the mailman), Wayne Anthony (undertaker).

The title comes from the lament of a shearer's neglected wife: 'Friday night, too tired; Saturday night, too drunk; Sunday, too far away.' The setting is an outback sheep station in 1956; Foley, the gun shearer, joins a new

432 *Sunday Too Far Away* John Ewart (*c*), Jack Thompson (*second from r*)

shearing team and shares a room with Old Garth, a former top shearer who is now a drunkard and who mirrors a possible future for Foley. As the shearing season progresses, the team battles with the grossly inadequate cook; Old Garth dies, and Foley befriends the grazier's daughter. When the 'prosperity bonus' of a few pence per hundred sheep is withdrawn from the shearers' entitlements, they go on strike. The film ends as Foley and his team confront the non-union labour brought in by the graziers to complete the shearing.

The film was the first feature produced by the South Australian Film Corporation, established in 1972 by the state premier, Don Dunstan, to promote a commercially viable film industry in the state. The corporation was guaranteed the production of all state government films and was given authority to borrow funds to finance its own productions. Substantial investments were secured from the Australian Film Development Corporation for the $300 000 feature, and shooting began in March 1974. Made entirely on location near Port Augusta and Quorn in South Australia (with the same shearing shed on Carriewerloo Station used fifteen years earlier in *The Sundowners*), the production struck severe rains and floods and was completed behind schedule early in May. In the post-production phase, substantial cuts were made to the romantic sub-plot between Foley and the grazier's daughter, reducing the role of the girl to a few enigmatic appearances, and leaving a crucial scene (in which Foley breaks down and confesses his fears for the future) unmotivated and out of character. A scene in which Foley crashes his car and walks away from it in disgust was also moved from the end of the film to the beginning.

Carefully promoted by the S.A.F.C., the film established a record of critical success before its first commercial release. In March it won four major prizes in the Australian Film Awards, including a Golden Reel as best feature film, and was selected for screening in the Directors' Fortnight at the Cannes Festival, May 1975, where it was warmly welcomed by European critics. English critics seemed to find it easiest to appraise the film by comparison with familiar American standards: David Robinson in *The Times,* 21 May 1975, found the qualities of John Ford in the film's perception of 'a sort of grandeur in people of the most limited horizons and spirits'; and Ken Wlaschin in *Films and Filming,* August 1975, likened the film's view of male companionship to the work of Howard Hawks. The film went on to open the Sydney Film Festival on 1 June, and appeared at several overseas festivals later in the year.

After a lavish première in Adelaide on 15 June 1975, the film opened commercially the next day in the Warner Theatre, Adelaide. Interstate distribution was handled by Roadshow and the film quickly established a strong box-office record.

The director, Ken Hannam, was born in Melbourne and worked in radio as an actor and writer before starting in television in 1956 as a writer and later as a producer and director. In 1968 he went to London and worked extensively in television series such as *Z Cars* and *Dr Finlay's Casebook,* before returning to Australia in 1974 to direct *Sunday Too Far Away.*

433 The Man from Hong Kong

1975 BRIAN TRENCHARD SMITH

PC: The Movie Company (Sydney)/Golden Harvest (Hong Kong). EXEC P: Raymond Chow, John Fraser. P: David Hannay, André Morgan. SC: Brian Trenchard Smith. PH: Russell Boyd. ED: Ron Williams, Alan Lake. ART D: David Copping, Chien Shun. M: Noel Quinlan. SONGS: 'Sky high' by Des Dyer, Clive Scott, sung by Jigsaw; 'A man is a man is a man' by Noel Quinlan. P CO-ORD: Pom Oliver, T. C. Lau. ASST D: Hal McElroy, Chu Yut-hung. SD R: Cliff Curll. SD RE-R: Peter Fenton. STUNT CO-ORD: Peter Armstrong, Grant Page. MARTIAL ARTS INSTRUCTOR: Hung Kam-po. 103 mins. Colour. Scope.

CAST: Jimmy Wang Yu (Inspector Fang Sing-Ling), George Lazenby (Jack Wilton), Ros Spiers (Caroline Thorne), Hugh Keays-Byrne (Morrie Grosse), Roger Ward (Bob Taylor), Rebecca Gilling (Angelica), Frank Thring (Willard), Hung Kam-po (Win Chan), Grant Page (assassin), Deryck Barnes (Angelica's father), Bill Hunter (Peterson), Ian Jamieson (drug courier), Elaine Wong (Mei Ling), John Orcsik (Charles), André Morgan (rooftop guard).

Inspector Fang from Hong Kong arrives in Sydney to assist in the extradition of a Chinese drug-smuggler. When his charge is murdered, Fang remains in Australia to crack the narcotics ring. His target is Wilton, a powerful figure in the Sydney underworld, who uses a martial arts school as a cover for his operations. Using a hang-glider to bypass Wilton's defences, Fang confronts him in a violent showdown which results in Wilton's death.

The numerous martial arts films both starring and directed by Wang Yu in Hong Kong were renowned for the ingenuity and bloodiness of their violence, and *The Man from Hong Kong* sustained this image: weapons ranged from meat-hooks to javelins and the villain is dispatched with a hand grenade thrust into his mouth. From the opening scene of a kung fu fight on top of Ayers Rock intercut with a helicopter chasing a speeding car in the nearby desert, the emphasis is on comic-strip action, which the *Bulletin,* 13 September 1975, aptly described as 'live-action Tom and Jerry'.

The director, Brian Trenchard Smith, had long specialized in movie stunt work and in 1973 had made a prize-winning documentary for television, *The Stuntmen*. His work in *The Man from Hong Kong* displayed a good-humoured gusto that disarmed many critics, especially the British, who were less self-conscious about the film than the Australians, and Tony Rayns in the *Monthly Film Bulletin*, September 1975, found that it 'hits a note of throwaway excess that has eluded the recent [James Bond] movies'.

The film marked the first pre-production investment by the Greater Union Organization since *Sons of Matthew* (1949). John Fraser, the general manager of B.E.F. Distributors (a subsidiary of Greater Union), co-produced the film with the Hong Kong company of Golden Harvest. An investment was also received from the Australian Film Development Corporation, and a total of $535 000 was spent on the production.

In July 1975, the film was released in the U.S.A. by Twentieth Century-Fox under the title, *The Dragon Flies*. Distribution in Asia was handled by Cathay, and in Britain by Rank. In Australia, B.E.F. opened the film simultaneously at two Sydney theatres, the Rapallo and the Metro King's Cross, on 4 September. Publicity was helped by a theme song that became a popular hit, and the emphasis on hang-gliding helped to stimulate a growing interest in the sport in Australia. An R certificate from the Australian censor prohibited a large proportion of the youth market (those under 18 years of age) from seeing the film, and box office trading in Australia was less than anticipated. Overseas revenue, however, was strong, and Asian earnings especially put the film comfortably into profit.

433 *The Man from Hong Kong* Jimmy Wang Yu

434 *The Great MacArthy* Barry Humphries (*l*), John Jarratt

434 The Great MacArthy

1975 DAVID BAKER

PC: Stoney Creek Films. P: David Baker. EXEC. P: Richard Brennan. ASSOC P: Alan Benjamin. SC: John Romeril. From the novel, *A Salute to the Great McCarthy*, by Barry Oakley. PH: Bruce McNaughton. CAM OP: Gale Tattersall, Keith Wagstaff. ED: John Scott. ART D: David Copping. M: Bruce Smeaton. PM: Michael Martorana. ASST D: Hal McElroy. SD R: Ron Green. 93 mins. Colour.

CAST: John Jarratt (MacArthy), Judy Morris (Miss Russell), Kate Fitzpatrick (Andrea), Sandy Macgregor (Vera), Barry Humphries (Colonel Ball-Miller), John Frawley (Webster), Colin Croft (Tranter), Chris Haywood (Warburton), Colin Drake (Ackerman), Ron Frazer (Twentyman), Max Gillies (Stan), Dennis Miller (MacGuinness), Lou Richards (Lou Arnold), Jack Dyer (Jack Diehard), Jim Bowles (Les), Bruce Spence (Bill Dean), Peter Cummins (Rerk), Cul Cullen (MacArthy senior), Maurie Fields (company director), Laidley Mort (Henry), Tim Robertson (Herb), Sally Conabere (nurse), Jon Finlayson (Vincent), Max Meldrum, Bill Garner, John Derum, Luigi Villani, Burt Cooper.

MacArthy is a country football hero kidnapped by the South Melbourne club and made a star player in the city. The chairman of the club, Colonel Ball-Miller, gives MacArthy a job in one of his companies and tries to improve him with night school. There he is seduced by the English teacher, Miss Russell, who introduces him to the world of high culture. As his popularity grows, MacArthy takes part in a television commercial as Batman and injures both himself and Colonel Ball-Miller's fiery daughter, Andrea. In hospital, MacArthy and Andrea become passionate lovers, despite their plaster casts, and are soon married. Their relationship equally quickly breaks down, and the Colonel insists on divorce, threatening to ruin MacArthy's football career if he does not co-operate. MacArthy refuses to give up his claim to the family fortune, and goes on strike in the middle of a game. With the loyal support of Miss Russell, he stands firm against all the forces that the Colonel can muster.

David Baker saw MacArthy as a fundamentally 'recessive' character, moving 'through a dramatic landscape teeming with

Dickensian-style grotesques'. Characters like Ackerman, an ageing clerk with a passion for bird-mimicry and flying experiments; Vera, a hysterical Jewish girl; Warburton, the office clown; Tranter, a predatory homosexual television producer—all briefly involve a wide-eyed MacArthy in their own eccentric worlds and then disappear from the film. Baker's gallery of weird characters, the persistently frenetic action, and the aggressive bad taste of some of the humour, confounded many critics, who reacted strongly against the film. On the other hand, Phillip Adams in the *Age*, 31 January 1976, deplored such reactions for their 'mean spirited' attitude and acclaimed the film's subtle undertone of humanity.

Shot in mid-1974 for $250 000 (of which half was provided by the Australian Film Development Corporation), the film was released by Seven Keys at the height of the 1975 football season, opening at the Athenaeum Theatre, Melbourne, on 7 August. Financial return was minimal.

435 The Box

1975 PAUL EDDEY

PC: Crawford Productions. P: Ian Jones. SC: Tom Hegarty. STORY: Tom Hegarty, Ray Kolle. PH: Wayne Williams. CAM OP: David Eggby. ED: Philip Reid. ART D: Leslie Binns. MUSIC ED: Gary Hardman. PM: David Lee. ASST D: Geoff Morrow. SD R: Gary Wilkins. 100 mins. Colour.

CAST: Barrie Barkla (Max Knight), Fred Betts (Sir Henry Usher), Belinda Gilbin (Kay Webster), Ken James (Tony Wild), Paul Karo (Lee Whiteman), George Mallaby (Paul Donovan), Tracy Mann (Tina), Judy Nunn (Vicki Stafford), Lois Ramsey (Mrs Hopkins), Ken Snodgrass (Jack O'Brien), Geraldine Turner (Lindy Jones), Luigi Villani (Mick), Robin Ramsay (Bruce Madigan), Cornelia Frances (Dr S. M. Winter), Keith Lee (Price), Marilyn Vernon (Ingrid O'Toole), Graham Kennedy (himself).

The television serial, *The Box*, about the daily crises in the work of a busy television station, had been produced regularly since early 1974 by Crawford Productions in Melbourne. A feature film spin-off was prompted largely by the relative financial success in 1974 of a feature based on a rival serial, *Number 96*. Like *Number 96*, *The Box* retained the characters of the serial and used the freer censorship of the cinema to lace the film with nudity, but it was a substantially more ambitious production, making an effort to tell a coherent story and aiming for an acceptable technical standard by shooting on 35 mm with a reasonable budget. The Australian Film Development Corporation contributed substantially towards the budget of $300 000, and the film was shot over a four-week period early in 1975.

The film's fictional television station, UCV-12, is in financial difficulty; an efficiency drive is launched by the managing director, Sir Henry Usher, and a female systems expert, Dr S. M. Winter, is called in to advise. Desperate attempts are made by the staff to impress Dr Winter but they go sadly awry. A feature film, *Manhunt* (looking very much like one of Crawford's own television police dramas), is being shot to try to boost the station's income, but the star, Tony Wild, is so disaster-prone that the film finally has to be reconceived as a comedy. Eventually the paths of the main characters cross in a series of hotel bedroom mix-ups and seductions, and after getting drunk for the first time in her life, Dr Winter is persuaded to report favourably on the work of the studio staff.

435 *The Box*

Distributed by Roadshow, it opened at the Albert Cinema, Brisbane, on 8 August 1975.

436 Picnic at Hanging Rock

1975 PETER WEIR

PC: Picnic Productions. A McElroy and McElroy production in association with Pat Lovell. SC: Cliff Green. From the novel by Joan Lindsay. PH: Russell Boyd. CAM OP: John Seale. ED: Max Lemon. ART D: David Copping. ARTISTIC ADVISER TO DIRECTOR: Martin Sharp. COSTUME DES: Judith Dorsman. ORIGINAL M: Bruce Smeaton. ASST D: Mark Egerton. P ASST: Pom Oliver. SD R: Don Connolly. 115 mins. Colour.

CAST: Rachel Roberts (Mrs Appleyard), Dominic Guard (Michael Fitzhubert), Helen Morse (Diane de Poitiers), Jacki Weaver (Minnie), Vivean Gray (Miss McCraw), Kirsty Child (Dora Lumley), Anne Lambert (Miranda), Karen Robson (Irma), Jane Vallis (Marion), Christine Schuler (Edith), Margaret Nelson (Sara), John Jarratt (Albert), Ingrid Mason (Rosamund), Martin Vaughan (Ben Hussey), John Fegan (Doctor McKenzie), Wyn Roberts (Sergeant Bumpher), Gary McDonald (Constable Jones), Frank Gunnell (Edward Whitehead), Peter Collingwood (Colonel Fitzhubert), Olga Dickie (Mrs Fitzhubert), Kay Taylor (Mrs Bumpher), Tony Llewellyn-Jones (Tom), Faith Kleinig (cook), Jenny Lovell (Blanche), Janet Murray (Juliana).

Picnic at Hanging Rock is a tale of mystery and menace in a sunny Australian landscape. Its story of late-Victorian schoolgirls and a teacher who vanish while exploring the volcanic outcrop of Hanging Rock offers many tantalizing possibilities: the suggestion of a time warp (sounds of the search for the girls are heard before they are lost), the dreamlike haze of a hot summer's day in the bush that makes things seem not quite what they are, and the awe-inspiring power of the Australian bush, which alienates some and hypnotically absorbs others.

The mysteries of Joan Lindsay's book were scrupulously cultivated by the film-makers. Weir created a thorough network of visual, verbal and aural imagery which deepened the mystery: flower symbolism, scars that appear on the foreheads of sympathetic characters, the singing of 'Rock of Ages', haunting panpipe music, and much more, supported its animistic force. Enigma also surrounded the source of the story: the public was encouraged by both the novelist and the film-makers to believe that the disappearance had actually happened.

436 *Picnic at Hanging Rock*

The book was first published in 1967 and the screen rights secured by Patricia Lovell in 1973. After two years in search of funds, the production began in February 1975 with backing from the Australian Film Development Corporation, B.E.F. Distributors, and the South Australian Film Corporation, whose investment was conditional upon the film being shot substantially in South Australia. The total budget was around $450 000. The six-week shooting schedule began with scenes at Hanging Rock in Victoria followed by work in South Australia, at the historic mansion of Martindale Hall near Mintaro (for exteriors of the school building), and in the S.A.F.C.'s studio in Adelaide. The British actress Vivien Merchant was cast as the unstable headmistress of the girls' school, but fell ill shortly before her arrival in Australia and her place was taken by the Welsh actress, Rachel Roberts. Distributed by B.E.F., the film had its world première at the new Hindley cinema complex in Adelaide on 8 August 1975. It became an immediate commercial

436 *Picnic at Hanging Rock* Karen Robson (*c*)

and critical landmark in Australian cinema. Its popularity in Australia was followed by international critical acclaim at Cannes in May 1976, and it readily found sales in England and Europe, and later in the U.S.A.

On the strength of its success, Patricia Lovell quickly became one of Australia's busiest producers. She had had long experience in television, working as a compere of a children's programme, *Mr Squiggle*, for the Australian Broadcasting Commission, as a reporter on the current affairs programme, *Today*, for the Seven network, and as an actress in series such as *Skippy* and *Homicide*.

Cliff Green, too, found his career greatly boosted by the film. It was his first screenplay for a feature film, but he had previously written prolifically for television and radio, including serials, children's programmes and documentaries for the ABC, and for three years had been a staff writer for Crawford Productions in Melbourne preparing episodes of *Homicide* and *Matlock Police*. He later worked as a freelance writer and contributed episodes to many ABC series, including *Rush* and *The Norman Lindsay Festival*. A quartet of plays by Green, under the group title of *Marion*, was televised by the ABC in 1974 and attracted much attention for their perceptive portrayal of a young schoolteacher (played by Helen Morse) in a small country town.

437 Pure S

1975 BERT DELING

PC: Apogee Films. P: Bob Weiss. SC: Bert Deling and the cast. PH: Tom Cowan. ED: John Scott. PM: Larry Meltzer, Russell Kirby. SD: Lloyd Carrick. 83 mins (including 6 mins of introductory music). Colour. 16mm.

CAST: Gary Waddell (Lou), Ann Heatherington (Sandy), Carol Porter (Gerry), John Laurie (John), Max Gillies (Dr Wolf), Tim Robertson (TV interviewer), Helen Garner (Jo), Phil Motherwell.

Pure S is the episodic story of four young heroin addicts in their journey through Melbourne's drug sub-culture in search of their next drug supply. Bert Deling consciously directed the action as a comedy, with rapid-fire dialogues in the manner of Howard Hawks, violent colours, and actors in constant hectic motion. His aim was to communicate the hysteria of the drug-taker's life-style, and because 'most people who see *Pure S* are looking into an alien world we thought comedy would make that process a little easier'. Not all audiences appreciated the style—the hard rock music, the coarse language, lingering close-ups of vascular injections—and a critic in the Melbourne *Herald*, 3 May 1976, tagged it 'the most evil film that I've ever seen' and found the comedy 'as appropriate as a musical about Auschwitz'. The Commonwealth film censors responded initially by banning the film altogether, and then releasing it with an R certificate provided that the title was changed from the original *Pure Shit* (slang for refined heroin). But the film had a power to polarize opinion, and reactions that recognized the dramatic validity of Deling's approach came from several sources. Bob Ellis found it 'a gutter-hugging but oddly homeric account' of the junkies' life, with dialogue 'strangely close in spirit, if not in slang or cadence, to that of the great Neil Simon—sharp and lean and pugnacious' (*Nation Review*, 31 March-6 April 1977).

The film's budget of $28 000 was partly provided by the Film, Radio and Television Board of the Australia Council, and partly by the Buoyancy Foundation, an organization to help drug-takers. The aim was to make a film to counter the government-produced anti-drug films, which failed either to communicate the realities of the drug scene or to reach people with drug problems. It premièred at the Perth Film Festival on 15 August 1975, but because of its censorship problems did not open commercially until 7 May 1976 at the Playbox Cinema, Melbourne.

438 The Golden Cage

1975 AYTEN KUYULULU

PC: Independent Artists. P: Ilhan Kuyululu. SC: Ayten Kuyululu, Ismet Soydan. SCRIPT ED: Harold Lander. PH: Russell Boyd. ED: David Huggett. ART D: Sonia Hofmann. M: Mary Vanderby (restaurant scenes), Aspidistra (rock music and lyrics). PM, ASST D: Phil Noyce. PRE-P: Ian Stocks. SD R: Carlo Tachi. SECOND UNIT (Turkey): D: Molkan Kayhan. PH: Hami Sami Cosar. SD R: Attila Aksu. 70 mins. Colour. 16 mm.

CAST: Sait Memisoglu (Ayhen), Ilhan Kuyululu (Murat), Kate Shiel (Sarah), Ron Haddrick (rich man), Michelle Fawdon (guitar player), Emel Ozden (girl in Istanbul), Kerry-Ann Scott (girl in tavern), Kate Williams (girl in disco), Caesar (pianist), David Elfick (man at party), Moi-Moi (Asian waitress), Margaret Sneddon (old woman), Michael Nassar (barman), Frank Shields (wine waiter), Sonia Hofmann and Roz Radin (models), Ron Owen (film director).

This simply constructed tragedy traces the lives of two Turkish migrants in Australia. The older of the two, Murat, works hard and saves money to buy a truck, but eventually uses his savings to visit Turkey to celebrate his sister's wedding. The other, the handsome and restless Ayhen, has an affair with an Australian girl, Sarah. Ayhen wants to marry her but his family opposes the idea because he is a Muslim and she is an 'infidel'; Sarah refuses to give up her own religion for his, and they gradually grow apart. When Ayhen finds that Sarah is to bear his child, he insists violently that she marry him, but she adamantly refuses. The relationship ends in despair and suicide.

Filmed primarily in Sydney, with occasional inserts of documentary footage from Turkey, *The Golden Cage* was produced with the aid of $22 500 from the Film, Radio and Television Board of the Australia Council. Much of the dialogue was shot in Turkish and subtitled in English.

The director and her husband, Ilhan, migrated from Turkey to Sweden in 1964, where she made a 57-minute television film, *The Outsiders*, about the problems of Turkish migrants in Sweden. In 1971 they came to Australia and settled in Sydney. Ayten Kuyululu sang in the Australian Opera Company, and with her husband, established the Australian Turkish People's Playhouse, performing plays for the Turkish community in Sydney. Her first Australian film was *A Handful of Dust* (1973), a 40-minute story of a middle-aged woman's involvement in a blood vendetta. Ayten and Ilhan Kuyululu played the leading roles themselves, and Ilhan later took one of the leading roles in *The Golden Cage*.

The film was shot in March and April 1975 and was first screened in Australia as part of the International Women's Film Festival in August and the following months, but Australian theatrical and television companies showed no interest in handling it.

439 How Willingly You Sing

1975 GARRY PATTERSON

PC: Inch Films. P, ED, GRAPHICS: Garry Patterson. SC: Garry Patterson and cast. PH: Peter Tammer. M: arranged by Robert Patterson, performed by The Inner Circle. P ASST: Jim Robertson. SD: Spence Williams. VIDEO: Ruben Mow. 89 mins. Colour. 16mm.

CAST: Garry Patterson (Simon Dore), Isaac Gerson (the Astrologer), Jim Robertson (the Cop), Jerry Powderly (the Psychiatrist), Morris Gradman (the Wandering Jew), Braham Glass (the Mother), Allan Levy (the Revolutionary), Pat Longmore.

This 16mm narrative film, produced with the aid of $12 000 from the Experimental Film and Television Fund, was the personal work of Garry Patterson, a young architecture graduate, cartoonist and stage actor. His previous films included a 38-minute 'mimed excursion into the Cinema of the Absurd', *Retreat . . . Retreat* (1971), which won two prizes at the 1971 Australian Film Awards. *How Willingly You Sing* is a loosely structured fantasy expressing an absurd, comic view of the world, and centring on the eccentric screen persona of Patterson himself: he dominates nearly every scene, playing the banjo, talking to his 'misguided' psychiatrist, being advised by a white-haired astrologer, and searching for a Wandering Jew who holds the key to the salvation of the world. Patterson himself described the narrative as 'a character's futile and fruitless search to find himself within society and on society's terms. [His experiences] simply reinforce his misguided and typically Australian belief that everything is okay'.

After a première at the Perth Film Festival in August 1975, the film screened from 10 September to full houses during a three-week season at the Melbourne Co-op Cinema. Colin Bennett in the *Age*, 12 September 1975, admired the 'Lewis Carroll logic' and Patterson's 'well-timed sense of the absurd', but felt the need for more discipline to focus the film's ideas. Patterson subsequently worked prolifically in super 8mm, making documentaries and political films in Melbourne.

440 **Down the Wind**

1975 KIM McKENZIE, SCOTT HICKS

PC: Chrysalis Films. P: Scott Hicks. SC: Kim McKenzie. PH: Gus Howard. ED, WILDLIFE PH: Kim McKenzie, Scott Hicks. M: Mozart, Neil Young. P ASST: Paul Arlauskas, Kerry Heysen. SD: Peter Barker. 70 mins. 16mm. Colour.

CAST: David Cameron (Simon Jess), Penne Hackforth-Jones (Sara), Ross Thompson (Tom), Christina Mackay (Tina), Rod Mullinar (Reg), Christine Schofield (receptionist).

A young photographer, Simon Jess, accepts an assignment he does not really want, to shoot some backgrounds in the Snowy Mountains for a forthcoming fashion display. He abruptly departs for the mountains, leaving behind a comfortable lifestyle and a bewildered girlfriend, Sara. He dabbles half-heartedly in the social life of a mountain ski resort, then disappears into the wilds, pursuing a majestic falcon with which he has developed an all-consuming identification.

Apart from occasional cut-aways to Sara and her attempts to come to terms with Simon's restlessness, the film primarily forms a protracted metaphor with Simon's pursuit of fulfilment represented in his quest for the wild falcon. His own surname, Jess, is itself a falconry term, and the film stresses a line from a poem about the bird: 'I'd whistle her up and let her down the wind to prey at fortune.' In his search through the alpine bush for the bird, Simon is stunned in a fall and the branches enclose his figure like a nest; and the film ends abruptly as he reaches the peak of a mountain after a long climb to the falcon's nest, and he attains the elation of spirit he has long been seeking.

The film was the second of two joint projects by the South Australian film-makers, Kim McKenzie and Scott Hicks. Both were in their early twenties when the films were made, and both had recently graduated from the Drama Department at Flinders University in Adelaide. Their first film, *The Wanderer*, was completed in 1974 and screened at the Adelaide Film Festival, where it won an award for the best South Australian film in the festival. This 16mm film about a young man torn between university and life on the road prefigured the themes of *Down the Wind*, and featured two of the same cast members, Ross Thompson and Penne Hackforth-Jones. *Down the Wind* followed in 1975, completed on 16mm for $22 000, mostly provided by the Film, Radio and Television Board of the Australia Council. Scenes were shot in the Mount Kosciusko region and the Adelaide hills, and the first of the film's rare screenings was held in Adelaide on 28 August 1975. McKenzie subsequently joined the film unit of the Australian Institute for Aboriginal Studies in Canberra, and Hicks became an assistant director with the South Australian Film Corporation.

441 *Plugg* Peter Thompson

441 **Plugg**

1975 TERRY BOURKE

PC: Romac Productions. EXEC P: Robert Roget, Peter McNamara. P: Ninki Maslansky. ASSOC P: Terry Bourke, Rod Hay. SC: Terry Bourke. PH: Brian Probyn. ED: Rod Hay. ART D: Barry Adler. M: Bob Young. PM: Patrick Clayton. ASST D: Gerry Letts. SD R: Phil Judd. TITLES: Yoram Gross. STUNTS: Peter West, Frank Lennon. 88 mins. Colour.

CAST: Peter Thompson (Horatio Plugg), Norman Yemm (Inspector Closer), Cheryl Rixon (Kelli Kelly), Reg Gorman (Constable Hector), Joseph Furst (Judge Fraudenheist), Allan Cassall (Herman Cavanagh), David Vallen (Arab Barabbas), Phil Cleary (Big Mick Hendlebreyer), Bob Maguire (Percy Hazelwood), Michael Kent (Mark Adler), Edgar Metcalfe (Claude Marshall-Enright), Pat Skevington (Estelle Marshall-Enright), Helen O'Grady (Gwen Farrington), Max Bartlett (prosecutor), Robbie McGregor (hotel manager), Sid Plummer (Birdy Thorne), Georgina Danielle (body dancer), Robyn Aylward (Barabbas's secretary), Josie Mackay (massage madame), Raymond Long (defense counsel), Patrick Clayton (jury foreman), Eric Reade (court clerk), Chic Stringer (boudoir bouncer).

This slapstick sex comedy was the third exploitation feature by Terry Bourke and Rod Hay. The story follows the misadventures of an incompetent private detective named Plugg who is assigned to watch a suspect escort agency. In pursuit of Plugg comes a disaster-prone policeman, Inspector Closer, and a series of chases take the characters though a massage parlour, a nude swimming pool party, and a motel where illicit assignations take place.

Produced in Perth for $100 000, the film opened there on 3 October 1975 at the Grand Theatre. Seasons elsewhere were scattered and brief.

442 Scobie Malone

1975 TERRY OHLSSON

PC: Kingcroft Productions. P: Casey Robinson. ASSOC P: John Shaw. SC: Casey Robinson, Graham Woodlock. From the novel, *Helga's Web*, by Jon Cleary. PH: Keith Lambert. ED: Bill Stacey. P DES: Bill Hutchinson. M: Peter Clarke. SONG: sung by Kerrie Biddell. SD: David McConnachie. 98 mins. Colour.

CAST: Jack Thompson (Scobie Malone), Judy Morris (Helga Brand), Shane Porteous (Russ), Jacqueline Kott (Norma Halidon), James Condon (Walter Halidon), Joe Martin (Jack Savanna), Cul Cullen (Captain Bixby), Noel Ferrier (Mr Sin), Walter Sullivan (Police Inspector), Max Meldrum (scientific officer), Ken Goodlet (Premier), Joe James (Attorney General), Victoria Anoux, Zoe Salmon.

The first attempt to film one of Jon Cleary's Scobie Malone stories was *The High Commissioner*, made in England by Ralph Thomas in 1968, with Rod Taylor as Scobie. In this second film, Scobie investigates the life of a high-class call girl whose battered corpse has been found in the Sydney Opera House. His inquiries lead him to the upper levels of the government where he finds the murderer safely protected by political allies.

Casey Robinson, an American scriptwriter with a long line of major Hollywood credits, including *Dark Victory* (1939) and *King's Row* (1942), had settled in Australia in semi-retirement. Finance for the $300 000 production was partly supplied by the Australian Film Development Corporation, and shooting began in February 1975. The director, Terry Ohlsson, had made documentaries and commercials for many years, mostly for Kingcroft Productions in Sydney. This, his first feature, was released through Regent and premièred in Brisbane at the Albert Theatre on 3 October 1975. Few critics had anything positive to say about it, and box-office returns were poor.

443 The Removalists

1975 TOM JEFFREY

PC: Margaret Fink Productions. P, DESIGN: Margaret Fink. ASSOC P, PM: Richard Brennan. SC: David Williamson, from his own play. PH: Graham Lind. SET DESIGN: Bill Hutchinson. ED: Anthony Buckley. M: Galapagos Duck. ASST D: Michael Lake. SD R: Ken Hammond. SD ED: Martin Clarke. 93 mins. Colour.

CAST: Peter Cummins (Sergeant Simmonds), John Hargreaves (Constable Ross), Jacki Weaver (Marilyn Carter), Kate Fitzpatrick (Kate Mason), Martin Harris (Kenny Carter), Chris Haywood (the removalist).

Constable Ross, fresh from police training school, reports for his first day of work at a suburban police station run by the cynical Sergeant Simmonds. While Simmonds instructs Ross in the realities of life in the force, they become involved in a violent argument between a naïve woman and her boorish husband, after the woman's arrogant sister bullies her into reporting that she has been bashed.

The film closely followed the structure of David Williamson's play about authority and violence, first performed at La Mama, Melbourne, in 1971. Most of the dialogue was retained, as were the two basic sets of the police station and a small flat in a housing estate: rather than 'open up' the play with exterior scenes, the film-makers opted for a highly mobile camera to record the action indoors. Shooting took place in mid-1974 at the Ajax Studios, Bondi, with a budget of about $250 000, including a major investment from the Australian Film Development Corporation. It was the first film produced by Margaret Fink, and she was actively involved in the creative control of the film, not solely its administration. With her director, Tom Jeffrey, she achieved a subdued monochromatic effect in the lighting and colour that reinforced the bleakness of Williamson's theme.

Tom Jeffrey had worked extensively in television with the Australian Broadcasting Commission and in England with the BBC. In 1969 he directed the ABC television serial,

443 *The Removalists* Peter Cummins

Pastures of the Blue Crane, and in 1973 joined Air Programs International in Sydney. *The Removalists* was his first feature. It was released belatedly through Seven Keys on 16 October 1975 at the Century Theatre, Sydney, but it failed to attract the same popularity as Williamson's play. Reviews were generally favourable, with P. P. McGuinness in the *National Times*, 6-11 October 1975, welcoming it in the context of a current surfeit of 'nostalgia' films as a drama 'set firmly and unapologetically in the real Australia', and praising Peter Cummins and John Hargreaves for portraying 'on the one hand the callousness and hysteria of long failure and on the other the callowness and cowardice of the new recruit'.

444 Solo Flight

1975 IAN MILLS

P, SC: Ian Mills. PH: Gordon Glenn. ED: Kevin Stott. M: Sibelius. PM: Patricia Robbins. SD: Lloyd Carrick. CHIEF TECHNICIAN: Shaw Tan. ASST TECHNICIANS: Alan Walton, Ian Armet. 75 mins. Colour. 16mm.

CAST: Fiona Russell (the housewife), Don Barker, Sid Jennings, John Ley, James Bond, David Maher, John Tants, Sandra Tants, Ina Bertrand.

A housewife, alienated from her husband and her dull suburban existence, starts to take flying lessons, and briefly faces the possibility of an affair with a young man from the flying club. At the same time she dreams of an idyllic Eden where she and her friends live in harmony with nature and with each other. As the film ends the woman takes her first solo flight and soars high into the air, while in her mind she is transformed and liberated into another dimension of life.

This experiment in narrative structure was dominated by its dream sequences, with their emotional accompaniment of Sibelius's Second Symphony, their concentration on romantic images of nature, and with the dream people themselves, robed in sackcloth and moving slowly and silently in formation through the bush. Shot on 16mm for about $12 000 (partly provided by the Experimental Film and Television Fund), the film was screened briefly at the Melbourne Co-op Cinema in October 1975.

Mills, a former producer-director with the Australian Broadcasting Commission, was a lecturer in the Media Centre at La Trobe University, Melbourne, when the film was made.

445 Protected

1975 ALESSANDRO CAVADINI

P: Carolyn Strachan. PH: Fabio Cavadini. ED: Ronda MacGregor. Colour. 16mm. 55 mins.

Narrators: Don Brady, Robert Hughes.

Designed partly to record for Aborigines an episode of multi-tribal resistance against white domination, and partly to inform white audiences about conditions on Aboriginal reserves in Queensland, *Protected* was a passionate protest against the 'protective' legislation in Queensland under which Aborigines lost their basic freedoms and were subjected to physical and mental abuse. The film told the story of a strike in June 1957 when the Aborigines on the Palm Island reserve, off the north Queensland coast, refused to work or obey orders from white officials. The strike was broken when seven of the Aboriginal leaders were forcibly transferred to other reserves, but the issues at the heart of the strike remained unchanged.

In June 1974, with the aid of a sympathetic white film crew, the experiences leading up to and during the strike were relived by members of the Palm Island community. The film arose from the film-makers' contact with Aborigines from Queensland then living in

445 *Protected*

Redfern, Sydney. Invited to Palm Island to tell the story of the reserve, Alessandro Cavadini and Carolyn Strachan initially used video equipment to explore ideas from the film in a 'workshop' environment. During shooting, few scenes were rehearsed, and actions were filmed as they arose from discussions. The roles of the Aborigines in the strike were played either by relatives of the people involved or by themselves. The white officials were played by citizens from Townsville, on-shore from the island.

The first screening was held on Palm Island on 11 November 1975, and a print owned by the community was screened widely through reserves in Queensland. In June 1976 it was presented at the Sydney Film Festival as a finalist in the Greater Union Awards. Subsequent distribution was primarily through co-operatives and non-commercial outlets.

Cavadini came to Australia from Italy in 1969, after working for nine years in film animation. He spent several years as a freelance animator and cameraman, and in 1972 produced and directed *Ningla-a-na*, a documentary about the Aboriginal Embassy in Canberra and the attempts by the government to remove it. Australian distribution of *Ningla-a-na* was arranged by Carolyn Strachan, a former audiovisual librarian and television production assistant in Sydney. After working together on *Protected*, Cavadini and Strachan made a companion film, *We Stop Here* (1977), a record of stories told by old Aborigines in northern Queensland about early attempts by white settlers to massacre and poison their tribe.

446 Inn of the Damned

1975 TERRY BOURKE

PC: Terryrod Productions. P: Terry Bourke, Rod Hay. ASSOC P: Peter Medich, Roy Medich. SC: Terry Bourke. PH: Brian Probyn. CAM OP: Peter James, Richard Wallace. ED: Rod Hay. ART D: Gary Hansen. M: Bob Young. PM: Pat Clayton. ASST D: Mark Egerton. SD R: Tim Lloyd, Bob Hayes. GRAPHICS: Yoram Gross. STUNTS: Peter Armstrong. SECOND UNIT PH: Andrew Fraser, Alan Grice. 118 mins. Colour.

CAST: Dame Judith Anderson (Caroline Straulle), Alex Cord (Cal Kincaid), Michael Craig (Paul Melford), Joseph Furst (Lazar Straulle), Tony Bonner (Trooper Moore), John Meillon (George Parr), John Morris (Martin Cummings), Robert Quilter (Biscayne), Diana Dangerfield (Mrs Millington), Carla Hoogeveen (Beverley), Don Barkham (Sergeant Malone), John Nash (the Colonel), Phillip Avalon (Alfred), Lionel Long (search horseman), Gordon Glenwright (Squire Grimstead), Nat Levison (undertaker), Louis Wishart (Arnold), Reg Gorman (coach co-driver), George Pollack (Mad Mick Marriott), Linda Brown (Peaches), Anna King (coach passenger), Hilary Bamberger (Mrs Bennett), Graham Ware (coachdriver), Graham Corry (Andrew Millington).

Like Terry Bourke's previous feature, *Night of Fear* (1973), *Inn of the Damned* was originally a one-hour script intended for his projected television series, *Fright*, and again relied on violence as a box-office gimmick. In an old wayside inn in north-eastern Victoria in 1896, a crazed woman and her apparently mute husband take vengeance on society for the death of their children, years before, at the hands of an escaped convict. After many murders have taken place, an American bounty hunter comes to investigate the mysterious happenings at the inn, and during a long night of violence, he manages to end the rampage of the old couple.

The production was beset by open conflict between the producers and their principal backers (the Australian Film Development Corporation), spiralling costs and a long delay between completion and Australian release. Shooting began early in November 1973, with location work in the Blue Mountains near Sydney (standing in for the Gippsland area of Victoria), and interiors in the Artransa Studios, Sydney. It was released by Roadshow on 13 November 1975 at the Paris Theatre, Sydney, for a two-week season.

447 Nuts, Bolts and Bedroom Springs

1975 GARY YOUNG

PC: Garron International. P, SC: Gary Young. PH: Mal Pollard. P ASST: Steve Mills, Rob Aaron. SD: John Lennon, John True. TITLES: Eric Porter. 72 mins. Colour.

CAST: Gary Young (Fred), Steve Michaels, Val Moore, Lyn Samson, Adrian Penning, Steve Sweeney, Wendy Talbot, Russ Mulcahy, Kim Newman, Don Evans, Carol Lane, Barbara Jackson.

The producers issued the following synopsis: 'Fred is a guy that just can't get "It". . . . He gets the "knockback" from his wife, gets sprung with the luscious, curvy chick next door, perved on while hard at it in the car, attacked at a "blue" movie and so it goes on.'

This low-budget ($45 000) sexploitation movie was shot on 35mm and financed entirely by Garron International. To attract sceptical city exhibitors, the producer-director-actor, Gary Young, attempted, with some success, to establish a commercial record for the film in rural areas, beginning with a season in November 1975 at the Westview Drive-in Theatre, Dubbo, N.S.W.

Gary Young had previously made *Wheels on Fire* (1973), a 66-minute documentary in 35mm about drag racing and hot-rod cars.

448 The Lost Islands

1975 BILL HUGHES

PC: O-Ten Network/Paramount Pictures. P: Roger Mirams. ASSOC P, SC: Michael Laurence. PH: David Gribble. ED: Ross Simmons. ART D: Owen Williams. M: Bob Young. SONG: 'Lost islands', composed and sung by Michael Caulfield. PM: Peter Appleton. ASST D: Michael Midlam. SD R: Jack Friedman. 73 mins. Colour.

CAST: Tony Hughes (Tony), Jane Vallis (Anna), Robert Edgington (David), Amanda Ma (Sui Ying), Chris Benaud (Mark), Margaret Nelson (Helen Quinn), Rodney Bell (Aaron Quinn), Ric Hutton (Prime Minister), Michael Aitkens (Quig), Ron Blanchard (Quel), Michael Howard (Jason Quinn), Willie Fennell (Quizzle), Cornelia Frances (Mrs Quinn), Frank Gallagher, Ted Ogden, Ron Haddrick.

Five youngsters are shipwrecked on a tropical island where they find the descendants of eighteenth-century colonists who know nothing of modern times and live in a feudal state governed by a despotic ruler.

The adventures of the children on the island formed the basis of a 26-episode television series, *The Lost Islands*, largely shot in and around Sydney by the O-Ten television network in conjunction with Paramount Pictures of the U.S.A. The series was intended for world-wide television distribution, and the nationalities of the five children accordingly ranged across the globe—American, Australian, Chinese, English and German.

While the series was still in production, three of the early episodes were edited together to form a 35mm feature, released around Australia during the Christmas holidays, opening at the Capitol Theatre, Sydney, on 11 December 1975. The series commenced on Australian television in February 1976.

448 *The Lost Islands*

449 *Ride a Wild Pony* Robert Bettles in the grip of Michael Craig

449 Ride a Wild Pony

1975 DON CHAFFEY

PC: Walt Disney Productions. EXEC P: Ron Miller. P: Jerome Courtland. SC: Rosemary Anne Sissons. From the novel *A Sporting Proposition* by James Aldridge. PH: Jack Cardiff. SUP ED: Peter Boita. ED: Mike Campbell. ART D: Robert Hilditch. M: John Addison. PM: Peter Appleton. ASST D: Mark Egerton. SD R: John Heath. 88 mins. Colour.

CAST: Michael Craig (James Ellison), John Meillon (Mr Quayle), Robert Bettles (Scotty Pirie), Eva Griffith (Josie Ellison), Graham Rouse (Bluey Waters), Alfred Bell (Angus Pirie), Ron Haddrick (J. C. Strapp), Peter Gwynne (Sergeant Collins), Melissa Jaffer (Mrs Pirie), Kate Clarkson (Jeannie Quayle), John Meillon Jnr (Kit Quayle), Lorraine Bayly (Mrs Ellison), Wendy Playfair, Elizabeth Alexander, Jessica Noad, Neva Carr Glyn, Harry Lawrence, Les Foxcroft, John Fegan.

The first feature made in Australia by the Walt Disney organization was an unpretentious outdoors adventure set in the 1920s, about the rivalry between two children for ownership of a pony. One is the wilful son of a poor migrant farmer, the other the pampered crippled daughter of a wealthy horsebreeder. Their dispute over the pony leads to a legal battle, which temporarily divides the local community.

The British director, Don Chaffey, who had directed several previous features for Disney, staged most of the film on location in the small town of Chiltern, near Wodonga in northern Victoria. $50 000 was spent on giving the town a 1920s atmosphere: the main street was covered with dirt, several building façades were constructed, and existing buildings repainted. With a total budget of over $1 000 000, shooting began in October 1974, using a substantially Australian crew and only two non-Australian performers (Michael Craig, and the child actress, Eva Griffith, daughter of the British actor, Kenneth Griffith).

On 2 November 1975 B.E.F. gave the film a festive children's preview simultaneously in five state capitals and commercial seasons followed on 26 December in most states.

450 **End Play**

1976 TIM BURSTALL

PC: Hexagon Productions. P, SC: Tim Burstall. ASSOC P: Alan Finney. Based on the novel by Russell Braddon. PH: Robin Copping. CAM OP: Dan Burstall. ED: David Bilcock. ART D: Bill Hutchinson. M: Peter Best. SONG: sung by Linda George. PM, ASST D: Ross Dimsey. SD R: Des Bone. 114 mins. Colour.

CAST: George Mallaby (Robert Gifford), John Waters (Mark Gifford), Ken Goodlet (Inspector Cheadle), Robert Hewitt (Sergeant Robinson), Delvene Delaney (Janine Talbot), Kevin Miles (Charlie Bricknall), Charles Tingwell (Dr Fairburn), Walter Pym (Stanley Lipton), Sheila Florance (Mavis Lipton), Adrian Wright (Andrew Gifford), Belinda Giblin (Margaret Gifford).

A young female hitch-hiker is murdered on a remote stretch of highway in rural Victoria. Two brothers who live nearby arouse the attention of the police; one is Mark, a merchant seaman on leave, and the other, Robbie, an embittered paraplegic confined to a wheelchair. Both brothers act suspiciously, but it is uncertain whether each is seeking an alibi for himself or is trying to protect the other from arrest.

In adapting the setting of Russell Braddon's book from England to Australia, Burstall wrote (in a press release) of his interest in several 'very Australian' qualities in the characters. Not least among these was the 'ambiguous attitude' of Robbie towards the police, which Burstall saw as an Australian rather than a British characteristic. But above all, Burstall expressed interest in the 'naked and exposed relationship' between the brothers, with their suave manners thinly concealing 'a kind of directness and fairness that . . . is unlikely to be found in an English context'. The film emerged less as a straight whodunit than as a thriller observing the long and bizarre process of disposing of the corpse, and the tensions between the two suspects. It was above all an actors' piece, and it introduced two actors with strong television followings in their first major cinema roles: John Waters (from the Australian Broadcasting Commission series, *Rush*) as the introverted foil to George Mallaby (from *Homicide* and *The Box*) as the paraplegic.

With a total production cost of $294 000, the film was shot in January 1975, almost a year before its commercial release through Roadshow at the Mayfair Theatre, Sydney, and at a Hoyts Midcity Cinema in Melbourne, on 1 January 1976.

450 *End Play* John Waters

451 Caddie

1976 DONALD CROMBIE

PC: Anthony Buckley Productions. P: Anthony Buckley. SC: Joan Long. From the autobiography by 'Caddie'. PH: Peter James. ED: Tim Wellburn. ART D: Owen Williams. COSTUME DES: Judith Dorsman. M: Patrick Flynn. PM: Ross Matthews. ASST D: Hal McElroy, Janet Isaac, Steve Knapman. SD R: Des Bone. 103 mins. Colour.

CAST: Helen Morse (Caddie), Takis Emmanuel (Peter), Jack Thompson (Ted), Jacki Weaver (Josie), Melissa Jaffer (Leslie), Ron Blanchard (Bill), Drew Forsythe (Sonny), Kirrili Nolan (Esther), Lynette Curran (Maudie), June Salter (Mrs Marks), John Ewart (Paddy Reilly), John Gaden (solicitor), Jane Harders (Vikki), Phillip Hinton (John Marsh), Mary Mackay (Mater), Lucky Grills (pawnbroker), Robyn Nevin (Black Eye), Simon Hinton (Terry Marsh), Marianne Howard (Ann Marsh), Pat Everson (Mrs Norris), Carmel Cullen (pianola woman), Brian Nyland (dole clerk), Willie Fennell (doctor), Les Foxcroft (Mr Norris), Jack Allen (saloon pianist).

Based on the autobiography of a Sydney barmaid published pseudonymously in 1953, the film reconstructs her life between 1925 and 1932, after she leaves her adulterous husband to fend for herself and her two small children. Working as a barmaid, she falls in love with a Greek migrant, Peter, but their life together is disrupted when family obligations force him to return to Greece. In the depths of the Depression, Caddie's income is barely enough to live on, and she falls victim to malnutrition and nervous exhaustion. Help comes from a friendly 'rabbit-o' whose family share their meagre lot with her until she is well again. Always resilient and resourceful, Caddie now takes another job as barmaid, handling S.P. betting on the side, and gradually her life begins to look more hopeful.

With its loving attention to period detail (achieved on a tight budget of less than $400 000) the film was marked by the amiable spirit of its portrait of ordinary people and their life in the Depression. The film was shot on forty locations in the older parts of inner Sydney, with pub interiors staged at the old Cinesound studio at Rozelle. The period feeling was enriched by the film-makers' close familiarity with Australian cinema from the 1920s. Perhaps more than any other Australian producers or writers, Tony Buckley and Joan Long were able to benefit from their extensive research into Australian film traditions, and films like *Sunshine Sally* (1922), studied in the pre-production period, contributed much to *Caddie*'s image of old Sydney.

Finance was raised from the Australian Film Development Corporation, the *Australian Women's Weekly*, the Nine television network, the Secretariat for International Women's Year, and Roadshow (who distributed the film), and shooting began late in 1975. It was released on 9 April 1976 as one of the opening programmes in Greater Union's Pitt Centre cinema complex in Sydney. In less than a year it had grossed over $2 000 000 from the Australian box-office and from overseas sales, and the investors were able to recoup their inital outlay. Much of the success was due to the central performance of Helen Morse, and the film thrust her into prominence as a local star. P. P. McGuinness in the *National Times*, 19-24 April 1976, commented that she and her co-stars had created portraits of 'authentic Australian women, with absolutely correct accent and intonation', and had contributed 'immeasurably to [the film's] very firm feeling of local habitation'. The reputation of the film was aided by its participation at overseas festivals, including San Sebastian, where it won two major awards, including best actress (Helen Morse).

Anthony Buckley, Joan Long and Don Crombie were partners in the production company. Buckley was one of the most experienced feature film editors in Australia and had privately produced several 16mm films including a survey of Australian film history, *Forgotten Cinema* (1967), and *Snow, Sand and Savages* (1973) on the life of Frank Hurley. *Caddie* was the first feature directed by Don Crombie; he had previously spent some ten years at Film Australia, and also a short period with the South Australian Film Corporation, where he had directed a much-praised television drama, *Who Killed Jenny Langby?* (1974), and the pilot for a television series, *Stacey's Gym* (1974). It was also the first feature written by Joan Long, an experienced documentary script-writer with a long career at Film Australia. Three of her major scripts there won awards from the Australian Writers' Guild: *Paddington Lace* (1971), a popular short fiction film directed by Chris McCullugh, and two studies of the early years of the Australian film industry, *The Pictures that Moved* (1969) and *The Passionate Industry* (1973), the last of which she also directed. In 1976 she produced her second feature screenplay, *The Picture Show Man* (released in 1977).

451 *Caddie* Helen Morse (*r*)

452 Illuminations

1976 PAUL COX

P: Tibor Markus. SC: Paul Cox. ASST P: Roderick McNicoll. PH: Paul Cox, Brian Gracey. ED: Paul Cox, Russell Hurley. ART D: Alan Stubenrauch. MD: Alex Berry. ASST D: Bernard Eddy. SD: Russell Hurley. 74 mins. Colour. 16mm.

CAST: Gabriella Trsek (Gabi), Tony Llewellyn-Jones (Tony), Norman Kaye (Gabi's father), Sheila Florance, Athol Smith, Tibor Markus, Robert Trauer, Elke Neidhardt.

When her father dies, a young woman becomes preoccupied with death and 'the infinite'. During a visit to the country, she attempts to kill herself, but recovers to experience a regeneration of her love for life. She also starts to share a more alert and sensitive relationship with her lover, and their relationship is enriched by their growing self-knowledge and freedom from conventional anxieties about life and death.

Illuminations was the culmination of a large body of metaphysical cinema produced over the preceding decade by Paul Cox. In most of his films ideas were expressed through complex image structures rather than verbally, and similarly, dialogue in *Illuminations* is limited to surface exchanges, while the visuals are tense with compact symbolic intention. An obsessive concentration on details in the setting serves both as metaphor for the characters' inner experiences and as a key to mood. While some critics seemed baffled by the lack of literal content, others, such as Andrew Mackay in the Melbourne *Herald*, 19 May 1976, responded positively to the emotional expressiveness of the images: 'a simple story of love, life and death [with] several gently moving moments . . . Paul Cox's fascination with colours, textures and patterns illuminates the film with a warm assertion of life.'

The film was dedicated to its producer, Tibor Markus, who died soon after its completion. Partial finance was provided by the Film, Radio and Television Board of the Australia Council and the film was released through the film-makers' co-operatives, with a month-long season at the Melbourne Co-op Cinema commencing on 7 May 1976.

452 *Illuminations* Gabriella Trsek

Cox was born in the Netherlands in 1940 and came to Australia in 1963 as a professional still photographer. He began making 16mm films in 1965 as a means of personal expression rather than as a commercial venture, and his work included *Mirka* (1970), a portrait of an eccentric Melbourne artist and doll-maker, Mirka Mora (mother of Philippe), *The Journey* (1972), a sombre narrative exploring the loneliness of a middle-aged man haunted by the past, and *We Are All Alone, My Dear* (1977), a short documentary about an old woman in a rest home for the aged.

453 Betty Blokk-buster Follies

1976 PETER BATEY

EXEC P: Eric Dare. A Reg Livermore production. MD: Mike Wade. 120 mins. Colour.

CAST: Reg Livermore, the Baxter Funt band, the Reginas.

This film record of Reg Livermore's popular one-man stage show was photographed in the Bijou Theatre, Balmain, in Sydney, late in 1975. Apart from a few shots of the audience in the theatre and of Livermore making up and waiting in the wings, it concentrates on his stage performance as he presents a series of comic and sad character sketches and songs, accompanied by the five-piece Baxter Funt band, and the vocal trio, the Reginas. The characters include the bare-bottomed Betty Blokk-buster, a German parlour-maid who entertained the troops during the war; an old man who recalls his youth as a fashionable male model; and Vaseline Amalnitrate, a football star who joins the Australian Ballet.

Opening at the Village Twin Cinema, Brisbane, on 6 July 1976, the film was shown widely around Australia but did not attract the popularity of the stage show.

454 Mad Dog Morgan

1976 PHILIPPE MORA

PC: Motion Picture Productions. P: Jeremy Thomas. ASSOC P: Richard Brennan. SC: Philippe Mora. Based on the book *Morgan* by Margaret Carnegie. PH: Mike Molloy. CAM OP: John Seale. ED: John Scott. ART D: Robert Hilditch. M: Patrick Flynn. ABORIGINAL SONGS, DIDGERIDOO: David Gulpilil. P SUP: Peter Beilby. PM: Jenny Woods. ASST D: Michael Lake, Chris Maudson. SD R: Ken Hammond. SD RE-R: Peter Fenton. STUNTS: Grant Page. 102 mins. Colour. Scope.

CAST: Dennis Hopper (Daniel Morgan), Jack Thompson (Detective Manwaring), David Gulpilil (Billy), Frank Thring (Superintendent Cobham), Michael Pate (Superintendent Winch), Wallas Eaton (Macpherson), Bill Hunter (Sergeant Smith), John Hargeaves (Baylis), Martin Harris (Wendlan), Robin Ramsay (Roget), Graeme Blundell (Italian Jack), Gregory Apps (Arthur), Liza Lee-Atkinson (barmaid), Elaine Baillie (farm girl), Don Barkham (Morrow), Kurt Beimel (Dr Dobbyn), David Bracks (McLean), Liddy Clark (Alice), Peter Collingwood (Judge Barry), Peter Cummins (Gibson), John Derum (Evans), Gerry Duggan (Martin), Max Fairchild (prisoner), Chuck Faulkner (Sergeant Montford), Judith Fisher (Mrs Warby), Alan Hardy (Bob), Isobel Harley (Mrs Macpherson), David John (John Evans), Norman Kaye (swagman), Hugh Keays-Byrne (Simon), Kevin Leslie (Maples), Robert McDarra (parole officer), David Mitchell (Haley), Christoper Pate (Roget's assistant), Grant Page (Maginnity), Philip Ross (Watson), Bruce Spence (Heriot), Peter Thompson (Mayor), Roger Ward (trooper), Ken Weaver (Bond).

This portrait of the bushranger Dan Morgan, who roamed the Riverina and northern Victoria during the gold rush days of the 1860s, was based on twelve years of research by Margaret Carnegie. Morgan had a public reputation as a maniacal killer, but the film attempted to break through the legend to present Morgan as a poor Irish victim of a violent society and a repressive colonial administration. Morgan, paranoid, wild-eyed and rootless, is driven into his life of crime after witnessing the bloody massacre of Chinese on the goldfields and being unjustly arrested and abused for six years in prison. With an Aboriginal boy, Billy, as his sole friend and ally, he is hounded to ever more desperate acts of retaliation by a sadistic police superintendent, Cobham, and is eventually killed in a police ambush.

The film was shot entirely on location in Morgan's own territory around the New South Wales-Victoria border, and included scenes in his actual cave hide-out, deep in the bush of the Yambla Range. The central role was played by the American method actor, Dennis Hopper, who clearly identified with Morgan's outrageous mockery of convention and authority. As Philippe Mora, the director, later stated, Hopper 'brought an insanity to the role, and an intensity that most actors would have found impossible to create'. As played by Hopper, Morgan became the most colourful and dangerous of screen bushrangers, softened by his love for Billy, and his loneliness and self-pity. Other characters in the film, however, emerged as somewhat two-dimensional, especially the arch-villain Cobham, played by Frank Thring as a grotesque, fat and evil animal, reminiscent of Charles Laughton's performance in *Island of Lost Souls* (1932).

Financed jointly by private investors and the Australian Film Commission, the $450 000 production was shot on a tight six-week schedule commencing on 27 October 1975. It screened at Cannes in May 1976 and won an award there as the best Western. Distribution in Australia was handled by B.E.F., and screenings at the Sydney and Melbourne Film Festivals in June were followed by a commercial première at Greater Union's Pitt Centre, Sydney, on 9 July. Despite the generous support of critics and an active publicity campaign, the film failed to attract the public: a reputation for violence, based on its violent emotions and its occasional bursts of gore, did little to help it. In the U.S.A., too, the film's results were mediocre, despite the prestige of a major New York opening on 22 September.

Philippe Mora was born in 1949, the son of a prominent art dealer, George Mora, and an artist, Mirka Mora. At La Trobe University in 1967 he co-founded the magazine *Cinema Papers* with Peter Beilby. Encouraged by his parents to paint, Mora went to England to work as an artist, especially in comic-strip idioms, and he contributed to the satirical *Oz* magazine. His first feature was a homage to the gangster genre, *Trouble in Molopolis*, made in London in 1970. In 1972-3 in England he made a feature-length documentary *Swastika*, compiling footage from the 1930s and the war to examine Hitler's public image. In 1974, he made another compilation documentary about America in the Depression, *Brother Can You Spare a Dime*, and like *Swastika*, it attracted international press coverage. He was 26 when shooting began on *Mad Dog Morgan*.

455 The Fourth Wish

1976 DON CHAFFEY

PC: Galaxy Productions/South Australian Film Corporation. P: John Morris. ASSOC P: Matt Carroll, Jill Robb. SC: Michael Craig. PH: Geoff Burton. CAM OP: Gale Tattersall. ED: G. Turney-Smith. ART D: David Copping. M: Tristan Carey. PM: Matt Carroll. ASST D: Mark Egerton, Steve Knapman. SD R: Barry Brown. 105 mins. Colour.

CAST: John Meillon (Casey), Robert Bettles (Sean), Robyn Nevin (Connie), Brian Anderson (Wally), Julie Dawson (Hannah), Ann Haddy (Dr Kirk), Michael Craig (Dr Richardson), Max Wearing (specialist), Brian James (Jarvis), Donald Crosby (priest), Cul Cullen (Patcheck), Ron Haddrick (Harbord), Julie Hamilton (Jenny), Les Foxcroft (Ross), Moishe Smith (Roger).

Casey is a blue-collar worker who learns that his twelve-year-old son, Sean, has leukemia and has only a few months to live. Casey leaves his job to devote himself to making his son's remaining months as happy as possible. The boy makes three wishes, which Casey tries to fulfil in his own abrasive way: the first is for a dog, Roger, which brings Casey into conflict with his landlord; the second is for a reunion with his wife, Connie, who had deserted Casey eight years earlier; and the third is to meet the Queen. In trying to fulfil Sean's wishes and cope with the tragic crisis in his life, Casey discovers resources of strength and love in himself that enable him to face the future without despair.

The screenplay by Michael Craig, the British actor-writer permanently resident in Australia, was based on a three-part television play which the Australian Broadcasting Commission had produced in mid-1974. John Meillon had starred in the television production, and with Craig and the sometime Disney director, Don Chaffey, formed a company, Galaxy Productions, to co-produce the film with the South Australia Film Corporation for a relatively low budget of $240 000. Other investors were the Seven television network and the Australian Film Commission. Shooting began in Adelaide early in November 1975 with Robert Bettles in the role of Sean, originally played by Mark Shields-Brown on television. The world première was held in Adelaide on 15 July. Reviews were mixed: the Melbourne *Herald*, 10 September 1976, objected to the film's 'shameless manipulation' of emotions, but Mike Harris in the *Australian*, 24 July 1976, commended the 'shrewdness' of the production, finding it 'superbly schmaltzy' and 'immensely affecting'.

455 *The Fourth Wish* John Meillon (*l*), Robert Bettles

456 Fantasm

1976 RICHARD BRUCE [Richard Franklin]

PC: TLN Film Productions. EXEC P: Leon Gorr, Ted Mulder. P: Antony I. Ginnane. SC: Ross Dimsey. From an idea by Antony I. Ginnane. PH: Vince Monton. ED: Ford Footpole [Tony Patterson]. UNIT M: Tom Hamell (U.S.A.). SD R: Neil Rozenski (U.S.A.), Paul Clark (Australia). 90 mins. Colour.

CAST: Dee Dee Levitt (Abby), Maria Arnold (Barbara), Bill Margold (husband), Gretchen Gayle (Gabrielle), Rene Bond (Dianne), Al Williams (rapist), Con Covert (transvestite), Mara Lutra (Felicity), Uschi Digart (Super Girl), Maria Welton (Iris), John Holmes (Neptune), Mary Gavin (Belle), Gene Allan Poe (son), Robert Savage (visitor 1), Kirby Hall (visitor 2), Shayne (Celeste), Sue Doloria (Harriet), Al Ward (teacher), Clement St George (Satanist), Serena (victim), John Bluthal (Professor Jurgen Notafreud).

With its sights set firmly on the soft-core pornographic market, *Fantasm* presented ten of the alleged most common sexual fantasies of women in the 1970s, including sex in the beauty salon, fruit fetishism, and lesbianism in a sauna, with each episode introduced by a German psychiatrist, Professor Jurgen Notafreud. Because of difficulties in finding a cast in Australia, Antony Ginnane, Richard Franklin (working under the pseudonym of Richard Bruce) and Vince Monton went to Los Angeles to shoot the film, using professional stars of the American pornographic industry. The production cost was low ($50 000) and the film was shot on 16mm in a rapid ten-day schedule (one fantasy sequence per day). Linking scenes with the professor were shot back in Australia. The Australian distributor, Filmways, subsequently invested in the film by funding the preparation of 35mm prints from the 16mm original. Probably with the intention of provoking a censorship controversy, Filmways premièred the film at the Capri Cinema, Brisbane, on 16 July 1976; although the Commonwealth censor had passed the film (after four minor cuts) with an R certificate, the Queensland Film Review Board promptly banned the film in that state, in line with its policy of ridding Queensland of the worst extremes of screen pornography. With its

456 *Fantasm* Mara Lutra, John Holmes

notoriety boosted by the Queensland ban, the film became a solid commercial success elsewhere in Australia. Sales at the Cannes Festival in May had already covered most of the production cost, and by the end of the year, Ginnane stated that the film's financial backers had recorded a 200 per cent return on their investment. A sequel followed in 1977.

457 Queensland

1976 JOHN RUANE

PC: Film Noir Productions. P: Chris Fitchett. SC: John Ruane, Ellery Ryan. PH: Ellery Ryan. ED: Mark Norfolk. PM: Adrian Pickersgill. ASST D: Peter Gawler. SD R: Brett Southwick. 52 mins. Colour. 16mm.

CAST: John Flaus (Doug), Bob Karl (Aub), Alison Bird (Marge), Tom Broadbridge (Mick), Jack Mobbs (Ern), Gary Metcalf (foreman), Frank Lewis (Shagger), Fred Greenwood (Bill), Les Carter (bum), John Bishop (Peter), Patricia Condon (Di), Manuel Bugeja (foreigner), Lloyd Hall (Charlie), Barbara Barber (waitress), Glad Folie (Mrs Ern).

Doug is a factory worker living a withdrawn existence in a gloomy Melbourne suburb. He spends his free time in the pub, at the greyhound races and sharing a bleak room with an invalid pensioner, Aub. For Doug, Queensland represents an ideal of a new life—sunshine, a decent job and an escape from monotony. The film follows his fumbling and futile attempts to re-establish contact with Marge, a woman he used to live with and whom he still loves, and to organize their departure together for Queensland in his battered Holden car.

The film was made for $12 000 (with assistance from the Experimental Film and Television Fund), while John Ruane was a film student at the Swinburne College of Technology in Melbourne. The difficult role of Doug was played by the film theorist and

457 *Queensland* Bob Karl (*l*), John Flaus

lecturer, John Flaus: a shambling hulk never without a boyish hopefulness, and quietly, pathetically, refusing to accept his lot as anything more than a temporary downturn. After a prize-winning appearance in the 1976 Australian Film Awards, *Queensland* was released through the co-operative movement and the Vincent Library. It opened at the Melbourne Co-op Cinema on 27 July 1976 and quickly established a reputation as one of the more substantial and emotionally mature of the low-budget independent features.

458 *Oz* Joy Dunstan as Dorothy

458 Oz

1976 CHRIS LÖFVEN

PC: Count Features. P: Chris Löfven, Lyne Helms. ASSOC P: Jane Scott. SC: Chris Löfven. PH: Dan Burstall. ADDITIONAL PH: Vince Monton. ED: Les Luxford. ART D: Robbie Perkins. OPTICAL EFFECTS: Larry Wyner. M: Ross Wilson. SONGS: 'Living in the land of Oz', 'Greaseball', 'The mood', 'Who's gonna love you tonight', writen and sung by Ross Wilson; 'You're driving me insane', written by Baden Hutchins, sung by Graham Matters; 'Our warm tender love', written by Gary Young, sung by Joy Dunstan; 'Beatin' around the bush', and 'Glad I'm living here', written by Wayne Burt, sung by Jo Jo Zep and the Falcons. PM: Lyne Helms. ASST D: Walter Boston. SD RE-R: Peter Fenton. STUNTS: Graham Matherick. 103 mins. Colour.

CAST: Joy Dunstan (Dorothy), Graham Matters (Wally/the Wizard/record salesman/tram conductor/doorman/face at party), Bruce Spence (bass player/surfie), Michael Carman (drummer/mechanic), Gary Waddell (guitarist/bikie), Robin Ramsay (Good Fairy), Paula Maxwell (Jane), Ned Kelly (bouncer/truckie), Lorraine West (waitress), Beris Underhill (receptionist).

Oz is a 'rock'n'roll road movie' with the narrative structure of *The Wizard of Oz* (1939). Dorothy is now a groupie in search of the king of rock performers, the Wizard; the Straw Man is a vague and gentle surfie, the Tin Man a country car mechanic, and the Lion a timid and self-pitying bikie dressed in fearsome black leather.

In the 1960s, Chris Löfven had been Australia's most consistently productive teenage film-maker, producing a number of short 16mm anecdotes that won prizes and honours at home and abroad. In 1971 he completed a long 'diary' film, *Part One; 806* (65 mins), in which he presented a free flow of images about his life and friends in Melbourne, followed by *Part Two; the Beginning* (11 mins), in which his friends were reborn into an idyllic new world. In 1971 he went to England and worked for three years as a freelance film editor. His aim in *Oz* was to cater for the 16-24 age group audience, which he believed Australian producers had unjustly ignored, and he drew heavily on current youth culture, with groupies, surfies, motorbikes and Holden cars, bizarre clothing boutiques, and above all pop music, with numerous songs on the soundtrack and an extravagant live concert finale. Löfven himself had long been closely involved in rock music and had played with a Melbourne band for some time. To prepare the sound-track he chose Ross Wilson, a singer-songwriter, formerly a member of the successful Daddy Cool group and later producer of records by the Skyhooks.

458 *Oz* Gary Waddell as the Lion

With a budget of $150 000, provided jointly by the Australian Film Commission and Greater Union, the film was shot in the summer heat of early 1976, using principally young technicians trained in television and commercials. The film opened in Melbourne at the Chelsea Theatre on 30 July 1976, but was not a marked success. Subsequently, however, it was released profitably in the U.S.A. by Inter Planetary Pictures, under the title of *20th Century Oz*, shortened by fifteen minutes and with the music re-mixed into four-track stereo sound.

459 The Devil's Playground

1976 FRED SCHEPISI

PC: The Film House. P, SC: Fred Schepisi. PH: Ian Baker. ART D: Trevor Ling. ED: Brian Kavanagh. M: Bruce Smeaton. PM: Greg Tepper. ASST D: Mal Bryning, Rhonda Schepisi. SD R: Don Connolly. SD ED: Edward McQueen-Mason. 107 mins. Colour.

CAST: Arthur Dignam (Brother Francine), Nick Tate (Brother Victor), Simon Burke (Tom Allen), Charles McCallum (Brother Sebastian), John Frawley (Brother Celian), Jonathan Hardy (Brother Arnold), Gerry Duggan (Father Hanrahan), Peter Cox (Brother James), John Diedrich (Fitz), Thomas Keneally (Father Marshall), Sheila Florance (Mrs Sullivan), Anne Phelan and Jillian Archer (girls in pub), Gerda Nicolson (Mrs Allen), John Proper (Mr Allen), Bill Kelly (farmer), Vicki Bray (Miss Weatherhead), Hannah Govan (Miss Doyle), Danee Lindsay (Lynette), Michael Carman (Nigel Ryan), Iain Murton (Brian Anderson), Alan Cinis (Waite), Warren Coleman (Westaway), Gary Pixton (Tomkin), Richard Morgan (Smith), Rowan Currie (Casey), Wayne Comley (Mahoney), Michael David (Turner), Marc Gough (Brown), Andrew Court (Woolmore), Brett Murphy (Tierman), Deborah, Janine, Quentin and Jason Schepisi (Allen children).

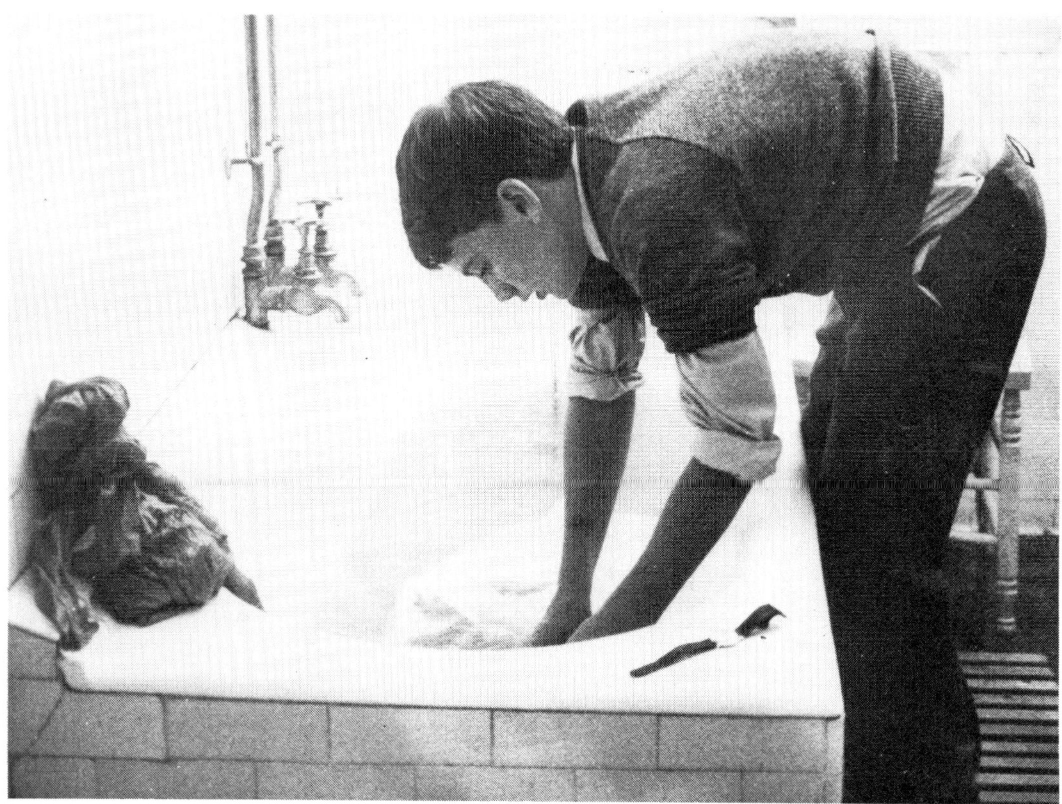

459 *The Devil's Playground* Simon Burke

The Devil's Playground is a study of life in a Catholic seminary college in the early 1950s. The effect of rigid discipline, sanctioned by religious authority, is observed both on the boys, in their tortuous adjustment to puberty, and on the brothers of the teaching order, some of whom have yet to accept their physical and emotional inability to live up to the absolute strictures of their order.

Much of the screenplay was autobiographical, based on Fred Schepisi's own Catholic upbringing and the time he spent in a seminary college in his early 'teens. He had spent several years preparing the screenplay for this his first feature, and had previously directed (among innumerable sponsored shorts and commercials) a short story on a similar theme, *The Priest*, an episode in the portmanteau film, *Libido* (1973). *The Priest* had been written by Thomas Keneally, and Keneally took a key role in *The Devil's Playground* as a priest who oozes cheerful bonhomie but preaches hell-fire and damnation.

Shot in 1975 on location in the stately home and formal gardens of Werribee Park, near Melbourne, the film cost $300 000 and was financed primarily by the Australian Film Commission and Schepisi's own company, the Film House. Distributed by Schepisi himself, it opened in Melbourne at the Bryson Cinema on 12 August 1976 and attracted strong commercial results. The film had been selected to screen in the Directors' Fortnight at the Cannes Festival in May 1976; in June it had won most of the important prizes in the Australian Film Awards, and in the same month had been presented at the Sydney and Melbourne Film Festivals with extraordinary audience and critical acclaim. A few reservations expressed by critics—especially over a heavily stressed performance by Arthur Dignam, whose 'portrait of celibacy gone mad [was] all staring eyes and starting nerves' (*Bulletin*, 21 August 1976—were overshadowed by the welcome given to the film for its emotional force and perceptions about boyhood. P. P. McGuinness in the *National Times*, 6-11 September 1976, applauded its 'remarkable degree of psychological truth' and its sensitive central portrait of the artist as a young boy: Simon Burke 'is the appropriate mix of charm and awkwardness, sniggering embarrassment and simple goodness, which makes the part into one of the really memorable child portraits of the cinema'.

459 *The Devil's Playground*

460 The Trespassers

1976 JOHN DUIGAN

PC: Vega Film Productions. EXEC P, ASST D: Richard Brennan. P, SC: John Duigan. ASSOC P: Graham Ducker. PH: Vince Monton. ED: Tony Patterson. ART D: Gillian Armstrong. M: Bruce Smeaton. PM: Lynne Gailey. SD R: Lloyd Carrick. SD MIX: Peter Fenton. 91 mins. Colour.

CAST: Judy Morris (Dee), Briony Behets (Penny), John Derum (Richard), Hugh Keays-Byrne (Frank), Peter Carmody (Ted), Camilla Nicoll (Jenny), Diana Greentree (Angela), David Kendall (Peter), John Frawley (Captain Williams), Max Gillies (publisher), Peter Stratford (interviewer), Phil Motherwell (draft resister), Cliff Ellen (barman), Syd Conabere (Harry), Chris Haywood (Sandy), Merle Keenan (Madge), Murielle Salter (Merle), Jock Campbell (Dr MacDonald), Des Fitzgerald (Mr Jongeblood), Lorraine Milne (pianist), John Orcsik (Cedric), Peter Thompson (schoolteacher), Ross Thompson (Terry), John Bowman (Mark).

Three people are entangled in romantic conflict against a background of the anti-Vietnam-war movement in 1970. Richard is a successful political journalist living in Melbourne with an intellectual, Penny, and at the same time having an affair with Dee, an independent-minded actress with an alternative theatre group. When the two women meet accidentally, they become friends and go on a seaside holiday together where their relationship becomes closer. When Richard arrives to visit them he finds himself barely tolerated by either woman.

John Duigan's second feature was more coherent than his first, *The Firm Man* (1975), and its best scenes, between the two women, were played with warmth and conviction, and their sympathetic relationship was far more credible than either of their relationships with Richard. Shooting took place on location in Melbourne and in the south Gippsland area of Victoria, with funding partly from the Australian Film Commission. Distributed by Filmways, the film premièred as the opening attraction at the Australian Film Institute's new cinema, the Longford, Melbourne, on 18 August 1976.

461 Surrender in Paradise

1976 PETER COX

PC: Paradise Pictures. P, SC: Peter Cox. PRODUCTION ASSOCIATES: Chris Collier, Evan Ham. PH: Don McAlpine. ED: Bob Blasdall, Peter Cox. M: Ralph Tyrell. PM: Nicola Kospartov. ASST D: Toivo Lember. SD: Jan Murray. 92 mins. Colour. 16mm.

CAST: Ross Gilbert (Rusty Swan), Errol O'Neill (Sergeant Rutter), Carolyn Howard (Valda), Rod Wissler (Cecil), Gaye Pool (Dulcie), Bill Reynolds (Brown), Robb Ireland (Mortlake), Harry Gibbs (Green), Gavin Patterson (Frankie), Jeff Blow (Black), Hazel Howson (Mrs Swan), Norman Hardy (Simpson), Chris Collier (Thorald), Greg McCart (doctor), Don McAlpine ('Raw Meat').

Around the turn of the century, a bushranger, Rusty Swan, receives a message that his mother is dying, and sets off with his girlfriend, Valda, and his partner-in-crime, Cecil, to visit her. Pursued by a posse led by Sergeant Rutter, the three travellers experience a time-warp and the chase leads them to modern-day Surfers Paradise. There they discover cars, television and the tourist industry, and stage a violent showdown with their pursuers on a beach crowded with indifferent holiday-makers.

Publicized as Queensland's first feature film since Chauvel's *Greenhide* (1926), this 16mm production employed both amateurs and professionals in its cast and crew. Two-thirds of its cost of around $30 000 was provided by the Film, Radio and Television Board of the Australia Council. Shooting took place in November and December 1975, using locations in the country near Brisbane, and on the Queensland Gold Coast. The world première was held at the Schonell Theatre, Brisbane, on 4 October 1976. Interstate screenings were rare and it did not reach Sydney until mid-1978. The young director, Peter Cox, had graduated in architecture from the University of Queensland, where he had worked in student theatre. He had also made several short 16mm films before embarking on his first feature.

462 Don's Party

1976 BRUCE BERESFORD

PC: Double Head Productions. P: Phillip Adams. ASSOC P: David Barrow. SC: David Williamson, from his own play. PH: Don McAlpine. ED: William Anderson. ASST D: Mike Martorana. SD R: Des Bone. SD ED: Lyn Tunbridge. SD MIX: Peter Fenton. 90 mins. Colour.

CAST: Ray Barrett (Mal), Clare Binney (Susan), Pat Bishop (Jenny), Graeme Blundell (Simon), Jeanie Drynan (Kath), John Gorton (himself), John Hargreaves (Don), Harold Hopkins (Cooley), Graham Kennedy (Mack), Veronica Lang (Jody), Candy Raymond (Kerry), Kit Taylor (Evan).

462 *Don's Party* Ray Barrett (*l*), John Hargreaves

On election day, 25 October 1969, Don and Kath throw a party to celebrate what they hope will be the first Labor Party victory in twenty years. The film is less about politics than about the people at the party: as the optimism of the Labor supporters degenerates into the bitterness of defeat, the party also degenerates into an early morning alcoholic haze and the painful exchange of home truths.

David Williamson's highly successful play was only marginally altered for the screen (by Williamson himself), although until shortly before production began it had been intended to re-set the film in December 1975 at the time of the Whitlam-Fraser electoral contest. Attempts to 'open up' the action were also abandoned in the final screenplay, and although off-stage bedroom scenes now appeared on-screen, and a new scene was added of a nude swim in a neighbour's backyard pool, the bulk of the film was set resolutely inside Don's house to sustain the tensions and claustrophobia of the party.

Several of the cast had already worked in the play. Ray Barrett had played the lecherous lawyer Cooley in the London production but appeared instead in the film as the ageing ex-academic, Mal. Barrett was born in Brisbane and had acted widely on the Australian stage and radio before going to England in 1958; there he became internationally known in the long-running television series *The Troubleshooters*, and played in numerous theatrical, film and television roles before returning to Australia in 1975. Graeme Blundell, who had produced the first stage production of *Don's Party* at the Pram Factory, Melbourne, in August 1971, was now cast against his Alvin Purple image as the nervous conservative, Simon. Graham Kennedy, one of the most popular of all Australian television personalities, appeared as an ineffectual deserted husband with a sexual kink. The former child star of *Long John Silver* (1954), Kit Taylor, was cast as a hot-tempered dentist cheated of his woman by Cooley. As in much of Williamson's work, the female characters tended to be colourless and the female cast—including Pat Bishop, who had played Kath in the first Sydney production, and Veronica Lang who had played Jody in London—were generally overshadowed by the more boisterous and perceptively drawn males. A brief appearance by the former Prime Minister, John Gorton, was affectionately conceived as a tribute to the support he had given in the late 1960s for government funding of the arts.

In 1973, Jack Lee, a veteran British director resident in Australia, began working with Phillip Adams to mount the production, but delays were caused by Adams's commitments with the Australia Council. Shooting eventually began in January 1976 under the direction of Bruce Beresford, with the action staged at night and virtually in sequence over a five-week period, using a house in the Sydney suburb of Westleigh as the main location. Private investors in the $270 000 production included several independent exhibitors who handled the first release of the film in Canberra, Melbourne and Sydney, thereby substantially reducing distribution fees; the remainder of the production cost was covered by the Australian Film Commission and a small investment from Twentieth Century-Fox. Distribution was handled directly by Phillip Adams for the initial city releases, with Twentieth Century-Fox taking over the film for suburban and country areas.

A world première was somewhat perversely held during an arts festival at the New South Wales country town of Queanbeyan on 10 November 1976, and it opened commercially at the Center Cinema, Canberra, on 17 November.

463 Storm Boy

1976 HENRI SAFRAN

PC: South Australian Film Corporation. P: Matt Carroll. ASSOC P: Jane Scott. SC: Sonia Borg. From the novel by Colin Thiele. PH: Geoff Burton. CAM OP: Ross Nichols. ED: G. Turney-Smith. ART D: David Copping. M: Michael Carlos. LOCATION M: Beverley Davidson. ASST D: Ian Goddard, Ian Jamieson. SD R: Ken Hammond. TECHNICAL ADVISER: Grant Page. PELICAN TRAINER: Gordon Noble. 87 mins. Colour.

CAST: Greg Rowe (Storm Boy), Peter Cummins (Hideaway Tom), David Gulpilil (Fingerbone Bill), Judy Dick (Miss Walker), Tony Allison (ranger), Michael Moody (boat master), Graham Dow (Edwards), Frank Foster-Brown (Lynch), Eric Mack (Jones), Michael Caulfield and Paul Smith (hunters), Hedley Cullen (Marina manager), children from the Port Elliot Primary School.

This story of a boy's friendship with a wild pelican had already reached a large audience as a novel and school text. Its narrative simplicity and healthy respect for the natural environment were retained in the film, with a romantic portrait of a boy growing up close to nature and isolated from the disciplines and disillusionments of more conventional childhoods.

The setting was the Coorong, in south-eastern South Australia, a saltwater inlet one hundred miles long and a haven for bird life. For several months before production, three pelicans were trained by Gordon Noble, and when shooting began in May 1976 they proved sufficiently co-operative for work to proceed according to a tight four-week schedule. Exteriors were shot near Goolwa, a town opposite the head of the Coorong, and interiors in the South Australian Film Corporation's studio at Norwood, Adelaide. The cast was led by Greg Rowe, eleven years old at the time of filming, and previously untrained in acting. David Gulpilil played a supporting role as an Aboriginal youth who camps in the wildlife sanctuary and teaches Storm Boy about the land, the sea and the Aboriginal people.

The $320 000 production, jointly funded by the South Australian Film Corporation, the

463 *Storm Boy* Greg Rowe (*l*), David Gulpilil

Australian Film Commission and the Seven television network, opened at the Fair Lady Theatre, Adelaide, on 19 November 1976 and became an immediate commercial success. Release in other states followed in mid-1977, again with remarkable box-office results. Overseas sales proliferated, and it was the first Australian film to attract a major distributor in Japan. Most critics strongly supported the film, both at home and abroad, and in England the *Monthly Film Bulletin*, February 1978, praised it as 'A beautifully crafted film for children . . . With its simple, direct story-line, fine acting and marvellously photographed scenes of natural beauty, *Storm Boy* is the best movie of its kind for some little time.'

The director, Henri Safran, was born in Paris in 1932 and came to Australia in 1960 to work with the Australian Broadcasting Commission as a producer of television documentaries and drama. He became an Australian citizen in 1963 but returned to Europe in 1966 to work in British television as a director in series such as *The Troubleshooters* and *Softly Softly*. His first film back in Australia was *Listen to the Lion* (not released until 1977).

464 Barney

1976 DAVID WADDINGTON

PC: Columbia Pictures. P: David Waddington, John Williams. SC: Colin Drake. PH: Richard Wallace. CAM OP: Ross Nichols. ED: Rod Hay. M: Tommy Tycho. SONGS: lyrics by Roy Lister, sung by Julie Anthony. PM: Les White. ASST D: Chris Maudson, Michael Carlton. SD R: Ken Hammond. STUNT CO-ORD: Larry McGarry. 84 mins. Colour.

CAST: Brett Maxworthy (Barney Dawson), Sean Kramer (Rafe Duggan), Lionel Long (Charles Dawson), Spike Milligan (Hawker), Jack Allen (Sergeant), Robert Quilter (Lieutenant McMahon), Shirley Cameron (Florence), Jackie Rees (Maria), Rob Steele (Trooper Perrin), Danny Adcock (Trooper Hayes), Mike Preston (O'Shaughnessy), Terry Redell (First Mate of Lady Jane), Jim Clifford (Trooper Dunn), Ron Ratcliff (rich man), Judy Connelli (woman in shop), Herbie Nelson (Smithy), Al Thomas (Aaron), Larry McGarry (Trooper), Andy Clark (Trooper), Jerry Thomas (Morgan), Dieter Chidel (Benson), Alex Pope (Riley), Bodie Leigh (first man), Colin Petersen (second man).

Barney is a bland 'family film' set in the 1880s. A small boy named Barney, a wombat named Amanda, and a roguish Irish convict named Rafe are the sole survivors of a shipwreck. The trio set out for Ballarat, where Barney's father works. On the way they meet two gipsy women who drug Rafe and try to steal Barney's money. Later Rafe is wrongly accused of horse-theft and is imprisoned; Barney contrives his escape, and a chase ensues through the bush. Only with the aid of an eccentric wandering hawker do Barney, Rafe and Amanda manage to evade the police. After a final brief adventure with bushrangers, Barney is reunited with his father, and Rafe rides off on his white steed to seek new adventures.

The cast was led by Brett Maxworthy, a twelve-year-old boy with some experience in pop music and children's television shows. His co-star, an Irish-born comedian, Sean Kramer, had been working in Australian television since the mid-1960s in drama series such as *Homicide* and *Luke's Kingdom* and the game show *Almost Anything Goes*. The original Smiley of 1956, Colin Petersen, took a bit-part to symbolize Columbia's hopes that

Barney would find the same success as the earlier film.

The film cost an estimated $230 000, provided jointly by Columbia and the Australian Film Commission. Shooting began in May 1976 using locations on the New South Wales coast and at the Australiana Village at Wilberforce near Sydney. The director, David Waddington, was in his late twenties and had worked primarily in television in Sydney and in the production of sponsored documentaries. The film was released widely in Australia by Columbia for the Christmas holidays, commencing in Melbourne at a Hoyts Midcity Cinema on 16 December 1976, but commercial results were well below expectations.

465 Deathcheaters

1976 BRIAN TRENCHARD SMITH

PC: Trenchard Productions/D. L. Taffner (Australia). EXEC P: Richard Brennan. P, STORY: Brian Trenchard Smith. ASSOC P: John Fitzgerald. SC: Michael Cove. PH: John Seale. ED: Ron Williams. ART D: Darrel Lass. M: Peter J. Martin. TITLE SONG: sung by Kerrie Biddell. PM: Lyn McEnroe, Betty Barnard. ASST D: Lyn McEnroe, Chris Maudson. STUNT CO-ORD: Grant Page. 96 mins. Colour.

CAST: John Hargreaves (Steve Hall), Grant Page (Rodney Cann), Margaret Gerard (Julia Hall), Noel Ferrier (Mr Culpepper), Judith Woodroffe (Gloria), Ralph Cotterill ('un-civil' servant), John Krummel (Anticore director), Drew Forsythe (battle director), Brian Trenchard Smith (hit and run director), Michael Aitkens (police driver), Roger Ward and Wallas Eaton (police sergeants), Dale Aspin (lady car driver), Peter Collingwood (Mr Langham), Chris Haywood (butcher), Ann Semler (Lina), Max Aspin and David Bracks (bank robbers), Reg Evans (army sergeant), Vincent Ball (naval intelligence officer), Lito Hernandez (chief of Hernandez' guards), Ziggy (Bismarc).

Two ex-Vietnam commandos now doing stunt work for television are recruited by a government security organization to raid the island stronghold of a Filipino racketeer and secure incriminating papers from his safe. With the aid of numerous explosions, the two men secure the papers and escape from the island's guards in a hang-glider, launched by a giant catapult.

Squeezing high 'production values' out of a small budget of $150 000, the film was aimed firmly at young audiences, offering them non-stop action and bloodless violence, a strong element of flippant, dare-devil comedy and a touch of comical sex. Finance was provided jointly by the Australian Film Commission, the Nine television network, Roadshow Distributors, Trenchard's own company and his television marketing agent, D. L. Taffner (Australia) Pty Ltd. The film was shot on 16mm and blown up to 35mm for release in Sydney over a four-week period in mid-1976. Highlights included a scene high on the outside wall of the Hilton Hotel in Sydney, the scaling of the 300-foot sheer face of North Head (leading to the island fortress), and the crash-landing of the hang-glider into the sea, where the heroes are picked up by a submarine.

The director's long preoccupation with stuntwork had characterized most of his television productions and feature films. He had often worked with the local stunt expert, Grant Page, and now gave him his first starring role. An outstanding athlete and sportsman, Page had served in the Australian Army as a commando for four years before entering the local television and film industry as a stuntman. The principal 'feminine interest' was provided by Trenchard's wife, the American-born Margaret Gerard, making her film debut after minor stage work in the U.S.A.

Deathcheaters was released around Australia during the Christmas holidays, beginning on 16 December 1976 at the Valley Twin Cinema, Brisbane. The Melbourne *Herald*, 24 December 1976, expressed reservations about its 'sexism, racism [and] mindless violence', but most critics accepted it at face value as 'sheer Saturday morning action-adventure escapism'.

466 Eliza Fraser

1976 TIM BURSTALL

PC: Hexagon Productions. P: Tim Burstall. ASSOC P: Alan Finney. SC: David Williamson. PH: Robin Copping. CAM OP: Dan Burstall. ED: Edward McQueen-Mason. ART D: Leslie Binns. M: Bruce Smeaton. PM: Michael Lake, Michael Midlam. ASST D: Michael Lake, Tom Burstall. SD R: Des Bone. SD MIX: Peter Fenton. STUNTS: Graham Matherick, Grant Page, Heath Harris, Bill Stacey. 127 mins. Colour.

CAST: Susannah York (Eliza Fraser), Trevor Howard (Captain Foster Fyans), Noel Ferrier (Captain James Fraser), John Castle (Captain Rory McBryde), John Waters (David Bracefell), Abigail (buxom girl), Gerard Kennedy (Martin Cameron), Arna-Maria Winchester (Mrs Cameron), Charles Tingwell (Duncan Fraser), Gus Mercurio (Darge), Lindsay Roughsey (Euenmundi), George Mallaby (Lieutenant Otter), Carole Skinner (Mrs Shortland), Vicki Bray (Mrs Annie Fraser), Martin Harris (John Graham), Leon Lissek (sergeant), Graham Matherick (flogger), Dennis Miller (Fyan's cook), Bruce Spence (Bruce McIver), John Frawley (Brown), Bill Hunter (Youlden), Sean Scully (Elliott), Serge Lazareff (Doyle), Martin Phelan (Stone), John Cobley (Hodge), Ingrid Mason (Mrs Otter), Peter Hammill (copy-boy), Alan Finney (sideshow spruiker), David Phillips (first mate), Fabian Muir (Johnny).

On 21 May 1836 the *Stirling Castle* is wrecked on the Australian coast on the way from Sydney to Singapore. The ship's captain, James Fraser, and his wife Eliza, are stranded and spend months living with Aborigines. Captain Fraser is later killed by convicts from Moreton Bay, but Eliza is rescued with the help of a convict escapee, Bracefell, who is also living with the Aborigines. Eliza returns to Sydney and makes a fortune telling a highly sensational version of her experiences in carnival sideshows.

Both the story and the location of Fraser Island, with its long sweeps of white sand and thick matted scrub, had inspired many artists: Patrick White wrote a novel, *A Fringe of Leaves* (London, 1976), on the subject and Sidney Nolan painted a series of pictures there. The first version of a screenplay was written by Burstall in 1969 and later found competition in a proposed British production to star either Vanessa Redgrave or Julie Christie. Because of the apparent imminence of the rival film,

Burstall's production was brought forward ahead of schedule, and shooting started in March 1976. The production was highly ambitious, with overseas stars, and a crowded ten-week schedule that took in locations in three states, from the reconstructed gold-mining town of Sovereign Hill near Ballarat and other locations in Victoria, to the old penal settlement of Trial Bay, north of Newcastle, and finally to Fraser Island itself. About 120 Aborigines from Mornington Island in the north of Queensland were flown to Fraser Island for the film, since the island no longer supported its own Aboriginal population. The budget was originally quoted at about $750 000 but expenses soared, and rain and unexpected physical difficulties on Fraser Island forced the cost to about $1 200 000. Finance was raised from Hexagon and a consortium of Melbourne businessmen, as well as $375 000 from the Australian Film Commission. Distribution was handled by Roadshow, and Australia-wide release was arranged through Hoyts Theatres on 16 December 1976. Returns on the home market were less than anticipated (some $600 000 in film hire by the end of 1977), and after *High Rolling* (1977), Hexagon ceased production.

After many months of energetic publicity promising Australia's most expensive and flamboyant production, a mixed critical response reflected a certain degree of disappointment. Burstall and Williamson had attempted to pitch the story in the rollicking style of *Tom Jones* with Eliza as an aggressive and lusty comic heroine, but some local critics reacted strongly against the treatment. Keith Connolly in *Cinema Papers* wrote: 'The story of Eliza Fraser, which . . . is a human drama of epic proportions, emerges in the film as a jejune comedy of terrors [The] film pads Eliza's story with elements as uncomfortably disparate—and irrelevant—as bedroom farce, ironic social comment, film noir, a knockabout brawl, even a cops 'n' robbers chase.' The cast received more praise, and the *Australian*, 18 December 1976, singled out Noel Ferrier as 'the one real delight of the film. His subtle, unexaggerated portrayal of the bumbling old captain [with] his stiff upper lip and sagging rotund belly wavering under culture shock, catches a mood of semi-serious, witty romp that the rest of the film attempts but never achieves.'

466 *Eliza Fraser* George Mallaby (*l*), John Castle

467 Let the Balloon Go

1976 OLIVER HOWES

PC: Film Australia. P: Richard Mason. ASSOC P: Jim McElroy. SC: Richard Mason, Ivan Southall, Oliver Howes. ADDITIONAL DIALOGUE: Cliff Green. From the novel by Ivan Southall. PH: Dean Semler. ED: Max Lemon. ART D: David Copping. M: George Dreyfus. PM: Rod Freedman. ASST D: Elizabeth Knight, Phil Noyce. SD R: Don Connolly. SD ED: Greg Bell. STUNTS: Grant Page. 78 mins. Colour.

CAST: Robert Bettles (John Sumner), Jan Kingsbury (Mrs Sumner), John Ewart (Constable Baird), Bruce Spence (Acting Fire Chief Gifford), Ben Gabriel (Mr Sumner), Ken Goodlet (Major Fairleigh), Ray Barrett (Dr McLeod), Sally Whiteman (Mamie), Matthew Wilson (Cecil), Terry McQuillan (Harry), Nigel Lovell (parson), Babette Stephens (Mrs Braithwaite), Brian Anderson, Charles Metcalfe, Philip Ross, Scott Griffiths, Goff Vockler, Bob Lee.

This children's story, complete with a bright-red fire engine, a flour-bomb fight and a colourful collection of eccentric adults, was based on a prize-winning novel by Ivan Southall, a prolific Australian writer of children's literature. The central character is John Sumner, a young boy growing up in 1917 in a small town in rural New South Wales. He wears a leg brace and suffers from mild epilepsy, and is cosseted by an over-protective mother. The theme, that a balloon is not a balloon until you let it go, emerges gradually as John makes determined attempts to break free of his mother's domination: he causes constant mischief around the town and eventually climbs the tallest tree to prove that he is capable of behaving like a normal boy.

The sentimental plot was relieved by its comical adults—a pompous policeman, an incompetent fire chief, and a rambunctious retired Major. The story also included a long slapstick sequence, in Keystone Kops style, of a mock battle between the home defence corps of neighbouring towns, which the children disrupt with flour bombs and water hoses.

The film was produced for about $400 000 by Film Australia, mainly on location at the New South Wales country town of Carcoar. Distributed by Twentieth Century-Fox, it opened at the Town Theatre, Sydney, on 16 December 1976, screening at matinees only. It was also sold widely overseas, including a sale to the elusive American market.

468 Summer of Secrets

1976 JIM SHARMAN

PC: Secret Picture Productions. P: Michael Thornhill. SC: John Aitken. PH: Russell Boyd. CAM OP: Gale Tattersall. ED: Sara Bennett. ART D: Jane Norris. M: Cameron Allan. P ASST: Ross Matthews. ASST D: Errol Sullivan. SD ED: Greg Bell. SD MIX: Peter Fenton. 102 mins. Colour.

CAST: Arthur Dignam (Doctor Beverley Adams), Rufus Collins (Bob), Nell Campbell (Kym), Andrew Sharp (Steve), Kate Fitzpatrick (Rachel), Jude Kuring (shop assistant).

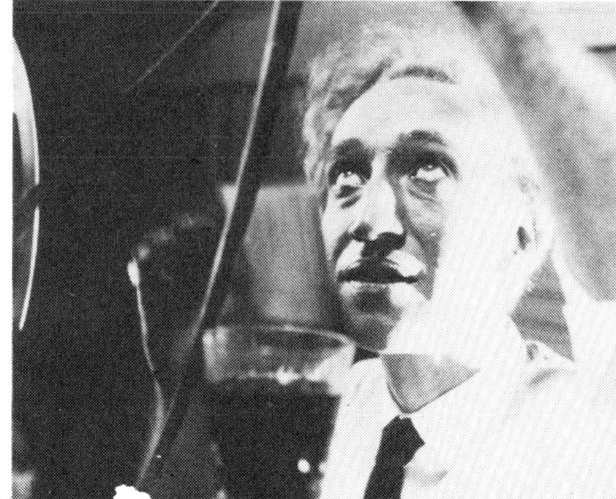

468 *Summer of Secrets* Arthur Dignam

A young man, Steve, returns with his girlfriend, Kym, to a remote beach where he had spent a happy childhood. Together they stumble onto the activities of a reclusive doctor, Beverley Adams, who is experimenting fanatically with the brain and with memory. Gradually Steve realizes that the doctor has discovered the secret of life itself and that he intends to restore his dead wife, Rachel, to life. As Rachel slowly comes alive, the doctor discovers to his horror that his attempts to reshape the past have failed, and that reality offers something quite different.

Although the story suggested kinship with Sharman's previous film, *The Rocky Horror Picture Show* (1975), it submerged its elements of the fantastic in an extraordinarily long and repetitious exposition and in much sombre discussion of vague abstractions. As P. P. McGuinness in the *National Times* 10-15 January 1977, commented: 'It is a pity that the plot development and the various devices and surprises . . . add up to something as silly as they do. For from time to time there are passages in the film which really work, and show that, hidden away among the nonsense, are the elements of what could have been a really good horror film.'

The film was shot late in 1975 under the working title of *The Secret of Paradise Beach* and cost some $370 000, provided by the Australian Film Commission and G.U.O. Film Distributors. It opened quietly at the Rapallo Theatre, Sydney, on 24 December 1976, and received a generally hostile press and an uninterested public. In March it surprised its detractors by winning two of the main prizes at a festival of science fiction films in Paris.

469 **Break of Day**

1976 KEN HANNAM

PC: Clare Beach Films. P: Pat Lovell. ASSOC P: Cliff Green, Geoff Burton. SC: Cliff Green. PH: Russell Boyd. ED: Max Lemon. ART D: Wendy Dickson. M: George Dreyfus. PM: Pom Oliver. ASST D: Mark Egerton, Mark Turnbull, Steve Andrews. SD R: Don Connolly. SD MIX: Peter Fenton. SD ED: Greg Bell. 112 mins. Colour.

CAST: Sara Kestelman (Alice Hughes), Andrew McFarlane (Tom Cooper), Ingrid Mason (Beth), Tony Barry (Joe), Eileen Chapman (Susan), John Bell (Arthur), Ben Gabriel (Mr Evans), Dennis Olsen (Roger), Geraldine Turner (Sandy), Maurie Fields (Lou), Malcolm Phillips (Robbie), Sean Myers (David), Kate Ferguson (Jean).

469 *Break of Day* Andrew McFarlane (*l*), Sara Kestelman

In 1920, in the quiet country town of Tetlow, a restless young war veteran, Tom Cooper, is distracted from the mundane demands of his life by a visiting artist, Alice Hughes. Her liberated Bohemian attitudes intrigue Tom and he neglects his pregnant wife and his work in order to be with Alice. She is drawn to him in turn as a symbol of Anzac manhood. When a group of Alice's extroverted friends arrive from the city, Tom gradually realizes that their standards are foreign to him. He finally returns to his routine existence, sadder but with a growing self-awareness.

Shooting began in April 1976, with the old gold-mining town of Maldon in central Victoria as the main location. The film cost a little over $500 000 to produce, including investments by the Australian Film Commission, the Victorian government (its first feature venture), the Nine television network, and the film's distributor, G.U.O. The world première was held at the Bercy Cinema, Melbourne, on 31 December 1976. Although it had a potential wealth of themes—small-town attitudes towards an independent woman, the myth of Anzac heroism, and more—the film emerged as a leisurely pastoral romance, with one of its central sequences, a country cricket match, created with such loving detail that 'one can almost taste the hot scones and catch a whiff of the beer tent' (*Herald*, 8 January 1977). Despite the effectiveness of such scenes, the film became the focus of a critical reaction against an apparent surfeit of 'nostalgia' films: 'I'm beginning to wonder if we're ever going to see contemporary Australia on the screen' (*Australian*, 22 January 1977).

470 Raw Deal

1977 RUSSELL HAGG

PC: Homestead Films. P: Russell Hagg, Patrick Edgeworth. ASSOC P: Jenny Henry. SC: Patrick Edgeworth. PH: Vince Monton. ED: Tony Patterson. ART D: Jon Dowding. COSTUME DES: Clare Griffin. M: Ronald Edgeworth. TITLE SONG: sung by Margret Roadknight. SD R: Gary Wilkins. 94 mins. Colour.

CAST: Gerard Kennedy (Palmer), Gus Mercurio (Ben), Rod Mullinar (Alex), Christopher Pate (Dick), Hu Pryce (Ned), John Cousins (Sir Charles), Michael Carman (Sir Frederick), Norman Yemm (O'Neil), Gary Day, David Ravenswood, Reg Evans, Bethany Lee, Briony Behets, Anne Pendlebury, David Cameron.

An opening title states: 'Australia has never known revolution. Perhaps this is why.' In the 1870s a nervous colonial administrator hires Palmer, an English bounty hunter, and Ben, an American gun salesman, to eliminate a marauding army of Irish Catholic revolutionaries in their desert stronghold. Palmer and Ben recruit a team of three gunmen to help them and the mission is successfully accomplished. They return to collect their pay from the government, but find themselves in a trap set by treacherous officials. A bloody gunfight ensues but Palmer and Ben manage to escape and set off to start a new life in America.

Despite its opening title, the film had no pretensions to being anything more than an action-packed Western with the most tenuous relationship to Australian history. Critics had fun trying to categorize it, variously proposing 'the witchetty Western', 'pie 'n' sauce cowboy', 'Kangaroo-western' and the 'Plucky Country oater'. The $450 000 production was shot on location at Sunbury, Victoria, and Mungo, N.S.W., by the company responsible for two Australian Western series for television, *Cash and Company* and *Tandarra.* The director, Russell Hagg, was born in Melbourne in 1938 and worked on student films and revues at the University of Melbourne before graduating in architecture and embarking on a career as a designer in British feature films. He returned to Australia to join Crawford Productions as a script-writer, and in 1973 directed the first episode of *Cash and Company*, which he co-produced with the British-born writer, Patrick Edgeworth. Finance for their first feature was raised from the Australian Film Commission, the Victorian government, the Seven television network, G.U.O. Film Distributors, and other private investors. It opened quietly in Sydney and Melbourne on 4 February 1977.

470 *Raw Deal* Gerard Kennedy (*l*), Gus Mercurio

471 The Singer and the Dancer

1977 GILLIAN ARMSTRONG

P: Gillian Armstrong. SC: John Pleffer, Gillian Armstrong. Based on the short story 'Old Mrs Bilson' by Alan Marshall. PH: Russell Boyd. ART D: Sue Armstrong. ED: Nicholas Beauman. M: Robert Murphy. PM: Errol Sullivan. SD: Laurie Fitzgerald. 52 mins. Colour. 16mm.

CAST: Ruth Cracknell (Mrs Bilson), Elisabeth Crosby (Charlie), Russell Keifel (Pete), Jude Kuring (Mrs Herbert), Gerry Duggan (doctor), Julie Dawson (Mrs Rogers), Kate Sheil (young Mrs Bilson), Rob Steele (Jim Bilson), Kerry Walker (Rose Buckley).

An old woman, treated as a simple-minded invalid by her family, periodically escapes to sit by the river and listen to the races on her radio. There she befriends Charlie, a young woman from the city who has come with her husband to seek a new life in the country. The two women talk about their lives, and it becomes clear to them both that their experiences are parallel: both are abused by unfaithful and boorish husbands, and yet both are totally dependent on their men for any form of social fulfilment.

This slow and melancholy study of the surrender of two women to destinies determined by their men was the first long narrative film by Gillian Armstrong, a young film-maker in her mid-twenties. She had previously directed several documentaries and short stories, including *One Hundred a Day* (1973) from another story by Alan Marshall, and *Gretel* (1973) from a story by Hal Porter, both made while she was a student at the Film and Television School in Sydney, and perhaps most notably, *Smokes and Lollies* (1975), a documentary about fourteen-year-old girls, made for the South Australian Film Corporation. *The Singer and the Dancer* was shot late in 1975, with two weeks on location at Picton, south of Sydney. The $27 000 production, largely funded by the Film, Radio and Television Board of the Australia Council, was shown at the Sydney Film Festival in June 1976, where it won the Greater Union award

471 *The Singer and the Dancer* Ruth Cracknell

for best narrative film. Ruth Cracknell later won the Sammy Award for best actress. Columbia agreed to distribute the film theatrically, with 35mm prints blown up (at the Australian Film Commission's expense) from the 16mm original, and it opened at the Australia Cinema, Melbourne, in April 1977. Despite strong critical support, publicity was poor and it ran for only two weeks. Later, in July, the Australian Film Commission sponsored a season at the Union Theatre, Sydney University, and it played to capacity houses.

472 **The FJ Holden**

1977 MICHAEL THORNHILL

PC: FJ Films. P: Michael Thornhill. ASSOC P: Jenny Woods, Errol Sullivan. SC: Terry Larsen, Michael Thornhill. DIALOGUE: Terry Larsen. PH: David Gribble. CAM OP: Frank Hammond. ED: Max Lemon. ART D: Monte Fieguth, Lissa Coote. M: Jim Manzie. MUSIC CONSULTANT: Ken Quinnell. UNIT M: Pom Oliver. ASST D: Errol Sullivan. SD R: Don Connolly. SD MIX: Peter Fenton. 105 mins. Colour.

CAST: Paul Couzens (Kevin), Eva Dickinson (Anne), Carl Stever (Bob), Gary Waddell (Deadlegs), Graham Rouse (sergeant), Karlene Rogerson (Cheryl), Vicki Arkley (Chris), Robert Baxter (senior constable), Colin Yarwood (Brian), Sigrid Thornton (Wendy), Ray Marshall (Mr Sullivan), Maggie Kirkpatrick (Betty Armstead), Harry Lawrence (security guard).

Kevin is an apprentice motor mechanic in the western suburbs of Sydney. With his mate, Bob, he spends his spare time drinking and cruising around the streets in his canary yellow FJ model Holden, looking for girls. One day he meets Anne, a girl who works in a large shopping complex, and they spend some time together, visiting each other's homes, going to a classy restaurant, racing the Holden with other cars on a disused road, and making love in the back seat of the car. One day Kev gets drunk and tries to make love with Anne while Bob is watching. Anne throws them out of the house and when she later refuses to be pacified, Kev becomes aggressive and causes a minor fracas at a party. The police are called but Kev escapes in his car and spends the night drinking with Bob and nursing his hurt feelings. He returns home at dawn to find the police waiting.

Derived from a series of comic poems by Terry Larsen, Thornhill's adaptation replaced the humour with an austere and grim description of a conformist society. The film was, in some ways, an extension of Thornhill's first feature, *Between Wars* (1975), and depicted a society in which the individual offered no resistance to the forces of social unity, and in which alternative courses of action were absent.

The $318 000 production was backed financially by G.U.O. Film Distributors and

472 *The FJ Holden* Carl Stever (*l*), Paul Couzens

the Australian Film Commission. The non-professional leading players came from the western suburbs of Sydney, and the film was shot there in November and December 1976. With a rock music score and a title song aimed at the top 40, it was promoted actively as a film for the youth market. The world première was held simultaneously at the Chullora Drive-in and the Rapallo Theatre, Sydney, on 29 April 1977. The Australian Film Board of Review gave the film an M rating ('for mature audiences'), but some states objected to the film's sex and strong language, and exercised their right to override the Commonwealth decision. In Queensland, South Australia, Western Australia and Tasmania it was released with an R certificate, restricting its audience to people over 18 years of age.

473 The Picture Show Man

1977 JOHN POWER

PC: Limelight Productions. P, SC: Joan Long. Inspired by Lyle Penn, 'Penn's Pictures on Tour'. PH: Geoff Burton. CAM OP: Bill Grimmond. ART D: David Copping. COSTUME DES: Judith Dorsman. ED: Nicholas Beauman. M: Peter Best. PM: Sue Milliken. ASST D: Mark Egerton. SD R: Ken Hammond. STUNTS: Grant Page. 98 mins. Colour.

CAST: Rod Taylor (Palmer), John Meillon (Mr Pym), John Ewart (Freddie), Harold Hopkins (Larry), Patrick Cargill (Fitzwilliam), Yelena Zigon (Madame Cavalli), Gary McDonald (Lou), Sally Conabere (Lucy), Judy Morris (Miss Lockhart), Donald Crosby (Major Lockhart), Dolore Whiteman (Mrs Summers), Jeanie Drynan (Mrs Duncan), Tony Barry (policeman), Gerry Duggan (open-air theatre secretary), Ernie Bourne (bookie).

473 *The Picture Show Man* From the left, John Meillon, John Ewart, Rod Taylor, Gary McDonald

Maurice Pym is a travelling cinema operator in the 1920s, covering the backroads of northern New South Wales with his son Larry and his dapper pianist, Freddie. The film follows their adventures with women, horses, motor vans, inflammable film and new-fangled sound equipment, and above all, with a brash American rival who intrudes into their territory and threatens to steal their livelihood.

After seeing Joan Long interviewed on television about her documentary on early Australian cinema, *The Passionate Industry*

(1973), Lyle Penn sent her a manuscript that he had written about his experiences as a youth on the road with his travelling showman father, which he had been unable to have published. Joan Long used this manuscript as a basis for her fictional screenplay, and drew also on her own extensive research into Australian cinema history. In 1975 she formed her own production company and secured funding from the Australian Film Commission, the New South Wales government, the Women's Film Fund, and a number of private investors. Shooting took place in the last months of 1976 on location in the New England plains around Tamworth, and in the river country near Grafton, N.S.W. It was the first feature to be directed by John Power, after a distinguished career in television. He had produced current affairs and documentary programmes for the Australian Broadcasting Commission, including a prize-winning documentary on Dr Evatt, *Like a Summer Storm* (1972). In 1973 he directed, also for the ABC, a highly praised dramatized documentary, *Billy and Percy*, about W. M. Hughes and his secretary Percy Deane, for which he won the best director award in the 1975 Australian Film Awards.

In reaction against what she regarded as the excessive 'earnestness' of films by many of her Australian contemporaries, Joan Long set out to make an unashamedly lighthearted film in which the characters displayed 'a typically Australian philosophical resilience in the face of adversities' (letter to the authors, June 1978). The film was rich in colourful characters, with flamboyant performances from both John Meillon and John Ewart. It also revived the long forgotten tradition of the squatter's daughter in the character of Lucy, who combined expert horsemanship with self-assurance in romance.

Distributed by Roadshow, the film opened on 5 May 1977 at Village Theatres' East End complex in Melbourne. Local critical reaction was mixed, but in the 1977 Australian Film Awards the film figured prominently with prizes for art direction and costume design, and for best supporting actor (John Ewart). The music score also won an award, and the song, 'Tap tap' (performed by Pym as an interlude in his movie shows), became a minor hit. In the U.S.A. it was selected as one of the ten best films of 1977 by the National Board of Review, and it was screened with popular success at the 1977 London Film Festival.

474 Phil Noyce

474 Backroads

1977 PHILLIP NOYCE

PC: Backroads Productions. P: Phillip Noyce. ASSOC P, ASST D: Elizabeth Knight. SC: John Emery, Phillip Noyce and the cast. PH: Russell Boyd. ED: David Huggett. M: Robert Murphy. SONGS: 'Tarpaulin muster' and 'They say it's a crime' composed by Dougie Young; 'Backroads' composed and sung by Zac Martin. UNIT M: Kevin Smith. SD R: Lloyd Carrick. SD MIX: Julian Ellingworth. 61 mins. Colour. 16mm.

CAST: Bill Hunter (Jack), Gary Foley (Gary), Zac Martin (Joe), Terry Camilleri (Jean-Claude), Julie McGregor (Anna).

Jack, a white vagrant, and Gary, a young Aboriginal, steal a 1962 Pontiac Parisienne and head off around the dusty roads of western New South Wales. They steal booze, rifles and fancy clothes, and pick up a trio of fellow-travellers—Gary's uncle Joe from a reserve near Bourke, a French hitch-hiker whom Jack regales with his worst xenophobia, and an embittered woman who has deserted her role as mother and wife in the city to lose herself in the outback. When Joe drunkenly shoots a stranger, they are pursued by police, and Joe and Jack are arrested; Gary tries to escape but is hunted down and killed.

Although the action is redolent of the 'road movie' genre, the film becomes, in the dialogues between Gary and Jack, an angry polemical statement about white responsibility for black poverty and destitution. It was the first feature film in which Aborigines made a major creative contribution (other than acting), and Gary Foley's participation was central to the construction and content of the film: an activist closely involved in the upsurge of black political consciousness in the 1970s, Foley assisted with the direction of the black actors and monitored the film's expression of the black viewpoint. At his insistence, the ending of the film was re-written: originally Jack and Gary were to reach Sydney in their car and find themselves caught in a giant traffic jam, but Foley preferred the despair of an ending in which the whites shoot him down like a hated animal.

474 *Backroads* Bill Hunter (*l*), Zac Martin

Filmed on location around Bourke and Brewarrina in western New South Wales, the film cost a low $30 000, partly provided by the Creative Development Branch of the Australian Film Commission. It was screened at the 1977 Sydney Film Festival in June, and with an R certificate for its language, it opened at the Union Theatre, University of Sydney, on 27 June 1977.

One of the boldest of the younger Australian feature film directors, Noyce was born in Griffith, N.S.W., in 1950. He began making experimental films in 1968 with *Better to Reign in Hell*, a violent psycho-drama, followed by several short 16mm films exploring structural ideas. He was manager of the Sydney Filmmakers' Co-op from 1970 to 1972, and in 1973 became one of the first group of students at the Film and Television School in Sydney. There he made a short film, *Caravan Park* (1973), from a story by John Emery (screenwriter of *Backroads*), and *Castor and Pollux* (1974), a film contrasting the lives of a group of hippies with a gang of bikies, which Bob Ellis in *Nation Review*, 26 April-2 May 1974, called 'one of the most savagely iconoclastic and bawdily vivacious documentaries ever made'. In 1976 he completed another boldly structured and outspoken documentary, *God Knows Why But It Works*, for Film Australia (from an idea by the producer, Richard Mason), and after *Backroads* made his first 35mm feature, *Newsfront*, released in 1978.

475 Out Of It

1977 KEN CAMERON

P, SC: Ken Cameron. PH: David Gribble. ED: David Huggett. M: Robert Murphy. PM: Michael Jacob. ASST D: Ron Owen. SD R: Carlo Tonti. SD MIX: Phil Judd. 50 mins. 16mm. Colour.

CAST: Glenn Mason (Larry), Chris Haywood (Warren), George Spartels (Tony), Martin Harris (Boyle), Terry Camilleri (Jacko), Saviour Sammut (Ferret), Arna-Maria Winchester (hitch-hiker), Margaret Nelson (Wendy).

Three friends in the industrial suburbs of Sydney, bored both by unemployment and by the jobs available to them, drift from stripping stolen cars to assisting in a clumsy warehouse robbery. To avoid the police, they decide to drive north along the coast, perhaps as far as Coolangatta in Queensland. They find themselves worrying about things back at home, and they don't really enjoy the journey. Gradually they split up: one goes back to Sydney, another falls into the hands of the police, and the third wanders back unsure what to do next, but with fond memories of something exciting that almost happened in his life.

This portrait of three young men in a state of listless depression was marked by the affection of the director for his characters, and by his tight control over the film. It was close in some ways to the spirit of Longford's *The Sentimental Bloke*, with sequences mounting unobtrusively towards a rounded character study, with a strong sense of physical location, and with a sharp ear for the self-deprecatory humour of the trio. Sandra Hall wrote in the *Bulletin*, 16 July 1977: 'The film is animated by the characterisations—three rich and funny studies in larrikinism at its most uncertain . . . Perhaps the main value of the film is its humor, the kind not seen in Australian cinema since *Sunday Too Far Away*.'

Shot over a three-week period in October 1975, and completed for less than $24 000, *Out Of It* was the first major film by Ken Cameron. It was slow to gain attention, and was overshadowed initially by more flamboyant works. It won second place in the

475 *Out of It* George Spartels

Greater Union Awards at the 1977 Sydney Film Festival (the winner was *Listen to the Lion*), and opened publicly as a support to *Backroads* at the Union Theatre, University of Sydney, on 27 June. Subsequent distribution was through the Sydney Filmmakers' Co-operative. Cameron, a former secondary school teacher, released his second 16mm feature in June 1978—*Temperament Unsuited*—about the problems of a student teacher (played by Steve Spears) trying to work in a conservative high school.

476 The Love-Letters from Teralba Road

1977 STEPHEN WALLACE

P: Richard Brennan. SC: Stephen Wallace. SCRIPT ED: Moya Wood. PH: Tom Cowan. CAM ASST: Martha Ansara. ED: Henry Dangar. PROPS, COSTUMES: Joanna Collard. M: Ralph Schneider. ASST D: Sandie Richardson, Stuart Green. SD: Laurie Fitzgerald. SD MIX: Peter Fenton. 50 mins. Colour. 16mm.

CAST: Kris McQuade (Barbara), Bryan Brown (Len), Gia Carides (Maureen), Joy Hruby (Len's mother), Kevin Leslie (Barbara's father), Ashe Venn (Norma), Don Chapman (foreman).

Len is a storeman in Newcastle, quick-tempered and in ill health. His wife, Barbara, has gone to Sydney to live with her father and sister after Len has beaten her in a drunken rage. Len writes to her asking forgiveness and his letters express love and tenderness. But when they meet to discuss the future of their marriage they have little to say to each other and soon quarrel. Back in Newcastle, Len continues to write, proposing to get a job transfer to Sydney and asking Barbara to find them a flat of their own where they can start their lives together again.

The film's psychological observations—of two people fantasizing about a marriage that has not worked, and able only to express their deeper feelings indirectly—were based on letters that the director, Stephen Wallace, had found in an old house. Setting his story in the industrial wastelands of Newcastle and in a poor working-class suburb of Sydney, Wallace directed the film unobtrusively and gave his leading players the maximum freedom to develop credible portrayals of two people caught at their most vulnerable. The film was made cheaply, for around $25 000, with financial assistance from the Creative Development Branch of the Australian Film Commission. At the 1977 Australian Film Awards it won three prizes, including the gold award for best short fiction film, and an award for photography. After presentation at the 1977 Sydney Film Festival, it opened at the Union Theatre, University of Sydney, on 26

476 *The Love-letters from Teralba Road* Bryan Brown, Kris McQuade

July. It was Wallace's first major film; he had previously made several short 16mm fiction films and had worked at Film Australia as a production assistant and later as director and writer of short documentaries.

477 High Rolling

1977 IGOR AUZINS

PC: Hexagon Productions. P: Tim Burstall. ASSOC P: Alan Finney. SC: Forrest Redlich. PH: Dan Burstall. ED: Edward McQueen-Mason. M: Sherbet. PM: Tom Binns. ASST D: Tom Burstall. SD R: Barry Brown. 85 mins. Colour.

CAST: Joseph Bottoms (Tex), Grigor Taylor (Alby), Judy Davis (Lynn), John Clayton (Arnold), Wendy Hughes (Barbie), Sandy Macgregor (Susie), Simon Chilvers (sideshow boss), Gus Mercurio (Ernie), Robert Hewitt (Frank), Roger Ward (Lol), Peter Cummins (bus-driver), Gil Tucker (shooter), Christine Amor (teenage girl), Katy Morgan (young girl), Chantal Contouri (bus hostess), Terry Gill (waiter), Marilyn Vernon (teenage girl), Mario Milano (country fighter), Terry Norris (farmer), Paul Young (shooter), Steven Millichamp (bouncer), Peter Thompson (fat man), Sean Scully (policeman).

Tex, an American carnival hand, and Alby, an Australian tent boxer, drift around coastal Queensland. They steal a car and a marijuana hoard from a homosexual, Arnold, and pick up a sixteen-year-old hitch-hiker, Lynn. At Surfers Paradise, Tex and Alby spend their money getting drunk in a night-club, and make an unsuccessful attempt to pick up two singers. Pursued by thugs sent by Arnold, they 'hijack' a tourist bus in order to get more money. A fierce chase ensues, but Tex and Alby survive and, joined by Lynn, they set off once more on the road.

A 'road movie' with a soundtrack by the pop group, Sherbet, *High Rolling* set itself firmly in the sunshine and sleaziness of the Queensland coast. As Sandra Hall wrote in the *Bulletin*, 3 September 1977: 'it catches the essence of the Gold Coast's appeal as the place where young Australians go for their first taste of a measure of the high life away from home. Surfers [Paradise] has ready-made myths, tatty though they are, and Auzins and Redlich make the most of them.' Produced for around $400 000, with an imported American star, it was the first feature by a Melbourne television director, Igor Auzins. He had joined Crawford Productions in 1969 and worked as a cameraman and, after 1971, as director on *Division Four*, *Homicide* and other series. He became producer of *Homicide* in 1974 but left Crawford when the series was abandoned. As a freelance director he made documentaries for the South Australian Film Corporation, numerous television commercials, and also telemovies for Reg Grundy Productions and other companies. Distributed by Roadshow, *High Rolling* opened on 4 August 1977 at Village theatres around Australia.

477 *High Rolling* Grigor Taylor (*l*), Joseph Bottoms (*r*)

478 The Getting of Wisdom

1977 BRUCE BERESFORD

PC: Southern Cross Films. P: Phillip Adams. SC: Eleanor Witcombe. From the novel by Henry Handel Richardson. PH: Don McAlpine. CAM OP: Gale Tattersall. ED: William Anderson. P DES: John Stoddart. ART D: Richard Kent. M: Franz Schubert, Sigismund Thalberg, Arthur Sullivan; piano played by Sarah Grunstein. PM: Russel Karel. ASST D: Michael Lake. SD R: Des Bone, Gary Wilkins. SD MIX: Peter Fenton. 100 mins. Colour.

CAST: Susannah Fowle (Laura), Hilary Ryan (Evelyn), Terence Donovan (Tom Macnamara), Patricia Kennedy (Miss Chapman), Sheila Helpmann (Mrs Gurley), Candy Raymond (Miss Zielinski), Barry Humphries (Reverend Strachey), John Waters (Reverend Shepherd), Julia Blake (Isabella Shepherd), Dorothy Bradley (Miss Hicks), Kay Eklund (Mrs Rambotham), Max Fairchild (Mr O'Donnell), Jan Friedl (Miss Snodgrass), Diana Greentree (Maisie Shepherd), Maggie Kirkpatrick (Sarah), Monica Maughan (Miss Day), Kerry Armstrong (Kate), Celia de Burgh (M.P.), Kim Deacon (Lilith), Alix Longman (Chinky), Jo-Anne Moore (Tilly), Amanda Ring (Cupid), Janet Shaw (Bertha), Karen Sutton (Pin), Sigrid Thornton (Maria).

Laura Tweedle Rambotham is an ebullient country girl who is sent to an exclusive boarding school in Melbourne at the turn of the century. Despite her yearning to be accepted, she finds it difficult to conform to the expected standards of decorum and taste. During her second year she causes excitement among the girls by fabricating a story about a secret romance between herself and the school's young minister, Reverend Shepherd. Later she forms a close attachment to a sophisticated older girl, Evelyn, with whom she practises music and shares her deepest feelings. When Evelyn leaves, Laura reacts by throwing herself furiously into her studies and in the final examinations she wins both the literary and music prizes. At the final school assembly she defiantly plays an emotional piece of music of her own choice and later, outside the school gates, takes off her hat and gloves and runs energetically across the parklands.

478 *The Getting of Wisdom* Susannah Fowle with bat

This portrait of an eccentric, strong-willed girl, her attempts to be a 'lady', and her eventual survival, untainted, through a strict formal education, was the second film to be made from Henry Handel (née Ethel) Richardson's semi-autobiographical novels. The first had been *Rhapsody* (1954), an M.G.M. production, starring Elizabeth Taylor, based on the novel *Maurice Guest,* about Laura's experiences in Europe on a music scholarship. Far more faithfully adapted, Beresford's film was written by Eleanor Witcombe, an Australian author of plays for radio and theatre and episodes for television series, including *Number 96* and *Seven Little Australians.* The $525 000 production was shot in Victoria as the first enterprise by the new Victorian Film Corporation. Locations included the Methodist Ladies' College, Melbourne, for the exteriors of the school, Mandeville Hall for interiors, and the town of Eddington near Bendigo in central Victoria as Laura's home town. Additional investment came from the Australian Film Commission and the Nine television network, and shooting took place in January and February 1977. The leading role was given to a Melbourne schoolgirl, Susannah Fowle, in her first professional acting role. Altogether, some 6000 girls were auditioned for the school pupil roles. Other parts were played by Barry Humphries, who returned to Australia from London for a rare straight role as the sanctimonious school principal, and Hilary Ryan, an American-born actress with British stage experience, as Laura's idol, Evelyn.

Distributed by Roadshow, the film opened at the Bryson Cinema, Melbourne, on 17 August, and with the support of critics and educational authorities (the book was a set school text) it had substantial seasons in all states. In May 1978 it was presented in the Directors' Fortnight at the Cannes Film Festival.

479 Journey Among Women

1977 TOM COWAN

PC: Ko-An Film Productions. P: John Weiley. SC: Tom Cowan, John Weiley, Dorothy Hewett and cast. STORY, PH: Tom Cowan. CAM ASST: Malcolm Richards, Jeni Thornley. ED: John Scott. M: Roy Ritchie. COSTUMES: Norma Moriceau. PROPS: Sally Campbell. DIRECTOR OF ACTORS' WORKSHOPS: Adam Salzer. SD R: Jef Doring. SD ED: Greg Bell. 93 mins. Colour.

CAST: Jeune Pritchard (Elizabeth Harrington), Nell Campbell (Meg), Diana Fuller (Bess), Lisa Peers (Charlotte), Jude Kuring (Grace), Robyn Moase (Moira), Michelle Johnson (Bridget), Rose Lilley (Emily), Lillian Crombie (Kameragul), Therese Jack (Kate), Kay Self (Sheila), Helenka Link (Jane), Ralph Cotterill (Corporal Porteous), Martin Phelan (Captain Richard McEwan), Tim Elliot (Doctor Hargreaves).

In the late eighteenth century, in a remote Australian penal colony, the refined young daughter of a judge-advocate, Elizabeth Harrington, determines to do something to improve conditions for a group of twelve recalcitrant women convicts who are kept in appalling conditions of squalor and are abused by the guards. When the women manage to escape, Elizabeth goes with them. The bush is wild and trackless, and the women have no food or maps, and no specific destination. Stumbling across a hidden distillery they celebrate their escape in an orgy of drunkenness, to Elizabeth's growing horror. A young Aboriginal girl, Kameragul, shows them how to survive in the bush, but Elizabeth is over-

479 *Journey Among Women*

come with fever and malnutrition. The youngest member of the group, Emily, nurses her back to health and helps to liberate her from the inhibitions of her past life. Months pass, and the colony hears vague reports of a tribe of Amazons living and hunting in the bush. When Emily is raped and murdered by two men, Elizabeth helps the group to take revenge and the men are killed. Soldiers led by Elizabeth's former fiancé, Captain McEwan, attempt to round up the women. To forestall an attack, Elizabeth agrees to go back to the colony, but persistently spurns McEwan. Twisted by hate, he returns to the bush to kill the women, but the women retaliate and McEwan dies in a bushfire. Back in the colony, Elizabeth continues to feel affinity with the wild women and seeks to find freedom in her own more complex world.

Despite its early colonial setting, the film was very much an exploration of contemporary issues, and the historical context served mainly to heighten the extremes of social repression against which the women rebel. As the producer, John Weiley, wrote, the film 'uses the mirror of the past to focus on the obsessions of today—the independence of women—civilization against nature—freedom against responsibility'. The film relied heavily on improvisation, and the cast lived in camps in the bush for six weeks in the winter of 1976, in an attempt to lead the life of the characters they were playing, and to discover through experience and discussion how the women might have reacted to freedom and to each other. Their home in the wilderness was established on the banks of the Hawkesbury River, near Berowra, north of Sydney.

Shot on 16mm for a total cost of $150 000, the film was subsequently taken for distribution by G.U.O. and blown up to 35mm. It attracted controversy in the media for its aggressive theme and acquired a reputation for lesbianism and nudity, which contributed to its good commercial results when it opened at the Rapallo Theatre, Sydney, on 18 August 1977.

480 Listen to the Lion

1977 HENRI SAFRAN

PC: Stockton Ferri Films. P, SC, ART D: Robert Hill. PH: Malcolm Richards. ED: Mervyn Lloyd. M: Michael Carlos. PM: Ian Goddard. SD R: Bob Hayes. 52 mins. Colour. 16mm.

CAST: Wyn Roberts (Hunter), Barry Lovett (one-legged man), Syd Heylen (Hunter's friend), John Derum (evangelist), Alan Penney, Paul O'Laughlin and Kevin Leslie (men at tip), Richard Gilbert, Paul Johnston, Ron Morse and Jean du Bois (people in tunnel), Les Foxcroft (night shelter man), Richmond Young (constable), Joseph Dicker and Steven Warren (crematorium workers).

The last hours in the life of a Sydney derelict: lying drunk in an alley he is beaten by thugs and severely injured; a friend helps him to find refuge in a night shelter and as he lies dying, he has an 'out of body' experience and sees himself flying about the room. After the cremation of his corpse, his sightless body returns to the footpath and he stands beating a drum, unheeded by passers-by.

The film was devised by Robert Hill, a journalist and later production assistant at Film Australia. He spent months researching the life of homeless people in Sydney, exploring their social codes and visiting the flop-houses, abandoned buildings and parks where they lived. Henri Safran, recently returned from England, was signed to direct, and a substantial part of the $36 000 budget was provided by the General Production Fund of the Australian Film Commission. Safran subsequently directed *Storm Boy* for the South Australian Film Corporation (released before *Listen to the Lion* in 1976). In June 1977 the film won two awards at the Sydney Film Festival: best film in the fiction section of the Greater Union Awards, and the Rouben Mamoulian Award for 'the most distinguished Australian short film'. It opened commercially at the Union Theatre, University of Sydney, on 5 September.

480 *Listen to the Lion* Wyn Roberts (*l*), Barry Lovett

481 Summerfield

1977 KEN HANNAM

PC: Clare Beach Films. P: Pat Lovell. ASSOC P: Pom Oliver. SC: Cliff Green. PH: Mike Molloy. CAM OP: Gale Tattersall. ED: Sara Bennett. ART D: Graham Walker. M: Bruce Smeaton. ASST D: Mark Egerton. SD: Ken Hammond, Gary Wilkins. 91 mins. Colour.

CAST: Nick Tate (Simon Robinson), John Waters (David Abbott), Elizabeth Alexander (Jenny Abbott), Michelle Jarman (Sally Abbott), Charles Tingwell (Dr Miller), Geraldine Turner (Betty), Max Cullen (Jim), Sheila Florance (Miss Gleeson), Isobel Harley (Miss Tucker), Joy Westmore (Mrs Shields), Adrian Wright (Peter Flynn), Barry Donnelly (Sergeant Potter), David Smeed (Mark), Max Fairchild (Joe Baxter).

A schoolteacher appointed to a small coastal town becomes curious about the unexplained disappearance of his predecessor. While investigating the mystery, he is drawn into the strange world of a reclusive family living on a near-by island estate called Summerfield. There he discovers secrets that bring tragedy to the quiet life of the town.

Shot on location at the town of Cowes and around Western Port, Victoria, the film was marked by its striking physical setting, with 'lovingly posed pictures of silver sea and pastel coastline' (*Age*, 17 October 1977). The $560 000 production was financed jointly by the Australian Film Commission, G.U.O. Film Distributors, the Victorian Film Corporation, and private investors. Shooting took place in the first months of 1977, and it opened at the Pitt Centre, Sydney, on 30 September. Much of the critical reaction was hostile, especially to the structure of the plot, but the *Sydney Morning Herald* (1 October 1977) wrote more positively of it as 'a brooding, atmospheric film of high quality', and most critics reserved at least some praise for the film's visual attractions and for the cast.

482 Inside Looking Out

1977 PAUL COX

PC: Illumination Films. P: Bernard Eddy, Paul Cox. ASSOC P: Tony Llewellyn-Jones. SC: Paul Cox, Susan Holly Jones. PH, ED: Paul Cox. CAM OP: Peter Tammer, Brian Gracey. ART D: Alan Stubenrauch. M: Norman Kaye. ASST D: Bernard Eddy. SD R: Russell Hurley. 88 mins. Colour.

CAST: Briony Behets (Elizabeth), Tony Llewellyn-Jones (Robert), Norman Kaye (Alex), Elke Neidhardt (Marianne), Juliet Bacskai (babysitter), Dani Eddy (Dani), Jean Campbell (neighbour).

The marriage of Robert and Elizabeth has degenerated into a barren state of truce, and both have lost sight of whatever originally brought them together. Robert is an ambitious journalist and Elizabeth a devoted mother, but both occupations serve as retreats from the marriage rather than as a source of enrichment. The film presents episodes from a week in their life, exploring each character's refusal or inability to acknowledge the emptiness of their relationship.

A study of the distress that can underlie modern marriage in a world of material plenty, Paul Cox's first 35mm feature continued the metaphysical preoccupations of his earlier 16mm work. P. P. McGuinness welcomed it as 'an accurately observed slice of modern urban life . . . one of the small number of tiny budget films which are, on the sidelines of the main industry, doing much more to portray and comment on our contemporary society than the mainstream industry' (*National Times*, 5-10 December 1977). The Australian Film Commission invested $23 000 in the production, approximately half of the total cost. After premières at the Sydney and Melbourne Film Festivals in June 1977, the film opened commercially at a Sydney suburban cinema, the Dendy Crows Nest, on 24 November.

481 Patricia Lovell and Ken Hannam during the shooting of *Summerfield*

483 Blue Fire Lady

1977 ROSS DIMSEY

PC: Australian International Film Corporation. P: Antony I. Ginnane. ASSOC P: Bill Fayman. SC: Bob Maumill. PH: Vince Monton. ART D: John Powditch. ED: Tony Patterson. M: Mike Brady. PM: Barbie Taylor. ASST D: Geoff Morrow. SD R: Gary Wilkins. 96 mins. Colour.

CAST: Cathryn Harrison (Jenny), Mark Holden (Barry), Peter Cummins (McIntyre), Marion Edward (Mrs Gianini), Lloyd Cunnington (Mr Grey), Irene Hewitt (Mrs Bartlett), Syd Conabere (Mr Bartlett), Philip Barnard-Brown (Stephen), Gary Waddell (Charlie), John Wood (Gus), John Ewart (Mr Peters), Rollo Roylance (reporter), John Murphy (veterinarian), Telford Jackson (chief steward), Roy Higgins (Kelvin Clegg), Bill Collins (broadcaster), Jack Mobbs (postman).

Jenny Grey, a country girl who loves horses, is sent away to the city because her father is embittered by the death of his wife in a riding accident. Jenny takes a job as a stable hand at the racetrack and is given charge of a troublesome filly, Blue Fire Lady. When the horse is auctioned by her owner because of her intractable behaviour, Jenny manages to buy her, with the surprise help of her father. Under Jenny's loving attention, Blue Fire Lady goes on to win a major award at an important gymkhana.

This 'unobjectionable piece of *Schoolgirl's Own*' (*Age* 20 January 1978) was produced with entirely private funds for a total budget of $231 000. Shooting took place in and around Melbourne over a five-week period in August and September 1977, with race scenes staged at the Caulfield track. The leading role was played by the teenage English actress, Cathryn Harrison (grand-daughter of Rex Harrison), supported by the Australian singer-songwriter, Mark Holden, as a university student who becomes her friend. The prominent Australian jockey Roy Higgins also appeared in the film, along with many other people from the Victorian racing world. Distributed by Filmways (who had invested in the film), it opened in Adelaide on 9 December 1977 and screened widely during the school holiday period.

The director, Ross Dimsey, was born in Melbourne on 16 October 1943. He worked in the British and American film industries from 1965 and returned to Melbourne in 1968 to work as assistant director and production manager on several features, and to write and direct numerous commercials and sponsored documentaries. He also wrote the screenplay for the two *Fantasm* films (1976 and 1977), and in 1973 directed a feature-length version of Jack Hibberd's play *Dimboola*, which was never released.

484 The Mango Tree

1977 KEVIN DOBSON

PC: Pisces Productions. P, SC: Michael Pate. ASSOC P, ASST D: Michael Lake. Based on the novel by Ronald McKie. PH: Brian Probyn. CAM OP: Peter Moss. ED: John Scott. ART D: Leslie Binns. COSTUME DES: Pat Forster. M: Marc Wilkinson. PM: Tom Binns. SD R: Barry Brown. 104 mins. Colour. Scope.

CAST: Christopher Pate (Jamie Carr), Geraldine Fitzgerald (Grandma Carr), Robert Helpmann (the Professor), Gerard Kennedy (Preacher Jones), Gloria Dawn (Pearl), Carol Burns (Maudie Plover), Barry Pierce (Angus McDonald), Diane Craig (Miss Pringle), Ben Gabriel (Wilkenshaw), Gerry Duggan (Scanlon), Jonathan Atherton (Stinker Hatch), Tony Bonner (Captain Hinkler), Tony Foley (Private Davis), Tony Barry, Terry McDermott.

With a hearty, folksy sentiment redolent of Hollywood's Deep South, this 'family film' set in the 'Deep North' of Australia opens on Christmas Eve in a small town in northern Queensland towards the end of the First World War. Grandma Carr (played by the New York actress, Geraldine Fitzgerald) is a benevolent matriarch, known and loved by all in the town, and doing her best to help her grandson, Jamie, through the emotional turmoil of adolescence. With wide-eyed enthusiasm, Jamie learns about life from a gallery of characters around him: 'the Professor', a seemingly hopeless drunk who gives him wisdom and friendship; a sadistic schoolteacher who outrages his sense of justice; a French teacher who tenderly gives him his first sexual experiences; a pioneer aviator, Captain Hinkler, who comes a hero to the town and takes Jamie for a flight in his Tiger Moth; and 'the Preacher', a fundamentalist driven by a blind sense of righteousness into madness and murder. Through it all Jamie grows towards emotional maturity, and after the death of his beloved grandmother, he manfully sets out to build his own future in the city.

484 *The Mango Tree* Christopher Pate, Diane Craig

The $650 000 production was shot almost entirely on location in northern Queensland, in the small town of Gayndah, at Mount Perry and Cordalba, and in the country around the sugar centre of Bundaberg. Finance was raised from the Australian Film Commission, G.U.O. Film Distributors, and the Bundaberg Sugar Company, and shooting took place over a seven-week period from late April 1977. Much expense was saved by Bundaberg residents making available their homes and heirlooms as part of the period setting. After a world première there on 13 December, the film opened in Sydney and Melbourne on 16 December for long summer holiday seasons. The young director, Kevin Dobson, making his first feature while still in his mid-20s, had worked extensively in television, including several years with Crawford Productions in Melbourne, where he edited and subsequently directed numerous episodes of *Matlock Police*, in which Michael Pate had starred. Later, as a freelance director, he had made a telemovie, *Gone to Ground* (1977), a thriller starring Charles Tingwell.

485 Dot and the Kangaroo

1977 YORAM GROSS

PC: Yoram Gross Film Studios. P: Yoram Gross. ASSOC P: Sandra Gross. DIRECTOR OF VOICES: Mary Madgwick. SC: John Palmer, Yoram Gross. From the novel by Ethel Pedley. ANIMATION PH: Graham Sharpe. LIVE ACTION PH: Frank Hammond. ED: Rod Hay, Klaus Jaritz. ART D: Sandra Gross. CHARACTER DESIGN, STORYBOARD: Laurie Sharpe. ANIMATORS: Sue Beak, Cam Ford, Peter Gardiner, Rowl Greenhalg, Athol Henry, Greg Ingram, Richard Jones, Wallace Logue, Peter Luschwitz, Vivienne Ray, Laurie Sharpe, Richard Slapczynski. M: Bob Young. SONGS: lyrics by John Palmer, Marion von Adlerstein, Bob Young. PM: Sue Field. SD R: Phil Judd (dialogue), Maurie Wilmore (music). 86 mins. Colour.

VOICES: Barbara Frawley (Dot), Joan Bruce (the Kangaroo), Spike Milligan (Mr Platypus), June Salter (Mrs Platypus), Ross Higgins (Willie Wagtail), Lola Brooks, Peter Gwynne, Ron Haddrick, Richard Meikle, George Assang, Kerrie Biddell, John Derum, Kevin Golsby, Nola Lester, Sue Walker, Noel Brophy, Ann Haddy, Robina Baird.

Dot, the little daughter of an outback settler, is lost one day in the bush. She befriends a big female red kangaroo who helps her to find her way home. Carrying Dot in her pouch, the kangaroo travels through the bush, meeting many characters including a platypus, a koala and a kookaburra. After many adventures, Dot finally returns home and the kangaroo goes back to the bush.

This simple story, first published in 1899 and adapted into a play in 1924, was chosen after a long search through Australian children's literature. The search was undertaken when the producers, Yoram and Sandra Gross, decided to make a distinctively Australian animated feature for the world children's market. The eventual concept was unusual, with animated characters superimposed over live-action backgrounds. A detailed storyboard was prepared and the complex task of shooting backgrounds to synchronize with the drawings was tackled in the Blue Mountains and at Jenolan Caves. Laurie Sharpe, an animator with twenty years' experience in Australia and overseas, designed the characters, conceiving them as simultaneously animal and human, and the work of animation was sublet to various artists in Sydney, working separately in their own studios, rather than in a group 'factory'. The drawings and backgrounds were merged by a process of 'aerial image photography', a variation on rear-projection, in which the backgrounds were projected frame-by-frame under the individual cells, and the composite image photographed by an overhead camera. The entire film took about twelve months to complete, and it cost a low total of around $250 000 (two-thirds of which was provided by the Australian Film Commission). Australian distribution was handled directly by Hoyts Theatres, and it opened at their Entertainment Centre, Sydney, on 15 December 1977 for matinee screenings during the school holidays. Earlier in the year it won the main prize for children's films at the Tehran Film Festival.

Yoram Gross was born in Poland in 1926. He studied music at Krakow University and worked as an assistant in Polish feature film production before emigrating to Israel in 1950. There he worked on advertising and animated films, including a feature-length puppet film, *Joseph the Dreamer* (1960). He came to Australia in the late 1960s and formed a film company in Sydney with his Israeli wife, Sandra. Together they made numerous documentary and advertising films and occasional animated experiments. In 1975 they wrote a book, *The First Animated Step*, surveying the history of animation, and made a film of the same title, intended to introduce school audiences to basic principles of the art.

486 The Last Wave

1977 PETER WEIR

PC: Ayer Productions. P: Hal McElroy, Jim McElroy. SC: Peter Weir, Tony Morphett, Petru Popescu. STORY: Peter Weir. PH: Russell Boyd. CAM OP: John Seale. P DES: Goran Warff. ART D: Neil Angwin. SPECIAL EFFECTS: Monty Fieguth, Robert Hilditch. ED: Max Lemon. M: Charles Wain. PM: Ross Matthews. ASST D: John Robertson. SD R: Don Connolly. SD MIX: Greg Bell. 106 mins. Colour.

CAST: Richard Chamberlain (David Burton), Olivia Hamnett (Annie Burton), David Gulpilil (Chris Lee), Fred Parslow (Reverend Burton), Vivean Gray (Dr Whitburn), Nandjiwarra Amagula (Charlie), Walter Amagula (Gerry Lee), Roy Bara (Larry), Cedric Lalara (Lindsey), Morris Lalara (Jacko), Peter Carroll (Michael Zeadler), Athol Compton (Billy Corman), Hedley Cullen (Judge), Michael Duffield (Andrew Potter), Wallas Eaton (morgue doctor), Jo England (baby sitter), John Frawley (policeman), Jennifer de Greenlaw (Zeadler's secretary), Richard Henderson (prosecutor), Penny Leach (schoolteacher), Merv Lilley (publican), John Meagher (morgue clerk), Guido Rametta (Guido), Malcolm Robertson (Don Fishburn), Greg Rowe (Carl), Katrina Sedgwick (Sophie Burton), Ingrid Weir (Grace Burton).

While defending a group of urban Aborigines in a murder case, a lawyer, David Burton, becomes convinced that the killing had tribal significance. As he investigates the life of the Aborigines involved, he begins to have dreams and premonitions, which he slowly comes to comprehend. With the reluctant help of the Aborigines, he learns that the remains of an ancient civilization still exist far below the streets of Sydney, and that his dreams are signifying the imminent destruction of the city by a giant tidal wave.

Before exploring the mysteries of the forgotten civilization, the film establishes a mood of supernatural foreboding through a series of climatic disturbances—a freak hailstorm in the desert, unusually severe coastal storms, and later a fall of black rain—which are gradually linked by the lawyer to his premonitions of a future apocalypse. Water recurs as an image of menace, growing more and more relentless until the lawyer's final confrontation with the substance of his dream on a deserted beach near the city. A distinction is made between the Aboriginal 'dreamtime' and the Western

486 *The Last Wave* Richard Chamberlain (*l*), David Gulpilil

concept of 'real time' and this distinction becomes increasingly central to the film as the lawyer slowly realizes his psychic affinity with the dreamtime world and his increasing need to be initiated into the secrets of tribal lore. The film also explores the plight of Aborigines in urban society, and above all, it is dominated by the charismatic performances of two full-blood Aborigines, the experienced actor David Gulpilil and a tribal leader from Groote Eylandt, Nandjiwarra Amagula.

The $810 000 production was shot in March and April 1977 in Adelaide and Sydney. Finance was raised from the Australian Film Commission, the South Australian Film Corporation, and from the advance sale to United Artists of the rights for several English-speaking territories. With the American market in mind, the producers worked with an American writer, Petru Popescu, on the screenplay, and imported Richard Chamberlain to star in the leading role. After prize-winning presentations at the Paris and Tehran film festivals in November, the film opened in Sydney, Melbourne and Adelaide on 15 December to generally favourable reviews. Overseas distribution was widespread and the film attracted solid returns in the U.S.A. after its release there in January 1979.

487 **Summer City**

1977 CHRISTOPHER FRASER

PC: Avalon Films/Summer City Productions. P, SC: Phillip Avalon. PH: Jerry Marek. ED: David Stiven. ART D: Jann Harris. M: Phil Bitkis. PM: Lionel Slutzkin. ASST D: Michael Carlton. SD R: Bill Pitt. 85 mins. Colour.

CAST: John Jarratt (Sandy), Phillip Avalon (Robbie), Steve Bisley (Boo), Mel Gibson (Scollop), Debbie Forman (Caroline), James Elliot, Abigail, Ward Austin.

Conceived as a 'road movie', with both action and comedy for the teenage market, *Summer City* was set in the rock-and-roll era of the early 1960s, complete with clips from Brian Henderson's television show, *Bandstand*, songs by Australian rock-and-roll stars on the sound-track, and an appearance by the disc jockey Ward Austin. Four young men set off up the coast in their old Chevy for a weekend of surfing and fun. They stop at a country dance where Boo, a loud-mouthed 'lady-killer', seduces a 14-year-old girl, Caroline. As they travel on, fighting breaks out in the group, and when Boo is confronted by Caroline's father, a crazed war veteran with a rifle, the scene is set for violence and bloodshed.

The film was shot cheaply on 16mm (later blown-up to 35mm) for $200 000, provided entirely by private investors. Shooting began in October 1976, with locations on the coast near Sydney and Newcastle, especially at the small town of Catherine Hill Bay, 80 miles north of Sydney. The writer, producer and co-star was Phillip Avalon, a model and actor who had previously written, produced and acted in a telemovie, *The Double Dealer* (1975), about drug-trafficking and 'the white slave trade'. Avalon and his associates distributed and promoted the film themselves through independent cinemas, with a première at the Century Theatre, Sydney, on 22 December 1977.

488 Fantasm Comes Again

1977 ERIC RAM [Colin Eggleston]

PC: Australian International Film Corporation. EXEC P: Robert F. Ward, Mark Josem, P: Antony I. Ginnane. ASSOC P: Leon Gorr. SC: Robert Derrière [Ross Dimsey]. PH: Vince Monton. ED: Tony Patterson. ART D: Anthony Brockliss. M: John Mol. PM, ASST D: Tom Jacobson. SD R: Neil Rozensky, Don Boardman. 94 mins. Colour.

CAST: Angela Menzies-Wills (Libbie), Clive Hearne (Harry), Uschi Digart (Leslie), Rick Cassidy (Mr Bates), Liz Wolfe (Rita), Rosemarie Bem (Cindy), Urias S. Cambridge (Bob), Rainbeaux Smith (Carol), Peter Kurzon (Ted), Lois Owens (Alice), Mike Stapp (rapist), Michael Barton (Miss Peabody), Suzy A. Star (Penny), Dee Dee Levitt (Bianca).

A cub reporter, Libbie, is assigned to her paper's sexual advice column. She is initiated into the job by a crusty old journalist, Harry, who tells her about the wide variety of experiences submitted by the readers—among them, sex in a threesome at a drive-in theatre, sex in a gymnasium, and sex in a library where the 'Silence Please' sign gives the male librarian an advantage over the female readers.

This sexploitation sequel to *Fantasm* (1976) again had linking scenes (the story of the reporter) shot in Australia, but the bulk of the film was shot by the Australian director and photographer in Los Angeles with stars of the American soft-core pornographic cinema. It was the first feature by Colin Eggleston (using the pseudonym of Eric Ram), formerly a story editor and director of television series for Crawford Productions in Melbourne. Financed entirely with private funds, the $80 000 production was released by Filmways (one of the main investors in the film) at their Dendy Cinema in Collins Street, Melbourne, on 26 December 1977.

488 *Fantasm Comes Again* Uschi Digart, Dee Dee Levitt

Appendix A: Film preservation in Australia

One of the earliest attempts by the Commonwealth government to preserve film was made in 1915 when prints of two wartime propaganda films, *Will They Never Come?* and *The Hero of the Dardanelles*, were lodged in the Federal parliamentary library in Melbourne. Neither film survived in its entirety, however, since responsibility for long-term preservation was beyond the scope of any library in Australia until several decades later.

Despite pleas by interested members of the public and a few in the film trade, film preservation did not receive any formal recognition until 1937, when the Commonwealth government set up the National Historic Film and Speaking Record Library as part of the Parliamentary Library. This initial government action prompted the collection of a few selected newsreels for preservation. After this modest start, work was suspended because of the war, and in the early 1950s the Film Division of the National Library of Australia took over the task of preservation. The Film Division had been established in 1946 as one of several non-commercial government film distribution libraries created in the immediate post-war years to provide films for schools and universities.

During the 1950s the Film Division staff began to locate, acquire and restore old Australian films. The work was carried out by staff in between the demands of their job in the Division's distribution activity, and the film archival function of preservation received little official support within the Library until the late 1960s. The advances that were made were due almost entirely to the dedication and stubborn persistence of Rod Wallace, Larry Lake and a few other librarians, in the unpromising climate of a moribund film production industry and a general cultural and academic disregard for film as a medium of historical value or artistic expression. Action by Lake and Wallace ensured the survival of important films such as Longford's *The Sentimental Bloke* (1919) and *On Our Selection* (1920), as well as the early work of Charles Chauvel.

The embryonic archive within the Film Division of the National Library grew slowly. In the late 1960s, government support for film production, together with the emergence of film studies in schools and universities, and a growing interest from the film trade in old Australian films that could be sold to television, created a greater awareness of the need for a properly functioning archive. In 1973 a separate staff unit was established within the National Library to build upon the work of the Film Division and develop the National Film Archive. Under the guidance of librarians self-trained in film work, including Rod Wallace, Ray Edmondson and Karen Foley, the Archive rapidly expanded to become a vital part of the Australian film community. Staff were sent overseas for the study of preservation procedures, and internationally accepted standards were rigorously adopted.

Throughout its development, the Film Archive's work was made more complex by its attachment (for administrative and historic reasons) to the National Library, a body primarily concerned with books and papers, in which specialized collections of non-book materials such as film and recorded music were traditionally of secondary importance. The Archive's work in the 1970s was further complicated by the emergence of other bodies that claimed film archival functions, which threatened confusion in acquisition policies and procedures and a regression in preservation standards. In response to the limitations on the National Film Archive created by its relationship with the National Library, and to the threat of competition in a field that could not afford rivalry for technical and financial reasons, a group was formed in 1975 to press for increased government support for the Archive and for its autonomy. This group, the Association for a National Film and Television Archive, succeeded in drawing some wider public attention to the needs of the Film Archive and helped to achieve the maintenance of the Archive's position in the years of cutback in the staffing and funding of government services that occurred after the election of the Fraser government in December 1975.

Today the Archive not only provides film producers with footage (subject to copyright controls) and information, but also services numerous researchers in a wide variety of fields. The restoration of feature films such as *Silks and Saddles* (1921), *The Breaking of the Drought* (1920) and *Jedda* (1955) from deteriorated originals have made these films available for renewed public screenings and have demonstrated the world standard of the Australian archive. In 1978 the Archive held some 14 000 titles, including about 200 Australian feature films, 3000 issues of *Cinesound Review*, *Movietone News* and other newsreels, hundreds of documentary films, episodes from television series, and commercials, as well as a growing number of feature films from other countries deposited in the Archive by producers for use there by students and other researchers.

Appendix B: Bibliographical note

In the preparation of this book, searches were made of many city and country newspapers, and film and theatre periodicals. Interviews with many film pioneers were recorded, production papers examined whenever available, and voluminous correspondence conducted with film-makers. Where possible, film-makers personally checked the accuracy of the entries on their films.

Detailed references to the source material on individual films have been lodged with the National Film Archive in Canberra, and copies can be readily obtained from there. In the present text we have included references only for those items from which we have made direct quotations.

Copies of tape-recorded interviews, production papers and memorabilia have also been deposited with the National Film Archive and are available there, subject to restrictions imposed by the original donor or interviewee.

Among the periodicals and newspapers, particularly heavy use was made of the following publications.

Everyones (Sydney), a weekly film trade paper, published in Sydney from 1921 to 1937. Edited for many years by Gayne Dexter, the paper often took a strong independent editorial line on issues relating to industry practices. Dexter was not afraid of attacking the American distribution majors, and for several months, early in 1935, the magazine was boycotted by the American distributors after Dexter spoke out against their stranglehold over the market.

Film Weekly (Sydney), a much more conformist industry paper, published in Sydney from 1927 to 1972. It reflected the mainstream opinion in the film trade, and was uncritical and euphoric about commercial achievements, but up to the 1950s it provided an invaluable record of the work of the exhibition and distribution trade, as well as of feature film production. After the mid-1950s it declined along with the industry itself under the impact of television, and became even more of an uncritical publicity vehicle for the major distribution companies.

Theatre Magazine (Sydney), a monthly publication, from 1904 to 1926, which provided detailed information on theatre and film, especially Australian activity.

Picture Show (Sydney), a fan magazine monthly, from 1919 to 1923, which included much detail on Australian film people.

Australian Variety and Show World (Sydney), another early trade monthly, published from 1913 to 1921, then incorporated in *Everyones.*

Referee (Sydney), a weekly sports newspaper, which carried a film and theatre trade page for several years; it proved a useful source for information on Australian production from 1911 to 1915.

The Sun (Sydney). For a daily newspaper, the *Sun* employed an unusually frank film critic from around 1917 into the early 1920s. Its anonymous critic (or critics) assessed films from a moralistic but sophisticated aesthetic viewpoint that was rare in the Australian press at this time.

Sydney Morning Herald. Although slow to start any form of regular film criticism, by the late 1920s and through the 1930s this daily newspaper published anonymous reviews (many by Kenneth Wilkinson) that, like items in the *Sun,* adopted a stern moral tone in disparaging Hollywood and the American influence on Australian culture.

From the 1940s onwards, film criticism in Australia's daily press was generally innocuous, with a few notable exceptions, such as Colin Bennett in the *Age* (Melbourne), who, throughout the 1960s, provided a strong voice in favour of local production initiatives and encouraged a more enlightened attitude by governments to film culture. From the mid-1970s, film criticism and discussion of the industry improved in the quarterly *Cinema Papers* and in the weekly press, including the *Bulletin* (the articles of Sandra Hall) and the *National Times* (the articles of P. P. McGuinness).

Among archival records, particular use was made of the film censorship files from the 1910s and 1920s in the correspondence of the Chief Secretary's Office, New South Wales, held by the Archives Authority of New South Wales, Sydney. In the Australian Archives, Canberra, the literary copyright files of the Commonwealth Patent Office were examined for the period up to 1930, and proved a valuable source for stills and scripts for a number of early films.

Among publications, the work of Eric Reade stands out as a pioneering effort in the documentation of Australian film history. The following items are listed for further reading.

Baxter, J., *The Australian Cinema* (Sydney, 1970)

Bertrand, I., *Film Censorship in Australia* (Brisbane, 1978)

Dunn, M., *How They Made Sons of Matthew* (Sydney, 1949)

Hall, K. G., *Directed by Ken G. Hall* (Sydney, 1977)

Kathner, R., *Let's Make a Movie* (Sydney, 1946)

Legg, F., *The Eyes of Damien Parer* (Adelaide, 1963)

Legg, F. and Hurley, T., *Once More on my Adventure* (Sydney, 1966)

Porter, H., *Stars of Australian Stage and Screen* (Adelaide, 1965)

Reade, E., *The Australian Screen* (Melbourne, 1976)

Thornhill, M., *The Australian Cinema? (Current Affairs Bulletin,* 18 December 1967)

Wasson, M., *The Beginnings of Australian Cinema* (Australian Film Institute, Melbourne, 1964)

Index

Note The titles of the 488 films covered in the book, and their numbers, are set in bold type. All other films mentioned in the book are set in italics. The figures given, in all cases, refer to **film numbers,** not page numbers—except the roman numerals I to VII, which refer to the seven period introductions in the book.